OUT OF THE BACKGROUND

READINGS ON CANADIAN NATIVE HISTORY

second edition

Edited by

Ken S. Coates
University of Waikato, New Zealand

&

Robin Fisher
University of Northern British Columbia

COPP CLARK LTD.
TORONTO

P9-BJA-479

ISBN: 0-7730-5533-9

publisher: Jeff Miller
managing editor: Barbara Tessman
editor: Bay Ryley
design: Susan Hedley, Liz Nyman
cover design: Kyle Gell
typesetting: Carol Magee
printing and binding: Metropole Litho Inc.

Canadian Cataloguing in Publication Data

Main entry under title:

Out of the background: readings on Canadian native history

(New Canadian readings)
2nd ed.
Includes bibliographical references.
ISBN 0-7730-5533-9

1. Indians of North America - Canada - History. 2. Indians of North America - Canada - Cultural assimilation - History. 3. Indians of North America - Canada - Government relations.   I. Coates, Kenneth, 1956– II. Fisher, Robin, 1946– . III. Series.
E78.C2098 1996   971'.00497   C95-932098-9

COPP CLARK LTD.
2775 Matheson Blvd. East
Mississauga, Ontario
L4W 4P7

Printed and bound in Canada

1 2 3 4 5   5533-9   00 99 98 97 96

FOREWORD

○

The study of Canadian aboriginal history, a generation ago the province of a few scholars, today is one of the burgeoning fields of study in Canadian history. Undergraduates take courses, graduate students research and write Masters' and Doctoral theses, and scholars publish a continuing flood of books and articles. The field has grown so fast and produced so much high quality work in a few years that access to the best new work has become difficult for all but specialists with good libraries close at hand.

Hence this new edition of *Out of the Background*. Those interested in the development of the field of aboriginal history need only compare the first edition of this book, published in 1988, with this one. The number of new articles of recent date should readily demonstrate how the field has developed and turned in new directions. There is no reason to believe that this process of exploration and revision of older approaches will cease.

This is all to the good. The more scholars, the more new approaches, the more exciting aboriginal history is for those who teach and study it. *Out of the Background*, ably edited by Robin Fisher and Ken S. Coates, two of the leading figures in the field, presents a fine sample of the best of this new work in an easy-to-use and attractive format.

J.L. Granatstein
General Editor

CONTENTS

○

PAUL TENNANT ○ Cut-offs, Claims Prohibition, and the Allied Tribes, 1916–27 ____ 279

BRIDGET MORAN ○ Justa: A First Nations Leader (Dakelhne butsowhudilhzulh'un) ____ 297

DANIEL FRANCIS ○ Marketing the Imaginary Indian ____ 310

DANIEL PAUL ○ The Twentieth Century and the Failure of Centralization: A Micmac Perspective ____ 320

HARRY ASSU WITH JOY INGLIS ○ Renewal of the Potlatch at Cape Mudge ____ 353

J.R. MILLER ○ Great White Father Knows Best: Oka and the Land Claims Process ____ 367

ROBIN FISHER ○ Judging History: Reflections on the Reasons for Judgment in *Delgamuukw v. B.C.* ____ 391

FURTHER READING ____ 402

INTRODUCTION

○

When we compiled the articles for the first edition of *Out of the Background*, we were impressed with the richness and diversity of the historical literature. From an isolated spot on the margins of Canadian historiography, writing on Native history expanded greatly through the 1970s and 1980s. The last seven years have seen a continuation of this tend—Canadian historical writing on First Nations is currently one of the most dynamic academic fields in this country, drawing together scholarly disciplines and diverse cultural perspectives.

Non-Native interest in First Nations peoples, history, and cultures remains very strong. Significant markets for aboriginal art—from west coast argylite carvings to Inuit silk-screen prints—have been established. First Nations musicians, such as the Montagnais group Kashtin and Inuit singer Susan Aglukark, have found warm and receptive audiences, plus a regular spot in the annual Juno awards celebrating excellence in Canadian music. The lessons and nuances of Native spirituality have intrigued a large number of non-Native observers, including New Agers, members of Christian denominations (some of whom have gone beyond apologies for past wrongs to a welcoming of Native spirituality), and spiritual seekers. In the past, purveyors of mass culture presented aboriginal themes in stereotypic terms and First Nations peoples as caricatures, like Tonto of Lone Ranger fame. While elements of this pattern remain, television programs like "North of 60" and "Northern Exposure," "Medicine River," and movies like "Black Robe," and "Clearcut" have made a determined effort to portray indigenous cultures in a more accurate fashion.

This fascination with aboriginal cultures has now been joined by increased concern for the challenges facing contemporary First Nations peoples and communities. Biting criticism of government policies, reserve conditions, and patterns of Canadian racism and discrimination appear regularly on the television, radio, and in the bookstores. There is, if anything, a mini-industry developing around the exposure of aboriginal suffering and government mismanagement of indigenous affairs. Publications by and about First Nations people appear regularly, and it would be seriously incorrect to claim that aboriginal issues are ignored by the mainstream media.

Aboriginal Canada has been transformed in the past twenty years, and with it the political and social fabric of the country at large. Consider a partial list of the major aboriginal developments and issues of the past few years: Elijah Harper and the collapse of the Meech Lake Accord, the Mohawk stand-off at Oka, the resolution of the Council for Yukon Indians land claim, extended debate about the aboriginal provisions in the flawed and ultimately unsuccessful Charlottetown constitutional accord, the establishment of a Royal Commission on Aboriginal Peoples, the controversial decision by Justice Alan MacEachern in the historical Delgamuth case (involving the Gitskan We'etsewewten people), an unprecedented acceleration of the process of returning to aboriginal self-government, indigenous involvement in reversing the decision to halt major resource development projects (including the James Bay hydro-electric development in Quebec and the Kemano Completion Project in British Columbia), and the exposure of deteriorating social conditions at Davis Inlet, Labrador. Indeed, an extensive list of complex issues related to First Nations continues to have a prominent place on the nation's political and public affairs agenda.

It is difficult to gauge the impact of recent scholarship on the debates outlined above. Academics have emerged as public commentators on aboriginal land claims and self-government, and many work behind the scenes with aboriginal, government, and private sector groups. However, most scholars interested in First Nations issues work through the less public forums of the university classroom, conference presentations, scholarly journals, and the publication of the academic monograph. Some of the latter have found a sizeable audience; Paul Tennant's prize-winning *Aboriginal People and Politics* spent a long period on the BC best-seller lists, historical surveys by J.R. Miller and Olive Dickason attracted far more attention than is the norm for academic texts; Bruce Trigger's work on the Huron deservedly won wide acclaim, and Julie Cruikchank's *Life Lived Like a Story*, a collaboration with three Yukon First Nations women, provided a large audience with an innovative means of approaching and understanding the experience of indigenous people.

The development of Canadian historical writing on First Nations people is marked by more than simply a growth in volume. While several themes, most noticeably the pre-1900 fur trade, government policy, and missionary activity continue to attract attention, historians have also explored in new directions. Hitherto neglected topics—the role of Native women, patters of inter-racial social relations, environmental aspects of indigenous culture and indigenous-newcomer relations, disease and indigenous health, twentieth-century social and economic developments, the direct impact of residential schools on indigenous peoples, and patterns of aboriginal protest to newcomer encroachment and government policy—have attracted historical investigators.

There has also been a geographic broadening of the historiography of First Nations. Through the 1960s and 1970s, historical literature tended to focus on the prairie west and the early history of central Canada. Led by scholars like W.L. Morton, Bruce Trigger, Cornelius Jaenan and A.J. Ray, most historians investigated the pre-1870 Hudson's Bay Company territories and the history of the Huron and Iroquois of New France. This research provided an impressive methodological and conceptual foundation for future work, which expanded to British Columbia (initially through the work of Robin Fisher), the Maritimes (following a major monograph by L.F.S. Upton) and the Canadian North (through the writings of K.S. Coates and Kerry Abel). The historiography has become truly national in scope, affording new opportunities to compare developments in different parts of the country and to focus more attentively on the role of indigenous cultures in determining patterns of social, cultural, and economic change.

Despite this proliferation of fine writing in the field, enormous historiographical gaps remain. Academics have documented comparatively little about twentieth-century developments related to First Nations (particularly the post-World War II period), despite the fact that there is no shortage of detailed government and other records relating to this era. Other (not time-specific) areas in need of further exploration include health care and demographic change, family structure and relations inside indigenous communities, First Nations-newcomer social relations, the historical experience of urban aboriginals, the persistence and evolution of indigenous spirituality, the involvement of First Nations people in the wage or market economy, technology and the transformation of indigenous life-ways, and the survival of aboriginal languages and cultures in the face of North American popular culture.

Perhaps the greatest challenge is a methodological one. Historical scholarship has traditionally placed the greatest value on written documents (qualitative and quantitative), asserting that these sources are more reliable than other historical records. A growing number of scholars are testing this assumption, and are looking as well to physical and artistic evidence of changes in aboriginal culture. Even more, responding to First Nations communities, non-Native researchers have discovered the incredible richness and vitality of aboriginal oral tradition—living history—and have been provided access to this important but previously ignored source of historical documentation.

The articles collected in the second edition of *Out of the Background* represent a cross-section of writing on First Nations in Canada. We have attempted to include a variety of historical and historiographical themes, to cover major developments in the various regions of the country, and to provide examples of the many different methods that scholars have used in an attempt to understand aboriginal history. In attempting to mix the old and the new and to examine a large number of central themes in the writing of Native history, we have had to leave out many important works of scholarship. We hope that readers will pursue these studies through the reference contained in the individual essays or through the guide to further reading at the end of the book.

As the historical literature produced since we published the first edition of *Out of the Background* in 1988 reveals, this is a dynamic and important field. The essays in this collection are designed to introduce readers to the historiographical vitality of this field and to encourage further research and reading in the area. Just as contemporary events continuously reshape our assessment of the history of First Nations in Canada, so too does historical writing reconfigure our understanding of the events, personalities, and processes that created the social, economic, cultural, and political conditions currently facing the aboriginal people in this country. It is our greatest hope that this book contributes to a search for knowledge and awareness—the necessary aspects of that attempt to address the present and future needs of the First Nations of Canada.

THE ROAD TO AFFLUENCE:
A REASSESSMENT OF EARLY HURON
RESPONSES TO EUROPEAN CONTACT[◇]

BRUCE G. TRIGGER

o

Until recently, ethnologists and ethnohistorians believed that the detailed European accounts of Huron life that were produced between 1616 and 1650 were descriptions of a native culture essentially unaltered by European contact. It was acknowledged that Huron culture probably had been enriched and their life transformed in superficial ways by the acquisition of European trade goods, but these changes were not seen as altering their prehistoric culture to any significant degree.[1] This paper reassesses that position and argues for a dramatic effect on Huron life, caused by the growing affluence of the protohistoric period of indirect trade.

The view of changes being superficial reflected the continuing influence of Ralph Linton's distinction between directed and nondirected cultural change.[2] It was widely believed that changes that came about as a result of indirect contact, or in situations where the indigenous people were politically and militarily dominant, were unlikely to disrupt native societies; on the contrary, by means of such changes these societies were able to realize their full cultural potential. Only when Europeans deliberately sought to alter native styles of life and had the power to do so did cultural change become disruptive. This view remains popular and in some cases may be appropriate.[3]

◇ Reprinted with permission from *Affluence and Cultural Survival: 1981 Proceedings of the American Ethnological Society*, ed. Richard F. Salisbury and Elisabeth Tooker (American Ethnological Society, 1984), 12–25.

THE ARCHAEOLOGICAL RECORD

This interpretation, as it pertained to the Hurons, seems to be confirmed in many respects by archaeologists. Prior to European goods reaching southern Ontario, the Hurons, like other Northern Iroquoian-speaking groups, were dependent upon a horticultural economy. Extended families lived in longhouses and their villages sometimes had over 1000 inhabitants. These villages had to be relocated every ten to twenty years, as fields and nearby sources of firewood became exhausted. Many of them were palisaded and located on bluffs, which suggests that warfare was already prevalent. There is also evidence that prisoners were being tortured and that the bones of dead Hurons were being interred periodically in village ossuaries.[4] Nearby villages formed small tribal clusters.[5] Councils had evolved to co-ordinate the activities of at least the larger villages and tribal groupings.[6] All of this was similar to the historic period. The Hurons claimed in 1640 that two of their tribes, the Attignawantans and Attigneenongnahacs, had formed the nucleus of their confederacy over 200 years before. By contrast, two other tribes, the Arendahronons and the Tahontaenrats, joined only about the beginning of the seventeenth century,[7] following a period that recent archaeological research shows to have been one of unexpectedly great sociocultural change. During that period Huron villages, unlike those of the Five Iroquois Nations, had altered their overall distribution, contracting northward and westward to cluster along the small rivers flowing north into Georgian Bay. Communities and tribal clusters split and merged as part of this process,[8] most likely as localized clan segments—the Hurons' most durable social and political units—realigned themselves. It is likely that the historically known tribes of the Huron confederacy developed only after the Huron had relocated in their seventeenth-century homeland. By contrast, the resilience of clan and moiety affiliations of the Hurons and Tionontatis after their dispersal in 1649 suggests that these groupings, which had social and religious functions, were less responsive to major geographical shifts of location.[9]

All recorded Iroquoian societies in the seventeenth century, including the Hurons, viewed war and trade as alternative forms of intertribal relations. Neighboring tribal groupings either were at peace and traded with each other or engaged in blood feuds of varying intensity. Warfare was essential, since it was the most important way in which Iroquoian men acquired individual prestige.[10] There was also much rivalry between peace, or council, chiefs and war chiefs, even though both types usually came from the same lineages. The former normally had a vested interest in maintaining peaceful relations and trade with neighboring tribes, while the war chiefs sought opportunities to attack them. The latter were supported by the young men, who were anxious to win personal prestige and who viewed the efforts of council chiefs and older men to curtail warfare, not as prudence, but an effort to prevent them from challenging their elders. The relative power of council chiefs and war chiefs tended to vary as the political situation changed.[11] If we assume that similar relations applied in the sixteenth century, the archaeological records of trade and warfare may tell us about the shifting patterns of political power among the Hurons at that time.

TRADE BEFORE 1609

Archaeologists generally have believed that there was only a limited amount of trade among Iroquoian groups prior to the protohistoric period. A likely exception was the trade between the Hurons, some of whom had lived in northern Simcoe County from earliest times, and the Nipissings, which seems to have been based on the exchange of Huron surplus produce for furs, fish and meat. Elsewhere, the presence of only small amounts of native copper from the Lake Superior region and shells from the Eastern Seaboard of the United States suggests that individual Iroquoian villages remained relatively isolated and that intertribal trade was restricted, although it may have been increasing in late prehistoric times.[12] Exotic goods are also rare in prehistoric Huron ossuaries, which generally seem to have been lined with mats rather than with beaver-skin robes as they were in the historic period.

Direct trade between the Hurons and the French began in 1609, bringing with it the period of recorded history. Trigger summarizes the growth of direct trade between Europeans and native peoples during the sixteenth century.[13] Small amounts of European goods seem to have been passing from one native group to another this far inland already in the first half of the sixteenth century. Some may have reached the Iroquoians from the East Coast of the United States, which was visited intermittently by European explorers, traders, and colonists, but their most reliable and important source was the lower St. Lawrence Valley, where there was a gradual increase in the volume of trade throughout the sixteenth century. European goods were passed from one native group to another. In 1535 native copper was being traded along a route that ran from Lake Superior eastward to Lake Nipissing and the Ottawa Valley and then across the forests of southern Quebec to Tadoussac.[14] A return exchange of European goods could have reached the Hurons by way of the Kichesipirinis, an Algonkin tribe of the upper Ottawa Valley, and the neighboring Nipissings, who must have passed some of them along to their Huron trading partners living at the southeastern corner of Georgian Bay. Ridley shows that close ties had existed between the Nipissings and some Hurons since the earliest development of a horticultural economy in southern Ontario.[15]

The upper St. Lawrence seems to have been less important as a trade route. Though the Stadaconans, or St. Lawrence Iroquoians living in the Quebec City area, obtained limited amounts of European goods before 1534, probably in return for furs,[16] the Hochelagans, who lived on Montreal Island, seem not to have been involved in such trade.[17] No convincing evidence of European goods has so far been found in St. Lawrence Iroquoian sites farther up the St. Lawrence Valley. Suspected European goods have turned out to be made of native copper.[18] It is possible that the St. Lawrence Iroquoians living west of Montreal had been dispersed prior to the 1530s.

Documents reveal that later in the sixteenth century Algonkin traders carried European goods up the St. Lawrence Valley to various groups living around the rim of Lake Ontario, including the Hurons of the Trent Valley. This route was closed, around the beginning of the seventeenth century, as a result of Five Nations attacks directed against Algonkins living in the lower part of the Ottawa Valley. It remained closed until after the final dispersal of the Hurons.[19]

The earliest European goods to reach southern Ontario were restricted both in variety and volume. They included rare iron celts, iron awls, and fragments of cut-up brass kettles that were bent by the Indians to make metal beads. It appears that communities that were located close to major trade routes had readier access to these goods than did other groups. Especially during the early stages, some communities probably received no European goods. While the Hurons in Simcoe County continued to exchange their surplus corn, as well as nets and tobacco first with the Nipissings and later with various Ottawa Valley Algonkin groups, they now also seem to have traded beaver skins, which they continued to trap within their tribal territories until they became depleted about 1630.[20] There is evidence that some Iroquoian groups relocated during the late sixteenth century in order to be closer to good beaver-hunting grounds. One example is the Tionontatis, who moved north into their seventeenth-century homeland in order to be able to hunt beaver in the nearby swamps at the head of the Grand River.[21] Huron communities fragmented when some of their inhabitants decided to move to new locations, while other groups joined together in areas favorable for hunting or trading for European goods.[22]

By 1615, the Hurons were trading corn and European goods for beaver skins with the Algonkins, Nipissings, and Ottawas and European goods for fancy furs and other native luxury goods with the Tionontatis and Neutrals of southwestern Ontario. They were also obtaining wampum directly from the Susquehannocks of Pennsylvania, an Iroquoian group with whom they had concluded an alliance against their common enemies, the Five Nations. This expansion of intertribal trade in native luxury goods late in the sixteenth century appears to have been stimulated by the fur trade.

The Hurons and their neighbors quickly realized that European metal cutting tools, including arrowheads, were technologically and militarily superior to their own stone implements. Yet in the course of the sixteenth century Huron social and political organization underwent changes that seem out of proportion to the utilitarian significance of the small amounts of European goods that they were obtaining. As I observed in *The Children of Aataentsic*, "what appears in the archaeological record as a few scraps of metal seems in fact to have been a sufficient catalyst to realize certain potentials for development that were inherent in prehistoric Huron society, but which otherwise might never have come to fruition."[23] At this period the exotic and perhaps magical properties of these scarce goods and the prestige of possessing them probably remained of greatest importance. Their scarcity may also have enhanced the desire to obtain corresponding categories of native luxuries.

PROTOHISTORIC WARFARE

Recent interpretations of protohistoric Iroquoian warfare depended heavily upon pottery analysis. Foreign-style pottery found in small amounts in a village site, especially if trace-element analysis shows it to be made of local clays,[24] may indicate that it was manufactured by women captured from a foreign group. Reciprocal presence of foreign-style pottery in two groups more likely indicates mutual bloodfeud and raiding than it does peaceful trade. Imported pottery, especially if it occurs only in particular sections of villages, may attest the forcible or voluntary relocation of extended families as a result of warfare.[25] With caution, such evidence can be used, along with European descriptions of warfare patterns after 1603, to infer the nature of conflict during the preceding century.

On the basis of such pottery distributions, P.G. Ramsden suggests that the disappearance of the St. Lawrence Iroquoians was the final result of wars waged between them and some Huron groups.[26] He proposes that the St. Lawrence Iroquoians at first supplied the Hurons with European goods, but later either cut off this trade or were unable to supply them with enough goods. As a result, the Hurons decided to disperse them and trade directly with the Europeans. Thus the numerically weaker St. Lawrence Iroquoians were destroyed. St. Lawrence Iroquoian artifacts identified in some presumably late sixteenth-century Huron sites are those used by women and not men. Pipes and bone artifacts of St. Lawrence types are said to be absent, which suggests that the men had been killed by the Hurons. Significant amounts of domestic pottery indicate that large numbers of St. Lawrence Iroquoian women had been taken prisoner by the Hurons.[27]

Yet the earliest pottery evidence of contacts, and probably warfare, between St. Lawrence Iroquoians and Hurons clearly precedes the presence of European goods on Huron sites. In addition, European goods are not securely attested on any St. Lawrence Iroquoian sites in the upper St. Lawrence Valley; which could mean that most of the St. Lawrence Iroquoians were dispersed by the early sixteenth century, leaving only those groups that Jacques Cartier encountered at Montreal and around Quebec. The Hurons do not seem to have had a strong motive for attacking and destroying their remaining eastern neighbors in order to gain access to European goods. In part or in whole, they were able to obtain these goods from Algonkian-speaking groups by way of Georgian Bay without them having to pass through St. Lawrence Iroquoian territory. There is also no evidence that the St. Lawrence River west of Quebec City was a major artery of trade while the St. Lawrence Iroquoians lived there. If the Hurons living in the Trent Valley attacked the remaining St. Lawrence Iroquoians in order to remove them as middlemen, why was there no sign of a Huron presence along the St. Lawrence when Champlain explored the river in 1603 or anytime prior to what the French and the Hurons agreed was their first direct encounter in 1609? Why also at this time were Mohawk and Oneida warriors raiding the St. Lawrence Valley below Montreal, preventing the Hurons and Algonkins from using the upper valley, and also raiding the lower Ottawa Valley in order to seize European goods? Champlain's observations seem to accord with early accounts that claim it was the Five Nations (probably specifically the Mohawks and Oneidas) who dispersed the remaining St. Lawrence Iroquoians after 1570 in an effort to capture European axes and other goods from neighboring tribes and probably to gain access to the European trading station at Tadoussac.[28]

If some St. Lawrence Iroquoians sought refuge with the Hurons living in the Trent Valley, oral traditions recorded by the French suggest that others joined a branch of the Petite Nation, an Algonkin tribe living in the lower part of the Ottawa Valley.[29] These refugee groups may have played a vital role in forging the close links that existed in the early historic period between the Petite Nation and the Arendahronon tribe of the Hurons. As long as some, if not all, of the ancestors of the Arendahronons continued to live in the Trent Valley, French goods were probably brought up the St. Lawrence Valley to them by the Petite Nation, who in turn may have obtained them from the Kichesipirinis. After the upper St. Lawrence Valley was closed as an artery of communication by the Five Nations and the Arendahronons moved into Simcoe County, the Petite Nation continued to visit and trade with them by way of Lake Nipissing. Early in the seventeenth century, large numbers of Algonkins were spending each winter living and trading in the Huron country. This trading alliance gradually involved the Hurons in the Algonkins' wars against the Oneidas and the Mohawks, Five Nations groups with whom they had probably formerly had little contact. A few Huron warriors were with the Algonkin and Montagnais war party that, accompanied by Champlain, fought with the Mohawks on the shore of Lake Champlain in 1609. Probably in 1613, and certainly in 1615 and 1638, large war parties made up of Hurons and Algonkins attacked these two eastern Five Nations tribes.[30]

Little is known about warfare among neighboring Iroquoian groups in southern Ontario in prehistoric times, although it may have been common. Ceramic analysis provides little evidence of warfare or of any other kind of mutual contact between the Hurons and the Seneca and Cayuga tribes of the Five Nations prior to about 1550. It is true that by 1609 warfare with these tribes was a significant factor in Huron life. Yet it is questionable that all Hurons had moved north into Simcoe County before 1600 to avoid the attacks of the Five Nations.[31] Even when the Hurons informed Champlain that they had abandoned the Trent Valley in response to Five Nations warfare[32] this does not necessarily mean that they moved into Simcoe County to avoid Five Nations attacks on their villages. Rather it suggests that when the Five Nations cut the trade route running up the St. Lawrence, along which the Algonkins were supplying the Hurons living in the Trent Valley with European goods, these groups may have moved north into Simcoe County to be closer to the Georgian Bay route, which remained open.[33] While this explanation acknowledges Five Nations warfare as one reason for the clustering of all Huron groups in northern Simcoe County by the beginning of the seventeenth century, it interprets the primary aim of this relocation as being to have continuing access to familiar trading partners.

PROTOHISTORIC POLITICAL CHANGE

The precise movements bringing together the population that constituted the Huron confederacy in the historic period are not yet known. One can, however, speculate about the social and political processes that accompanied these moves. As Huron groups shifted north, they must have settled on land that had belonged to the ancestors of the Attignawantan and Attigneenongnahac tribes, whose villages in historic times were confined to the western part of northern Simcoe County. All of the land to the south and east that had been abandoned by Huron settlement remained Huron hunting territory. Yet we do not know to what degree these areas were thrown open to use by all Hurons or were reserved for their former inhabitants. Presumably, the Attignawantans and Attigneenongnahacs received some compensation for relinquishing their own land for settlement by other Huron groups. The newcomers would also have had to learn about the northern trade routes from the original inhabitants of Simcoe County and required the latter's consent in order to use them. As the Huron population became more densely settled, trade for skins and meat with northern hunting groups became an essential part of their economy. We do not know to what degree the newcomers' gaining permission to settle near Georgian Bay and to trade directly with the north was a peaceful process or one that involved intimidation or even conflict between various Huron groups. The Hurons spoke about waging fierce wars in late protohistoric times against the neighboring Tionontatis.[34] They may have had similar conflicts with the Neutrals.[35] These wars ended when the Hurons began to supply European goods to these groups on a regular basis. Neither was ever allowed to join the Huron confederacy, however, or to use the Hurons' northern trade routes.

Archaeologists have not yet traced the origins of the historic Huron tribes, although I have already remarked that none of them seems precisely equivalent to local village clusters observed at an earlier date. The archaeological record suggests that the Huron confederacy was greatly expanded, if (contrary to Huron traditions) it did not come into existence, around the end of the sixteenth century.[36] The councils that managed the affairs of the Huron tribes and confederacy were probably extensions of an older system of village government. Such tribal governments as had existed in the past must have been greatly extended and elaborated as the Huron confederacy expanded to embrace its final membership. The expanded tribal association and the denser Huron settlement pattern required new and more elaborate hierarchies of chiefs and the development of more complex rituals of consultation than had existed previously. Such patterns could not develop without much discussion and bargaining.

While the details remain unclear, the late sixteenth century must have been a period of rapid social and political change for the Hurons. This would have produced considerable tension and an unknown amount of warfare. While the Huron confederacy suppressed such warfare as had previously existed among the Hurons, and expanding trading patterns ultimately eliminated it between them and the Tionontatis and Neutrals, new alliances, possibly new forms of economic competition, and the continuing search for individual prestige created new conflicts with all of the tribes of the Five Nations. Although Huron trading networks had expanded with tribes living to the north and south, during the sixteenth century the volume of intertribal trade remained limited by comparison with trade in the historic period.[37] Only a relatively small number of Hurons would have been engaged in such trade. Hence, during the protohistoric period, expanding trade probably enhanced the power of council or peace chiefs far less than the tensions and dislocations of that period enhanced the power of the war chiefs. Yet we must enquire why this is not reflected in any obvious way in later French descriptions of Huron society.

HISTORIC TRADE, 1609–15

The first direct contact between Hurons and French occurred in 1609.[38] That summer, Ochasteguin, an Arendahronon chief, and some of his men accompanied their Petite Nation trading partners to the St. Lawrence ostensibly to join Champlain on an expedition against the Mohawks. The Kichesipirini Algonkins, seeking to remain significant middlemen in the trade between the French and the Huron, sought to discourage the conclusion of a formal trading alliance between them. Nevertheless, in 1611, the chiefs of the recently expanded Huron confederacy council secretly sent presents to Champlain inviting him to visit the Huron country to conclude an alliance with them. In spite of strenuous Kichesipirini opposition, Champlain was able to visit the Huron country in 1615, where a large joint Huron and Algonkin raiding party had assembled to attack the Oneidas or Onondagas. While allegedly going there to join this war party, Champlain was able to visit each Huron village and conclude a formal alliance with its chiefs.[39]

Between 1609 and 1615, the allocation of rights to trade with the French created a major political problem for the Hurons. According to their traditional practice, the right to control the use of a trade route belonged to the man who had first pioneered it, or possibly to the leader of his clan segment. This individual had the right to charge other traders for the privilege of using his route, although there was no effective mechanism for enforcing this.[40] Thus, although Ochasteguin had pioneered the trade with the French, in later years it was Atironta, the highest ranking chief of his tribe, who was the principal trading partner of the French. Even so, direct trade with the French was far too important for one man or even one tribe to control and soon all Huron groups were demanding a share of it. Prior to 1611, the Arendahronons shared the right to trade with the French not only among their own headmen but also with all the headmen in the other tribes of the Huron confederacy. Atironta preserved only his role as the chief Huron ally of the French. Each of the Huron council chiefs now had his own right to trade with the French. It was in that capacity that the many Huron chiefs collectively and individually concluded their alliance with Champlain. Most of the trading with the French was done by the Attignawantans, the largest and most prestigious tribe of the Huron confederacy.

HISTORIC POLITICAL CHANGE, 1615-29

Once the Hurons began to trade directly with the French, they were able to obtain a greater amount and variety of European goods than ever before. The Ottawas and Nipissings became satellites of the Hurons, in the sense that these groups collected furs from bands to the west and north, which in turn they traded with the Hurons for cornmeal and European goods, rather than seeking to obtain the latter directly from the French. The unaccustomed wealth that began to reach the Huron country at this time must have greatly enhanced the prestige of the council, or peace chiefs, who either personally traded with the French and with neighboring Indian groups or received substantial presents in return for sanctioning others to do so. This permitted these chiefs to redistribute large amounts of exotic goods, and especially goods of European origin, to their kin, clients, and other Hurons generally.

The increasing economic importance of the Huron peace chiefs and a period of relative tranquillity, both among the Huron tribes and in their relations with their neighbors, including the Five Nations, must have helped these chiefs to regain their prestige at the expense of the war chiefs. It no doubt also helped to stabilize the Huron government after a period of marked instability and rapid change. A possible reminder of the use that the council chiefs had made of the developing trade with the French to recover their authority was the apparently deprecatory nicknames, such as "big stones" and "stay-at-homes," that Jean de Brébeuf recorded in 1636 the Hurons were now applying to their headmen.[41]

The year 1615 marked the beginning of a 15-year period of considerable stability for the Hurons. Their economic life was greatly enriched by trade, but the Huron country was not flooded with European goods. The 800 miles of canoe travel and portages that separated it from the French trading posts along the St. Lawrence River precluded obtaining enough European goods to satisfy fully the growing needs and wants of a large Huron population. By 1630, the Hurons had also exhausted the beaver stock of their own tribal territories and henceforth had to obtain all the furs they traded with the French from other native groups, often in return for new or second-hand European goods. Hence the Hurons never possessed the vast numbers and array of European goods that tribes, such as the Mohawks, who lived closer to European trading posts were able to obtain.[42] Nevertheless, rituals such as the Ononharoia, or winter festival, and the periodically celebrated Feasts of the Dead seem to have been considerably elaborated, as a means both of redistributing goods and of promoting social solidarity. As the latter ritual grew more elaborate, large amounts of goods were exchanged between the community that was burying its dead prior to relocation and the other Huron groups as well as foreign trading partners who were invited to participate as guests. Large numbers of furs, kettles and other trade goods were also buried with the dead or destroyed in the course of this ritual. Obtaining metal cutting tools speeded the work of forest clearance, made it easier to use large posts to construct houses and palisades, and stimulated the elaboration of traditional arts and crafts, such as bone working. Broken metal kettles provided raw material for more extensive metal working, using techniques applied in prehistoric times to native copper. The Hurons and neighboring Iroquoian tribes also modified iron tools for their own purposes.[43] The metal arrowheads that they either purchased from the French or made out of fragments of metal kettles could pierce traditional Iroquoian body armor and hence were essential for keeping militarily abreast of the Five Nations. Yet, while the Hurons clearly recognized the advantages of possessing European cutting tools and metal kettles, the limited supply of these goods kept pottery making and the manufacture of stone and bone tools alive until after the dispersal of the Huron confederacy.

There is no evidence that the right of peace chiefs to control trade routes or to distribute much of the goods brought to the Huron country was being challenged by other Huron traders. Clan solidarity remained an important factor in Huron life. There is also no evidence that these chiefs were attempting to hoard surplus wealth as an end in itself. Their prestige continued to be validated by the redistribution of such wealth. Individuals who refused to participate whole-heartedly in such activities still risked being suspected or even accused of witchcraft.[44] All of this suggests that while Huron social and political structure existed on a vaster scale than in prehistoric times, it continued to be founded upon essentially traditional role concepts. Warfare with the Five Nations continued at a moderate pace but does not appear to have undermined the power of the council chiefs at this period.

Nevertheless, archaeological data make it clear that much of what seems "traditional" in historic Huron society represented a restoration of stability and, in particular, of the roles played by the council chiefs after a long period of change and dislocation. By comparison with 50 years earlier, the Huron settlement pattern had been greatly altered, so that all Huron people were living in close proximity to one another. New tribal structures seem to have emerged, the confederacy was vastly expanded, if, indeed, it had not come into being in the interval, trading networks had proliferated and the volume of trade vastly increased, and crafts and ritual life had been enriched. The new social order was based on an expanded application of principles that must already have been present and applied in embryonic form in Huron society in prehistoric times and, in this sense, was traditional. Yet the new Huron society was larger and more complex than it had been previously and the process of expansion must have been extremely stressful even if the final result was stable. The whole process was nondirected, in the sense that Europeans had not deliberately sought to influence it. The main dislocations had occurred prior to direct contact with them and while the supply of European goods remained extremely limited. The period of relative affluence that followed direct contact was thus a period of renewed stability.

MISSION PERIOD AND DECLINE, 1634-49

The moderately well-documented period of prosperity and stability came to an end in 1629 with the temporary expulsion of the French from Quebec by English privateers. This disrupted Huron trading relations and led to a period of renewed crisis in intertribal relations in eastern Canada. The return of the French to the Huron country in 1634 was followed by a series of epidemics that by 1640 had halved the population of the Hurons and of neighboring peoples. There is no evidence of similar epidemics earlier in the seventeenth century in this region.[45] In the course of these epidemics, many of the most experienced chiefs, ritualists, and craftsmen perished. This was followed by increasingly severe attacks by the Five Nations, who were anxious to acquire more furs by raiding and expanding their hunting territories to the north. Finally, the coercive element that the Jesuits forced French traders and government officials to introduce into French-Huron relations in an effort to Christianize the Hurons put additional strain on their political and cultural life prior to their dispersal by the Five Nations in 1649.

CONCLUSIONS

No one can doubt the need to interpret ethnographic data in an historical perspective. Yet, especially for the early phases of direct and indirect contact between Europeans and native peoples, only archaeological data can provide adequate historical context. The Hurons, as they were described by European visitors between 1615 and 1650, seemed to be a traditional society, largely unaffected by the presence of European traders in North America. Yet archaeological data reveal that major changes in Huron settlement patterns took place during the century preceding the earliest French descriptions of Huron culture. It seems that these shifts were brought about mainly by a desire to secure and maintain access to sources of European goods. The social and political changes associated with these shifts in settlement must have been accompanied by much uncertainty and tension and probably by overt conflict. Clearly not all change that occurs independently of European control and direction is easy and peaceful. It is also of interest that the main period of crisis preceded the increased flow of European goods into the Huron country that began after the Huron started to trade directly with the French in 1609.

By contrast, the period from 1615 to 1629 was one of social and political stability, accompanied by a higher level of affluence and cultural florescence. The new society remained traditional in the sense that redistribution was highly valued, peace chiefs had reconsolidated their leading role in co-ordinating Huron life, and Huron political behavior remained noncoercive. Yet Huron society was co-ordinated on a larger scale than it had been formerly and the dense nucleation of the Huron population created a social environment not found among the Five Nations, whose tribes continued to live in separate clusters as they had done in prehistoric times. Although the scale of Huron society and Huron cultural life was greatly altered, the new society was able to cope with relative affluence and, indeed, had used this affluence to achieve an impressive level of social and political stability. Yet their achievements were doomed to destruction in 1649 by the Five Nations' need for more abundant supplies of beaver pelts, intertribal and international competition, and French interference in Huron life in support of Jesuit mission policy.

NOTES

1. Elisabeth Tooker, *An Ethnography of the Huron Indians, 1615–1649*, Bureau of American Ethnology Bulletin, no. 190 (1964), 4; Bruce G. Trigger, *The Huron: Farmers of the North* (New York, 1969).

2. Ralph Linton, ed., *Acculturation in Seven American Indian Tribes* (New York, 1940), 501–2; E.H. Spicer, ed., *Perspectives in American Indian Cultural Change* (Chicago, 1961), 519–20.

3. Trigger, *The Children of Aataentsic: A History of the Huron People to 1660*, 2 vols. (Montreal, 1976); Robin Fisher, *Contact and Conflict: Indian–European Relations in British Columbia, 1774–1890* (Vancouver, 1977); Toby Morantz, "The Fur Trade and the Cree of James Bay" in *Old Trails and New Directions*, ed. C.M. Judd and A.J. Ray (Toronto, 1980), 39–58.

4. J.V. Wright, *The Ontario Iroquois Tradition*, National Museum of Canada Bulletin, no. 210 (Ottawa, 1966).

5. P.G. Ramsden, *A Refinement of Some Aspects of Huron Ceramic Analysis*, Mercury Series, no. 68 (Ottawa: Archaeological Survey of Canada, 1977).

6. Trigger, "Inequality and Communication in Early Civilizations," *Anthropologica* 18 (1976): 30–34.

7. Reuben Gold Thwaites, *The Jesuit Relations and Allied Documents*, (Cleveland, 1896–1901), 16:227–29.

8. Ramsden, *Refinement*.

9. Trigger, *Children of Aataentsic*, 825.

10. Trigger, *The Huron*, 42–53.

11. Thwaites, ed., *Jesuit Relations*, 15:53.

12. W.A. Ritchie, *The Archaeology of New York State* (New York, 1965), 293.

13. Trigger, "Sixteenth Century Ontario: History, Ethnohistory and Archaeology," *Ontario History* 72 (1979): 205–23.

14. H.P. Biggar, *The Voyages of Jacques Cartier*, Publications of the Public Archives of Canada, no. 11 (Ottawa, 1924), 106, 171.

15. Frank Ridley, "The Frank Bay Site, Lake Nipissing, Ontario," *American Antiquity* 20 (1954): 40–50.

16. Trigger, *Children of Aataentsic*, 214.

17. Biggar, *Voyages of Jacques Cartier*, 160–61.

18. J.F. Pendergast and J.V. Wright, personal communications.

19. Trigger, *Children of Aataentsic*, 233–34.

20. Gabriel Sagard, *Histoire du Canada*, 4 vols. (Paris, 1866), 585.

21. Ramsden, *Refinement*, 274.

22. Ibid., 292, 286.

23. Trigger, *Children of Aataentsic*, 245.

24. Trigger, et al., "Trace-Element Analysis of Iroquoian Pottery," *Canadian Journal of Archaeology* 4 (1980): 119–45.

25. Ramsden, "Late Iroquoian Occupations of South-Central Ontario," *Current Anthropology* 20 (1979): 597–98.

26. Ramsden, *Refinement*, 293.

27. Wright, *Ontario Prehistory: An Eleven-Thousand Year Archaeological Outline* (Ottawa: National Museum of Man, 1972), 90; and *Quebec Prehistory* (Toronto, 1979), 71–75; Ramsden, *Refinement*, 293.

28. Trigger, "Hochelaga: History and Ethnohistory" in *Cartier's Hochelaga and the Dawson Site*, ed. J.F. Pendergast and B.G. Trigger (Montreal, 1972), 71–92.

29. Trigger, *Children of Aataentsic*, 225–27.

30. Ibid., 275, 308–15, 559–60.

31. C.E. Heidenreich, "The Indian Occupance of Huronia, 1600–1650" in *Canada's Changing Geography*, ed. R.L. Gentilcore (Scarborough, ON., 1967), 16.

32. H.P. Biggar, ed., *The Works of Samuel de Champlain* (Toronto, 1922–36), 3:59.

33. Trigger, "The Historic Location of the Hurons," *Ontario History* 54 (1962): 137–48.

34. Thwaites, ed., *Jesuit Relations*, 20:43.

35. G.M. Wrong, ed., *The Long Journey to the Country of the Hurons* (Toronto, 1939), 151.

36. Tooker, *Ethnography of the Huron Indians*, 3–4.

37. T.F. McIlwraith, "Archaeological Work in Huronia, 1946: Excavations near Warminster," *Canadian Historical Review* 27 (1946): 400.

38. Trigger, *Children of Aataentsic*, 246–47.

39. Ibid., 246–301.

40. Thwaites, ed., *Jesuit Relations*, 10:223–25.

41. Ibid., 231–33.

42. J.F. Jameson, ed., *Narratives of New Netherlands, 1609–1664* (New York, 1909), 141.

43. Charles Garrad, "Iron Trade Knives on Historic Petun Sites," *Ontario Archaeology* 13 (1969): 3–15.

44. Trigger, *Children of Aataentsic*, 423–25.

45. Cf. J.A. Dickinson, "The Pre-contact Huron Population: A Reappraisal," *Ontario History* 72 (1980): 173–79.

THROUGH ANOTHER GLASS DARKLY:
EARLY INDIAN VIEWS OF EUROPEANS

JAMES AXTELL

○

By the principles of their craft, ethnohistorians sooner or later get around to examining both sides of their various cultural frontiers. For a long time, anthropologists dominated the discipline and devoted most of their attention to the study of Indian groups, past and present. With the increasing participation of historians in the early 1970s, ethnohistory has expanded its purview to treat the other side of the frontier, but somewhat more critically than Western or Turnerian frontier historians of previous generations were wont to do.

One group of historians who have shown a sustained interest in Indians, or at least the *idea* of Indians, are intellectual historians, who have written extensively on the changing views of Indians held by European and American observers. But until the mid-70s, they did not write systematically about Indian views of the white man. Cornelius Jaenen broke this impasse in 1974 with an article on "Amerindian Views of French Culture in the Seventeenth Century," published in the *Canadian Historical Review*. It was soon followed by James Ronda's "'We Are Well As We Are': An Indian Critique of Seventeenth-Century Christian Missions," which appeared in the *William and Mary Quarterly* in January 1977. It is no coincidence that both authors are ethnohistorians, for only ethnohistorians know the Indians, as individuals, well enough to imagine that they, as well as whites, had an intellectual history worth reconstructing.

◇ Reprinted with permission from *After Columbus: Essays in the Ethnohistory of Colonial North America* (New York: Oxford University Press, 1988).

○

For centuries, European explorers and settlers have taken their lumps from historians for having mistreated the Indians of North America. Much of the indictment, some of it written by contemporaries of the actors, has stood up well even on appeal to modern historical judges. But recently the indictment has taken a new twist in which the invaders are accused of not even having *seen* the Indians clearly and realistically. Instead, the critics charge, they saw them at best (in Shakespeare's overworked phrase) "through a glass darkly"; at worst, they never saw them at all but only tawny reflections of their own self-projections and neuroses, as in a mirror. In any event, the European's "ethnocentrism," their monolithic concept of "savagism," whether noble or ignoble, so clouded their vision that the human and cultural reality of native life was almost never recognized and less seldom acknowledged. Inevitably, this ethnological blindness led to constant misunderstanding and violence.[1]

Exploration of the various conquest mentalities is all to the good, provided we do not commit the fallacy of intellectual determinism, of attributing historical change solely to ideas.[2] But we should also realize that such a procedure is only half that required by the working principles of ethnohistory. If ideas have consequences when they are translated by will into action, it is imperative that we examine the reigning ideas of all parties, European *and* native. For if the intruders were driven to act partly by their particular mental constructs of the natives, the natives' behavior in turn must have been similarly motivated by their mental images of the Europeans. If we do not have some idea of what was in the Indians' minds and imaginations as they confronted the intruders, we will never fathom why they acted as they did in different circumstances. The consequence of that ignorance will be to reduce them to inscrutable inhumanity, without feelings, ideas, or expectations. But we must avoid the lazy and unhelpful tactic of attributing their behavior to an indigenous brand of "ethnocentrism." As members of cultures, *all* people are ethnocentric. Our task is to discover the particular configuration of ideas and values that makes each culture distinctive.

We must be equally careful to speak of plural Indian perceptions and not to homogenize them prematurely into a stereotypical "Indian" response. The natives, no less than the Europeans, were divided by politics, gender, age, rank, and status. And they met Europeans at different times in different places under different circumstances. The perception of a young Iroquois girl whose first white person was a gentle missionary walking alone and unarmed into her village was obviously different from that of an older Micmac warrior who was greeted by cannon shot from the first sailing ship he ever saw.

Nevertheless, while it may no longer be permissible to speak of "the primitive mind," as previous generations of anthropologists were wont to do, the various Eastern Woodland groups who met the earliest waves of Europeans shared enough mental habits and conceptual modes to give their responses a striking degree of similarity. Undoubtedly, tribal reactions to the intruders differed, but largely as a result of specific and immediate socio-cultural circumstances rather than conceptual frameworks. So we are as justified in generalizing about a century of Eastern Woodland—"Indian"—views of intrusive Europeans as we are about "European" views of the New World and its inhabitants.

Yet our evidence for native views poses special challenges. Since the Indians of North America had no writing systems, they have left us virtually no first-hand accounts of their early perceptions of white men. But they did not fail to register their views for later historians. The first source is the descriptions of early European explorers and colonists, who witnessed—through their own distorting lenses—the Indians' behavior toward them, from which we can cautiously deduce certain attitudes and emotions. Second, these same Europeans and later ethnographers recorded native myths and stories about the Indians' first meetings with Europeans. Even when collected long after the event, oral traditions accurately convey cultural details and the emotional ambience of those initial encounters. Related to oral tradition are the first names given by the natives to the white men. The characteristics highlighted by these names are a valuable index to native images and values. Europeans also made an appearance in native art, where the material projects images as vividly as words do. And finally, the White Man appears in native humor, which reflects persistent attitudes and durable stereotypes.

Indians formed opinions about Europeans not only in North America but in Europe as well. From Columbus's first voyage onward, European explorers had a propensity for plucking human souvenirs from the beaches and riverbanks of the New World. A few were taken to the slave markets of Spain, others to the monasteries of France, some to audiences with heads of state, others to learn a language to enable them to serve as interpreters upon their return, all to satisfy the curiosity of the homebound and to be impressed in turn by the splendors of "civilization."[3] Those who survived the round trip had strong feelings about their experiences and their hosts or captors. These feelings they conveyed to their countrymen, and we are fortunate to be able to eavesdrop on a few of their frank relations.

Even before the first white men appeared they may have impressed themselves upon the Indian imagination. Shamans who were thought capable of seeing into the future and other prescient people may have prophesied the coming of the Europeans. I say "may have" because these prophecies were recorded only after contact with the newcomers. A Powhatan shaman in Virginia predicted that "bearded men should come & take away their Country & that there should none of the original Indians be left, within an hundred & fifty years."[4] During the lethal plague that preceded the arrival of the Plymouth pilgrims in 1620, a Nauset Indian on Cape Cod dreamed of the advent of "a great many men" dressed in what proved to be English-style clothes. One of them, dressed all in black, stood on an eminence with a book in his hand and told the assembled Indians that "God was _moosquantum_ or angry with them, and that he would kill them for their sinnes. . . ."[5]

More prevalent were oral traditions regarding the Europeans' arrival, a few collected shortly after contact, most of them several centuries later. In 1633 a young Montagnais related the story his grandmother had told him of the Indians' astonishment at seeing a French ship for the first time. Like many natives before and after, they thought it was a "moving Island." Having seen the men aboard, however, the Montagnais women began to prepare wigwams for them, "as is their custom when new guests arrive," and four canoes bade the strangers welcome. The French gave them a barrel of ship's biscuits and probably offered them some wine. But the natives were appalled that these people "drank blood and ate wood" and promptly threw the tasteless biscuits into the St. Lawrence. Obviously more impressed by French technology than cuisine, the Montagnais henceforth called the French *ouemichtigouchiou*, "men in a wooden canoe or boat."[6]

The Micmacs were equally unimpressed by French fare. When the first Frenchmen arrived in the Gaspé, the Micmacs "mistook the bread which was given them for a piece of birch tinder." When wine was proffered, the natives became convinced that the strangers were "cruel and inhuman, since in their amusements . . . they drank blood without repugnance. . . . Therefore they remained some time not only without tasting it, but even without wishing to become in any manner intimate, or to hold intercourse, with a nation which they believed to be accustomed to blood and carnage."[7]

Further west, an Ojibwa prophet dreamed that

> men of strange appearance have come across the great water. They have landed on our island [North America]. Their skins are white like snow, and on their faces long hair grows. These people have come across the great water in wonderfully large canoes which have great white wings like those of a giant bird. The man have long and sharp knives, and they have long black tubes which they point at birds and animals. The tubes make a smoke that rises into the air just like the smoke from our pipes. From them come fire and such terrific noise that I was frightened, even in my dream.

At once a flotilla of trusted men was sent through the Great Lakes and down the St. Lawrence to investigate. On the lower river they found a clearing in which all the trees had been cut down, which led them to conjecture that "giant beavers with huge, sharp teeth had done the cutting." The prophet disagreed, reminding them of the long knives in his dream. Knowing that their stone-headed axes could not cut such large trees as smoothly, the were "filled with awe, and with terror also." Still more puzzling were "long, rolled-up shavings" of wood and scraps of "bright-coloured cloth," which they stuck in their hair and wound around their heads. Further down the river they finally came upon the white-faced, bearded strangers with their astonishing long knives, thunder tubes, and giant winged canoes, just as the prophet had predicted.

Having satisfied their curiosity and fulfilled the prophet's dream, the Indians returned home with their trophies; each villager was given a small piece of cloth as a memento. To impress their neighbors, the Ojibwas followed an old custom. Just as they tied the scalps of their enemies on long poles, "now they fastened the splinters of wood and strips of calico to poles and sent them with special messengers" from one tribe to another. Thus were these strange articles passed from hand to hand around the whole lake, giving the natives of the interior their first knowledge of the white men from Europe.[8]

The Indians regarded the Europeans' ability to fashion incredible objects and make them work less as mechanical aptitude than as spiritual power. When the Delawares, who once lived along the New Jersey-New York coast, met their first Dutch ship, they concluded that it was a "remarkably large house in which the Mannitto (the Great or Supreme Being) himself was present." Thinking he was coming to pay them a visit, they prepared meat for a sacrifice, put all their religious effigies in order, and staged a grand dance to please or appease him. Meanwhile, the tribal conjurers tried to fathom his purpose in coming because their brethren were all "distracted between hope and fear." While preparations were being made, runners brought the welcome news that the visitors were humans like themselves, only strangely colored and oddly dressed. But when the Dutchmen made their appearance, graced the assembly with a round of liquor, and distributed iron and cloth gifts, the natives were confirmed in their original belief that every white man was an "inferior Mannitto attendant upon the Supreme Deity"—the ship's captain—who "shone superior" in his red velvet suit glittering with gold lace.[9]

The earliest French and English explorers who were the objects of native awe corroborated native testimony, despite some suggestion that the Indians were struck most forcefully by other European characteristics. Some Indians appeared to be fascinated by the whiteness of European skin. On Arthur Barlowe's reconnaissance of Roanoke Island in 1584, the natives "wondred mervelously when we were amongest them, at the whitenes of our skinnes, every conveting to touch our breastes, and to view the same."[10] Sixty years earlier, one of Verrazzano's sailors was nearly drowned trying to swim with some small gifts to a group of Indians on the same Outer Banks. Before returning him safely to the ship, the natives "placed him on the ground in the sun . . . and made gestures of great admiration, looking at the whiteness of his flesh and examining him from head to foot."[11]

The close examination the Indians occasionally gave the explorers' chests, faces, and arms, however, may have been focused on the skin's hairiness rather than its pallor. Mariners, after all, were likely to be deeply suntanned after a spring or summer cruise of several weeks. Most Indians, by contrast, were relatively hairless, and the little they grew was assiduously plucked or singed. Understandably, European beards and tufted chests held an ugly fascination for them. Before they laid eyes on a white man, the Potawatomis and Menominees around Green Bay believed the French to be a "different species from other men" because they were "covered with hair," not because their skin was a shade or two lighter.[12] By the same token, the caresses Jacques Cartier received from Algonquians on the Gaspé in 1534 were given less because he was white-skinned than to thank him for the presents he had just given. By the time he reached the Iroquoian village of Hochelaga on Montreal Island the following year, he had learned that "rubbing . . . with their hands" was a traditional native greeting, not one reserved for white visitors.[13]

The first Europeans, however, were no ordinary guests, and their friendly reception owed much to the native belief that they were spiritually powerful men, gods (as the Europeans put it) or *manitous* (in Algonquian parlance) like the Indians' own shamans and conjurers. The sources of their power were chiefly two. The first was their reputation among the Indians as purveyors or preventers of disease, exactly comparable to native shamans, who were also thought to wield powers of life and death. Jacques Cartier was asked to lay hands on all the sick and handicapped of Hochelaga as if, he said, "Christ had come down to earth to heal them." In 1665 a Jesuit priest found himself held in similar regard to the natives of Michigan and Wisconsin. When he advised a Fox man to have his dangerously ill parents bled, the man poured powdered tobacco over the priest's gown and said, "Thou art a spirit; come now, restore these sick people to health; I offer thee this tobacco in sacrifice."[14] The priest at least came off better than the first French captain who sailed to the Menominees on Lake Michigan: he had tobacco ground into his forehead.[15]

At the same time, the Indians believed that all spiritual power was double-edged: those who could cure could also kill. Only powerful "spirits" possessed the ability to bewitch or to counteract another's witchcraft. When they inadvertently carried deadly European diseases into the North Carolina coastal region, the English colonists at Roanoke were deified by their hosts for their ability to kill Indians at a distance and to remain unscathed themselves. "There could at no time happen any strange sicknesse, losses, hurtes, or any other cross unto [the natives]," wrote Thomas Harriot, the expedition's Indian expert, "but that they would impute to us the cause or meanes thereof for offending or not pleasing us." The Indians had extra cause to worry when four or five towns that had practiced some "subtle devise" against the English were ravaged by an unknown disease shortly after the colonists' departure. The English allies under chief Wingina deduced that the havoc was wrought by "our God through our meanes, and that wee by him might kil and slaie whom wee would without weapons and not come neere them. . . . This marvelous accident in all the countrie," explained Harriot, "wrought so strange opinions of us, that some people could not tel whether to thinke us gods or men," particularly when no Englishman died or was even especially sick.[16]

The second and more important source of the white man's power in native America was his technological superiority. The Indian's acquaintance with it began well before 1524, when Verrazzano cruised the eastern waters from the Carolinas to Maine. On an "Arcadian" coast somewhere south of New York harbor, a handsome, naked Indian man approached a group of the French sailors and showed them a burning stick, "as if to offer us fire." But when the Europeans trumped his hospitality by firing a matchlock, "he trembled all over with fear" and "remained as if thunderstruck, and prayed, worshiping like a monk, pointing his finger to the sky; and indicating the sea and the ship, he appeared to bless us."[17]

Not without reason, European iron weapons continued to impress the natives who saw them in action for the first time. When Pierre Radisson and Nicolas Perrot travelled among the Indians of Wisconsin in the middle years of the seventeenth century, the natives literally worshipped their guns, knives, and hatchets by blowing sacred smoke over them, as a sacrifice to the spirits within. To Perrot the Potawatomi elders said, "Thou art one of the chief spirits, since thou usest iron; it is for thee to rule and protect all men. Praised be the Sun, who has instructed thee and sent thee to our country."[18]

Weapons were of paramount importance to the feuding native polities of North America, but metal objects of any kind, cloth goods, and cleverly designed or sizable wooden objects also drew their admiration. Thomas Harriot put his finger on the primary cause of the Indians' initially exalted opinion of the white strangers when he noted that

> most things they sawe with us, as Mathematicall instruments, sea compasses, the vertue of the loadstone in drawing iron, a perspective glasse whereby was shewed manie strange sightes, burning glasses, wildefire woorkes, gunnes, bookes, writing and reading, spring clocks that seeme to goe of themselves, and manie other things that wee had, were so straunge unto them, and so farre exceeded their capacities to comprehend the reason and meanes how they should be made and done, that they thought they were rather the works of gods than of men, or at the leastwise they had bin given and taught us of the gods.[19]

The Sioux, Illinois, and Seneca Indians among whom the Recollect priest Louis Hennepin journeyed during the early 1680s frequently clapped their hands over their mouths in astonishment at such things as printed books, silver chalices, embroidered chasubles, and iron pots, all of which they designated as "spirits."[20] In the 1630s the natives of southern New England considered a windmill "little less than the world's wonder" for the whisking motion of its long arms and its "sharp teeth biting the corn," and the first plowman "little better than a juggler" or shaman. Being shown the iron coulter and share of the plow, which could "tear up more ground in a day than their clamshells [hoes] could scrape up in a month," they told the plowman "he was almost Abamacho, almost as cunning as the Devil."[21]

The white man's varied powers were celebrated in the generic names given to him by different native groups. The Narragansetts of Rhode Island called all Europeans "Coatmen" or "swordmen." The Mohawks of New York referred to the Dutch as "Iron-workers" or "Cloth makers," while the Hurons called the French *Agnonha*, "Iron People." In northern New England the Pocumtucks knew the French as "Knife men," just as the Virginians and later all Americans were known as "Longknives." The long-robed Recollect missionaries obviously made less impression on the Montagnais, who referred to them as "Those dressed like women." Their evangelical rivals, the Jesuits, were known less derisively as "Black Robes," and by the Hurons as "The men called charcoal."[22]

Native characterizations of Europeans also received material expression in Indian artifacts, particularly effigy combs and pipes and wampum belts. Probably in the seventeenth century, the Iroquois made a belt to mark the sight of the first "pale faces." (Samuel Champlain and two consorts clashed with a war party of Mohawks on Lake Champlain in 1609, but they were probably not the Europeans commemorated.) Unlike several eighteenth-century belts, it does not feature European figures. Rather it consists of four groups of three purple-beaded, diagonal lines, indicating props or supports of the Longhouse, the symbol of the League of Five Nations. The tradition that has come down with the belt suggests that either the Dutch or the English pledged military support to the Iroquois against their enemies, and perhaps vice versa.[23]

Throughout the colonial period, most belts employed geometrical shapes as a cultural vocabulary of mnemonics—diamonds, squares, and pentagons as tribes or nations, diagonals as agreements and mutual aid pacts, long lines as paths or messages. But by the eighteenth century the colonists were occasionally pictured as recognizably human figures. Missionaries invariably held or stood near crosses, but most Europeans wore frock coats and tall, wide-brimmed hats. A few of the purple-beaded newcomers were distinguished from their Indian companions on the belts by their white hearts.[24]

The Senecas of western New York fixed the image of the white man (never woman) when they carved delicate antler combs and molded clay pipes. The first European to make his appearance on a Seneca comb was probably a Dutchman, who was carved in frock coat and hat at the Steele site, where one village of Senecas lived between 1625 and 1645. Most of the trade goods reaching the Senecas at this time came from Dutch traders at Fort Orange on the Hudson. On a site occupied about thirty years later, the natives had begun to sculpt men in Dutch-style hats on pipes, carve mounted Europeans on antler combs, and cast lead in the shape of behatted Dutchmen. At the nearly contemporaneous Boughton Hill site, Europeans on horseback were favorite features on antler combs. Standing or mounted, most white men by then held long guns at their side, symbolizing their technological superiority as well as their potential threat to native sovereignty.[25]

The threats to native land and liberty came from many different directions. The white-hearted or guileful white man on wampum belts had analogues in Indian humor. Most of these stories are found in colonial or early national collections of American folk anecdotes, so they may not reflect only Indian sources of humor. But they do emanate from a double source, "the play of Yankee humor on racial mingling, and the Indian's own sense of wit and shrewdness."[26] Even when the morphology of the tales resembles European precedents, they accurately convey Indian attitudes toward the intruders in their midst.

One such story describes how the early colonists asked their generous native hosts for a small parcel of land upon which to settle, the size merely of a cow's hide. Having seen a cow on board the settlers' ship, the Indians readily agreed. As soon as the bargain was concluded, however, the settlers

ed a bull, their largest, cut the skin into a thin continuous strip, and mea-
red out a huge piece of ground. In other versions the seat of a chair was
caned for the same nefarious purpose.[27]

Another anecdote about sharp dealing featured a white trader who sold
Indian a packet of gunpowder, telling him that it contained the seeds of
ine, wheatlike grain. The gullible Indian planted and tended his new
eds" carefully, but with no results. Some time later the trader demanded
the Indian the settlement of an overdue account, to which the Indian
lied, "Me pay you when my powder grow."[28] That this kind of story
ce had a real grain of truth makes it no less effective. In 1622, after
echancanough's warriors killed 347 Virginia colonists in a sudden upris-
ng and confiscated many arms and ammunition, he ordered most of the
gunpowder planted in expectation that he could "draw therefrom the like
increase, as of his Maize or Corne, in Harvest next."[29]

As the natives increasingly were forced to conform to colonial expectations and institutions, they must have taken pleasure in the telling of anecdotes in which they outwitted white authorities. When one New England
Indian was hailed before a justice of the peace for trespass and sabbath-
breaking, he demanded a receipt for the fine he paid. The justice was somewhat surprised by the request but agreed to furnish the receipt if the culprit
could show his need for it. The Indian explained in his humblest manner:

> 'Tis best to have things sure; for perhaps, by and by, you die; an
> Indian being a little tougher, perhaps, I live a little longer; then I
> die, and go up to God's house and knock. "Ah! who comes there?"
> I must tell, it won't do to tell lies dere. "Well, have you settled for
> cutting the tree on the sabbath day?" Yes, sir. "Where is your
> receipt?" I haven't any.—Then I must go away, along down from
> God's house, to HELL, to get a receipt of you, sir; but if you will
> give me one now, sir, it will save me all dat trouble.[30]

The Indians got an eyeful of European behavior in North America, but
many colonial officials felt that the colonists who interacted with the natives
most frequently were not outstanding models of Western "civilization." So
from time to time they shipped carefully selected natives off to Europe to
view the white man at his best, with the expectation that upon their return
they would spread the gospel of European superiority throughout their
native villages. Among the earliest Indian tourists were three Tupinambas,
who were taken from their native Brazil to Rouen in 1562. Although they
were South Americans, their responses to Europe were remarkably similar
to those of their northern brethren who followed. After talking with King
Charles IX, the twelve-year-old monarch, someone asked them what they
found most amazing about *la belle France*. Their first observation was "they
thought it very strange that so many grown men, bearded, strong, and
armed, who were around the king [his Swiss guard] should submit to obey
a child, and that one of them was not chosen to command instead." And
second, "they had noticed that there were among us men full and gorged
with all sorts of good things, and that their other halves were beggars at
their doors, emaciated with hunger and poverty; and they thought it

strange that these needy halves could endure such an injustice, and did not take the others by the throat, or set fire to their houses."[31]

A half-century later, Savignon, an eighteen-year-old Huron lad, made a similar trip to France with Champlain and had much the same reaction as did his Tupi predecessors. When he returned to Canada in 1611, he was deemed a liar by his tribesmen when he tried to describe the marvels he had seen, such as a "coach drawn by six or eight horses" and "a striking clock." Savignon "well remembered the good cheer he had enjoyed in France," particularly his presentation at the court of Louis XIII, and "boasted of it everywhere." Yet "he never had the wish to return" because of the social institutions and behavior he had seen. "Often when he saw two men quarrelling without coming to blows or killing one another, [he] would mock at them, saying that they were nought but women, and had no courage." He and his tribesmen deplored "the great number of needy and beggars" in France, attributing it to lack of charity, and blamed the French clergy, "saying that if [they] had some intelligence [they] would set some order in the matter, the remedies being simple." Even more alarming to Huron sensibilities was Savignon's report that "among the French, men were whipped, hanged and put to death without distinction of innocence or guilt." This persuaded the Hurons not to send their children to Quebec for schooling at the hands of the Recollects.[32]

Another visitor used some of his time in England to dispel one of his countrymen's dominant myths about the colonists. Uttamatomakkin, one of Powhatan's trusted councillors who accompanied Pocahontas to England in 1616, was amazed "at the sight of so much corn and trees in his journey from Plymouth to London." He, like many Indians, imagined that the dearth of these vital articles had brought the English to America.[33] When the Narragansetts asked Roger Williams why the English came to their country, they answered themselves, saying "It is because you want *firing*: for they," Williams explained, "having burnt up the *wood* in one place . . . are faine to follow the wood; and so to remove to a fresh new place for the woods sake."[34]

While the Indians were constantly making dismaying discoveries about the intruders, the Europeans were no less busy trying to lay open the secret springs of native behaviour and culture. One of the rudest revelations the Europeans had was that the Indians—allegedly savage, poor, and un-lettered—had a terrific superiority complex, not only at first contact but long after. When the French landed in Acadia in 1610, they were astounded to discover that the local Micmacs thought themselves "better, more valiant and more ingenious" than the French, and even "richer." After eighty years of contact with the French, and even "richer." After eighty years of contact with the French, the Micmacs had not changed their opinion. "There is no Indian," said a Micmac chief, "who does not consider himself infinitely more happy and more powerful than the French."[35] A New England sagamore, dressed in his finery with "six naked Indian spatterlashes at his heels for his guard," wrote one early observer, "thinks himself little inferior to the great Cham. He will not stick to say he is all one with King Charles.

He thinks he can blow down castles with his breath and conquer kingdoms with his conceit."[36] The Iroquois were no different. According to an eighteenth-century Englishman who know them well, "they seem always to have Lookd upon themselves as far Superiour to the rest of Mankind and accordingly Call themselves *Ongwehoenwe*, i.e. Men Surpassing all other men."[37]

Although the natives were quick to acknowledge the superiority of certain items of European technology, particularly metal implements and woven cloth, they were most reluctant to praise the life that the white men made from them. They simply preferred their own. To give but one example, the Micmacs could not understand the French fetish for large, permanent houses. Why, they asked, "do men of five to six feet in height need houses which are sixty to eighty?" They much preferred the sensibleness of Indians "who carry their houses and their wigwams with them so that they may lodge wheresoever they please, independently of any seignior whatsoever." They were infinitely happier than the grasping strangers, they said, because "we are very content with the little we have."[38]

After considerable travel among the Indians of North Carolina, John Lawson knew it to be true. "There is one Vice very common every where, which I never found amongst them," he noted in 1709, "which is Envying other Mens Happiness. . . . Of this Sin I cannot say I ever saw an Example, though they are a People that set as great a Value upon themselves, as any sort of Men in the World." Because the Indians of North America valued "natural Vertues and Gifts" rather than material possessions, they did not envy the white men with their insatiable appetites for land, wealth, and power. Because, as Montaigne observed, "each man calls barbarism whatever is not his own practice," they clung to their own ways as long as possible, finding comfort as well as efficiency in the familiar.[39]

The mystery we should like to solve is how, in the face of inexplicable and uncontrollable diseases, admitted technological inferiority, demographic inundation, loss of land and power, and aggressive religious and cultural proselytizing, the Indians managed to sustain their magnificent, if disconcerting, self-regard. If we could solve that, we would possess the key to understanding the depth and range of their early feelings and attitudes toward the European intruders.

NOTES

1. James Axtell, "Bronze Men and Golden Ages: The Intellectual History of Indian-White Relations in Colonial America," *Journal of Interdisciplinary History* 12 (1982): 663–75.

2. David Hackett Fischer, *Historians' Fallacies: Toward a Logic of Historical*
Thought (New York, 1970), 195–200. Fischer calls it the "idealist fallacy."

3. James Axtell, *The Invasion Within: The Contest of Cultures in Colonial North America* (New York, 1985), 24, 27, 55–56; Olive Patricia Dickason, *The Myth of the Savage and the Beginnings of French Colonialism in*

28 JAMES AXTELL

the Americas (Edmonton, 1984), ch. 10; above ch. 9, 148–52.

4. Edmund Berkeley and Dorothy Smith Berkeley, eds., *The Reverend John Clayton: ... His Scientific Writings and Other Related Papers* (Charlottesville, 1965), 39, Clayton to Dr Nehemiah Grew, 1687.

5. William S. Simmons, *Spirit of the New England Tribes: Indian History and Folklore, 1620–1994* (Hanover, NH, 1986), 66–67, 71.

6. Reuben Gold Thwaites, ed., *The Jesuit Relations and Allied Documents* (Cleveland, 1896–1901), 5:119–21 (hereafter cited as *JR*); Father Gabriel Sagard, *The Long Journey to the Country of the Hurons* [Paris, 1632], ed. George M. Wrong, trans. H.H. Langton (Toronto: Champlain Society, 1939), 79.

7. Father Chrestien Le Clercq, *New Relation of Gaspesia* [Paris, 1691], ed. and trans. William F. Ganong (Toronto: Champlain Society, 1910), 109.

8. Ella Elizabeth Clark, ed., *Indian Legends of Canada* (Toronto, 1960), 150–51. This story was told by a member of the Bear clan in 1855.

9. John Heckewelder, *History, Manners, and Customs of the Indian Nations Who Once Inhabited Pennsylvania and the Neighbouring States* [1818], ed. William G. Reichel (Philadelphia, 1876), 71–75. Heckewelder received this story from an intelligent Delaware man at the end of the eighteenth century.

10. David Beers Quinn, ed., *The Roanoke Voyages, 1584–1590*, Hakluyt Society Publications, 2d ser. 104–5 (London, 1955), 111–12 (continuous pagination).

11. Lawrence G. Wroth, *The Voyages of Giovanni da Verrazzano* (New Haven, 1970), 135.

12. Emma Helen Blair, ed. and trans., *The Indian Tribes of the Upper Mississippi Valley and Region of the Great Lakes*, (Cleveland, 1911), 1:309.

13. H.P. Biggar, ed., *The Voyages of Jacques Cartier*, Publications of the

Public Archives of Canada 11 (Ottawa, 1924), 56, 62, 162–63.

14. Ibid., 165; Louis Phelps Kellogg, ed., *Early Narratives of the Northwest, 1634–1699*, Original Narratives of Early American History (New York, 1917), 129, 155–56.

15. Walter James Hoffman, "The Menomini Indians," Bureau of American Ethnology, *14th Annual Report* (Washington, DC, 1896), pt. 1: 214–16 at 215.

16. Quinn, *Roanoke Voyages*, 378–79.

17. Wroth, *Voyages of Verrazzano*, 137.

18. Blair, *Indian Tribes of the Upper Mississippi*, 1:308–9; Kellogg, *Early Narratives of the Northwest*, 45–46.

19. Quinn, *Roanoke Voyages*, 375–76.

20. *Father Louis Hennepin's Description of Louisiana* [Paris, 1683], trans. Marion E. Cross (Minneapolis, 1938), 82, 96, 98, 105, 108–9, 130.

21. William Wood, *New England's Prospect* [London, 1634], ed. Alden T. Vaughan (Amherst, MA, 1977), 96.

22. Roger Williams, *A Key into the Language of America* (London, 1643), 59; Bruce G. Trigger, *The Children of Aataentsic: A History of the Huron People to 1660*, 2 vols. (Montreal, 1976), 307, 360, 617–18 (continuous pagination); Gordon M. Day, *The Mots loups of Father Mathevet*, National Museum of Man, Publications in Ethnology 9 (Ottawa, 1975), 353 n. 424; Arthur Woodward, "The 'Long Knives,'" *Indian Notes* [Heye Foundation], 5, 1 (Jan. 1928): 64–79; Gabriel Sagard-Théodat, *Histoire du Canada* (Paris, 1636), 465; Axtell, *The Invasion Within*, 109.

23. Noah T. Clarke, "The Wampum Belt Collection of the New York State Museum," 24th Report of the Director of the Division of Sciences and the State Museum, *New York State Museum Bulletin* 288 (Albany, NY, 1931), 85–121 at 90, 109.

24. Ibid., 108, 109; Tehanetorens, *Wampum Belts* (Onchiota, NY: Six Nations Indian Museum, n.d.), 61, 62, 66.

25. Rochester Museum and Science Center, Rochester, NY, collections from the Steele, Dann, and Boughton Hill sites; "Excavations on Boughton Hill," 16th Report of the Director . . . 1919, *NY St. Mus. Bull.*, 227–28 (Albany, NY, 1921), 11–13 and plates.

26. Richard M. Dorson, "Comic Indian Anecdotes," *Southern Folklore Quarterly* 10 (1946): 113–28 at 113.

27. Ibid., 121.

28. Ibid., 123.

29. Susan Myra Kingsbury, ed., *The Records of the Virginia Company of London* (Washington, DC, 1906–35), 3:556.

30. Dorson, "Comic Indian Anecdotes," 124.

31. Donald M. Frame, trans., *The Complete Works of Montaigne* (Stanford, 1948), 159.

32. Sagard, *Histoire du Canada*, 241–42, 275–76, 291; Marc Lescarbot, *The History of New France* [Paris, 1609],

trans. W.L. Grant, intro. H.P. Biggar, (Toronto: Champlain Society, 1907–14), 3:22.

33. Samuel Purchas, *Hakluytus Posthumus, or Purchas His Pilgrimes* (Glasgow, 1905–07), 19:118–19.

34. Williams, *Key into the Language*, 59–60.

35. *JR*, 1:173–77; Le Clercq, *New Relations of Gaspesia*, 106.

36. Wood, *New England's Prospect*, 85.

37. The Letters and Papers of Cadwallader Colden, 8, *Collections of the New-York Historical Society* (New York, 1937), 67:279, Rev. Henry Barclay to Colden, 7 Dec. 1741.

38. Le Clercq, *New Relation of Gaspesia*, 103–4.

39. John Lawson, *A New Voyage to Carolina* [London, 1709], ed. Hugh Talmage Lefler (Chapel Hill, 1967), 206; Frame, *Complete Works of Montaigne*, 152.

THE EUROPEAN IMPACT ON THE CULTURE OF A NORTHEASTERN ALGONQUIAN TRIBE: AN ECOLOGICAL INTERPRETATION ⬦

CALVIN MARTIN

○

As the drive for furs, known prosaically as the fur trade, expanded and became more intense in seventeenth-century Canada, complaints of beaver extermination became more frequent and alarming. By 1635, for example, the Huron had reduced their stock of beaver to the point where the Jesuit Father Paul Le Jeune could declare that they had none.[1] In 1684 Baron Lahontan recorded a speech made before the French governor-general by an Iroquois spokesman, who explained that his people had made war on the Illinois and Miami because these Algonquians had trespassed on Iroquois territory and overkilled their beaver, "and contrary to the Custom of all the Savages, have carried off whole Stocks both Male and Female."[2] This exploitation of beaver and other furbearers seems to have been most intense in the vicinity of major trading posts and among the native tribes most affected by the trade (the Montagnais Huron, League Iroquois, Micmac, and others[3]), while those tribes which remained beyond European influence and the trade, such as the Bersimis of northeastern Quebec, enjoyed an abundance of beaver in their territories.[4]

Even before the establishment of trading posts, the Micmac of the extreme eastern tip of Canada were engaged in lively trade with European fishermen. Thus areas that were important in the fishing industry, such as Prince Edward Island, the Gaspé Peninsula, and Cape Breton Island, were cleaned out of moose and other furbearers by the mid-seventeenth century.[5]

⬦ *William and Mary Quarterly*, 3d ser., 31 (1974): 3–26. Reprinted with permission from the author. The author would like to thank Professors Wilbur R. Jacobs, Roderick Nash, and Albert C. Spaulding for their helpful comments and criticisms of this article.

Reviewing this grim situation, Nicolas Denys observed that game was less abundant in his time than formerly; as for the beaver, "few in a house are saved; they [the Micmac] would take all. The disposition of the Indians is not to spare the little ones any more than the big ones. They killed all of each kind of animal that there was when they could capture it."[6]

In short the game which by all accounts had been so plentiful was now being systematically overkilled by the Indians themselves. A traditional explanation for this ecological catastrophe is neatly summarized by Peter Farb, who conceives of it in mechanistic terms:

> If the Northeastern Athabaskan and Northern Algonkian Indians husbanded the land and its wildlife in primeval times, it was only because they lacked both the technology to kill very many animals and the market for so many furs. But once white traders entered the picture, supplying the Indians with efficient guns and an apparently limitless market for furs beyond the seas, the Indians went on an orgy of destruction.

The Indian, in other words, was "economically seduced" to exploit the wildlife requisite to the fur trade.[7]

Such a cavalier dismissal of northeastern Algonquian culture, especially its spiritual component, renders this explanation superficial and inadequate. One can argue that economic determinism was crucial to the course of Algonquian cultural development (including religious perception) over a long period of time. Yet from this perspective European contact was but a moment in the cultural history of the Indians, and it is difficult to imagine that ideals and a life-style that had taken centuries to evolve would have been so easily and quickly discarded merely for the sake of improved technological convenience. As we shall see, the entire Indian-land relationship was suffused with religious considerations which profoundly influenced the economic (subsistence) activities and beliefs of these people. The subsistence cycle was regulated by centuries of spiritual tradition which, if it had been in a healthy state, would have countered the revolutionizing impact of European influence. Tradition would doubtless have succumbed eventually, but why did the end come so soon? Why did the traditional safeguards of the northeastern Algonquian economic system offer such weak resistance to its replacement by the exploitive European-induced regime?

When the problem is posed in these more comprehensive terms, the usual economic explanation seems misdirected, for which reason the present article will seek to offer an alternative interpretation. The methodology of cultural ecology will be brought to bear on the protohistoric and early contact phases of Micmac cultural history in order to examine the Indian-land relationship under aboriginal and postcontact conditions and to probe for an explanation to the problem of wildlife overkill.[8]

Cultural ecology seeks to explain the interaction of environment and culture, taking the ecosystem and the local human population as the basic units of analysis.[9] An ecosystem is a discrete community of plants and animals, together with the nonliving environment, occupying a certain space and time, having a flow-through of energy and raw materials in its operation, and composed of subsystems.[10] For convenience of analysis, an ecosystem can be separated into its physical and biological components, although one should bear in mind that in nature the two are completely intermeshed in complex interactions. And from the standpoint of cultural ecology, there is a third component: the metaphysical or spiritual.

The ecosystem model of plant and animal ecologists is somewhat strained when applied to a human population, although, as Roy A. Rappaport has demonstrated in his *Pigs for the Ancestors*, the attempt can be very useful.[11] The difficulties encountered include the assignment of definite territorial limits to the area under consideration (resulting in a fairly arbitrary delimitation of an ecosystem), the quantification of the system's energy budget and the carrying capacity of the land, and the identification of subsystem interrelations. Assigning values to variables becomes, in many instances, quite impossible.

The transposition of the ecosystem approach from cultural anthropology to historical inquiry complicates these problems even further, for the relationships between a human population and its environment are seldom amenable to rigorous quantitative analysis using historical documents as sources. Yet this is certainly not always so. In the case of the fur trade, for example, one may in fact be able to measure some of its effects on the environment from merchants' records—showing numbers of pelts obtained from a region over a certain time period—and also from lists of goods given to the Indians at trading posts and by treaties. Even when available, such records are too incomplete to satisfy the rigorous demands of the ecologists, but to say that they are of limited value is not to say that they are useless.

Few historians have used the ecological model in their work.[12] Recognizing the need for the environmental perspective in historiography, Wilbur R. Jacobs recently observed that

> those who hope to write about such significant historical events [as the despoiling of the American west] . . . will need a sort of knowledge not ordinarily possessed by historians. To study the impact of the fur trade upon America and her native people, for instance, there must be more than a beginning acquaintance with ethnology, plant and animal ecology, paleoecology, and indeed much of the physical sciences.[13]

In the case of the northeastern Algonquian, and the Micmac in particular, the fur trade was but one factor—albeit an important one—in the process of acculturation. Long before they felt the lure of European technology, these littoral Indians must have been infected with Old World diseases carried by European fishermen, with catastrophic effects. Later, the Christian missionaries exerted a disintegrative influence on the Indians' view of and relation to their environment. All three of these factors—disease, Christianity, and technology—which may be labeled "trigger" factors, must be assessed in terms of their impact on the Indians' ecosystem.[14]

Among the first North American Indians to be encountered by Europeans were the Micmacs who occupied present-day Nova Scotia, northern New Brunswick and the Gaspé Peninsula, Prince Edward Island, and Cape Breton Island. According to the Sieur de Dièreville, they also lived along the lower St. John River with the Malecites, who outnumbered them.[15] For our present purposes, the Micmac territory will be considered an ecosystem, and the Micmac occupying it will be regarded as a local population. These designations are not entirely arbitrary, for the Micmac occupied and exploited the area in a systematic way; they had a certain psychological unity or similarity in their ideas about the cosmos; they spoke a language distinct from those of their neighbors; and they generally married within their own population. There were, as might be expected, many external factors impinging on the ecosystem which should also be evaluated, although space permits them only to be mentioned here. Some of these "supralocal" relations involved trade and hostilities with other tribes; the exchange of genetic material and personnel with neighboring tribes through intermarriage and adoption; the exchange of folklore and customs; and the movements of such migratory game as moose and woodland caribou. The Micmac ecosystem thus participated in a regional system, and the Micmac population was part of a regional population.[16]

The hunting, gathering, and fishing Micmac who lived within this Acadian forest, especially along its rivers and by the sea, were omnivores (so to speak) in the trophic system of the community. At the first trophic level, the plants eaten were wild potato tubers, wild fruits and berries, acorns and nuts and the like. Trees and shrubs provided a wealth of materials used in the fashioning of tools, utensils and other equipment.[17] At the time of contact, none of the Indians living north of the Saco River cultivated food crops. Although legend credits the Micmac with having grown maize and tobacco "for the space of several years,"[18] these cultigens, as well as beans, pumpkins, and wampum (which they greatly prized), were obtained from the New England Algonquians of the Saco River area (Abnakis) and perhaps from other tribes to the south.[19]

Herbivores and carnivores occupy the second and third trophic levels respectively, with top carnivores in the fourth level. The Micmac hunter tapped all three levels in his seasonal hunting and fishing activities, and these sources of food were "to them like fixed rations assigned to every moon."[20] In January, seals were hunted when they bred on islands off the coast; the fat was reduced to oil for food and body grease, and the women made clothing from the fur.[21] The principal hunting season lasted from February till mid-March, since there were enough marine resources, especially fish and mollusks, available during the other three seasons to satisfy most of the Micmac's dietary needs. For a month and a half, then, the Indians withdrew from the seashore to the banks of rivers and lakes and into the woods to hunt the caribou, moose, black bear, and small furbearers. At no other time of the year were they so dependent on the caprice of the weather: a feast was as likely as a famine. A heavy rain could ruin the beaver and caribou hunt, and a deep, crustless snow would doom the moose hunt.[22]

Since beaver were easier to hunt on the ice than in the water, and since their fur was better during the winter, this was the chief season for taking them.[23] Hunters would work in teams or groups, demolishing the lodge or cutting the dam with stone axes. Dogs were sometimes used to track the beaver which took refuge in air pockets along the edge of the pond, or the beaver might be harpooned at air holes. In the summer hunt, beaver were shot with the bow or trapped in deadfalls using poplar as bait, but the commonest way to take them was to cut the dam in the middle and drain the pond, killing the animals with bows and spears.[24]

Next to fish, moose was the most important item in the Micmac diet, and it was their staple during the winter months when these large mammals were hunted with dogs on the hard-crusted snow. In the summer and spring, moose were tracked, stalked and shot with the bow; in the fall, during the rutting season, the bull was enticed by a clever imitation of the sound of a female urinating. Another technique was to ensnare the animal with a noose.[25]

Moose was the Micmacs' favorite meat. The entrails, which were considered a great delicacy, and the "most delicious fat" were carried by the triumphant hunter to the campsite, and the women were sent after the carcass. The mistress of the wigwam decided what was to be done with each portion of the body, every part of which was used. Grease was boiled out of the bones and either drunk pure (with "much gusto") or stored as loaves of moose-butter;[26] the leg and thigh bones were crushed and the marrow eaten; the hides were used for robes, leggings, moccasins, and tent coverings;[27] tools, ornaments, and game pieces were made from antlers, teeth and toe bones, respectively.[28] According to contemporary French observers, the Micmac usually consumed the moose meat immediately, without storing any, although the fact that some of the meat was preserved rather effectively by smoking it on racks, so that it would even last the year, demonstrates that Micmac existence was not as hand-to-mouth as is commonly believed of the northeastern Algonquian.[29] Black bear were also taken during the season from February till mid-March, but such hunting was merely coincidental. If a hunter stumbled upon a hibernating bear, he could count himself lucky.[30]

As the lean months of winter passed into the abundance of spring, the fish began to spawn, swimming up rivers and streams in such numbers that "everything swarms with them."[31] In mid-March came the smelt, and at the end of April the herring. Soon there were sturgeon and salmon, and numerous waterfowl made nests out on the islands—which meant there were eggs to be gathered. Mute evidence from seashore middens and early written testimony reveal that these Indians also relied heavily on various mollusks, which they harvested in great quantity.[32] Fish was a staple for the Micmac, who knew the spawning habits of each type of fish and where it was to be found. Weirs were erected across streams to trap the fish on their way downstream on a falling tide, while larger fish, such as sturgeon and salmon, might be speared or trapped.[33]

The salmon run marked the beginning of summer, when the wild geese shed their plumage. Most wildfowl were hunted at their island rookeries; waterfowl were often hunted by canoe and struck down as they took to flight; others, such as the Canadian geese which grazed in the meadows, were shot with the bow.[34]

In autumn, when the waterfowl migrated southward, the eels spawned up the many small rivers along the coast. From mid-September to October the Micmac left the ocean and followed the eels, "of which they lay in a supply; they are good and fat." Caribou and beaver were hunted during October and November, and with December came the "tom cod" (which were said to have spawned under the ice) and turtles bearing their young.[35] In January the subsistence cycle began again with the seal hunt.

As he surveyed the seasonal cycle of these Indians, Father Pierre Biard was impressed by nature's bounty and Micmac resourcefulness "These then, but in a still greater number, are the revenues and incomes of our Savages; such, their table and living, all prepared and assigned, everything to its proper place and quarter."[36] Although we have omitted mention of many other types of forest, marine and aquatic life which were also exploited by the Micmac, those listed above were certainly the most significant in the Micmacs' food quest and ecosystem.[37]

Frank G. Speck, perhaps the foremost student of northeastern Algonquian culture, has emphasized that hunting to the Micmacs was not a "war upon the animals, not a slaughter for food or profit."[38] Denys's observations confirm Speck's point: "Their greatest task was to feed well and to go a-hunting. They did not lack animals, which they killed only in proportion as they had need of them."[39] From this, and the above description of their effective hunting techniques, it would appear that the Micmac were not limited by their hunting technology in the taking of game. As Denys pointed out,

> the hunting by the Indians in old times was easy for them. . . . When they were tired of eating one sort, they killed some of another. If they did not wish longer to eat meat, they caught some fish. They never made an accumulation of skins of Moose, Beaver, Otter, or others, but only so far as they needed them for personal use. They left the remainder [of the carcass] where the animals had been killed, not taking the trouble to bring them to their camps.[40]

Need, not technology, was the ruling factor, and need was determined by the great primal necessities of life and regulated by spiritual considerations. Hunting, as Speck remarks, was "a *holy occupation*";[41] it was conducted and controlled by spiritual rules.

The bond which united these physical and biological components of the Micmac ecosystem, and indeed gave them definition and comprehensibility, was the world view of the Indian. The foregoing discussion has dealt mainly with the empirical, objective, physical ("operational") environmental model of the observer; what it lacks is the "cognized" model of the Micmac.[42]

Anthropologists regard the pre-Columbian North American Indian as a sensitive member of his environment, who merged sympathetically with its living and nonliving components.[43] The Indian's world was filled with superhuman and magical powers which controlled man's destiny and nature's course of events.[44] Murray Wax explains

> To those who inhabit it, the magical world is a "society," not a "mechanism," that is, it is composed of "beings" rather than

"objects." Whether human or nonhuman, these beings are associated with and related to one another socially and sociably, that is, in the same ways as human beings to one another. These patterns of association and relationship may be structured in terms of kinship, empathy, sympathy, reciprocity, sexuality, dependency, or any other of the ways that human beings interact with and affect or afflict one another. Plants, animals, rocks, and stars are thus seen not as "objects" governed by laws of nature, but as "fellows" with whom the individual or band may have a more or less advantageous relationship.[45]

For the Micmac, together with all the other eastern subarctic Algonquians, the power of these mysterious forces was apprehended as "manitou"—translated "magic power"—much in the same way that we might use the slang word "vibrations" to register the emotional feelings emanating (so we say) from an object, person, or situation.[46]

The world of the Micmac was thus filled with superhuman forces and beings (such as dwarfs, giants, and magicians), and animals that could talk to man and had spirits akin to his own, and the magic of mystical and medicinal herbs—a world where even inanimate objects possessed spirits.[47] Micmac subsistence activities were inextricably bound up within this spiritual matrix, which, we are suggesting, acted as a kind of control mechanism on Micmac land-use, maintaining the environment within an optimum range of conditions.

In order to understand the role of the Micmac in the fur trading enterprise of the colonial period, it is useful to investigate the role of the Micmac hunter in the spiritual world of precontact times. Hunting was governed by spiritual rules and considerations which were manifest to the early French observers in the form of seemingly innumerable taboos These taboos connoted a sense of cautious reverence for a conscious fellow-member of the same ecosystem who, in the view of the Indian, allowed itself to be taken for food and clothing. The Indian felt that "both he and his victim understood the roles which they played in the hunt; the animal was resigned to its fate."[48]

That such a resignation on the part of the game was not to be interpreted as an unlimited license to kill should be evident from an examination of some of the more prominent taboos. Beaver for example, were greatly admired by the Micmac for their industry and "abounding genius"; for them, the beaver had "sense" and formed a "separate nation."[49] Hence there were various regulations associated with the disposal of their remains: trapped beaver were drawn in public and made into soup, extreme care being taken to prevent the soup from spilling into the fire; beaver bones were carefully preserved, never being given to the dogs—lest they lose their sense of smell for the animal—or thrown into the fire—lest misfortune come upon "all the nation"—or thrown into rivers—"because the Indians fear lest the spirit of the bones . . . would promptly carry the news to the other beavers, which would desert the country in order to escape the same misfortune." Likewise, menstruating women were forbidden to eat beaver, "for the Indians are convinced, they say, that the beaver, which has sense, would no longer allow itself to be taken by the Indians if it had been eaten by their unclean daughters." The fetus of the beaver, as well as that of the bear, moose, otter, and porcupine was reserved for the old men, since it was believed that a youth who ate such food would experience intense foot pains while hunting.[50]

Taboos similarly governed the disposal of the remains of the moose—what few there were. The bones of a moose fawn (and of the marten) were never given to the dogs nor were they burned, "for they [the Micmac] would not be able any longer to capture any of these animals in hunting if the spirits of the martens and of the fawns of the moose were to inform their own kind of the bad treatment they had received among the Indians."[51] Fear of such reprisal also prohibited menstruating women from drinking out of the common kettles or bark dishes.[52] Such regulations imply cautious respect for the animal hunted. The moose not only provided food and clothing, but was firmly tied up with the Micmac spirit-world—as were the other game animals.

Bear ceremonialism was also practised by the Micmac. Esteem for the bear is in fact common among boreal hunting peoples of northern Eurasia and North America, and has the following characteristics: the beast is typically hunted in the early spring, while still in hibernation. It is addressed, when either dead or alive, with honorific names; a conciliatory speech is made to the animal, either before or after killing it, by which the hunter apologizes for his act and perhaps explains why it is necessary; and the carcass is respectfully treated, those parts not used (especially the skull) being ceremonially disposed of and the flesh consumed in accordance with taboos. Such rituals are intended to propitiate the spiritual controller of the bears so that he will continue to furnish game to the hunter.[53] Among the Micmac the bear's heart was not eaten by young men lest they get out of breath while traveling and lose courage in danger. The bear carcass could be brought into the wigwam only through a special door made specifically for that purpose, either in the left or right side of the structure. This ritual was based on the Micmac belief that . . . women did not "deserve" to enter the wigwam through the same door as the animal. In fact, we are told that childless women actually left the wigwam at the approach of the body and did not return until it had been entirely consumed.[54] By means of such rituals the hunter satisfied the soul-spirit of the slain animal. Of the present-day Mistassini (Montagnais) hunter, Speck writes that "should he fail to observe these formalities an unfavorable reaction would also ensue with his own soul spirit, his 'great man' . . . as it is called. In such a case the 'great man' would fail to advise him when and where he would find his game. Incidentally the hunter resorts to drinking bear's grease to nourish his 'great man.'"[55] Perhaps it was for a similar reason that the Micmac customarily forced newborn infants to swallow bear or seal oil before eating anything else.[56]

If taboo was associated with fishing, we have little record of it; the only explicit evidence is a prohibition against the roasting of eels, which if violated, would prevent the Indians from catching others. From this and from the fact that the Restigouche division of the Micmac wore the figure of a salmon as a totem around their neck, we may surmise that fish, too, shared in the sacred and symbolic world of the Indian.[57]

Control over these supernatural forces and communication with them were the principal functions of the shaman, who served in Micmac society as an intermediary between the spirit realm and the physical. The lives and destinies of the natives were profoundly affected by the ability of the shaman to supplicate, cajole, and otherwise manipulate the magical beings and powers. The seventeenth-century French, who typically labeled shamans (or *buowin*) frauds and jugglers in league with the devil, were repeatedly amazed at the respect accorded them by the natives.[58] By working himself into a dreamlike state, the shaman would invoke the manitou of his animal helper and so predict future events.[59] He also healed by means of conjuring. The Micmac availed themselves of a rather large pharmacopeia of roots and herbs and other plant parts, but when these failed they would summon the healing arts of the most noted shaman in the district. The illness was often diagnosed by the *buowin* as a failure on the patient's part to perform a prescribed ritual; hence an offended supernatural power had visited the offender with sickness. At such times the shaman functioned as a psychotherapist, diagnosing the illness and symbolically (at least) removing its immediate cause from the patient's body.[60]

It is important to understand that an ecosystem is holocoenotic in nature: there are no "walls" between the components of the system, for "the ecosystem reacts as a whole."[61] Such was the case in the Micmac ecosystem of precontact times, where the spiritual served as a link connecting man with all the various subsystems of the environment. Largely through the mediation of the shaman, these spiritual obligations and restrictions acted as a kind of control device to maintain the ecosystem in a well-balanced condition.[62] Under these circumstances the exploitation of game for subsistence appears to have been regulated by the hunter's respect for the continued welfare of his prey—both living and dead—as is evident from the numerous taboos associated with the proper disposal of animal remains. Violation of taboo desecrated the remains of the slain animal and offended its soul-spirit. The offended spirit would then retaliate in any of several ways, depending on the nature of the broken taboo: it could render the guilty hunter's (or the entire band's) means of hunting ineffective, or it could encourage its living fellows to remove themselves from the vicinity. In both cases the end result was the same—the hunt was rendered unsuccessful—and in both it was mediated by the same power—the spirit of the slain animal. Either of these catastrophes could usually be reversed through the magical arts of the shaman. In the Micmac cosmology, the overkill of wildlife would have been resented by the animal kingdom as an act comparable to genocide, and would have been resisted by means of the sanctions outlined above. The threat of retaliation thus had the effect of placing an upper limit on the number of animals slain, while the practical result was the conservation of wildlife.

○

The injection of European civilization into this balanced system initiated a series of chain reactions which, within a little over a century, resulted in the replacement of the aboriginal ecosystem by another. From at least the beginning of the sixteenth century, and perhaps well before that date, fishing fleets from England, France, and Portugal visited the Grand Banks off Newfoundland every spring for the cod, and hunted whale and walrus in the Gulf of St. Lawrence.[63] Year after year, while other, more flamboyant men were advancing the geopolitical ambitions of their emerging dynastic states as they searched for precious minerals or a passage to the Orient, these unassuming fishermen visited Canada's east coast and made the first effective European contact with the Indians there. For the natives' furs they bartered knives, beads, brass kettles, assorted ship fittings, and the like,[64] thus initiating the subversion and replacement of Micmac material culture by European technology. Far more important, the fishermen unwittingly infected the Indians with European diseases, against which the natives had no immunity. Commenting on what may be called the microbial phase of European conquest, John Witthoft has written:

> All of the microscopic parasites of humans, which had been collected together from all parts of the known world into Europe, were brought to these [American] shores, and new diseases stalked faster than man could walk into the interior of the continent. Typhoid, diphtheria, colds, influenza, measles, chicken pox, whooping cough, tuberculosis, yellow fever, scarlet fever, and other strep infections, gonorrhea, pox (syphilis), and smallpox were diseases that had never been in the New World before. They were new among populations which had no immunity to them. . . . Great epidemics and pandemics of these diseases are believed to have destroyed whole communities, depopulated whole regions, and vastly decreased the native population everywhere in the yet unexplored interior of the continent. The early pandemics are believed to have run their course prior to 1600 A.D.[65]

Disease did more than decimate the native population; it effectively prepared the way for subsequent phases of European contact by breaking native morale and, perhaps even more significantly, by cracking their spiritual edifice. It is reasonable to suggest that European disease rendered the Indian's (particularly the shaman's) ability to control and otherwise influence the supernatural realm dysfunctional—because his magic and other traditional cures were now ineffective—thereby causing the Indian to apostatize (in effect), which in turn subverted the "retaliation" principle of taboo and opened the way to a corruption of the Indian-land relationship under the influence of the fur trade.

Much of this microbial phase was of course protohistoric, although it continued well into and no doubt beyond the seventeenth century—the time period covered by the earliest French sources. Recognizing the limitations of tradition as it conveys historical fact, it may nevertheless be instructive to examine a myth concerning the Cross-bearing Micmac of the Miramichi River which, as recorded by Father Chrestien Le Clercq, seems to illustrate the demoralizing effect of disease. According to tradition, there was once a time when these Indians were gravely threatened by a severe sickness; as was their custom, they looked to the sun for help. In their extreme need a "beautiful" man, holding a cross, appeared before several of them in a dream. He instructed them to make similar crosses, for, as he told them, in this symbol lay their protection. For a time thereafter these Indians, who believed in dreams "even to the extent of superstition," were very religious and devoted in their veneration of this symbol. Later, however, they apostatized:

> Since the Gaspesian [Micmac] nation of the Cross-bearers has been almost wholly destroyed, as much by the war which they have waged with the Iroquois as by the maladies which have infected this land, and which, in three or four visitations, have caused the deaths of a very great number, these Indians have gradually relapsed from this first devotion of their ancestors. So true is it, that even the holiest and most religious practices, by a certain fatality attending human affairs, suffer always much alteration if they are not animated and conserved by the same spirit which gave them birth. In brief, when I went into their country to commence my mission I found some persons who had preserved only the shadow of the customs of their ancestors.[66]

Their rituals had failed to save these Indians when threatened by European diseases and intergroup hostilities; hence their old religious practices were abandoned, no doubt because of their ineffectiveness.

Several other observers also commented on the new diseases that afflicted the Micmac. In precontact times, declared Denys, "they were not subject to diseases, and knew nothing of fevers."[67] By about 1700, however, Dièreville noted that the Micmac population was in sharp decline.[68] The Indians themselves frequently complained to Father Biard and other Frenchmen that, since contact with the French, they had been dying off in great numbers. "For they assert that, before this association and intercourse [with the French], all their countries were very populous, and they tell how one by one the different coasts, according as they have begun to traffic with us, have been more reduced by disease." The Indians accused the French of trying to poison them or charged that the food supplied by the French was somehow adulterated. Whatever the reasons for the catastrophe, warned Biard, the Indians were very angry about it and "upon the point of breaking with us, and making war upon us."[69]

To the Jesuit fathers, the solution to this sorry state of affairs lay in the civilizing power of the Gospel. To Biard, his mission was clear:

> For, if our Souriquois [Micmac] are few, they may become numerous; if they are savages, it is to domesticate and civilize them that we have come here; if they are rude, that is no reason that we

should be idle; if they have until now profited little, it is no wonder, for it would be too much to expect fruit from this grafting, and
to demand reason and maturity from a child.

In conclusion, we hope in time to make them susceptible of
receiving the doctrines of the faith and of the christian and catholic
religion, and later, to penetrate further into the regions beyond.[70]

The message was simple and straightforward: the black-robes would
enlighten the Indians by ridiculing their animism and related taboos, discrediting their shamans, and urging them to accept the Christian gospel.
But to their chagrin the Indians proved stubborn in their ancient ways, no
matter how unsuited to changing circumstances.[71]

Since the advent of European diseases and the consequent disillusion-
ment with native spiritual beliefs and customs, some Indians appear to
have repudiated their traditional world view altogether, while others clung
desperately to what had become a moribund body of ritual. We would suppose that the Christian message was more readily accepted by the former,
while the latter group, which included the shamans and those too old to
change, would have fought bitterly against the missionary teachings.[72] But
they resisted in vain for, with time, old people died and shamans whose
magic was less potent than that of the missionaries were discredited.[73] The
missionary was successful only to the degree that his power exceeded that
of the shaman. The nonliterate Indian, for example, was awed by the magic
of handwriting as a means of communication.[74] Even more significant was
the fact that Christianity was the religion of the white man, who, with his
superior technology and greater success at manipulating life to his advantage, was believed to have recourse to a greater power (manitou) than did
the Indian. Material goods, such as the trading articles offered the Indians
by the French were believed by the native to have a spirit within, in accord
with their belief that all animate and inanimate objects housed such a spirit
or power.[75] Furthermore, there were degrees of power in such objects,
which were determined and calibrated in the Indian mind by the degree of
functionalism associated with a particular object.[76] For example, the
Micmac believed that there was a spirit of his canoe, of his snowshoes, of
his bow, and so on. It was for this reason that a man's material goods were
either buried with him or burned, so that their spirits would accompany his
to the spirit world, where he would have need of them. Just as he had
hunted in this physical world, so his spirit would again hunt the game spirits with the spirits of his weapons in the land of the dead.[77] Denys described
an incident which emphasized the fact that even European trading goods
had spirits, when he related how the brass kettle was known to have lost its
spirit (or died) when it no longer rang when tapped.[78] Thus Christianity,
which to the Indians was the ritual harnessing all of this power, was a
potent force among them. Nevertheless, the priests who worked among the
Indians frequently complained of their relapsing into paganism, largely
because the Micmac came to associate Christianity and civilization in general with their numerous misfortunes, together with the fact that they never
clearly understood the Christian message anyway, but always saw it in
terms of their own cosmology.[79]

As all religious systems reflect their cultural milieux, so did seventeenth-century Christianity. Polygamy was condemned by the French missionaries as immoral, the consultation of shamans was discouraged, the custom of interring material goods was criticized, eat-all feasts were denounced as gluttonous and shortsighted, and the Indians were disabused of many of their so-called superstitions (taboos).[80] The priests attacked the Micmac culture with a marvellous fervor and some success.[81] Although they could not have appreciated it, they were aided in this endeavor by an obsolescent system of taboo and spiritual awareness; Christianity merely delivered the coup de grace.

The result of this Christian onslaught on a decaying Micmac cosmology was, of course, the despiritualization of the material world. Commenting on the process of despiritualization, Denys (who was a spectator to this transformation in the mid-seventeenth century) remarked that it was accomplished with "much difficulty"; for some of the Indians it was achieved by religious means, while others were influenced by the French customs, but nearly all were affected

> by the need for the things which come from us, the use of which has become to them an indispensable necessity. They have abandoned all their own utensils, whether because of the trouble they had as well to make as to use them, or because of the facility of obtaining from us, in exchange for skins which cost them almost nothing, the things which seemed to them invaluable, not so much for their novelty as for the convenience they derived therefrom.[82]

In the early years of the fur trade, before the establishment of permanent posts among the natives, trading was done with the coast-wise fishermen from May to early fall.[83] In return for skins of beaver, otter, marten, moose, and other furbearers, the Indians received a variety of fairly cheap commodities, principally tobacco, liquor, powder and shot (in later years), biscuit, peas, flour, assorted clothing, wampum, kettles and hunting tools.[84] The success of this trade in economic terms must be attributed to pressure exerted on a relatively simple society by a complex civilization and, perhaps even more importantly, by the tremendous pull of this simple social organization on the resources of Europe.[85] To the Micmac, who like other Indians measured the worth of a tool or object by the ease of its construction and use, the technology of Europe became indispensable. But as has already been shown, this was not simply an economic issue for the Indian; the Indian was more than just "economically seduced" by the European's trading goods.[86] One must also consider the metaphysical implications of Indian acceptance of the European material culture.

European technology of the sixteenth and seventeenth centuries was largely incompatible with the spiritual beliefs of the eastern woodland Indians, despite the observation made above that the Micmacs readily invested trading goods with spiritual power akin to that possessed by their own implements. As Denys pointed out, the trade goods which the Micmac so eagerly accepted were accompanied by Christian religious teachings and

French custom, both of which gave definition to these alien objects. In accepting the European material culture, the natives were impelled to accept the European abstract culture, especially religion, and so, in effect, their own spiritual beliefs were subverted as they abandoned their implements for those of the white man. Native religion lost not only its practical effectiveness, in part owing to the replacement of the traditional magical and animistic view of nature by the exploitive European view, but it was no longer necessary as a source of definition and theoretical support for the new Europe-derived material culture. Western technology made more "sense" if it was accompanied by Western religion.

Under these circumstances in the early contact period, the Micmac's role within his ecosystem changed radically. No longer was he the sensitive fellow-member of a symbolic world; under pressure from disease, European trade, and Christianity, he had apostatized—he had repudiated his role within the ecosystem. Former attitudes were replaced by a kind of mongrel outlook which combined some native traditions and beliefs with a European rationale and motivation. Our concern here is less to document this transformation than to assess its impact on the Indian–land relationship. In these terms, then, what effect did the trade have on the Micmac ecosystem?

The most obvious change was the unrestrained slaughter of certain game. Lured by European commodities, equipped with European technology, urged by European traders,[87] deprived of a sense of responsibility and accountability for the land, and no longer inhibited by taboo, the Micmac began to overkill systematically those very wildlife which had now become so profitable and even indispensable to his new way of life. The pathos of this transformation of attitude and behavior is illustrated by an incident recorded by Le Clercq. The Indians, who still believed that the beaver had "sense" and formed a "separate nation," maintained that they "would cease to make war upon these animals if these would speak, howsoever little, in order that they might learn whether the Beavers are among their friends or their enemies."[88] Unfortunately for the beaver, they never communicated their friendliness. The natural world of the Indian was becoming inarticulate.

It is interesting to note that Dièreville, who observed the Micmac culture at the beginning of the eighteenth century, was the only witness to record the native superstition which compelled them to tear out the eyes of all slain animals. Somehow, perhaps by some sort of symbolic transference, the spirits of surviving animals of the same species were thereby blinded to the irreverent treatment accorded to the victim; otherwise, through the mediation of the outraged spirits, the living would no longer have allowed themselves to be taken by the Indians.[89] The failure of the earlier writers to mention this particular superstition suggests that it was of fairly recent origin, a result of the overexploitation of game for the trade. To the Micmac mind, haunted by memories of a former time, the practice may have been intended to hide his guilt and ensure his continued success.

Together with this depletion of wildlife went a reduction of dependency on the resources of the local ecosystem. The use of improved hunting equipment, such as fishing line and hooks, axes, knives, muskets, and iron-tipped arrows, spears, and harpoons,[90] exerted heavier pressure on the resources of the area, while the availability of French foodstuffs shifted the position of the Micmac in the trophic system, somewhat reducing his dependency on local food sources as it placed him partly outside of the system. To be sure, a decreasing native population relieved this pressure to a degree, but, according to evidence cited above, not enough to prevent the abuse of the land.

Other less obvious results of the fur trade were the increased incidence of feuding and the modification of the Micmac settlement patterns to meet the demands of the trade. Liquor, in particular brandy, was a favorite item of the trade—one for which the Indians "would go a long way."[91] Its effects were devastating. Both Jean Saint-Vallier (François Laval's successor as bishop of Quebec) and Biard blamed liquor as a cause for the increased death rate of the natives. Moreover, it was observed that drunkenness resulted in social disintegration as the Indians became debauched and violent among themselves, and, at times, spilled over into the French community which they would rob, ravage, and burn. Drunkenness also provided a legitimate excuse to commit crimes, such as murdering their enemies, for which they would otherwise be held accountable.[92]

European contact should thus be viewed as a trigger factor, that is, something which was not present in the Micmac ecosystem before and which initiated a concatenation of reactions leading to the replacement of the aboriginal ecosystem by another.[93] European disease, Christianity, and the fur trade with its accompanying technology—the three often intermeshed—were responsible for the corruption of the Indian-land relationship, in which the native had merged sympathetically with his environment. By a lockstep process European disease rendered the Indian's control over the supernatural and spiritual realm inoperative, and the disillusioned Micmac apostatized, debilitating taboo and preparing the way for the destruction of wildlife which was soon to occur under the stimulation of the fur trade. For those who believed in it, Christianity furnished a new, dualistic world view, which placed man above nature, as well as spiritual support for the fur trade, and as a result the Micmac became dependent on the European marketplace both spiritually and economically. Within his ecosystem the Indian changed from conservator to exploiter. All of this resulted in the intense exploitation of some game animals and the virtual extermination of others. Unfortunately for the Indian and the land, this grim tale was to be repeated many times along the moving Indian-white frontier. Life for the Micmac had indeed become more convenient, but convenience cost dearly in much material and abstract culture loss or modification.

The historiography of Indian-white relations is rendered more comprehensible when the Indian and the land are considered together: "So intimately is all of Indian life tied up with the land and its utilization that to think of Indians is to think of land. The two are inseparable."[94] American Indian history can be seen, then, as a type of environmental history, and perhaps it is from this perspective that the early period of Indian–white relations can best be understood.

NOTES

1. Reuben Gold Thwaites, ed., *The Jesuit Relations and Allied Documents: Travels and Explorations of the Jesuit Missionaries in New France, 1610–1791* (1896–1901; reprint, New York, 1959), 8:57.

2. Baron Lahontan, *New Voyages to North America . . . An Account of the Several Nations of that vast Continent. . . ,* ed. Reuben Gold Thwaites (Chicago, 1905), 1:82.

3. Thwaites, ed., *Jesuit Relations,* 5:25; 6:297–99; 8:57; 40:151; 68:47, 109–11; 69:95, 99–113.

4. Ibid., 8:41.

5. Nicolas Denys, *The Description and Natural History of the Coasts of North America (Acadia),* ed. and trans. William F. Ganong (Toronto, 1908), 1:187, 199, 209, 219–20.

6. Ibid., 432, 450.

7. Peter Farb, *Man's Rise to Civilization as Shown by the Indians of North America from Primeval Times to the Coming of the Industrial State* (New York, 1968), 82–83.

8. See Wilson D. Wallis and Ruth Sawtell Wallis, *The Micmac Indians of Eastern Canada* (Minneapolis, 1955), for a thorough ethnographic study of the Micmac, Jacques and Maryvonne Crevel, *Honguedo ou l'Histoire des Premiers Gaspesiens* (Quebec, 1970), give a fairly good general history of the Micmac during the seventeenth century, together with a description of the fishing industry.

9. Julian H. Steward, "The Concept and Method of Cultural Ecology" in his *Theory of Culture Change: The Methodology of Multilinear Evolution* (Urbana, IL, 1955), 30–42; and Andrew P. Vayda and Roy A. Rappaport, "Ecology, Cultural and Noncultural" in *Introduction to Cultural Anthropology: Essays in the Scope and Methods of the Science of Man,* ed. James A. Clifton (Boston, 1968), 494.

10. W.D. Billings, *Plants, Man, and the Ecosystem,* 2nd ed. (Belmont, CA, 1970), 4.

11. Roy A. Rappaport, *Pigs for the Ancestors: Ritual in the Ecology of a New Guinea People* (New Haven, CT, 1968).

12. Among the few who have are William Christie MacLeod, "Conservation Among Primitive Hunting Peoples," *Scientific Monthly* 43 (1936): 562–66, and Alfred Goldsworthy Bailey in his little-known book, *The Conflict of European and Eastern Algonkian Cultures, 1504–1700,* 2nd ed. (Toronto, 1969).

13. Wilbur R. Jacobs, *Dispossessing the American Indian: Indians and Whites on the Colonial Frontier* (New York, 1972), 25.

14. Billings, *Plants, Man, and the Ecosystem,* 37–38.

15. Sieur de Dièreville, *Relation of the Voyage to Port Royal in Acadia or New France,* trans. Mrs. Clarence Webster, ed. John Clarence Webster (Toronto, 1933), 184. According to the editor, p. 216, the Malecites later replaced the Micmacs living along the St. John, the latter withdrawing to Nova Scotia. See also Diamond Jenness, *The Indians of Canada,* 3rd ed. (Ottawa, 1955), 267.

16. See Rappaport, *Pigs for the Ancestors,* 225–26. If the present article were intended as a more rigorous analysis of the Micmac ecosystem, we would report on the topography of this region, on the soil types, the hydrological characteristics, the climate, the influence of the ocean, and the effects of fires caused by lightning. But since neither the Micmac nor the first Europeans had any appreciable effect on these physical variables—except perhaps that of water relations—we shall pass over the physical environment and go on to the biological. Suffice it to say that the water of numerous rivers and streams was regulated in its flow by beaver dams

throughout much of this region, and Indian beaver hunting and trapping certainly upset this control.

17. For a thorough discussion of Micmac plant and animal use see Frank G. Speck and Ralph W. Dexter, "Utilization of Animals and Plants by the Micmac Indians of New Brunswick," Washington Academy of Sciences, *Journal* 41 (1951): 250–59.

18. Father Chrestien Le Clercq, *New Relation of Gaspesia, with the Customs and Religion of the Gaspesian Indians,* ed. and trans. William F. Ganong (Toronto, 1910), 212–13; Thwaites, ed., *Jesuit Relations,* 3:77; Marc Lescarbot, *The History of New France,* trans. W.L. Grant (Toronto, 1907), 3:93, 194–95. Lescarbot asserts that the Micmac definitely grew tobacco, most likely the so-called wild tobacco, *Nicotiana rustica* (ibid., 252–53).

19. Lescarbot, *History of New France,* 2:323–25; 3:158.

20. Thwaites, ed., *Jesuit Relations,* 3:77–83.

21. Ibid., Denys, *Description of North America,* 2:403; Lescarbot, *History of New France,* 3:80; Le Clercq, *New Relation of Gaspesia,* 88–89, 93; Dièreville, *Relation of the Voyage to Port Royal,* 146.

22. Lescarbot, *History of New France,* 3:219–20, and Thwaites, ed., *Jesuit Relations,* 3:77–79.

23. Lescarbot, *History of New France,* 3:222–24. See Horace T. Martin, *Castorologia, or the History and Traditions of the Canadian Beaver* (Montreal, 1892), for a good treatise on the beaver.

24. Le Clercq, *New Relation of Gaspesia,* 276–80; Dièreville, *Relation of the Voyage to Port Royal,* 133–34; Denys, *Description and Natural History,* 2:429–33; Lescarbot, *History of New France,* 3:222–24.

25. Lescarbot, *History of New France,* 3:220–22; Denys, *Description and Natural History,* 2:426–29; Le Clercq, *New Relation of Gaspesia,* 274–76. Speck and Dexter place caribou

before moose in order of importance, but they cite no evidence for such ranking. Speck and Dexter, "Utilization of Animals and Plants by Micmacs," 255.

26. Le Clercq, *New Relation of Gaspesia,* 118–19.

27. Ibid., 93–94; Denys, *Description and Natural History,* 2:412; Lescarbot, *History of New France,* 3:133; Speck and Dexter, "Utilization of Animals and Plants by Micmacs," 255.

28. Speck and Dexter, "Utilization of Animals and Plants by Micmacs," 255.

29. Le Clercq, *New Relation of Gaspesia,* 116, 119; Dièreville, *Relation of the Voyage to Port Royal,* 131; Thwaites, ed., *Jesuit Relations,* 3:107–9.

30. Denys, *Description and Natural History,* 2:433–34.

31. Thwaites, ed., *Jesuit Relations,* 3:79.

32. Ibid., 81; and Speck and Dexter, "Utilization of Animals and Plants by Micmacs," 251–54.

33. Lescarbot, *History of New France,* 3:236–37, and Denys, *Description and Natural History,* 2:436–37.

34. Le Clercq, *New Relation of Gaspesia,* 92, 137; Lescarbot, *History of New France,* 3:230–31; Denys, *Description and Natural History,* 2:435–36.

35. Thwaites, ed., *Jesuit Relations,* 3:83.

36. Ibid.

37. Le Clercq, *New Relation of Gaspesia,* 109–10, 283; and Denys, *Description and Natural History,* 2:389, 434.

38. Frank G. Speck, "Aboriginal Conservators," *Audubon Magazine* 40 (1938): 260.

39. Denys, *Description and Natural History,* 2:402–3.

40. Ibid., 426.

41. Speck, "Aboriginal Conservators," 260. Italics in original.

42. Rappaport, *Pigs for the Ancestors,* 237–38; and Vayda and Rappaport, "Ecology, Cultural and Non-cultural," 491.

43. See, for example, the writings of Speck, especially "Aboriginal Conservators," 258–61; John Witthoft, "The American Indian as Hunter," *Pennsylvania Game News* 39 (Feb.–April, 1953); George S. Snyderman, "Concepts of Land Ownership among the Iroquois and their Neighbors," *Bureau of American Ethnology Bulletin*, no. 149, ed. William N. Fenton (Washington, DC, 1951), 15–34; Robert F. Heizer, "Primitive Man as an Ecological Factor," Kroeber Anthropological Society, *Papers* 13 (1955): 1–31. See also William A. Ritchie, "The Indian and His Environment," *Conservationist* (Dec.–Jan. 1955–56): 23–27; Gordon Day, "The Indian as an Ecological Factor in the Northeastern Forest," *Ecology* 24 (1953): 329–46; MacLeod, "Conservation," 562–66.

44. Witthoft, "American Indian" (March 1953), 17.

45. Murray Wax, "Religion and Magic" in *Introduction to Cultural Anthropology*, ed. Clifton, 235.

46. See William Jones, "The Algonkin Manitou," *Journal of American Folk-Lore* 18 (1905): 183–90, and Frederick Johnson, "Notes on Micmac Shamanism," *Primitive Man* 16 (1943): 58–59.

47. See Stansbury Hagar, "Micmac Magic and Medicine," *Journal of American Folk-Lore* 9 (1896): 170–77, and Johnson, "Notes on Micmac Shamanism," 54, 56–57, who report that such beliefs in the supernatural and spiritual survive even in modern times, although in suppressed and attenuated form. Le Clercq, *Relation of New Gaspesia*, 187, 209, 212–14; and Denys, *Description and Natural History*, 2:117, 442.

48. Witthoft, "American Indian" (Feb. 1953), 16.

49. Dièreville, *Relation of the Voyage to Port Royal*, 139, and Le Clercq, *New Relation of Gaspesia*, 225–29, 276–77.

50. Le Clercq, *New Relation of Gaspesia*, 225–29.

51. Ibid., 226.

52. Ibid., 227–29.

53. Witthoft, "American Indian" (March 1953), 16–22; A. Irving Hallowell, "Bear Ceremonialism in the Northern Hemisphere," *American Anthropologist*, new series 28 (1926): 1–175.

54. Le Clercq, *New Relation of Gaspesia*, 227.

55. Frank G. Speck, "Mistassini Hunting Territories in the Labrador Peninsula," *American Anthropologist*, new series 25 (1923): 464. Johnson, "Notes on Micmac Shamanism," 70–72, distinguishes between the Montagnais, Wabanaki, and Micmac ideas of the "soul."

56. Le Clercq, *New Relation of Gaspesia*, 88–89; Dièreville, *Relation of the Voyage to Port Royal*, 146; Lescarbot, *History of New France*, 3:80.

57. Denys, *Description and Natural History*, 2:430, 442; and Le Clercq, *New Relation of Gaspesia*, 192–93.

58. Denys, *Description and Natural History*, 2:417–18; and Le Clercq, *New Relation of Gaspesia*, 215–18.

59. Thwaites, ed., *Jesuit Relations*, 2:75; Le Clercq, *New Relation of Gaspesia*, 215–16; George H. Daugherty, Jr., "Reflections of Environment in North American Indian Literature" (PhD thesis, University of Chicago, 1925), 31; Johnson, "Notes on Micmac Shamanism," 71–72.

60. Le Clercq, *New Relation of Gaspesia*, 215–18, 296–99; Denys, *Description and Natural History*, 2:415, 417–18; Hagar, "Micmac Magic," 170–77. Denys, *Description and Natural History*, 2:418, observed that most of these ailments were (what we would call today) psychosomatic in origin.

61. Billings, *Plants, Man, and the Ecosystem*, 36.

62. Thwaites, ed., *Jesuit Relations*, 2:75.

63. H.P. Biggar, *The Early Trading Companies of New France: A Contribution to the History of Commerce and Discovery in North America* (1901; reprint New York, 1965), 18–37.

64. John Witthoft, "Archaeology as a Key to the Colonial Fur Trade," *Minnesota History* (1966): 204–5.

65. John Witthoft, *Indian Prehistory of Pennsylvania* (Harrisburg, PA, 1965), 26–29.

66. Le Clercq, *New Relation of Gaspesia*, 146–52. The Recollet fathers, especially Father Emanuel Jumeau, were able to cause a renaissance of the old traditional religion by encouraging these people to look to the cross once more for their salvation, although, of course, this time it was the Christian cross. We should bear in mind that the cross was an art motif common among non-Christian people, and of independent origin from that of the Christian cross. Whether the cross mentioned in this particular tradition was of Christian or aboriginal origin should make little difference, for the story still serves to illustrate the process of apostatization.

67. Denys, *Description and Natural History*, 2:415. Estimates of the aboriginal population of North America at the time of European contact are constantly being revised upward. Henry F. Dobyns, "Estimating Aboriginal American Population: An Appraisal of Techniques with a New Hemispheric Estimate," *Current Anthropology* 7 (1966): 395–416, placed the figure at a controversial and fantastically high total of 9 800 000 natives.

68. Dièreville, *Relation of the Voyage to Port Royal*, 116. See Thwaites, ed., *Jesuit Relations*, 1:177–79.

69. Thwaites, ed., *Jesuit Relations*, 3:105–7.

70. Ibid., 1:183.

71. Ibid., 2:75–77; 3:123; and Le Clercq, *New Relation of Gaspesia*, 193, 220, 224–25, 227, 239, 253. See also Denys, *Description of North America*, 2:117, 430, 442.

72. Notice that when a custom in any society becomes a mere formality and loses its practical meaning, it is easily discarded when challenged by detractors, who may or may not replace it with something more meaningful. See Le Clercq, *New Relation of Gaspesia*, 206, 227, and Lescarbot, *History of New France*, 3:94–95.

73. Jean Baptiste de la Croix Chevrières de Saint-Vallier, *Estat Présent de l'Eglise et de la Colonie Françoise dans la Nouvelle France, par M. l'Evêque de Québec* (Paris, 1688), 36–37; and Thwaites, ed., *Jesuit Relations*, 2:75–77. See Le Clercq, *New Relation of Gaspesia*, 220–21, where he speaks of converting a noted shaman to Christianity. André Vachon, "L'Eau-de-Vie dans la Société Indienne," Canadian Historical Association, *Report of the Annual Meeting* (1960), 22–32, has observed that the priest replaced the shaman and sorcerer in Indian society by virtue of his superior powers. By discrediting his Indian counterparts (and rivals), the priest became the shaman-sorcerer (i.e., a source of both good and evil power).

74. Lescarbot, *History of New France*, 3:128, and Le Clercq, *New Relation of Gaspesia*, 133–35.

75. Le Clercq, *New Relation of Gaspesia*, 209, 213–14, and Bailey, *Conflict of European and Eastern Algonkian Cultures*, 47.

76. Denys, *Description and Natural History*, 2:439.

77. Le Clercq, *New Relation of Gaspesia*, 187, 209, 212–14, 238–39, 303; Lescarbot, *History of New France*, 3:279, 285; Thwaites, ed., *Jesuit Relations*, 1:169; Denys, *Description and Natural History*, 2:437–39; Dièreville, *Relation of the Voyage to Port Royal*, 161.

78. Denys, *Description and Natural History*, 2:439–41.

79. Le Clercq, *New Relation of Gaspesia*, 125, 193; and Thwaites, ed., *Jesuit Relations*, 1:165. See ibid., 2:89, where baptism was understood by the Micmac (of Port Royal, at least) "as a sort of sacred pledge of friendship and alliance with the French."

80. Lescarbot, *History of New France*, 3:53–54; Denys, *Description and Natural History*, 2:117, 430, 442; Le

Clercq, *New Relation of Gaspesia*, 116; Dièreville, *Relation of the Voyage to Port Royal*, 161; Thwaites, ed., *Jesuit Relations*, 3:131–35. See ibid., 2:75–77, where the shamans complain of having lost much of their power since the coming of the French.

81. Le Clercq observed that since the introduction of Christianity and especially baptism the manitou had not afflicted them to the degree that he did formerly. See Le Clercq, *New Relation of Gaspesia*, 225. See also 229–33, where cases are recorded of native men and women who seemed to feel a divine call and ordination, representing themselves as priests among their fellows.

82. Denys, *Description and Natural History*, 2:440–41.

83. Samuel de Champlain, *The Voyages of the Sieur de Champlain of Saintoge . . .*, vol. 1 of *The Works of Samuel de Champlain*, ed. and trans. H.P. Biggar (Toronto, 1922), passim; and Thwaites, ed., *Jesuit Relations*, 3:81.

84. Lescarbot, *History of New France*, 2:281–82, 323–24; 3:158, 168, 250; Thwaites, ed., *Jesuit Relations*, 3:75–77; Le Clercq, *New Relation of Gaspesia*, 93–94, 109; Dièreville, *Relation of the Voyage to Port Royal*, 132–33, 139–41.

85. Harold A. Innis, *The Fur Trade in Canada: An Introduction to Canadian Economic History*, rev. ed. (Toronto, 1956), 15–17.

86. Farb, *Man's Rise to Civilization*, 82–83.

87. See Thwaites, ed., *Jesuit Relations*, 1:175–77, and Denys, *Description and Natural History*, 2:439, for mention of the French lust for furs.

88. Le Clercq, *New Relation of Gaspesia*, 276–77. See also Dièreville, Relation of the Voyage to Port Royal, 139.

89. Dièreville, *Relation of the Voyage to Port Royal*, 161.

90. Lescarbot, *History of New France*, 3:191–92; and Denys, *Description and Natural History*, 2:399, 442–43.

91. Dièreville, *Relation of the Voyage to Port Royal*, 174, and Denys, *Description and Natural History*, 2:172, 443–52. If we are to believe Craig MacAndrew and Robert B. Edgerton, *Drunken Comportment: A Social Explanation* (Chicago, 1969), 111, the Micmac encountered by Jacques Cartier along the shores of Chaleur Bay in 1534 were the first historically documented North American tribe to receive European liquor.

92. Saint-Vallier, *Estat Présent*, 36–37, 42; Thwaites, ed., *Jesuit Relations*, 3:105–9; Denys, *Description and Natural History*, 2:443–52; Dièreville, *Relation of the Voyage to Port Royal*, 166; Le Clercq, *New Relation of Gaspesia*, 244–45, 254–57. The subject of North American Indian drinking patterns and problems has been the topic of much debate from the seventeenth century to the present. The best scholarship on the subject, which has by no means been exhausted, is contained in MacAndrew and Edgerton, *Drunken Comportment*; Vachon, "L'Eau-de-Vie," 22–32; Nancy Oestreich Lurie, "The World's Oldest On-Going Protest Demonstration: North American Indian Drinking Patterns," *Pacific Historical Review* 40 (1971): 311–32.

93. Billings, *Plants, Man, and the Ecosystem*, 37–38.

94. See John Collier's report on Indian affairs, 1938, in the *Annual Report of the Secretary of the Interior* (Washington, DC, 1938), 209–11, as quoted by Wilcomb Washburn, ed., *The Indian and the White Man* (Garden City, NY, 1964), 394.

VOICES OF DISASTER: SMALLPOX AROUND THE STRAIT OF GEORGIA IN 1782 ◊

COLE HARRIS

o

Well, its a good thing to study these things back, you know. Like the way the people died off.

—Jimmy Peters, 1986[1]

The old Indians grow quite pathetic sometimes when they touch upon this subject. They believe their race is doomed to die out and disappear. They point to the sites of their once populous villages, and then to the handful of people that constitute the tribe of today, and shake their heads and sigh.

—Charles Hill-Tout, 1904[2]

Demographic collapse, in short, led to widespread settlement discontinuity. To grasp the implications of such discontinuity, one must imagine what almost total depopulation would mean in Italy or Spain ca. 1500—silent villages, decaying cities, fields lying waste, orchards overgrown with brush.

—Karl W. Butzer, 1992[3]

It is now clear that Europeans carried diseases wherever they went in the Western Hemisphere and that among genetically similar peoples with no immunity to introduced viruses and bacteria, the results were catastrophic.[4] In the century or so after Columbus the population of the Western

◊ Reprinted with permission from *Ethnohistory* 41, 4 (Fall 1994): 591–626. Drafts of this article have benefited from comments by Karl Butzer, Daniel Clayton, Julie Cruikshank, Jody Decker, Robert Galois, Averil Groeneveld-Meijer, Richard Inglis, Phil Keddie, Shirley Leon, George Lovell, Richard Mackie, Sonny McHalsie, Daniel Marshall, Bruce Miller, Gordon Mohs, Matthew Sparke, and Wayne Suttles. Research has been supported by a grant from the Social Sciences and Humanities Research Council of Canada.

Hemisphere fell by some 90 percent according to current estimates.[5] For all the tyrannies of conquerors and colonists, diseases apparently had far more telling demographic effects.

In British Columbia little is known about contact-related disease and depopulation. Whites have told other stories, ethnographers have encouraged native informants to describe "traditional" ways, and the few recorded native accounts of disease usually have been treated as myths. Today, as political debates about native government and land claims intensify and appeals proceed through the courts, questions of disease and depopulation are explicitly repoliticized—which does not make listening easier.[6] For a society preoccupied with numbers, scale, and progress, more people imply fuller, more controlled occupation of land. Thus, it has been in the interest of non-natives to suggest small pre- or early contact native populations and in the interest of natives to suggest much larger ones. A disinterested position may not exist. Yet there are native accounts of disease, many of them long predating current political and legal calculations, as well as numerous references to disease by white explorers and traders.

In this essay, I consider Coast Salish accounts of pre-contact smallpox around the Strait of Georgia, the body of water between southern Vancouver Island and the mainland, and in adjacent parts of Puget Sound and the lower Fraser valley (Figure 1). Even today there may be more smallpox stories in circulation, or fragments of stories partly remembered, but these are the ones that have been recorded and made public. A comparison of these native stories with early white accounts suggests that, in different ways and from different vantage points, they describe the same events. From this insight, coupled with information from the plains, I conclude that smallpox reached the Strait of Georgia in 1782 and that its effects were devastating. I then discuss whether useful estimates of immediate pre-smallpox population are possible, and end by asking why this epidemic has been so invisible and what it means that whites have lived for several generations alongside the Coast Salish without understanding— without apparently wanting to understand—that their numbers had been decimated by smallpox before Vancouver and Galiano sailed up the Strait of Juan de Fuca.

Although the introduction of smallpox to the Strait of Georgia was part of a hemispheric tragedy, there is no simple line from the late-fifteenth-century Caribbean to the late-eighteenth-century Northwest Coast. The course, effects, and social construction of disease were different in each place. The Strait of Georgia and the larger Northwest Coast have their own stories to tell—to which I come as a geographer mindful of another geographer's adage that one cannot know a place very well without locating its people.[7] To enquire where people lived in what is now southern British Columbia at the beginning of the nineteenth century is to encounter smallpox; ongoing continental debates about disease, depopulation, and the contact process; and the politics of land in contemporary British Columbia.

Surviving native accounts of the arrival of smallpox are scattered and fragmentary. The great late-nineteenth- and early-twentieth-century ethnographers of Northwest Coast cultures did not work among the Coast Salish; the major ethnographic story collections do not come from these peoples.

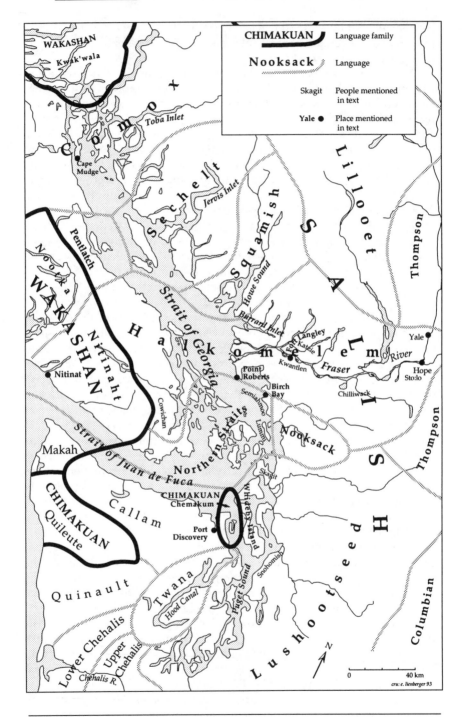

FIGURE   1   *THE STRAIT OF GEORGIA*
(AFTER SUTTLES AND KINKADE)

Nor did the ethnographers have pre- and early-contact diseases in mind and, therefore, ask questions that would have elicited information about them. Generation after generation the elderly died, cultures changed, and, eventually, oral traditions thinned. What is left are short references and, condensed and often rephrased, a few whole accounts. All the material cited here has been written down, and it is impossible to reconstruct the circumstances of the stories or the intentions of the tellers. Often an account has been translated by one person and then recorded in summary form by another. In Jan Vansina's phrase, they are "mutilated messages" that present every opportunity for misunderstanding.[8] And yet, these surviving fragments are powerful and generally consistent with each other.

Erna Gunther, writing on the Clallam, (south coast of the Strait of Juan de Fuca) and Homer Barnett, writing on the Coast Salish of British Columbia, either heard no stories about early epidemics or did not record them.[9] Wilson Duff, writing on the Sto:lo (along the lower Fraser well above its mouth) considered that early epidemics probably had reached the Sto:lo but had no information about them.[10] On the other hand, W. W. Elmendorf, ethnographer of the Twana (Hood Canal in Puget Sound) learned that his informants' grandparents "lived at times of disastrous epidemics." The most severe, he was told, was very early, "perhaps about 1800," and came from the south via the Lower Chehalis; "from the Twana it passed north to the Klallam and peoples on southern Vancouver Island."[11] Wayne Suttles, writing on the Lummi (southeastern Strait of Georgia) reported that according to "native tradition" smallpox arrived before George Vancouver in 1792; "several villages were completely wiped out, while all suffered losses."[12]

Other accounts are fuller, though somewhat filtered by white constructions. In the mid-1890s a Vancouver woman, Ellen Webber, asked the Kwantlen about a large unoccupied midden approximately a quarter of a mile long, one hundred feet wide and, at its center, some twenty feet deep along the north bank of the Fraser River forty kilometers from its mouth. She published her findings "as they were given to me" (but largely in her own words) in *The American Antiquarian*. Apparently the village was more than six hundred years old and had contained six hundred prosperous people. Attacks from the north had always been fended off, usually with stones piled in cairns along the riverbank in front of the village."[13] But one year the raiders came in such numbers that their canoes blackened the river. Even so, the Kwantlen defended their village ferociously. The river ran red with blood. Then, as a Kwantlen victory seemed assured, some of their enemy attacked from the rear.

> Now all was confusion. Many were killed, and many women were taken slaves. A few escaped to the woods, where they remained in hiding two or three days. Then, with the children, they came out, and with sad hearts they laid away their dead. . . . But misfortune followed the little band of survivors. In the swamp, near the village lived a fearful dragon with saucer-like eyes of fire and breath of steam. The village was apparently regaining its former strength when this dragon awoke and breathed upon the children. Where

his breath touched them sores broke out and they burned with the heat, and they died to feed this monster. And so the village was deserted, and never again would the Indians live on that spot.[14]

Until almost Webber's day, people "remembered and respected the dragon" and when passing the swamp crossed to the other side of the river and paddled softly and silently so as not to waken it. "Accursed is the one who awakens the dragon, he and all his people; for the sore-sickness will surely be their punishment."[15]

In 1896 Charles Hill-Tout, former theology student at Oxford and then master of an Anglican college in Vancouver, visited the Squamish "through the kindness of the Roman Catholic bishop" to record their history and cosmology.[16] The chiefs produced "the old historian of the tribe," Mulks, decrepit, blind, and "about 100 years old." He spoke only archaic Squamish, which Hill-Tout could not understand, and which Mulks uttered "in a loud, high-pitched key" that his Squamish listeners followed with rapt attention. Every ten minutes or so, the translator offered a précis, not a fifth, Hill-Tout estimated, of what the old man had said. The story began with the creation of the world out of the water, and continued with accounts of a flood from which only one couple survived and of a winter that did not end and during which all but two, a man and his daughter, died of starvation. In each case the land was repeopled, and "the people learned to forget the terrible punishment the Great Spirit had sent upon their forefathers." Then,

one salmon season the fish were found to be covered with running sores and blotches, which rendered them unfit for food. But as the people depended very largely upon these salmon for their winter's food supply, they were obliged to catch and cure them as best they could, and store them away for food. They put off eating them till no other food was available, and then began a terrible time of sickness and distress. A dreadful skin disease, loathsome to look upon, broke out upon all alike. None were spared. Men, women and children sickened, took the disease and died in agony by hundreds, so that when the spring arrived and fresh food was procurable, there was scarcely a person left of all their numbers to get it. Camp after camp, village after village, was left desolate. The remains of which, said the old man, in answer to my queries on this head, are found today in the old camp sites or midden-heaps over which the forest has been growing for so many generations. Little by little the remnant left by the disease grew into a nation once more, and when the first white men sailed up the Squamish in their big boats, the tribe was strong and numerous again.[17]

In 1936 Old Pierre, then about seventy-five years old, told the ethnographer Diamond Jenness a similar story (although more influenced by the missionaries).[18] Old Pierre, a Katzie, lived along the Pitt River, a tributary of the lower Fraser two days' paddle from the Squamish. The time came, he said, when the land was "overcrowded." When people "gathered at the

Fraser River to fish, the smoke from their morning fires covered the country with a pall of smoke." Then the "Lord Above" sent rain that fell until most of the mountains were covered and most people had drowned. After the flood, the population multiplied again and "the Lord Above . . . saw that once more they were too numerous in the land." "Then in the third month (October) of a certain year snow began to fall." Soon every house was buried. Nine months passed "before the snow melted completely from the house-tops." Half the people died of starvation. A third time the population grew, and then came smallpox. Old Pierre's account is the most explicit surviving pre-contact description of the disease around the Strait of Georgia.

> After many generations the people again multiplied until for the third time the smoke of their fires floated over the valley like a dense fog. Then news reached them from the east that a great sickness was travelling over the land, a sickness that no medicine could cure, and no person escape. Terrified, they held council with one another and decided to send their wives, with half the children, to their parents' homes, so that every adult might die in the place where he or she was raised. Then the wind carried the smallpox sickness among them. Some crawled away into the woods to die; many died in their homes. Altogether about three-quarters of the Indians perished.
>
> My great-grandfather happened to be roaming in the mountains at this period, for his wife had recently given birth to twins, and, according to custom, both parents and children had to remain in isolation for several months. The children were just beginning to walk when he returned to his village at the entrance to Pitt Lake, knowing nothing of the calamity that had overtaken its inhabitants. All his kinsmen and relatives lay dead inside their homes; only in one house did there survive a baby boy, who was mainly suckling at its dead mother's breast. They rescued the child, burned all the houses, together with the corpses that lay inside them, and built a new home for themselves several miles away.
>
> If you dig today on the site of any of the old villages you will uncover countless bones, the remains of the Indians who perished during this epidemic of smallpox. Not many years later Europeans appeared on the Fraser, and their coming ushered in a new era.[19]

Farther upriver, among the Sto:lo, echoes of similar events linger to this day. Albert Louis heard of a flood before the whites came, then smallpox. "It killed, oh, half the Indians all around the Fraser River there."[20] Dan Milo, almost one hundred years old in 1962, spoke of a village (Kilgard) where everyone died save one boy who settled down with a girl who was the only survivor from a village nearby.[21] In the village of Sxwoxwiymelh ("a lot of people died at once"), according to Susan Peters, twenty-five to thirty people died each day and were buried in one of the larger pit houses.[22] Patrick Charlie said that everyone there died of smallpox and that the houses were burned down.[23] In 1986 Jimmy Peters, who grew up after

World War I in the village of Yale at the foot of the Fraser Canyon, remembered elders who tried to keep children away from the houses collapsed on the dead and the burial grounds, and the children who, curious and uncomprehending, sneaked off there anyway.

> Things that the old timers did years ago, we're not supposed to touch it even kickwillie [pit] houses. And where they were buried. A lot of them died in that place. And just buried in there. . . . Chickenpox, smallpox, killed them all off. And they just died there. And we're not supposed to go there and touch them. A lot of times we used to go up there and dig out and see what they used to use years back. Like rock bowls, or rock knives, wood chisels, you know. But they'd tell me. "Don't you go there. Somedays, some nights you'll dream about that, and you might not live long," he says. They're too sacred. You leave them there. You're not supposed to touch anything that they owned years back.[24]

Sometime in the 1920s, Ayessic, chief at Hope, a village fifty kilometers below Yale on the Fraser, told the antiquarian and collector C.F. Newcombe about the first whites to descend the river. "News came from above . . . that men of different race were coming." Troubled, "the people came together and it was decided to try to please the newcomers." After they had painted their bodies "with red fungus paint (soquat)," messengers were sent to invite the strangers at Big Canyon "to come down." " They found them there camping with a number of boxes and packs which were thought to hold smallpox or miracle medicine."[25]

In the 1960s a fisherman (Nick Stevens) at the mouth of the river remembered his native grandfather's account of smallpox among the Cowichan on Saltspring Island. There, "according to the stories handed down," smallpox came on the south wind, and the people could not get "the clean north wind to blow the foul disease away." The south wind blew all winter "until most of the tribe were dead and there were too few left to bury their bodies." The survivors took the corpses to a small island near Fulford harbor, "placing their remains in crevices in the rocks, covering them with flat stones." When, as boys, Nick Stevens and his brother found a skull on the island their grandfather flew into a rage. "Take it back where you found it, he roared. It will bring us bad luck."[26]

In a slightly different category is *Indians of Skagit County*, by Martin Sampson, a Swinomish chief, published in 1972. Relying partly on oral tradition, Sampson describes a "first epidemic in the 1700s," which he identifies as smallpox, that killed a great many coastal people but did not reach the upper Skagit.[27]

Ample ground exists for disagreement about the meaning of these fragments. They may not all refer to the same epidemic, their dating would be expected to be uncertain, some of their elements (for example, floods) recur in stories told in many cultures, and some of their analytical categories are anachronistic introductions. At the same time, many point to an eighteenth-century epidemic, and two have an explicit chronological marker: the epidemic preceded whites. Descriptions of the disease fit smallpox (though measles is probably not excluded. Yet these fragments, coming from many different performance situations, appear to describe the same event and are broadly congruent with other event from outside the oral tradition.

The European record of the lands and peoples around the Strait of Georgia begins in 1790 when the Spaniard Manuel Quimper sailed through the Strait of Juan de Fuca as far as the San Juan Islands. Encountering small numbers of natives almost wherever he went, he estimated that there were five hundred people in the Strait and a thousand at its southwestern entrance near Núñez Gaona (Neah Bay). Some of these people, he thought, had been drawn from the outer coast by the great quantities of "seeds" (camas?) available in the strait.[28] The next year, the commander at Nootka, Francisco Eliza, continued the Spanish survey through most of El Gran Canal de Nuestra Sra del Rosario (the Strait of Georgia). Again, he saw many people at the entrance to the Strait of Juan de Fuca and mentioned native settlements here and there around the Gran Canal del Rosario. Along the south shore of the Strait of Juan de Fuca natives "from outside" came from time to time "to trade boys"; at the edge of all the beaches were "skeletons fastened to poles."[29] The next year both British (Vancouver) and Spanish (Galiano, Valdes) expeditions circumnavigated Vancouver Island, surveying and mapping as they went. The Spanish wrote appreciatively about the natives but offered few comments on native settlements or numbers. They found deserted and inhabited villages in the Gulf Islands and inhabited villages near rivers at the head of some inlets and at several other places. Beyond Johnstone Strait, on the northeast coast of Vancouver Island, the Nuchaimuses (Nimpkish) were a "populous tribe."[30]

The British, who had more officers and a little more time than the Spaniards and were more inclined to treat natives as objects for investigation, provided a good deal more information. Reaching the southeastern end of the Strait of Juan de Fuca, Vancouver began to find deserted villages, and human skeletons "promiscuously scattered about the beach, in great numbers." After local surveys in the ships' boats, his officers made similar reports; it seemed, Vancouver wrote, as if "the environs of Port Discovery were a general cemetery for the whole of the surrounding country." In some of the deserted villages "the habitations had now fallen into decay; their inside, as well as a small surrounding space that appeared to have been formerly occupied, were overrun with weeds." There were also "lawns" on eminences fronting the sea, which Vancouver thought might have been sites of former villages; in a few of them the framework of houses remained. In Vancouver's mind, "each of the deserted villages was nearly, if not quite, equal to contain all the scattered inhabitants we saw."[31] As the expedition continued into Puget Sound, it found more of the same.

> During this Expedition we saw a great many deserted Villages, some of them of very great extent and capable of holding many human Inhabitants—the Planks were taken away, but the Rafters stood perfect, the size of many a good deal surprised us, being much larger in girth than the Discovery's Main mast. A Human

face was cut on most of them, and some were carved to resemble the head of a Bear or Wolf—The largest of the Villages I should imagine had not been inhabited for five or six years, as brambles and bushes were growing up a considerable height.[32]

In a "favoured" land that was "most grateful to the eye" there were not many people.[33] "We saw only the few natives which are mentioned, silence prevailed everywhere, the feathered race, as if unable to endure the absence of man, had also utterly deserted this place."[34]

The expedition continued north, and found more deserted villages along the eastern shore of the Strait of Georgia. At Birch Bay there was "a very large Village now overgrown with a thick crop of Nettles and bushes."[35] There were deserted villages in Burrard Inlet, Howe Sound, and Jervis Inlet, and only occasional "small parties of Indians either hunting or fishing [that] avoided us as much as possible."[36] Farther north, Toba Inlet "was nearly destitute of inhabitants," although there was a deserted but well-fortified village that "seemed so skillfully contrived and so firmly and well executed as rendered it difficult to consider the work of the untutored tribes we had been accustomed to meet."[37] Only as the expedition traveled into and through Johnstone Strait did it encounter a country that was "infinitely more populous than the shores of the gulf of Georgia."[38]

While Vancouver considered that deserted villages and numerous human skeletons "do not amount to a direct proof of the extensive depopulation they indicate," he and his officers thought that the lands around Puget Sound and the Strait of Georgia had been recently and severely depopulated.[39] Archibald Menzies, the expedition's botanist, estimated that "the inhabitants of this extensive Country [apparently Puget Sound] did not appear to us on making every allowance of computation from the different Villages and strolling parties that were met with to exceed one thousand in all, a number indeed too small for such a fine territory."[40] Peter Puget gave the same figure.[41] All agreed that the cause or causes of depopulation could not be established, but variously speculated that they might have been disease, warfare, or population movements associated with seasonal hunting and fishing or the maritime fur trade on the outer coast.

DISEASE

Vancouver reported near Port Discovery that "several of their stoutest men had been seen perfectly naked, and contrary to what might have been expected of rude nations habituated to warfare their skins were mostly unblemished by scars, excepting such as the smallpox seemed to have occasioned, a disease which there is great reason to believe is very fatal amongst them."[42] Farther south, in Hood Canal, he recognized "one man, who suffered very much from the small pox. This deplorable disease is not only common, but it is greatly to be apprehended is very fatal amongst them, as its indelible marks were seen on many; and several had lost the sight of one eye, which was remarked to be generally the left, owing most likely to the virulent effects of this baneful disorder."[43] Later, near Whidbey Island,

Vancouver reported that Puget had met some very unwelcoming Indians: "In their persons they seemed more robust than the generality of the inhabitants; most of them had lost their right eye, and were much pitted with the small pox."[44] Puget himself wrote: "The Small pox must have had, and most terribly pitted they are; indeed many have lost their Eyes and no Doubt it has raged with uncommon Inveteracy among them but we never saw any Scars with wounds, a most convincing proof in my Mind of their peaceable Disposition."[45] The Spaniards did not report signs of smallpox.

The next Europeans in the region were Simon Fraser's overland party in 1808. Fraser mentioned smallpox once: "The small pox was in the camp [a native village some two hundred kilometers from the mouth of the Fraser River] and several Natives were marked with it."[46] David Thompson, on the lower Columbia three years later, was asked: "Is it true that the white men . . . have brought with them the Small Pox to destroy us . . . is this true and are we all soon to die."[47] The fur trader Ross Cox, who spent two months at the mouth of the Columbia in 1814, said that the natives remembered smallpox with "a superstitious dread."[48] John Work, a member of a Hudson's Bay Company (HBC) expedition sent from the Columbia in 1824 to explore the lower Fraser, noted that an old chief near the mouth of the Fraser River seemed to be marked with smallpox.[49] The next year a Scottish botanist, John Scouler, visited the Strait of Georgia in an HBC ship and saw an elderly, pockmarked native in the "retinue" of the Cowichan chief "Chapea" at Point Roberts, just south of the mouth of the Fraser. He had seen no other direct evidence of smallpox on the Northwest Coast.

> The rarity of such an occurrence at once indicated the fatality of the disease and the dread they entertain of it. This epidemic broke out among them in 17— and soon depopulated the eastern coast of America, and those on the Columbia were not secure behind the Rocky Mountains, and the ravages of the disease were only bounded by the Pacific Ocean. The Cheenooks to the present time speak of it with horror, and are exceedingly anxious to obtain that medicine which protects the whites, meaning vaccination. Such is the dread of this disease that when about to plunder the tribes of the interior, they have been deterred by the threat of disseminating smallpox among them.[50]

Three years later the Hudson's Bay Company established Fort Langley on the lower Fraser; in the fort journal (1827–30) and in the correspondence associated with the fort's early years, physical evidence of smallpox is not mentioned.[51]

RAIDING

At the time of the Fort Langley journal the peoples around Georgia Strait and Puget Sound lived in terror of raids from the Yaclewtas (Lequiltok), a Kwakwa̱ka'wakw people from northern Vancouver Island. Armed with muskets obtained directly or indirectly from Nawittee, a maritime fur-trade center at the northern end of Vancouver Island, the Lequiltok killed or captured many Coast Salish people in the 1820s. The fact that Vancouver's journals mention fortified villages and beacons (watchtowers?) "so frequently erected in the more southerly parts of New Georgia," and that abundant archaeological evidence exists of fortified, pre-contact sites around the Strait of Georgia, imply that raiding had been common before 1792.[52] The many native accounts of these raids are difficult to date, but at least in the Kwantlen story reported by Ellen Webber a raid from the north was followed by smallpox, which, in turn, was followed by the coming of whites. Myron Eells, a missionary in Puget Sound, reported a story, which he probably heard sometime between 1875 and 1879, of a pitched and apparently pre-contact battle near Victoria between warriors from most of the Puget Sound tribes and "the British Columbia Indians" (probably the Lequiltok). The British Columbia Indians won, and "only a few of the defeated Indians ever lived to return; in some cases only three or four of a tribe."[53] Undoubtedly raiding was widespread before 1792, with often drastic local effects. Whether it could lay waste to a region as large as the lands around Puget Sound and the Strait of Georgia, especially before 1792 when few if any raiders had firearms, is another matter.

POPULATION MOVEMENTS

Twentieth-century ethnographies of people such as the Clallam (Gunther), Twana (Elmendorf), and Lummi (Suttles)—who occupied territories where the Vancouver expedition found many deserted villages—describe seasonal migrations.[54] Early in the spring small groups left coastal winter villages to fish, to dig clams, to gather edible plants, or to hunt along coasts nearby. The Lummi went to the eastern San Juan Islands to dig camas and clams, to fish for spring salmon and halibut, and to hunt; the Twana dispersed around the shores of Hood Canal. Some old people usually remained in the winter village where, through the spring and summer, groups returned intermittently and briefly to leave dried fish or roots. In late July some of the eastern Clallam went to Hood Canal to take dog salmon. In September most of the Lummi gathered at fishing weirs a short distance up the Nooksack River. Such seasonal rounds did not take most people far from their winter village or the coast. The Twana named the shores of Hood Canal in great detail and the interior very sparsely. Certainly, the ethnographies describe early- to mid-nineteenth-century practices that, it has been argued recently, were even more local in the 1790s.[55] In either case, almost everyone who wintered around Puget Sound and the Strait of Georgia would have been scattered in small groups along the coast fairly near their winter villages when the Vancouver expedition passed through.

John Scouler was the first to suggest that a failure to understand the native seasonal round was "the cause of the mistake into which the very accurate C. [aptain] Vancouver fell, concerning the apparent depopulation of the coast."[56] Scouler himself thought, incorrectly, that natives "retreat to the interior of the country" from the end of September to the beginning of

April, and then returned to the coast where, by Scouler's own logic, Vancouver should have found them. There is no evidence that native seasonal rounds took people away in May and June from the coastlines that Vancouver and his officers explored and mapped.

Another possibility, however, is raised in the journals: that peoples from these inland waters had moved to the outer coast to trade directly with Europeans. If they had, there is no record of it in the ethnographies. Nor would peoples along or en route to the outer coast readily make room for intruding traders, much less for entire communities. The characteristic continental pattern of the fur trade is the opposite; groups well placed to trade directly with Europeans sought to monopolize such contacts by keeping others away.[57]

o

Native oral traditions and the texts of European explorers and traders provide largely independent records of late-eighteenth-century disease and depopulation around the Strait of Georgia. Besides their distinct cultural contexts, the two accounts are differently positioned in relation to the events they describe. The one grows out of the curiosity and ignorance of outsiders and the durability of writing; the other, out of the intimacy of experience and the shifting nature of oral tradition. Yet the contents of one seem to be broadly reproduced in that of the other. The two sets are mutually reinforcing and undoubtedly address the same horrendous event: late pre-contact depopulation around the Strait of Georgia and Puget Sound caused principally by smallpox.

The outbreak of smallpox was part of a pandemic that broke out in central Mexico in 1779 and quickly spread.[58] In 1780–81 it devastated the Guatemalan Highlands and a decade later reached southern Chile, enabling the Spaniards to expand into an area they had been unable to conquer for 250 years.[59] The New Mexican pueblos were hit in 1780; from there, transported indirectly by horse, smallpox diffused rapidly northward to affect all groups on the northern plains and, by early 1782, the forest Cree north and west of lake Manitoba.[60] From there it soon reached the Chipewyans. According to David Thompson, who was on the plains a few years later, "From the Chipeways it extended over all the Indians of the forest to its northward extremity and by the [Dakota] Sioux over all the Indians of the Plains and crossed the Rocky Mountains."[61] The same epidemic affected groups around the Great Lakes. Thompson, who estimated that half to three-fifths of the people on the northern plains died, talked with an Orcadian employee (from Orkney) of the Hudson's Bay Company who had witnessed the devastation: stinking tents in which all were dead, bodies eaten by wolves and dogs, "survivors in such a state of despair and despondence that they could hardly converse with us." "The countries were in a manner depopulated."[62] Twenty-three years later, when Lewis and Clark reached the middle Missouri, they found the "fallen down earth of the houses" and the scattered bones of men and animals in empty villages.[63]

An elderly man at Fort Cumberland on the North Saskatchewan River told Thompson that a war party of Nahathaway (upper Churchill and Saskatchewan River Cree) Indians had contracted the disease from the Snake (Shoshone).[64] William Tomison, the trader at Cumberland House on the North Saskatchewan River, understood that the disease had reached the Shoshone from the Spaniards.[65] Certainly, smallpox was among the Shoshone in 1781. From a major rendezvous in southwestern Wyoming, the Shoshone traded with the Flathead, Nez Perce, Walla Walla, and various peoples along the Snake River.[66] Any of these trading connections could have brought smallpox to the lower Columbia. So could parties of Flatheads, Pend d'Oreille, Nez Perce, and others that crossed the Rockies to hunt and raid along the upper Missouri.[67] In 1840 Asa Smith, a Congregational missionary, reported that sixty or seventy years before smallpox had reached the Nez Perce this way, "very few surviving the attack of the disease."[68] In 1829 the Hudson's Bay Company trader John Work reported "a dreadful visitation of smallpox" on the Columbia Plateau near Fort Colvile that, he estimated, had occurred fifty or sixty years before. The Jesuit missionary Gregory Mengarini reported smallpox among the Flathead at about the same time.[69]

It is clear, as Scouler reported in 1825, that smallpox reached the lower Columbia from the east. A decade earlier on the Columbia, Ross Cox drew on the same body of common knowledge:

> The disease first proceeded from the banks of the Missouri. It travelled with destructive rapidity as far north as Athabasca and the slaves of Great Slave Lake, crossed the Rocky Mountains at the sources of the Missouri, and having fastened its deadly venom on the Snake Indians [Shoshone], spread its devastating course to the northward and west-ward, until its frightful progress was arrested by the Pacific Ocean.[70]

So, in the 1840s did John Dunn, another fur trader. Smallpox, he said, "had nearly dispeopled the whole of the northern continent of its native inhabitants."[71] Breaking out "between the sources of the Missouri and the Mississippi . . . it spread its devastation northward as far as Athabasca, and the three horns of the Great Slave Lake; and westward across the Rocky Mountains to a short distance along the shores of the north Pacific. . . . Numbers of tribes were totally swept away; or reduced to a few scattered and powerless individuals. The remnants of many others united; and formed a new and heterogeneous union."[72]

As James Mooney suggested years ago, the diffusion of the epidemic from this direction probably dates its arrival along the lower Columbia to 1782.[73] From the lower Columbia it spread north, probably via the Cowlitz and lower Chehalis Rivers, to Puget Sound and in 1782–83 affected most if not all the peoples around Puget Sound and the Strait of Georgia.[74] It extended as far north as Nitinat on the west coast of Vancouver Island, to perhaps Cape Mudge on the east coast of Vancouver Island, and up the Fraser River well into the canyon (Figure 2).[75] It may have stopped because it struck in winter; devastated populations may no longer have been infectious when mobility increased in the spring. The mortality rate will never be known, but given evidence from the plains that this was hemorrhagic smallpox and the dense, previously unaffected populations it encountered on the west coast, Old Pierre's estimate of three-quarters may well be conservative.[76]

In my view, and contrary to Robert Boyd, who has recently and usefully reopened the study of epidemics on the Northwest Coast, there was not a second smallpox epidemic in Puget Sound and around the Strait of Georgia in 1801.[77] Boyd's evidence for a second epidemic—Elmendorf's informants, Old Pierre, and Fraser's report—is consistent with a single epidemic in 1782. Moreover, by the time the Astorians and Northwesters arrived on the lower Columbia visible evidence of smallpox had become rare. Ross Cox, at Fort George in 1812 and for several years thereafter, reported that those bearing traces of smallpox were "nearly extinct."[78] John Scouler saw only one such face during a year on the lower Columbia and the Northwest Coast in the mid-1820s; John Work saw one pockmarked face on the Fraser in 1824.[79] Hudson's Bay Company traders, who usually reported evidence of smallpox, did not mention smallpox in the Fort Langley Journal (1827–30) or fort correspondence because they saw no trace of it (which may suggest a particularly high mortality rate in 1782. among affected children or that the peoples who came to trade and fish along the lower Fraser had not brought the elderly with them). Had there been a smallpox epidemic in 1801, evidence would still have been abundantly at hand less than a generation later and would have been reported. In a sense, however, Boyd is right about the limited coastal range of "the epidemic of 1801," although his map approximately describes the epidemic of 1782. Smallpox had appeared among the Tlingit in the 1770s but, as is pointed out below, there is no evidence that there was a coastwide epidemic in 1775. In 1862 there certainly was, but this time government officials and missionaries had vaccinated most of the Coast Salish and few of them died.[80]

It might now appear possible to estimate the regional population just prior to smallpox, especially as, in 1830, Archibald McDonald, chief trader at Fort Langley, compiled a census of the peoples around Puget Sound and the Strait of Georgia.[81] Positing a sexually balanced population and a normal age distribution after 1782, no ecological constraints on population growth, and cultural pressure to build up the population (therefore high birthrates), it would seem possible to work back from 1830 to an estimate of the population just after the epidemic. This figure multiplied by the rate of population loss in 1782 would give the pre-epidemic population. However, it is not known whether other European diseases reached the region soon after 1782 (gonorrhea came with the traders to Fort Langley in 1827 but may already have reached the area). It is not known whether raiding was a major demographic factor (though in this period there is reason to think that it was). The mortality rates for 1782 are only estimates. The census of 1830 is very approximate. And so on. No solid ground exists anywhere.

Other approaches to estimating pre-contact populations are not more promising.[82] It hardly seems possible, in this region of great ecological variety, general abundance, and occasional dearth, to estimate usefully the

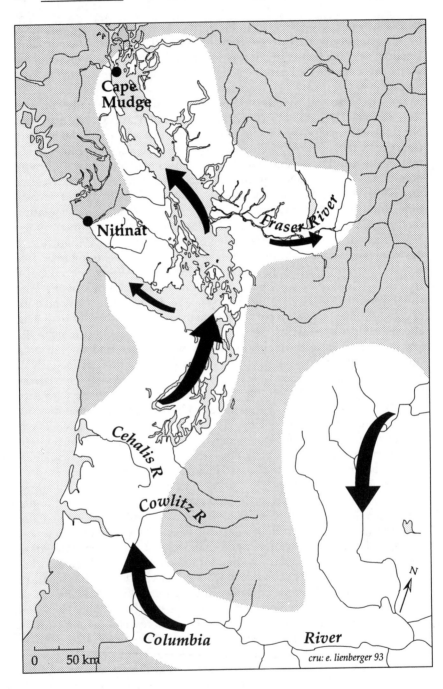

FIGURE 2   *APPROXIMATE DISTRIBUTION OF
SMALLPOX, 1782*

regional ecological carrying capacity for peoples of late-eighteenth-century Coast Salish technology. Perhaps it can be said only that, given a mild, humid climate, the resources of river and sea, and the capacity of migrating salmon to transfer a portion of the food chain of the whole North Pacific Ocean to local fishing sites, there was more nonagricultural food on the Northwest Coast than anywhere else on the continent, and perhaps more in and around the lower Fraser River than elsewhere on the Northwest Coast. Nor, given the methodological problems of inferring population density from archaeological evidence, can archaeology soon provide reliable estimates.[83] If the diseases that shortly followed smallpox were known (they are not), medical predictions of rates of infection and mortality could be made. The rate of population decline around the Strait of Georgia inferred from the nineteenth-century censuses (1830, 1839, 1852, 1876, 1877, 1881) could be projected back to 1780, but this projection takes no account of the disastrous first effects of European infectious diseases. In short, none of these approaches suggests a calculation or a research strategy that might be expected to yield a fairly reliable estimate of the pre-smallpox population around the Strait of Georgia.

I return, therefore, to opinions from the past. Vancouver and his officers thought the region was depopulated. Thirty-five years later, the Hudson's Bay Company traders at Fort Langley were amazed at the numbers of people about. Canoes passed up and down river "by Hundreds," or "in great numbers."[84] In 1828, 550 canoes of Cowichan and 200 of Squamish came down from the Fraser Canyon. A three-quarter-mile-long Cowichan fishing village sat on the south bank of Lulu Island, and a Nanaimo village, only somewhat smaller, was a few miles below the fort.[85] Often, from the trader's perspective, "a great many Indians" were hanging around.[86] Archibald McDonald, chief trader at Fort Langley, noted, "The Indian population in this part of the world is very great."[87]

The census he submitted in 1830 reported native men around the Strait of Georgia, Puget Sound, and along the lower Fraser River. It had been made "by repeated examination of the Indians themselves," and particularly, for Fraser populations, of Sopitchin, a "chief" from a village at the foot of the Fraser Canyon. McDonald was surprised at the high figures in the canyon but, as he had seen many people there in 1828 (when descending the river with Governor Simpson) and knew Sopitchin's estimates for the lower Fraser to be reliable, was inclined to accept them. This census, combined with the 1835 census of the Kwakwaka'wakw by the Hudson's Bay Company trader W. F. Tolmie, yields a map—the indirect product of two HBC traders and several native "chiefs"—of the distribution of population from the head of Puget Sound to the northern end of Vancouver Island in the 1830s (Figure 3).[88]

Although the map omits some peoples altogether, its general patterns are clear. There were dense populations in the Fraser Canyon and in parts of Queen Charlotte Strait. Elsewhere the numbers were modest. Along the lower Fraser River, a rich source of food, there were few winter residents.[89] Most of the peoples the traders commented on came seasonally to the river

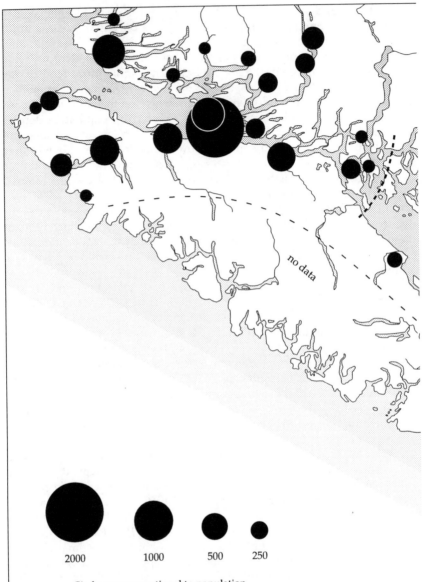

2000   1000   500   250

Circles are proportional to population.
For Kwakwaka'wakw no. of houses x 25 (Tolmie)
for rest, no. of men x 4 (McDonald).

- - -   Boundary between McDonald and
        Tolmie censuses

0   10 km

FIGURE 3   HBC CENSUS OF STRAIT OF GEORGIA
            AND EXTENSIONS, 1830s

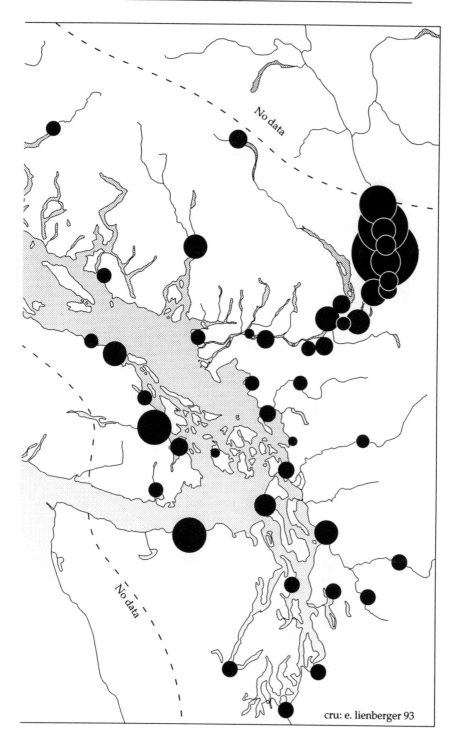

No data

No data

cru: e. lienberger 93

from around the Strait. On the coast of Puget Sound, the region that had so charmed Vancouver and his officers and in which there was such a quantity and diversity of accessible foods, the population was less than twenty-five hundred, well above Menzies' and Puget's estimates of one thousand, but still small in so favored an area.[90] The map is what, in hindsight, it could only be: an approximate picture of populations that had recovered somewhat from a devastating smallpox epidemic fifty years before. Estimates of population density are relative. For Hudson's Bay Company traders used to sparse boreal populations, there were a lot of people around; for those who knew what the population had been, there were all too few.

In the native memory there was a time when the land was densely settled. Even before the flood, according to Old Pierre, "Families settled on the mountains, on the plains, and on the sea-shore, wherever they could find food, for the land was overcrowded." After they recovered from the flood they were again "too numerous on the land."[91] According to Bob Joe, a Sto:lo, the population in the Chilliwack area was formerly "a thousand to one, comparing the population today."[92] Agnes Kelly said there had been "thousands" of people nearby at Agassiz.[93] Such estimates cannot he taken literally; more useful, perhaps, is an inventory of former Sto:lo and Southern Thompson villages from which a map of winter villages from Koia'um in the north (where in 1808 Fraser saw evidence of smallpox) to just below the modern city of Chilliwack can be prepared (Figure 4).[94] The data in the inventory are largely from ethnographic sources, collected over the years and supplemented by archaeological site surveys. Although the map has been prepared cautiously, it is uncertain whether all village sites were occupied each winter; if they were not then the map probably exaggerates the density of late-eighteenth-century winter settlement along this stretch of the Fraser River.

Yet it is intriguing, especially when considered in relation to data from the 1830 census (Figure 5). The distribution of population in 1830 does not correspond to the earlier distribution of villages. The Chilliwack River, along which, apparently, there had been some twenty-five villages, was largely deserted in 1830. Calculations are tempting. If the average population of a village was 150 people, then before the smallpox epidemic at least 15,000 people inhabited the area shown in Figure 4. There are obvious ambiguities about the number and size of inhabited villages, but it does seem clear that this section of the Fraser River once supported far more people than are indicated in the census of 1830 or than white settlers and ethnographers have supposed.

The demographic outlines of the fifty years after 1780 around the Strait of Georgia and Puget Sound are, I think, fairly clear. A large, dense, and probably demographically unstable population was devastated by smallpox in the winter of 1781–82 or 1782–83.[95] The great majority of the people died. Although recovery was retarded by Lequiltok riding and, perhaps, by other European diseases, the regional population had risen substantially by 1830 but not nearly to its pre-smallpox level.

Depopulation created vacuums that drew in surrounding people. Some of those who had not been able to live on the Fraser River could now do so.

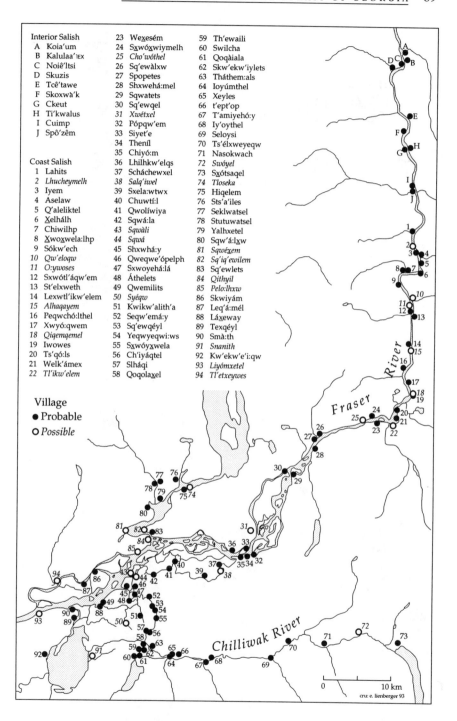

Interior Salish
A Koia'um
B Kalulaa'ᴵᴱˣ
C Noiê'ltsi
D Skuzis
E Tcê'tawe
F Skoxwà'k
G Ckeut
H Ti'kwalus
I Cuimp
J Spô'zêm

Coast Salish
1 Lahits
2 *Lhucheymelh*
3 Iyem
4 Aselaw
5 Q'aleliktel
6 X̱elhálh
7 Chiwilhp
8 X̱wox̱wela:lhp
9 Sókw'ech
10 *Qw'eloqw*
11 *O:ywoses*
12 Sx̱wótl'áqw'em
13 St'elxweth
14 Lexwtl'ikw'elem
15 *Alhaqayem*
16 Peqwchó:lthel
17 Xwyó:qwem
18 *Qiqemqemel*
19 Iwowes
20 Ts'qó:ls
21 Welk'ámex
22 *Tl'ikw'elem*

23 Wex̱esém
24 Sx̱wóx̱wiymelh
25 *Cho'wóthel*
26 Sq'ewàlxw
27 Spopetes
28 Shxwehá:mel
29 Sqwatets
30 Sq'ewqel
31 *Xwétxel*
32 Pópqw'em
33 Siyet'e
34 Thenfl
35 Chiyó:m
36 Lhilhkw'elqs
37 Scháchewxel
38 *Salq'iwel*
39 Sxela:wtwx
40 Chuwtf:l
41 Qwolíwiya
42 Sqwá:la
43 *Sqwàli*
44 *Sqwá*
45 Shxwhá:y
46 Qweqwe'ópelph
47 Sxwoyehá:lá
48 Áthelets
49 Qwemilits
50 *Syéqw*
51 Kwikw'alith'a
52 Seqw'emá:y
53 Sq'ewqéyl
54 Yeqwyeqwi:ws
55 Sx̱wóyx̱wela
56 Ch'iyáqtel
57 Slháqi
58 Qoqolax̱el

59 Th'ewaili
60 Swilcha
61 Qoqàiala
62 Skw'ekw'iylets
63 Tháthem:als
64 Ioyúmthel
65 Xeyles
66 t'ept'op
67 T'amiyehó:y
68 Iy'oythel
69 Seloysi
70 Ts'élxweyeqw
71 Nasokwach
72 *Swóyel*
73 Sx̱ótsaqel
74 *Tloseka*
75 Hiqelem
76 Sts'a'iles
77 Seklwatsel
78 Stutuwatsel
79 Yalhxetel
80 Sqw'á:lx̱w
81 *Sqwéx̱em*
82 *Sq'iq'ewilem*
83 Sq'ewlets
84 *Qithyil*
85 *Pelo:lhxw*
86 Skwiyám
87 Leq'á:mél
88 Láx̱eway
89 Texqéyl
90 Smà:th
91 *Snanith*
92 Kw'ekw'e'i:qw
93 *Liyómxetel*
94 *Tl'etxeywes*

Village
● Probable
○ *Possible*

F I G U R E   4   *WINTER VILLAGES, MID–LATE*
EIGHTEENTH CENTURY

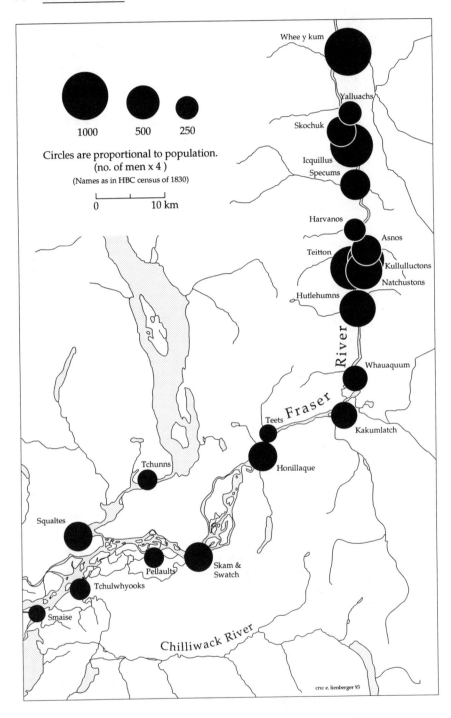

cru: e. lienberger 93

FIGURE 5   *HBC CENSUS, SMAISE TO WHEE Y KUM, 1830*

The evidence is unclear, but some surviving Katzie may have moved out of the Pitt River to settle on the Fraser; surviving upriver Chilliwack may have moved down to the rich sloughs on the Fraser floodplain.[96] It is quite possible—though no evidence exists one way or another—that space opened on the lower Fraser at this time for the Cowichan and Nanaimo fishing villages that were reported in the 1820s. The people in Mud Bay, just south of the Fraser, were wiped out, and the Semiahmoo moved north, occupying this territory. Similar relocations occurred on the San Juan Islands and on the south coast of Vancouver Island.[97] More generally, depopulation contributed to interregional political instability as the depleted Coast Salish became more vulnerable to Lequiltok raiding.[98] In the longer run, the Coast Salish, who once were the most numerous people on the Northwest Coast, became relatively invisible in their own territory. Other peoples came to exemplify Northwest Coast culture both to the outside world and to the newcomers in the towns and countrysides that emerged around Puget Sound and the Strait of Georgia. Such relative neglect has partly to do with urbanization patterns; the particular secrecy with which the Coast Salish treated their stories, songs, and ceremonies; and the influence of Franz Boas; but it has also to do with early, profound depopulation. As the Swinomish chief Martin Sampson put it, the whites encountered "a people trying to recover from a devastating blow."[99]

ɔ

How is it that the smallpox epidemic of 1782 is not part of the lore of modern British Columbia, especially as it was identified, quite precisely, more than eighty years ago? In a short piece on the native population of North America published in the *Bulletin* of the Bureau of American Ethnology in 1910, James Mooney concluded that smallpox had reached the Pacific from the plains in 1782; in his more elaborate survey, published posthumously in 1928, he suggested that this epidemic was "very destructive throughout southern British Columbia."[100] Yet as late as 1964 the anthropologist Wilson Duff, in *Indian History of British Columbia*, used Hudson's Bay Company and later Dominion censuses to calculate that 70 000 people lived in what is now British Columbia in 1835.[101] Although Duff knew that there had been smallpox among the Tlingit, Haida, and Coast Tsimshian, and suspected it in the south, his estimate of the precontact population of British Columbia—"at least 80,000 and probably somewhat more"—largely discounted smallpox as a demographic influence. Most earlier ethnographers ignored the possibility of pre- or early contact epidemics of infectious European diseases; even as late as 1965 Philip Drucker thought that "the first devastating smallpox epidemic probably occurred in the middle 1830s."[102] Among contemporary scholars, Robin Fisher doubts much of the evidence for early smallpox."[103] James R. Gibson has spelled out the archival case for smallpox among the Tlingit and adjacent peoples in 1835–38 and, as noted above, Robert Boyd has argued an important, if jumbled, case for smallpox epidemics in 1775 and 1801.[104] Overall, academic scholarship has approached with great hesitation the idea that native societies were decimated by disease just before or soon after Europeans arrived on the Northwest Coast.

But why? The question has wide ramifications, and I can only sketch components of an answer.

It is important to recognize that the early-conflict Northwest Coast does not have a common epidemiological history, unlike the plains where, with the advent of the horse, diseases could be carried quickly over great distances. On the coast, people lived geographically circumscribed lives, traveling to local or regional resource procurement and trading sites, but not, until the establishment of Fort Victoria, drawn into contact with most other coastal peoples. When smallpox broke out in Victoria in 1867 and nervous officials sent natives home, a mechanism was at hand as never before for the diffusion of smallpox throughout the Northwest Coast. Smallpox had broken out among the Tlingit in the 1770s and had reached the lower Columbia from the east in 1782, but the two outbreaks were unconnected. Cook saw no signs of smallpox at Nootka in 1778, nor did the Spaniards in 1789–92, nor did the maritime fur traders. Smallpox was not there nor, from the evidence, anywhere else on the west coast of Vancouver Island north of Nitinat in the late eighteenth century.[105] Nor had it reached the northeast coast of the island. In 1841 Governor Simpson, traveling through Johnstone Strait in the Hudson's Bay Company's steamer the Beaver, found that the Quakeolths (Kwagulths, Kwakwaka'wakw) "had been exempted from the smallpox," a conclusion supported by the Vancouver journals and by Robert Galois's recent study of Kwakwaka'wakw settlement.[106] To grossly simplify the geography of early-contact disease, there were at least three broad epidemiological regions along the Northwest Coast: the Alaskan panhandle and north coastal British Columbia; the west coast of Vancouver Island and around Queen Charlotte Sound and Johnstone Strait; and the Strait of Georgia to the Columbia. If a common coastal pattern is assumed, then argument about different findings in different locations obscures both the complex geography of depopulation and particular demographic disasters, such as the smallpox epidemic of 1782–83. Eventually, a hundred years or more after contact, the demographic effects of introduced diseases among different populations may everywhere have been much the same— those who escaped smallpox in 1782 succumbing, they or their progeny, to other European introductions later—but, if this were so, there were many different local histories of depopulation.

Until the last generation, estimates of particular pre-contact populations—and therefore of particular epidemics and depopulations—have been approached within the widely held assumption that the contact population of North America (north of the Rio Grande) was about one million. Mooney divided his 1910 estimate of 1 150 000 as follows: U.S., 846 000; Canada, 220 000; Alaska, 72 000; Greenland, 10 000.[107] In his more elaborate estimates published posthumously in 1928, he "conservatively" estimated the pre-contact population of British Columbia at 86 000.[108] There were no other careful continental estimates. The influential Berkeley anthropologist, Alfred Kroeber, writing in 1939, thought that "until a new, equally systematic survey has been done, Mooney's figures should be accepted in toto," although in Kroeber's view they were "too high rather than too low" and would probably "shrink to around 900,000, possibly somewhat farther." Moreover, for Kroeber "the outstanding fact [about Mooney's figures] is the exceptional density on the Pacific coast."[109] This powerful orthodoxy survived well into the 1960s and beyond. Therefore, if early censuses pointed to a native population in British Columbia in the 1830s of about 70 000 (and if this number was an "exceptional density" in a country with a contact population of 220 000), pre-contact totals could not have been much higher. Such, precisely, was the box in which Wilson Duff and Philip Drunker found themselves. Given Mooney's, then Kroeber's, assumptions about Canadian and continental populations, there was not much demographic space for contact diseases on the Northwest Coast.

Nor, in a sense, was there ethnographic space. Salvage ethnography in the style of France Boas assumed traditional native cultures yielding to modern western cultures without much of interest in between. Therefore ethnographers in quest of the former sought out elderly people with good memories and wrote down as much of what they were told as possible, in so doing capturing, they thought, vanishing traditional ways. When field notes were worked up into books, there was an academic datum plane: traditional Northwest Coast culture. If the ethnographers asked their questions at the end of the nineteenth or early in the twentieth century, as many of them did, their informants remembered and described early– to mid-nineteenth-century societies. Ethnography transformed this slice of time into timeless traditional culture. Smallpox and other contact diseases posed two basic challenges to such procedures. First, they raised the possibility that informants' memories did not quite reach the traditional world. If smallpox or other diseases had disrupted societies before the most elderly informants remembered them, then traditional societies were simply out of ethnographic range. Ethnographic notebooks contained information about societies that were already somewhat transformed. Second, and even more telling, the concept of pre- or early-contact epidemics introduced the idea of time and began, however crudely, to situate native people historically. Native society before and after a devastating smallpox epidemic could not, presumably, be the same. The farther back in time epidemics were pushed—and the concept of change associated with them—the more they interfered with the idea of traditional culture, and the more impetus they gave to the idea of history. At the least, the Eurocentrism inherent in the assumption that native cultures were static would give way to another Eurocentrism: that native history began with a devastating European introduction. Beyond this was yet another assumption, that native societies changed like any others and generated multiple histories in which epidemics were embedded; but the ethnographers' view of native culture was more static and deflected them from the consideration of pre- and early-contact epidemics along the Northwest Coast.

The idea of disease-induced depopulation runs counter to the longheld conviction that Europeans brought enlightenment and civilization to savage peoples."[110] It turns the story of the contact process away from the rhetorics of progress and salvation and toward the numbing recognition of catastrophe. Progress wrestled from the wilderness by hard, manly work and registered by expanding settlements and population losses. The rhetoric of development begins to pale. The western idea of property coupled with an expanding world economy appear as agents of destruction as much as of creation. A linear view of progress fails, as it becomes harder to believe that European goods and a European God had rescued native peoples from want and ignorance. Ideologies and values that European transatlantic expansion had so powerfully reinforced lose authority. The whole European engagement with a New World, which was not new after all, begins to appear in a different light.

These sober thoughts were not what modern British Columbians or other recent North Americans proud of their achievements and intent on their futures wanted to hear. It was far more convenient to think that the native population had always been small and that those who remained would soon die off. In the late nineteenth and early twentieth centuries, as railways multiplied, speculations proliferated, boosterism filled the air, and the native populations dwindled, there was ample ground to think that both were true. By this time most natives lived on reserves as wards of the state, segregated from the mainstream of white society. To all intents and purposes they had become invisible, and their pasts, reduced to curious fragments in museums, were even more so. An immigrant racist white society was not interested in such pasts, scholarship was blinkered, and only a few elederly natives told stories that were easily construed as myths.

○

Now, some of the constraints are lifting. Hemispheric and continental pre-Columbian population estimates are far higher than in Mooney's or Kroeber's day; in their light, there is now room to consider that the population of British Columbia may have been greater than what seemed possible only a few years ago. Native peoples have not died out, and the continuing vitality of native societies coupled with their growing political and academic influence has considerably undermined the salvage ethnographers' bipolar model of culture. The broad critique of metatheory, positivist science, and one-point perspective, sustained over the last generation, has encouraged scholarship to articulate the long-hidden or suppressed accounts of relatively powerless people—women, ethnic minorities, peasants, refugees, as well as natives.[111] In addition, archival sources are more accessible than they were. For all these reasons, it is far easier now than it was even a short generation ago to discern infectious diseases in early-contact British Columbia. The picture that emerges is hardly surprising. Native people in the province were not spared what natives in the rest of the continent and hemisphere experienced. In the century or so after the first arrival of European infectious diseases, native populations throughout the Western Hemisphere commonly declined by some 90 percent; that, in all probability, was also the magnitude of decline in British Columbia. If so, then the population of the province on the eve of the first epidemics was well over two hundred thousand people, of whom more than fifty thousand lived around the Strait of Georgia and up the Fraser River to the limit of Coast Salish territory.[112] If population decline was on the order of 95 percent, then these figures are doubled.

In southern British Columbia the process of disease-related depopulation probably began with the smallpox epidemic of 1782.[113] Eventually, in recurring epidemics over approximately a century, smallpox visited all native groups in the province, some several times. However, it was only the most spectacular of a complex of European infectious diseases that together were far more devastating than any one alone. The eventual result, everywhere, was severe depopulation at precisely the time that changing technologies of transportation and communication brought more and more of the resources of the northwestern corner of North America within reach of the capitalist world economy. Here was an almost empty land, so it seemed, for the taking, and the means of developing and transporting many of its resources. Such was the underlying geographical basis of the bonanza that awaited immigrants to British Columbia.

Passing through the province by train just before World War I, Rupert Brooke, a poet as English as the ancient village of Grantchester where he lived, missed the dead and "the friendly presence of ghosts." Mountain breezes, he said, "have nothing to remember and everything to promise." This was a stranger's conceit. Jimmy Peters, who poked as a lad in the graves of his ancestors, knew otherwise. So did Charles Hill-Tout, who listened to Mulks, the old Squamish historian, and the Scowlitz elders who believed "their race is doomed to die out and disappear." Rupert Brooke was traveling through a profound settlement discontinuity, measured not, as it would have been in Europe, by decaying cities, wasted fields, and overgrown orchards, but by the abandonment of countless seasonal settlement sites, the unnaming and renaming of the land, and the belief of some that their world was coming to an end and of others that it was opening toward a prosperous future.

NOTES

1. Interview by Gordon Mohs and Sonny McHalsie with Elder Jimmy Peters, 29 September 1986, Sto:lo Heritage, Book 11A, Oral History Sto:lo Tribal Council, Sardis, BC. This essay owes much of its initial impetus to comments by Ruben Ware in *A Sto:lo Bibliography* (Sardis, BC, 1983) and to the remarkable collection of research materials in the Coqualeetza Resource Centre.

2. "Ethnological Report on the Stseelis (Chehalis) and Skaulits (Scowlitz) Tribes of the Halkomelem Division of the Salish of British Columbia," *Journal of the Royal Anthropological Institute* 34 (July–Dec. 1904). Reprinted in *The Salish People: The Local Contribution of Charles Hill-Tout*, vol. 3, *The Mainland Halkomelem*, ed. Ralph Maud (Vancouver, 1978), 100.

3. "The Americas before and after 1492: An Introduction to Current Geographical Research," *Annals of the Association of American Geographers* 82 (1992): 352.

4. On the medical implications of genetic similarity, see Francis L. Black, "Why Did They Die?" *Science* 258 (11 Dec. 1992): 1739–40.

5. For current estimates and reviews of estimates see William Denevan, "Native American Populations in 1492: Recent Research and Revised Hemispheric Estimate" in *The Native Population of the Americas in 1492*, 2nd ed. (Madison, WI, 1992), xvii–xxxviii; and Douglas H. Ubelaker, "North American Indian Population Size: Changing Perspectives" in *Disease and Demography in the Americas*, ed. J.W. Verano and D.H. Ubelaker (Washington, DC, 1992), 169–78.

6. One of the most contested judgments is *Delgamuukw et al. v the Queen, Reasons for Judgment,* Supreme Court of British Columbia, 8 March 1991.

7. Glenn Trewartha, "A Case for Population Geography," *Annals of the Association of American Geographers* 43 (June 1953): 71–97.

8. Vansina, *Oral Tradition as History* (Madison, WI, 1985), 83.

9. Gunther, *Klallam Ethnology,* University of Washington Publications in Anthropology, 1, 5 (Jan. 1927), 171–314; Barnett, *The Coast Salish of British Columbia* (Eugene, OR, 1955).

10. Duff, *The Upper Stalo Indians of the Fraser River of BC,* Anthropology in British Columbia, Memoir No. 1 (Victoria, 1952).

11. Elmendorf, *The Structure of Twana Culture,* Washington State University, Research Studies 28 (3), Monographic Supplement 2 (Pullman, WA, 1960), 272.

12. Suttles, "Post-Contact Culture Change among the Lummi Indians," *British Columbia Historical Quarterly* 18, 1–2 (1954): 42. In 1951 a Samish woman, Ruth Sheldon, then ninety-four years old, told Suttles that most of her people were wiped out by smallpox "about 300 years ago," a date that, allowing twenty years per generation, Suttles revises to 1770–90. Other information about disease that he gathered in the late 1940s and early 1950s from Semiahmo, Swinomish, and Katzie informants cannot be dated unambiguously to the eighteenth century. Suttles, personal communication, July 1993.

13. By Hydahs in this story, but Haida do not appear to have been on the South Coast before 1853. These raiders were probably Lequiltok, southern Kwakwa̲ka'wakw peoples.

14. E.C. Webber, "An Old Kwanthum Village—Its People and Its Fall," *American Antiquarian* 21 (Sept.–Oct. 1899): 309–14. "Dragon," presumably, is Ellen Webber's word.

15. Webber, *Museum and Arts Notes* 6, 3 (Sept. 1931): 119.

16. Hill-Tout, "Notes on the Cosmogony and History of the Squamish Indians of British Columbia" in *The Salish People: The Local Contribution of Charles Hill-Tout,* vol. 2, *The Squamish and the Lillooet,* ed. Ralph Maud (Vancouver, 1978). First published in *Transactions, Royal Society of Canada,* 2nd ser., 3 (1897): sec. 2. Franz Boas collected a somewhat similar Squamish story about a sequence of disasters caused by fire, flood, and finally smallpox and winter. "Later Qa' is sent the smallpox and one winter with deep snow to the people as punishment for their wickedness" ("Indian Legends of the North Pacific Coast of America Collected by Franz Boas" [typescript], trans. by Deitrich Bertz for the BC Indian Languages Project [1977], 92, Special Collections, University of British Columbia Library). T.P.O. Menzies, curator of the Vancouver City Museum, heard a version of Mulk's story from Chief George in North Vancouver in June 1934 (British

Columbia Archives and Records Society [BCARS], Newcombe Family Papers, Add. MS 1077, vol. 44, folder 5).

17. Maud, *Salish People*, 2:22.

18. Jenness, *The Faith of a Coast Salish Indian*, Anthropology in British Columbia, Memoir 3 (1955), British Columbia Provincial Museum, Victoria, BC.

19. Ibid., 34.

20. Interview by Oliver Wells with Albert Louis, 28 July 1965, in "Sto:lo Villages, Encampments, and Settlements," Sto:lo Tribal Council (1987), 160.

21. Wells, *The Chilliwacks and Their Neighbors* (Vancouver, 1987), 40. Albert Louie, n. 21, told much the same story.

22. "Sto:lo Villages, Encampments, and Settlements."

23. Interview by Wilson Duff, Yale University, summer 1950, BCARS, Stalo Notebook 1, Victoria, BC.

24. Interview by Gordon Mohs and Sonny McHalsie with Elder Jimmy Peters, 29 September 1986.

25. BCARS, Add. MS 1077, Newcombe Family Papers, Series 2, Ethnological Volume 44, folder 1.

26. "Are All Fishermen Superstitious?" *Fisherman* (Vancouver), 20 March 1964, 15.

27. Sampson, *Indians of Skagit County*, Skagit County Historical Series, No. 2, Skagit County Historical Society (Mount Vernon, WA, 1972), 25.

28. "Quimper's Journal" in Henry Raup Wagner, *Spanish Explorations in the Strait of Juan de Fuca* (Santa Ana, CA, 1933), 129–32; also Wayne Suttles, "They Recognize No Superior Chief: The Strait of Juan de Fuca in the 1790s" in *Culturas de la Costa Noroeste de America*, ed. J.L. Peset (Madrid, 1989), 251–64.

29. "Extract of the Navigation Made by the Pilot Don Juan Pantoja" in Wagner, *Spanish Explorations*, 185–88.

30. "Voyage of the Sutil and Mexicana" in Wagner, *Spanish Explorations*, esp. 254, 289, 293. On the Spanish route through Johnstone Strait see Robert Galois, *Kwakwaka'wakw Settlements, 1775–1920: A Geographical Analysis and Gazetteer* (Vancouver, 1994).

31. William Kaye Lamb, ed., *A Voyage of Discovery to the North Pacific Ocean and Round the World, 1791–1795* (London, 1984), 2:516–17, 538.

32. T. Manby Journal, Dec. 1790–June 1793, William Robertson Coe Collection, Yale University, 43; photocopy in W. Kaye Lamb Papers, Special Collections, University of British Columbia, Box 1.

33. Puget Journal, Adm 55, 27, 133–34, Public Record Office, London; photocopy in W. Kaye Lamb Papers.

34. James Johnstone Log Book, 2 Jan. 1792, 20 May 1792, 176; photocopy in W. Kaye Lamb Papers, Box 4. This point was obviously discussed; Archibald Menzies, the expedition's botanist, put it this way: "In his excursion . . . we saw only the few Natives I have already mentioned, silenced and solitude seemed to prevail over this fine and extensive country, even the feathered race, as if unable to endure the stillness that pervaded everywhere had in great measure abandoned it and were therefore very scarce." C.F. Newcombe, ed., *Menzies' Journal of Vancouver's Voyage, April–Oct. 1792* (Victoria, 1923), 40.

35. Newcombe, *Menzies' Journal*, 53.

36. T. Manby Journal, 12 June.

37. Lamb, *Voyage of Discovery*, 603–4.

38. Ibid., 613.

39. Ibid., 538.

40. Newcombe, *Menzies' Journal*, 49.

41. Puget Journal, 133–34.

42. Lamb, *Voyage of Discovery*, 540.

43. Ibid., 528.

44. Ibid., 559.

45. Puget Journal, 34.

46. W. Kaye Lamb, ed., *The Letters and Journals of Simon Fraser, 1806–1808* (Toronto, 1960), 94.

47. R. Glover, ed., *Thompson's Narrative, 1774–1812* (Toronto, 1962), 367.

48. Ross Cox, *Adventures on the Columbia River* (London, 1831), 1: 314.

49. John Work's Journal, 18 Nov. 1824–30 Dec. 1824, A/B/40/W89.2A, BCARS.

50. Dr John Scouler's Journal of a Voyage to N. W. America," *Quarterly of the Oregon Historical Society* 6 (June 1905): 303–4.

51. Fort Langley Journal, 27 June 1827–30 July 1830, BCARS.

52. Lamb, *Voyage of Discovery*, 603. See, for example, Donald H. Mitchell, "Excavations at Two Trench Embankments in the Gulf of Georgia Region," *Syesis* 1 (1–2): 29–46; and Gary Coupland, "Warfare and Social Complexity on the Northwest Coast" in *Cultures in Conflict: Current Archaeological Perspectives*, ed. D.C. Tkaczuk and B.C. Vivian (Calgary, 1989), 205–41. Defensive sites began to be built around the Strait of Georgia about one thousand years ago, and some were maintained into the nineteenth century (Grant Keddie, Archaeologist at Royal BC Museum, Victoria, personal communication, June 1993).

53. Eells, *The Indians of Puget Sound: The Notebooks of Myron Eells* (Seattle, WA, 1985), 24.

54. Gunther, *Klallam Ethnology*, esp. 195, 196, 214; Elmendorf, *The Structure of Twana Culture*, esp. 260–64; Wayne Suttles, "Post-Contact Culture Change among the Lummi Indians," *British Columbia Historical Quarterly* 18, 1–2 (1954): esp. 53–54.

55. The ethnographic record has been taken to describe pre-contact patterns of settlement and seasonal migration. However, Richard Inglis and James Haggarty have argued recently that on the west coast of Vancouver Island the pre-contact settlement pattern was one of many small villages, each occupied by a house group that depended on very local resources. See "Pacific Rim National Park Ethnographic History," Microfiche Report Series 257, Environment Canada (1986).

56. "Dr John Scouler's Journal," 198.

57. A tendency that can be observed from the earliest days of the St Lawrence fur trade. See for example, R. Cole Harris, ed., and Geoffrey J. Matthews, cart., *Historical Atlas of Canada*, vol. 1, *From the Beginning to 1800* (Toronto, 1987), 84, pl. 35.

58. Ann F. Ramenofsky, *Vectors of Death: The Archaeology of European Contact* (Albuquerque, NM, 1987), 130; H.F. Dobyns, "Estimating Aboriginal American Population: An Appraisal of Techniques with a New Hemispheric Estimate," *Current Anthropology* 7 (1966): 395–416.

59. W. George Lovell, *Conquest and Survival in Colonial Guatemala: A Historical Geography of the Cuchumatán Highlands, 1500–1821* (Montreal, 1992), 154–57; Fernando Casanuava, "Smallpox and War in Southern Chile in the Late Eighteenth Century" in *Secret Judgments of God: Old World Disease in Colonial Spanish America*, ed. N.D. Cook and W. George Lovell (Norman, OK, 1991), 183–212.

60. S.F. Cook, "Smallpox in Spanish and Mexican California, 1770–1845," *Bulletin of the History of Medicine* 7 (1939): 153–94; M. Simmons, "New Mexico's Smallpox Epidemic of 1780–1781," *New Mexico Historical Review* 41 (1966): 319–26; Arthur J. Ray, *Indians in the Fur Trade: Their Role as Trappers, Hunters, and Middlemen in the Lands Southwest of Hudson Bay, 1660–1870* (Toronto, 1974), 105–8; Jody F.

Decker, "Tracing Historical Diffusion Patterns: The Case of the 1780–1782 Smallpox Epidemic among the Indians of Western Canada," *Native Studies Review* 4, 1–2 (1988): 1–24; and "Depopulation of the Northern Plains Natives," *Social Science and Medicine* 33, 4 (1991): 381–96.

61. Glover, *Thompson's Narrative*, 236.

62. Ibid., 235–36.

63. Rueben Gold Thwaites, ed., *Original Journals of the Lewis and Clark Expedition, 1804–1806* (New York, 1904), 1:202; cited in Ramenofsky, *Vectors of Death*, 128–29. Lewis and Clark were told that "smallpox destroyed the greater part of the [Mandan] nation and reduced them to one large village and Some Small ones, all the nations before this maladey was afraid of them, after they were reduced the Seaux and other Indians waged war, and Killed a great many, and they moved up the Missourie" (Original Journals, 1:220).

64. Glover, *Thompson's Narrative*, 49.

65. Decker, "Tracing Historical Diffusion Patterns," 12.

66. William R. Swagerty, "Indian Trade in the Trans-Mississippi West to 1870" in *Handbook of North American Indians*, ed. Wilcomb E. Washburn, vol. 4, *History of Indian-White Relations* (Washington, DC, 1988), 352.

67. Clark Wissler, "Material Culture of the Blackfoot Indians," *Anthropological Papers of the American Museum of Natural History*, 5, 1 (New York, 1910), 13.

68. The quotes from Smith and Work are cited in Robert Boyd, "The Introduction of Infectious Diseases among the Indians of the Pacific Northwest, 1774–1874" (PhD thesis, University of Washington, 1985), 78–80.

69. Mengarini, *Recollections of the Flathead Mission: Containing Brief Observations, Both Ancient and Contemporary, Concerning This Particular Nation* (Glendale, CA, 1977), 193–94.

70. Cox, *Adventures on the Columbia River*, 1:312–13.

71. Dunn, *The Oregon Territory and the British North American Fur Trade* (Philadelphia, 1845), 84–85.

72. Ibid.

73. Mooney, "Population," Bureau of American Ethnology Bulletin 30 (Washington, DC, 1910).

74. Elmendorf was told that the disease came from the Lower Chehalis River via the Satsop people. Elmendorf, *The Structure of Twana Culture*, 272.

75. Hoskins, in F.W. Howay, *Voyages of the "Columbia" to the Northwest Coast, 1787–1790 and 1790–1793* (Boston, 1941), 196; Boit, in Howay, 371. This estimate is approximate. It accords generally with Vancouver's observations in 1792 and with George Simpson's in 1841 that the Qwakeolths had never been affected by smallpox. Simpson, *Narrative of a Journey around the World during the Years 1841 and 1842* (London, 1847), 1:189.

76. Decker, "Tracing Historical Diffusion Patterns," 16–17.

77. Boyd, "The Introduction of Infectious Diseases," 71–111; and "Demographic History, 1774–1874" in *Handbook of North American Indians*, ed. Wayne Suttles, vol. 7, *Northwest Coast* (Washington, DC, 1990), 137–38.

78. Cox, *Adventures on the Columbia River*, 1:314.

79. Even on the Columbia as early as 1814 pockmarked faces were becoming uncommon; Cox noted that "the vestiges . . . were still visible on the countenances of the elderly men and women." Ibid., 1:312.

80. It was reported that Roman Catholic missionaries vaccinated

"upward of 12 000 Indians on the Lower Fraser" (*New Westminster Columbian*, 29 April 1863), and that government officials vaccinated some 1200 natives at Lytton (ibid., 25 June 1862). A few natives along the Harrison River and at Douglas contracted the disease, but there was no epidemic along the Lower Fraser at this time. Beyond Lytton the picture was very different.

81. Archibald McDonald to Governor and Council, Northern Dept. of Rupert's Land, 25 Feb. 1830, HBCA, D.4/123 fos. 66–72 (microfilm reel 3M53). Printed, with some errors of transcription, in Mary K. Cullen, "The History of Fort Langley, 1827–96," *Canadian Historic Sites: Occasional Papers in Archaeology and History*, no. 20 (Ottawa, 1979), 82–89.

82. For a survey of methodologies of population reconstruction, see Noble David Cook, *Demographic Collapse: Indian Peru, 1520–1620*, vol. 1 (Cambridge, 1981).

83. Ramenofsky, *Vectors of Death*, is a brave attempt. See also Cook, *Demographic Collapse*.

84. Fort Langley Journal, 27 June 1827–30 July 1830, BCARS.

85. John Work's Journal, 19 Dec. 1824.

86. Such comments abound in the Fort Langley Journal.

87. McDonald to Governor and Council, 25 Feb.1830.

88. *The Journals of William Fraser Tolmie, Physician and Fur Trader* (Vancouver, 1963), 317–20.

89. Michael Kew, "Salmon Availability, Technology, and Cultural Adaptation in the Fraser River Watershed" in *A Complex Culture of the British Columbia Plateau: Traditional Stl'atl'imx Resource Use*, ed. Brian Hayden (Vancouver, 1992).

90. The figure includes all coastal peoples listed south of the Fraser River around Puget Sound as far as, but not including, the Clallam. The census total is 570 men, a figure I have multiplied by four. This territory may cover approximately the same area for which Puget and Menzies provided estimates.

91. Jenness, *The Faith of a Coast Salish Indian*, 33.

92. Interview by Oliver Wells with Bob Joe, 8 Feb.1962, in Wells, *The Chilliwacks and Their Neighbors*, 54.

93. Interview by Gordon Mohs with Agnes Kelly, 7 July 1986, in Sto:lo Heritage, Book 11A.

94. The Southern Thompson villages (Koia'um to Spo'zem) are based largely on inventories compiled by James Teit, Charles Hill-Tout, and Gilbert M. Sproat. See Cole Harris, "The Fraser Canyon Encountered," *BC Studies* 94 (Summer 1992): 5–28. The Sto:lo villages are based largely on "Stolo Villages, Encampments, and Settlements," an inventory prepared by Gordon Mohs and Sonny McHalsie for the Sto:lo Tribal Council and derived from site-by-site considerations of available ethnographic and archaeological evidence.

95. A dense nonagricultural population living close to the technical-ecological limit of the food supply appears to be vulnerable to sudden catastrophes or "die-offs." See Ester Boserup, "Environment, Population, and Technology in Primitive Societies" in *The Ends of the Earth: Perspectives on Modern Environmental History*, ed. Donald Worster (New York, 1988), 22–38; and Ezra B.W. Zubrow, *Prehistoric Carrying Capacity: A Model* (Menlo Park, CA, 1975). The many stories about a succession of disasters and depopulations should not be dismissed.

96. All of these movements are poorly understood, and their connections to small-pox-related depopulations are open to debate. On the Katzie, see Suttles, Katzie *Ethnographic Notes*, Anthropology in British Columbia, Memoir No. 2 (Victoria, 1955), 8–11; on the Chilliwack, see Duff, *The Upper Stalo Indians on the*

Fraser River of BC, 43–45; on the Semiahmoo, see Suttles, "Economic Life on the Coast Salish of Haro and Rosario Straits" (PhD thesis, University of Washington, 1951), 29.

97. Suttles, "Post-Contact Culture Change among the Lummi Indians," 42–43.

98. Galois, Kwakwaka'wakw Settlements, intro., sec. D. In the 1920s Diamond Jenness learned that smallpox had decimated the Saanich Indians of southeastern Vancouver Island about 1780 and had crippled their resistance to enemy raids ("The Saanitch Indians of Vancouver Island," typescript, n.d., BCARS, 56). I thank Dan Clayton for bringing this reference to my attention.

99. Sampson, *Indians of Skagit County*, 1.

100. Mooney, "The Aboriginal Population of America North of Mexico," Smithsonian Miscellaneous Collection, vol. 80, no. 7 (Washington, DC, 1928). For a discussion of the basis of Mooney's calculations see Douglas H. Ubelaker, "The Sources and Methodology for Mooney's Estimates of North American Indian Populations" in *The Native Population of the Americas in 1492*, 2nd ed., ed. William Denevan (Madison, WI, 1992), 243–92.

101. Duff, *The Indian History of British Columbia*, vol. 1, *The Impact of the White Man*, Anthropology in British Columbia, Memoir No. 5 (Victoria, BC, 1964), 39, 44.

102. Drucker, *Cultures of the North Pacific Coast* (San Francisco, 1965), 188–89.

103. Fisher, *Contact and Conflict: Indian-European Relations in British Columbia, 1774–1890* (Vancouver, 1977), 22–23.

104. Gibson, "Smallpox on the Northwest Coast, 1835–1838," *BC Studies* 56 (Winter 1982–83): 61–81; Boyd, "The Introduction of Infectious Diseases," 71–111.

105. Except possibly in Quatsino Sound where there is an enigmatic and isolated reference to disease and death. See E. Curtis, *The North American Indian*, vol. 10, *The Kwakiutl* (1915; rpt. facs. ed., New York, 1970), 305.

106. Simpson, *Narrative*, 189; Galois, Kwakwaka'wakw Settlements.

107. Mooney, "Population," 286–87.

108. Mooney, "Aboriginal Population."

109. Kroeber, *Cultural and Natural Areas of Native North America*, vol. 38, 4th ed. (Berkeley, CA, 1963 [1939]), 132, 134.

110. A good introduction to the literature on these questions is Daniel T. Reff, *Disease, Depopulation, and Culture Change in Northwestern New Spain, 1518–1764* (Salt Lake City, UT, 1991), chap. 1.

111. For example, there is clearly a relationship between the striking work of the subaltern historians on the dispossessed in India and the spate of recent attempts to articulate native voices in the Americas. See Ranajit Guha and Gayatri Chakravorty Spivak, eds., *Selected Subaltern Studies* (New York, 1988).

112. The census of Canada lists the native population of British Columbia as follows: 1881, 25 661; 1091, 25 488; 1911, 20 134; 1921, 22 377. None of these figures should be taken as more than a low-side approximation, but, together, they are the most accurate available representation of the native population of the province a little more than a century after contact. If the population had declined by 90–95 percent during these years, then its pre-contact level was in the 200 000–400 000 range. In this case the calculation is for Coast Salish in British Columbia and is derived from the nominal 1881 census, District 187, Div. 7, and District 189, Div. A2. Counting native people on the non-native as well as the native rolls, there were 5452 Coast Salish around the Strait of Georgia in 1881, a figure that is then assumed to be roughly 5–10 percent of the pre-epidemic population.

113. Henry Dobyns has argued for the hemispheric smallpox pandemic in the 1520s in *Their Number Became Thinned: Native American Population Dynamics in Eastern North America* (Knoxville, TN, 1983), but Daniel T. Reff's work on northwestern Mexico and the southwestern United States provides, I think, strong evidence against a sixteenth-century epidemic in the northern Cordillera. However, the case has been argued: see Sarah Campbell, "Post-Columbian Culture History in the Northern Columbia Plateau: AD 1500–1900" (PhD thesis, University of Washington, 1989).

PERIODIC SHORTAGES, NATIVE WELFARE, AND THE HUDSON'S BAY COMPANY, 1670–1930 ⬥

ARTHUR J. RAY

o

Today, various forms of government assistance provide the principal sources of income for many northern Canadian native settlements, thereby supporting a welfare society. It is widely believed that this modern welfare society emerged recently, as the fur trade declined and was no longer able to provide native people with the income they needed to obtain basic necessities. The historical chronologies that have been most widely used by ethnologists reflect this belief. The most recent example is the chronology employed as the framework in the Smithsonian Subarctic Handbook, which dates the end of the "stabilized fur and mission stage," the end of the era of fur-trade society in other words, at 1945. This was the time when the so-called "modern era" began, when, it is thought, "the Canadian government began to assume direct responsibility for native health, education, and welfare needs long neglected."[1] When reflecting upon this conceptualization of the economic history of native peoples, one must question whether it is a

⬥ This excerpt is reprinted with permission of the publisher from *The Subarctic Fur Trade: Native Social and Economic Adaptations* by Shepherd Krech III (Vancouver: UBC Press 1984). All rights reserved by the Publisher. The author would like to thank the Social Sciences and Humanities Research Council of Canada and the Faculty Grants Committee of the University of British Columbia for financial assistance they provided to help defray research expenses. I would like to thank the Hudson's Bay Company for permission to consult and quote from their archives. Finally, I would like to express my appreciation to Mrs. Shirlee Anne Smith, Hudson's Bay Company Archivist, and Professor I.M. Spry for commenting on earlier drafts of this paper. The author, of course, is responsible for its contents.

valid and useful way to view the cultural and economic transformations that have taken place in the north.[2] Does it, for example, give a proper appreciation of the continuities of northern Indian cultures and the roots of contemporary native economic problems? To answer this and related questions it is necessary to examine the problems of resource shortages in the north and the ways in which the native peoples and the incoming European traders dealt with them.

Today, opinions are divided whether hunting, fishing, and gathering societies generally faced a problem of chronic starvation—the more traditional viewpoint—or whether they were the original affluent societies, as Marshall Sahlins has suggested. Sahlins does not deny that occasional starvation plagued hunters and gatherers, but, as he points out, more advanced horticulturalists and farmers faced this problem as well. Of greater importance, Sahlins posits that demand for basic commodities is curtailed in "primitive economies" and brought into line with available resources. He further argues that only a relatively small amount of time is devoted to basic subsistence pursuits.[3]

In Sahlins's terms it is clear that the parkland-grassland bison hunters, the barren ground caribou hunters, the Ojibwa fishing villagers, the Iroquoian horticulturalists, and the wood bison-moose hunters of the Peace River country could probably be classified as "affluent." All had reasonably stable food resources that normally exceeded the requirements of the local populations. The situation of hunters of the full boreal forest at the time of contact is more uncertain. For this region, references abound concerning food shortages during the early years of contact. The problem with such accounts, however, is that native complaints of privation were part of their bargaining strategy, and therefore Indians not infrequently exaggerated their actual situation. This is not meant to suggest that Indians did not experience real hardships; rather, that it is risky to accept all such accounts at face value without carefully considering the contexts in which they were made.

More to the point, it is clear that native people had developed resource management and redistribution strategies in the pre-contact period which served to minimize the risk of severe privation as a consequence of localized short-term scarcities of basic staples. Traditionally, most native groups had the capability of exploiting a wide range of resources even in areas where hunting activities were highly focused on single species such as the grassland bison, moose, or barren ground caribou. If these primary game were not readily available, secondary ones such as red deer (wapiti), woodland caribou, and beaver were pursued.[4] Furthermore, in many areas, such as the flanks of the shield uplands, the parklands, and the northern transitional forests, the seasonal hunting cycle took groups on lengthy migratory routes that exposed them to a wide variety of ecological niches, any one of which could be resorted to in times of need. Furthermore, these cycles of movement lessened the risk of overhunting any single locality. The need for spatial flexibility in pre-contact big-game economies was recognized in the territorial control system that emerged. As E.S. Rogers has shown, in the boreal forest, native groups tended to hunt in the same areas every year—their hunting range. However, if game was scarce in that range, they could temporarily hunt on the lands of their neighbours to obtain basic necessities.[5] On the other hand, hunting or trapping for essentially commercial purposes was not permitted under the hunting range system.

While potential scarcity was minimized by exploiting diverse ranges (parkland-grassland, parkland-boreal forest, shield upland-Hudson Bay lowland, and northern transitional forest-tundra) and by having the capability to hunt a number of different species of game, the possibility of serious shortages stemming from unusual weather conditions, forest fires, and faunal epidemics still existed. To deal with these occasional hard times, native economies were structured to reinforce co-operation and sharing. Under such a system, general reciprocity was the dominant mode of internal exchange. Individuals were expected to share whatever surpluses they had with their families, close relatives, and members of their band. Indeed, as European traders learned, aid was often extended to strangers. According to the rules of general reciprocity, one did not expect an immediate return for aid rendered nor was any economic value placed on the obligation. The reciprocal obligation that accrued was generalized. The giver simply expected help in return when he was in need. In this way, general reciprocity served to knit groups together by a series of mutual obligations to render aid. This increased the survival chances of all members of the group. Sharing basic necessities of life with neighbouring groups was accomplished through the hunting-range system described above. To reinforce the co-operative orientation of their cultures, most groups, except perhaps those in the grassland area, negatively sanctioned the hoarding of wealth by individuals.[6] This does not mean that Indians were not interested in gaining access to wealth. Rather, individuals derived prestige from wealth by giving it away. For instance, generosity was a virtue that was expected of all chiefs or "captains," as the Europeans called them. It appears that most Indian trading captains distributed their wealth to their followers, thereby enhancing their social position.[7]

The fur trade negatively affected Indian economies in two fundamental ways. It served to increase the risk of serious resource shortages for native groups. At the same time, it increasingly undermined their ability to deal with this problem. For example, the fur trade tended to favour economic specialization among all native groups who took part in it. One of the earliest forms of specialization involved commercial trapping. Native people had always taken furs for their own use in making clothing. Probably the best known example was the use of beaver pelts to make beaver robes and coats. Indians began to hunt more selectively when they trapped for commercial purposes, often choosing furs that fetched the best prices. Initially, beaver and marten loomed large in the trade.

Very quickly, another specialty emerged: engaging in the trade as middlemen. Indians who became middlemen devoted little or no time to commercial trapping activities. Instead, they obtained furs from other Indian groups in exchange for trade goods they had acquired from Europeans. Middlemen often travelled great distances to carry on this exchange. It meant that less time could be spent than traditionally had been the case in food-gathering activities in the summer. To compensate, food supplies had to be secured from Europeans, from other Indian groups, or by increasing the role of women and children in food-gathering activities.

Still other groups specialized by becoming commercial hunters who supplied trading posts with provisions or "country produce," as it was called. Probably the most notable early examples of these types of groups were the homeguard Indians of the Hudson Bay lowlands—Cree at Moose Factory, Fort Albany, Fort Severn, York Factory, and Fort Churchill in the early years and Chipewyan at the latter post by the late eighteenth century; Ojibwa in the region between Lake Superior and Lake of the Woods, who supplied wild rice and, later, corn; and plains-dwelling Assiniboine, Blackfoot, and Cree, who supplied pemmican in the Parkland area.[8] Indeed, by the early nineteenth century, the number of Indians who specialized as commercial hunters was probably very large, given the proliferation of trading posts that took place during the period of intensive competition and considering that each post received a sizeable portion of its foods from local natives.

The commercialization of native economies and the concomitant specialization of resource orientation began to favour a shift in traditional attitudes toward sharing among unrelated groups. Though it appears that bands continued to be willing to share basic survival resources with their neighbours, to define survival needs clearly became increasingly difficult. For instance, in the precommercial era it was easy to determine how much hunting of any given species was necessary for a group to meet its immediate requirements for food, clothing, and shelter. But with the advent of the fur trade and the growing dependence on imported technologies, it was no longer a simple task to define need. Rather than directly applying an aboriginal technology to the local environment to obtain food, clothing, and shelter, the Indians, through the process of technological replacement, were increasingly caught in the trap of having to buy the tools that they needed to hunt, fish, and trap, to say nothing of utensils, blankets, and cloth. Native groups thus faced a problem whose impact on resource use was circular and cumulative. Items of European origin that originally were basically novel or luxury articles—firearms, hatchets, knives, and kettles, to name a few—became essentials. Partly for this reason, despite a traditional conservational attitude—in the sense that animals were hunted only to the degree that they were needed for food or clothing—once they began to trade, Indians overexploited many of their environments in response to the demands of an open-ended market.

The implications of this development for interband relations, resource use, and group survival can perhaps best be illustrated by examining the situation of the Blackfoot and their neighbours. In the 1750's, Anthony Henday accompanied a group of the Assiniboine and Cree who travelled from York Factory to the lands of the Blackfoot. Henday learned from his companions that the Blackfoot would allow them to hunt bison freely. The situation with regard to beaver was more complex, however. Henday tried to persuade the Assiniboine and Cree accompanying him to trap beaver. They refused. Not only was trapping unnecessary, since trading in the spring would give them more furs than they could carry in their canoes, but they indicated that the Blackfoot would kill them if they trapped beaver in Blackfoot territory.[9] Curiously, perhaps, subsequent entries in Henday's journal indicate that his Indian companions were trapping beaver. However, the women were using the pelts to make winter clothing.[10] In short, the Blackfoot prohibition related only to commercial trapping. The prohibition caused no hardship for the Assiniboine and Cree at this time because the Blackfoot provided more furs for trade than the former middlemen needed to satisfy their trade good requirements and allowed them to collect the furs they needed to survive the winter.

A century later the situation had changed drastically. Many former luxuries had become necessities. Growing trapping pressures led to the serious depletion of many fur-bearing animals in the area. Fortunately, while animal populations were under growing stress, the fur trade offered Indians of the parkland-grassland area an alternative economic opportunity. Bison could be commercially hunted to meet the burgeoning provision requirements of the fur trade. This was a significant development for the Blackfoot and their confederates as well as for their former trading partners, the Assiniboine and Cree. The expansion of the fur-trade operations of the Hudson's Bay and the North West Companies had displaced the Assiniboine and Cree from their middleman positions and provided the Blackfoot with direct access to European trading posts. For this reason, the Assiniboine and Cree who lived in the parkland became suppliers of provisions. By selling pemmican and grease to the traders, they could still obtain the European articles that they formerly obtained through their prairie trading networks.[11]

The commercialization of the buffalo hunt had several unfortunate results. Hunting pressures began to deplete this once abundant food resource. By the 1850's, bison ranges were beginning to contract. Increasingly, Assiniboine and Cree groups were forced to encroach on Blackfoot lands in pursuit of the dwindling herds. As the bison diminished in numbers, they became more valuable. Also, bison were absolutely essential for the highly specialized economies that had developed among the plains Assiniboine, Blackfoot, and Cree. Not surprisingly, the Blackfoot were no longer willing to share this resource with their neighbours.[12] They now competed with the Assiniboine and Cree for control over a valuable commercial subsistence resource that was in rapid decline. Consequently, persistent hostility developed between the Assiniboine-Plains Cree and the Blackfoot.[13]

The growing unwillingness of the Blackfoot to share their territory occurred in many other areas of Rupert's Land as an outgrowth of resource depletion. For instance, by 1821 beaver and other valuable fur-bearing animals were becoming scarce throughout the woodlands between James Bay and the Churchill River. Hudson's Bay Company traders and Indians alike began to see the need for conservation. However, the traditional tenure system was not well suited to a situation in which scarcity had become a chronic and widespread problem instead of an occasional and localized one. When certain Indian bands attempted to husband the fur resources in their hunting and trapping ranges by curtailing trapping activities, their neighbours frequently moved in and collected the furs.[14] While this might have been appropriate according to old customs, it meant that conservation schemes were virtually impossible to implement when the need for them arose. Local Indian bands apparently grew resentful of the incursions of their neighbours for trapping, but the band organization of the Subarctic offered no effective means of rationalizing access to or use of resources that were being depleted at an accelerating rate. The situation was particularly complicated with respect to beaver. This animal had always been a secondary source of food after moose and woodland caribou. With the destruction of these two big-game animal populations because of overhunting, beaver took on added significance in the provision quest of groups living in the boreal forest. Thus, beaver was not purely the commercial resource that some other fur bearers, such as marten, mink, and otter, were.[15]

Under the direction of Sir George Simpson, the Hudson's Bay Company attempted to use its considerable economic power to introduce a conservation programme. In areas where it held a monopoly, it began to exert pressures on local bands to restrict their trapping activities to assigned territories. The company's efforts were effective only in those areas where caribou populations had already declined sharply, forcing the Indians to shift to food sources that were less mobile, usually fish and hare.[16] In other places, particularly in districts where competition persisted, such as along the American border, encroachment of bands on each other's territories continued to be a vexing problem and the subject of considerable commentary in Hudson's Bay Company correspondence.[17]

Thus, as resources became valuable commercially and in turn more scarce as a result of heavy hunting and trapping, more rigid and spatially restrictive land-tenure systems began to emerge. The hunting range was supplanted by the system of band territories in many areas by the middle of the nineteenth century. During the late nineteenth century and the early part of this century, the trap line replaced this system in most of the woodland areas. In this way the mobility of the native peoples was increasingly curtailed.

Resource depletions depressed native economies in another important way. By the early nineteenth century, reduction of game had forced many woodland groups living south and east of the Churchill River to rely more intensively on less valuable fur-bearing animals, such as muskrat, and on alternative sources of food, such as hare and fish. This trend increased the hardships that several groups experienced because many of these less valuable species, fish excepted, exhibited more erratic fluctuations in their population cycles. For example, beaver and marten populations vary less from high point to low point, enjoy greater population wave lengths, and endure less erratic cycles than do muskrat and hare. Because of resource depletion, Indians were forced to spend more time hunting and trapping species of lesser value and more uncertain yield. In the 1820's Governor Simpson remarked, not surprisingly, that the Ojibwa living in the muskrat country of the lower Saskatchewan River area had a feast-and-famine economy, owing to oscillations in the population of this aquatic animal.[18]

Similarly, in areas where hare had become the dominant food source in the late nineteenth and early twentieth centuries, native economies were on a very precarious footing. This was especially true of the Hudson Bay-James Bay lowlands. When hare populations dropped sharply, Indians were forced to divert their attentions from trapping to the food quest.[19] Consequently, fur returns from posts like Moose Factory and Fort Albany exhibit great fluctuations. These variations are often more a consequence of the changing availability of hare than a reflection of the population cycles of the principal fur bearers (various fox) in the area.[20] Only those Indians who had access to a good fishery, usually sturgeon or whitefish, escaped the hardships that resulted from overdependence on hare.

The plight of Indians who took up residence in the Hudson Bay-James Bay lowland area was not brought about solely by overhunting. It was also in part the consequence of a major alteration that they made in their pre-contact ecological cycle. As noted earlier, prior to European penetration into the region, Indians apparently did not inhabit the lowlands throughout the year. There simply was not enough game. Therefore, they only visited the region during the summer to hunt geese and to fish, retreating to the Shield uplands in winter. Nevertheless, the arrival of the Hudson's Bay Company and the establishment of trading posts on the shores of Hudson and James Bays meant that a need developed for post hunters. These hunters were particularly important for the spring and autumn goose hunts, and geese became one of the principal ingredients in the men's diet at the posts.[21] But to obtain a maximum return on the fall hunt, Indians often had to remain in the lowlands near the posts long after they normally would have returned inland to hunt and trap. In this way, specialization as post hunters favoured the permanent occupation of the Hudson Bay-James Bay lowlands and curtailed the spatial mobility of the Cree and Chipewyan who were involved. In essence, they discontinued the aboriginal practice of moving through their hunting range to seasonal surpluses, and instead developed a symbiotic relationship with the Hudson's Bay Company post where regional surpluses were stockpiled (see Figure 1). When the Indians faced privation, usually in the winter, they turned to the company for relief, which was always provided.

Even when Indian groups did not attach themselves to trading posts as provision suppliers, involvement in the fur trade often curtailed the exploitation of a diverse environment in favour of a new scheme that was more narrowly focused and riskier in terms of the food quest. For example, as noted above, the Chipewyan originally occupied the food-rich northern transitional forest-tundra zone, where they subsisted principally on moose and barren ground caribou.[22] This was not prime fur country, however. As the Chipewyan were drawn into the fur trade in the eighteenth century, bands responded in three ways. Some drew near to Fort Churchill and became post hunters, with results that have already been described. Others became middlemen. Still others began to trap. Both of the latter two groups

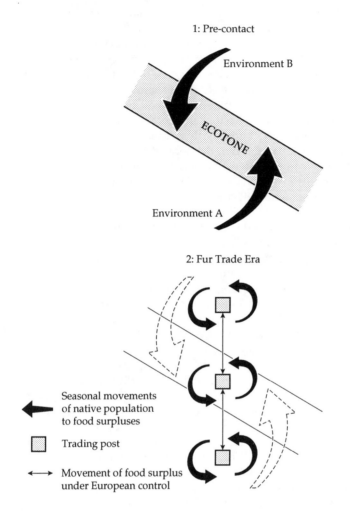

1: Pre-contact

Environment B

ECOTONE

Environment A

2: Fur Trade Era

Seasonal movements
of native population
to food surpluses

Trading post

Movement of food surplus
under European control

FIGURE 1   *CHANGING SPATIAL ECOLOGY OF THE
NORTH*

were drawn southwestward into the boreal forest where furs were more
plentiful. These forests were located northeast of Great Slave, Athabasca,
and Reindeer Lakes. However, while this ecozone was a better trapping
environment, it was not as well stocked with game as their aboriginal
homeland had been.[23] The increased population pressure on local resources
that would have been the consequence of this historical migration must
have further undermined the ability of these micro-environments to support a sound big-game economy.

When these developments are considered together, it is clear that one of
the most far-reaching aspects of European expansion into the north

involved overturning basic aboriginal ecological strategies. While pre-contact Indian bands often followed extensive migration circuits to take advantage of seasonal food surpluses, Europeans were unable to adopt this approach. Trade required the maintenance of large, spatially fixed settlements, together with rigid time schedules for cargo shipments along set routeways. This meant that the European companies had to devise sophisticated logistical systems that could move food from surplus areas to their posts for storage and redistribution. Needless to say, this was a revolutionary ecological strategy for northern Canada.

Generally, the significance of this revolution has been overlooked. Surely it was as important as the technological innovations that were introduced to the native economies, but most attention has been addressed to this latter issue. By being able to move large stocks of food from surplus areas (the grasslands, the Peace River country, the fisheries on the edge of the Shield, and wild rice areas) and by importing it from eastern North America and Europe, the traders not only managed to maintain their posts, but also increasingly were able to sustain native populations in many areas that were either initially marginal in terms of provisions or became so because of over-hunting. Indeed, as the late nineteenth century progressed, country provisions became more unreliable in most areas of historic Rupert's Land, and foodstuffs imported from eastern Canada and Europe or purchased from the developing prairie farming community of Red River had to be counted on more and more. Throughout the old area of Rupert's Land native peoples grew to depend on the trading posts for food. This dependence emerged partly out of necessity and partly out of the deliberate policy of the Hudson Bay Company. As noted, when country food stocks declined, native people had to spend more time searching for food; therefore, they had less time to devote to trapping activities. To combat this trend, in many areas the Hudson's Bay Company imported flour and sold it well below cost to the Indians.[24] It was hoped that this subsidy would encourage trapping. The policy was generally effective, although it served to further reduce native self-sufficiency in subsistence and to orient their diet toward a much higher starch intake than had been the case traditionally.

As native vulnerability to shortages of basic staples increased, the European traders were better able to manipulate them to serve their own interests. After 1821, one of the principal concerns of the Hudson's Bay Company involved maintaining a sufficiently large and low-cost labour force in the regions south and east of the Churchill River to assure that a profitable fur trade would continue. This meant that large scale emigration of native people from seriously depleted areas, such as the Nelson and Hay Rivers territories, to non-fur-producing regions, such as the Red River Colony, was strongly discouraged.[25] Furthermore, company hiring policies largely excluded Indians from occupations that involved work during the winter trapping season.[26] Instead, Indians were generally employed during the summer when they were hired to man boat brigades and carry on unskilled maintenance work around posts or to serve as hunters and fishermen. Significantly, there never were enough of these low-paying seasonal jobs to hire all who might have wished to be employed. Therefore, the practice developed of awarding summer jobs only to the most reliable hunters and trappers, mainly those who had paid their debts. Housing was also often provided for them at the post.[27] In this way, the employment practices of the Hudson's Bay Company were specifically designed to encourage Indians to remain in the traditional hunting and trapping sector of the economy well beyond the time that many were finding it difficult to do so.

Additional support for, and control of, native people was achieved by the extension of credit as well as by the distribution of gratuities. The former was made available to able-bodied adult males; the latter to widows, orphans, the aged and the infirm. The use of credit in the fur trade can be traced back to the earliest days of the Hudson's Bay Company's operations. By advancing to Indians outfits of goods, the company, and other traders as well, hoped to secure the future returns of hunts; credit, as well as gratuities, served to tide Indians over during times of poor hunting and trapping. Thus, from the beginning, debt and gratuities became essential to the fur trade. When European competition for Indians' furs was modest and the fur market steady or rising, the system was not too costly, and it gave Europeans greater control over the Indians.[28]

The debt-gratuity system became increasingly troublesome for the fur traders as time passed. When Indians specialized economically, and as resource depletion became an ever more serious problem, Indians grew more vulnerable to shortages of food and low fur returns. Hard times occurred with increasing frequency, and in some areas, such as the Hudson Bay-James Bay lowlands, inadequate supplies of food had become a chronic problem by the turn of this century.[29] While traditional sharing practices continued to operate within Indian bands, deprivation could only be alleviated by increasingly resorting to the Hudson's Bay Company posts for gratuities and credit. At the same time, the ability, and perhaps willingness, of Indians to repay their debts seems to have diminished.

Reflecting these changing conditions, by the late nineteenth century the Hudson's Bay Company adopted a policy of discounting the face value of all Indian debts by 25 percent at the time they were issued. Thus, for every 100 Made Beaver (MB) of credit issued to an Indian only 75 MB was entered into the account books. Furthermore, any credit outstanding after one year was written off as a bad debt.[30]

The company could well afford to write off debts in this fashion. The standards of trade that it used to value goods and furs allowed for a very considerable gross profit margin.[31] Indeed, it could be argued that the standards not only served to underwrite the credit/gratuity system, but that they increasingly made it necessary. For instance, the resource base continued to decline to the point that in some areas native purchasing power was no longer adequate to serve basic Indian consumer requirements. The Hudson's Bay Company could have relieved the plight of the Indians by lowering the prices it charged for staple items or by advancing the prices it paid for furs. James Ray, the district manager for James Bay, considered this option as a solution to the problems that native people at Great Whale River faced in the early 1920's. He rejected this course of action as others had done before him. In explaining his decision, he wrote: "Beyond the slight reductions mentioned (for ammunition which has been selling at 100 percent of cost landed price) I am not in favour of reducing our selling prices for it would be difficult to raise them again when better times shall come to the natives. So it seems the only solution, if it can be called a solution, to the problem is for us to go on advancing to these peoples as if for debt, though they have little hope of ever paying it. . . . If we continue as I proposed, the debt system as a means of keeping the natives alive during the lean years, the Company may in some small measure—be reimbursed by the amounts the natives may be persuaded to pay when the fat years shall come again and in the main, I imagine it will be more easily handled than any system of gratuity we may devise."[32] Thus, Ray preferred the large scale use of credit instead of resorting to a system of more flexible prices or to straightforward welfare.

Indians living in the southern James Bay area and the Montreal Department had been aware for some time that the Hudson's Bay Company's practice of issuing credit in the form of relatively high priced merchandise was aggravating their economic hardships. Therefore, when the Canadian Pacific Railroad was built, opening the southern portions of Rupert's Land to renewed competition in the late nineteenth century, Indians began to pressure the Hudson's Bay Company traders to give them credit in the form of cash advances, that is, consumer loans. The Indians intended to take this money to the "line" where they could buy their outfits at reduced prices. Indeed, some were said to be prepared to go as far as Montreal and Trois Rivières to get cheaper goods.[33] Not surprisingly, the company traders did not willingly comply with this request. Non-payment of credit in goods represented a potential loss of something less than 50 percent of face value of the loan. Furthermore, as Inspecting Officer P. McKenzie noted in 1890, "There is no profit to be made in cash advances to Indians in large amounts even supposing they . . . pay up their accounts in full every year."[34]

Of fundamental importance, the extensive use of credit under near monopoly conditions favoured the persistence of a credit/barter economy, using the Made Beaver standards. It was not simply the result of Indian conservatism or an inability on their part to operate in a monetized economy. It served the company's interest to conduct the trade in this fashion until the late nineteenth century. Holding a near monopoly, the Hudson's Bay Company was able to maintain high prices, pay low seasonal wages, and put the Indians under an obligation to it through the extension of credit.

By the final quarter of the nineteenth century the old order was, however, coming under increasing stress. The construction of the Canadian Pacific Railroad along the southern periphery of Rupert's Land not only increased competition, but it also brought a new kind of competitor. Rather than bartering furs for goods as in the past, increasingly, company opponents paid cash for the Indians' returns.[35] The Indians were able to take the money and search out the best prices for the commodities they needed. Traditionally, the prices of trade goods had been relatively constant and most bargaining was focused on the values assigned to furs and country provisions. Direct competition in trade good prices began in most areas of southern and southwestern Rupert's Land in the 1870's with the signing of treaties. Treaty payments injected cash into the local economies and encouraged small travelling pedlars to compete with the Hudson's Bay Company for the treaty money. The building of the Canadian Pacific Railroad thus served to accelerate a new trend by offering small fur buyers and merchants relatively cheap access to the north. The Indians benefited by being able to seek out the best prices for furs and goods rather than having to continue to deal with a single company which largely monopolized fur purchases and goods sales in most areas of the north.

Reflecting this new development, by 1899 the Hudson's Bay Company employed cash and barter standards in all districts except Mackenzie River, and Fur Trade Commissioner C.C. Chipman recommended that steps be taken immediately to introduce it to that district.[36] As Map 1 shows, by 1922–23 a significant portion (6–35 percent) or the merchandise transactions of the fur-trade division of the Hudson's Bay Company consisted of cash sales. In the Lake Huron, Lake Superior, and Athabasca areas, competition was strong and major inroads were being made into the old credit/barter system of trade.

As competition escalated, the issuing of credit became risky once again as it had been in the days of sharp rivalry between the Hudson's Bay and North West Companies in the period from 1790 to 1821. A significant number of Indians simply preferred to deal with whoever offered the best prices for furs in the spring, regardless of whether or not they owed debts to someone else. Consequently, to offset the growing number of bad debts, in the 1890's the Hudson's Bay Company began a concerted effort to curtail the use of credit in the hope of eventually operating the business on a basis of ready barter or cash. This objective was given the highest priority in so called "frontier districts," or areas open to intensive competition. Such districts included all areas lying within fifty miles of a railway line. Indeed, Indians adjacent to the line were regarded as unreliable because they roamed up and down it looking for the best prices.[37]

Other pressures were also mounting that encouraged the Hudson's Bay Company to curtail the credit/barter trade and to seek relief from the escalating expenses it was incurring giving gratuities to sick and destitute Indians. When fur returns were at a sufficiently high volume, the rate of advance built into the standard of trade provided the company with a gross profit margin that was sufficient to cover overhead costs and assure it an ample net return. By the late nineteenth century, however, the turnover at many posts had declined to the point where this was no longer the case. As Map 2 shows, by the early 1920's, the Hudson's Bay Company registered net losses in three of its more southerly trading districts. Furthermore, the net gains made in the Moose River and Athabasca districts were relatively small and were based largely on the operations of a few posts that did not experience strong competition.

In the late 1870's and early 1880's, York Factory, one of the company's oldest posts, had so taxed its local environment during its heyday that the

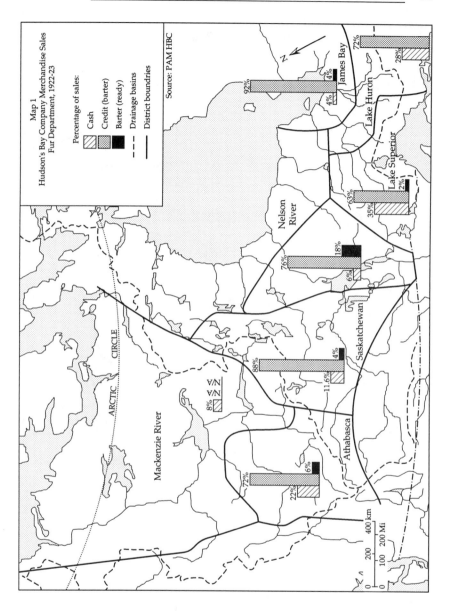

Map 1
Hudson's Bay Company Merchandise Sales
Fur Department, 1922-23

Percentage of sales:
Cash
Credit (barter)
Barter (ready)
Drainage basins
District boundries

Source: PAM HBC

trading returns or the local Indians were no longer sufficient to cover the post's operating expenses. W.J. Fortescue, who was in charge of the post at that time, thought the Indians there should be encouraged to enter into treaty negotiations with the government. Fortescue believed this arrangement desirable because the Indian's welfare would then become a government responsibility.[38] In addition, the annuity payments would constitute a new source of revenue for the company.[39] Thus, by the late nineteenth century, some interest in having the government assume the growing burden of Indian welfare needs was beginning to develop within the company.

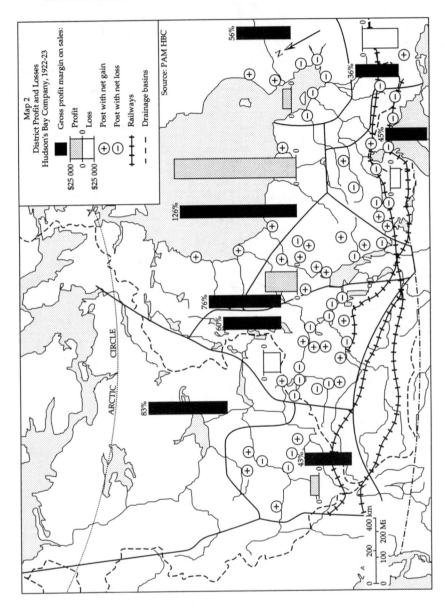

Map 2
District Profit and Losses
Hudson's Bay Company, 1922-23

Gross profit margin on sales:

Profit
Loss

Post with net gain
Post with net loss
Railways
Drainage basins

Source: PAM HBC

While Fortescue was somewhat ahead of his time in making this suggestion, by the early part of this century the government was beginning to
underwrite these expenses even outside treaty areas. For example, in the
James Bay district, where company gratuity expenses were particularly
large compared to other regions, the Hudson's Bay Company frequently
submitted bills for this cost to the government. The government usually
paid them.[40] In this way, the process of transferring responsibility for a welfare system that was an integral part or the fur trade from the company to
the government began in the late nineteenth century. It happened slowly

because the government was not eager to assume this burden. And, for humanitarian as well as practical business reasons, the Hudson's Bay Company could not simply abolish the practice of providing gratuities to needy Indians before alternative arrangements had been made. The company's predicament in this regard was illustrated by the problems that it faced in the Richmond Gulf area in 1924. In that year the Hudson's Bay Company provided over $31 000 in assistance in the form of gratuities, unpaid advances, and sick and destitute accounts. In discussing what should be done about the problem, District Manager James Ray noted: "it is true that the natives are our assets, that we must keep them alive for future profits even though we carry them at a loss till such time shall come. On occasion we have taken large profits out of the post as the following figures will show; Outfit 249 (1919) profit $51,724, Outfit 250 profit $250,497, (year of high realizations) Outfit 251 profits $1,017. (Year when slump in prices occurred) Outfit 252 profit $46,141. Outfit 253 profit $99,430. But the question arises, is it consistent with good business to go on assisting these people to the sum of $25,000 a year till such times as good tax years return to us? There are limits to what the Company may consider generous and judicious treatment."[41]

Clearly the company faced a dilemma. Resources were seriously depleted in the Richmond Gulf area and the natives were reduced to a heavy dependence on two species: hare to serve as food; fox as fur. When either failed, the Indians were destitute. When hare and fox were plentiful, the Indians lived well and the company reaped handsome profits. Similar circumstances prevailed elsewhere.

From the company's economic position, the ideal solution would have the government assume the financial burden of carrying the Indians through lean years. Then, despite deteriorating conditions, the company would be free to continue to prosecute the fur trade on a highly profitable basis. This eventually transpired, and by the 1940's the government was heavily involved in a wide variety of welfare programmes for native people. From the point of view of the traders, one of the negative aspects of this development—a problem apparently not forseen by Fortescue—was the loss of their control over the local Indian populations. Unlike the company's scheme, government assistance did not carry any obligation to hunt and trap.

From this discussion it is clear that the modern welfare society of the north is not a post-World War II phenomenon. It is deeply rooted in the fur trade. The welfare system was a necessary by-product of several processes: economic specialization by native peoples, a concomitant decreasing spatial mobility, European control of food surpluses and the depletion of resources. Reinforcing these were the labour policies, wage schedules, and standards of trade that assured the Hudson's Bay Company large gross profit margins in good years under near monopoly conditions, but that also allowed native peoples only a marginal return. Some scheme for the additional redistribution of excess profits to the Indians in the form of gratuities and "debt" to supplement their meagre returns from hunting and trapping was absolutely essential. Otherwise, the company could not have stemmed a migration of Indians from the boreal woodlands, and the loss of this labour force would have seriously undermined the prosecution of the trade in many districts south and east of the Churchill River.

Finally, it is clear that we must reconsider the stereotype of the Indian as essentially conservative economically. By holding a virtual monopoly on most aspects of the northern economy until the last quarter of the nineteenth century, the Hudson's Bay Company was the key determinant for development and change. In many areas of the north, it was in the company's interest and ability to perpetuate the use of a credit/barter or truck system until the late nineteenth century. The arrangement discouraged, and often prevented, Indians from leaving this part of the primary resource sector of the economy, even in regions where resources were so depleted that only marginal livelihoods could be sustained. The system failed to encourage the spread of the cash economy through cash buying of furs, partly to insure a higher gross profit margin and partly to minimize losses from bad debts. In summary, the Hudson's Bay Company was partly responsible for limiting the ability of Indians to adjust to the new economic circumstances at the beginning of this century. Debt-ridden, repeatedly blocked from alternative opportunities for over a century, and accustomed to various forms of relief over two centuries, Indians became so evidently demoralized in this century, but the groundwork for this was laid in the more distant past.

NOTES

1. June Helm, Edward S. Rogers, and James G.E. Smith, "Intercultural Relations and Cultural Change in the Shield and Mackenzie Borderlands" in *Handbook of North American Indians*, vol. 6, *Subarctic*, gen. ed. W.C. Sturtevant, ed. June Helm. (Washington, DC: Smithsonian Institution, 1981), 149.

2. Charles A. Bishop and Arthur J. Ray, "Ethnohistoric Research in the Central Subarctic: Some Conceptual and Methodological Problems," *Western Canadian Journal of Anthropology* 4 (1970): 116–44; Shepard Krech III, "The Influence of Disease and the Fur Trade on Arctic Drainage Lowlands Dene, 1800–50," *Journal of Anthropological Research* 39 (1983): 123–46.

3. Marshall Sahlins, *Stone Age Economics* (Chicago: Aldine, 1972), 1–100. Some ethnologists question whether even big-game hunters like the Caribou Eater Chipewyan could be said to have had an aboriginal affluent society. See James G.E. Smith, "Economic Uncertainty in an 'Original Affluent Society': Caribou and Caribou-Eater Chipewyan Adaptive Strategies," *Arctic Anthropology* 15, 1 (1978): 66–68.

4. Arthur J. Ray, *Indians in the Fur Trade* (Toronto: University of Toronto Press, 1974), 27–50.

5. Edward S. Rogers, *The Hunting Group—Hunting Territory Complex Among the the Mistassini* (Ottawa: National Museum of Canada Bulletin 195, 1963).

6. After the horse was adopted into the northern plains culture in the early eighteenth century (for Canada), it became a symbol of wealth and Indians did try to accumulate as many as possible. However, it is uncertain whether or not this was simply a post-contact development or was built on earlier traditions.

7. Arthur J. Ray and Donald B. Freeman, *Give Us Good Measure*

(Toronto: University of Toronto Press, 1978), 63–69.

8. Ray, *Indians in the Fur Trade*, 51–57; Ray and Freeman, *Give Us Good Measure*, 39–51; Wayne D. Moodie, "Agriculture and the Fur Trade" in *Old Trails and New Directions*, ed. C. Judd and A.J. Ray (Toronto: University of Toronto Press, 1980), 272–90.

9. L.J. Burpee, ed. *Journal of Journey Performed by Anthony Hendry: to Explore the Country Inland and to Endeavour to Increase the Hudson's Bay Company Trade, A.D. 1754–55*, Royal Society of Canada, series 3, vol. 1, sec. 2 (1907), 91–122.

10. Ibid.

11. Ray, *Indians in the Fur Trade*, 131–35.

12. Ibid, 223–26.

13. This situation had apparently developed sometime after 1774, judging from the account of M. Cocking, who visited the Blackfoot territory in 1772–73. Trade between the Assiniboine-Cree was still going on. However, shortly thereafter, the inland expansion by the Nor'Westers and the Hudson's Bay Company upset this arrangement.

14. Arthur J. Ray, "Some Conservation Schemes of the Hudson's Bay Company, 1821–50: An Examination of the Problems of Resource Management in the Fur Trade," *Journal of Historical Geography* 1, 1 (1975): 61–62; Charles A. Bishop, "The Emergence of Hunting Territories Among the Northern Ojibwa," *Ethnology* 9 (1970): 1–15; Krech in *The Subarctic Fur Trade: Native Social and Economic Adaptations* (Vancouver: University of British Columbia Press, 1984).

15. Ray, "Some Conservation Schemes of the Hudson's Bay Company," 65.

16. Ibid, 61; Bishop, "Hunting Territories Among the Northern Ojibwa," 10–14.

17. Many comments of this nature can be found in Governor Simpson's correspondence in the Hudson's Bay Company Archives (HBCA) A.12, Dr Irene M. Spy, personal communication 3 March 1981.

18. For discussion of animal population cycles, see C.G. Hewitt, *The Conservation of Wild Life in Canada* (New York: Charles Scribner and Sons, 1921). Simpson's observation is cited in Ray, *Indians in the Fur Trade*, 121.

19. According to the various documents dealing with the James Bay district between 1880 and 1920, one of the most common causes of poor fur returns was the failure of hare. See, for example, letters from Moose Factory to the Hudson's Bay Company Secretary, 1871–1889, Public Archives of Manitoba, Hudson's Bay Company Archives (hereinafter HBCA), A.11/47. In particular, the letter of 15 September 1890 noted the very poor return and claimed: "The causes of . . . falling off is attributed to scarcity of rabbit, the principal food of the Indians thus preventing them from hunting being occupied all of their time in procuring food. This is most apparent in Rupert River where the decline in these skins is no less than 900 percent. As you are probably aware this scarcity arises from disease, and is periodical running in a cycle of ten to eleven years, with 3 years of maximum and 3 years of minimum" (HBCA A.11/47).

20. This was also true inland on the Shield uplands of northern Ontario. See B.P. Winterhalder, "Canadian Fur Bearer Cycles and Cree-Ojibwa Hunting and Trapping Practices," *American Naturalist* 115, 6 (1980): 873–74.

21. Reflecting the importance of these hunts, the correspondence between the posts on the bay almost always commented on the success or failure of the local hunts. The record pertaining to York Factory indicates that geese were one of the cheapest provisions that could be obtained before 1880. Fortescue to Armit, York Factory, 1 Dec. 1880, HBCA A/119a, fo. 149.

22. Beryl G. Gillespie, "Territorial Expansion of the Chipewyan in the Eighteenth Century" in *Proceedings: Northern Athapaskan Conference 1971*, vol. 2, ed. A.M. Clark, National Museum of Man Mercury Series, Canadian Ethnology Service Paper no. 27 (Ottawa: Museums of Canada, 1975), 350–88.

23. C. Yerbury, personal communication.

24. For example, the Inspection Report for Cumberland District in 1886, recommended using cheap flour in the northern portion of district to discourage Chipewyans from hunting deer (HBCA D.25/1/1). Similar recommendations were made for other parts of the district.

25. Ray, *Indians in the Fur Trade*, 218.

26. Carol M. Judd, "Native Labour and Social Stratification in the Hudson's Bay Company's Northern Department, 1770–1870," *Canadian Review of Sociology and Anthropology* 17 (1980): 307.

27. William Anderson, Fort Albany, May, 1980 (personal communication). Mr. Anderson served as a company clerk in James Bay.

28. In the early years credit even may have been used to increase Indian fur outputs beyond the level that could have been achieved otherwise. In offering an historical overview of the fur trade, the Fur Trade Department Annual Report for 1929 included the following observation: "It was found then [after natives adopted European goods] that only sufficient game would be killed to meet the natives' own requirements, and so a plan was adopted to overcome that. Advances were given through the chief. These Chiefs and clans were a proud lot. . . . The clan with the largest advance was the most influential, and in order to remain influential all debt had to be paid" (HBCA A.74/43). Regarding the declining ability of the environment in some areas to cover these costs, see Fortescue (HBCA A.11/119a).

29. Beaver were said to be in steady decline as of the early 1890s. Other furs showed the normal cyclical variations. The problem was that the principal food was rabbit, which was said to run in ten- to twelve-year cycles with three years maxima and three years minima. The low points in the cycle frequently caused starvation (see footnote 19 above). Many other examples of the adverse effects of food shortages on trapping activities in this area between 1880 and 1930 could be cited. For example, Inspection Reports, 1888–90 (HBCA S 54/4–10); Annual Reports, 1890–94 (HBCA A.74/1–3); Fur Trade Reports 1912–24 (HBCA DFTR/1–19).

30. Rules and Regulations, London, 1887, rules 72–76 (HBCA D.26/3). These rules specified further that "doubtful" debts, those beyond current outfit but less than a year old, were to be entered in the accounts at 50 percent of original value.

31. On several occasions traders pointed out that the indebtedness of the Indians shown in their accounts did not represent the money actually owed the company, given that the debt was in terms of goods advanced and valued as per the standard of trade. The debts thus represented a loss of potential profit. As the inspection report for Bersimi in 1890 indicated, "the profit on goods (supposing the hunter or hunters been paying up pretty regularly for a few years previous) ought to be sufficient to prevent actual loss to the Company" (HBCA D.25/4).

32. Throughout the company's records, suggestions to lower prices are always turned down with the same explanation—that is, Indians would not allow them to be raised again (HBCA DFTR/19).

33. Indians dealt with CPR employees. Also, the railroad had a store car. In the Bersimis and Saguenay Districts cash advances had to be given to combat competition despite company opposition (HBCA D.25/4).

34. Of course, the profit margin would be reduced, given that it became a fur-cash transaction rather than fur and goods in which the company

extracted profit both ways (Inspection Report for Bersimis, 1890, HBCA D.25/4).

35. By 1898 cash tariffs and barter standards (MB) were in use in the southern portion of the Montreal, Southern, and Northern Departments. Hudson's Bay Company Commissioner C.C. Chipman indicated that the company would soon have to introduce it to the Mackenzie Department before opponents did, as had been the case elsewhere (HBCA A.12/FT 229/3).

36. Evidence for this can be obtained from a variety of sources. In 1880 W.J. Fortescue indicated that the MB tariff for goods was inelastic but that of furs was not (HBCA A.11/119a).

37. From the earliest years of the company's history there were efforts to curtail credit when competition was strong. The efforts usually were unsuccessful, and this was true in the 1880s also (Report for 1890, HBCA D.25/4).

38. Arthur J. Ray, "York Factory: The Crisis of Transition, 1870–80," *The Beaver* (Autumn 1982): 26–31.

39. A concerted effort was made in treaty areas to obtain as much of this money as was possible. Also credit was extended against Treaty payments (HBCA A.11/119a).

40. See HBCA A.12/FT 243/1 dealing with Destitute Indians and Treaties.

41. HBCA DFTR/19.

"WOMEN IN BETWEEN": INDIAN WOMEN IN FUR TRADE SOCIETY IN WESTERN CANADA[◆]

SYLVIA VAN KIRK

○

In attempting to analyse the life of the Indian woman in fur trade society in Western Canada, especially from her own point of view, one is immediately confronted by a challenging historiographical problem. Can the Indian woman's perspective be constructed from historical sources that were almost exclusively written by European men? Coming from a non-literate society, no Indian women have left us, for example, their views on the fur trade or their reasons for becoming traders' wives.[1] Yet if one amasses the sources available for fur trade social history, such as contemporary narratives, journals, correspondence and wills, a surprisingly rich store of information on Indian women emerges. One must, of course, be wary of the traders' cultural and sexual bias, but then even modern anthropologists have difficulty maintaining complete objectivity. Furthermore, the fur traders had the advantage of knowing Indian women intimately—these women became their wives, the mothers of their children. Narratives such as that of Andrew Graham in the late eighteenth century and David Thompson in the nineteenth, both of whom had native wives, comment perceptively on the implications of Indian-white social contact.[2] The key to constructing the Indian woman's perspective must lie in the kinds of questions applied to the data;[3] regrettably the picture will not be complete, but it is hoped that a careful reading of the traders' observations can result in a useful and illuminating account of the Indian woman's life in fur trade society.

The fur trade was based on the complex interaction between two different racial groups. On the one hand are the various Indian tribes, most importantly the Ojibway, the Cree and the Chipewyan. These Indians may

◆ Reprinted with permission from Canadian Historical Association, *Historical Papers* (1977), 31–46.

be designated the "host" group in that they remain within their traditional environment. On the other hand are the European traders, the "visiting" group, who enter the Northwest by both the Hudson Bay and St. Lawrence-Great Lakes routes. They are significantly different from the Indians in that they constitute only a small, all-male fragment of their own society. For a variety of factors to be discussed, this created a unique situation for the Indian women. They became the "women in between" two groups of males. Because of their sex, Indian women were able to become an integral part of fur trade society in a sense that Indian men never could. As country wives[4] of the traders, Indian women lived substantially different lives when they moved within the forts. Even within the tribes, women who acted as allies of the whites can also be observed; certain circumstances permitted individual women to gain positions of influence and act as "social brokers" between the two groups.

It is a major contention of this study that Indian women themselves were active agents in the development of Indian-white relations.[5] A major concern then must be to determine what motivated their actions. Some themes to be discussed are the extent to which the Indian woman was able to utilize her position as "woman in between" to increase her influence and status, and the extent to which the Indian woman valued the economic advantage brought by the traders. It must be emphasized, however, that Indian-white relations were by no means static during the fur trade period.[6] After assessing the positive and negative aspects of the Indian woman's life in fur trade society, the paper will conclude by discussing the reasons for the demise of her position.

○

Miscegenation was the basic social fact of the western Canadian fur trade. That this was so indicates active co-operation on both sides. From the male perspective, both white and Indian, the formation of marital alliances between Indian women and the traders had its advantages. The European traders had both social and economic reasons for taking Indian mates. Not only did they fill the sexual void created by the absence of white women,[7] but they performed such valuable economic tasks as making moccasins and netting snowshoes that they became an integral if unofficial part of the fur trade work force.[8] The traders also realized that these alliances were useful in cementing trade ties; officers in both the Hudson's Bay and North West companies often married daughters of trading captains or chiefs.[9] From the Indian point of view, the marital alliance created a reciprocal social bond which served to consolidate his economic relationship with the trader. The exchange of women was common in Indian society where it was viewed as "a reciprocal alliance and series of good offices ... between the friends of both parties; each is ready to assist and protect the other."[10] It was not loose morality or even hospitality which prompted the Indians to be so generous with their offers of women. This was their way of drawing the traders into their kinship circle, and in return for giving the traders sexual and domestic rights to their women, the Indians expected equitable privileges such as free access to the posts and provisions.[11] It is evident that the traders often did not understand the Indian concept of these alliances and a flagrant violation of Indian sensibilities could lead to retaliation such as the Henley House massacre in 1755.[12]

But what of the women themselves? Were they just pawns in this exchange, passive, exploited victims? Fur trade sources do not support this view; there are numerous examples of Indian women actively seeking to become connected with the traders. According to an early Nor'Wester, Cree women considered it an honour to be selected as wives by the voyageurs, and any husband who refused to lend his wife would be subject to the general condemnation of the women.[13] Alexander Ross observed that Chinook women on the Pacific coast showed a preference for living with a white man. If deserted by one husband, they would return to their tribe in a state of widowhood to await the opportunity of marrying another fur trader.[14] Nor'Wester Daniel Harmon voiced the widely held opinion that most of the Indian women were "better pleased to remain with the White People than with their own Relations," while his contemporary George Nelson affirmed "some too would even desert to live with the white."[15] Although Alexander Henry the Younger may have exaggerated his difficulties in fending off young Indian women, his personal experiences underline the fact that the women often took the initiative. On one occasion when travelling with his brigade in the summer of 1800, Henry was confronted in his tent by a handsome woman, dressed in her best finery, who told him boldly that she had come to live with him as she did not care for her husband or any other Indian. But Henry, anxious to avoid this entanglement partly because it was not sanctioned by the husband whom he knew to be insatiably jealous, forced the woman to return to her Indian partner.[16] A year or so later in the lower Red River district, the daughter of an Ojibway chief had more luck. Henry returned from New Year's festivities to find that "Liard's daughter" had taken possession of his room and "the devil could not have got her out."[17] This time, having become more acculturated to fur trade life, Henry acquiesced and "Liard's daughter" became his country wife. The trader, however, resisted his father-in-law's argument that he should also take his second daughter because all great men should have a plurality of wives.[18]

The fur traders also comment extensively on the assistance and loyalty of Indian women who remained within the tribes. An outstanding example is the young Chipewyan Thanadelthur, known to the traders as the "Slave Woman."[19] In the early eighteenth century after being captured by the Cree, Thanadelthur managed to escape to York Factory. Her knowledge of Chipewyan made her valuable to the traders, and in 1715–16, she led an H.B.C. expedition to establish peace between the Cree and the Chipewyan, a necessary prelude to the founding of Fort Churchill. Governor James Knight's journals gives us a vivid picture of this woman, of whom he declared: "She was one of a Very high Spirit and of the Firmest Resolution that ever I see any Body in my Days."[20]

Post journals contain numerous references to Indian women warning the traders of impending treachery. In 1797, Charles Chaboillez, having been warned by an old woman that the Indians intended to pillage his post, was able to nip this intrigue in the bud.[21] George Nelson and one of his men only escaped an attack by some Indians in 1805 by being "clandestinely assisted by the women."[22] It appears that women were particularly instrumental in saving the lives of the whites among the turbulent tribes of the Lower Columbia.[23] One of the traders' most notable allies was the well-connected Chinook princess known as Lady Calpo, the wife of a Clatsop chief. In 1814, she helped restore peaceful relations after the Nor'Westers had suffered a raid on their canoes by giving them important information about Indian custom in settling disputes. Handsome rewards cemented her attachment to the traders with the result that Lady Calpo reputedly saved Fort George from several attacks by warning of the hostile plans of the Indians.[24]

The reasons for the Indian women's action are hinted at in the traders' observations. It was the generally held opinion of the traders that the status of women in Indian society was deplorably low. As Nor'Wester Gabriel Franchère summed it up: "Some Indian tribes think that women have no souls, but die altogether like the brutes; others assign them a different paradise from that of men, which indeed they might have reason to prefer . . . unless their relative condition were to be ameliorated in the next world."[25] Whether as "social brokers" or as wives, Indian women attempted to manipulate their position as "women in between" to increase their influence and status. Certainly women such as Thanadelthur and Lady Calpo were able to work themselves into positions of real power. It is rather paradoxical that in Thanadelthur's case it was her escape from captivity that brought her into contact with the traders in the first place; if she had not been a woman, she would never have been carried off by the Cree as a prize of war. Once inside the H.B.C. fort, she was able to use her position as the only Chipewyan to her advantage by acting as guide and consultant to the Governor. The protection and regard she was given by the whites enabled Thanadelthur to dictate to Indian men, both Cree and Chipewyan, in a manner they would not previously have tolerated. Anxious to promote the traders' interests, she assaulted an old Chipewyan on one occasion when he attempted to trade less than prime furs; she "ketcht him by the nose Push'd him backwards & call'd him fool and told him if they brought any but Such as they ware directed they would not be traded."[26] Thanadelthur did take a Chipewyan husband but was quite prepared to leave him if he would not accompany her on the arduous second journey she was planning to undertake for the Governor.[27] It is possible that the role played by Thanadelthur and subsequent "slave women" in establishing trade relations with the whites may have enhanced the status of Chipewyan women. Nearly a century later, Alexander Mackenzie noted that, in spite of their burdensome existence, Chipewyan women possessed "a very considerable influence in the traffic with Europeans."[28]

Lady Calpo retained a position of influence for a long time. When Governor Simpson visited Fort George in 1824, he found she had to be treated with respect because she was "the best News Monger in the Parish"; from her he learned "More of the Scandal, Secrets and politics both of the out & inside of the Fort than from Any other source."[29] Significantly, Lady Calpo endeavoured to further improve her rank by arranging a marriage alliance between the Governor and her carefully raised daughter. Although Simpson declared he wished "to keep clear of the Daughter," he succumbed in order "to continue on good terms with the Mother."[30] Many years later, a friend visiting the Columbia wrote to Simpson that Lady Calpo that "'fast friend' of the Whites" was still thriving.[31]

As wives of the traders, Indian women could also manoeuvre themselves into positions of influence. In fact, a somewhat perturbed discussion emerges in fur trade literature over the excessive influence some Indian women exerted over their fur trader husbands. The young N.W.C. clerk George Nelson appears to have spent long hours contemplating the insolvable perplexities of womankind. Nelson claimed that initially Cree women when married to whites were incredibly attentive and submissive, but this did not last long. Once they had gained a little footing, they knew well "how to take advantage & what use they ought to make of it."[32] On one of his first trips into the interior, Nelson was considerably annoyed by the shenanigans of the Indian wife of Brunet, one of his voyageurs. A jealous, headstrong woman, she completely dominated her husband by a mixture of "caresses, promises & menaces." Not only did this woman render her husband a most unreliable servant, but Nelson also caught her helping herself to the Company's rum. Brunet's wife, Nelson fumed, was as great "a vixen & hussy" as the tinsmith's wife at the market place in Montreal: "I now began to think that women were women not only in civilized countries but elsewhere also."[33]

Another fur trader observed a paradoxical situation among the Chipewyan women. In their own society, they seemed condemned to a most servile existence, but upon becoming wives of the French-Canadian voyageurs, they assumed "an importance to themselves and instead of serving as formerly they exact submission from the descendants of the Gauls."[34] One of the most remarkable examples of a Chipewyan wife rising to prominence was the case of Madam Lamallice, the wife of the brigade guide at the H.B.C. post on Lake Athabasca. During the difficult winter of 1820–21, Madam Lamallice was accorded a favoured position because she was the post's only interpreter and possessed considerable influence with the Indians.[35] George Simpson, then experiencing his first winter in the Indian Country, felt obliged to give in to her demands for extra rations and preferred treatment in order to prevent her defection. He had observed that the Nor'Westers' strong position was partly due to the fact that "their Women are faithful to their cause and good Interpreters whereas we have but one in the Fort that can talk Chipewyan."[36] Madam Lamallice exploited her position to such an extent that she even defied fort regulations by carrying on a private trade in provisions.[37] A few years later on a trip to the Columbia,

Governor Simpson was annoyed to discover that Chinook women when married to the whites often gained such an ascendancy "that they give law to their Lords."[38] In fact, he expressed general concern about the influence of these "petticoat politicians" whose demands were "more injurious to the Companys interests than I am well able to describe."[39] The Governor deplored Chief Factor James Bird's management of Red River in the early 1820s because of his habit of discussing every matter "however trifling or important" with "his Copper Cold. [coloured] Mate," who then spread the news freely around the colony.[40] Too many of his officers, Simpson declared, tended to sacrifice business for private interests. Particular expense and delay were occasioned in providing transport for families. Simpson never forgave Chief Factor John Clarke for abandoning some of the goods destined for Athabasca in 1820 to make a light canoe for his native wife and her servant.[41]

It is likely that Simpson's single-minded concern for business efficiency caused him to exaggerate the extent of the Indian women's influence. Nevertheless, they do seem to have attempted to take advantage of their unique position as women "in between" two groups of men. This fact is supported by the traders' observation that the choice of a husband, Indian or white, gave the Indian woman leverage to improve her lot. Now she could threaten to desert to the whites or vice-versa if she felt she were not being well-treated: "She has always enough of policy to insinuate how well off she was while living with the white people and in like manner when with the latter she drops some hints to the same purpose."[42] Although Chipewyan women who had lived with the voyageurs had to resume their former domestic tasks when they returned to their own people, they reputedly evinced a greater spirit of independence.[43] Considerable prestige accrued to Chinook women who had lived with the traders; upon rejoining the tribes, they remained "very friendly" to the whites and "never fail to influence their connections to the same effect."[44]

From the Indian woman's point of view, material advantage was closely tied to the question of improved influence or status. The women within the tribes had a vested interest in promoting cordial relations with the whites. While George Nelson mused that it was a universal maternal instinct which prompted the women to try to prevent clashes between Indian and white,[45] they were more likely motivated by practical, economic considerations. If the traders were driven from the country, the Indian woman would lose the source of European goods, which had revolutionized her life just as much if not more than that of the Indian man. It was much easier to boil water in a metal kettle than to have to laboriously heat it by means of dropping hot stones in a bark container. Cotton and woolen goods saved long hours of tanning hides. "Show them an awl or a strong needle," declared David Thompson, "and they will gladly give the finest Beaver or Wolf skin they have to purchase it."[46]

Futhermore, it can be argued that the tendency of the Indians to regard the fur trade post as a kind of welfare centre was of more relevance to the women than to the men. In times of scarcity, which were not infrequent in

Indian society, the women were usually the first to suffer.[47] Whereas before they would often have perished, many now sought relief at the companies' posts. To cite but one of many examples: at Albany during the winter of 1706, Governor Beale gave shelter to three starving Cree women whose husband had sent them away as he could only provide for his two children.[48] The post was also a source of medical aid and succour. The story is told of a young Carrier woman in New Caledonia who, having been severely beaten by her husband, managed to struggle to the nearest N.W.C. post. Being nearly starved, she was slowly nursed back to health and allowed to remain at the post when it became apparent that her relatives had abandoned her.[49] The desire for European goods, coupled with the assistance to be found at the fur trade posts, helps to explain why Indian women often became devoted allies of the traders.

In becoming the actual wife of a fur trader, the Indian woman was offered even greater relief from the burdens of her traditional existence. In fact, marriage to a trader offered an alternative lifestyle. The fur traders themselves had no doubt that an Indian woman was much better off with a white man. The literature presents a dreary recital of their abhorrence of the degraded, slave-like position of the Indian woman. The life of a Cree woman, declared Alexander Mackenzie, was "an uninterrupted success[ion] of toil and pain."[50] Nor'Wester Duncan McGillivray decided that the rather singular lack of affection evinced by Plains Indian women for their mates arose from the barbarous treatment the women received.[51] Although David Thompson found the Chipewyan a good people in many ways, he considered their attitudes toward women a disgrace; he had known Chipewyan women to kill female infants as "an act of kindness" to spare them the hardships they would have to face.[52]

The extent to which the fur traders' observations represent an accurate reflection of the actual status of Indian women in their own societies presents a complex dilemma which requires deeper investigation. The cultural and class biases of the traders are obvious. Their horror at the toilsome burdens imposed upon Indian women stems from their narrow, chivalrous view of women as the "frail, weaker sex." This is scarcely an appropriate description of Indian women, particularly the Chipewyan who were acknowledged to be twice as strong as their male counterparts.[53] Furthermore, while the sharp sexual division of labour inflicted a burdensome role upon the women, their duties were essential and the women possessed considerable autonomy within their own sphere.[54] Some traders did think it curious that the women seemed to possess a degree of influence in spite of their degraded situation; indeed, some of the bolder ones occasionally succeeded in making themselves quite independent and "wore the breeches."[55]

A possible way of explaining the discrepancy between the women's perceived and actual status is suggested in a recent anthropological study of the Mundurucú of Amazonian Brazil. In this society, the authors discovered that while the official (male) ideology relegates women to an inferior, subservient position, in the reality of daily life, the women are able to

assume considerable autonomy and influence.[56] Most significantly, however, Mundurucú women, in order to alleviate their onerous domestic
duties, have actively championed the erosion of traditional village life and
the concomitant blurring of economic sex roles which have come with the
introduction of the rubber trade. According to the authors, the Mundurucú
woman "has seen another way of life, and she has opted for it."[57]

This statement could well be applied to the Indian woman who was
attracted to the easier life of the fur trade post. In the first place, she now
became involved in a much more sedentary routine. With a stationary
home, the Indian woman was no longer required to act as a beast of burden,
hauling or carrying the accoutrements of camp from place to place. The
traders often expressed astonishment and pity at the heavy loads which
Indian women were obliged to transport.[58] In fur trade society, the unenvi-
able role of carrier was assumed by the voyageur. The male servants at the
fort were now responsible for providing firewood and water, although the
women might help. In contrast to Indian practice, the women of the fort
were not sent to fetch home the produce of the hunt.[59] The wife of an officer, benefiting from her husband's rank, enjoyed a privileged status. She
herself was carried in and out of the canoe[60] and could expect to have all
her baggage portaged by a voyageur. At Fond du Lac in 1804 when the wife
of N.W.C. *bourgeois* John Sayer decided to go on a sugar-making expedition,
four men went with her to carry her baggage and provisions and later
returned to fetch home her things.[61]

While the Indian woman performed a variety of valuable economic
tasks around the post, her domestic duties were relatively lighter than they
had traditionally been. Now her energies were concentrated on making
moccasins and snowshoes. As one Nor'Wester declared, with the whites,
Indian women could lead "a comparatively easy and free life" in contrast to
the "servile slavish mode" of their own.[62] The prospect of superior comforts
reputedly motivated some Spokan women to marry voyageurs.[63] The ready
supply of both finery and trinkets which *bourgeois* and voyageurs were seen
to lavish on their women may also have had an appeal.[64] Rival traders
noted that luxury items such as lace, ribbons, rings, and vermilion, which
"greatly gain the Love of the Women," were important in attracting the
Indians to trade.[65] The private orders placed by H.B.C. officers and servants
in the 1790s, and later, include a wide range of cloth goods, shawls, garter-
ing, earrings and brooches for the women.[66] When taken by a trader *à la
façon du pays*, it became common for an Indian woman to go through a ritual
performed by other women of the fort; she was scoured of grease and paint
and exchanged her native garments for those of more civilized fashion. At
the N.W.C. posts, wives were clothed in "Canadian fashion" which consisted of a shirt, short gown, petticoat and leggings.[67]

The traders further thought that Indian women benefited by being freed
from certain taboos and customs which they had to bear in Indian society.
Among the Ojibway and other tribes, for example, the choicest part of an
animal was always reserved for the men; death it was believed would come
to any woman who dared to eat such sacred portions. The Nor'Westers paid

little heed to such observances. As Duncan Cameron sarcastically wrote: "I have often seen several women living with the white men eat of those forbidden morsels without the least inconvenience."[68] The traders were also convinced that Indian women welcomed a monogamous as opposed to a polygamous state. Polygamy, several H.B.C. officers observed, often gave rise to jealous and sometimes murderous quarrels.[69] It is possible, however, that the traders' own cultural abhorrence of polygamy[70] made them exaggerate the women's antipathy toward it. As a practical scheme for the sharing of heavy domestic tasks, polygamy may in fact have been welcomed by the women.

○

Thus far the advantages which the fur trade brought to Indian women have been emphasized in order to help explain Indian women's reactions to it. It would be erroneous, however, to paint the life of an Indian wife as idyllic. In spite of the traders' belief in the superior benefits they offered, there is evidence that fur trade life had an adverse effect on Indian women. Certainly, a deterioration in her position over time can be detected.

First there is the paradox that the supposedly superior material culture of the fur trade had a deleterious effect on Indian women. It was as if, mused Reverend John West, the first Anglican missionary, "the habits of civilized life" exerted an injurious influence over their general constitutions.[71] Apart from being more exposed to European diseases, the Indian wives of traders suffered more in childbirth than they had in the primitive state.[72] Dr. John Richardson, who accompanied the Franklin Expedition of the 1820s noted, that not only did Indian women now have children more frequently and over longer periods of time, but that they were more susceptible to the disorders and diseases connected with pregnancy and childbirth.[73] It was not uncommon for fur traders' wives to give birth to from eight to twelve children, whereas four children were the average in Cree society.[74]

The reasons for this dramatic rise in the birth rate deserve further investigation, but several reasons can be advanced. As recent medical research has suggested, the less fatiguing lifestyle and more regular diet offered the Indian wife could have resulted in greater fecundity.[75] The daily ration for the women of the forts was four pounds of meat or fish (one half that for the men);[76] when Governor Simpson jokingly remarked that the whitefish diet at Fort Chipewyan seemed conducive to procreation he may have hit upon a medical truth.[77] Furthermore, sexual activity in Indian society was circumscribed by a variety of taboos, and evidence suggests that Indian men regarded their European counterparts as very licentious.[78] Not only did Indian women now have sex more often, but the attitudes of European husbands also may have interfered with traditional modes of restricting family size. The practice of infanticide was, of course, condemned by the whites, but the Europeans may also have discouraged the traditional long nursing periods of from two to four years for each child.[79] In their view this custom resulted in the premature aging of the mothers,[80] but the fact that Indian children were born at intervals of approximately three years tends to support the recent theory that lactation depresses fertility.[81]

The cultural conflict resulting over the upbringing of the children must have caused the Indian women considerable anguish. An extreme example of the tragedy which could result related to the Chinook practice of head-flattening. In Chinook society, a flat forehead, achieved by strapping a board against the baby's head when in its cradle, was a mark of class; only slaves were not so distinguished. Thus it was only natural that a Chinook woman, though married to a fur trader, would desire to bind her baby's head, but white fathers found this custom abhorrent. The insistence of some fathers that their infants' heads not be flattened resulted in the mothers murdering their babies rather than have them suffer the ignominy of looking like slaves. Gradually European preference prevailed. When Governor Simpson visited the Columbia in the early 1820s, he reported that Chinook wives were abiding by their husbands' wishes and no cases of infanticide had been reported for some years.[82]

In Indian society, children were the virtual "property" of the women who were responsible for their upbringing;[83] in fur trade society, Indian women could find themselves divested of these rights. While the traders acknowledged that Indian women were devoted and affectionate mothers, this did not prevent them from exercising patriarchal authority, particularly in sending young children to Britain or Canada so that they might receive a "civilized" education.[84] It must have been nearly impossible to explain the rationale for such a decision to the Indian mothers; their grief at being separated from their children was compounded by the fact that the children, who were especially vulnerable to respiratory diseases, often died.[85]

It is difficult to know if the general treatment accorded Indian women by European traders met with the women's acceptance. How much significance should be attached to the views of outside observers in the early 1800s who did not think the Indian woman's status had been much improved? Some of the officers of the Franklin Expedition felt the fur traders had been corrupted by Indian attitudes toward women; Indian wives were not treated with "the tenderness and attention due to every female" because the Indians would despise the traders for such unmanly action.[86] The first missionaries were even stronger in denouncing fur trade marital relations. John West considered the traders' treatment of their women disgraceful: "They do not admit them as their companions, nor do they allow them to eat at their tables, but degrade them *merely* as slaves to their arbitrary inclinations."[87] Such statements invite skepticism because of the writers' limited contact with fur trade society, and in the case of the missionaries because of their avowedly hostile view of fur trade customs. Furthermore, the above statements project a European ideal about the way women should be treated, which apart from being widely violated in their own society, would have had little relevance for Indian women. It is doubtful, for example, that the Indian women themselves would have viewed the fact that they did not come to table, a custom partly dictated by the quasi-military organization of the posts, as proof of their debased positon.[88] The segregation of the sexes at meals was common in Indian society, but now, at least, the women did not have to suffice with the leftovers of the men.[89]

Nevertheless, there is evidence to suggest that Indian women were misused by the traders. In Indian society, women were accustomed to greater freedom of action with regard to marital relationships than the traders were prepared to accord them. It was quite within a woman's rights, for example, to institute a divorce if her marriage proved unsatisfactory.[90] In fur trade society, Indian women were more subject to arbitrary arrangements devised by the men. Upon retiring from the Indian Country, it became customary for a trader to place his country wife and family with another, a practice known as "turning off." Although there was often little they could do about it, a few cases were cited of women who tried to resist. At a post in the Peace River district in 1798, the Indian wife of an *engagé*, who was growing tired of wintering *en derouine*, absolutely rejected her husband's attempt to pass her to the man who agreed to take his place.[91] At Fort Chipewyan in 1800, the estranged wife of the voyageur Morin foiled the attempt of his *bourgeois* to find her a temporary "protector"; she stoutly refused three different prospects.[92] Indian women also did not take kindly to the long separations which fur trade life imposed on them and their European mates. Although the Indian wife of Chief Factor Joseph Colen was to receive every attention during his absence in England in the late 1790s, Colen's successor could not dissuade her from taking an Indian lover and leaving York Factory.[93]

Indian wives seem to have been particularly victimized during the violent days of the trade war when rivals went so far as to debauch and intimidate each other's women. In 1819 at Pelican Lake, for example, H.B.C. servant Deshau took furs from an N.W.C. servant and raped his wife in retaliation for having had his own wife debauched by a Nor'Wester earlier in the season.[94] A notorious instance involved the Indian wife of H.B.C. servant Andrew Kirkness at Isle à la Cross in 1810–11. In the late summer, this woman in a fit of pique had deserted her husband and sought refuge at the Nor'Westers' post. She soon regretted her action, however, for she was kept a virtual prisoner by the Canadians, and all efforts of the H.B.C. men to get her back failed. The upshot was that Kirkness himself deserted to the rival post, leaving the English in dire straits since he was their only fisherman. Kirkness was intimidated into remaining with the Nor'Westers until the spring with the threat that should he try to leave "every Canadian in the House would ravish his woman before his eyes." Eventually Kirkness was released, but only after his wife had been coerced into saying that she did not want to accompany him. As the H.B.C. party were evacuating their post, the woman tried to escape but was forcibly dragged back by the Nor'Westers and ultimately became the "property" of an *engagé*.[95]

Such abusive tactics were also applied to the Indians. By the turn of the century, relations between the Indians and the Nor'Westers in particular showed a marked deterioration. In what seems to have been a classic case of "familiarity breeding contempt," the Nor'Westers now retained their mastery through coercion and brute force and frequently transgressed the bounds of Indian morality. An especially flagrant case was the Nor'Westers' exploitation of Chipewyan women at its posts in the Athabasca district. By the end of the eighteenth century, they had apparently built up a nefarious traffic in these women; the *bourgeois* did not scruple at seizing Chipewyan women by force, ostensibly in lieu of trade debts, and then selling them to the men for large sums.[96] The situation became so bad that the Chipewyan began leaving their women behind when they came to trade, and when Hudson's Bay traders appeared on Lake Athabasca in 1792, the Indians hoped to secure their support and drive out their rivals. The English, however, were too weak to offer any effective check to the Nor'Westers, who continued to assault both fathers and husbands if they tried to resist the seizure of their women. Since they were not powerful enough to mount an attack, the Chipewyan connived at the escape of their women during the summer months when most of the traders were away. Resentful of their treatment, many of the women welcomed the chance to slip back to their own people so that the summer master at Fort Chipewyan was almost solely preoccupied with keeping watch over the *engagés'* women.[97] By 1800 at least one voyageur had been killed by irate Chipewyans, and the *bourgeois* contemplated offering a reward for the hunting down of "any d—nd rascal" who caused a Frenchman's woman to desert.[98]

The Indians appear to have become openly contemptuous of the white man and his so-called morality. A northern tribe called the Beaver Indians took a particularly strong stand. At first they had welcomed the Canadians but, having rapidly lost respect for them, now forbade any intercourse between their women and the traders.[99] Elsewhere individual hunters boycotted the traders owing to the maltreatment of their women.[100] Sporadic reprisals became more frequent. Whereas Indian women had previously played a positive role as a liaison between Indian and white, they were now becoming an increasing source of friction between the two groups. Governor Simpson summed up the deteriorating situation: "It is a lamentable fact that almost every difficulty we have had with Indians throughout the country may be traced to our interference with their Women or their intrigues with the Women of the Forts in short 9 murders out of 10 Committed on Whites by Indians have arisen through Women."[101]

Although there is little direct evidence available, it is possible that the Indian women themselves were becoming increasingly dissatisfied with their treatment from the whites. In spite of the initiative which the women have been seen to exercise in forming and terminating relationships with the traders, there were undoubtedly times when they were the unwilling objects of a transaction between Indians and white men. Certainly not all Indian women looked upon the whites as desirable husbands, a view that was probably reinforced with experience. George Nelson did observe in 1811 that there were some Indian women who showed "an extraordinary predilection" for their own people and could not be prevailed upon to live with the traders.[102]

The increasing hostility of the Indians, coupled with the fact that in well established areas marriage alliances were no longer a significant factor in trade relations, led to a decline in the practice of taking an Indian wife. In fact in 1806, the North West Company passed a ruling prohibiting any of its employees from taking a country wife from among the tribes.[103] One of the significant factors which changed the traders' attitudes toward Indian women, however, was that they were now no longer "women in between." By the turn of the century a sizeable group of mixed-blood women had emerged and for social and economic reasons, fur traders preferred mixed-blood women as wives.[104] In this way the Indian women lost their important place in fur trade society.

The introduction of the Indian woman's perspective on Indian-white relations serves to underscore the tremendous complexity of inter-cultural contact. It is argued that Indian women saw definite advantages to be gained from the fur trade, and in their unique position as "women in between," they endeavoured to manipulate the situation to improve their existence. That the limits of their influence were certainly circumscribed, and that the ultimate benefits brought by the traders were questionable, does not negate the fact that the Indian women played a much more active and important role in the fur trade than has previously been acknowledged.

NOTES

1. The lack of written Indian history is, or course, a general problem for the ethnohistorian. Indeed, all social scientists must rely heavily on the historical observations of the agents of white contact such as fur traders, explorers and missionaries. Little seems to have been done to determine if the oral tradition of the Indians is a viable source of information on Indian–white relations in the fur trade period.

2. Glyndwr Williams, ed., *Andrew Graham's Observations on Hudson's Bay 1769–91*, vol. 27 (London: Hudson's Bay Record Society, 1969); Richard Glover, ed., *David Thompson's Narrative 1784–1812*, vol. 40 (Toronto: Champlain Society, 1962).

3. A fascinating study which indicates how the application of a different perspective to the same data can produce new insights is *Women of the Forest* by Yolanda and Robert Murphy (New York, 1974). Based on field work conducted twenty years earlier in Amazonian Brazil, the authors found that by looking

at the life of the Mundurucú tribe from the woman's point of view, their understanding of the actual as opposed to the official functioning of that society was enlarged.

4. Marriages between European traders and Indian women were contracted according to indigenous rites derived from Indian custom. For a detailed explanation, see Sylvia Van Kirk, "'The Custom of the Country': An Examination of Fur Trade Marriage Practices" in *Essays in Western History*, ed. L.H. Thomas (Edmonton, 1976), 49–70.

5. See Murphy, *Women of the Forest*, chap. 6 for a useful comparison. Mundurucú women actively welcomed the social change brought about by the introduction of the rubber trade into their traditional economy.

6. An instructive study of the Indians' economic role in the fur trade is provided by Arthur Ray in *Indians in the Fur Trade* (Toronto, 1974). He shows that the Indian played a much more active, although chang-

ing role in the dynamics of the fur trade than had previously been acknowledged.

7. HBC men were prohibited from bringing women to Hudson Bay. It was not until the early nineteenth century that the first white women came to the Northwest.

8. In 1802, HBC men defended their practice of keeping Indian women in the posts by informing the London Committee that they were "Virtually your Honors Servants." Hudson's Bay Company Archives (hereafter HBCA), B.239/b/79, fos. 40d–41. For a discussion of the important economic role played by native women in the fur trade, see Sylvia Van Kirk, "The Role of Women in the Fur Trade Society of the Canadian West, 1700–1850" (PhD thesis, University of London, 1975).

9. HBCA, Albany Journal, 24 Jan. 1771, B.3/a/63, f. 18d; Connolly vs. Woolrich, Superior Court, 9 July 1867, *Lower Canada Jurist* 11 (1867): 234.

10. Charles Bishop, "The Henley House Massacres," *The Beaver* (Autumn 1976): 40.

11. Ibid., 39. For a more technical look at the socio-economic relationship between the Indians and the traders, see the discussion of "balanced reciprocity" in Marshall Sahlins, *Stone Age Economics* (Chicago, 1972), ch. 5.

12. In this instance the Indian captain Woudby attacked Henley House because the master was keeping two of his female relatives but denying him access to the post and its provisions.

13. Alexander Henry, *Travels and Adventures in Canada and the Indian Territories 1760–1766*, ed. Jas Bain (Boston, 1901), 248.

14. Alexander Ross, *The Fur Hunters of the Far West* (London, 1855), 1:296–97.

15. W. Kaye Lamb, ed., *Sixteen Years in the Indian Country: The Journal of Daniel Williams Harmon 1800–1816* (Toronto, 1957), 29; Toronto Public Library (hereafter TPL), George Nelson Papers, Journal 1810–11, 24 April 1811, 42.

16. Elliot Coues, ed., *New Light on the Early History of the Greater North West: The Manuscript Journals of Alexander Henry and David Thompson 1799–1814* (Minneapolis, 1965), 71–73.

17. Ibid., 163.

18. Ibid., 211.

19. For a detailed account of the story of this woman, see Sylvia Van Kirk, "Thanadelthur," *The Beaver* (Spring 1974): 40–45.

20. Ibid., 45.

21. Public Archives of Canada (hereafter PAC), Masson Collection, Journal of Charles Chaboillez, 13 Dec. 1797, 24.

22. TPL, Nelson Papers, Journal and Reminiscences 1825–26, 66.

23. Ross, *Fur Hunters*, 1:296.

24. Coues, ed., *New Light*, 793; Frederick Merk, ed., *Fur Trade and Empire: George Simpson's Journal, 1824–25* (Cambridge, MA, 1931), 104.

25. Gabriel Franchère, *Narrative of a Voyage to the Northwest Coast of America 1811–14*, ed. R.G. Thwaites (Cleveland, OH, 1904), 327.

26. Van Kirk, "Thanadelthur," 44.

27. Ibid., 45.

28. W. Kaye Lamb, ed., *The Journals and Letters of Sir Alexander Mackenzie* (Cambridge, 1970), 152.

29. Merk, *Fur Trade and Empire*, 104.

30. Ibid., 104–5.

31. HBCA, R. Crooks to G. Simpson, 15 March 1843, D. 5/8, f. 147.

32. TPL, Nelson Papers, Journal 1810–11, 41–42.

33. TPL, Nelson Papers, Journal 1803–04, 10–28 *passim*.

34. PAC, Masson Collection, "An Account of the Chipwean Indians," 23.

35. E.E. Rich, ed., *Simpson's Athabasca Journal and Report 1820–21* (London: Hudson's Bay Record Society, 1938), 1:74.

36. Ibid., 231.

37. HBCA, Fort Chipewyan Journal 1820–21, B.39/a/16, fos. 6–21d, passim.

38. Merk, *Fur Trade and Empire*, 99.

39. Ibid., 11–12, 58.

40. HBCA, George Simpson's Journal 1821–22, D. 3/3, f. 52.

41. Rich, ed., *Simpson's Athabasca Journal*, 23–24; see also Merk, *Fur Trade and Empire*, 131.

42. PAC, Masson Collection, "Account of Chipwean Indians," 23–24.

43. Ibid., 23.

44. Ross, *Fur Hunters*, 1:297.

45. TPL, Nelson Papers, Journal and Reminiscences 1825–26, 66. Nelson claimed that around 1780 some Indian women had warned the Canadian pedlars of impending attack because in their "tender & affectionate breast (for women are lovely all the world over) still lurked compassion for the mothers of those destined to be sacrificed."

46. Glover, ed., *David Thompson's Narrative*, 45. Cf. with the Mundurucú women's desire for European goods, Murphy, *Women of the Forest*, 182.

47. Samuel Hearne, *A Journey to the Northern Ocean*, ed. Richard Glover (Toronto, 1958), 190.

48. HBCA, Albany Journal, 23 Feb. 1706, B.3/a/1, f. 28.

49. Ross Cox, *The Columbia River*, ed. Jane and Edgar Stewart (Norman, OK, 1957), 377.

50. Lamb, ed., *Journals and Letters*, 135.

51. A.S. Morton, *The Journal of Duncan McGillivray . . . at Fort George on the Saskatchewan 1794–95* (Toronto, 1929), 60.

52. Glover, ed., *David Thompson's Narrative*, 106.

53. Hearne, *Journey to the Northern Ocean*, 35: "Women," declared the Chipewyan chief Matonabee, "were made for labour; one of them can carry, or haul, as much as two men can do."

54. There has been a trend in recent literature to exalt the Indian woman's status by pointing out that in spite of her labour she had more independence than the pioneer farm wife. See Nancy O. Lurie, "Indian Women: A Legacy of Freedom," *The American Way* 5 (April 1972): 28–35.

55. Morton, *Journal of Duncan McGillivray*, 34; L.R.F. Masson, *Les Bourgeois de la Compagnie du Nord-Ouest* (n.p., 1889), 1:256.

56. Murphy, *Women of the Forest*, 87, 112.

57. Ibid., 202.

58. Lamb, ed., *Journals and Letters*, 254; Glover, ed., *David Thompson's Narrative*, 125.

59. PAC, Masson Collection, Journal of John Thomson, 15 Oct. 1798, 10.

60. J.B. Tyrrell, *Journals of Samuel Hearne and Philip Turnor 1774–92* (Toronto: Champlain Society, 1934), 21:252.

61. Michel Curot, "A Wisconsin Fur Trader's Journal 1803–04," *Wisconsin Historical Collections* 20 (1911): 449, 453.

62. TPL, Nelson Papers, Journal 1810–11, 41, and Reminiscences, Part 5, 225.

63. Cox, *Columbia River*, 148.

64. Coues, ed., *New Light*, 914; Ross, *Fur Hunters*, 11:236.

65. Tyrrell, *Journals of Samuel Hearne*, 273.

66. HBCA, Book of Servants Commissions, A. 16/111 and 112 passim.

67. Lamb, ed., *Sixteen Years*, 28–29.

68. Masson, *Les Bourgeois*, 2: 263.

69. Hearne, *Journey to the Northern Ocean*, 80; Williams, ed., *Andrew Graham's Observations*, 158.

70. Alexander Ross, *Adventures of the First Settlers on the Oregon or Columbia River* (London, 1849), 280–81: Glover, ed., *David Thompson's Narrative*, 251.

71. John West, *The Substance of a Journal during a residence at the Red River Colony 1820–23* (London, 1827), 54.

72. The traders were astonished at the little concern shown for pregnancy and childbirth in Indian society, see for example Lamb, ed., *Journals and Letters*, 250 and Williams, ed., *Andrew Graham's Observations*, 177.

73. John Franklin, *Narrative of a Journey to the Shores of the Polar Sea 1819–22* (London, 1824), 86.

74. Ibid., 60. The Indian wives of Alexander Ross and Peter Fidler, for example, had thirteen and fourteen children respectively.

75. Jennifer Brown, "A Demographic Transition in the Fur Trade Country," *Western Canadian Journal of Anthropology* 6, 1 (1976): 68.

76. Cox, *Columbia River*, 354.

77. J.S. Galbraith, *The Little Emperor* (Toronto, 1976), 68.

78. TPL, Nelson Papers, Reminiscences, Part 5, 225.

79. Brown, "A Demographic Transition," 67.

80. Margaret MacLeod, ed., *The Letters of Letitia Hargrave* (Toronto: Champlain Society, 1947), 94–95; Alexander Ross, *The Red River Settlement* (Minneapolis, 1957), 95, 192.

81. Brown, "A Demographic Transition," 65.

82. Merk, *Fur Trade and Empire*, 101.

83. Williams, ed., *Andrew Graham's Observations*, 176, 178.

84. Ross, *Adventures of the First Settlers*, 280; W.J. Healy, *Woman of Red River* (Winnipeg, 1923), 163–66.

85. Lamb, ed., *Sixteen Years*, 138, 186.

86. Franklin, *Narrative of a Journey*, 101, 106.

87. West, *Substance of a Journal*, 16.

88. Cox, *Columbia River*, 360.

89. Hearne, *Journey to the Northern Ocean*, 57.

90. Williams, ed., *Andrew Graham's Observations*, 176.

91. PAC, Masson Collection, Journal of John Thomson, 19 Nov. 1798, 20.

92. Masson, *Les Bourgeois*, 2:384–85. We are not told whether she also escaped being sold when the brigades arrived in the spring as the *bourgeois* intended.

93. HBCA, York Journal, 2 Dec. 1798, B.239/a/103, f. 14d.

94. HBCA, Pelican Lake Journal, 18 Jan. 1819, D. 158/a/1, f. 7d.

95. This account is derived from HBCA, Isle à la Crosse Journal, B.89/a/2, fos. 5–36d passim.

96. Tyrrell, *Journals of Samuel Hearne*, 446n, 449.

97. Ibid., 449–50.

98. Masson, *Les Bourgeois*, 2:387–88.

99. Lamb, ed., *Journals and Letters*, 255; Rich, ed., *Simpson's Athabasca Journal*, 388.

100. PAC, Masson Collection, Journal of Ferdinand Wentzel, 13 Jan. 1805, 41.

101. Merk, *Fur Trade and Empire*, 127.

102. TPL, Nelson Papers, Journal 1810–11, 41–42.

103. W.S. Wallace, *Documents relating to the North West Company* (Toronto: Champlain Society, 1934), 22:211. This ruling was not enforced in outlying districts such as the Columbia. Even after the union in 1821, Governor Simpson continued to favour the formation of marital alliances in remote regions as the best way to secure friendly relations with the Indians, see Rich, ed., *Simpson's Athabasca Journal*, 392.

104. For a discussion of the role played by mix-blood women in fur trade society, see Van Kirk, "Role of Women in Fur Trade Society."

PROPHETS, PRIESTS, AND PREACHERS: GLIMPSES OF DENE HISTORY ✧

KERRY ABEL

○

By mid-nineteenth century, relations between the Dene and the fur traders appear to have been stabilizing and a new era of peace unfolding. A prosperous and well-adjusted society was emerging to the mutual advantage of all parties. The HBC had no interest in disrupting the fundamental relationship between the Dene and the land; trapping furs fit well into the Dene economy and world-view. Certainly the HBC was anxious to encourage greater participation in fur trapping and those people who took up the challenge found that their lives were somewhat changed, but the HBC had avoided almost entirely any interference in matters of religion or spiritual belief. At mid-century, however, both the Dene and the HBC were challenged with the arrival of a number of European and Canadian missionaries. The activities and impact of these men and women form one of the most intriguing chapters in Dene history.

Since their earliest contacts with Europeans and Canadians, the Dene had been aware that the fur traders held very different religious views. Regular Sunday services were introduced at Fort Chipewyan in 1823; families of the fur traders were encouraged to attend either an Anglican or Roman Catholic service, and there is evidence that Native visitors to the post also occasionally joined in.[1] The HBC did not promote religious activity among the First Nations, however, and although the Métis who lived among the Dene undoubtedly talked about religion, little formal or consistent information about Christianity would have reached the Dene. Nevertheless, they were very curious indeed about Euro-Canadian spiritual beliefs.

✧ Reprinted with permission from Kerry Abel, *Drum Songs: Glimpses of Dene History* (Montreal: McGill-Queen's University Press, 1993), 113–44.

People had probably heard rumours about missionaries among their southern neighbours, for a major expansion of mission effort was just then getting under way in the northwest. Events can be traced back to the period 1818 to 1820, when the Church of England and the Roman Catholic Church had both established parishes at the Red River settlement. Although the churches initially had sent clergy to minister to the non-Native members of the fur trade community, they quickly developed an interest in proselytizing non-Christians, so that church activities began to spread beyond the limits of Red River farms. In fact, interest in mission work was inherent in the organizations that were contributing to the establishment of churches in the northwest. The Oblates of Mary Immaculate (OMI) were a Roman Catholic order that had been founded in France in 1826 by Eugene de Mazenod, who hoped to revitalize the faith in a country torn by the French Revolution and to reinforce the authority of the papacy as part of a general movement in Europe called ultramontanism. The OMI had responded first to a call for clergy in Quebec and then in Red River. The Protestant church at Red River was encouraged in large part through the efforts of the Church Missionary Society (CMS), an evangelical organization composed of members of the Church of England who were dedicated to reforming their church through a return to simplicity of worship and belief in the fundamental doctrine of salvation by faith in Jesus Christ. In the minds of most members of the CMS, Roman Catholics were just as heathen as any non-Christian; hence the history of mission work in the northwest is as much a story of competition between sects as it is a story of missions to the Dene.

Both the OMI and the CMS represented very particular interpretations of the Christian message, although both societies emerged within the context of the late eighteenth-century upheaval in Europe, and both were critical of their parent churches for having grown complacent and corrupt. Interestingly enough, the founders of both societies had concluded that the solution to humanity's problems lay in deepened personal spirituality. Both approached their mission work with a highly organized battle plan, which included teaching missionaries the Native languages and stressing the central importance of preaching in imparting information and stirring people to respond to the Christian message with their hearts and souls. Education was central to their plans, for people had to be capable of reading Christian literature for themselves in order to understand the principles of Christian family life.

The work based at Red River received its first impetus to expand north and west through a curious series of events that began outside Red River and involved a third mission organization. In 1840 the Wesleyan Methodist Society sponsored four new missionaries for the northwest. Among them were Robert Rundle and James Evans. Evans, an energetic and enthusiastic man who had family connections with the HBC at Fort Simpson, established the mission headquarters at Norway House. It was during his stay there that Robert Rundle learned about the Athabasca and Mackenzie districts and resolved to visit them once he was established at Fort Edmonton, which was to be his mission home. Rundle was the first of the Methodist missionaries to visit the Dene when in the spring of 1842 he found a

Chipewyan camp on the banks of the Athabasca River. Unable to speak the language, however, Rundle was uncertain whether the Chipewyan family understood his purpose.

Rundle's visits must have aroused curiousity among the northern people, however, for the following year, a delegation of Métis (which possibly included some Chipewyan and Slavey people) travelled to Peace River to enquire about clergy. Abbé J.B. Thibeault of the Roman Catholic church at Red River resolved to visit them and obtained permission from the HBC to accompany the boat brigade north in 1844. James Evans at Norway House decided that the visit would be a disaster, and in the words of Letitia Hargrave, "Mr. Evans rushed to MacKenzies River by a short cut to be before hand with Monr Thibaut who as I said was taking his ease in Dugds brigade."[2] The hurried trip turned tragic at Île-a-la-Crosse when Evans's companion died under suspicious circumstances and the missionary was forced to turn back.

Abbé Thibeault's mission voyage was more successful. The priest was apparently welcomed enthusiastically by the Métis "freemen" who were living in the Athabasca District, and thus, when the first two Oblate clergy arrived in the Diocese of St. Boniface shortly afterward, Bishop Provencher sent one of them, young Alexandre Taché, north on what became an annual visit to the Cree and the Chipewyan of the Athabasca District. In 1848 a group of Métis from Great Slave Lake met Taché and asked for their own priest. In 1850 or 1851, a party from Great Slave Lake arrived at Fort Chipewyan to hear Father Henri Faraud, subsequently inviting him to visit their country.[3] When Faraud obliged the following spring, he claimed to have found a gathering of 1600 to 1800 Native people at Fort Resolution awaiting his visit.[4] With these successful overtures, Bishop Provencher approached the HBC for formal permission to augment the number of priests in the Athabasca and begin a permanent mission in the Mackenzie River District.

The HBC was not enthusiastic at the prospect. Since 1825, the Northern Council had been supporting the Roman Catholic and Protestant missions at Red River, believing that the church presence was in the "best interests of the Settlement,"[5] while the London Committee had put on record its belief that "zealous and faithful ministers of religion are powerful auxiliaries to the Civil Authorities in the maintenance of that peace and order on which [the] happiness of Society depends so much."[6] However, George Simpson, the governor of the Northern Department, had rather more ambivalent feelings about the utility of missions in general and their place in the interior in particular. He feared that the clergy would become a competing political force in the northwest, outside the control of the HBC.[7] He believed that the demands of the churches for transportation and supplies would become an expensive inconvenience for the company, and he was afraid that the missionaries would pull the Natives away from their fur-trapping pursuits and thus cut into the company's profits.[8] Above all, he was concerned about the role missionaries from Red River might play in assisting the Métis traders in the northwest. The fact that Athabasca Métis were so enthusiastic about inviting priests alarmed some HBC traders, who felt that connections through the church would simply facilitate trade links just then developing among the Métis through their family connections at Red River. Nevertheless, Simpson and his council accepted he London Committee's instructions and agreed to continue the policy of offering free transportation and accommodation to missionaries until such time as the churches were able to construct their own buildings.

The Roman Catholic mission at Fort Chipewyan could not expand immediately, however, because of a lack of funds and shortage of personnel. Finally, in 1858, the Oblates were ready to visit the more remote posts. Father Henri Grollier applied to the HBC for permission to accompany the spring boat brigade to Fort Simpson, his request supported by several Roman Catholic employees at that post who were anxious to have their marriages recognized and their children baptized. With this flurry of Roman Catholic activity, the Anglican church at Red River was suddenly roused. Although their clergy had been discussing expansion into the northwest for some time, their proposals had been vague and not well received by some of the church hierarchy. However, the realization that the Roman Catholics were about to gain a real foothold in the "far" north alarmed their evangelical sensitivities. Immediately, the Reverend James Hunter applied to the HBC for a passage of his own in the spring boat brigade. So it was that a Roman Catholic missionary and an Anglican missionary arrived together at Fort Simpson in the summer of 1858.

The first season of mission work on the Mackenzie was a sad story indeed from the viewpoint of the Christian message of brotherly love. Both Hunter and Grollier were difficult and determined men, steeped in the prejudices of their day and desperately anxious to outbid one another for the souls of Mackenzie River. They competed with tricks and false rumours, and as chief factor Bernard Ross noted, "The clashing of rival sects has stirred up McKenzies River Stagnation!"[9] That year, most of the "mission" work was really pastoral work directed at the fur traders and their families, but the missionaries quickly expanded their efforts to reach the Dene throughout their homeland."[10]

Both priests and ministers realized that their first task was to learn the Native languages. When Father Grollier visited the Mackenzie in 1858, he already spoke Chipewyan and was apparently also understood by the Slavey, an advantage not shared by the Anglican missionary James Hunter. Grollier's successors took great pains to acquire at least one of the Dene languages, and every effort was made to translate hymns, and catechisms into these languages using an adaptation of the syllabic system originally devised by James Evans for use among the Cree. The Anglicans also worked at translations of the Bible, since their theology emphasized the necessity for each individual to read the Word of God for him- or herself. Some of the priests also took considerable interest in learning about Dene beliefs and customs; Father Emile Petitot gained a substantial reputation in France through his published anthropological studies based on his observations and conversations with people throughout the northwest.

For the Roman Catholics, a typical mission week would include twice daily services with one high mass on Sunday. Their prayer services were both teaching vehicles and religious celebrations, including hymn singing, recitation of the rosary, a sermon (in French, Chipewyan or Slavey, and "Métis-French"), and a Native prayer.[11] In between these services, the priests would visit the Dene tents, teaching and answering questions as well as offering medical assistance. Once a Native person had learned certain rudiments of the faith, he or she would be offered baptism. Syllabic catechisms and printed prayers were circulated to those who understood the syllabic system. Rosaries and medals were given to those who attended services or instruction; calendars for keeping track of Sundays and other holy days were distributed for the Natives' use while they were travelling in the bush. Particular celebrations were staged on important feast days such as Christmas, Easter, Immaculate Conception Day (December), and the Assumption of the Virgin Mary (August). Adults who observed these ceremonies and other church doctrine would make their first communion some two or three years after baptism.

While much teaching was done orally or through pictures, the Oblate mission also stressed its literacy program. The Dene were almost uniformly enthusiastic about learning the secrets of written communication. Most of the early literacy work was with adults, but with the arrival of the Sisters of Charity of Montreal (Grey Nuns) in 1867, the emphasis shifted to teaching children. Classes for the Dene children did not provide a European-style education; rather they received instruction in Christian beliefs and morality, as one of the sisters explained:

> Our little mission in the McKenzie has worked since the beginning of its foundation to raise young people in all innocence and to lead them ... ultimately to form all-Christian families who will maintain civilisation and above all, the faith ... Future generations might produce vocations for the priesthood or religious life; what is important at the moment is to develop good mothers who understand the obligations of their position. All our care and all our efforts are directed at this vitally important goal.[12]

A large school at Providence was established with the first pupils drawn primarily from among the children of HBC employees, but the sisters were soon entrusted with increasing numbers of orphaned or abandoned children from Dene bands, so that by 1889 the number of orphans in their care exceeded the number of other students. These children were taught reading, writing, and elementary arithmetic, but most lessons were moral and religious training.

In 1853 Eugene de Mazenod issued a statement of "Instructions on Foreign Missions" that told Oblates that "every means" should be used "to bring the nomad tribes to abandon their wandering life and to build houses [and] cultivate fields."[13] The Athabasca-Mackenzie missionaries never really followed these orders, however, primarily because the missionaries themselves quickly learned that a sedentary, agricultural life was extremely difficult in the north. Their own gardens frequently failed, and they relied heavily on fish for food, like the people to whom they were ministering. Second, the northern missions took their directions increasingly from St Boniface (Red River) where Archbishop Taché followed Provencher's early lead in emphasizing spiritual conversion rather than cultural or economic change. As a result, the Oblate priests in the nineteenth century accommodated their work to the Dene annual round rather than encouraging cultural change in an unrealistic and improbable direction. Children in the Providence school were taught skills not unlike those taught by their parents, and were returned to their bands to pursue a hunting and trapping livelihood as what might be called "Christian hunters."[14] Both the Oblates and the Grey Nuns believed that Christianity could be quite viable in a hunting culture; hunters could be good Christians without becoming farmers. In fact, the case was sometimes even made that the bush life was preferable, since it "nearly always keeps the members of the same family together, and therefore away from many occasions of sin."[15] In other words, people living in the bush could avoid the increasing numbers of non-Natives in the north, and thus avoid the influence of Protestants or of "godless" behaviour. Nevertheless, the Roman Catholic missionaries did seek changes in those elements of Dene society they believed were incompatible with Christian values. In particular, they opposed infanticide, polygamy, shamanic activities, and what they perceived as cruelty to women.[16]

The approach of the CMS to its northern missions has also been misunderstood. One of the fundamental principles of the society was the belief that its goal was to establish indigenous Native churches that would be "self-supporting, self-governing, self-extending."[17] The missionary was to act merely as a catalyst to assist in the founding of such a church, and then he would withdraw from the field entirely. The society was also firm in its belief that its work was that of evangelizing only; funds were not available for schools (except for training Native ministers), for hospitals, or for other "social work." If a missionary wanted to undertake any of these projects, he would have to solicit funds independently of the CMS.

Just as the Oblate mission had not followed instructions from France in their entirety, the CMS missionaries in Athabasca-Mackenzie also developed their own approaches. The missionaries established small day schools at their missions to teach reading and writing so that people could read the Gospel for themselves. For a brief time, the mission also supported a home for orphaned children at Great Bear Lake and a small asylum at Fort Simpson. A model farm and "industrial school" was founded at Vermilion in 1879–80, although it never succeeded in attracting many students.[18] Funds for these projects came from sources other than the CMS, including money raised in Canada. A more successful diocesan school was established at Fort Resolution and moved to Hay River in 1895. Here, day students, several boarders, and a number of Sunday school pupils were taught to read and write using books written in Slavey (using both syllabic and Roman characters). However, the Native church policy of the CMS was not given any sort of realistic trial in the north because of the rather eccentric concerns of William Carpenter Bompas, who was consecrated bishop in 1873. Bompas was dogmatically evangelical and feared that a Native church would drift far from its evangelical moorings; he also had little faith in the ability of Dene catechists and missionaries. It was not until after Bompas had left the diocese that the first Native deacons were ordained.

While the Oblate mission had suffered from internal disputes to some extent, the CMS mission had much more serious problems. There was never a clear sense of direction or consistency of purpose. During Bompas's term of office, there was a confused swing between purely evangelical proselytizing and directed cultural change programs. His attempts to teach Dene children to settle down to agricultural or industrial pursuits received so little interest from the Dene and almost no financial support from Canada and England that he was never able to attempt his experiments on any significant scale. Only the work of Robert McDonald among the Gwich'in was more consistent. By 1890 the CMS was admitting that most people in Athabasca-Mackenzie were at least nominally Roman Catholic, and the society could no longer justify the expense of maintaining the Anglican mission. The Anglican Church in Canada had little interest in the work, so that when the CMS began to reduce its grants early in the twentieth century, the northern missions were left to teeter precariously on the edge of bankruptcy for many years.[19]

Given the nature of both the OMI and CMS, many popular stereotypes about their work in the nineteenth century prove to be quite inaccurate. Both societies were more interested in preaching and spiritual salvation than they were in inducing material cultural change. Both stressed the use of Native languages in their work. Neither achieved much success in attracting Dene students to their schools. Most pupils were the Métis offspring of fur trade families; few "bush" Natives participated and those who did come attended only sporadically and seldom for more than one or two years. Nevertheless, both societies introduced a fundamental challenge to the Dene. The missionaries claimed that they were bringing the sole religious truth and that those who accepted their message would have to make changes in their lives. In particular, the missionaries opposed polygamy, infanticide, and the ease with which the Dene terminated marriage arrangements. Furthermore, the missionaries were teaching more than the "pure" message of the Gospels. They linked Christianity to a European world view that included different ideas about the status of women, patterns of work and leisure, sexual customs, gambling, and even what constituted acceptable humour. They also provided a very different model of religious leadership.

How then did the Dene respond to these strangers in their midst? Initially, they welcomed the missionaries with customary hospitality and demonstrated a keen interest in what the clergy had to say. "Most of them listen with attention & some of them with evident interest," reported W. D. Keeve from Fort Simpson in 1869.[20] At Providence, Father Émile Grouard noted that he was "charmed by the liveliness with which the Indians gather at the sound of the bell."[21] The novelty of the mission even seemed to be drawing the Dene away from their normal pursuits, as Bernard Ross of the HBC lamented: "Cadien says that if the Priest does not visit Fort Rae, there will be no point in sending Hoole with the Indians to the cariboux country, as the natives will most probably resort to Fort Resolution for the purpose of obtaining instruction."[22] While the Anglicans were unwilling to baptize anyone until considerable instruction had been given, the Oblates were delighted at the number of Dene who agreed to be baptized early in their encounters. By 1865 about one-third of the population around Fort Simpson and nearly four-fifths of the Providence population had been baptized by the priests.[23]

It was not long before the number of baptisms suddenly fell off and the missionaries began to complain about the Natives' "laziness" and "indifference" towards mission teaching. At Fort Liard in 1872, the Rev. W.D. Keeve reported that he had attempted to teach a group of people, "but when, after making a few common place remarks, I pulled out my Indian book, they all got up and left the room."[24] Mgr Isidore Clut was profoundly disturbed by these changes, particularly among the Providence people who had once been the Oblates' greatest hope. When he asked one chief why his people had lost interest, "the chief replied to me that one of our Fathers, seeing that they were persisting in their evil conduct, had threatened them with hell if they did not change . . . [so they] got it into their heads to try to go to heaven without the help of the priest."[25]

What had happened to cause this change of heart? It is important to realize that the Dene were responding to the missionaries just as they responded to their own shamans and prophets.[26] After all, the missionaries claimed (like shamans) that they had a special ability to proclaim mysteries invisible to other people, that they had special channels of communication with the unseen world, and that they had the power to better people's lives. Thus, the Dene reacted in much the same way as they would when one of their own people proclaimed such points: they listened, they looked for practical proof, they might accept the teaching for a time, and then they would look to other leaders if the first one's powers seemed to fail. As one member of the Mountain people explained to an Anglican minister about his encounters with a priest, "At first I thought the Holy Father was like God, then I believed him to be like Satan but now I think he is a fool."[27] Nevertheless, the Dene were always careful to show consideration and respect for the missionaries, just as they would towards a shaman, because of the possibility that the individual might be able to cause them harm. As David Kirkby of the CMS reported, "In a few hearts among the Indians I believe there are some real feelings towards God, but for the most part they are very indifferent. They attend prayers, it is true, but I believe from either a 'superstitious' motive . . . or to please their ministers."[28]

Church ceremonies were often requested by the Dene in a manner indicating that such ceremonies were being interpreted within the context of traditional beliefs, not that the Dene had experienced an inward spiritual conversion as the priests and ministers had hoped. People frequently asked for the sign of the cross to be made over an ailing relative or to be used to prevent illness, without understanding its symbolism for the missionaries or having accepted other elements of Christian teaching.[29] Mgr Grandin was once asked for a supply of holy oil so that a band could perform the ceremony of baptism themselves for protection while out in the bush.[30]

This response to the missionaries also meant that the Dene felt free to transfer allegiances between the churches or between individual missionaries if one proved "stronger" than the other, leading the missionaries to lament the Natives' apparent ability to "possess two minds in the matter of

Religion."[31] A typical mission scene was described by W.D. Reeve, who was visiting a party of Dogrib camped outside Fort Simpson:

> I was tired last night but found it impossible to sleep owing to the noise made by the Indians who commenced gambling & beating the drums as soon as I laid down . . . I told them it was wrong to gamble on Sunday & tried to dissuade them but unsuccessfully . . . I returned to the other lodge, & during a lull in the game asked them if we should have prayers. They at once consented & were quiet & attentive during the service, but soon after its conclusion they were gambling as earnestly as ever.[32]

The first real test of power for the missionaries arose in a devastating epidemic of scarlet fever that swept through the district in 1864–65. Unable to provide much in the way of medical assistance, the missionaries devoted considerable effort to comforting the sick and baptizing those who had requested it in the hope of inducing a recovery. Of course, many who had been baptized later died, and fathers Petitot and Grouard noted that the Fort Simpson people were not only losing interest in their religious teaching, but were also exhibiting actual fear of the priests. Grouard discovered that he was being held responsible for the death of a man whom he had baptized, and the world was being circulated that "the Catholic religion and the baptism of the Priest are causing death."[33] The Anglicans encountered the same difficulty. W.D. Reeve reported a few years later at Fort Simpson that "one man has turned Roman Catholic on account of some fancied slight during the time of the fever, and because his wife and two children died."[34] Between 1865 and 1871, the number of baptisms at Providence and Simpson dropped dramatically, as the Dene turned to their own spiritual leaders for help in time of crisis.

Disease was not only the test of spiritual power. Game shortages also provided periods of crisis to challenge priest and shaman alike. When one Oblate priest scolded a man for reverting to magical practices after having been baptized, he received the reply that the man "could not see his relatives suffer from hunger and do nothing while he knew he could make the caribou come by his incantations."[35] Once again, practical results were the Dene test for new ideas.

A second reason the Natives began to reject the mission teaching involved a fundamental difference in philosophy. The Anglicans in particular based their appeal on the belief that man was sinful by nature and could be saved only by faith through the propitiation of Jesus Christ. The Dene, while they might believe that breaking moral laws could result in punishment, could never be convinced that they were fundamentally bad. W.D. Reeve noted their reluctance to learn a prayer for the forgiveness of sins; "one old woman said the Indians have no sins, they always walk 'straight,' and therefore there was no need for that petition,"[36] he recorded. "From a few observations that I have made I think it is a difficult matter to convince these Indians that their hearts are naturally sinful."[37] Since the missionaries were unable to convert the Dene to an acceptance of this first step in the chain of Christian theological thinking, it is hardly surprising that they began to encounter resistance to their other ideas.

Some Dene rejected the Christian message because it did not seem logical or consistent to them. One visitor to Fort Simpson recounted an incident in which a Native man asked the priest for a two-dollar loan and then deposited the money on the offering plate at the next day's service with considerable display. After some time, the priest asked the man to repay the loan. The man responded that he had already repaid it, on the offering plate in church. When the priest protested that such money was not for him, but for God, the Native replied, that "God did not need the money, that he was rich," and that the priest himself had recently preached that where "God lived all the streets were made of gold," so the priest would be wiser to keep the money himself.[38]

In another instance, a man who had initially accepted the Christian message rejected it after a long period of illness. William Spendlove of the CMS reported, "He tells me he finds it difficult to understand how God should afflict him who tried to serve him while many are well in health whose lives are sinful."[39] To this man, the Native explanation for the nature of illness seemed more convincing because it had practical proof. Others rejected the mission teaching because it had practical proof. Others rejected the mission teaching because the non-Native themselves did not seem to be following it. Indeed, the missionaries were acutely aware of the fact that other Euro-Canadians in the north, far from being pristine examples of Christian living, appeared to be members of a society that proclaimed certain moral values as laws but then failed utterly to follow them. The conflict was only too obvious to the Dene. Furthermore, some Dene resented what they considered the hypocrisy of the missionaries in preaching morality while themselves breaching laws the Natives considered equally important. One visitor to Fort Simpson expressed his disgust with the Oblates and announced he was leaving their flock after "they asked his children indecent questions respecting himself, his wife etc." during confession.[40]

Related to this problem of inconsistency was the problem of mission-educated children. Even one of the Anglican missionaries realized that the schools seemed to be encouraging behavior that ran counter to fundamental Christian values, and that as a consequence the Natives were accusing them of deliberate deception: "Civilized life, Christian treatment &c. actually unfit them for 'camp life' and the demeanour of their parents becomes distasteful hence they disobey and dispise them. . . . Consequently the Missionary is supposed to have done them harm when he has spent much time and patience doing them good . . . the more they know of kind treatment[,] right and wrong[,] the sooner they disrespect parents."[41] While supposedly being taught to respect their elders, the children were returning to their parents less respectful than ever. The Dene disapproved, and for many years, few of their children were sent to mission schools by parents who failed to see the advantages materialize as promised.

Probably the most important reason for the decreasing interest that followed the Dene's initial curiosity was their growing realization of the fundamental differences between the Europeans and themselves. The Natives soon noted that the missionaries (and the Anglicans in particular) were very much one-sided in their demands, exhibiting none of the reciprocity that the Dene valued so highly in interpersonal relationships. The missionaries' rudeness in this regard was both perplexing and annoying to the Dene. When Father Grouard attempted to intervene in a dispute over a woman at Fort Liard in 1866, one of the Dene leaders visited him later to say, "Why do you interfere in something which is none of your business? When you pray down there in your lodge, we leave you alone; leave us alone as well, to manage our affairs as we see fit."[42] When W.W. Kirkby appealed for converts, he was told, "If you want us to adopt your prayers, here is the condition we make for it. You are a married man, you have sons and daughters; very well, consent to take our daughters as wives for your sons, and give your daughters as wives for ours. Maybe then we will have faith in your words."[43]

A different understanding of reciprocity and obligation also created problems at the missions. The Grey Nuns lamented that some people expected to receive payment for leaving their children at the mission school,[44] while the CMS mission also despaired that the Natives would ever contribute either to the mission *per se* or to the education of their children. As one incident recounted by W.D. Reeve at Fort Simpson illustrates, the Dene were not prepared to share the European view of the proper nature of the relationship between the clergy and their flocks: "A brother of the youngest orphan boy at the mission tried to take him away this evening . . . the child has been under the care of the missionary ever since he was born & the man has not contributed an ounce of meat for his support, but because the child has on a new suit of leathern clothes he wishes to take him away . . . [and] teach him to hunt."[45]

In fact, the attitude of the Dene towards sending their children to the mission schools repeated an earlier situation in the culture contact scenario almost exactly. From the beginning of the HBC involvement with Native peoples in the fur trade, the Natives had agreed to permit traders to take Native wives only if the traders provided some service to the women's families in return. As one Albany post servant had explained, the Natives believed that since "ye Englishemen . . . Keeped there Women, they had a Right to there Victuals."[46] In exactly the same way, the Dene expected return favours for allowing the missionaries the privilege of sharing their children. Far from accepting the mission teaching as a gift bestowed upon them, as the missionaries believed it to be, the Dene demonstrated a response the churchmen found inexplicable. W. Spendlove noted the difficulty of gathering the Slavey at Fort Simpson for prayer, but realized that "in a few days they will 'wait upon Bishop' to beg, or as they think[,] to do him a favour."[47] In another case, Spendlove was struggling to attract more Dene children and orphans into the mission schools. He had no success at all until one day, when a delegation of Natives paid him a visit

> to enquire how many children we had given up for God and for the sake of the Gospel? I told them seven. [Spendlove had seven children.] How many boys and girls was the next question asked? 5 boys and 2 girls was the reply. After a long and serious talk among themselves they said we will do the same and when the Bishop's boat comes up you will see the same number and kind put on

board ready to embark I agreed to their parents' request to accompany them to Fort Simpson.[48]

When the missionaries dismissed such requests for reciprocity as ludicrous, the Dene were clearly offended and became resentful of the one-sided demands of the clergy. As the initial Dene interest diminished, the priests and ministers became increasingly perplexed about what was wrong. Because they failed to understand Dene traditions of reciprocity and and social obligation, they attributed their difficulties with the Natives to a range of problems quite removed from reality. The most common explanation, advanced by both Anglicans and Roman Catholics, was that the Natives were being misled by the underhanded tactics of the opposing church. "The Roman priests are most unprincipled in their dealings with the Indians," lamented David Kirkby. "They stir up, instead of smothering their superstitious feelings . . . horrifying them with the dreadful consequences of disobedience."[49] The Roman Catholics, in turn, complained that "gifts, promises, threats: nothing was spared to pervert the neophytes . . . With the gold of the Bible Societies, [the Protestant ministers] bought souls more than converting them."[50] Both sides mistakenly believed that the Dene were confused by the opposition and were unable to make the "rational" choice.

The missionaries' second most common conclusion was that the Native people were intellectually or socially slow to realize the "proper" state of religious organization and behaviour. They described those tribes that proved more responsive to mission teaching as more intelligent, and those who resisted as stupid or lazy.[51] The ethnocentrism of these nineteenth-century Europeans was such that they assumed anyone who saw the world differently must be somehow backward or underdeveloped.

For their part, those people who had become disenchanted with the missionaries and their messages decided to use the missions to their own advantage, even if only in a small way, which might mean a visit to the church in order to receive gifts of tea and tobacco. During times of hardship, small children could be left conveniently at the missions, where they could be housed for the winter. The exchange was the privilege of having the child, if only temporarily. For that privilege and trust, the missions were expected to provide good care and payment with food and clothing. More importantly, the Dene looked to the missionaries as sources of information about Europeans and their society. They were particularly curious about the manufacture of trade goods and anxious to know the secrets of the society that could produce such goods.[52] The Dene eagerly acquired reading and writing skills, partly so that they might secure better trade advantages by cultivating relationships with individual HBC men and partly so that they could disseminate information about that trade. While the HBC traders willingly shared some aspects of their lives with the Dene, they were reluctant to discuss other aspects, such as the economics of the trade, in order to protect their position. The Dene therefore turned to the missionaries as potential informants, and not surprisingly, they were not particularly interested in "Native catechists" like Allen Hardisty of the CMS. During his first year of work at Fort Simpson, Hardisty was not the success the society had hoped he would be among his own people. As W.D. Reeve mused, "I sincerely hope . . . that this has been owing more to his position than his disposition. There are several young men about his own age, & others, who remember that but a few years ago he was as ignorant as themselves, & who, instead of being pleased to be taught by him, resent the idea of him 'setting himself up' as a teacher."[53]

Bishop Bompas seems to have been partially aware of the attitude, explaining that the Native people "do not much value one of their own countrymen as teacher, for they had not sufficient trust in their attainments & they seem to view Christianity as a message from the White man's God.[54] Not only did the Dene want to hear about Christianity from the Euro-Canadians, but they were unwilling to accept the teaching of young men who had not proven their spiritual powers to the community.

Finally, there were some very practical and tangible reasons for the declining Dene interest in mission teaching. Both the CMS and the OMI began to insist on certain preconditions for baptism, most notably the abandoning of polygamy by the prospective recipient. Quite apart from the issue of unnecessary culture change, which would naturally be resisted, the Natives were faced with an acutely painful and personal dilemma. How could a man abandon his "extra" wife or wives; who would hunt for them? And how was a man to choose which wife to keep? As one Yukoner explained to an ethnographer, "You know how people sometimes had two wives? Minister say, that's wrong. Choose one they say. Imagine that; live with two women all that time, have to choose one. That's hard, I think."[55] The priests and ministers seemed to have been quite insensitive to the problem. It is hardly surprising that the Dene began to lose interest in such an unresponsive and inflexible system.

Nevertheless, after periods of initial interest and then declining attention, the missionaries gradually became accepted as part of life in the north. Christian rituals and practices became widely known and almost as widely performed. More Dene were labelling themselves as followers of the Christian faith, so that by the 1890s both mission societies began to perceive that their role had changed. Pastoral care and the stimulation of those already grounded in Christian beliefs gradually replaced the emphasis on conversion. The Dene began to incorporate certain elements of mission teaching into their lives, and relationships with the churches became more congenial and regularized.

However, it is still not clear whether the Dene were becoming assimilated into Euro-Canadian culture and whether they had completely accepted the Christian value system. The missionaries themselves were most cautious in making any such claims, even after forty years of effort. As Bishop Bompas explained to the CMS in 1891, "You use a strange argument for handing over these Missions to Canadians that many of the Indians have now been Christians for many years, as though the work was already done, when it is yet hardly begun. In Mackenzie River I fear there are very few real Christians though many professing ones. Our work has been so far a failure."[56] Non-church observers expressed similar hesitation at declaring the Dene "Christianized." "Whether or not they [the missionaries] actually do any good, as far as spiritual enlightenment goes," mused traveller Michael H. Mason, "I do not feel qualified to say. I think that the missionaries over-estimate their success in making genuine converts."[57]

Some of the most important evidence about the Dene response to the mission presence comes from the records of a number of so-called Prophet Movements that appeared throughout the region from time to time, causing considerable consternation among the priests and ministers. Similar movements have been observed among Native societies across North America in the culture contact situation, and anthropologists have developed a number of theories concerning them. Sometimes these movements are described simply as attempts to syncretize (unify and reconcile) traditional and Christian religious values and practices.[58] Others prefer to name them "crisis cults" in the sense that they represent a collective response to a "chronic or acute crisis" of some kind.[59] Perhaps the best-known analysis of the phenomenon is that of Anthony F.C. Wallace, who called them "revitalization movements,"[60] making that term a standard in ethnohistorical literature. Wallace has interpreted many of these movements as attempts to rebuild a shattered community, such as the Handsome Lake phenomenon among the divided Iroquois Confederacy (1799–1815).

Religious movements had been observed among the Dene long before the coming of the missionaries. For example, at Fort Chipewyan in 1813, the Chipewyan people instigated "a conspiracy" to kill all the whites in the district when an influential man "prophesied that there would soon be a complete change in the face of their country; that fertility and plenty would succeed to the present sterility; and that the present race of white inhabitants, unless they became subservient to the Indians, would be removed, and their places filled by other traders, who would supply their wants in every possible manner."[61]

The first mission report of a northern prophet movement came from Alexandre Taché after his 1859 visit to Île-à-la-Crosse. A young man there claimed that he was the son of God, spoke in tongues, and urged his family followers to destroy all their possessions. He proclaimed that he had received a revelation from God in which "the heavens stooped down and the earth drew near until all came within the compass of his tent, and a voice revealed to him the will of God which had not been made known before to any man."[62] He said he had learned that man could achieve eternal life here on earth, and he had a magical bag of powerful articles to help himself and his followers. Interest in his teaching lasted several years.

Several smaller groups formed among the Dene during the early 1860s. At Portage la Loche, two sons of an ex-shaman (who had been baptized by the Oblates) claimed to have been visited by three gods: the Creator, Jesus, and Mary. One of the young men explained that during this visit many truths had been revealed to them; the attending priest described his lengthy oration as a mixture of Christian and "pagan" beliefs. This revelation apparently did not attract as many followers as the earlier one at Île-à-la-Crosse.[63] At about the same time, Father Clut at Fort Chipewyan reported the presence of a man who also claimed to have talked to God and the angels and therefore to be wiser than the priest in such matters. In particular, he declared that polygamy, adultery, and fornication were no longer to be considered wicked.[64]

Emile Petitot reported that these manifestations occurred at nearly every post in the district in one form or another. One of his own personal experiences involved a couple of seers at Fort Good Hope in 1878 who prophesied that a great flood would sweep away the mission and trading post at that place, destroying all the white man's buildings. Another man named Ekèrichli had required his people to bow before him, confess their sins to him, and be rebaptized by him. His reputation among many of his followers was somewhat tarnished, however, when a year later his own wife claimed to have had a dream vision in which it was revealed to her that Ekèrichli was a great liar and that she was the Blessed Virgin sent to the people to bring them back to God.[65] At Fort Simpson William Spendlove reported on one man who had emerged from a four-day trance to tell his people the secrets of the unseen world he had visited. He prepared an elaborate painting on a deer skin to represent the future world, hoping that the Indians would use this deer to teach each other after his death. "In the spring he died as he had said," Spendlove marvelled, "to the sorrow of all his friends who almost worshipped him. The parchment was brought here this spring for the Bishop and it is really wonderful."[66]

All of these prophets demonstrated a continuity with traditional Dene religious activities but also expressed various degrees of toleration for European Christianity. The concept of heaven was merged with the aboriginal concept of a place where spirits dwelt; hence the Christian idea of an afterlife was maintained as compatible with Dene beliefs. The Dene added their own belief that gifted people could visit this unseen world while still alive. Jesus Christ and the Virgin Mary (as well, sometimes, as the rest of the saints) were readily accepted as great spirits like those with whom the Dene were already acquainted. The man who claimed that he was the son of God and the woman who believed she was a reincarnated Mary demonstrated the immediacy with which the Dene viewed the role of these spirits in the world. Some of the prophets urged their followers to abandon Christian artifacts and beliefs completely, while other prophets were willing to adopt certain new ideas. Specific objections were raised most commonly against mission teaching on the marriage relationship, sexual taboos, and the ban on Sunday work, while smaller matters, such as the performance of religious ceremonies after dark, might also be criticized. One man rejected the Roman Catholic mass as a legitimate religious ceremony but accepted other aspects of that faith. Often the prophets were speaking against both the white man's religion and his economic demands. Thus, some of the Kutcha-Kutchin (Yukon Flats Gwich'in) believed in the future coming of a Native "messiah" who would rid the country of all white men (missionaries and traders both) while allowing his people to keep tea, tobacco, and metal implements.[67]

One frequently noted call was for the abandoning of the practice of using dogs in teams or singly for labour.[68] The significance of this concern is not clear, but there are two possible explanations. The first is related to the use of dogs as beasts of burden. The Dogrib believed themselves to have descended from a dog, and other northern groups demonstrated considerable respect for canines, calling them brother and relatives. The introduction of dog teams through the Euro-Canadian traders may have been viewed with considerable distaste by the Dene and held as symbolic of the difference between outsiders and Dene. Hence, the oft-repeated call for an end to using dogs may have represented a general dissatisfaction with many elements of European culture. The second possible explanation is even more intriguing. Historian Jacqueline Peterson has suggested that the Ojibwa may have been encouraging the adoption of certain Ojibwa beliefs throughout the west at the beginning of the nineteenth century. Had knowledge of their White Dog ceremony also reached the Mackenzie District? The question is a fascinating one meriting more research.[69]

The missionaries interpreted these prophet movements in several ways. Most often, the prophets were dismissed as insane or mentally unbalanced.[70] On occasion, though, they might be seen as genuine cases of possession by the devil, as Father de Krangué interpreted the behaviour of a young man at Fort Simpson in 1871.[71] Father Grouard, on the other hand, believed them to be simply traditional "jongleurs," or medicine men, who "instinctively" understood the dangers the missionaries posed to their power and prestige, and who "became the unyielding enemies of the priest, using all possible means to hinder his work."[72] The Anglicans seemed to have been less aware of the actual content of these movements, making few references to them in their journals; when they were noted, the activities of the Natives were attributed to fanaticism induced by superstitious Roman Catholic teachings.

None of these "movements" was long-lasting, nor did any attract significant numbers of followers. In this sense, they were quite consistent with the traditional loose leadership patterns of Dene society and with that society's toleration for individual autonomy. On the other hand, the fact that these movements continued to appear throughout the period in question, and over a wide geographical area, suggests that dissatisfaction and even outright opposition to the mission teaching were active and widespread. The Dene were scarcely passive recipients of European lessons in religion, morality, and culture as many western observers have claimed.

However, a number of specific Christian rites and ceremonies found favour among the Dene. Baptism received the most attention in the mission records, probably because the Roman Catholics viewed it as the mark of conversion and the Anglicans saw it as the beginning of a Christian life. The Dene certainly do not appear to have interpreted the ceremony in the same way. After a visit to Fort Rae, Mgr Grandin reported the following incident, which illustrates one of the Native interpretations very well: "A chief came urging me to baptise the shirt of one of his hunters who was dying too far off for me to be taken to him. Two mothers, whose children had died without being baptized, begged me to baptize their tiny bonnets. Devastated at not being successful on this point, they begged me to take these bonnets and keep them safe."[73]

To some, baptism was a magical ceremony that would protect a person or his or her soul from evil, much as the purpose of the shaman's performances had done. Hence, baptism was frequently requested during times of illness or other hardship. Others submitted to baptism as a means to show respect for the missionary or to forge an alliance with a man of spiritual power, and thus in one sense to protect themselves from potential malevolence.[74] A northern chief wanted to have his son baptized with the name "Jesus Christ," but when Bishop Grandin opposed the choice, the chief defended it with this explanation: "I did that so that Jesus Christ will continue to remember him."[75]

Most of the missionaries did not seem to be aware of the way the Dene viewed baptism or church attendance; only David N. Kirkby of the CMS seems to have grasped something of the truth. As he wrote to the society, "They are not irreligious, for in private conversation they will often tell one how much they desire the good will of God." But he went on to lament, "As I judge, an Indian attends Church from three motives. (I) If the Minister says the prayers over him, it will be a kind of charm from evil (2) to please the Minister (3) and, I am afraid, last of all, to please God."[76]

Another aspect of the Christian faith in which the Dene participated, perhaps even more enthusiastically, was the Roman Catholic confessional. When a member of a small band died, Father Grouard noted the desire of the remainder of the group to demonstrate their penitence.[77] Emile Petitot made numerous references in his writing to the Dene acceptance of the confessional. It is hardly surprising. As Petitot and others had observed, Dene shamans had made use of the confession as part of their religious observances before the arrival of the missionaries. Petitot attributed the greater interest demonstrated by the Dene in Roman Catholicism to this similarity of belief and practice: "This conformity between our blessed religion and several of their ancient practices will doubtless be for them a preservative against the poison of Protestantism, where they find neither confession nor fasting; similarly the correlation between their traditions and the Mosaic was one of the factors which affirmed their faith in the words of the priest."[78]

The Dene appear to have considered the confessional as one of the most important elements of the Roman Catholic faith. When the Grey Nuns first arrived at Athabasca, the Natives crowded round them curiously, demanding to know whether they said Mass, and whether they heard women's confessions particularly.[79] There seems to have been little difference between the Dene interpretation of confession and that of the priests. It was one small area of effective communication.

Prayers and music were also accepted by the Dene as a part of religious ceremonies. Many northern visitors commented on the sight of Indians saying grace before meals or praying before a hunting expedition.[80] The missionaries recognized the appeal of hymns and made every effort to incorporate music into the religious services: the Grey Nuns at Providence had a harmonium, William Spendlove played the concertina at Fort Simpson, while Charlotte Bompas played the harmonium to the "great delight and astonishment" of the Fort Norman people.[81] Both churches translated hymns into Slavey, Gwich'in, and Chipewyan so that the words would be meaningful to the congregations. Music was an important part of the Dene's lives, as has been noted, particularly in relation to the acquisition of spiritual power. It is not surprising, then, that they so readily accepted the use of music in European religion. What is particularly interesting, however, is the fact that the Natives were not always convinced of the power or utility of those foreign hymns. In 1866 Emile Petitot recorded a conversation with one man who professed faith in the Trinity, Jesus Christ, Mary, and the Saints but rejected Christian hymns, preferring instead a traditional Dene chant of two syllables that he believed had been revealed by God to a sick person.[82] The chants given to individuals might be sources of power for them alone, so it is consistent with precontact beliefs that the Natives should continue to search for their own songs rather than accept only those provided by the missionaries. Nevertheless, just as a shaman might give his song to another, so some of the Dene appear to have accepted the power of mission hymns. As one told Emile Petitot, all his children had died, but "if I have a book of hymns, I will sing, and that will console me."[83]

Finally, the Dene responded enthusiastically to the Roman Catholic crucifixes, rosaries, medals, and pictures the priests provided to them during instruction or after baptism. The Evangelical Anglicans, who refused to use such objects, found this interest frustrating and annoying, but as one of their missionaries astutely noted, "There is a great hankering for the medals & crucifixes given by the priests. They are looked upon, for the most part, in the light of powerful charms which protect them from some evil thing."[84] The items provided by the priests became additions to the personal medicine bundles carried by many of the northern people.

In other aspects of religious practice, however, Dene beliefs were quite different from those of the missionaries, and communication and exchange became more awkward. Perhaps one of the greatest contrasts between Dene tradition and European expectation concerned the role of women in society. During the first years of mission work in the north, few women came to the trading posts, remaining behind in the camps while the men conducted the spring and autumn trades. When the missionaries finally began to see the Native women, they initially found it very difficult to gain a hearing among them. One of the Anglican ministers concluded rather unkindly that the women's diffidence was due to the fact that they were "dull of comprehension, & apparently less eager to learn than the men." Besides, he added, "they have not come in contact with civilized people so much as the men, hence the difficulty of making them understand."[85] Father Grouard's observations at Providence were perhaps a little more to the point:

> I began regular morning and evening exercises, and I had the great pleasure of seeing all the Indians come to hear me with the exception of the women who kept to the lodges . . . because up to now they imagined that religion was only for the men and that they had only to suffer in silence the brutalization to which the [illegible] and the ignorance of the Indians has reduce them. I have made

every effort to get them to come to me; and thanks to God, I have succeeded. It was necessary for me to appear very severe with them and even to scold them sharply because they seemed very little concerned with what I told them at first ... Nevertheless, several appeared happy with what I told them that the good Lord's prayer is just as good for women as it is for men, and I would like to send them to heaven just as much as their husbands.[86]

Once the women overcame their initial hesitation about the missions, they appear to have become some of the most enthusiastic participants, following a pattern that mission societies have observed in a number of cultures throughout the world. The women agreed to act as translators and language instructors; they also quickly exploited the new possibilities opened for them once they had the moral support of the missionaries. As Faraud reported from Great Slave Lake, his first marriage ceremony proved to be something of a surprise for everyone concerned. When he asked the bride if she would take the groom as her husband, she promptly replied in the negative, explaining that she had been taken from her father by force and abused by her spouse. "The priest comes to tell us that God gives Woman the same liberty as Man," she told the bewildered groom, "I want to enjoy this liberty; I don't want you at all." According to the priest, the assembly was initially horrified at such an outburst, but after some consideration agreed that she was a brave woman who might have a valid point.[87]

It also seemed that women were reluctant to speak freely to the male ministers and priests. In this regard, both mission groups found that the presence of non-Native women was most important. As noted above, some Natives looked on the Grey Nuns as a sort of "woman's priest," and William Spendlove remarked proudly on the success his wife had among the women, who were all rather "shy" with him.[88]

The changing relative position of men and women at the missions is reflected in the baptismal statistics. For the CMS at Fort Simpson in the 1860s, the ratio of adult male baptisms to adult female baptisms was almost 2 to 1; at Fort Norman for the same period, it was 6 to 1.[89] By the 1890s, however, there had been a dramatic change. At Fort Norman, for example, there were no adult men baptized at all, while four women received the sacrament.[90] It would seem that eventually, more women were exposed to intensive religious teaching, since the number of girls at the Providence school always exceeded the number of boys, whether the count is made among the orphaned children or among the regular students.[91]

What effect these changes had on the Native women, or how their husbands responded, can not be conclusively determined. Emile Petitot believed that religion transformed the "pitiful" lives of the Dene women, reflecting, "Ah! I now understand why women are more religious than men; why Jesus was followed above all by women ... why the principal consolations of the priest are furnished him by the feminine portion of his flock. Religion is necessary to man, but it is indispensible to the happiness of woman, if she does not want to be disparaged."[92] He was not more specific in describing the changes Christian faith might bring, however. It is not clear whether he meant that belief in the promise of the Christian heaven made the burdens of women's lives easier to bear, or whether he observed actual material changes in the women's lives and relationships. One twentieth-century observer believed that the Dene women had become "more emancipated" and increasingly likely to "rule the roost,"[93] but the word of one rather unreliable observer can scarcely be taken as conclusive evidence.

The conflict between the Roman Catholic and Protestant missions in the north has sometimes been used as an explanation for the indifference of the Dene to European religion in general.[94] However, according to Native religious tradition, a reaction of confusion and alienation on the part of the Dene was unlikely. Contests of influence and power were traditionally part of the shaman's life, and the Protestant or Catholic missionary's opposing claims to possess "The Truth" about God were no different from any shaman's claim. Surveyor John H. Lefroy was probably close to an understanding of the situation when he commented on the conflict between the Anglican and Methodist missionaries at The Pas. "The Indians . . . looked upon it precisely as they do on the disputes of their medicine men," wrote Lefroy. "He whose medicine is strongest gets the victory."[95]

What "medicine," then, did the Dene expect from the missionaries? Most importantly, they hoped for the prevention and cure of illnesses, just as they expected their own religious leaders to provide such practical services. Neither mission group was prepared to trust solely to the efficacy of prayer in this important matter, and medical services became a major part of their work—a "handmaid" to the preaching of the Gospel, as Bishop Bompas put it. However, there is little evidence to suggest that the medical aid offered by the missionaries was particularly successful. Both the Roman Catholics and Anglicans believed fervently in the theories of "homeopathic" medicine, according to which a disease could be cured by the administration of small doses of medication that produced symptoms like those of the disease itself. The Oblates had kits made up containing drugs for common illnesses and a booklet describing their applications.[96] The utility of such medicines is certainly rather doubtful, and even many Europeans did not share the enthusiasm of the system's proponents. As Augusta Morris, companion to Bishop Bompas's wife, complained in her diary, "I have been feeling *really* ill the last few days & seem to be getting weaker daily & my face shows it. The worst of it is there are no proper tonics here & Mr. Camsell had none, so I am forced to take *homeopathic* medicines, in which I have no faith, in order to satisfy Mrs. B[ompas]."[97]

Nevertheless, the availability of medicines at the missions appeared to have held a considerable attraction for the Natives. Early in the mission work, Father Grollier urged the appointment of a nursing sister to the north, "for then the whole District would come to her and thus Religion would spread."[98] W.D. Reeve reported that news of medicine spread quickly and would draw "quite a number of applicants" for its benefits.[99] Sometimes, however, these applicants had no particular faith in the European medicine but were merely desperate for any assistance at all. As William Spendlove noted in his journal, he was visited one day by a Native man who had come a considerable distance seeking medicine for a dying child. "He has tried the

'Medicine Man' and his own equally useless remedies," Spendlove wrote, "but applies to me as a last resource."[100] It is therefore important not to over-state the value placed by the Dene on the medical assistance provided by the missions.

The link between the religious leader and the healer of the sick was, of course, a natural one in the Dene cultural context. Consequently, the missionaries found it easy to attract attention through their medical offerings, and they could elicit spiritual responses from their patients at the same time. A successful treatment would be proof of the missionary's "power," and Mgr Faraud observed, "The cure of the body is almost always followed by the cure of souls."[101] In other words, the missionary who proved his powers through medical cures would, in all likelihood, gain an adherent. Illness was greatly feared by the Dene. "When an Indian is sick," commented William Spendlove, "he becomes exceedingly nervous & thinks he is going to die hence the most hardened sinner will often listen to the Gospel."[102]

The risk in all this, however, was inevitably revealed when the European medicine failed. Then the Dene would abandon the missions, just as they would abandon an ineffective shaman. During a major scarlet fever epidemic, for instance, attendance at the Nativity Mission at Fort Chipewyan dropped as word was spread that those who entered the priests' chapel would die.[103] Furthermore, the Dene sometimes interpreted their illnesses as having been deliberately caused by the missionaries through a spirit of malevolence, just as a Dene shaman could induce disease in someone who had angered him. W.D. Reeve became rather alarmed when a Fort Nelson man accused him of having "made bad medicine" against him or someone in his tribe, and had threatened that "if any of his people died in consequence, when he came again in spring he would shake hands with [Mr Brass of the HBC] in a different fashion to what he was then doing."[104]

When the Canadian government assisted the OMI in the construction of the north's first modern hospital at Fort Smith in 1913–14, the Dene were faced for the first time with the foreign concept of separating the treatment of disease from active appeal to the spirits. Needless to say, it was some time before the hospital was accepted. As Bishop Breynat recalled, people would not bring their sick relatives to it until all other hopes for a cure had been tried. "Little by little, following the obtaining of positive results," he noted, "they began to appreciate its benefits."[105]

Besides the provision of medicine, the Dene also looked to the missions for services of another kind, services that the missions were not prepared to offer. Essentially, the Dene hoped to develop economic ties through trade with the mission stations, realizing that the needs of these posts provided an alternate source of manufactured goods of the HBC, as well as a means to circumvent the company's debt system.

The company was well aware of the potential threat to its monopoly posed by the missions, and was constantly on guard in the Athabasca and Mackenzie districts for any sign that the missionaries were trading with the Natives. William L. Hardisty, chief factor at Fort Simpson, hoped that if the

HBC offered generous terms for transporting mission goods, the missions would be less inclined to employ Natives for transport (thereby giving the Natives an opportunity to take furs out of the district for trade), Hardisty also offered some flexibility in prices for provisions, hoping the missions would purchase what they needed from the company rather than trading with the Natives to obtain a better price.[106] Nevertheless, the Oblate missions in particular found it to their advantage to trade with the Natives directly, since (unlike the CMS missions) very little of their support came in the form of material goods and the order attempted to make each post as self-sufficient as possible. The HBC soon realized that the missions were bound to conduct some trade by necessity, and thus the absolute enforcement of its monopoly was impossible. Therefore, it attempted to reach a general agreement with the missions on the subject. In 1863 Hardisty wrote to Bishop Grandin, requesting his co-operation in the matter:

> The Indians will scarcely give us any [grease] at all now, owing to their receiving Ribbons & other fineries at the Mission in exchange for Grease. My reason for drawing your attention to this subject is not that I wish to deprive you or your Missionaries of this essential article of food—but that, you may give such instructions to your Missionaries as may insure to us at least a part of the Grease which the Indians procure by means of the Ammunition which they receive from us. By giving only Tobacco and Ammunition in exchange for Grease, as we do, I think the grievance complained of might be removed.[107]

Matters remained on an uneasy footing for many years. Although the missionaries did not wish to cross swords with the HBC, they believed that trade was vital to the maintenance of the missions, and also realized the political danger of offending a Native by refusing to trade with him, thereby also losing the opportunity to offer him religious teaching.[108] The Dene were quick to take advantage of the missionaries' attempts to be diplomatic. As an Oblate historian recorded later, they were "perpetually begging" for gifts or provisions, calling the priests "unreasonable and avaricious" for withholding anything, since they had only to "send a little bit of paper into the 'Great countries'" and it would "bring them back a cargo."[109]

The Dene also played the Roman Catholics against the Protestants, claiming that the priest (or minister) freely offered gifts of tea, sugar, and tobacco, so that the minister (or priest) had only to do likewise to gain an adherent. As a result, each group believed that the other was bribing the Indians with such gifts.

While some of this economic activity may be taken entirely at face value (that is, some Natives may have been visiting the missions solely for the purposes of trade), there may be another element involved. As Abraham Rotstein proposed in an important article, "Trade and Politics: An Institutional Approach,"[110] Native societies in eastern North America built their trade relationships with the Europeans on a pre-existing superstructure of political alliances, councils, and gestures such as gift exchanges and ceremonial behaviour. Economic life as a separate aspect of human activity did not exist for them as it did in European culture, but was rather intimately intertwined with politics and social life. Very much the same argument can be made in relation to the roles of the missionary and religion in the northwest. The Euro-Canadians seemed adept at separating the religious and economic spheres of activity; indeed, the Hudson's Bay Company demanded that they be separated. The Dene, on the other hand, made no such distinction, either in their own holistic world-view or in their approach to the European presence among them. Just as the activities of the shaman could be used for economic or political ends and an individual could safeguard his or her spiritual integrity by forming an alliance with a powerful person, the Dene attempted to form similar relationships with the missionaries. Hence, trade activities and social reciprocity were used by the Natives as an integral part of this interaction. And as David Kirkby observed, the missionaries were unable to enforce their own peculiar view of sharply delineated occupations. The Dene refused to accept that the missionary's purpose among them was "purely spiritual."[111]

This concept is demonstrated time and again throughout the period of mission activity. When Mgr Clut visited a camp outside Providence to investigate why religious interest there had been declining, the leader explained his reasons, but then added that "because I had taken the trouble to come to see them in their camp, they would change their resolve, and make an effort to save themselves by the Missionaries, offices; that, in order to keep them, they would give them provisions."[112] The priest's gesture in coming to their camp had been interpreted by these Natives as a sign of exchange with which they were prepared to reciprocate, in this case with an economic gesture of providing food. In fact, the missionaries themselves began to realize that gifts of tobacco and other gestures of alliance and reciprocity were a necessary part of their work, however distasteful such might be to their inherited cultural sensitivities. The practice of gift presentation at Christmas and New Year's became widespread in the north, when the Natives would congregate at the posts for dancing, celebration, and a ritual visit to both mission establishments.[113] It was a minor concession on the part of the missions, but one of great importance to the Dene.

No discussion about the Dene response to missions would be complete without an acknowledgment of the very important role played by the Métis population in that relationship. Most of the northern Métis were Roman Catholics, and many seem to have had some understanding of that faith before the arrival of the priests,[114] probably through the teaching of parents. The Métis became important allies of the priests, explaining the faith to the bush Natives with whom they were in contact. In fact, the priests found the Métis more amenable to their requests for financial aid and contributions of food for the missions, more likely to send their children to the mission schools, and more willing to act as language instructors for newly arrived priests. They might also act as champions of the Roman Catholic faith. When Father Gascon first visited Fort Liard, he was grateful for the assistance of the wife of one of the HBC servants, a Métisse known locally as "la bonne femme Houle." She apparently worked as a crew leader on the company's Liard-Simpson boat route, giving orders that made her "a terror both to whites and to Indians.[115] After visiting Red River and receiving instruction from the Grey Nuns there, she returned to the district "as bold for religion as ever she had been for the fur trade, or paganism."[116]

The Anglican missionaries were not particularly successful in finding allies among northerners of mixed ancestry. In fact, they seldom made the distinction between Natives and Métis, preferring to label anyone who was not Christian as "heathen." W.D. Reeve was assisted briefly in his attempts to learn Slavey by Betsy Brough, wife of an HBC servant at Fort Simpson, and another Métis named Cadien provided translation services from time to time; but the Anglicans frequently bewailed the advantage held by the Oblates in their Métis assistants. They have great auxiliaries in the French half-breeds whose influence over the Indians is very great," reported Reeve, "In fact, I am told they do even more than the priests to make the Indians Romanists."[117]

Reeve was quite correct in his observation that most of the Dene chose to ally themselves with the Roman Catholic mission. The reasons for this choice can only be guessed at from this distant time. Certainly, the Roman Catholic missionaries professed many concepts not much different from Dene tradition. The confessional, the charismatic religious specialist, the concept of fasting, and the wide range of saints/spirits who could intervene in the course of events may have been referred to with a different vocabulary, but the concepts were similar. On the other hand, the Anglicans professed some beliefs that were also like Dene traditions. The evangelical emphasis on the individualism of the conversion experience and on the ability of every person to address the unseen world directly, without the intermediary of a priest, were certainly in keeping with Dene beliefs. Furthermore, Anglican ministers were free to marry, and the Dene considered marriage a crucial means of alliance and reciprocity. Hence it is not surprising that the Gwich'in still remember that CMS missionary Robert McDonald married a local woman and thereby committed himself to the community.[118] There may very well be a connection between that marriage and the fact that the Gwich'in are the only Dene who today generally identify themselves as Anglican. The Anglican missions also tended to be more closely linked with the HBC in the north, for although the company's official policy was impartiality, most of its officers in the Athabasca and Mackenzie districts were Anglicans who enjoyed an uneasy relationship with the Roman Catholic priests.[119] The Anglican missions were usually situated closer to the HBC posts than were the Roman Catholic missions, and the attitudes of the HBC officers were frequently quite public. Therefore, those Dene anxious for political alliance or trade advantages with the HBC might have been drawn to the Anglican missions.

Nevertheless, other factors proved to be more important to the Dene, attracting them instead to the Roman Catholic missions. The Anglican missions, particularly under the direction of Bishop Bompas, made unyielding demands on the Dene and expected greater changes before baptism. Such conditions must have seemed quite unreasonable to the Dene, who saw baptism as merely a sign of goodwill. Second, the Anglicans never had sufficient funds, personnel, or consistent organizational ability to establish and maintain social services in the north. The Roman Catholics provided more medical care and maintained a large orphanage at Providence that became a highly valued institution because it provided an alternative to infanticide in times of hardship. Third, the Oblates made more of an effort to understand Dene traditions and cultural values, tending in the process to demonstrate a greater sympathy towards them. Furthermore, the Oblates were more willing to tolerate these traditional ideas among the people who asked for baptism or took communion. The Oblates did not see a fundamental conflict between Christianity and the hunting economy, while some of the CMS missionaries broke from their own society's goals and argued that agriculture and "industrial" training were necessary to a Christian outlook. Fourth, the Anglican religious practices were different from those of the Dene in several significant ways. As evangelicals, the CMS missionaries strongly rejected the use of pictures, medals, rosaries, crucifixes, and other religious objects in both public and private devotions. The Oblates, on the other hand, encouraged the use of such items as part of their traditional methods of reaching nonliterate audiences. Because the Dene associated these objects with personal power, the Anglican refusal to supply them must have seemed most peculiar and suspicious. Were the ministers refusing to share their power or their secrets? The behaviour of the priests was in some ways more consistent with Dene expectations and their ideas more consistent with Dene traditions. In addition, the priests enjoyed the support of most of the northern Métis, who could translate the new concepts more clearly for the Dene than English ministers, with their halting attempts, could. It is hardly surprising, then, that the Dene were more interested in what the priests had to say.

By the turn of the century, mission and government statistics proclaimed that the Dene had been Christianized. Dene Christianity was, however, a unique version of the faith, reflecting a range of individual responses to the challenges posed by the missionaries. Some people adopted specific elements of Christian practice that appeared to be more useful or successful than the paths taught them by their old spirit-mentors. The careful observance of prayers before meals, for example, became a widespread practice.[120] Others expressed themselves to the missionaries in ways the Europeans approved, and yet could cling inwardly to their old beliefs. During his travels around Great Slave Lake, Warburton Pike noted that the Yellowknife "are very particular in observing all the outward signs" of Roman Catholicism, but that "any mischance is put down to 'bad' medicine' . . . [and] there are several miracle-workers and foreseers of the future" in the district.[121] The Dene also tended not to want to press their beliefs on others. As W.D. Reeve was told, "they understood well themselves" but "would not be able to explain it clearly to others."[122] Some people responded to the missionaries as they would to any shaman, willingly following the mission teachings as long as they proved useful in daily life and going their own way when those teachings lost their utility. Always a highly practical people, the Dene were willing to accept what "worked." Still other people rejected Christian ideas entirely, either through avoidance or through active opposition by forming a rival group of followers.

In the long term, many elements of Christian belief and practice have been incorporated into the lives of the majority of Dene, although the adoption of a new religious vocabulary and new forms of religious practice has not always changed other Dene activities associated with a more traditional view of the spirit world. When anthropologist June Helm visited "Lynx Point" in the 1950s, she discovered that the old blood taboos, such as avoiding menstruating women or treating animal blood with great respect, were universally upheld; she could find no relationship between Dene concepts of right and wrong and the Christian doctrines of divine law and punishment; and she noted that the traditional custom of discarding a deceased person's property was still observed.[123] While today many Dene attend Roman Catholic church services, several observers have noted that participation is scarcely emphasized, so that, as one put it, "the service just carried on, the priest and teachers doing it their way, while the Indians did it theirs."[124] An anthropologist who visited the Chipewyan community of Snowdrift between 1968 and 1972 noted that the belief in $i^n k^n nze$ (or the spiritual power of individuals) was still prevalent among young and old alike.[125] Furthermore, he believed that some people considered Roman Catholicism to be "something essentially alien to the Indian way of life," something "imposed on the village from the outside" and not "an essential and integral part of their everyday life." One man told him that the church did not maintain a priest at Snowdrift permanently because "there is not enough money to be made from the people" there. The anthropologist noted that others seemed to view the church as a source of potential income akin to the HBC or the Canadian government.[126]

Thus, while the Dene accepted some aspects of the mission teachings in the nineteenth century, their world view was not undermined completely. They refused to accept the European compartmentalization of various aspects of human endeavour, such as politics, economics, and religion. And they refused to accept the European distinction between the sacred and the profane or between human beings and the natural environment. In practical terms as well, the missionaries did not cause significant change in the nineteenth century. They failed to attract many Dene to their schools, and few Dene found gardening to their taste. Life on the land, flexible marriage partnerships, and continuing respect for individual decision making were still a part of Dene life.

NOTES

1. James Keith, Fort Chipewyan, Nov. 1823, HBCA B.39/a/22, fos. 39, 4od, 47.

2. Letitia Hargrave to Florence Mactavish, York Factory, 9 Sept. 1844, in *The Letters of Letitia Hargrave*, ed. Margaret MacLeod

(Toronto: Champlain Society, 1947), 188.

3. A.A. Taché to M. Dawson, Red River, 7 Feb. 1859, in *Les Missions des Oblats* 2, 6 (June 1863): 172.

4. Joseph-Étienne Champagne, *Les Missions catholiques dans l'ouest*

canadien, 1818–75 (Ottawa: Éditions des Études Oblats, 1949), 85.

5. Minutes of the Northern Council for 2 July 1825, quoted in Arthur S. Morton, *A History of the Canadian West to 1870–71* (Toronto: University of Toronto Press, 1973 [1939]), 635.

6. Governor and Committee to George Simpson, 5 April 1827, HBCA A.6/27, fo. 240.

7. See Gaston Carrière, "L'Honorable Compagnie de la Baie-d'Hudson et les missions dans l'Ouest canadien," *Revue de l'Université d'Ottawa* 36 (1966): 15–39, 232–57; Frank A. Peake, "Fur Traders and Missionaries: Some Reflections on the Attitudes of the HBC Towards Mission Work Amongst the Indians," *Western Canadian Journal of Anthopology* 3, 1 (1972): 72–93.

8. George Simpson to Benjamin Harrison, 10 March 1825, in CMS North West America Mission Incoming Letterbooks 1822–62, C.1/M, NA microfilm reel no. A77.

9. Letter to George Simpson, 28 Nov. 1858, HBCA D.5/47, fo. 640.

10. For an account of the expansion of this work, see John Webster Grant, *Moon of Wintertime: Missionaries and the Indians of Canada in Encounter Since 1534* (Toronto: University of Toronto Press, 1984), 96–109.

11. Journal of Father Lecorre, Sept. to Dec. 1876, published in *Les Missions des Oblats* 15, 60 (Dec. 1877).

12. Letter from Sister Ward, Providence, 4 Sept. 1878, published in *Circulaire mensuelle* 1, 13 (March 1979). My translation.

13. Quoted in Margaret M. Whitehead, "Missionaries and Indians in Cariboo: A History of St Joseph's Mission, Williams Lake, BC" (MA thesis, University of Victoria, 1979), 21.

14. See Robert J. Carney, "The Native-Wilderness Equation: Catholic and Other School Orientations in the Western Arctic," Canadian Catholic Historical Association, *Study*

Sessions 48 (1981): 61–78; and Kerry M. Abel, "The Drum and the Cross: An Ethnohistorical Study of Mission Work among the Dene, 1858–1902" (PhD thesis, Queen's University, 1984).

15. Pierre Duchaussois, *The Grey Nuns in the Far North, 1867–1917* (Toronto: McClelland & Stewart, 1919), 70.

16. For histories of the OMI mission, see P.E. Breton, *Au pays des Peaux-de-Lièvres: J.M. Patrick Kearney, OMI* (St Hyacinthe, PQ: Arthur Douville, 1962); P.E. Breton, *Vital Grandin, OMI* (Paris: Librairie Arthème Fayard, 1960); Champagne, *Les Missions catholiques*; Pierre Duchaussois, *Mid Snow and Ice: The Apostles of the Northwest*, trans. Thomas Dawson from *Aux glaces polaires* (Ottawa: OMI, [1937]); Duchaussois, *The Grey Nuns*; Grant, *Moon of Wintertime*; A.G. Morice, *History of the Catholic Church in Western Canada* (Toronto: Musson Book Co., 1910); A. Philpot, *Le Frère Alexis Reynard: Premier apôtre inconnu du Grand Nord canadien* (Lyon: Oeuvre Apostolique, 1931); and numerous articles by Gaston Carrière.

17. CMS, *Proceedings* (1891–92), 22.

18. Only one was enrolled on opening day, and students spent an average of just one year at the school. See "Materials Relating to the Irene Training School," Provincial Archives of Alberta, A.281/98.

19. For histories of the CMS mission, see T.C.B. Boon, *The Anglican Church from the Bay to the Rockies* (Toronto: Ryerson Press, 1962); Boon, "William West Kirkby: First Anglican Missionary to the Loucheux," *The Beaver*, Outfit 295 (Spring 1965): 36–43; Ian A.L. Getty, "The Failure of the Native Church Policy of the CMS in the Northwest" in *Religion and Society in the Prairie West*, ed. Richard Allen, Canadian Plains Studies no. 3 (Regina, 1974), 19–34; Jean Usher, "Apostles and Aborigines: The Social Theory of the Church

Missionary Society," *Histoire sociale/Social History* 7 (April 1971): 28–52; Usher, *William Duncan of Metlakatla*, Publications in History no. 5 (Ottawa: National Museums of Canada, 1974); Grant, *Moon of Wintertime*.

20. Annual Letter to CMS, Fort Simpson, 29 Nov. 1869, NA microfilm reel no. A98.

21. Émile Grouard to Sister Marie Colombe, Providence, 10 Nov. 1864, AD HPF 4191.C74R124.

22. Bernard Ross to Laurence Clarke, Fort Simpson, 1 Jan. 1859, quoted in Peake, "Fur Traders and Missionaries," 84.

23. Based on figures in Sylvio Lesage, "Sacred Heart Mission, 1858–1959," typescript copy in Archives Deschatelets, Ottawa, BPC 513.L62; James Anderson, "1855 Census of the Population of the Mackenzies River District," NA MG 19/A29, for Fort Simpson, and Emile Petitot, "On the Athabasca District of the Canadian North-West Territory," Proceedings of the Royal Geographical Society, Nov. 1883, for Providence.

24. W.D. Reeve, Fort Simpson Journal, 19 Sept. 1872, CMS C.1/0, NA microfilm reel no. A100.

25. Letter from Mgr Isadore Clut, Providence, 8 Aug. 1976, published in *Les Missions des Oblats* 16, 61 (March 1878): 11. My translation.

26. Charlotte Bompas was one of the few Europeans to recognize this fact. "An Indian is apt to look upon all 'yaltis' (praying men) as more or less 'medicine men,'" she wrote in a letter to England in 1901, although she was referring primarily to the role of the physical rather than the spiritual healer. See S.A. Archer, comp., *A Heroine of the North: Memoirs of Charlotte Selina Bompas, 1830–1917* (London: Society for Promoting Christian Knowledge, 1929), 172.

27. William Spendlove, "A Wild Red Indian Tamed," unpublished chapter from his memoirs, PAA MR.250/1.

28. Kirkby to C.C. Fenn, Fort Simpson, 19 June 1890, CMS C.1/0, NA microfilm reel no. A116.

29. For instance, Émile Grouard reported on a visit to some "Nahanni" Indians who had no understanding of his message and did not respond to his speeches for several days and nights until one woman asked to have the sign of the cross made over her children to protect them. Letter to Sister Marie Colombe, Providence, 3 Dec. 1872, AD HPF 4191.C75R134.

30. Journal of Mgr Grandin, June 1862–April 1863, published in *Les Missions des Oblats* 5, 18 (June 1866): 220–21.

31. Words of W. Spendlove, Fort Simpson Journal, June–Dec. 1884, entry for 1 Aug., CMS C.1/0, NA microfilm reel no. A112.

32. W.D. Reeve, Fort Simpson Journal, Nov. 1872–Nov. 1873, entry for 19 Jan. 1873, CMS C.1/0, NA microfilm reel no. A100.

33. Quoted in Lesage, "Sacred Heart Mission," 9.

34. W.D. Reeve, Fort Simpson Journal, entry for 3 Sept. 1869, CMS C.1/0, NA microfilm reel no. A99.

35. Martha M.C. McCarthy, "The Missions of the Oblates of Mary Immaculate to the Athapaskans, 1846–1870: Theory, Structure, and Method" (PhD thesis, University of Manitoba, 1981), 305. Based on a letter from Séguin to Taché, 1 June 1887.

36. Fort Simpson Journal, entry for 9 June 1878, CMS C.1/0, NA microfilm reel no. A103.

37. Fort Simpson Journal, entry for 19 Aug. 1870, CMS C.1/0, NA microfilm reel no. A99.

38. Elihu Stewart, *Down the Mackenzie and up the Yukon in 1906* (London: Bodley Head, 1913), 240–41.

39. W. Spendlove, Fort Simpson Journal, entry for 8 May 1882, CMS C.1/0, Original Letters, Incoming 1880–1900, NA microfilm reel no. A110.

40. W.D. Reeve, Fort Simpson Journal, entry for 20 Jan. 1870, CMS C.1/0, NA microfilm reel no. A99. Reeve later noted that these "vile questions" were "too disgusting to be written down."

41. William Spendlove to CMS, Fort Simpson, n.d. (received 3 March 1884), CMS C.1/0, NA microfilm reel no. A111.

42. Émile J.B.M. Grouard, *Souvenirs de mes soixante ans d'apostolat dans l'Athabaska-Mackenzie* (Lyon, Winnipeg: OMI, 1923), 100. My translation.

43. Ibid., 99. My translation.

44. Duchaussois, *The Grey Nuns*, 74. Mgr Clut recounts an incident of 1874 in which he bargained with a Yellowknife Indian to get him to give up a young girl with whom he was cohabiting. The price eventually agreed upon was a bonnet, some fish, a comb, and some ammunition. Letter from Clut to OMI published in *Les Missions des Oblats* 14, 53 (March 1976): 22–26.

45. W.D. Reeve, Fort Simpson Journal, entry for 28 April 1872, CMS C.1/0, NA microfilm reel no. A100.

46. Quoted by Glyndwr Williams, "The Hudson's Bay Company and the Fur Trade, 1670–1870," *The Beaver*, Outfit 314 (1983): 69.

47. W. Spendlove, Fort Simpson Journal, entry for 6 Aug. 1884, CMS C.1/0, NA microfilm reel no. A112.

48. Manuscript by W. Spendlove, "Suffer the Little Children," PAA MR.250/1.

49. Kirkby to C.C. Fenn, Fort Simpson, 19 June 1890, CMS C.1/0, NA microfilm reel no. A116.

50. R.P. Th. Ortolan, *Les Oblats de Marie Immaculée durant le premier siècle de leur existence* (Paris: Librairie St Paul, 1914), 3:262–63.

51. For example, the Anglicans thought that the Gwich'in were "more intelligent and very anxious to learn," according to Diary of Augusta Morris, Fort Norman, 9 Dec. 1881, HBCA Z.13/1. The Slavey, on the other hand, were lacking "intellectual powers" or the ability to think in abstract terms, according to D.N. Kirkby's Report from Fort Norman, 4 Feb. 1888, CMS C.1/0, NA microfilm reel no. A115. The Gwich'in were receptive to the Anglicans, while the Slavey were not.

52. D.N. Kirkby, Report from Fort Norman, 4 Feb. 1888, CMS C.1/0 NA microfilm reel no. A115.

53. W.D. Reeve, Annual Report for 1874, quoted in Kerry M. Abel, "The South Nahanni River Region, NWT (1820–1972): Patterns of Socio-Economic Transition in the Canadian North" (MA thesis, University of Manitoba, 1980), 72.

54. Bishop Bompas to C.C. Fenn, Peace River, 12 Nov. 1882, CMS C.1/0, NA microfilm reel no. A111.

55. Quoted in Julie Cruikshank, *Athapaskan Women: Lives and Legends*, National Museums of Canada, Canadian Ethnology Service Paper no. 57 (Ottawa, 1979), 24.

56. Bishop Bompas to C.C. Fenn, Fort Norman, 2 May 1891, copy in PAA MR 170/2.

57. Michael Mason, *The Arctic Forests* (London: Hodder and Stoughton, 1924), 61.

58. June Helm and Eleanor Leacock, "The Hunting Tribes of Subarctic Canada" in *North American Indians in Historical Perspective*, ed. Eleanor Leacock and Nancy O. Lurie (New York: Random House, 1971), 368.

59. Definition of Weston LaBarre, cited in Robert R. Janes and J.H. Kelley, "Observations on Crisis Cult

Activities in the Mackenzie Basin" in *Problems in the Prehistory of the North American Subarctic*, ed. J. Helmer, S. Van Dyke, and F.J. Kense (Calgary: University of Calgary Archaelogy Association, 1977), 153.

60. Particularly in A.F.C. Wallace, *The Death and Rebirth of the Seneca* (New York: Random House, 1969) and "Revitalization Movements: Some Theoretical Considerations," *American Anthropologist* 58 (1956): 264–81.

61. John Franklin, *Journey to the Shores of the Polar Sea in 1819–22, with a brief account of the second journey in 1825–27* (London: John Murray, 1829), 2:44–45; and W.F. Wentzel to Roderick McKenzie, 18 Feb. 1814, in L.R. Masson, *Les bourgeois de la compagnie du nord-ouest, 1889–90* (New York: Antiquarian Press Reprint, [1960]), 1:109.

62. Journal of CMS missionary Robert Hunt, NA microfilm reel no. A90, 5 June 1859 and 11 June 1859. Also Alexandre Taché, *Vingt années des missions*, 120–22, cited in McCarthy, "The Missions of the Oblates," 309–13. Also see Breton, *Vital Grandin*, 118.

63. Valentin Vegreville to Alexandre Taché, 29 July 1860, Archives of the Archbishopric of St Boniface, TO 120–21, cited in McCarthy, "The Missions of the Oblates," 314–15.

64. Father Clut to Father Vegreville, 28 Dec. 1860, NA M2073, cited in McCarthy, "The Missions of the Oblates," 315–16.

65. Petitot to OMI, Fort Good Hope, 1 June 1878, published in *Les Missions des Oblats* 17, 65 (March 1879): 6–8.

66. W. Spendlove to CMS, Fort Simpson, 30 Nov. 1880, CMS C.1/0, NA microfilm reel no. A109.

67. Reported in Michael Mason, *The Arctic Forests*, 61.

68. For example, John Franklin, *Journey to the Shores of the Polar Sea*, 2:60,

230; Father Seguin to Father Clut, Fort Good Hope, 4 Feb. 1874, AD G-LPP2686, cited in McCarthy, "The Missions of the Oblates," 321.

69. Jacqueline Peterson, paper presented to the Twentieth Annual Conference of Algonkianists, Hull, Quebec, Oct. 1988.

70. Father Clut to Mgr Faraud, 16 Dec. 1861, cited in Gaston Carrière, "The Oblates and the Northwest, 1845–61," *Canadian Catholic Historical Association, Study Sessions, 1970,"* 54.

71. Lesage, "Sacred Heart Mission," 14.

72. Grouard, *Souvenirs*, 59–60. My translation.

73. Journal of Mgr Grandin, June 1862–April 1863, published in *Les Missions des Oblats* 5, 18 (June 1866): 220–21. My translation.

74. D.N. Kirkby to C.C. Fenn, Fort Simpson, 19 June 1890, CMS C.1/0, NA microfilm reel no. A116.

75. Journal of Bishop Grandin at Fort Rae, *Les Missions des Oblats*, June 1866, 221.

76. D.N. Kirkby to C.C. Fenn, Fort Simpson, 29 Nov. 1890, CMS C.1/0, NA microfilm reel no. A116.

77. Father Grouard to Father Sardou (Procurer General), Nativity Mission, 25 Aug. 1890, published in *Les Missions des Oblats* 28, 112 (Dec. 1890): 445.

78. Emile Petitot, "Étude sur la nation Montagnais," Fort Good Hope, 1 July 1865, published in *Les Missions des Oblats* 6, 24 (Dec. 1867): 508.

79. Sister Lapointe to Mlle Symns, 8 June 1868, AD Historical Documents of the Grey Nuns of Montreal, microfilm reel no. 89.

80. For example, Frank Russell, *Explorations in the Far North* (Iowa City: State University of Iowa, 1898).

81. Diary of Augusta E. Morris, entry for 5 Nov. 1881, HBCA Z.13/1.

82. Emile Petitot to R.P. Fabre, *Les Missions des Oblats* 6 (1867), quoted by McCarthy, "The Missions of the Oblates," 318.

83. Emile Petitot to OMI, Providence, 31 Aug. 1862, published in *Les Missions des Oblats* 2, 6 (June 1863): 224.

84. D.N. Kirkby to C.C. Fenn, Fort Simpson, 19 June 1890, CMS C.1/0, NA microfilm reel no. A116.

85. W.D. Reeve, Annual Letter, Fort Simpson, 17 July 1878, CMS C.1/0, NA microfilm reel no. A103.

86. Father Grouard to Sister Marie Colombe, Providence, 3 Dec. 1872, AD HPF 4191.C75R. My translation.

87. Faraud's memoirs, in Fernand-Michel, ed., *Dix huits ans chez les sauvages*, 157–58. My translation.

88. For example, W. Spendlove, Fort Simpson Journal, entry for 21 Dec. 1884, CMS C.1/0, NA microfilm reel no. A113; and W. Spendlove to C.C. Fenn, Fort Resolution, 24 July 1890, CMS C.1/0, NA microfilm reel no. A116. Charlotte Bompas was also remembered for her work with Dene women. See Archer, *A Heroine of the North*.

89. Compiled from "List of Fort Simpson Indians, 1860–1871," PAA MR.2/1; and Fort Norman Mission Register, PAA MR.1/1.

90. Ibid.

91. Compiled from various sources in the Oblate Archives Deschâtelets. It is possible more girls were sent to school as a substitute for the practice of female infanticide or because parents considered that young girls were less needed at home than boys.

92. Emile Petitot, *En Route pour la mer glaciale* (Paris: Letouzey, 1888), 377–78.

93. Edgar Laytha, *North Again for Gold* (New York: Frederick A. Stokes, 1939), 43–44.

94. For example, Abel, "The Drum and the Cross," 72; George Simpson to HBC Governor and Committee, 25 Nov. 1841, quoted in *London Correspondence Inward from Sir George Simpson, 1841–42*, ed. Glyndyr Williams and John S. Galbraith (London: Hudson's Bay Record Society, 1973), 79; Morris Zaslow, *The Opening of the Canadian North, 1870–1914* (Toronto: McClelland & Stewart, 1971), 70.

95. J.H. Lefroy to Anthony?, Fort Chipewyan, 11 Nov. 1843, in *In Search of the Magnetic North: A Soldier-Surveyor's Letters from the North-West, 1843–44*, ed. G.F.G. Stanley (Toronto: Macmillan, 1955), 74.

96. McCarthy, "The Missions of the Oblates," 271ff.

97. Fort Resolution, 11 March 1883, HBCA Z.13/2. McCarthy, in her "The Missions of the Oblates," 273–74, claims Bishop Bompas believed the homeopathic system used by the priests to be as "deceptive as their religion," citing NA microfilm reel no. A83, 9 Dec. 1867, but his wife obviously disagreed, and by this time, Bompas may also have changed his mind.

98. Father Grollier to Alexandre Taché, 18 July 1861, Archives of the Archbishopric of St Boniface, TO675, quoted in McCarthy, "The Missions of the Oblates," 272.

99. W.D. Reeve, Fort Simpson Journal, entry for 1 Oct. 1872, CMS, C.1/0, NA microfilm reel no. A100.

100. Fort Simpson Journal, entry for 17 May 1885, CMS C.1/0, NA microfilm reel no. A113.

101. Letter of 9 Jan. 1862, quoted in McCarthy, "The Missions of the Oblates," 272.

102. W. Spendlove, Fort Simpson Journal, entry for 4 March 1882, CMS C.1/0, NA microfilm reel no. A110.

103. Mgr Faraud to R.P. Fabre, 15 Nov. 1865, published in *Les Missions des Oblats* 6 (1867): 355–56. Also quoted in McCarthy, "The Missions of the Oblates," 317.

104. W.D. Reeve, Fort Simpson Journal, entries for 1 Oct. 1872 and 10 Feb. 1873, CMS C.1/0, NA microfilm reel no. A100.

105. Gabriel Breynat, *Cinquante ans aux pays des neiges* (Montreal: Fides, 1945–48), 2:271, footnote.

106. W.L. Hardisty to William Mactavish, Fort Simpson, 27 Nov. 1869, HBCA B.200/b/37, 228–29.

107. W.L. Hardisty to Bishop Grandin, Fort Simpson, 28 Nov. 1863, HBCA B.200/b/35, fo. 18.

108. D.N. Kirkby, Report for Holy Trinity Mission, Fort Norman, 4 Feb. 1888, CMS C.1/0, NA microfilm reel no. A115.

109. Duchaussois, *The Grey Nuns*, 72–73.

110. Abraham Rotstein, "Trade and Politics: An Institutional Approach," *Western Canadian Journal of Anthropology* 3, 1 (1972): 1–28.

111. Report from Fort Norman, 4 Feb. 1888, CMS C.1/0, NA microfilm reel no. A115.

112. Letter from Father Clut to OMI, Providence, 8 Aug. 1876, published in *Les Missions des Oblats* 16, 61 (March 1878): 11.

113. See, for example, a description of these traditions in Archer, *A Heroine of the North*; W.D. Reeve's Fort Simpson Journal for 1870s, such as the entry for 1 Jan. 1873, CMS C.1/0, NA microfilm reel no. A100; Russell, *Explorations in the Far North*, 99ff, and others.

114. Taché reported on his first visit to Athabasca that he met "Indians" there who had never seen a priest yet knew French prayers. In McCarthy, "The Missions of the Oblates," 277.

115. Duchaussois, *Mid Snow and Ice*, 239.

116. Ibid., 240.

117. W.D. Reeve, Annual Letter, Fort Simpson, June 1890, CMS C.1/0, NA microfilm reel no. A99.

118. Cruikshank, *Athapaskan Women*.

119. For example, at Fort Simpson in 1858.

120. Russell, *Explorations in the Far North*, 162–63.

121. Warburton Pike, *The Barren Ground of Northern Canada* (London: Macmillan, 1892), 120–21.

122. W.D. Reeve, Fort Simpson Journal, 4 March 1870, CMS C.1/0, NA microfilm reel no. A99.

123. June Helm, *The Lynx Point People: The Dynamics of a Northern Athapaskan Band*, National Museum of Canada, Bulletin 176 (Ottawa, 1961), 117–20.

124. Hugh Brody, *Maps and Dreams: A Journey into the Lives and Lands of the Beaver Indians of Northwest Canada* (Vancouver: Douglas & McIntyre, 1981), 79. See also John J. Honigmann, *Ethnography and Acculturation of the Fort Nelson Slave*, Yale University Publications in Anthopology no. 33 (1946), 135; James W. VanStone, *The Snowdrift Chipewyan* (Ottawa: Northern Coordination and Research Centre, Department of Northern Affairs and Natural Resources, 1963), 103–4.

125. David M. Smith, *I^{n}ko^{n}ze: Magico-Religious Beliefs of Contact-Traditional Chipewan [sic] Trading at Fort Resolution, NWT*, Mercury Series Ethnology Paper no. 6 (Ottawa: National Museum of Man, 1973), 20.

126. VanStone, *The Snowdrift Chipewyan*, 103.

CANADA'S SUBJUGATION OF THE
PLAINS CREE, 1879–1885 ⬧

JOHN L. TOBIAS

○

One of the most persistent myths that Canadian historians perpetuate is that of the honourable and just policy Canada followed in dealing with the Plains Indians. First enunciated in the Canadian expansionist literature of the 1870s as a means to emphasize the distinctive Canadian approach to and the unique character of the Canadian West,[1] it has been given credence by G.F.G. Stanley in his classic *The Birth of Western Canada*,[2] and by all those who use Stanley's work as the standard interpretation of Canada's relationship with the Plains Indians in the period 1870–85. Thus students are taught that the Canadian government was paternalistic and far-sighted in offering the Indians a means to become civilized and assimilated into white society by the reserve system, and honest and fair-minded in honouring legal commitments made in the treaties.[3] The Plains Indians, and particularly the Plains Cree, are said to be a primitive people adhering to an inflexible system of tradition and custom, seeking to protect themselves against the advance of civilization, and taking up arms in rejection of the reserve system and an agricultural way of life.[4] This traditional interpretation distorts the roles of both the Cree and the Canadian government, for the Cree were both flexible and active in promoting their own interests, and willing to accommodate themselves to a new way of life, while the Canadian government was neither as far-sighted nor as just as tradition maintains. Canada's principal concern in its relationship with the Plains Cree was to establish control over them, and Canadian authorities were willing to and did wage war upon the Cree in order to achieve this control.

Those who propagate the myth would have us believe that Canada began to negotiate treaties with the Indians of the West in 1871 as part of an overall plan to develop the agricultural potential of the West, open the land

⬧ *Canadian Historical Review* 64, 4 (December 1983): 519–48. Reprinted by permission of University of Toronto Press Incorporated.

for railway construction, and bind the prairies to Canada in a network of commercial and economic ties. Although there is an element of truth to these statements, the fact remains that in 1871 Canada had no plan on how to deal with the Indians and the negotiation of treaties was not at the initiative of the Canadian government, but at the insistence of the Ojibwa Indians of the North-West Angle and the Saulteaux of the tiny province of Manitoba. What is ignored by the traditional interpretation is that the treaty process only started after Yellow Quill's band of Saulteaux turned back settlers who tried to go west of Portage la Prairie, and after other Saulteaux leaders insisted upon enforcement of the Selkirk Treaty or, more often, insisted upon making a new treaty. Also ignored is the fact that the Ojibwa of the North-West Angle demanded rents, and created the fear of violence against prospective settlers who crossed their land or made use of their territory, if Ojibwa rights to their lands were not recognized. This pressure and fear of resulting violence is what motivated the government to begin the treaty-making process.[5]

Canada's initial offer to the Saulteaux and Ojibwa Indians consisted only of reserves and a small cash annuity. This proposal was rejected by the Ojibwa in 1871 and again in 1872, while the Saulteaux demanded, much to Treaty Commissioner Wemyss Simpson's chagrin, farm animals, horses, wagons, and farm tools and equipment. Simpson did not include these demands in the written treaty, for he had no authority to do so, but he wrote them down in the form of a memorandum that he entitled "outside promises" and which he failed to send to Ottawa. Thus, the original Treaties 1 and 2 did not include those items the Saulteaux said had to be part of a treaty before they would agree to surrender their lands. Only in 1874, after the Indian leaders of Manitoba became irate over non-receipt of the goods that Simpson had promised them, was an inquiry launched, and Simpson's list of "outside promises" discovered and incorporated in renegotiated treaties in 1875.[6] It was only in 1873 after the Ojibwa of the North-West Angle had twice refused treaties that only included reserves and annuities, that the government agreed to include the domestic animals, farm tools, and equipment that the Ojibwa demanded. After this experience Canada made such goods a standard part of later treaties.[7]

Just as it was pressure from the Indians of Manitoba that forced the government of Canada to initiate the treaty process, it was pressure from the Plains Cree in the period 1872–75 that compelled the government of Canada to continue the process with the Indians of the Qu'Appelle and Saskatchewan districts. The Plains Cree had interfered with the geological survey and prevented the construction of telegraph lines through their territory to emphasize that Canada had to deal with the Cree for Cree lands.[8] The Cree had learned in 1870 about Canada's claim to their lands, and not wanting to experience what had happened to the Indians in the United States when those people were faced with an expansionist government, the Cree made clear that they would not allow settlement or use of their lands until Cree rights had been clearly recognized. They also made clear that part of any arrangement for Cree lands had to involve assistance to the Cree in developing a new agricultural way of life.[9]

In adopting this position, the Cree were simply demonstrating a skill that they had shown since their initial contact with Europeans in 1670. On numerous occasions during the fur trade era, they had adapted to changed environmental and economic circumstances, beginning first as hunters, then as provisioners and middlemen in the Hudson's Bay Company trading system, and finally adapting from a woodland to parkland–prairie buffalo hunting culture to retain their independence and their desired ties with the fur trade.[10] Having accommodated themselves to the Plains Indian culture after 1800, they expanded into territory formerly controlled by the Atsina, and as the buffalo herds began to decline after 1850, the Cree expanded into Blackfoot territory.[11] Expansion was one response to the threat posed by declining buffalo herds; another was that some Plains Cree bands began to turn to agriculture.[12] Thus, when the Cree learned that Canada claimed their lands, part of the arrangement they were determined to make and succeeded in making was to receive assistance in adapting to an agricultural way of life. So successful were they in negotiating such assistance that when the Mackenzie government received a copy of Treaty 6 in 1876 it accepted the treaty only after expressing a protest concerning the too-generous terms granted to the Cree.[13]

While willing to explore the alternative of agriculture, three Cree leaders in the 1870s sought means to guarantee preservation of the buffalo-hunting culture as long as possible. Piapot (leader of the Cree-Assiniboine of the region south of the Qu'Appelle River), and Big Bear and Little Pine (leaders of two of the largest Cree bands from the Saskatchewan River district) led what has been called an armed migration of the Cree into the Cypress Hills in the latter 1860s. All three men were noted warriors and Big Bear and Piapot were noted religious leaders, but their prowess was not enough to prevent a Cree defeat at the Battle of the Belly River in 1870,[14] and as a result they explored the alternative of dealing with the government of Canada, but in a manner to extract guarantees for the preservation of Cree autonomy. They were determined to get the government to promise to limit the buffalo hunt to the Indians—a goal that Cree leaders had been advocating since the 1850s.[15] When Big Bear met with Treaty Commissioner Alexander Morris at Fort Pitt in September 1876, he extracted a promise from Morris that non-Indian hunting of the buffalo would be regulated.[16]

Big Bear refused to take treaty in 1876, despite receiving Morris's assurances about the regulation of the hunt. Little Pine and Piapot also did not take treaty when the treaty commissions first came to deal with the Cree. Oral tradition among the Cree maintains that all three leaders wished to see how faithful the government would be in honouring the treaties,[17] but equally important for all three leaders was their belief that the treaties were inadequate and that revisions were necessary. Piapot thought Treaty 4 (the Qu'Appelle Treaty) needed to be expanded to include increased farm equipment and tools, and to stipulate that the government had to provide mills, blacksmith and carpentry shops and tools, and instructors in farming and the trades. Only after receiving assurances that Ottawa would consider these requests did Piapot take treaty in 1875.[18] Big Bear and Little Pine objected to Treaty 6 (Fort Pitt and Carlton) because Commissioner Morris had made clear that in taking treaty the Cree would be bound by Canadian law. To accept the treaties would mean being subject to an external authority of which the Crees had little knowledge and upon which they had little influence. Neither Big Bear nor Little Pine would countenance such a loss of autonomy.

Big Bear had raised the matter of Cree autonomy at Fort Pitt in 1876 when he met Commissioner Morris. At that time Big Bear said: "I will make a request that he [Morris] save me from what I most dread, that is the rope about my neck. . . . It was not given to us to have the rope about our neck."[19] Morris and most subsequent historians have interpreted Big Bear's statements to be a specific reference to hanging, but such an interpretation ignores the fact that Big Bear, like most Indian leaders, often used a metaphor to emphasize a point. In 1875, he had made the same point by using a different metaphor when he spoke to messengers informing him that a treaty commission was to meet with the Cree in 1876. At that time Big Bear said "We want none of the Queen's presents: when we set a foxtrap we scatter pieces of meat all around, but when the fox gets into the trap we knock him on the head; we want no bait. . . ."[20] A more accurate interpretation of Big Bear's words to Morris in 1876 is that he feared being controlled or "enslaved," just as an animal is controlled when it has a rope around its neck.[21] In 1877, when meeting with Lieutenant-Governor David Laird, Little Pine also stated that he would not take treaty because he saw the treaties as a means by which the government could "enslave" his people.[22]

The importance of these three leaders cannot be underestimated, for they had with them in the Cypress Hills more than 50 percent of the total Indian population of the Treaty 4 and 6 areas. By concentrating in such numbers in the last buffalo ranges in Canadian territory, the Cree were free from all external interference, whether by other Indian nations or by the agents of the Canadian government—the North-West Mounted Police.[23] Recognizing that these men were bargaining from a position of strength, Laird recommended in 1878 that the government act quickly to establish reserves and honour the treaties. He was aware that the Cypress Hills leaders had the support of many of the Cree in treaty, and that many of the Cree leaders were complaining that the government was not providing the farming assistance promised. As the number of these complaints increased, so did Cree support for Big Bear and Little Pine.[24]

The Cree were concerned not only about the lack of assistance to farm, but when Canadian officials were slow to take action to regulate the buffalo hunt, Big Bear, Piapot, and Little Pine met with Blackfoot leaders and with Sitting Bull of the Teton Sioux in an attempt to reach agreement among the Indian nations on the need to regulate buffalo hunting.[25] These councils were also the forum where Indian leaders discussed the need to revise the treaties. On learning about the Indian council, the non-Indian populace of the West grew anxious, fearing establishment of an Indian confederacy which would wage war if Indian demands were rejected.[26] However, an Indian confederacy did not result from these meetings, nor was agreement reached on how the buffalo were to be preserved, because the Cree, Sioux, and Blackfoot could not overcome their old animosities towards one another.[27]

When in 1879 the buffalo disappeared from the Canadian prairies and Big Bear and Little Pine took their bands south to the buffalo ranges on the Milk and Missouri rivers, most of the other Cree and Assiniboine bands also went with them. The Cree who remained in Canada faced starvation while awaiting the survey of their reserves and the farming equipment that had been promised. Realizing that many of the Cree were dying, the government decided that those who had taken treaty should be given rations. As well, the government appointed Edgar Dewdney to the newly-created position of Commissioner of Indian Affairs for the North-West Territory; a farming policy for the western reserves was introduced; a survey of Cree reserves was begun; and twelve farming instructors were appointed to teach the Indians of the North-West.[28]

The new Indian Commissioner quickly sought to use rations as a means of getting control over the Cree. In the fall of 1879 he announced that rations were to be provided only to Indians who had taken treaty. To get the Cree into treaty more easily and to reduce the influence of recalcitrant leaders, Dewdney announced that he would adopt an old Hudson's Bay Company practice of recognizing any adult male Cree as chief of a new band if he could induce one hundred or more persons to recognize him as leader. He expected that the starving Cypress Hills Cree would desert their old leaders to get rations. As a means of demonstrating Canada's control over the Cree, Dewdney ordered that only the sick, aged, and orphans should receive rations without providing some service to one of the government agencies in the West.[29]

Dewdney's policies seemed to work, for when the Cree and Assiniboine who had gone to hunt in Montana returned starving, their resolve weakened. Little Pine's people convinced their chief to take treaty in 1879, but when Big Bear refused to do the same, almost half of his following joined Lucky Man or Thunderchild to form new bands in order to receive rations.[30]

Taking treaty to avoid starvation did not mean that the Cree had come to accept the treaties as written; rather they altered their tactics in seeking revisions. Believing that small reserves were more susceptible to the control of the Canadian government and its officials, Big Bear, Piapot, and Little Pine sought to effect a concentration of the Cree people in an Indian territory similar to the reservation system in the United States. In such a territory the Cree would be able to preserve their autonomy or at least limit the ability of others to control them; they would be better able to take concerted action on matters of importance to them.[31]

Soon after taking treaty Little Pine applied for a reserve in the Cypress Hills, twenty-seven miles north-east of the North-West Mounted Police post of Fort Walsh. Piapot requested a reserve next to Little Pine's, while ten other bands, including most of the Assiniboine nations, selected reserve sites contiguous to either Little Pine's or Piapot's and to one another.[32] If all these reserve sites were granted, and if Big Bear were to take treaty and settle in the Cypress Hills, the result would be the concentration of much of the Cree nation and the creation of an Indian territory that would comprise most of what is now south-western Saskatchewan.

Unaware of the intention of the Cree and Assiniboine leaders, Canadian officials in the spring of 1880 agreed to the establishment of a reserve for all the Canadian Assiniboine and reserves in the Cypress Hills for each of the Cree bands that wished them. In 1880, the Assiniboine reserve was surveyed, but the other Indian leaders were told that their reserves would not be surveyed until the following year.[33] In the interim, most of the Cree went to the buffalo ranges in Montana.

The Cree effort to exploit the remaining American buffalo ranges caused them much trouble. The Crow, the Peigan, and other Indian nations with reservations in Montana were upset by competition for the scarce food resource, and these people threatened to break the treaties they had made with the American government and to wage war on the Cree if the American authorities did not protect the Indian hunting ranges. These threats were renewed when the Cree began to steal horses from the Crow and Peigan. To add to their difficulties, American ranchers accused the Cree of killing range cattle. American officials, not wishing trouble with their Indians and wishing to placate the ranchers, informed the Cree that they would have to return to Canada. Most Cree bands, aware that if they did not leave voluntarily the American government would use troops to force them to move north, returned to the Cypress Hills.[34]

They returned to find that Canadian officials were now aware of the dangers to their authority posed by a concentration of the Cree. A riot at Fort Walsh in 1880, which the police were powerless to prevent or control, assaults on farming instructors who refused to provide rations to starving Indians, and rumours that the Cree were planning a grand Indian council to discuss treaty revisions in 1881 all caused the Indian Commissioner much concern.[35] To avoid further difficulties over rations, in late 1880 Dewdney ordered that all Indians requesting rations be given them, regardless of whether the supplicant was in treaty.[36] There was little that the government could do at this time about the proposed Indian council or the concentration of Cree in the Cypress Hills.

In the spring of 1881, Cree bands from all regions of the Canadian prairies left their reserves to go south to meet with Little Pine and Big Bear. Even the new bands Dewdney had created were going to the council in American territory. What was also disconcerting to Canadian officials were the reports that Big Bear and Little Pine, who had gone to Montana to prepare for the council, had reached an accommodation with the Blackfoot and had participated in a joint raid on the Crow. To all appearances the Blackfoot, the Indian confederacy the Canadian government most feared, would be part of the Indian council.[37]

The Indian council was not held because the raid on the Crow led American officials to intervene militarily to force the Cree to return to Canada. With Montana stockmen acting as militia units, the American army prevented most Cree and Assiniboine bands from entering the United States. As well, the American forces seized horses, guns, and carts, and

escorted the Cree to Canada.[38] The Cree-Blackfoot alliance did not materialize, for soon after the raid on the Crow, young Cree warriors stole horses
from the Blackfoot and thereby destroyed the accord that Little Pine and Big
Bear were attempting to create.[39]

The actions of the American military in 1881 were extremely beneficial
to Canada. Not only did the Americans prevent the holding of the Indian
council, but by confiscating the guns and horses of the Cree, the Americans
had dispossessed the Cree of the ability to resist whatever measures the
Canadian authorities wished to take against them. The Canadian authorities
also benefited from Governor-General Lorne's tour of the West in 1881, for
many of the Cree bands that had gone to the Cypress Hills in the spring
went north in late summer to meet Lorne to impress upon him the inadequacy of the treaties and the need to revise them.[40] Thus, Lorne's tour prevented the concentration of most of the Cree nation in the Cypress Hills.

The threat posed to Canadian authority in the North-West by concentration of the Cree was clearly recognized by Dewdney and other Canadian
officials in late 1881. They saw how the Cree had forced officials to placate
them and to ignore their orders in 1880 and 1881. This convinced both
Dewdney and Ottawa that the Cree request for contiguous reserves in the
Cypress Hills could not be granted. Dewdney recognized that to grant the
Cree requests would be to create an Indian territory, for most of the Cree
who had reserves further north would come to the Cypress Hills and
request reserves contiguous to those of the Cypress Hills Cree. This would
result in so large a concentration of Cree that the only way Canada could
enforce its laws on them would be via a military campaign. To prevent this,
Dewdney recommended a sizeable expansion of the Mounted Police force
and the closure of Fort Walsh and all government facilities in the Cypress
Hills. This action would remove all sources of sustenance from the Cree in
the Cypress Hills. Dewdney hoped that starvation would drive them from
the Fort Walsh area and thus end the concentration of their force.[41]

Dewdney decided to take these steps fully aware that what he was doing
was a violation not only of the promises made to the Cypress Hills Indians in
1880 and 1881, but also that by refusing to grant reserves on the sites the
Indians had selected, he was violating the promises made to the Cree by the
Treaty Commissions in 1874 and 1876, and in the written treaties.
Nevertheless, Dewdney believed that to accede to the Cree requests would be
to grant the Cree de facto autonomy from Canadian control, which would
result in the perpetuation and heightening of the 1880–81 crisis. Rather than
see that situation continue, Dewdney wanted to exploit the opportunity presented to him by the hunger crisis and disarmament of the Cree to bring them
under the government's control, even if it meant violating the treaties.[42]

In the spring of 1882 the Cree and Assiniboine were told that no further
rations would be issued to them while they remained in the Cypress Hills.
Only if the Indians moved north to Qu'Appelle, Battleford, and Fort Pitt
were they to be given assistance, and at those locations only treaty Indians
were to be aided. The Mounted Police were ordered to stop issuing rations
at Fort Walsh and the Indian Department farm that had been located near
Fort Walsh was closed. Faced with the prospect of starvation, without

weapons or transport to get to the Montana buffalo ranges, and knowing that if they were to try to go south the Mounted Police would inform the American military authorities, many Cree and all the Assiniboine decided to go north.[43] Even Big Bear discovered that his people wanted him to take treaty and move north. In 1882, after taking treaty, he, along with Piapot and Little Pine, promised to leave the Cypress Hills.[44]

Only Piapot kept his promise and even he did not remain long at Fort Qu'Appelle. By late summer of 1882, Piapot was back in the Cypress Hills complaining about how he had been mistreated at Qu'Appelle, and making the Cree aware of how they could lose their autonomy if the government could deal with them as individual bands.[45] On hearing this report, the other Cree leaders refused to leave the Fort Walsh region and insisted upon receiving the reserves promised them in 1880 and 1881. North-West Mounted Police Commissioner Irvine feared a repetition of the incidents of 1880 if he refused to feed the Cree and believed that the hungry Cree would harass the construction crews of the Canadian Pacific Railway for food, which would lead to confrontation between whites and Indians which the police would be unable to handle and which in turn might lead to an Indian war. Therefore Irvine decided to feed the Cree.[46]

Dewdney and Ottawa were upset by Irvine's actions. Ottawa gave specific instructions to close Fort Walsh in the spring of 1883. When Irvine closed the fort, the Cree faced starvation. As it was quite evident that they could not go to the United States, and as they would not receive reserves in the Cypress Hills, the Cree moved north. Piapot moved to Indian Head and selected a reserve site next to the huge reserve set aside for the Assiniboine. Little Pine and Lucky Man moved to Battleford and selected reserve sites next to Poundmaker's reserve. Big Bear went to Fort Pitt.

The move to the north was not a sign of the Cree acceptance of the treaties as written, nor of their acceptance of the authority of the Canadian government. Big Bear, Little Pine, and Piapot were aware that the other Cree chiefs were dissatisfied with the treaties, and were also aware that if they could effect concentration of the Cree in the north they would be able to preserve their autonomy, just as they had done in the Cypress Hills in the 1879–81 period. Therefore, the move to the north was simply a tactical move, for no sooner were these chiefs in the north than they once again sought to effect a concentration of their people.

By moving to Indian Head, Piapot had effected a concentration of more than 2000 Indians. This number threatened to grow larger if the council he planned to hold with all the Treaty 4 bands to discuss treaty revisions were successful. Commissioner Dewdney, fearing the results of such a meeting in 1883, was able to thwart Piapot by threatening to cut off rations to any Indians attending Piapot's council and by threatening to arrest Piapot and depose any chiefs who did meet with him. Although Dewdney, in 1883, prevented Piapot holding a large council by such actions, Piapot was able to get the Treaty 4 chiefs to agree to meet in the late spring of 1884 for a thirst dance and council on Pasquah's Reserve, near Fort Qu'Appelle.[47]

While Piapot was organizing an Indian council in the Treaty 4 area, Big Bear and Little Pine were doing the same for the Treaty 6 region. Little Pine and Lucky Man attempted to effect a concentration of more than 2000 Cree on contiguous reserves in the Battleford district, by requesting reserves next to Poundmaker, whose reserve was next to three other Cree reserves, which in turn were only a short distance from three Assiniboine reserves. Another 500 Cree would have been located in the Battleford area if Big Bear's request for a reserve next to Little Pine's site had been granted. Only with difficulty was Dewdney able to get Big Bear to move to Fort Pitt.[48] However, he was unable to prevent Big Bear and Little Pine from sending messengers to the Cree leaders of the Edmonton, Carlton, and Duck Lake districts to enlist their support for the movement to concentrate the Cree.[49]

Dewdney was convinced that the activities of Big Bear, Piapot, and Little Pine were a prelude to a major project the Cree planned for the following year, 1884. He was also aware that his ability to deal with the impending problem was severely limited by decisions taken in Ottawa. The Deputy Superintendent-General of Indian Affairs, Lawrence Vankoughnet, was concerned about the cost of administering Dewdney's policies, and he ordered reductions in the level of assistance provided to the Cree and in the number of employees working with the Cree.[50] In making these decisions, Ottawa effectively deprived Dewdney of his major sources of intelligence about the Cree and their plans. It also deprived Dewdney of a major instrument in placating the Cree—the distribution of rations to those bands which co-operated.

Vankoughnet's economy measures led to further alienation of the Cree. In some areas, notably in the Fort Pitt, Edmonton, and Crooked Lakes regions, farming instructors were assaulted and government storehouses broken into when Indians were denied rations. The incident on the Sakemay Reserve in the Crooked Lakes area was quite serious, for when the police were called upon to arrest those guilty of the assault, they were surrounded and threatened with death if they carried out their orders. Only after Assistant Indian Commissioner Hayter Reed had agreed to restore assistance to the Sakemay band to the 1883 level and had promised not to imprison the accused were the police allowed to leave with their prisoners.[51]

The violence that followed the reductions in rations convinced Dewdney that starving the Cree into submission was not the means to control them. He wanted to use coercion, but this required an expansion of the number of police in the West. Therefore, he recommended that more men be recruited for the Mounted Police. In addition, Dewdney wanted to ensure that jail sentences were given to arrested Indians so that they would cause no further problems. Having seen the effects of incarceration on Indians, Dewdney was convinced that this was the means to bring the Cree leaders under control. However, what was needed in his opinion were trial judges who "understood" Indian nature at first hand and who would take effective action to keep the Indians under control. Therefore, Dewdney wanted all Indian Department officials in the West to be appointed stipendiary magistrates in order that all Indian troublemakers could be brought to "justice" quickly. As Dewdney stated in his letter to Prime Minister John A.

Macdonald: "The only effective course with the great proportion [of Indian bands] to adopt is one of sheer compulsion. . . ."[52]

Dewdney used the policy of "sheer compulsion" for only a few months in 1884. He found that his efforts to use the Mounted Police to break up the Indian councils and to arrest Indian leaders only led to confrontations between the Cree and the police. In these confrontations the police were shown to be ineffectual because they were placed in situations in which, if the Cree had been desirous of initiating hostilities, large numbers of Mounted Police would have been massacred.

The first incident which called the policy of compulsion into question was the attempt to prevent Piapot from holding his thirst dance and council in May 1884. Assistant Commissioner Hayter Reed, fearing that the council would result in a concentration of all the Treaty 4 bands, ordered Police Commissioner Irvine to prevent Piapot from attending the council. Irvine was to arrest the chief at the first sign of any violation of even the most minor law. To be certain that Piapot broke a law, Reed promised to have an individual from Pasquah's reserve object to the council being held on that reserve in order that the accusation of trespass could be used to break up the meeting, which all the bands from Treaty 4 were attending.[53]

With a force of fifty-six men and a seven-pounder gun, Irvine caught up with Piapot shortly before the chief reached Pasquah's reserve. Irvine and the police entered the Indian camp at 2 A.M., hoping to arrest Piapot and remove him from the camp before his band was aware of what happened. However, when they entered the camp, the police found themselves surrounded by armed warriors. Realizing that any attempt to arrest the chief would result in a battle, Irvine decided to hold his own council with Piapot and Reed. This impromptu council agreed that Piapot should receive a new reserve next to Pasquah, in return for which Piapot would return to Indian Head temporarily.[54]

The agreement reached between Piapot and Irvine and Reed was a victory for Piapot. By getting a reserve at Qu'Appelle again, Piapot had approximately 2000 Cree concentrated on the Qu'Appelle River, and he was able to hold his council and thirst dance, for after going to Indian Head, he immediately turned around and went to Pasquah's. Reed and Irvine were aware of Piapot's ruse, but did nothing to prevent his holding the council, for they were aware that the Cree at Qu'Appelle were prepared to protect Piapot from what the Indians regarded as an attack on their leader. Realizing the effect that an Indian war would have on possible settlement, and that the police were inadequate for such a clash, the Canadian officials wished to avoid giving cause for violent reaction by the Cree.[55] Piapot acted as he did because he realized that if any blood were shed the Cree would experience a fate similar to that of the Nez Percés, Blackfoot, and Dakota Sioux in those peoples' conflicts with the United States.

Dewdney and the police were to have a similar experience when they attempted to prevent Big Bear from holding a thirst dance and council at Poundmaker's reserve in June 1884. Dewdney feared that Big Bear's council, to which the old chief had invited the Blackfoot and all the Indians from

Treaty 6, would result in a larger concentration of Cree than Little Pine had already effected at Battleford. Dewdney also believed that he had to undo what Little Pine had accomplished, and refused to grant Little Pine and Lucky Man the reserve sites they had requested next to Poundmaker. Big Bear was again told that he would not be granted a reserve in the Battleford district. Dewdney believed that the Cree chiefs would ignore his order to select reserve sites at some distance from Battleford, and that this could be used as a reason for arresting them. To legitimize such actions on his part, Dewdney asked the government to pass an order-in-council to make it a criminal offence for a band to refuse to move to a reserve site the Commissioner suggested.[56] In order to avoid violence when he attempted to prevent Big Bear's council and ordered the arrests of Lucky Man and Little Pine, Dewdney instructed the Indian agents at Battleford and Fort Pitt to purchase all the horses, guns, and cartridges the Cree possessed. He increased the size of the police garrison at Battleford and ordered the police to prevent Big Bear from reaching Battleford.[57]

All Dewdney's efforts had little effect, for Big Bear and his band eluded the police, reached Battleford, and held their thirst dance. The Cree refused to sell their arms, and even the effort to break up the gathering by refusing to provide rations had no result other than to provoke another assault on a farm instructor on 17 June 1884. When the police sought to arrest the farm instructor's assailant, they were intimidated into leaving without a prisoner. When a larger police detachment went to the reserve on 18 June, the police were still unable to make an arrest for fear of provoking armed hostilities. Only on 20 June, when the thirst dance had concluded, were the police able to arrest the accused and only then by forcibly removing him from the Cree camp. This was done with the greatest difficulty for the police were jostled and provoked in an effort to get them to fire on the Cree. That no violence occurred, Superintendent Crozier, in charge of the police detachment, attributed to the discipline of his men and to the actions of Little Pine and Big Bear, who did all that was humanly possible to discourage any attack on the police.[58]

The events at Battleford frightened all parties involved in the confrontation. Big Bear was very much disturbed by them, for he did not want war, as he had made abundantly clear to Dewdney in March 1884, and again to the Indian agent at Battleford, J.A. Rae, in June. However, he did want the treaties revised and establishment of an Indian territory.[59] Agent Rae was thoroughly frightened and wanted Dewdney and Ottawa to adopt a more coercive policy designed to subjugate the Cree. Superintendent Crozier argued for a less coercive policy, for unless some accommodation were reached with the Cree, Crozier believed that out of desperation they would resort to violence.[60]

On hearing of the events of May and June 1884, Ottawa decided that Dewdney, who was now Lieutenant-Governor in addition to being Indian Commissioner, was to have complete control over Indian affairs in the North-West Territories. As well, the Prime Minister informed Dewdney that more police were being recruited for duty in the West and that the Indian

Act was being amended to permit Dewdney to arrest any Indian who was on another band's reserve without the permission of the local Indian Department official.[61] Dewdney was thus being given the instruments to make his policy of compulsion effective.

Dewdney did not, however, immediately make use of his new powers. He still intended to prevent concentration of the Cree, and rejected the requests Big Bear, Poundmaker, Lucky Man, and others made for a reserve at Buffalo Lake, and later rejected Big Bear's, Little Pine's, and Lucky Man's renewed requests for reserves next to Poundmaker's.[62] However, rather than following a purely coercive policy, Dewdney adopted a policy of rewards and punishments. He provided more rations, farming equipment, oxen, ammunition, and twine, and arranged for selected Cree chiefs to visit Winnipeg and other large centres of Canadian settlement. If the Cree were not satisfied with his new approach, he would use force against them. To implement this new policy, Dewdney increased the number of Indian Department employees working on the Cree reserves, for he wanted to monitor closely the behaviour of the Indians, and, if necessary, to arrest troublesome leaders.[63]

While Dewdney was implementing his new policy, the Cree leaders continued their efforts to concentrate the Cree in an exclusively Indian territory. Little Pine went south to seek Blackfoot support for the movement.[64] Big Bear, Lucky Man, and Poundmaker went to Duck Lake for a council with the Cree leaders of the Lower Saskatchewan district. The Duck Lake council, attended by twelve bands, was initiated by Beardy and the chiefs of the Carlton District. Beardy, who acted as spokesman for the Carlton chiefs, had been relatively inactive in the Cree movements in the 1881-83 period. He, however, had been the most vehement critic of the government's failure to deliver the farm materials promised by the treaty commissioners. In the 1877-81 period, Beardy was a man of little influence in the Carlton area, but when Mistawasis and Ahtahkakoop, the principal Cree chiefs of the Carlton District came to share his views, Beardy's standing among the Carlton Cree rose dramatically.[65]

The Duck Lake Council, called by Cree leaders whom Dewdney thought were loyal and docile, and of which the Commissioner had no foreknowledge, was a cause of much concern. Especially vexing was the detailed list of violations of the treaty for which the Cree demanded redress from the government. The Cree charged that the treaty commissioners lied to them when they said that the Cree would be able to make a living from agriculture with the equipment provided for in the treaties. However, rather than provide all the farming goods, what the government did, according to the Cree, was to withhold many of the cattle and oxen; send inferior quality wagons, farm tools, and equipment; and provide insufficient rations and clothes, and no medicine chest. The petition closed with the statement expressing the Cree sentiment that they had been deceived by "sweet promises" designed to cheat them of their heritage, and that unless their grievances were remedied by the summer of 1885, they would take whatever measures necessary, short of war, to get redress.[66]

Dewdney originally assumed, as did some newspapers across the West, that the Duck Lake Council was part of a plot by Louis Riel to foment an Indian and Metis rebellion. Dewdney's assumption was based on the fact that the Duck Lake Council was held a short time after Riel had returned to Canada. It was also known that Riel had attended it, and that he had advocated such an alliance and a resort to violence when he had met with the Cree in Montana in 1880.[67] Further investigation, however, made quite clear that Riel had little influence on the Cree. To allay the growing concern about the possibility of an Indian war, Dewdney had Hayter Reed issue a statement that nothing untoward was happening and that there was less danger of an Indian war in 1884 than there had been in 1881. Privately Dewdney admitted to Ottawa and his subordinates in the West that the situation was very serious.[68] After both he and Dewdney had met with Cree leaders throughout the West and after carefully assessing the situation, Hayter Reed stated that the government had nothing to fear from the Cree until the summer of 1885. What Reed and Dewdney expected at that time was a united Cree demand to renegotiate treaties.[69]

What Reed and Dewdney had learned on their tours of the Battleford, Edmonton, Carlton, and Qu'Appelle districts in the fall of 1884 was that Big Bear, Piapot, and Little Pine were on the verge of uniting the Cree to call for new treaties in which an Indian territory and greater autonomy for the Cree would be major provisions. In fact, throughout the summer and fall of 1884 Little Pine attempted, with limited success, to interest the leaders of the Blackfoot in joining the Cree movement for treaty revision. Little Pine had invited the Blackfoot to a joint council with the Cree leaders on Little Pine's reserve scheduled for the spring of 1885.[70] If the Blackfoot joined the Cree, Ottawa's ability to govern the Indians and control the West would be seriously jeopardized.

At the moment that the Cree movement seemed on the verge of success, Big Bear was losing control of his band. As he told the assembled chiefs at Duck Lake in the summer of 1884, his young men were listening to the warrior chief, Little Poplar, who was advocating killing government officials and Indian agents as a means of restoring Cree independence. Big Bear feared that if Little Poplar's course of action were adopted the Cree would fight an Indian war that they were certain to lose.[71]

Dewdney was aware of Little Poplar's growing influence on the young men of Big Bear's and the Battleford Assiniboine bands; however, he wished to wait until after January 1885 before taking any action, because after that date the new amendments to the Indian Act would be in effect. These amendments could be used to arrest and imprison Little Pine, Little Poplar, Big Bear, and Piapot, and thereby, Dewdney hoped, destroy the movements these chiefs led.[72] In anticipation of confrontations in 1885, Dewdney ordered that the guns and ammunition normally allotted to the Cree so they could hunt for food be withheld. In addition, Indian councils were prohibited, including the one scheduled for Duck Lake in the summer of 1885, to which all the Cree in Treaty 6 had been invited. Arrangements were made to place the Mounted Police at Battleford under Dewdney's command, and serious consideration was given to placing an artillery unit there also.[73]

To get improved intelligence, Dewdney hired more men to work as Indian agents with the Cree. These men were given broad discretionary powers and were to keep the Commissioner informed on Cree activities. As well, English-speaking mixed-bloods, many of whom had worked for the Hudson's Bay Company and had the confidence of the Cree, were hired as farm instructors. There would now be a farm instructor on each Cree reserve, with explicit instructions to keep the Indian Agent informed of what was happening on his reserve. Staff who had personality conflicts with any of the Cree leaders were either transferred or fired. Only Thomas Quinn, Indian Agent at Fort Pitt and his farming instructor, John Delaney, were not removed before March 1885, although both were slated for transfer.[74]

Dewdney found that his most important staffing move was the employment of Peter Ballendine, a former Hudson's Bay Company trader much trusted by the principal Cree leaders. Ballendine's job was to ingratiate himself with Big Bear and report on that chief's comings and goings. Ballendine won the confidence of Big Bear and reported upon how wrong Dewdney's earlier efforts to break up Big Bear's band had been. Because so many of Big Bear's original followers joined either Lucky Man, Thunderchild, or Little Pine's bands, Big Bear by 1884 was left with only the most recalcitrant opponents of the treaty. These individuals were only luke-warm in support of their chief's non-violent efforts to get the treaty revised. They favoured instead the course of action advocated by Little Poplar. Ballendine believed that the government could expect trouble from the Big Bear and Little Poplar bands. However, Ballendine emphasized that there was little danger of a Cree-Metis alliance, for the Cree were refusing to meet with the Metis, and were rejecting all entreaties from the Metis suggesting the two should make common cause. Instead the Cree, under the leadership of Big Bear, Beardy, and Little Pine, were planning their own council for the summer of 1885.[75]

Ballendine also developed a new source of information in Poundmaker, who was also acting as a police informer. It was from Poundmaker that Dewdney and the police learned that Little Pine was attempting to involve the Blackfoot in the summer of 1884, and wanted to do so in January 1885, but was prevented from doing so because of temporary blindness—a possible sign of malnutrition from the hunger that most Cree experienced in the extremely harsh winter of 1884–85. Little Pine had sought to get Poundmaker to encourage Crowfoot to join the Cree movement but Poundmaker refused to aid Little Pine, and when Little Pine recovered from his blindness, he went south to meet with Crowfoot. [76]

While Little Pine met with Crowfoot, Big Bear was being challenged for the leadership of his band by his son Imases, also called Curly, and by one of his headmen, Wandering Spirit. These two men were spokesmen for the younger men of Big Bear's Band, and wanted to work with Little Poplar. In the winter of 1885, Little Poplar was journeying constantly between Pitt and

Battleford enlisting support for his plan of action. Although Ballendine could not get precise information on Little Poplar's plans, he did report that by March 1885 Big Bear had asserted himself and that the influence of Imases and Wandering Spirit had seemed to wane.[77]

On the basis of these and similar reports, Dewdney and the police were convinced that, although a number of councils were expected in 1885, no violence was to be anticipated from the Cree. Nevertheless, Dewdney wished to prevent the Cree from holding their councils. His strategy was to make the Cree satisfied with the treaties. He therefore admitted in February 1885 that the government had violated the treaties and ordered delivery to the Cree of all goods the treaties had stipulated. In addition, he ordered a dramatic increase in their rations. If this failed to placate them he planned to arrest their leaders, use the police to keep the Cree on their reserves, and to depose any chief who attempted to attend an Indian council.[78]

Dewdney had the full support of Ottawa for his policy of arresting Cree leaders. The only reservations the Prime Minister expressed were that Dewdney have sufficient forces to make the arrests and that he provide enough evidence to justify the charges of incitement to an insurrection. Macdonald also volunteered to communicate with the stipendiary magistrates to assure their co-operation in imposing long prison terms for any Cree leader convicted of incitement.[79] Macdonald was willing to provide this assistance because Dewdney had earlier complained that he could not use preventive detention of Indian leaders because the magistrates "only look at the evidence and the crime committed when giving out sentences," rather than taking into consideration the nature of the man and the harm that he might do if he were released at an inopportune time.[80] All these preparations were complete when word reached Dewdney of the Metis clash with the Mounted Police at Duck Lake in March 1885.

The Riel Rebellion of 1885 provided Dewdney with a new instrument to make his coercive policy effective. The troops sent into the North-West to suppress the Rebellion could be used to destroy the Cree movement for an Indian territory. The Cree themselves would provide the excuse Dewdney needed virtually to declare war on the bands and leaders who had led the Cree movement for treaty revision. During March 1885, the Cree did engage in some acts of violence that Dewdney chose to label acts of rebellion.

These acts were unrelated to the Cree movement for treaty revision. In fact, these acts that led to the subjugation of the Cree were committed by persons not involved with the Cree movement for autonomy. It is one of the ironic quirks of history that the leaders of the Cree movement had little or nothing to do with the events which would destroy that movement to which they had devoted ten years of their lives. Nevertheless, they would be held responsible for the actions of their desperate and hungry people. To heighten the irony, it was the Metis movement, from which the Cree had held aloof, which would give Dewdney the excuse to use military force to subjugate the Cree.

The Duck Lake clash coincided with a Cree Council on Sweetgrass Reserve. The council of the Battleford area Cree had been called to consider how they could press for increased rations. When word reached the Cree at Sweetgrass of the clash at Duck Lake, they felt that circumstances would make Indian Agent Rae willing to grant them more rations. Thus the Cree, taking their women and children with them to demonstrate their peaceful intent, set out for Battleford. Fear and panic prevailed at Battleford, for on learning of the Crees' approach, the town's citizens assumed that the Cree had thrown in their lot with the Metis. The town was evacuated; most townspeople took refuge in the Mounted Police post.[81]

When the Cree arrived at Battleford they found the town abandoned They sent word to the police post that they wished to speak to the Indian Agent, who refused to leave the safety of the post. The Cree women, seeing the abandoned stores and houses filled with food, began to help themselves. Then, fearing arrest by the police, the Cree left town. On the way back to their reserves, as well as on their way to town, the Cree assisted a number of Indian Department employees and settlers to cross the Battle River to get to the police post, thus demonstrating the pacific nature of their intentions.[82]

Rather than returning to their individual reserves, the Cree went to Poundmaker's, for as the leader in the Battleford district to whom the government had shown much favour in the past, Poundmaker was seen as the man best able to explain to the government what had happened at Battleford. A second significant reason was the deaths of two prominent Cree leaders: Red Pheasant, the night before the Cree left for Battleford, and Little Pine, the night they returned. As it was the practice of the Cree to leave the place where their leaders had expired, both bands left their reserves and went to Poundmaker's, who, given the fears the whites had concerning a Cree and Metis alliance, might possibly defuse any crisis. Thus, in March 1885, Poundmaker became the spokesman of the Battleford Cree. [83]

No sooner were the Cree at Poundmaker's than they were joined by the local Assiniboine, who insisted that a soldier's (war) tent be erected, for events at the Assiniboine reserves convinced them that an attack on the Indian camp was imminent. The Assiniboine explained that when word had reached them of the Duck Lake fight, a few of their young men sought revenge on farming instructor James Payne, who was blamed for the death of a girl. The girl's male relatives killed Payne and murdered farmer Barney Tremont. The Assiniboine now assumed that the Canadian authorities would behave in a similar manner to the Americans and blame all Indians for the actions of a few individuals.[84]

Erection of the soldier's tent meant that the warriors were in control of the camp and that Poundmaker and the civil authorities had to defer to them. It was at this time that the Metis appeal for aid was received. The Cree refused to assist the Metis, although they expected an attack on their camp. Watches were set on the roads, and protection was offered to the Metis at Bresaylor for the settlers there had earned the enmity of the Batoche Metis. As long as no military or police forces came towards the Cree camp, the Cree remained on their reserves and did not interfere with anyone going to or leaving Battleford. The Mounted Police detachment from Fort Pitt and Colonel Otter's military unit arrived in Battleford without encountering any Indians. Nevertheless, reports from the police and local officials maintained that the town was under siege.[85]

While the Battleford Cree were preparing their defences, Big Bear's band was making trouble for itself. Big Bear was absent from his camp when the members of his band heard about the fight at Duck Lake. Wandering Spirit and Imases sought to use the opportunity presented by the Metis uprising to seek revenge for the insults and abuses perpetrated against the Cree by Indian Agent Thomas Quinn and Farming Instructor Delaney. Quinn had physically abused some of the Indian men, while Delaney had cuckolded others before he brought a white bride to Frog Lake in late 1884. Big Bear's headmen demanded that the two officials open the storehouse to the Cree, and when they refused to do so, they were murdered. This set off further acts of violence that resulted in the murder of all the white men in the camp save one.[86]

On his return to camp Big Bear ended further acts of violence. Although unable to prevent a minor skirmish between his young men and a small police patrol, he convinced his warriors to allow the police detachment at Fort Pitt to withdraw from the post without being attacked and to guarantee safety to the civilian residents of the Frog Lake and Fort Pitt regions. Big Bear then led his people north, where he hoped they would be out of harm's way and not engage in further acts of violence.[87]

Beardy also lost control of his band. He and the neighbouring One Arrow band had reserves next to Batoche. Before the clash with the police, the Metis had come to the One Arrow Reserve, captured Farming Instructor Peter Thompkins, and threatened the Cree band with destruction unless the Cree aided the Metis. Some of the younger men of One Arrow's band agreed to do so.[88] The Metis made the same threat against Beardy and his band, and although a few of his young men joined the Metis, Beardy and most of his people remained neutral.[89] It is doubtful that the Cree would have aided the Metis without the threat of violence. Earlier, the Cree of the Duck Lake region had threatened hostilities against the Metis, for the Metis had settled on One Arrow's Reserve and demanded that the government turn over to them some of One Arrow's Reserve. Ottawa, fearing the Metis more than the Cree in 1880, acquiesced. Over the next four years, one task of the local Indian Agent and the police was to reconcile the Cree with the Metis of the Batoche region.[90]

The Cree acts of violence in March 1885 were the excuse Dewdney needed to justify the use of troops against them. He maintained that the Battleford, Fort Pitt, and Duck Lake Cree were part of the Riel Rebellion. Privately, Dewdney reported to Ottawa that he saw the events at Battleford and Frog Lake as the acts of a desperate, starving people and unrelated to what the Metis were doing.[91] In fact, Dewdney had sought in late March to open negotiations with the Battleford Cree, but Rae refused to meet the Cree leaders. Subsequent efforts to open negotiations ended in failure because there was no way to get a message to Poundmaker, and after

Colonel Otter's attack on the Cree camp any thought of negotiations was dropped.[92]

Publicly Dewdney proclaimed that the Cree were part of the Metis uprising. He issued a proclamation that any Indian who left his reserve was to be regarded as a rebel.[93] As well, to intimidate Piapot and the Treaty 4 Cree, Dewdney stationed troops on their reserves. To prevent an alliance of Blackfoot and Cree, Dewdney announced that he was stationing troops at Swift Current and Medicine Hat. Dewdney took these steps, as he confided to Macdonald, because he feared that the Cree might still attempt to take action on their own cause, and he was concerned because in the previous year the Cree had attempted to enlist the Blackfoot in the movement to revise the treaties.[94]

The military commander in the North-West, General F.D. Middleton, was not as concerned about the problems with the Cree. He wanted to concentrate his attention on the Metis. Although he did send troops under Colonel William Otter to Swift Current, he refused to order them to Battleford to lift the alleged siege until he received word of the Frog Lake massacre. Otter was then ordered to lift the "siege" and protect Battleford from Indian attack, but he was not to take the offensive. At the same time General Thomas Strange was ordered to bring Big Bear under control.

Otter reached Battleford without seeing an Indian. He was upset that he and his troops would not see action. He therefore proposed that he attack the Indian camp at Poundmaker's Reserve. Middleton vetoed the plan, but Dewdney welcomed it as a means to bring the Cree under government control. Taking the Lieutenant-Governor's approval to be paramount to Middleton's veto, Otter launched his attack. The engagement, known as the Battle of Cut Knife Hill, almost ended in total disaster for Otter's force. Only the Cree fear that they would suffer the same fate as Sitting Bull after the Battle of the Little Big Horn saved Otter's troops from total annihilation.[95]

The tale of the subsequent military campaigns against the Cree by Strange and Middleton and the voluntary surrenders of Poundmaker and Big Bear is found in detail in Stanley's *Birth of Western Canada* and Desmond Morton's *The Last War Drum*. With Big Bear and Poundmaker in custody, Dewdney prepared to use the courts in the manner he had planned before the Riel Rebellion. Both Cree leaders were charged with treason-felony, despite Dewdney's knowledge that neither man had engaged in an act of rebellion. Eyewitnesses to the events at Fort Pitt, Frog Lake, and Battleford all made clear that neither chief was involved in the murders and looting that had occurred. In fact, many of these people served as defence witnesses.[96] As Dewdney informed the Prime Minister, the diaries and letters of the murdered officials at Frog Lake showed that until the day of the "massacre" there was "no reason to believe that our Indians were even dissatisfied much less contemplated violence."[97] Ballendine's reports indicated that there were no plans for violence, that the Cree were not involved with the Metis, and that they planned no rebellion. Dewdney believed that the Cree had not "even thought, intended or wished that the uprising would reach the proportion it has. . . . Things just got out of control."[98] As Dewdney related to the Prime Minister, had the people living in the region not been new settlers from the East, and had they not fled in panic, much of the "raiding" and looting would not have occurred. In regions where people had not abandoned their homes no raiding occurred.[99] Therefore, the charges against Big Bear and Poundmaker were designed to remove the leadership of the Cree movement for revision of the treaties. They were charged to elicit prison sentences that would have the effect of coercing the Cree to accept government control. The trials were conducted to have the desired result, and both Big Bear and Poundmaker were convicted and sentenced to three years in Stoney Mountain Penitentiary.[100] Neither man served his full term, and both died a short time after their release from prison.

By the end of 1885, Dewdney had succeeded in subjugating the Cree. Big Bear was in prison, Little Pine was dead, and Piapot was intimidated by having troops stationed on his reserve. Dewdney had deprived the Cree of their principal leaders and of their autonomy. He used the military to disarm and impoverish the Cree by confiscating their horses and carts; he increased the size of the Mounted Police force, and used the police to arrest Cree leaders who protested against his policies; he broke up Cree Bands, deposed Cree leaders, and forbade any Indian to be off his reserve without permission from the Indian Agent.[101] By 1890, through vigorous implementation of the Indian Act, Dewdney and his successor, Hayter Reed, had begun the process of making the Cree an administered people.

The record of the Canadian government in dealing with the Cree is thus not one of honourable fair-mindedness and justice as the traditional interpretation portrays. As Dewdney admitted in 1885, the treaties' promises and provisions were not being fulfilled, and Dewdney himself had taken steps to assure Canadian control over the Cree, which were themselves violations of the treaties. Thus, he had refused to grant the Cree the reserve sites they selected; he had refused to distribute the ammunition and twine the treaties required. His plans for dealing with the Cree leaders were based on a political use of the legal and judicial system, and ultimately he made use of the military, the police, and the courts in a political manner to achieve his goal of subjugating the Cree. Only by ignoring these facts can one continue to perpetuate the myth of Canada's just and honourable Indian policy from 1870 to 1885.

NOTES

1. Douglas Owram, *Promise of Eden: The Canadian Expansionist Movement and the Idea of the West, 1856–1900* (Toronto, 1980), 131–34.

2. G.F.G. Stanley, *The Birth of Western Canada: A History of the Riel Rebellions* (Toronto, 1960).

3. Ibid., 206–15.

4. Ibid., vii–viii, 196, 216–36. It should be noted that the traditional interpretation of a Cree rebellion in association with the Metis has been challenged by R. Allen, "Big Bear," *Saskatchewan History* 25 (1972); W.B.

Fraser, "Big Bear, Indian Patriot," *Alberta Historical Review* 14 (1966): 1–13; Rudy Wiebe in his fictional biography, *The Temptations of Big Bear* (Toronto, 1973) and in his biography of Big Bear in the *Dictionary of Canadian Biography* (hereafter DCB), vol. 11, 1881–90 (Toronto, 1982), 597–601; and Norma Sluman, *Poundmaker* (Toronto, 1967). However, none of these authors deals with Canada's Indian policy, and none examines what the Cree were doing in the period 1876–85.

5. Alexander Morris, *The Treaties of Canada with the Indians of Manitoba and the North-West Territories* (Toronto, 1880), 37; Public Archives of Manitoba (hereafter PAM), Adams G. Archibald Papers.

6. Public Archives of Canada (hereafter PAC), Indian Affairs Files, RG 10, vol. 3571, file 124–2; also vol. 3606, file 2036. See also Morris, *Treaties of Canada*, 25–43 and 126–27, for a printed account of the negotiations and the texts of the original and renegotiated treaties, 313–20, 338–42. Two articles by John Taylor, "Canada's Northwest Indian Policy in the 1870s: Traditional Premises and Necessary Innovations" and "Two Views on the Meaning of Treaties Six and Seven" in *The Spirit of Alberta Indian Treaties*, ed. Richard E. Price (Montreal, 1980), 3–7 and 9–45 respectively, provide a good account of the Indian contribution and attitude towards the treaties.

7. Morris, *Treaties of Canada*, 44–76; on 120–23 Morris demonstrates how he had to make Treaty 3 the model for the Qu'Appelle Treaty to get the Saulteaux and Cree of the Qu'Appelle River region to accept what he originally offered them. Compare Treaties 1–6 to see what the government was forced to concede. Also see Taylor's "Traditional Premises" for Indian contributions to the negotiation process.

8. PAC, RG 10, vol. 3586, file 1137, Lieutenant-Governor Morris to Secretary of State for the provinces,

13 Sept. 1872; vol. 3576, file 378, entire file; vol. 3609, file 3229; vol. 3604, file 2543; vol., 3636, 6694–1.

9. PAC, RG 10, vol. 3612, file 4012, entire file; PAM, Archibald Papers, W.J. Christie to George W. Hill, 26 April 1871; Archibald to Secretary of State for the Provinces, 5 Jan. 1872; also letters in note 15; William Francis Butler, *The Great Lone Land* (Rutland, VT, 1970), 360–62, 368; PAC, MG 26A, John A. Macdonald Papers, vol. 104, entire volume; PAM, Archibald Papers, Joseph Howe to Archibald, 30 June 1872; PAM, Alexander Morris Papers, Lt Governor's Collection, Morris to Minister of the Interior, 7 July 1873; PAC, RG 10, vol. 3625, file 5366, Morris to Minister of the Interior, David Laird, 22 July and 4 Aug. 1875; vol. 3624, file 5152, Colonel French, Commissioner of the NWMP to the Minister of Justice, 6 and 19 Aug. 1875; Morris, *Treaties of Canada*, 170–71; PAC, RG 10, vol. 3612, file 4012, entire file; PAM, Adams G. Archibald Papers, Petition of James Seenum to Archibald, 9 Jan. 1871, and attached letters of Kehewin, Little Hunter, and Kiskion; Archibald to Secretary of State for the provinces, 5 Jan. 1872.

10. Two excellent studies of the Cree in the pre-1870 era are those by Arthur J. Ray, *Indians in the Fur Trade: Their Role as Hunters, Trappers, and Middlemen in the Lands Southwest of Hudson Bay 1660–1870* (Toronto, 1974), and David G. Mandelbaum, *The Plans Cree*, vol. 37, Anthropological Papers of the American Museum of Natural History, Pt 2 (New York, 1940).

11. Ibid. An excellent study of the Cree expansion is the unpublished MA thesis by John S. Milloy, "The Plains Cree: A Preliminary Trade and Military Chronology, 1670–1870" (Carleton University, 1972); also Henry John Moberly and William B. Cameron, *When Fur Was King* (Toronto, 1929), 208–12, describes part of the last phase of this movement. The shrinking

range of buffalo and how the Cree reacted are also discussed in Frank Gilbert Roe, *The North American Buffalo: A Critical Study of the Species in Its Wild State* (Toronto, 1951), 282–333.

12. Henry Youle Hind, *Narrative of the Canadian Red River Exploring Expedition of 1857 and of the Assiniboine and Saskatchewan Exploring Expedition of 1858* (Edmonton, 1971), 1:334; Irene Spry, *The Palliser Expedition: An Account of John Palliser's British North American Expedition, 1857–1860* (London, 1964), 598–60; Viscount Milton and W.B. Cheadle, *The Northwest Passage by Land, Being the Narrative of an Expedition from the Atlantic to the Pacific* (Toronto, 1970), 66–67; Edwin Thompson Perry, *Five Indian Tribes of the Upper Missouri: Sioux, Arickaras, Assiniboine, Crees, Crow* (Norman, OK, 1969), 99–137; J. Hines, *The Red Indians of the Plains: Thirty Years' Missionary Experience in Saskatchewan* (Toronto, 1916), 78–80, 88–91.

13. Morris, *Treaties of Canada*, 77–123 and 168–239, discusses the negotiations of Treaties 4 and 6 with the Cree and how he was forced to modify his offer. Also described is the Cree concern about their land. The reaction of the Mackenzie government is detailed in PAC, RG 10, vol. 3636, file 6694-2 and in particular, Minister of the Interior Report to Privy Council, 31 Jan. 1877 and order-in-council, 10 Feb. 1877.

14. Milloy, "The Plains Cree," 250–62; Alexander Johnson, *The Battle at Belly River: Stories of the Last Great Indian Battle* (Lethbridge, 1966).

15. Hind, *Narrative*, 1:334, 360–61, carries reports of Mistickoos or Short Stick's comments on a council of Cree leaders that resolved to limit white and Metis hunting privileges. Viscount Milton and W.B. Cheadle, *The Northwest Passage by Land*, 66, 67, contains comments on the Cree determination to limit non-Indian involvement in the hunt. PAM, Adams G. Archibald Papers, letter no. 200, Macdonald to Archibald,

14 Feb. 1871; letter no. 170, English halfbreeds to Archibald, 10 Jan. 1871, all stress that Cree were taking action to limit non-Indian involvement in the buffalo hunt.

16. Morris, *Treaties of Canada*, 241.

17. Interview with Walter Gordon, Director of the Indian Rights and Treaties Program, Federation of Saskatchewan Indians, March 1974. Poundmaker made a similar statement in an interview quoted in "Indian Affairs," *Saskatchewan Herald*, 2 Aug. 1880. The importance of Big Bear, Piapot, and Little Pine cannot be underestimated, for of those Cree chiefs who took treaty only Sweetgrass had the standing of these men, and Sweetgrass died within a few months of taking treaty.

18. Morris, *Treaties of Canada*, 84–87. More detailed information on the adhesions of Piapot and Cheekuk is to be found in PAC, RG 10, vol. 3625, file 5489, W.J. Christie to Laird, 7 Oct. 1875.

19. Morris, *Treaties of Canada*, 240. See 355 for the clauses in Treaty 6 respecting acceptance of Canadian laws.

20. Ibid., 174.

21. Fraser, "Big Bear, Indian Patriot," 76–77 agrees that Big Bear was not referring specifically to hanging but to the effect the treaty would have on the Cree.

22. PAC, RG 10, vol. 3656, file 9093, Agent Dickieson to Lt-Gov. Laird, 14 Sept. 1877.

23. PAC, RG 10, vol. 3648, file 8380; vol. 3655, file 9000, Laird to Minister of the Interior, 9 May 1878.

24. PAC, RG 10, vol. 3655, file 9000, Laird to Minister of the Interior, 9 May 1878; vol. 3636, file 9092, Laird to Superintendent-General, 19 Nov. 1877; vol. 3670, file 10771, Laird to Minister of the Interior, 12 Nov. 1878; vol. 3672, file 10853, Dickieson to Meredith, 2 April 1878; vol. 3656, file 9092, Inspector

James Walker to Laird, 5 Sept. 1877; Department of Indian Affairs and Northern Development (hereafter DIAND), Ottawa, file 1/1-11-3, Laird to Minister of the Interior, 30 Dec. 1878; Dickieson to Laird, 9 Oct. 1878; Walker to Laird, 4 and 26 Feb. 1879.

25. PAC, RG 10, vol. 3655, file 1002, Laird to Minister of the Interior, 9 May 1878; vol. 3672, file 19853, Dickieson to Vankoughnet, 26 July 1878; PAC, MG 26A, E.D. Clark to Fred White, 16 July 1879.

26. "News from the Plains," *Saskatchewan Herald*, 18 Nov. 1878; "From the Plains," *Saskatchewan Herald*, 5 May 1879; "Contradictory News from the West," *Fort Benton Record*, 31 Jan. 1879.

27. PAC, RG 10, vol. 3672, file 10853, M.G. Dickieson to Vankoughnet, 26 July 1878; *Opening Up the West: Being the Official Reports to Parliament of the North-West Mounted Police from 1874–1881* (Toronto, 1973), Report for 1878, 21.

28. PAC, RG 10, vol. 3704, file 17858, entire file; vol. 3648, file 162-2, entire file; vol. 3699, file 16580, order-in-council, 9 Oct. 1879; vol. 3766, file 22541; E.T. Galt to Superintendent-General of Indian Affairs, 27 July 1880; vol. 3730, file 26279, entire file; vol. 3757, file 21397, entire file.

29. House of Commons, *Sessional Papers*, 1885, vol. 17, report no. 3, 157; Edward Ahenakew, *Voices of the Plains Cree*, ed. Ruth Buck (Toronto, 1973), 26. Dewdney in adopting this tactic simply copied what the fur-trading companies had done in the past. The Cree tolerated such practices because they improved the opportunities to have better access to European goods. See Arthur J. Ray and Donald Freeman, *"Give Us Good Measure": An Economic Analysis of Relations between the Indians and the Hudson's Bay Company before 1763* (Toronto, 1978), passim. Ray, *Indians in the Fur Trade*, passim, deals with the same practice in the post-1763

period. Mandelbaum, *The Plains Cree*, 105–10 discusses the nature of Cree political organization and leadership that explains their acceptance of such practices.

30. Morris, *Treaties of Canada*, 366–67. DIAND, Treaty Annuity Pay Sheets for 1879. More than 1000 Plains Cree took treaty for the first time in 1879 under Little Pine, Thunderchild, and Lucky Man. Others from Little Pine's and Big Bear's bands had already taken treaty a year earlier as part of Thunder Companion's band, while others joined Poundmaker, and the three Cree bands settled in the Peace Hills. A portion of the Assiniboine also took treaty under Mosquito in 1878, while many of the northern Saulteaux who had followed Yellow Sky took treaty in 1878 under the leadership of Moosomin.

31. PAC, RG 10, vol. 3745, file 29506-4, vol. 2, Ray to Reed, 23 April 1883; vol. 3668, file 9644, Reed to Commissioner, 23 Dec. 1883. Although these materials refer to events in the Battleford district, as will be demonstrated, the tactics in 1883–84 were similar, if not exactly the same as those used in the Cypress Hills between 1879 and 1882. That they were not better recorded for the earlier period is due to the fact that the government had fewer men working with the Indians, and did not have as effective supervision in the 1879–82 period as it did at Battleford. Also much of the police and Indian Affairs material relating to this region in the 1879–82 period has been lost or destroyed.

32. PAC, RG 10, vol. 3730, file 36279, entire file; vol. 3668, file 10440, Agent Allen to L. Vankoughnet, 11 Nov. 1878; *Sessional Papers*, 1883, vol. 16, no. 5, 197; *Settlers and Rebels: Being the Reports to Parliament of the Activities of the Royal North-West Mounted Police Force from 1882–1885* (Toronto, 1973), Report for 1882, 4–6.

33. PAC, RG 10, vol. 3730, file 26219, Report of surveyor Patrick to

Superintendent-General, 16 Dec. 1880; vol. 3716, file 22546, Assistant Commissioner E.T. Galt to Superintendent-General, 27 July 1880; vol. 3757, files 31393 and 31333; vol. 3757, file 20034; PAC, MG 26A, vol. 210, Dewdney to Macdonald, 3 Oct. 1880.

34. PAC, RG 10, vol. 3652, file 8589, parts 1 and 2, entire file; vol. 3691, file 13893, entire file. *The Benton Weekly Record* throughout the spring and summer of 1880 carried reports of Cree and Assinboine horse-stealing raids, and reports of what the Cree were doing in Montana. On 7 May 1880, the paper carried an article entitled "Starving Indians," which was a strong denunciation of Canada's Indian policy and the effect it had on the Cree.

35. PAC, MG 26A, vol. 210, Dewdney to Macdonald, 29 Oct. 1880; *Saskatchewan Herald*, 14 Feb. 1881.

36. PAC, MG 26A, vol. 210, Dewdney to Macdonald, 26 Oct. 1880 and 23 April 1880; *Saskatchewan Herald*, 14, 28 Feb. 1881.

37. PAC, MG 26A, vol. 210, Dewdney to MacPherson, 4 July 1881; vol. 247, Galt to MacPherson, 14 July 1881; "Edmonton," *Saskatchewan Herald*, 12 Nov. 1881.

38. Ibid., also PAC, MG 26A, vol. 210, Dewdney to Macdonald, 19 June 1881; vol. 247, Galt to Vankoughnet, 16 July 1881; PAC, RG 10, vol. 3739; file 28748-1, Dewdney to Macdonald, 3 April 1882; Fred White to Minister of the Interior, 9 June 1882; Freylinghausen to Sackville-West, 9 June 1882. *Saskatchewan Herald*, 1 Aug. 1881; "Starving Indians," *Benton Weekly Record*, 14 July 1881; 25 August, 1 Sept., and 13 Oct. 1881.

39. PAC, RG 10, vol. 3739, file 28478-1, C.G. Denny to Commissioner, 24 Oct. 1881; vol. 3768, file 33642; vol. 3603, file 20141, McIlree to Dewdney, 21 June 1882; Glenbow Institute, Calgary, Edgar Dewdney Papers, vol. 5, file 57, Irvine to Dewdney, 24 June 1882; *Saskatchewan Herald*, 24 June 1882; *Edmonton Bulletin*, 17 June 1882.

40. PAC, RG 10, vol. 3768, file 33642, entire file.

41. PAC, MG 26A, vol. 210, Dewdney to Macdonald, 19 June 1881; vol. 247, Galt to Vankoughnet, 16 July 1881. *Saskatchewan Herald*, 1 Aug. 1881; "Starving Indians," *Benton Weekly Record*, 14 July 1881. See also *Benton Weekly Record*, 25 Aug., 1 Sept., and 13 Oct. 1881.

42. Morris, *Treaties of Canada*, 205, 218, 352–53.

43. PAC, RG 10, vol. 3604, file 2589, entire file. See also *Settlers and Rebels*, 1882 Report. See also Glenbow, Dewdney Papers, vol. 5, file 57, White to Irvine, 29 Aug. 1882; RG 10, vol. 3604, file 2589; "The Repatriated Indians," *Saskatchewan Herald*, 5 Aug. 1882; "From the South," *Saskatchewan Herald*, 21 May 1882; "Back on the Grub Pile," *Saskatchewan Herald*, 24 June 1882.

44. Glenbow, Dewdney Papers, vol. 5, file 57, Irvine to Dewdney, 24 June 1882 and 25 Sept. 1882; *Settlers and Rebels*, 1882 Report, 4, 5; *Sessional Papers*, 1883, vol. 16, no. 5, 197; PAC, RG 10, vol. 3604, file 2589; "Repatriated Indians," *Saskatchewan Herald*, 5 Aug. 1882.

45. "Repatriated Indians," *Saskatchewan Herald*, 5 Aug. 1882; Glenbow, Dewdney Papers, vol. 4, file 45, White to Dewdney, 12 Oct. 1882; *Saskatchewan Herald*, 14 Oct. 1882; "Big Bear and Others," and the "I.D.," *Edmonton Bulletin*, 21 Oct. 1882.

46. Glenbow, Dewdney Papers, vol. 4, file 45, White to Dewdney, 17 Oct. 1882; PAC, MG 26A, vol. 289, Vankoughnet to Macdonald, 2 Nov. 1882.

47. PAC, MG 26A, vol. 11, Dewdney to J.A. Macdonald, 2 Sept. 1883; PAC, RG 10, vol. 3682, file 12667, Dewdney to Superintendent-General, 28 April 1884.

48. PAC, RG 10, vol. 3668, file 10644, Reed to Commissioner, 23 Dec. 1883; Robert Jefferson, *Fifty Years on the Saskatchewan* (Battleford, 1929), 103.

49. PAC, RG 10, vol. 3668, file 10644, Reed to Commissioner, 23 Dec. 1883; *Edmonton Bulletin*, 9 Feb. 1884; *Saskatchewan Herald*, 24 Nov. 1883.

50. PAC, MG 26A, vol. 289, Vankoughnet to Macdonald, 4, 10 Dec. 1883; vol. 104, Deputy Superintendent-General, 27 Sept. 1883; Deputy Superintendent-General to Reed, 10 April 1884; vol. 212, Dewdney to Macdonald, 2 Jan. 1883 [sic! Given the contents of the letter, it is obvious Dewdney forgot that a new year had begun the previous day]; vol. 91, Dewdney to Macdonald, 24 July 1884; another letter but without a date, which was probably written in the first week of Aug. 1884; vol. 107, entire file; PAC, RG 10, vol. 3664, file 9843, entire file.

51. PAC, RG 10, vol. 3616, file 10181; Burton Deane, *Mounted Police Life in Canada: A Record of Thirty-One Years in Service, 1883–1914* (Toronto, 1973), 140–53; Isabell Andrews, "Indian Protest against Starvation: The Yellow Calf Incident of 1884," *Saskatchewan History* 28 (1975): 4–52; *Edmonton Bulletin*, 7 Jan., 3 Feb., 28 July, and 4 Aug. 1883.

52. Glenbow, Dewdney Papers, vol. 5, file 58, Dewdney to Superintendent-General, 29 Feb. 1884; PAC, MG 26A, vol. 211, Dewdney to Macdonald, 6 Oct. 1883; vol. 212, Reed to Dewdney, 15 Feb. 1884; Dewdney to Macdonald, 16 Feb. and 9 April 1884.

53. PAC, RG 10, vol. 3682, file 12667, Dewdney to Superintendent-General, 28 April 1884; vol. 3686, file 13168, entire file; vol. 3745, file 29506-4(2), Reed to Colonel Irvine, 18 May 1884.

54. PAC, RG 10, vol. 3745, file 29506-4(2), Reed to Irvine, 18 May 1884; Irvine to Comptroller Fred White, 27 May 1884; White to Vankoughnet, 19 May 1884.

55. PAC, RG 10, vol. 3745, file 29506-4(2), Agent Macdonald to Commissioner, 29 May 1884; vol. 3655, file 9026, Dewdney to Superintendent-General, 13 June 1884.

56. PAC, RG 10, vol. 3745, file 29506-4(2), Reed to Superintendent-General, 19 April 1884. Similar report in vol. 3576, file 309B. PAC, MG 26A, file 37, Dewdney to Macdonald, 3 May 1884. Dewdney's request and actions were contrary to what the Cree had been told about how reserve sites could be chosen, as were the government's actions in denying the Cree reserves in the Cypress Hills and forcing them to move north. See Morris, *Treaties of Canada*, passim; PAC, RG 10, vol. 3576, file 309B, Vankoughnet to Dewdney, 10 May 1884; MG 26A, vol. 104, Dewdney to Superintendent-General, 14 June 1884. Campbell Innes, "Fine Day Interview," *The Cree Rebellion of 1884: Sidelights of Indian Conditions Subsequent to 1876* (Battleford, 1926), 13–15; *Saskatchewan Herald*, 19 April and 17 May 1884.

57. PAC, RG 10, vol. 3576, file 309B, Reed to Superintendent-General, 19 April 1884; Reed to Vankoughnet, 19 April 1884; Ray to Commissioner, 23 April 1884; Reed to Superintendent-General, 20 May 1884; Glenbow, Dewdney Papers, vol. 3, file 36, Dewdney to Macdonald, 12 June 1884.

58. PAC, RG 10, vol. 3576, file 309B, Ray to Commissioner, 19, 21 June 1884; Crozier to Dewdney, 22 June 1884; Jefferson, *Fifty Years on the Saskatchewan*, 108–9; Innes, *The Cree Rebellion of 1884*, 13–17, 28.

59. PAC, RG 10, vol. 3576, file 309B, Ray to Commissioner, 28 June 1884; see also Rae to Dewdney, 9 June 1884; Innes, "McKay Interview," 44; PAC, RG 10, vol. 3576, file 309A, Dewdney to Ray, 5 July 1884.

60. PAC, RG 10, vol. 3576, file 309B, Ray to Dewdney, 23 June 1884; Crozier to Dewdney, 23 June 1884.

61. Glenbow, Dewdney Papers, vol. 3, file 37, Macdonald to Dewdney, 18 July 1884, 11 Aug. 1884, and 2 Sept. 1884; vol. 4, file 45, Macdonald to White, 15 Sept. 1884; PAC, RG 10, vol. 3576, file 309A, Vankoughnet to Dewdney, 27 July 1884.

62. PAC, RG 10, vol. 3576, file 309B, Ray to Commissioner, 30 June 1884; file 309A, Ray to Commissioner, 24, 29 July 1884; PAC, MG 26A, vol. 212, Dewdney to Macdonald, 14 July 1884 and J.A. MacRae to Commissioner, 7 Aug. 1884; vol. 107, Ray to Commissioner, 29 July 1884.

63. PAC, RG 10, vol. 3745, file 29506-4(2), Dewdney to Superintendent-General, 7 August 1884; vol. 3576, file 309A, Ray to Dewdney, 19 July 1884; PAC, MG 26A, vol. 104, Dewdney to Department, 19 July 1884.

64. PAC, RG 10, vol. 3576, file 309B, Ray to Commissioner, 30 June 1884; file 309A, Ray to Commissioner, 24, 29 July 1884; PAC, MG 26A, vol. 212, Dewdney to Macdonald, 14 July 1884; J.A. MacRae to Commissioner, 7 Aug. 1884; vol. 107, Ray to Commissioner, 29 July 1884.

65. PAC, MG 26A, vol. 107, Ray to Commissioner, 29 July and 2 Aug. 1884; J.A. MacRae to Commissioner, 29 July 1884.

66. PAC, RG 10, vol. 3697, file 15423, J.A. MacRae to Dewdney, 25 Aug. 1884.

67. PAC, RG 10, vol. 3697, file 15423, Reed to Superintendent-General, 23 Jan. 1885; Reed to Dewdney, 22, 25 Aug. 1884; PAC, MG 26A, vol. 107, J.A. MacRae to Commissioner, 29 July 1884; J.M. Ray to Commissioner, 2 Aug. 1884; MacRae to Commissioner, 5 Aug. 1884; vol. 212, MacRae to Commissioner, 7 Aug. 1884; PAC, RG 10, vol. 3756, file 309A, J.M. Ray

to Commissioner, 24, 25 July 1884; "Big Bear Rises to Speak," *Saskatchewan Herald*, 5 Aug. 1882; *Saskatchewan Herald*, 25 July, and 9 Aug. 1884.

68. PAC, RG 10, vol. 3576, file 309A, Commissioner to Ray, 7 Aug. 1884; Ray to Commissioner, 29 July 1884; see also in PAC, MG 26A, vol. 107; Glenbow, Dewdney Papers, vol. 6, file 69, Crozier to Comptroller, NWMP, 27 July 1884; PAC, MG 26A, vol. 212, Dewdney to Macdonald, 8 Aug. 1884.

69. PAC, MG 26A, vol. 107, Reed to Dewdney, 23, 24, 25 Aug., 4 Sept. 1884; Dewdney to Macdonald, 5 Sept. 1884.

70. PAC, RG 10, vol. 3576, file 309A, Begg to Commissioner, 20 Feb. 1885; "Indian Affairs," *Saskatchewan Herald*, 31 Oct. 1884.

71. Glenbow, Dewdney Papers, vol. 6, file 66, Reed to Dewdney, 4 Sept. 1884.

72. Statutes of Canada, 43 Vict., 27, "An Act to Amend the Indian Act, 1880," 12 April 1884; PAC, MG 26A, vol. 107, Dewdney to Macdonald, 24 Aug. 1884.

73. PAC, MG 26A, vol. 212, Reed to Dewdney, 7 Sept. 1884; vol. 107, Dewdney to Macdonald, 24 Aug. 1884.

74. PAC, RG 10, vol. 3576, file 309A, Reed to Dewdney, 12 Sept. 1884; vol. 3745, file 29506-4(2), Reed to Dewdney, 14 Sept. 1884; vol. 3704, file 17799, entire file; vol. 3664, file 9834 and 9843; vol. 3761, file 30836, entire file; Glenbow, Dewdney Papers, vol. 4, file 45, Reed to Dewdney, 12 Sept. 1884; vol. 4, file 47, Crozier to Comptroller, NWMP, 4 Nov. 1884; vol. 5, file 57, Crozier to Dewdney, 30 Jan. 1885.

75. PAC, RG 10, vol. 3582, file 749, Ballendine to Reed, 8 Nov. and 26 Dec. 1884.

76. PAC, RG 10, vol. 3582, file 949, P. Ballendine to Reed, 20 Nov., 26 Dec., 2 Jan. 1885; J.M. Ray to

Commissioner, 27 Dec. 1884; Crozier to Commissioner, NWMP, 14 Jan. 1885; vol. 3576, file 309A, Magnus Begg to Dewdney, 20 Feb. 1885; PAC, MG 26A, extract of Ray to Dewdney, 24 Jan. 1885. Ray, Ballendine, and Crozier when they reported on Little Pine mentioned that their principal source of information was Poundmaker, although Ballendine did get some of his information directly from Little Pine himself.

77. PAC, RG 10, vol. 3582, file 949, Ballendine to Reed, 10 Oct., and 26 Dec. 1884, and 2 Jan. and 16 March 1885; Ballendine to Dewdney, 19 March 1885; PAC, MG 26A, vol. 107, extract of Ray to Dewdney, 24 Jan. 1885. PAC, MG 271C4, Edgar Dewdney Papers, vol. 2, Francis Dickens to Officer Commanding, Battleford, 27 Oct. 1884.

78. PAC, MG 26A, vol. 117, Dewdney to Macdonald, 9 Feb. 1885; PAC, RG 10, vol. 3676, file 309A, Dewdney to Vankoughnet, 12 Feb. 1885.

79. PAC, RG 10, vol. 3705, file 17193, Vankoughnet to Dewdney, 5 Feb. 1885; Vankoughnet to Macdonald, 31 Jan. 1885; vol. 3582, file 949, Vankoughnet to Reed, 28 Jan. 1885; Glenbow, Dewdney Papers, vol. 3, file 38, Macdonald to Dewdney, 23 Feb. 1885.

80. PAC, RG 10, vol. 3576, file 309A, Dewdney to Vankoughnet, 12 Feb. 1885.

81. Jefferson, Fifty Years on the Saskatchewan, 125.

82. Ibid., 126–28; PAC, MG 26A, deposition, William Lightfoot to J.A. MacKay, 31 May 1885.

83. Jefferson, Fifty Years on the Saskatchewan, 127, 130, 138.

84. Innes, "Fine Day Interview," 185; Sluman, Poundmaker, 199–200, 184–85; Jefferson, Fifty Years on the Saskatchewan, 130–38.

85. Desmond Morton, The Last War Drum (Toronto, 1972), 98–102;

86. PAC, RG 10, vol. 3755, file 30973, Reed to Commissioner, 18 June 1881; see also material cited in note 72 above. William B. Cameron, Blood Red the Sun (Edmonton, 1977), 33–61, vividly describes the slaughter at Frog Lake.

87. Cameron, Blood Red the Sun, passim.

88. Charles Mulvaney, The History of the North-West Rebellion of 1885 (Toronto, 1885), 212–16; Settlers and Rebels, 1882 Report, 22, 26–27; PAC, RG 10, vol. 3584, file 1130, 1, Superintendent Herchmer to Dewdney, 5 April 1885.

89. Ibid.

90. PAC, RG 10, vol. 3697, file 15446, entire file; vol. 3598, file 1411, entire file; vol. 7768, file 2109-2; vol. 3794, file 46584.

91. PAC, MG 271C4, vol. 7, letters, Dewdney to White, March–April 1885. This correspondence reveals that in early April Dewdney believed that he had to deal with an Indian uprising. However, he did admit that this impression was based on scanty and often faulty or false information. By mid-April, Dewdney makes clear to White, the NWMP Comptroller, that he did not believe that he was dealing with either an Indian uprising or a rebellion.

92. PAC, MG 271C4, vol. 1, Dewdney to Begg, 3 May 1885; vol. 4, Dewdney to Middleton, 30 March 1885; RG 10, vol. 3584, file 1130, Dewdney to Ray, 7 May 1885; Jefferson, Fifty Years on the Saskatchewan, 128–33.

93. PAC, RG 10, vol. 3584, file 1120, Proclamation of 6 May 1885.

94. PAC, MG 26A, vol. 107, Dewdney to Macdonald, 6 April 1885.

95. Morton, The Last War Drum, 96–110.

96. Cameron, Blood Red the Sun, 195–204. Sandra Estlin Bingman,

"The Trials of Poundmaker and Big Bear," *Saskatchewan History* 28 (1975): 81–95, gives an account of the conduct of the trials and raises questions about their conduct, particularly the trial of Big Bear. However, Bingman apparently was unaware of Dewdney and Macdonald's efforts to use the courts and whatever other means possible to remove Cree leaders.

97. PAC, MG 26A, vol. 107, Dewdney to Macdonald, 3 June 1885.

98. Ibid.

99. Ibid.

100. Bingman, "The Trials of Poundmaker and Big Bear," 81–95.

101. A very good account of Dewdney's actions to bring the Cree under government control after 1885 is to be found in Jean Lamour, "Edgar Dewdney and the Aftermath of the Rebellion," *Saskatchewan History* 23 (1970): 105–16. For a discussion of the use of the Indian Act as a means of destroying Indian cultural autonomy see John L. Tobias, "Protection, Civilization, Assimilation: An Outline History of Canada's Indian Policy," *The Western Canadian Journal of Anthropology* 6 (1976). For a discussion of specific use of this policy against the Cree, and how the Cree reacted see John L. Tobias, "Indian Reserves in Western Canada: Indian Homelands or Devices for Assimilation" in *Approaches to Native History in Canada: Papers of a Conference held at the National Museum of Man, October, 1975*, ed. D.A. Muise (Ottawa, 1977), 89–103.

CATEGORIES AND TERRAINS OF EXCLUSION: CONSTRUCTING THE "INDIAN WOMAN" IN THE EARLY SETTLEMENT ERA IN WESTERN CANADA ✧

SARAH CARTER

○

In 1884 Mary E. Inderwick wrote to her Ontario family from the ranch near Pincher Creek, Alberta, where she had lived with her new husband for six months.[1] The letter provides a perspective on the stratifications of race, gender, and class that were forming as the Euro-Canadian enclave grew in the district of Alberta. Mary Inderwick lamented that it was a lonely life, as she was twenty-two miles from any other women, and she even offered to help some of the men near them to "get their shacks done up if only they will go east and marry some really nice girls." She did not consider the companionship of women such as "the squaw who is the nominal wife of a white man near us," and she had dismissed her maid, who had become discontented with her position as a servant. Inderwick had disapproved of a ball at the North-West Mounted Police (NWMP) barracks at Fort Macleod, despite the fact that it was "the first Ball to which the squaws were not allowed to go, but there were several half breeds." Commenting on the Aboriginal population that still greatly outnumbered the new arrivals, Inderwick wrote that they should have been "isolated in the mountains," rather than settled on nearby reserves, and that the sooner they became extinct the better for themselves and the country.

At the time of Mary Inderwick's arrival in the West the consolidation of Canada's rule was not yet secure. The Metis resistance of 1885 fed fears of a larger uprising, and an uncertain economic climate threatened the promise of a prosperous West. There was a sharpening of racial boundaries and categories in the 1880s and an intensification of discrimination in the Canadian

---

✧ Reprinted with permission from *Great Plains Quarterly* 13 (Summer 1993): 147–61.

West. The arrival of women immigrants like Mary Inderwick after the Canadian Pacific Railway was completed through Alberta in 1883 coincided with other developments such as the railway itself, the treaties, and the development of ranching and farming that were to stabilize the new order and allow the recreation of Euro-Canadian institutions and society. The women did not introduce notions of spatial and social segregation, but their presence helped to justify policies already in motion that segregated the new community from indigenous contacts.[2] The Canadian state adopted increasingly segregationist policies toward the Aboriginal people of the West, and central to these policies were images of Aboriginal women as dissolute, dangerous, and sinister.

From the earliest years that people were settled on reserves in western Canada, Canadian government administrators and statesmen, as well as the national press, promoted a cluster of negative images of Aboriginal women. Those in power used these images to explain conditions of poverty and ill-health on reserves. The failure of agriculture on reserves was attributed to the incapacity of Aboriginal men to become other than hunters, warriors, and nomads.[3] Responsibility for a host of other problems, including the deplorable state of housing on reserves, the lack of clothing and footwear, and the high mortality rate, was placed upon the supposed cultural traits and temperament of Aboriginal women. The depiction of these women as lewd and licentious, particularly after 1885, was used to deflect criticism from the behavior of government officials and the NWMP and to legitimize the constraints placed on the activities and movements of Aboriginal women in the world off the reserve. These negative images became deeply embedded in the consciousness of the most powerful socio-economic groups on the Prairies and have resisted revision.

The images were neither new nor unique to the Canadian West. In "The Pocahontas Perplex" Rayna Green explored the complex, many-faceted dimensions of the image of the Indian woman in American folklore and literature. The beautiful "Indian Princess" who saved or aided white men while remaining aloof and virtuous in a woodland paradise was the positive side of the image. Her opposite, the squalid and immoral "Squaw," lived in a shack at the edge of town, and her "physical removal or destruction can be understood as necessary to the progress of civilization."[4] The "Squaw" was pressed into service and her image predominated in the Canadian West in the late nineteenth century, as boundaries were clarified and social and geographic space marked out. The either/or binary left newcomers little room to consider the diversity of the Aboriginal people of the West or the complex identities and roles of Aboriginal women. Not all Euro-Canadians shared in these sentiments and perceptions. Methodist missionary John McDougall, for example, in 1895 chastised a fellow missionary author for his use of the term "squaw": "In the name of decency and civilization and Christianity, why call one person a woman and another a squaw?"[5] While it would be a mistake to assume a unified mentality among all Euro-Canadians, or, for example, among all members of the NWMP, it is nonetheless clear that the negative stereotype not only prevailed but was deliberately propagated by officials of the state.

EURO-CANADIAN SETTLEMENT OF THE WEST

Following the transfer of the Hudson's Bay Company territories to the Dominion of Canada in 1870, the policy of the federal government was to clear the land of the Aboriginal inhabitants and open the West to Euro-Canadian agricultural settlement. To regulate settlement the North-West Mounted Police (later Royal North-West and then Royal Canadian Mounted Police) was created and three hundred of them were dispatched west in 1874. A "free" homestead system was modeled on the American example, and a transcontinental railways was completed in 1885. To open up the West to "actual settlers," seven treaties with the Aboriginal people were negotiated from 1871 to 1877, and through these the government of Canada acquired legal control of most of the land of the West. In exchange the people received land reserves, annuities, and, as a result of hard bargaining by Aboriginal spokesmen, commitments to assist them to take up agriculture as their buffalo-based economy collapsed. A Department of Indian Affairs with headquarters in Ottawa was established in 1880, and in the field an ever-expanding team of Indian agents, farm instructors, and inspectors were assigned to implement the reserve system and to enforce the Indian Act of 1876. The people who had entered into treaties were wards of the government who did not have the privileges of full citizenship and were subject to a wide variety of controls and regulations that governed many aspects of life.

Much to the disappointment of the federal government, the West did not begin rapid development until the later 1890s. There were small pockets of Euro-Canadian settlement, but in 1885 in the district of Alberta, for example, the Aboriginal and Metis population was more than 9500 while the recent arrivals numbered only 4900.[6] All seemed hopeless, especially by the mid-1880s when immigration was at a near standstill. Years of drought and frost and problems finding suitable technique for farming the northern Plains account in part for the reluctance of settlers, and the 1885 resistance of the Metis in present-day Saskatchewan did little to enhance the image the government wished to project of the West as a suitable and safe home.

RESISTANCE TO SETTLEMENT

The Metis were people of mixed Aboriginal and European ancestry who regarded the Red River settlement (Winnipeg) as the heartland of their nation. It was here in 1869–70, under the leadership of Louis Riel, that the Metis first resisted Canadian imperialism, effectively blocking Ottawa's takeover of the West until they had been guaranteed their land rights, their French language, and their Roman Catholic religion. But the victory negotiated into the Manitoba Act of 1870 soon proved hollow as the Canadian government adopted a variety of strategies to ensure that the Metis did not receive the lands promised them, and many moved further West.[7] In their new territories the Metis again demanded land guarantees but when the Canadian government largely ignored their requests, they asked Louis Riel to lead another protest in 1884. The Canadian government dispatched troops west and defeated the Metis at Batoche in May 1885. Riel was found guilty of treason and was hanged, as were eight Aboriginal men convicted of murder.

Despite desperate economic circumstances and deep resentment over government mistreatment, few of the treaty people of the West joined the Metis resistance, although at a settlement called Frog Lake, in present-day Alberta, some young Cree men killed an Indian agent, a farm instructor, and seven others, and in the Battleford district two farm instructors were killed. This limited participation became a rationale for the increasingly authoritarian regime that governed the live of the treaty people. Anxious to see western development succeed in the face of all of the setbacks of the 1880s, the Canadian government restricted the Aboriginal population in order to protect and enrich recent and prospective immigrants.

DEVELOPMENT OF STEREOTYPES

Particularly irksome to many of the recently-arrived "actual settlers" was Aboriginal competition they faced in the hay, grain, and vegetable markets. Despite obstacles, many Aboriginal farmers had produced a surplus for sale. Settlers' particularly vocal and strident complaints led the government to curtail farming on reserves. To explain why underused reserves had become pockets of rural poverty, Indian Affairs officials claimed that Aboriginal culture and temperament rendered the men unwilling and unable to farm.

Plains women were also responsible: according to government pronouncements they were idle and gossipy, preferring tents to proper housing because tents required less work to maintain and could be clustered in groups that allowed visiting and gossip. Reports of the Superintendent General of Indian Affairs claimed that Indians raised dust with their dancing and the women's failure to clean it up spread diseases such as tuberculosis. Administrators blamed the high infant mortality rate upon the indifferent care of the mothers. The neglected children of these mothers grew up "rebellious, sullen, disobedient and unthankful."[8] While men were blamed for the failure of agriculture, women were portrayed as resisting, resenting, and preventing any progress toward modernization. As an inspector of Indian agencies lamented in 1908, "The women, here, as on nearly every reserve, are a hindrance to the advancement of the men. No sooner do the men earn some money than The women want to go and visit their relations on some other reserve, or else give a feast or dance to their friends. . . . The majority of [the women] are discontented, dirty, lazy and slovenly."[9]

The unofficial and unpublished reports of reserve life show that officials recognized that problems with reserve housing and health had little to do with the preferences, temperament, or poor housekeeping abilities of women. Because of their poverty the people were confined in large numbers in winter to what were little better than one-room and one-story huts or shacks that were poorly ventilated and impossible to keep clean, as they had dirt floors and were plastered with mud and hay. Tents and tipis might well have been more sanitary and more comfortable. One inspector of agencies noted in 1891 that women had neither soap, towels, wash basins, nor wash pails, and no means with which to acquire these.[10] Officials frequently noted that women were short of basic clothing but had no textiles or yarn to work with. Yet in official public statements, the tendency was to ascribe blame to the women rather than to draw attention to conditions that would injure the reputation of government administrators.

"LICENTIOUSNESS" AND GOVERNMENT OFFICIALS

Officials propagated an image of Aboriginal women as dissolute, as the bearers of sinister influences, to deflect criticism from government agents and policies. This image was evoked with particular strength in the wake of an 1886 controversy that focused upon the alleged "brutal, heartless and ostentatious licentiousness" of government officials resident in Western Canada.[11] The remarks of Samuel Trivett, a Church of England missionary on the Blood reserve in present-day southern Alberta, became the focus of the controversy. To a special correspondent for *The Mail* of Toronto, Trivett said that Indian women were being bought and sold by white men who lived with them without legally marrying them and then abandoned the offspring to life on the reserve.[12]

Trivett strongly hinted that some government agents were involved in licentious behavior, an accusation seized upon by critics of the administration of Indian affairs in western Canada. In the aftermath of the Metis resistance of 1885, opponents of John A. Macdonald's Conservatives amassed evidence of neglect, injustice, and incompetence and were delighted to add immortality to this list. In the House of Commons in April of 1886, Malcolm Cameron, Liberal Member of Parliament, delivered a lengthy indictment of Indian affairs in the West, focusing upon the unprincipled and unscrupulous behavior of officials of the Indian department. Cameron quoted Trivett and further charged that agents of the government, sent to elevate and educate, had instead acted to "humiliate, to lower, to degrade and debase the virgin daughters of the wards of the nation." He knew of one young Indian agent from England, unfit to do anything there, who was living on a reserve in "open adultery with two young squaws . . . revelling in the sensual enjoyments of a western harem, plentifully supplied with select cullings from the western prairie flowers."[13]

Cameron implicated members of the NWMP in this behavior, wondering why it was that over 45 percent of them were reported to have been under medical treatment for venereal disease. Cameron was not the first to raise the matter of police propriety in the House. Concern about possible improper relations between the police and Aboriginal women long predated the Trivett scandal and was one aspect of a larger debate in the press and in the House in the late 1870s over charges of inefficiency, lack of discipline, high desertion rates, and low morale in the force. Lieutenant-Governor of the North-West Territories David Laird alerted NWMP

Commissioner James Macleod in 1878 that reports about immoral conduct were in circulation: "I fear from what reports are brought me, that some of your officers at Fort Walsh are making rather free with the women around there. It is to be hoped that the good name of the Force will not be hurt through too open indulgence of that kind. And I sincerely hope that Indian women will not be treated in a way that hereafter may give trouble."[14]

Although Macleod and Assistant Commissioner A.G. Irvine denied that there was "anything like 'a regular brothel'" about the police posts, such reports persisted. In the House of Commons in 1880 Joseph Royal, a Manitoba Member of Parliament, claimed that the NWMP was accused of "disgraceful immorality" all over the West. Royal had evidence that at one of the police posts that winter there had been "an open quarrel between an officer and one of the constables for the possession of a squaw . . ." and that one officer slapped another "in the face on account of a squaw." Royal had been informed that "many members of the force were living in concubinage with Indian women, whom they had purchased from their parents and friends."[15] In 1886 public attention was once again drawn to police behavior. The Mail informed its readers that between 1874 and 1881 the police had "lived openly with Indian girls purchased from their parents" and only the arrival of settlers had compelled them to abandon or at least be "more discreet in the pursuit of their profligacy."[16]

There is little doubt that Trivett and other critics based their accusations of both the police and government officials on some foundation, but remaining evidence is scanty and scattered. Missionaries depended to a large extent on the goodwill of government and were rarely as outspoken as Trivett or John McLean, a Methodist missionary on the Blood reserve near Fort Macleod, who in 1885 characterized many reserve employees as utterly incompetent and urged the government to employ only married men, "of sterling Christian character."[17] But missionaries were instructed in 1886 by Edgar Dewdney, lieutenant-governor of the North-West Territories, not to voice their accusations to the newspapers "even if allegations against public officials were true," as this would do more harm than good, would affect mission work, and could be used to stir up political strife.[18] Government officials generally investigated reports of government misconduct themselves and this functioned to cover up or to mitigate such allegations. Similarly members of the NWMP themselves looked into any complaints about the force's behavior.

MARRIAGES OF ABORIGINAL WOMEN AND NWMP MEMBERS

There were members of the NWMP, especially among the earliest recruits of the 1870s and early 1880s, who formed relationships with Aboriginal and Metis women, as did a great many other male immigrants of these years. Some of these were marriages of long-standing, sanctioned by Christian ceremony or customary law. Lakota author/historian John O'Kute-sica noted that six "Red Coats" of the Wood Mountain Detachment in the early 1880s, married Lakota women from Sitting Bull's band, and most of the couples, such as Mary Blackmoon and Thomas Aspdin, lived together to old age and death. One couple, Archie LeCaine and Emma Loves War, separated because she did not wish to move to Eastern Canada.[19]

Other relationships were of a more temporary nature. Of course there were children. Cecil Denny for example, while a sub-inspector at Fort Macleod, had a daughter with Victoria Mckay, a part-Piegan woman who was the wife of another policeman, constable Percy Robinson.[20] Denny was forced to resign from the force in 1881 as a result of his involvement in a series of court cases that Robinson brought against him for "having induced his wife to desert him and also having criminal connections with her."[21] The child was raised by her mother on the American Blackfoot reservation. Assistant Surgeon Henry Dodd of the NWMP had a daughter who lived on one of the Crooked Lake reserves in the Qu'Appelle Valley. There is a record of this in the police files only because Dodd was granted leave to attend to her when she was very ill in 1889.[22]

D.J. Grier, who served three years with the NWMP beginning in 1877 at Fort Macleod, married Molly Tailfeathers, a Piegan woman, and together they had three children.[23] By 1887, however, Grier had remarried a white woman. For a short time the children from his first marriage lived with their mother on the Piegan reserve, but the two eldest were taken from her and placed in the care of Grier's parents, who had also settled in Fort Macleod. Grier was one of the most prominent men of the West. Renowned as the first commercial wheat grower in Alberta, he also served as mayor of Macleod for twelve years from 1901 to 1913.

ABUSE OF ABORIGINAL WOMEN

John O'Kute-sica wrote at length about one unsuccessful Wood Mountain customary marriage, that of his aunt Iteskawin and Superintendent William D. Jarvis, an Englishman with the original contingent who was dismissed from the force in 1881. According to O'Kute-sica his aunt consented to marry Jarvis because he promised that her brothers and sisters would have something to eat twice a day, and all of her people were in want and suffering. After only a few weeks of marriage Jarvis, in a jealous rage, publicly assaulted Iteskawin at a Lakota "Night Dance," an incident that strained relations between the two communities, and she immediately left him.[24] On most of the few occasions that Aboriginal women laid charges against policemen for assault or rape, their claims were hastily dismissed as defamation or blackmail.[25]

Some government employees resident on reserves clearly abused their positions of authority. In 1882, for example, Blackfoot Chief Crowfoot and his wife complained that the farm instructor on their reserve demanded sexual favors from a young girl in return for rations, and when an investigation proved this to be the case the man was dismissed.[26] Both the documentary and oral records suggest that several of the government employees that the Crees killed at Frog Lake and Battleford in the spring of 1885 were resented intensely because of their callous and at times brutal treatment of Aboriginal women. The farm instructor on the Mosquito reserve near Battleford, James Payne, was known for his violent temper—he once beat a young woman and threw her out of his house when he found her visiting his young Aboriginal wife. The terrified and shaken woman, who was found by her father, died soon after, and her grieving father blamed Payne, whom he killed in 1885.[27] Farm instructor John Delaney, who was killed at Frog Lake in 1885, laid charges against a man by the name of Sand Fly in 1881 so he could cohabit with Sand Fly's wife. Delaney first claimed that Sand Fly had struck him with a whip, and when this charge did not result in the desired jail sentence, Delaney claimed that the man had beaten his wife. The farm instructor then lived with Sand Fly's wife, and the general feeling in the district, shared by the local NWMP, was that "Mr. Delaney had the man arrested in order to accomplish his designs."[28] As a Touchwood Hills farm instructor told a visiting newspaper correspondent in 1885, the charges of immortality among farm instructors on reserves were in many instances too true, as "the greatest facilities are afforded the Indian instructor for the seduction of Indian girls. The instructor holds the grub. The agent gives him the supplies and he issues them to the Indians. Now you have a good idea of what semi-starvation is . . ."[29]

BLAMING ABORIGINAL WOMEN

The most vocal response to the accusations of Trivett and other critics was not to deny that there had been "immorality" in the West but to exonerate the men and blame the Aboriginal women, who were claimed to have behaved in an abandoned and wanton manner and were supposedly accustomed to being treated with contempt, to being bought and sold as commodities, within their own society. In defending the NWMP in 1880, the Toronto *Globe* emphasized that Aboriginal women had "loose morals" that were "notorious the world over" and that "no men in the world are so good as to teach them better, or to try to reform them in this respect." These sentiments were echoed again and again in the wake of the 1886 controversy. The editor of the Fort *Macleod Gazette*, a former NWMP, argued that whatever immorality there might have been came from the women themselves and from the customs of their society. They were prostitutes before they went to live with white men, who did not encourage this behavior but were simply "taking advantage of an Indian's offer." *The Mail* told readers that Aboriginal males had sold their wives and children in the thousands to soldiers and settlers since the time of the French fur trade in exchange for alcohol, and that with the arrival of the police a great deal had been done to end this situation.[30]

The *Gazette* stressed, incorrectly, that there was no marriage in plains societies, simply a little lively bartering with the father and a woman could be purchased for a horse or two. The argument that Aboriginal women were virtual slaves, first to their fathers, and then to their husbands, was called upon by all who wished to deflect criticism from government officials and the NWMP. In the House of Commons in April 1886 Sir Hector Langevin defended the record of the government against Cameron's charges of immorality. Langevin claimed that to Indians marriage was simply a bargain and a sale and that immortality among them long predated the arrival of government agents in the North-West.[31]

The government published its official response to the criticisms of Indian affairs in the North-West in an 1886 pamphlet entitled "The Facts Respecting Indian Administration in the North-West." A government official had again inquired into accusations about the misconduct of employees of the Indian department and, predictably, had found no evidence. The investigator, Hayter Reed, assistant commissioner of Indian affairs, was one of those unmarried officials who had been accused of having Aboriginal "mistresses" as well as a child from one of these relationships.[32] The pamphlet boldly asserted that Trivett was unable to come up with a shred of actual evidence, although the missionary vehemently denied this.[33] The pamphlet writer admitted that some men had acquired their wives by purchase, but claimed that this was the Indian custom, and that "no father ever dreams of letting his daughter leave his wigwam till he has received a valuable consideration for her." If the government stopped this custom, there would be loud protests, over and above the Indians' "chronic habit of grumbling." "The Facts" insisted that it was not fair to criticize the behavior of the dead, such as Delaney the Payne, who had "passed from the bar of human judgment."[34]

ENDANGERED WHITE WOMEN

The real danger was not to Indian women but to white women, who might again be dragged into horrible captivity if critics encouraged Indians in their exaggerated, misled notions. Two white women, Theresa Delaney and Theresa Gowanlock, had been taken hostage by Big Bear's band following the events at Frog Lake. There were a great number of Metis and Aboriginal women (and men) hostages as well, but outrage and indignation did not focus upon them. Although Delaney and Gowanlock were fed and housed as well as their captors, and released unharmed, the government publication played up the perils, hazards, and threat to the safety of these women and others who might move west. The women's account of their two months of captivity stressed the "savagery" of their captors, and the ever-present danger of "the fate worse than death."[35]

Following the period of heightened tensions within the Euro-Canadian community after the events of 1885 there was an increased emphasis upon the supposed vulnerability of white women in the West. Rumors circulated through the press that one of Big Bear's wives was a white woman being held against her will.[36] After a girl of about nine with fair hair and blue eyes was spotted on the Blackfoot reserve by an English artist accompanying Canada's governor general on a tour across the continent, in 1889, the story of a "captive" white child attracted international attention and calls for a rescue mission. Indignant outrage was expressed, especially in the Fort

Macleod newspaper, which called for prompt action to rescue the girl from "the horrible fate that is surely in store for her." The NWMP and Indian affairs officials assigned to look into the case knew all along that the child was not a captive at all but resided with her mother on the reserve. The captivity story functioned, however, to reaffirm the vulnerability of white women in the West and to provide a rationale for those wished to secure greater control over the Aboriginal population.[37]

THE IMAGE OF THE "SQUAW MAN"

The use of the term "squaw man" to denote men of the lowest social class became increasingly frequent during the later 1880s. There was disdain for those within the community who did not conform to the new demands to clarify boundaries. Police reports blamed "squaw men" for many crimes such as liquor offenses or the killing of cattle. S.B. Steele of the NWMP wrote from the Fort Macleod district in 1890 that the wives of these men "readily act as agents, and speaking the language, and being closely connected with the various tribes, their houses soon become a rendezvous for idle and dissolute Indians and half breeds, and being themselves in that debatable land between savagery and civilization possibly do not realize the heinousness and danger to the community. . . ."[38] The *Moosomin Courier* of March 1890 blamed the "squaw-men" for stirring up trouble with the Indians in 1885 and prejudicing them against policies that were for their own good.[39]

LIVES OF ABORIGINAL WOMEN

The overwhelming image that emerged from the 1886 "immorality" controversy was that of dissolute Aboriginal women. They, and the traditions of the society from which they came, were identified as the cause of vice and corruption in the new settlements of the prairie West. This was not an image shared or accepted by all Euro-Canadians in the West at all times, nor did the image bear resemblance to the lives of the vast majority of Aboriginal women. Women were not commodities that were bought, sold, or exchanged at will by men. Plains marriage practices entailed mutual obligations between the families of the couple and an on-going exchange of marriage-validating gifts.

Aboriginal oral and documentary sources suggest that in the early reserve years, particularly in the aftermath of the events of 1885, women provided essential security and stability in communities that had experienced great upheaval. In these years of low resources and shattered morale, the work of women in their own new settlements was vital, materially as well as spiritually. Cree author Joe Dion wrote that when spirits and resources were low on his reserve in the late 1880s "much of the inspiration for the Crees came from the old ladies, for they set to work with a will that impressed everybody."[40] Aboriginal women also provided considerable assistance to new immigrants, particularly women. They were important as midwives to some early immigrants and they helped instruct newcomers in the use of edible prairie plants and other native materials.[41] Aboriginal women formed what was described as a "protective society" around the women and children hostages in Big Bear's camp in 1885, keeping them out of harm's way, but this aspect of the drama was absent from the headlines of the day.[42]

CONSTRAINTS ON ABORIGINAL WOMEN

It was the image of Aboriginal women as immoral and corrupting influences that predominated in the non-Aboriginal society that was taking shape. Authorities used this characterization to define and treat Aboriginal women, increasingly narrowing their options and opportunities. Both informal and formal constraints served to keep Aboriginal people from the towns and settled areas of the prairies and their presence there became more and more marginal. While they may not have wished to live in the towns, their land-use patterns for a time intersected with the new order and they might have taken advantage of markets and other economic opportunities, but townspeople believed that Aboriginal people did not belong within the new settlements that were replacing and expelling "savagery."[43] Their presence was seen as incongruous, corrupting, and demoralizing. Classified as prostitutes, Aboriginal women were seen as particular threats to morality and health. An 1886 pamphlet of advice for emigrants entitled "What Women Say of the Canadian Northwest" was quick to reassure newcomers that Aboriginal people were seldom seen. The 320 women who responded to the question "Do you experience any dread of the Indians?" overwhelmingly replied that they rarely saw any. Mrs. S. Lumsden, for example, thought they were "hundreds of miles away with sufficient force to keep them quiet."[44]

Following the events of 1885, government officials as well as the NWMP made strenuous efforts to keep people on their reserves. A pass system required all who wished to leave to acquire a pass from the farm instructor or agent declaring the length of and reason for absence. A central rationale for the pass system was to keep away from the towns and villages Aboriginal women "of abandoned character who were there for the worst purposes."[45] There is evidence that some Aboriginal women did work as prostitutes.[46] Cree chiefs of the Edmonton district complained to the prime minister in 1883 that their young women were reduced by starvation to prostitution, something unheard of among their people before.[47] Officials attributed prostitution not to economic conditions but to what they insisted was the personal disposition or inherent immorality of Aboriginal women.[48] Classified as prostitutes, Aboriginal women could be restricted by a new disciplinary regime. Separate legislation under the Indian Act, and, after 1892, under the Criminal Code governed Aboriginal prostitution, making it easier to convict Aboriginal women than other women. As legal historian Constance Backhouse has observed, this separate criminal legislation, "with its attendant emphasis on the activities of Indians rather than whites, revealed that racial discrimination ran deep through the veins of nineteenth century Canadian society."[49]

The pass system was also used to bar Aboriginal women from the towns for what were invariably seen as "immoral purposes." Women who were found by the NWMP to be without passes and without means of support were arrested and ordered back to their reserves.[50] In March of 1886 the Battleford police dealt with one woman who refused to leave the town by taking her to the barracks and cutting off locks of her hair. Two years later the Battleford paper reported that

> during the early part of the week the Mounted Police ordered out of town a number of squaws who had come in from time to time and settled here. The promise to take them to the barracks and cut off their hair had a wonderful effect in hastening their movements.[51]

Accustomed to a high degree of mobility about the landscape, Aboriginal women found that the pass system not only restricted their traditional subsistence strategies but also hampered their pursuit of new jobs and resources. Government officials further limited the women's employment and marketing opportunities by advice such as that given by one Indian agent, who urged the citizens of Calgary in 1885 not to purchase anything from or hire Aboriginal people, so as to keep them out of the town.[52] The periodic sale of produce, art, and craftwork in urban or tourist areas could have provided income to women and their families, as did such sales for Aboriginal women in eastern Canada. Studies of rural women in western Canada suggest that in the prairie boom and bust cycle the numerous strategies of women, including the marketing of country provisions and farm products, provided the buffer against farm failure.[53] Aboriginal women were not allowed the same opportunities to market these resources.

The mechanisms and attitudes that excluded Aboriginal women from the new settlements also hampered their access to some of the services these offered. Jane Livingston, the Metis wife of one of the earliest farmers in the Calgary district, found that whenever there was a new policeman in Calgary, he would ask her and her children for passes and make trouble because of their appearance. On one occasion when a child was sick and she needed medicines from downtown Calgary, she rubbed flour into her face and "hoped I looked like a white Calgary housewife" so that the new police constable would not bother her about a pass.[54]

MURDERS OF ABORIGINAL WOMEN

Community reactions to the poisoning of one Aboriginal woman and the brutal murder of another in the late 1880s in southern Alberta reflect the racial prejudices of many of the recent immigrants. In 1888 Constable Alfred Symonds of the NWMP detachment of Stand Off was accused of feloniously killing and slaying a Blood woman by the name of Mrs. Only Kill by giving her a fatal dose of iodine. The woman had swallowed the contents of a bottle given to her by Symonds that apparently held iodine and had died the next morning. The same day she had also eaten a quantity of beans that had turned sour in the heat. Although Only Kill died on Wednesday morning, the matter was not reported to the coroner until late on Friday night. The coroner claimed that by this time the body was too decomposed for post mortem examination, and the coroner's jury decided that the deceased had come to her death either from eating sour beans or from drinking the fluid given to her by Symonds, who was committed to trial and charged with having administered the poison.[55] Constable Symonds was a popular and jocular cricketer and boxer, the son of a professor from Galt, Ontario.[56] In his report on the case, Superintendent P.R. Neale of the NWMP wrote to his superior, "I do not think any Western jury will convict him." Symonds appeared before Judge James F. Macleod, former commissioner of the NWMP, in August of 1888 but the crown prosecutor made application for "Nolle Prosequi," which was granted, and the prisoner was released.[57]

During the 1889 trials of the murderer of a Cree woman identified only as "Rosalie," who had been working as a prostitute, it became clear that there were many in Calgary who felt "Rosalie was only a squaw and that her death did not matter much."[58] Instead the murderer gained the sympathy and support of much of the town. The murder was a particularly brutal one, and the accused, William "Jumbo" Fisk, had confessed and given himself up to authorities, yet there were problems finding any citizens willing to serve on a jury that might convict a white man for such a crime. The crown prosecutor stated that he regretted having to conduct the case, as he had known the accused for several years as a "genial, accommodating and upright young man."[59] Fisk was a popular veteran of 1885, and he was from a well-established eastern Canadian family. At the end of the first of the Rosalie trials the jury astoundingly found the accused "Not Guilty." Judge Charles Rouleau refused to accept this verdict and he ordered a re-trial at the end of which Rouleau told the jury to "forget the woman's race and to consider only the evidence at hand," that "it made no difference whether Rosalie was white or black, an Indian or a negro. In the eyes of the law, every British subject is equal."[60] It was only after the second trial that Fisk was convicted of manslaughter and sent to prison for fourteen years at hard labor. The judge intended to sentence him for life, but letters written by members of parliament and other influential persons who had made representations to the court as to his good character, combined with a petition from the most respectable people of Calgary, persuaded him to impose the lesser sentence.

The people of Calgary tried to show that they were not callous and indifferent toward Rosalie by giving her "as respectable a burial as if she had been a white woman," although several months later the town council squabbled with the Indian Department over the costs incurred, as the department did not think it necessary to go beyond the costs of a pauper's funeral. As a final indignity Rosalie was not allowed burial by the priests in the mission graveyard, although she had been baptized into the Roman Catholic Church, because they regarded her as a prostitute who had died in sin. The lesson to be learned from the tragedy, according to a Calgary newspaper, was "keep the Indians out of town."[61]

ABORIGINAL WOMEN AND ANGLO-SAXON MORAL REFORMERS

There was an intensification of racial discrimination and a stiffening of boundaries between Aboriginal and newcomer in the late 1880s in western Canada. In part this may have been because the immigrants exemplified the increasingly racist ideas and assumptions of the British toward "primitive" peoples.[62] Like the Jamaica Revolt and the India Mutiny, the events of 1885 in western Canada sanctioned perceptions of Aboriginal people as dangerous and ungrateful and justified increased control and segregation.[63] Aboriginal women presented particular perils and hazards. The Metis of the Canadian West had fomented two "rebellions" in western Canada, so authorities wanted to discourage such miscegenation, which could potentially produce great numbers of "malcontents" who might demand that their rights and interests be recognized.[64]

A fervor for moral reform in Protestant English Canada also began to take shape in the later 1880s. Sexual immorality was a main target and racial purity a goal of the reformers.[65] There were fears that Anglo-Saxons might well be overrun by more fertile, darker, and lower people who were believed not to be in control of their sexual desires. Attitudes of the moral reformers toward the inhabitants of the cities' slums were similar to categorizations of "savages" as improvident, filthy, impure, and morally depraved. The 1886 accusations of Malcolm Cameron about the extent of venereal disease among the NWMP had led to an internal investigation of the matter, and although this proved that Cameron's claims were exaggerated, they were not entirely incorrect.[66] The concerns of the moral reformers, however, justified policies segregating Aboriginal and newcomer communities.

THE INVALIDATION OF MIXED MARRIAGES

Also at issue in the West at this time was the question of who was to control property and capital, who was to have privilege and respectability, and who was not. The possibility that the progeny of interracial marriages might be recognized as legitimate heirs to the sometimes considerable wealth of their fathers posed problems and acted as a powerful incentive for the immigrants to view Aboriginal women as immoral and accustomed to a great number of partners. With the arrival of Euro-Canadian women, Aboriginal wives became fewer, and there is evidence, just as Trivett had suggested, that in the 1880s husbands and fathers were leaving their Aboriginal wives and children for non-Aboriginal wives. D.W. Davis, for example, began his career in Alberta as a whiskey trader at the infamous Fort Whoop-Up, but by 1887 was elected as the first Member of Parliament for the Alberta district. He had a family of four children with a Blood woman by the name of Revenge Walker, but in 1887 he married an Ontario woman, Lillie Grier (sister of D.J. Grier), with whom he had a second family. Although Davis, like Grier, acknowledged the children of the earlier marriage and provided for their education, they were excluded from the economic and social elite in the non-Aboriginal community.[67]

While the validity of mixed marriages according to "the custom of the country" had been upheld in Canadian courts earlier in the nineteenth century, this changed with the influential 1886 ruling in *Jones v. Fraser*. The judge ruled that the court would not accept that "the cohabitation of a civilized man and a savage woman, even for a long period of time, gives rise to the presumption that they consented to be married in our sense of marriage."[68] In 1899 the Supreme Court for the North-West Territories decided that the two sons of Mary Brown, a Piegan woman, and Nicholas Sheran, a founder of a lucrative coal mine near Lethbridge, were not entitled, as next of kin, to a share of their father's estate, as the judge found that Sheran could have but did not legally marry Brown while they lived together from 1878 until Sheran's death in 1882.[69]

HAUNTED BY AN IMAGE

Negative images of Aboriginal women proved extraordinarily persistent. Their morality was questioned in a number of sections of the Indian Act. If a woman was not of "good moral character" for example, she lost her one-third interest in her husband's estate, and a male government official was the sole and final judge of moral character. As late as 1921 the House of Commons debated a Criminal Code amendment that would have made it an offense for any white man to have "illicit connection" with an Indian woman. Part of the rationale advanced was that "the Indian women are, perhaps, not as alive as women of other races in the country to the importance of maintaining their chastity." The amendment was not passed, as it was argued that this could make unsuspecting white men the "victims" of Indian women who would blackmail them.[70] By contrast, any critical reflections upon the behavior of early government officials and the police in western Canada did not survive beyond the controversy of the 1880s. Ideological constraints, combined with more formal mechanisms of control such as the pass system, succeeded in marginalizing Aboriginal women and in limiting the alternatives and opportunities available to them.

Local histories of the prairies suggest that by the turn of the century many of the settlements of the West had their "local Indian" who was tolerate on the margins or fringes of society and whose behavior and appearance was the subject of local anecdotes. "Old Dewdney" for example, an ancient, often flamboyantly dressed man, was a familiar sight in Fort Macleod. Local people exchanged stories about the exotic past of the old man and of their generosity and kindness toward him.[71] "Nikamoos" or the Singer camped each summer by herself on the trail to the Onion Lake reserve agency in Saskatchewan. Among the white community it was reputed that as a girl Nikamoos had run away with a policeman but that he had been compelled to leave her. The child she bore died and Nikamoos went insane.[72]

A solitary Indian woman known only as Liza camped on the outskirts of Virden, Manitoba, for many years until her disappearance sometime in the 1940s. By then Liza was thought to have been well over one hundred years old. She lived winter and summer in an unheated tent by the railroad tracks although she spent the long winter days huddled in the livery stable and also at times crept into the Nu-Art Beauty Parlour, where she sat on the floor in front of the window, warming herself in the sun. Liza smoked a corncob pipe as she shuffled about the streets and lanes of Virden, rummaging in garbage tins. She bathed under the overflow pipe at the water tower, sometimes clothed and sometimes not, and dried off by standing over the huge heat register in Scales and Rothnie's General Store. To an extent she was tolerated and even assisted; town employees shoveled out a path for her when she was buried under snow, and it was thought that the town fathers supplied her with food from time to time. Children were half fascinated and half frightened by this ancient woman. Old-timers believed that Liza was there well before the first settlers, that she was among the Sioux who had escaped the pursuing American army in 1876, that she received regular checks from the United States, and that she was capable of fine handwriting, where learned, no one knew.[73]

The presence of Liza, and the stories told about her, served to sharpen the boundaries of community membership and to articulate what was and what was not considered acceptable and respectable.[74] Liza was the object of both fascination and repugnance as she violated norms of conventional behavior, dress, and cleanliness, representing the antithesis of "civilized" prairie society. Although economically and socially marginal, Liza was symbolically important. Her role attests to the recurrent pattern through which the new society of the West gained in strength and identity and sought to legitimate its own authority by defining itself against the people who were there before them. Liza was a real person, but what she represented was a Euro-Canadian artifact, created by the settlement. The narratives circulated about Liza were not those she might have told herself—of the disasters that had stripped her of family and community, or perhaps of her strategies in adopting the character role—and this folklore reflected less about Liza than about the community itself. Her solitary life was unique and in contrast to the lives of Aboriginal women; Liza was not representative of a Lakota woman within Lakota society. Yet her presence on the margins of the settlement was tolerated and encouraged in the way these women were not, as she appeared to fit into the well-established category of the "squaw" that still served to confirm the Euro-Canadian newcomers in their belief that their cultural and moral superiority entitled them to the land that had become their home.

NOTES

1. Mary E. Inderwick, "A Lady and Her Ranch" in *The Best From Alberta History*, ed. Hugh Dempsey (Saskatoon: Western Producer Prairie Books, 1981), 65–77. In 1882 the North-West Territories were divided into four provisional districts named Assiniboia, Saskatchewan, Alberta, and Athabasca.

2. For an examination and critique of the argument that European women introduced segregation, see Margaret Strobel, *European Women and the Second British Empire* (Bloomington: Indiana University Press, 1991). See also essays by Ann Laura Stoler, "Carnal Knowledge and Imperial Power: Gender, Race

and Morality in Colonial Asia" in *Gender at the Crossroads of Knowledge: Feminist Anthropology in the Postmodern Era*, ed. Micaela di Leonardo (Berkeley: University of California Press, 1991), 51–101, and Stoler, "Rethinking Colonial Categories: European Communities and the Boundaries of Rule" in *Colonialism and Culture*, ed. Nicholas B. Dirks (Ann Arbor: University of Michigan Press, 1992), 319–52.

3. See Sarah Carter, *Lost Harvests: Prairie Indian Reserve Farmers and Government Policy* (Montreal: McGill-Queen's University Press, 1990).

4. Rayna Green, "The Pocahontas Perplex: The Image of Indian Women in American Culture" in *Unequal Sisters: A Multicultural Reader in U.S. Women's History*, ed. Ellen Carol DuBois and Vicki L. Ruiz (New York: Routledge, 1990), 15–21.

5. John McDougall, "A Criticism of 'Indian Wigwams and Northern Camp-Fires'" (n.p.: 1895), 12–13.

6. P.B. Waite, *Canada, 1874–1896: Arduous Destiny* (Toronto: McClelland & Stewart, 1971), 149.

7. D.N. Sprague, *Canada and the Metis, 1869–1885* (Waterloo, ON: Wilfrid Laurier Press, 1988).

8. Canada, *Sessional Papers*, Annual Report of the Superintendent General of Indian Affairs for the year ending 30 June 1898, xix, for the year ending 31 Dec. 1899, xxiii, xxviii, 166; *The Mail* (Toronto), 2 March 1889; Pamela Margaret White, "Restructuring the Domestic Sphere—Prairie Indian Women on Reserves: Image, Ideology and State Policy, 1880–1930" (PhD thesis, McGill University, 1987); quote taken from W.H. Withrow, *Native Races of North America* (Toronto: Methodist Mission Rooms, 1895), 114.

9. Canada, *Sessional Papers*, Annual Report of the Superintendent General of Indian Affairs for the year ending March 1908, 110.

10. Inspector Alex McGibbon's report on Onion Lake, Oct. 1891, National Archives of Canada (NA), Record Group 10 (RG 10), records relating to Indian Affairs, Black Series, vol. 3860, file 82, 319-6.

11. *The Globe* (Toronto), 1 Feb. 1886.

12. *The Mail* (Toronto), 23 Jan. 1886.

13. Canada, House of Commons *Debates*, Malcolm Cameron, Session 1886, vol. 1, 720–21.

14. As quoted in E.C. Morgan. "The North-West Mounted Police: Internal Problems and Public Criticism, 1874–1883," *Saskatchewan History* 26, 2 (Spring 1973): 56.

15. Canada, House of Commons *Debates*, 21 April 1880, Joseph Royal, Fourth Parliament, Second Session, 1638.

16. *The Mail*, 2 Feb. 1886.

17. John Maclean, "The Half-breed and Indian Insurrection," *Canadian Methodist Magazine* 22, 1 (July 1885): 173–74.

18. Edgar Dewdney to the Bishop of Saskatchewan, 31 May 1886, NA, RG 10, vol. 3753, file 30613.

19. John O'Kute-sica Correspondence, collection no. R-834, File 17(b), 15, Saskatchewan Archives Board (SAB).

20. *Blackfeet Heritage: 1907–08* (Browning: Blackfeet Heritage Program, n.d.), 171.

21. A.B. McCullough, "Papers Relating to the North West Mounted Police and Fort Walsh," Manuscript Report Series no. 213 (Ottawa: Parks Canada, Department of Indian and Northern Affairs, 1977), 132–33.

22. L. Herchemer to Comptroller, 23 May 1889, NA, RG 18, vol. 35, file 499–1889.

23. Personal Interview with Kirsten Grier, great-granddaughter of D.J. Grier, Calgary, 19 May 1993. See also *Fort Macleod—Our Colourful Past: A History of the Town of Fort Macleod from 1874 to 1924* (Fort Macleod, AB: Fort Macleod History Committee, 1977), 268–69.

24. O'Kute-sica Correspondence, 3.

25. See for example S.B. Steele to Commissioner, Fort Macleod, 20 July 1895, NA, RG 18, vol. 2182, file RCMP 1895 pt. 2, and Gilbert E. Sanders Diaries, 20 Oct. 1885, Edward Sanders Family Papers, M1093, file 38, Glenbow Archives.

26. F. Laurier Barron, "Indian Agents and the North-West Rebellion" in 1885 and After: Native Society in Transition, ed. F. Laurie Barron and James B. Waldram (Regina: Canadian Plains Research Center, 1986), 36.

27. Norma Sluman and Jean Goodwill, John Tootoosis: A Biography of a Cree Leader (Ottawa: Golden Dog Press, 1982), 37.

28. Hugh A. Dempsey, Big Bear: The End of Freedom (Vancouver: Douglas & McIntyre, 1984), 117. See also Saskatchewan Herald (Battleford), 14 and 28 Feb. 1881.

29. Newspaper clipping, "Through the Saskatchewan," n.p., n.d., N.A. William Henry Cotton Collection.

30. The Globe, 4 June 1880; Macleod Gazette (Fort Macleod, AB), 23 March 1886; The Mail, 2 Feb. 1886.

31. Canada, House of Commons Debates, Session 1886, vol. 1, 730.

32. William Donovan to L. Vankoughnet, 31 Oct. 1886, NA, RG 10, vol. 3772, file 34983.

33. The Globe, 4 June 1886.

34. The Facts Respecting Indian Administration in the North-West (Ottawa, 1886), 9, 12.

35. Theresa Gowanlock and Theresa Delaney, Two Months in the Camp of Big Bear (Parkdale: Parkdale Times, 1885).

36. Manitoba Sun (Winnipeg), 7 Dec. 1886.

37. Sarah Carter, "'A Fate Worse Than Death': Indian Captivity Stories Thrilled Victorian Readers: But Were They True?" The Beaver 68, 2 (April/May 1988): 21–28, Macleod Gazette quoted p. 22.

38. Canada, Sessional Papers, Annual Report of the Commissioner of the North West Mounted Police for 1890, vol. 24, no. 9, 62.

39. Moosomin Courier, 13 March 1890.

40. Joe Dion, My Tribe the Crees (Calgary: Glenbow-Alberta Institute, 1979), 114.

41. See Sarah Carter, "Relations Between Native and Non-Native Women in the Prairie West, 1870–1920," paper presented to the Women and History Association of Manitoba, Winnipeg, Feb. 1992.

42. Elizabeth M. McLean, "Prisoners of the Indians," The Beaver, Outfit 278 (June 1947): 15–16.

43. David Hamer, New Towns in the New World: Images and Perceptions of the Nineteenth Century Urban Frontier (New York: Columbia University Press, 1990), 17, 213.

44. "What Canadian Women Say of the Canadian North-West" (Montreal: Montreal Herald, 1886), 44.

45. L. Vankoughnet to John A. Macdonald, 15 Nov. 1883, NA, RG 10, vol. 1009, file 628, no. 596-635.

46. S.W. Horrall, "The (Royal) North-West Mounted Police and Prostitution on the Canadian Prairies," Prairie Forum 10, 1 (Spring 1985): 105–27.

47. Clipping from the Bulletin (Edmonton), 7 Jan. 1883, NA, RG 10, vol. 3673, file 10 986.

48. Canada, Sessional Papers, Annual Report of the Superintendent General of Indian affairs for the year ending 1906, 82.

49. Constance B. Backhouse, "Nineteenth-Century Canadian Prostitution Law: Reflection of a Discriminatory Society," Histoire sociale/Social History 18, 36 (Nov. 1985): 422.

50. Canada, Sessional Papers, Annual Report of the Commissioner of the North-West Mounted Police Force for the year 1889, reprinted in The New West (Toronto: Coles Publishing, 1973), 101.

51. *Saskatchewan Herald* (Battleford), 15 March 1886, 13 March 1888 (quoted).

52. *Calgary Herald*, 5 March 1885.

53. See for example Carolina Antoinetta J.A. Van de Vorst, "A History of Farm Women's Work in Manitoba" (MA thesis, University of Manitoba, 1988).

54. Lyn Hancock with Marion Dowler, *Tell Me Grandmother* (Toronto: McClelland & Stewart, 1985), 139.

55. *Macleod Gazette*, 18 July 1888.

56. John D. Higinbotham, *When the West Was Young: Historical Reminiscences of the Early Canadian West* (Toronto: Ryerson Press, 1933), 260–61.

57. R.C. Macleod, *The North-West Mounted Police and Law Enforcement, 1873–1905* (Toronto: University of Toronto Press, 1976), 145. See also NA, RG 18, vol. 24, file 667–1888.

58. Donald Smith, "Bloody Murder Almost Became Miscarriage of Justice," *Herald Sunday Magazine*, 23 July 1989, 13. Thanks to Donald Smith, Department of History, University of Calgary for allowing me to draw upon his sources on this case.

59. James Gray, *Talk To My Lawyer: Great Stories of Southern Alberta's Bar and Bench* (Edmonton: Hurtig Publishers, 1987), 7.

60. Rouleau quoted in Smith, "Bloody Murder,"15.

61. *Calgary Herald*, 24 July, 10 Sept. (quoted), 27 Feb., and 8 March (quoted) 1889.

62. See Christine Bolt, *Victorian Attitudes to Race* (Toronto: University of Toronto Press, 1971); Philip D. Curtin, *The Image of Africa: British Ideas and Action, 1780–1850* (Madison: University of Wisconsin Press, 1964); V.G. Kiernan, *The Lords of Human Kind: European Attitudes Toward the Outside World in the Imperial Age* (Middlesex: Penguin Books, 1972); Douglas A. Lorimer, *Colour, Class and the Victorians*

(Leicester University Press, Holmes and Meier Publishers, 1978); and Philip Mason, *Patterns of Dominance* (London: Oxford University Press, 1971).

63. Walter Hildebrandt, "Official Images of 1885," *Prairie Fire* 6, 4 (1985): 31–40.

64. This is suggested by Backhouse, "Nineteenth-Century Canadian Prostitution Law," 422.

65. Mariana Valverde, *The Age of Light, Soap, and Water: Moral Reform in English Canada, 1885–1925* (Toronto: McClelland & Stewart, 1991).

66. NA, RG 18, vol. 1039, file 87–1886, pt. 1.

67. Beverley A. Stacey, "D.W. Davis: Whiskey Trader to Politician," *Alberta History* 38, 3 (Summer 1990): 1–11.

68. Sylvia Van Kirk, *"Many Tender Ties": Women in Fur Trade Society, 1670–1870* (Winnipeg: Watson and Dwyer Publishing, 1980), 241, and Constance Backhouse, *Petticoats and Prejudice: Women and the Law in Nineteenth-Century Canada* (Toronto: Osgoode Society, 1991), chap. 1.

69. Brian Slattery and Linda Charlton, ed., *Canadian Native Law Cases* 3, 1891–1910 (Saskatoon: Native Law Centre, 1985), 636–44.

70. Canada, House of Commons *Debates*, Session 1921, vol. 4, 26 May 1921, 3908.

71. Fort Macleod History Committee, *Our Colourful Past*, 217–18.

72. Ruth Matheson Buck, "Wives and Daughters," *Folklore* 9, 4 (Autumn 1988): 14–15.

73. "Talk About Stories," *Anecdotes and Updates: Virden Centennial, 1982* (Virden: Empire Publishing, 1982), 57–59

74. Diane Tye, "Local Character Anecdotes: A Nova Scotia Case Study," *Western Folklore* 48 (July 1989): 196.

UPSETTING THE RHYTHMS:
THE FEDERAL GOVERNMENT
AND NATIVE COMMUNITIES
IN THE YUKON TERRITORY,
1945 TO 1973 ◇

KEN S. COATES

○

The last forty years have witnessed marked changes in the organization and function of Indian communities in the Yukon Territory. Before the collapse of the fur market in the late 1940s, most Yukon Indians maintained their nomadic habits, moving seasonally from fishing camp to trap-line. They were, after 100 years of contact, much changed from their precontact ancestors, but they retained their autonomy and relied on traditional means of social control. In the aftermath of World War II, the balance between Indian harvesters and the increasingly dominant non-Native sector of Yukon society shifted dramatically. The opening of new mines, expansion of existing towns and construction of roads into previously inaccessible corners of the territory, combined with a greatly increased federal presence in the territory, upset Yukon society and forced a reorganization of Indian life. Not since the first years of direct contact with Europeans had the Indians of the Yukon Territory faced such sweeping transformations. Within a decade, the foundations of their economy were uprooted, a new social and political superstructure imposed, and the very fabric of Native culture assailed.[1] The social and cultural dislocations attending this transformation have often been noted: serious alcohol problems, economic despair, reliance on government welfare payments, culturally insensitive health care, the establish-

◇ Reprinted with permission from *Northern Communities: The Prospects for Empowerment*, ed. Gurston Dacks and Ken Coates, Occasional Paper no. 25 (Edmonton: Canadian Circumpolar Institute [formerly the Boreal Institute for Northern Studies], University of Alberta, 1988), 11–22.

ment of an assimilationist education system, and family and community tensions. The litany of social ills helps illustrate the depth of the dislocations. It does not, however, explain the cause or timing of the changes.[2]

At the crux of the social upheaval was the destruction and re-creation of the northern Indian community. In the process of "bringing the northern Indians into the twentieth century,"—a common phrase among federal civil servants in the post-war period—the government systematically undermined the essence of Native social organization and life. The process was neither deliberate nor malicious. Most of the changes came unexpectedly, and as a result of policies designed to "improve the northern Indians' social and economic conditions. Whatever the intent, the government's programs nonetheless upset the rhythms of Native life in the Yukon Territory. In its place, government policies created new Indian communities, funded by welfare subsidies and administered by Department of Indian Affairs officials. An examination of this process in the Yukon Territory, 1945–1973, illustrates the nature of the reorientation, the problems that accompanied government programs, and the Natives' response to the restructuring of their lives.

The dominant goal of federal intervention in Yukon Native affairs was to alter the rhythms of Indian life. Beginning with the Hudson's Bay Company fur trade, which reached the region in the 1840s, the Yukon Natives had proved adept at responding to opportunities presented by white expansion. They participated enthusiastically in the trade, worked as guides and tripmen, sought temporary wage labour with the miners, and otherwise adapted to the new economic realities. The Natives were not, however, fully integrated into the emerging industrial order. White exclusionist policies, based on stereotypes of Native work abilities, limited opportunities for regular employment, but it was primarily the Indian preferences for a harvesting lifestyle that determined patterns of Native-white economic interaction.

These forces, in place before the Klondike Gold Rush, determined the nature of Indian response to white society in the North over the next half-century. Natives continued to work as casual labourers on the periphery of the industrial order, but only as determined by the dictates of harvesting. Most Yukon Indians followed a migratory pattern, representing an adaptation from the pre-contact norm of following the seasonal cycles of hunting, fishing, trapping and trading. Harvesting continued, in season, but the dictates of the fur trade economy, the season of riverboat travel on the Yukon River and tributaries (many Indians cut cordwood for the stern-wheelers), and the needs of the mining economy for casual labour also had to be taken into account.

Since hunting, trapping and fishing occurred away from white settlements, the continuation of harvesting ensured that most Natives, and not just those living in isolated areas, stayed away from those communities for much of the year. The situation frustrated missionaries and schoolteachers, who continually saw their efforts at Christianization and education eroded by the Natives' time in the bush. The parsimonious federal government, although providing modest assistance to Anglican and Catholic schools, refused to take a more integrative approach to Native affairs, preferring to leave the Indians as Indians. Their flexible lifestyle, which combined temporary access to the industrial economy and the stability of harvesting, proved quite persistent, surviving even the disruptions of the building of the Alaska Highway. The rhythms of Yukon Indian life, built around a viable fur trade, subsistence hunting and Native preference for harvesting over industrial labour, would face a new challenge in the 1950s.

This seasonal pattern, changed after the arrival of whites, left the structure of Native society substantially unaltered.[3] Most Natives spent much of the year, as they had in pre-contact times, in family or extended-family units. A number of families, loosely organized into bands, would gather together regularly for specific hunting or fishing tasks, most often the summer fishery, before breaking up again into family units when local resources could no longer support the larger group. As a nomadic, family-oriented people, the Yukon Indians lacked internally generated hierarchical controls; as with other hunting and gathering peoples, decision-making came through "an egalitarian system of largely consensual, informal authority."[4] Community controls traditionally worked through the avoidance of conflict and a non-hierarchical and flexible authority system. This situation fit well with the seasonal mobility and social flexibility of the Yukon Indians; it did not suit the changing plans of the federal government in the post-war period.

Before discussing the territorial situation in detail, it must be noted that the federally sponsored reorganization of Indian society was in no way unique to the Yukon Territory. From the 19th century, successive Canadian governments exhibited their displeasure with Native lifestyles by encouraging settlement on segregated reservations and assisting assimilation through education. On the western plains, the treaty process accelerated this transition forming permanent communities of previously nomadic peoples. The Natives did not always oppose the changes that accompanied treaties, reserves, annuity payments, and the like. There is increasing evidence of the Indians' willingness to adapt to new economic and social realities and to adopt new technologies or lifestyles that suited the altered conditions.[5] It is also clear that the federal government, acting primarily through the Department of Indian Affairs, did not always welcome or support Native attempts at integration. The officials seemingly believed that Natives had to be brought slowly toward the standards of white Canadian society.[6]

Although the government programs seldom met either official goals or Indian aspirations, they nonetheless reorganized Native society. The most visible symbol of this transformation was the Indian village—a seeming remnant of traditional days, but in fact a stark reminder of the inability of federal policy-makers to understand Native life. In its path-breaking report on social and economic conditions among the Canadian Indians, the Hawthorn Commission paid particular attention to this transition:

> For the first time, thousands of Indians found themselves living in permanent, sedentary communities with clearly defined spatial and social boundaries. A growing body of formal rules governing corporate land usage, residential rights, band leadership rights,

and so on, gave these mostly quite small communities a legal character and exclusiveness which stood in marked contrast to the traditional residential grouping.[7]

There was no such effort in the Yukon Territory until after World War II. Before that time, a combination of federal parsimony and limited interest in the Canadian North limited federal involvement in Indian affairs in the Yukon Territory. The government did not completely ignore the Indians; the Department of Indian Affairs appointed an Indian Agent in 1914. He, in turn, provided relief payments for the destitute and ensured that health services were available for those able to visit a physician's office in Whitehorse or Dawson City. In the main, however, the government recognized that the Indians wished to remain as harvesters, and realized further that a continuation of Indian seasonal mobility limited the demands on the federal coffers. Minor initiatives were taken to protect Native access to resources (provided such regulations did not interfere with mineral exploration) and residential reserves were surveyed near the principal non-Native centres. In the latter case, the purpose was not to attract Indian residents, but rather to ensure that Natives and whites did not live close together. For their part, the Yukon Indians did not protest government indifference. They enjoyed relatively unimpeded access to harvestable resources, the fur trade remained strong, and seasonal mobility continued as before.[8]

A series of events in the late 1940s, all outside the control of the Yukon Indians, conspired to upset the rhythms of Native life and to introduce a new era in federal-Indian relations. The transition started with a new national commitment to universal social welfare. Prodded by the Cooperative Commonwealth Federation on the political left and almost outmanoeuvred by the newly-minted Progressive Conservative Party on the right, the Liberal government of William Lyon Mackenzie King took a few tentative steps towards the creation of a universal welfare system. This program was national in scope, drawing Native people into a web of initiatives that paid no attention to their particular needs and aspirations. At the same time, a new commitment to the economically disadvantaged led the federal government to the specific realization that Native people had fallen far behind the rest of Canadian society. While government programs for all Canadians increased in the post-war period, therefore, many new initiatives targeted specifically at Native "problems" also emerged.[9]

This interventionism proved particularly trying for the Indians of the Yukon Territory. Having been all but ignored over the previous half-century, the Natives now faced the impact of national policies, country-wide initiatives for Indian people, and specific measures aimed at northern Natives. The transition from neglect to regular involvement was abrupt and disruptive. The government possessed substantial financial and legal resources in its attempts to restructure Native society; the Indians had little with which to respond, beyond a determination to remain as Indians and resist the assimilationist tendencies.

The process started, rather innocently, with the introduction of Mother's Allowance in 1944. Any Canadian parent with a child under the age of 16 years could receive the monthly payments of up to $5.00. Since most Natives in the Yukon Territory did not have access to schools, primarily due to family mobility, the government waived the requirement that school-age children be registered in and attending schools. At the same time, however, the government refused to trust Native parents to spend the money on the children as intended. Fearing that the Indians, having returned from several months in the bush, would "waste" the generous federal supplement, the government insisted on paying northern Natives "in kind" rather than by cheque. This allowed federal officials to dictate what the Indians could and could not buy. Canned milk and tomatoes, southern clothing and prepared baby foods were high on the list of authorized items, a clear indication of official disapproval of Native eating and clothing habits.[10]

Other programs offered in the immediate post-war period were similarly benign. The federal government established a pension for elderly Natives and a public health nurse to administer routine medical services and to provide health education. Similarly, doctors began regular visits to Native communities and a dentist provided dental clinics in isolated Native villages. The government conducted a major tuberculosis survey, and built an addition onto the Whitehorse General Hospital to house Indians with the disease. The government even established a trap-line registration program in 1950, hoping to protect Indian access to fur resources and to keep out southern interlopers.[11] The programs appeared to deal with the specific conditions of the Yukon Indians, promising to preserve their economic base— the fur trade—and to respond to the serious medical problems among the Native population.

The government had, as well, altered its long-standing opposition to offering welfare payments to northern Indians. In 1933, John Hawksley, the Yukon Indian Agent, offered a clear statement of government options in this area:

> The Indians, owing to changed circumstances, cannot afford to stay around the villages or leave their families while the men go away to hunt and trap, they are compelled to separate into small parties and live in the woods for the purpose of hunting and trapping in order to make a living. Opportunities of obtaining work from white people are very much reduced. To insist upon the Indian families staying in the village (which has been suggested) would mean that some of them would have to receive help in the way of provisions. It appears to be a much wiser policy to keep them independent, earning their own living, and they are less liable to get into bad habits.[12]

The government's concern rested on parsimony as much as interest in Indian "habits," but had ensured the continuation, for half a century, of a policy of actively discouraging relief payments.

Few Indians had required government assistance. From the early days of the fur trade, the Indians had linked occasional work for non-Native employers with trapping and subsistence hunting. They particularly valued seasonal activities, such as wood-cutting, big-game guiding, and packing, which provided a source of cash income but did not unduly disrupt mobility. This pattern continued through the building of the Alaska Highway.[13] Indians typically worked during the summer months—a slow time for harvesting but the key construction period—and returned to their hunting camps for the fall and winter. The seasonal round at Champagne in 1949 was typical. The Indians continued to trap and fish, moving as resources dictated. A few, mostly young men, found occasional work with the highway maintenance crews, but stayed only during the summer months.[14] For the Natives of the Yukon Territory, the resulting "mixed economy," a juxtaposition of subsistence harvesting and work for wages, represented the best response to territorial economic realities and their own cultural needs.[15]

The delicate balance of harvesting and wage employment collapsed in the late 1940s. A catastrophic decline in the fur trade undermined the foundation of the Indian economy. In both 1944 and 1945, Yukon fur trappers collected over $650 000 worth of pelts. Although the number of pelts traded increased dramatically over the next five years (from 87 000 in 1944–45 to 153 000 in 1949–1950), fur returns plummeted to less than a third of their earlier values. Yukon fur returns dropped to $144 000 in 1948–49, the lowest level in fifteen years.[16] The problem lay outside the Yukon Territory, as the increased catch figures attest. Declining prices and reduced demand wreaked havoc with the formerly stable trade, forcing Indians to seek other sources of income.[17] And this was not the end of the Indians' problems. Almost simultaneously, the termination of riverboat travel between Whitehorse and Dawson City—the last ship ran in 1955—eliminated the need for Indian woodcutters along the river.[18] For over fifty years, Natives had supplemented their earnings by cutting wood, an activity that blended well with their seasonal movements. But this too now ended, the victim of the new roads linking Whitehorse, Mayo and Dawson.

The timing of the economic collapse was auspicious, for it coincided with the expansion of the government's pension and welfare programs. The Indians needed money to supplement their declining returns and subsistence hunting; the government was prepared to offer the necessary support. The purse-strings, closely guarded for decades, had been loosened. New procedures permitted traders and missionaries in isolated districts to provide food and other supplies to needy Indians. Between 1940 and 1944, annual expenditures on relief averaged under $12 000. By 1949, that figure had jumped to over $30 000, and welfare spending tripled again to over $90 000 in 1954–1955. (Ten years later, the federal government spent over $200 000 on welfare payments to Yukon Indians).[19]

The option of securing income from other sources did exist, and federal agents encouraged Indians to seek employment with non-Native companies. Worried that Natives would become dependent upon the relief payments, the local Indian agent attempted to assist "the Indians to be self-supporting and reliant." As a result, financial assistance was provided "to Indians to assist them in possible worthwhile fields of endeavour, in preference to direct relief."[20] Ignoring that Indians in the Yukon Territory had been "self-supporting and reliant" for generations, federal officials sought to use the relief system to integrate the Natives into the broader territorial economy. The Department of Indian Affairs hired men to work on reserve housing projects and at the new experimental farm at Haines Junction. Money was loaned to Indians seeking to exploit commercial woodcutting opportunities or to find work driving dog teams. The local Indian Agents believed that such subsidies would eliminate the need for welfare payments, help break down discriminatory barriers facing the Yukon Indians, and undercut the Natives' continued seasonal movements. To many government officials, economic integration was the key to cultural change, and would encourage the rapid assimilation of Yukon Indians into the non-Native territorial society.[21] Those who tried to enter the industrial labour force, however, had little success. Prejudicial hiring practices ensured there were few jobs for those Indians trying to find more permanent positions.

By the mid-1950s, the Yukon Indians had come to depend on the pensions, Mother's Allowance, welfare grants and other forms of federal assistance now available. Reliance on government payments did not signify an acceptance of federal assimilationist policies. Despite the Department of Indian Affairs' best efforts to encourage industrial labour patterns, the Indians continued to prefer hunting and trapping. Government subsidies had become, in effect, a support payment for their nomadic lifestyle, replacing casual wage labour and allowing a continuing of seasonal mobility. The irony was obvious. Programs designed to integrate, educate and settle the Indians were instead providing the financial basis for the maintenance of the Natives' preferred subsistence lifestyle.

Federal officials noted the contradiction between intentions and the results. The Indians were not moving into the mainstream of the territorial society and economy, and showed little willingness to follow the federal government's assimilationist lead. More direct intervention was necessary if the Indians were to be "modernized" and trained for the realities of the "new North." The transition from offering assistance programs to Indians to taking a more active role in encouraging a restructuring of the Native lifestyle occurred in the mid-1950s. The government increased the financial resources available to the Yukon Indian agency, but even more importantly began to use the coercive powers at its disposal to ensure Indian compliance with federal plans.

The primary effort was directed at the children. In 1920, the federal government had given itself the legal authority to force Native attendance in schools.[22] This provision had not been enforced in the North, largely because the government had no desire to build and maintain a network of Indian day schools among the widely scattered nomadic bands. Officials similarly ignored the provision in the Mother's Allowance Act that required attendance at school. Signs of changing priorities in education first emerged in the late 1940s. The Department of Indian Affairs decided that the old policy of segregating Native children in Indian day and residential schools did not encourage proper educational development. A new policy called for the integration of Native and white children in provincial and territorial schools wherever possible. White residents in the Yukon Territory resisted this change, and urged the government to maintain a separate Indian school system. For children from isolated bands, such integration was impossible.

These children would be required to attend residential school. The new national priorities were applied in the Yukon Territory by the mid-1950s. The Mother's Allowance regulations were rigorously enforced. Parents unable to deliver their children to a day school on a regular basis were required to send them to either the Anglican residential school at Carcross or the Catholic school at Lower Post. Any families failing to comply faced a quick termination of Mother's Allowance payments.[23]

The Yukon Indians now faced a difficult choice. Nomadic patterns could be maintained if children were sent to residential school, but this required the very painful splintering of families. Conversely, families could remain together if at least one parent moved with the children to a village and remained there year-round. The father could continue to hunt and trap—albeit without the important assistance provided by his wife and children—but the rest of the family would have to remain near the school for the duration of the academic year.[24]

The Yukon Indians had resisted the pressure to move to sedentary villages. Without a viable fur trade and unable to find other methods of supplementing their subsistence harvests, however, they required the allowances, pensions and welfare payments the government now offered. Reluctantly, and with many family and group adaptations which permitted a continuation of harvesting activities, they began to move more permanently into the villages.[25]

Increased school attendance provides the best indication of the pace of this micro-urbanization. The number of students enrolled in Yukon Indian day schools tripled between 1940 and 1955. In 1950, the first year Native students entered the Yukon territorial school system, 21 children occupied desks in the predominantly white classrooms. Five years later, 110 Native children were in the system. Altogether, combining Indian day schools, residential schools and territorial public schools, the number of children enrolled jumped from 181 in 1945 to 387 in 1955. Equally important, attendance at these schools, as required by law, became increasingly regular. In 1940, 40% of those on the school lists missed each day; by 1955, almost 95% of registered students attended class.[26]

The content of the schooling these children received also changed. Before 1945, the government left responsibility for Indian education to the church, and expressed little interest in school programming. The missionary system proved very disruptive, offering little of benefit to the Indians and preparing them poorly for the life awaiting them in their villages. As the Indian children entered the day, residential and public schools in the 1950s, however, they discovered an even more aggressively assimilationist education system. The increasingly secular teaching corps ignored Native languages, taught "practical" industrial skills, and attempted to give the students a grounding in southern Canadian curricula. The effort offered little real preparation for the world the children would discover upon returning to their communities.[27]

Education was, understandably, the foundation of official attempts to reconstitute Native life in the Yukon Territory, but the federal government did not limit its efforts to this single program. Residential reserves had been established near the main towns early in the century. Most had been unused, or resorted to spasmodically, over the next four decades. The reserve question assumed new currency in the 1950s. The Territorial Indian Agent was asked to investigate the need for new reserves in areas facing development pressure. R.J. Meek requested a reserve for Ross River because "Recent mining discoveries in the area will probably create a change in the economic set-up of the Indians which up to this year (1953) has been based entirely on trapping and hunting."[28] Meek also requested a new reserve for Snag, recommended that the Fort Selkirk site be maintained and observed that the Indians did not need a reserve at Stewart River.[29] Through the 1950s, additional reserves were surveyed at Burwash, Old Crow, Upper Liard Bridge and Marsh Lake (The claim to several dormant reserve sites was re-established in this decade as well).[30]

A 1958 overview of the status of Yukon Indian reserves revealed that the reserve program had still not worked and that many of the Yukon bands remained semi-nomadic into the late 1950s. The report also spelled out the government's continuing intent to alter the residential patterns of the isolated bands. Regarding the Aishihik Band, the Superintendent of Indian Affairs noted "We will investigate the possibilities of these Indians moving from this remote area to the parcel of land reserved at Haines Junction." The Burwash Indians lived on private land, not the government reserve. It was hoped that they too could be moved. The members of the Champagne band faced similar pressure: "Some of the younger Indians are being encouraged to locate on the Haines Junction Reserve to improve employment opportunities and to be closer to services." Indians in the Dawson area, formerly of the Moosehide reserve, were moved into Dawson City and provided with government housing. Superintendent Jutras suggested that the Indians at White River and Ross River be consulted before their reserves were moved. The White River reserve was to be "close to the highway and services." The recommendation for the Ross River band noted, "These Indians derive their livelihood from trapping. They make their headquarters at Ross River, where they are at the mercy of one trader who charges high prices for food and gives low returns for furs. After consultation with the Indians, stake a few acres at Ross River as a village site and proceed with limited housing. This Ross River area is a welfare problem and the younger Indians are to be encouraged to move to Upper Liard Bridge permanently and transfer to that Band."[31]

The government's priorities were quite clear. Officials discouraged the Indians from pursuing a trapping and hunting lifestyle. Efforts were made to ensure permanent residence on a reserve, preferably one near schools and other services. Here was the essence of the federal attempt to upset the rhythm of Native life in the Yukon Territory. The reserve would become the work site, welfare and other support payments the controlling mechanisms, education and business programs the tools, and the Indians of the Yukon Territory the clay. Under the control of Department of Indian Affairs officials, Native society would be dismantled and reconstructed along suitable "Canadian" lines.

The new and artificial communities[32] that followed became the basis for subsequent government programming, and eventually for Native activism. The communities were not, however, the traditional or deliberate creation of their Indian members. As the Indians moved into the villages in the late 1950s and 1960s, they entered an alien environment, one that followed a different seasonal pattern, had different standards of leadership and unique mechanisms of social control. Traditional means of social control, which emphasized consensus and the avoidance of conflict, were not suited to the demands of sedentary communities. But the government had a solution here too, in the form of the band chief and council structure. As was noted in the Hawthorn Report, the imposition of institutional structures was not unique to the Yukon Indians: "[T]he band council device was not a spontaneous creation of the Indians, but one which was introduced from the outside; . . . the system was not congruent with Indian precedent or social organization in most cases."[33]

Although the band councils created the image of Native involvement, the reality was much different. A band-by-band study of management practices, conducted on behalf of the Council of Yukon Indians in 1971, revealed that only a few of the band managers had the training necessary to handle the tasks assigned to them. In most communities, including those where the managers fulfilled the functions expected of them, the Indian leaders had little authority.[34] The council system had not been intended to leave real power in the hands of Indian leaders. Instead, it provided an agency through which the government could deal with the whole group. Rather than serving as leaders in the Indian sense of the term, band chiefs and councils functioned as intermediaries, implementing government programs on occasion and representing the group's interests to the Department of Indian Affairs. Even in this one apparent gesture toward Indian autonomy, the government had in fact limited and even co-opted Native leadership, imposed yet another artificial structure, and reduced even further the power of traditional Indian means of social control.[35]

Since both the physical Indian village and the political structures designed to control the resultant "community" were created by non-Indian forces, it is not surprising that the communities had difficulty responding to the problems that followed. From the mid-1950s to the present, the standard indicators of social and economic distress all point to a serious crisis within the Yukon Indian communities. Unemployment rates are shockingly high (even if the returns from the non-wage economy are taken into consideration), alcohol and drug problems plague entire villages and political tensions remain.[36]

The transition to a sedentary lifestyle had not proceeded as the government had hoped. The move to the villages rested on the collapse of the fur trade and the availability of government financial aid programs; it was not predicated on an acceptance of the acculturative processes advocated by the government. The process of assimilation had run up against two impressive barriers: the discriminatory attitudes of the non-native community, which limited the Indians' integration into the broader society, and the Natives' unwillingness to conform to the model set out by the government. Natives in the Yukon Territory remained culturally and economically segregated, and the process of assimilation moved slowly.

Government policies generated much resentment. Much of the frustration has been vented internally, as evidenced in reports of domestic and community violence, drinking problems and other forms of self-destructive behaviour. In the late 1960s, however, Indian leaders turned their protests toward the government and the non-Native people of Canada. In a speech delivered in 1971, Chief Elijah Smith of the Yukon Native Brotherhood declared his desire to end "the welfare thinking of Indian Affairs and our people." Since the formation of the Yukon Native Brotherhood in 1968, and particularly through the land claims processes of the Yukon Native Brotherhood and the Council for Yukon Indians, Native people have repeatedly stated their intention to regain control over their lives and to eliminate the still-lingering residue of paternalism and assimilationism of government officials. Native elders remember only too well how recent the transition has been, and how different the community lifestyle of the 1980s is from the seasonal rhythms of the 1940s.

For the Council for Yukon Indians, community-level decision making is held out as the best hope of addressing the Natives' serious economic and social difficulties. Requests for Native social workers, economic development officers, and specially trained teachers reflect the interest in shifting the locus of power from civil servants' offices in Whitehorse and Ottawa to the communities themselves. The efforts at empowering Natives on a local level continue in other forums as well. The work of the Yukon Native Languages Project, which is helping to revitalize Indian languages through classroom instruction, the increased use of Native elders in instructional settings, and an Indian communication network (newspaper, radio and television) to enhance contact among Indian groups throughout the territory, all seek to give Natives the knowledge and skills necessary to sustain and protect their culture. The community empowerment is most noticeable in the current land claims negotiations. After the 1984 tentative accord was rejected by several bands, the federal government and the Council for Yukon Indians implemented a new process, which requires continuous consultation with the various communities, and mandates a land claims settlement that will address separately the specific concerns of each community.[37]

There is, ultimately, a great irony in the Indians' acceptance of the community as the basic unit of politics and culture in the new North. The forces of education, health care, work and government services brought the Indians into the settlements and gradually broke the rhythms of Native life. The altering of those rhythms, particularly without offering the Indians a culturally or economically viable alternative, created permanent settlements but also contributed significantly toward the many problems faced by the Natives in the post-war period. The emphasis on community decision making and administration represents an acceptance by the Indians, however grudging, of the post-war realities of life in the North. Indian leaders are not, however, seeking to recapture the past, or to resurrect the lifeways of the pre-World War II period, when seasonal mobility and residential flexibility allowed individuals and groups to adjust to changing social and economic conditions. Increased development, improved roads, Native migration within the territory and other changes in Yukon society have rendered recourse to old techniques largely ineffectual. As they plan for the future of their people, Native leaders face the reality that their options are limited by the changes of the past forty years, and that the agenda they must deal with is, similarly, very much a creation of the post-war period.

NOTES

1. The Yukon Indians were, of course, not alone. Indian and Inuit groups across the North faced similar changes, although the timing and scale of the transformation differed from place to place.

2. Scholars, particularly anthropologists, have commented extensively on the post World War II conditions in northern villages. For a good example of this work, see the special issue of *Anthropologica* NS 5, 1 (1963), which deals with aspects of Native communities in the North.

3. Marriages between Native women and white men upset the social balance somewhat, lowering the marrying age of women and raising the age for men.

4. Thomas Stone, "Flux and Authority in a Subarctic Society: The Yukon Miners in the Nineteenth Century," *Ethnohistory* 30, 4 (1983): 216.

5. John Tobias, "Canada's Subjugation of the Plains Cree," *Canadian Historical Review* 64 (1993): 4. As this related to other northern Indians see Ken Coates and William R. Morrison, "Treaty Five (1875-1908)," "Treaty Ten (1906)," "Treaty Eleven (1921)" (Ottawa: Treaties and Historical Research Centre, 1986). See also Fumoleau, *As Long as This Land Shall Last: A History of Treaty 9 and Treaty 11, 1870–1939* (Toronto: McClelland & Stewart, 1975).

6. John Tobias, "Protection, Civilisation, Assimilation: An Outline History of Canada's Indian Policy" in *As Long as the Sun Shines and the Water Flows: A Reader in Canadian Native Studies*," ed. Ian Getty and A.S. Lussier (Vancouver: University of British Columbia Press, 1983).

7. H.B. Hawthorn, ed. *A Survey of the Contemporary Indians of Canada: Economic, Political, Educational Needs and Policies*, Part II (Ottawa: 1968), 177.

8. Ken Coates, "Best Left as Indians: The Federal Government and the Indians of the Yukon, 1894–1950," *Canadian Journal of Native Studies* 4, 2 (1984).

9. Denis Guest, *The Emergence of Social Security in Canada* (Vancouver: University of British Columbia Press, 1980).

10. Indian Affairs Branch, *Annual Report*, 1945–48. Note that most other Indians in Canada (except those in the Northwest Territories) received their allowances by cheque.

11. Robert McCandless, *Yukon Wildlife: A Social History* (Edmonton: University of Alberta Press, 1985).

12. Public Archives of Canada, Yukon Territorial Records, RG 91, vol. 9, file 1491, John Hawksley to A.F. Mackenzie, 29 Aug. 1933.

13. Ken Coates, "The Alaska Highway and the Indians of the Southern Yukon, 1942–50: A Study of Native Adaptation to Northern Development" in *The Alaska Highway: Papers*

of the 40th Anniversary Symposium, ed. Ken Coates (Vancouver: University of British Columbia Press, 1985), 151–71.

14. Yukon Territorial Archives, Anglican Church Records, Champagne File. Anthony Guscoyne, Report to the Diocese of Yukon Upon the Present State of Champagne (YT), Mission Field, Summer 1949.

15. On the idea of the mixed economy, see Michael Asch, "Some Effects of the Late Nineteenth Century Modernization of the Fur Trade on the Economy of the Slavey Indians," *Western Canadian Journal of Anthropology* 4 (1976):7–15, and "The Ecological-Evolutionary Model and the Concept of the Mode of Production" in *Challenging Anthropology*, ed. D. Turner and G. Smith (Toronto: McGraw-Hill Ryerson, 1979). On the economy of the Yukon Indians, see Coates, "Best Left as Indians."

16. Kenneth Rea, *The Political Economy of the Canadian North* (Toronto: University of Toronto Press, 1968).

17. The collapse of the fur trade coincided with the introduction of the trap-line registration system. The Indians vigorously protested the $10 annual fee, claiming that it cut deeply into their already diminished returns. Their protests were ignored. See Robert McCandless, *Yukon Wildlife*, 142–148.

18. Gordon Bennett, "Yukon Transportation: A History," Canadian Historic Sites, Occasional Papers in Archaeology and History, 19 (1978): 146.

19. Indian Affairs Branch, *Annual Reports*, 1939–70.

20. Department of Indian Affairs, *Annual Report*, 1949, 200.

21. Department of Indian Affairs, *Annual Reports*, 1949–52.

22. Ken Coates, "A Very Imperfect Means of Education: Indian Day Schools in the Yukon Territory, 1890–1950" in *Indian Education in Canada*, vol. 1, *The Legacy*, ed. Jean

Barman, Y. Hebert, and D. McCaskill (Vancouver: University of British Columbia Press, 1985).

23. Indian Affairs Branch, Annual Report, 1946, 212; Department of Indian Affairs, RG 10, vol. 8762, file 906/25-1-005, pt. 1, R.J. Meek to Indian Affairs Branch, 8 Feb. 1950. Yukon Territorial Archives, Series 4, vol. 33, file 689, Rowat to Jeckell, 4 June 1945.

24. In remote areas, local schools were not provided until the 1960s. Sending children away permitted families to continue their harvesting activities. When the schools were eventually established, parents had to move into the towns. For an excellent discussion of this process in Ross River, see R.F. McDonnell, "Kasini Society: Some Aspects of the Social Organization of an Atha-baskan Culture Between 1900–1950" (PhD thesis, University of British Columbia, 1975); and Peter Dimitrov and Martin Weinstein, *So That the Future Will Be Ours* (Ross River, 1984).

25. This process has, erroneously, I believe, often been ascribed to the construction of the Alaska Highway. The Indians in the southern Yukon remained as mobile and as reluctant to settle on the reserves as did the Indians elsewhere in the district. The timing of their move to the villages was similar to that of Indian groups away from the highway. For the contrary view see Julie Cruikshank, "The Gravel Magnet: Some Social Impacts of the Alaska Highway on Yukon Indians" in *The Alaska Highway* ed. Ken Coates 172–87. See also Frank Duerden, *The Evolution and Nature of the Contemporary Settlement Pattern in a Selected Area of the Yukon Territory* (Winnipeg: University of Manitoba Centre for Settlement Studies, 1971).

26. Coates, "A Very Imperfect Means of Education."

27. Richard King, *The School at Mopass: A Problem of Identity* (Toronto: Holt, Rinehart and Winston, 1967). For the historical background on residential school education in the Yukon, see Ken Coates, "Betwixt and Between:

the Anglican Church and the Children of the Carcross (Chouttla) Residential School, 1910–55," *BC Studies* 62 (1984–85).

28. Indian Affairs and Northern Development, file 801-30-0-1, Meek to Arneil, 21 Oct. 1953.

29. Ibid.

30. Ibid; Indian Affairs and Northern Development, Bethune to Supt of Reserves and Trusts, Schedule of Lands Reserves for Indians, Yukon Territory, 14 May 1958.

31. Indian Affairs and Northern Development, file 801-30-0-1, Meek to Arneil, 21 Oct. 1953; Indian Affairs and Northern Development, Report of Jutras, Supt of Indian Affairs, Reserves (Yukon), 9 June 1958. On the government's subsequent programs at Ross River, see Dimitrov and Weinstein, *So That the Future Will Be Ours.*

32. Most northern communities were, of course, both new and artificial. Non-Natives coming north, however, carried widely shared expectations about the nature of community life and a general acceptance of the official mechanisms of social control.

33. Hawthorn, *A Survey of the Contemporary Indians,* 78.

34. H.J. Bredin, "Indian Bands of the Yukon Territory" (Council of Yukon Indians, 1971).

35. A 1973 government report indicated that all Yukon chiefs and councils were selected by "traditional" (as opposed to elected) means. They were not, however, performing traditional functions. The selection procedures have now changed, and chief and council elections now form part of Indian political life in the territory.

36. Ken Coates, "Indian Participation in the Economy," paper prepared for Yukon 2000 Conference, Sept. 1986.

37. Ibid.

DESPERATELY SEEKING ABSOLUTION: NATIVE AGENCY AS COLONIALIST ALIBI? ⋄

ROBIN BROWNLIE AND MARY-ELLEN KELM

o

In 1991, a British Columbia judge rejected the Gitksan Wet'suwet'en land claim, releasing a written judgment in which the potential political effect of historians' "expertise" was given clear expression. In this judgment, Chief Justice Allan MacEachern dismissed the evidence of anthropologists who testified in the Gitksan's favour on the grounds that they were "too closely associated with the plaintiffs."[1] Historians, on the other hand, were deemed far more credible due to their perceived impartiality as "collectors of archival, historical documents"; for this reason the judge remarked: "Generally speaking, I accept just about everything they put before me."[2] While some might evaluate this as a flattering tribute to the science of history and its Canadian practitioners, it seems to us that MacEachern has attributed to historians a degree of objectivity that is really unattainable, particularly in the politically charged field of Native-newcomer relations. None of us conducts research or formulates theses independently of either our life experience or the events currently taking place in society around us. These realities help determine the issues we examine, the questions we ask, and the ways in which we seek to answer them. The judge's assumptions about historical impartiality confront us with an urgent need to investigate the reality behind the traditional historian's neutral pose, to examine the premises on which the study of Native-newcomer relations is presently based, and to consider the agenda behind historical writings whether or not it is made explicit. For the implications of the Gitksan Wet'suwet'en land claims case are clear: published academic work is accessible to the larger, non-academic world, and conclusions, like facts, can be employed for political ends by anyone who has reason to construct a case. We owe it to ourselves, and to the people whose past we study, to approach our work with

⋄ *Canadian Historical Review* 75, 4 (1994): 543–56. Reprinted by permission of University of Toronto Press Incorporated.

an awareness of its political ramifications and a consciousness of our own location with respect to the subject matter. In the words of Adrienne Rich: "we cannot help making history because we are made of it, and history is made of people like us, carriers of the behavior and assumptions of a given time and place."[3] As historians, our engagement with the past cannot obscure our involvement with the present, despite MacEachern's wishful thinking.

With this in mind, we have undertaken an analysis of a recent trend in publications on Native-newcomer relations: the recognition of Native agency and the ways in which some historians are approaching the issue. We will examine three scholarly works: Douglas Cole and Ira Chaikin's *An Iron Hand upon the People: The Law against the Potlatch on the Northwest Coast* (Vancouver/Toronto: Douglas & McIntyre 1990); J.R. Miller's article "Owen Glendower, Hotspur, and Canadian Indian Policy," originally published in *Ethnohistory* 4 (1990), also in his anthology *Sweet Promises: A Reader on Indian-White Relations in Canada* (Toronto: University of Toronto Press 1991); and Tina Loo's paper in the *Canadian Historical Review*, "Dan Cranmer's Potlatch: Law as Coercion, Symbol, and Rhetoric in British Columbia, 1885–1951" (73, 2, 1992).

These three works are linked in their commitment to uncovering the role of Native agency in the relationship between Canada's First Nations and the Canadian government in the late nineteenth and early twentieth centuries. Cole and Chaikin, Loo, and Miller all examine the functioning of the law banning the potlatch, while Miller also looks at the pass system and residential schools, as elements of a general policy aimed at forced cultural change. In all three works, the authors conclude that despite the weight of the state's authority, the First Nations continued to assert themselves, to resist the power of colonialism, and to maintain the vibrancy of their cultures. In taking this approach, these scholars have contributed to the crucial process of dismantling the antiquated stereotype of Aboriginal people as passive victims in the era of settlement.

With this, we have no quarrel. The argument for Native agency is now nearly twenty years old in the writing of Canadian history and its use in understanding Aboriginal roles in the fur trade, for instance, is virtually undisputed.[4] Cole, Chaikin, Miller, and Loo are part of a larger group of Native historians who seek to show that Aboriginal people were able to act as well as react to the myriad of state and church initiatives that sought to eliminate the First Nations as economic, political, social, cultural, and religious forces within the nascent Canadian state.[5] Scholars have proven that the argument for Native agency is not misplaced in the settlement period even as they have shown the lengths to which state and church authorities went to ensure the dominance of non-Native society. Cole, Chaikin, Miller, and Loo break with the general trend in one significant way: they go beyond the argument for the recognition of Native agency to one that uses evidence of Native resilience and strength to soften, and at times to deny, the impact of colonialism, and thus, implicitly, to absolve its perpetrators. Though all four scholars seem to acknowledge the colonial oppression experienced by the First Nations, they nonetheless concur that through poor implementation, Native resistance, and the peculiarities of legal process, the negative effects of colonization were mitigated, even nullified. Further, in Tina Loo's paper, this approach is extended to making the argument that by calling forth resistance, the colonizers actually contributed to the empowerment of Aboriginal people. In the course of presenting their evidence for such claims, these writers gloss over the suffering of First Nations under federal "wardship," minimize the extent of the very real and observable damage inflicted on Aboriginal societies, and continually emphasize the altruistic intent of the colonizers. This trend in scholarly writing thus carries within it an insidious tendency to turn Native agency into colonialist alibi.[6]

This problem is perhaps most evident in Cole and Chaikin's work, *An Iron Hand upon the People*. The subject of the potlatch and its suppression has long been a contentious one in Canadian Native history, no doubt because, as the authors note, since the nineteenth century it has assumed a great symbolic significance for both Native and non-Native societies. No other institution better illustrated the gulf between indigenous cultures and the dominant imported one. In the potlatch, the religious, social, and economic values of the various Northwest Coast societies were holistically integrated, a fact that offended missionaries and government officials precisely because they recognized that these values were incompatible with the seamless assimilation of Aboriginal people into Euro-Canadian society. Through the facade of official rhetoric about concern for Native health, neglect of children and elders, or economic impoverishment due to potlatching shines the true motivation for criminalization of the institution. Contemporary commentators saw it as "inconsistent with all progress," progress being the adoption of Euro-Canadian values, work habits, and patterns of accumulation and consumption.[7] To stress this is in no way to imply malevolent intent on the part of those espousing the ban: the term "progress" summarized the panaceas of the age, expressing boundless faith in the future and in the potential of technology to solve all the problems of human existence. It must, however, be emphasized that most members of the Euro-Canadian population considered their own society demonstrably superior to all others and viewed this "fact" as a justification for imposing their culture on others whenever they were able. In this they differed from Aboriginal people, whose interest often lay in mutual reciprocity and respect in cultural exchange, a perspective that obviated the need to demonstrate cultural superiority.

It is in their approach to this central question of imposing cultural values that Cole and Chaikin reveal both the ambivalence of their own position and a Eurocentric bias that compels them to defend the motives of colonial society while denying First Nations an equal right to self-determination. The authors try, throughout the course of the book, to develop an ethical basis upon which to judge the potlatch law. Yet they remain unsuccessful because they delay defining their terms of reference. By the time they make this effort, they have already passed a number of subjective and apparently unconscious judgments.[8] Consistently, they justify the motives of colonial officialdom (although, oddly enough, not those of the missionaries) until they finally take the ethical stand that "we have to recognize a role for government, a right to intervene to secure some measure of conformity to its own customs and values and in pursuit of its goals."[9] This is a right that they do not accord to Native societies, for their defence of the campaign against the potlatch rests on the assertion that it represented a "system" that "itself was coercively intolerant of dissent."[10] Although they do not appear to recognize it, "by potlatch system" they in fact mean Northwest Coast Aboriginal cultures, in which the potlatch was, in most cases, deeply embedded and inseparable from the rest of the culture. Northwest Coast societies, then, unlike Euro-Canadian society, are defined as "coercively intolerant of dissent" when their members "intervene to secure some measure of conformity to [their] own customs and values and in pursuit of [their] goals."

The denial of such a right to potlatching societies stems from the authors' perception of them as being founded on false moral principles. Defending the suppression of the potlatch, Cole and Chaikin state: "the law could be justified to the extent that it sought to assist those victimized by a system that was itself sometimes coercive. To the extent that humans—children, the old and women—may have been victimized by a system that, sometimes from hygienic innocence, sometimes from the tyranny of male domination, sometimes from avarice, placed status and prestige above humanistic principles, the potlatch itself was morally wrong."[11] The crowning irony of this condemnation lies in the choice of moral standards. The authors vilify potlatching societies on the grounds of their alleged victimization of children, elders, and women through a male-dominated system based on transcendent avarice and the pursuit of status and prestige. This catalogue of evils bears remarkable resemblance to those decried by Euro-Canadian social reformers when they sought the improvement of their own Western, Christian, capitalist society. When Cole and Chaikin ignore this point, refusing to turn their moral scrutiny to the society of the anti-potlatchers, they leave the impression that the dominant culture was free of the faults attributed to the Northwest Coast societies and therefore that it was superior to them. In doing so, Cole and Chaikin seem to reveal an unstated ideological sympathy with the anti-potlatch campaign.

The decisive flaw in this work lies in the failure of the authors to appreciate their Eurocentric bias and to recognize the cultural integrity of Aboriginal societies. When traditional Native leaders objected to the campaign against the potlatch, they were consciously acting in defence of their entire way of life, just as the Christian converts who sought the law's enforcement did so in pursuit of their own goal—assimilation as an adaptive response to the colonial invasion. To utilize this disagreement within Native communities as an indication of the moral ambiguity of the potlatch, as Cole and Chaikin do, is a distortion because it ignores the fundamental significance of the struggle.[12] This was not an intellectual dispute over universal ethical principles, but rather an expression of the existential crisis caused within Aboriginal societies by the ongoing erosion of their subsistence base, the introduction of European diseases, and the missionary assault on their system of beliefs. This, it seems to us, is the issue that Cole and Chaikin wish to avoid. The anti-potlatch campaign is never adequately placed in its context as a key element of the "assault on indigenous culture," in spite of an introduction which acknowledges this broader program.[13] Although they take great pains to highlight the altruistic goals of anti-potlatchers, they are also immensely relieved that the potlatch never died out altogether, for had this occurred, the charge of cultural genocide would have been irrefutable. As it is, the resourcefulness of Native people in preserving elements of their culture has spared the colonizers from a success that would have been a disgrace to their descendants.

The argument of Native agency is thus very useful to Cole and Chaikin in diverting attention from the role of non-Natives in the suppression of Aboriginal cultures, but they apply it selectively. On the one hand, Native people are shown to be active participants in their destiny not only when they support the anti-potlatch law and lobby for its enforcement but also when they resist and adapt the potlatch to the hostile conditions of the ban. On the other hand, the right to political and moral self-determination, arguably the most significant form of agency, is withheld from the First Nations and, instead, accorded exclusively to the Canadian government.

J.R. Miller, in his article "Owen Glendower, Hotspur, and Canadian Indian Policy," takes a somewhat different tack. While he concluded with the caveat that his analysis should not be "read as arguing that interference and coercion did not occur,"[14] Miller devotes himself throughout the paper to proving that neither the pass system nor the law against Native ceremonial was enforceable, and that residential schools were not wholly pernicious institutions of cultural re-education. In his attempts to find a nuanced view of these policies, he produces a very contradictory picture. Like Cole and Chaikin, he argues that the effect of such bans on cultural practices were mitigated both by their limited potential for enforcement and by Native ingenuity in subverting them. This, of course, begs the question of the law's effectiveness: Why did Northwest Coast potlatchers change the structure of the potlatch to escape prosecution if the law was unenforceable and therefore non-threatening? Similarly, if residential schools were not as bad as we have been led to believe by their Native survivors, why were their students resisting, making repeated escape attempts, and destroying school property as Miller describes? If parents exerted significant control over curriculum and school regulations (at one school, that is, which Miller acknowledges as an isolated and extraordinary case), why were Native parents generally so dissatisfied with the education system and so reluctant to relinquish their children to it? If Native languages were, in fact, not always prohibited in the schools, why have so many former pupils testified to the loss of their ancestral tongues and traditions through their subjection to residential schooling?

It is when one poses this sort of question that one is struck by Miller's idiosyncratic application of his evidence. One example is his citation of Eleanor Brass's autobiography as proof that some Native students were first exposed to indigenous cultural practices at residential schools.[15] In fact, in her book Brass laments her inability to speak her people's language, which her parents (both graduates of a residential school) had chosen not to teach their children in part because they "thought we would be held back in school if they spoke nothing but Indian languages to us."[16] Although Brass later made efforts to develop proficiency in Cree, to her great regret her lack of sufficient exposure to it as a child proved an insurmountable barrier. Here is a case where two generations of residential schooling demonstrably resulted in the loss of the Native tongue; yet this thought-provoking autobiography is quoted in the context of Miller's contention that Native cultures were not always destroyed in residential institutions.

The author himself alludes to another source of the apparent contradiction when he comments on the deterrent effect the anti-potlatch law may have had. This is the only instance where he acknowledges the possibility that these policies might have produced results that are not found in documentary sources: namely, psychological ones. For even if the law was unevenly enforced, if agents did not always insist that Native children attend residential schools, if the pass system did stand largely as a dead letter, nonetheless, at any point—with a change of Indian agent, federal government, or legal code (over all of which the First Nations had little or no control)—these policies had the potential to become the coercive instruments they were meant to be. This threat alone is significant and cannot be ignored.

Further, when these policies *were* brought to bear, their impact was momentous, as survivors of the residential schools attest. Familial relationships were disturbed even when children were allowed home for the summer.[17] Indeed, it would be absurd to pretend that the occasional two-day stay with one's family was in any way comparable to growing up in its bosom. Languages *were* lost, in part due to residential schooling, and with them were lost the traditions that the elders could not share over linguistic barriers.[18] This was an avowed purpose of separating Native children from their families and cultures, and in a great many cases it was devastatingly effective. Moreover, while residential school training can be given some credit for inadvertently supply Native people with the skills to fight the Canadian government and therefore helping give rise to twentieth-century First Nations leadership (as in the case of Peter Kelly and Andrew Paull), the residential schools can also be blamed directly for leading to the deaths of many more Native people than were ever led to literacy and articulateness in Euro-Canadian terms. By the Department of Indian Affairs' own accounting, at least a quarter of all residential school students died while on school rolls or shortly thereafter from diseases, predominantly tuberculosis, that they contracted while in the institutions. Where post-schooling health could be plotted by the department's chief medical officer, the death rate was raised to 69 percent. When these statistics became public in 1907, Canadians were outraged. But even among those within the department who wanted residential schools abolished on health grounds, there was little will to take on the fight to change the system.[19] Poorly implemented as residential school policy may have been, the mere fact that it was policy made it resistant to revision. When Native parents fought against the confiscation of their children, they did so, in part, because they rightly feared that their children would not return unscathed. The great distances, both physical and cultural, between home community and residential school made it difficult for parents to protect their offspring from the dangers that faced them, both from disease and from institutional personnel. The sense of helplessness that ensued is only underscored by Miller's account of the violence inflicted by irate parents on school officials and teachers.[20] Rather than being evidence of parental influence over education, such instances show the frustrations of parents who were denied a consultative voice or access to effective control mechanisms within the education system.

A further inadequacy in Miller's analysis of residential schools is his tendency to concentrate on parents to the virtual exclusion of the institutional experience of children. This omission serves Miller's argument well, since children's influence over the residential schools was surely constrained. In the article, the frequency of escape attempts is cited as proof that the system could not be effective in assimilating Native people because so many removed themselves from its grasp. Yet, quite apart from the fact that even successful runaways—themselves a minority—often spent months, if not years, in the schools before finding an opportunity to liberate themselves, surely the most obvious conclusion to be drawn from such escapes is that the children found life in residential schools unendurable. And, in fact, it is hard to find anyone who was exposed to them who describes the experience as a wholly pleasant one, even when they recount no incidents of physical or sexual abuse.

As other researchers have found, Aboriginal people did sometimes benefit, directly or indirectly, from the education they received in the schools. But scholars, such as Jo-Anne Fiske, do not use this evidence, as Miller does, to dispute the assimilative and culturally invasive intentions of school administrators, but rather point to the scope for subversion both on the part of students and some instructors.[21] The residential schools may not have been monolithic instruments of colonial oppression, but they were designed to disrupt Native homelife, to promote abhorrence of Aboriginal tradition, and to train a body of semi-skilled, semi-literate labourers to fit into the capitalist labour market without displacing non-Native workers. The fact that Native people have long been aware of the ambivalent legacy of the schools does not, and should not, be taken to prove that the residential schools were not intended for and did not have the effect of cultural dislocation. For instance, Basil Johnston's book *Indian School Days* has been quoted on occasion as supporting the concept of residential schools. Yet he actually begins his account by stating: "Just as private schools have a place in the educational system, so do the residential schools, but under vastly different terms, conditions and formats from those that existed in the residential school as I first encountered it."[22] Johnston's account of residential school life at Spanish, Ontario is not wholly negative, yet he does not condone the educational system that operated under the assumption that Native children could only be adequately instructed when isolated from their homes and families.

These are factors and experiences that Miller either avoids or ignores in trying to find the shadings of a picture that has often been painted in stark contrasts. But a nuanced view, which acknowledges that the First Nations were not passive victims, must be built not only on evidence of Native strength but also on a complete and honest delineation of the forces they were confronting. To deny the full effects of residential schooling is to depreciate the power of the First Nations to withstand them. By ignoring the impact of such colonial policies, Miller trivializes the Native agency he seeks to highlight.

In a similar vein, Tina Loo wishes to show that the law is not merely a tool of coercion but also has creative and empowering potential even for those whose interests were not central to its formulation. Looking specifically at the prosecution of Dan Cranmer under the anti-potlatch law, Loo argues that certain facets of the legal process mediated the deleterious effect of the law and, in fact, worked to strengthen the authority of the First Nations who came into contact with it.

Her argument is based on two main premises: first, that the potlatch law can be seen as a distinct "site of struggle" and can be removed from the larger context of Native-white relations in British Columbia; and, second, that the law functions within a culture of argument in which those subject to the law are enabled to subvert the intentions of its formulators. She writes: "Because the power of argument is creative, because it is all about making a case, seeing the law in this way opens up the possibility that people who are subject to legal regulation can act as well as react. As will be discussed, the potlatch law was certainly oppressive (it had a coercive dimension) and symbolized colonial values, but the Indians who practised the ritual not only had success at avoiding prosecution, but they were also successful in arguing their cases before the court."[23]

Both premises, we believe, are problematic. First, Loo attempts to argue that the law can be removed from the context of Native-newcomer relations in British Columbia because it was not really about Aboriginal people at all, but rather was merely an expression of the desire of the recently established settler society to define itself. Given that the law, which was explicit in its intentions to facilitate the eradication of Native ceremony, was passed by the *federal* government at the instigation of Indian agents and missionaries, and that provincial settlers and their government were often opposed to the ban and ambivalent about its enforcement, Loo's argument here is unconvincing. Spurious though it may be, removing the functioning of the potlatch law from its assimilationist context enables Loo to conclude that, in the end, Native people *and their customary law* triumphed when the amended Indian Act of 1951 omitted all reference to the anti-potlatch provision. While the removal of the provision *was* a belated victory for Native people, it cannot be said that the customary law of the First Nations prevailed, since the potlatch was only one part of that law. On the contrary, since the establishment of colonial governments in Canada, Native people have been, and continue in most cases to be, ruled not by their own law but by the legal system of a foreign power. All of Loo's subsequent contentions about the power of legal argument must be read with an appreciation of that fact.

Second, the decontextualization of the law in this article permits Loo to make the following claim: "While the [Cranmer prosecution] is emblematic of their oppression, it has also come to represent a triumph. For the Alert Bay Kwakiutl, the outlawing of the potlatch and the 'confiscation' of their masks mark the beginnings of a political consciousness that has led them into the courts to resist the incursions of colonial society and to recover their land and cultural identity."[24] While one could certainly argue that the Kwakwaka'wakw hardly needed the banning of the potlatch to develop political consciousness, it is perhaps equally important to remind ourselves that the criminalization of Native culture also had the fundamental effect of removing the "site of struggle" between the First Nations and colonial society from circumstances that settlers and their government wished to avoid (such as armed insurrection) to one over which the non-Natives had a substantial degree of control—that is, the courts.[25]

Loo uses new and important evidence to show that, once in the courts, the Kwakwaka'wakw did not simply throw up their hands in the face of a foreign legal authority. Rather, drawing on an oratorical tradition and a willingness to understand the system with which they were confronted, they were able to draft arguments that were sophisticated and compelling. It is significant, as Loo points out, that the First Nations have never submitted to the colonial power, but have always tried to act in ways that would benefit themselves, their culture, and the generations to come. Their ability to create arguments and to act intelligently does not surprise us. In fact, it should be self-evident. Where we disagree with Loo is in her conclusion that Native ability to resist somehow diminished the coercive nature of the law. Under prosecution for potlatching, the First Nations were placed in a purely defensive position, confronting a powerful system that sought above all to legitimize itself. As Loo stresses in her analysis, the very existence of the ban forced the government to pursue convictions in order to preserve its authority. And this it clearly did, when the conviction was brought down and the potlatchers were given the offensive choice of either being imprisoned or ransoming their cultural heritage in exchange for their freedom. Fundamentally, we must wonder how it was that, despite the arguments created and the latitude that Loo claims is afforded legal interpretation by the culture of argument, Dan Cranmer and the other defendants' lost their case. The result of the trial, it seems, is beyond the scope of Loo's argument. The lingering words of the Cranmer prosecution were not ones of empowerment, but rather those of Herbert (Mecha) Martin drawn to our attention in the opening quotations of Loo's paper: "We suffered so."

The other argument advanced here for the empowering potential of the law is equally tenuous. The author contends that individual members of Native communities could benefit from the potlatch law by employing it against their fellows: "The agents' reports suggest that some Indians used the law to overthrow the entrenched hereditary system of rank and privilege that existed within some Native communities."[26] This assertion clearly rests on the premise we saw in Cole and Chaikin's work that potlatching societies victimized some of their members and that Euro-Canadian law was well adapted to restructure them to eliminate this problem. Yet the individuals who are cited as having taking this approach were, from the evidence presented, primarily victims not of Native culture but of the cultural breakdown that was taking place as a result of internal religious divisions caused by missionization. Jane Cook, for instance, who "took an active role in suppressing the potlatch," was of mixed parentage and had been raised by a Euro-Canadian missionary couple.[27] She has been described as "a formidable super-missionized woman" who "was deadset against all Indian ways, none of which she knew much about."[28] Her efforts cannot be seen as attempts to reform Kwakwaka'wakw society, but rather to destroy it. It is difficult to discern in this account any empowering effects for Jane Cook of her use of the law. Furthermore, through political and familial factions within the First Nations have used European technology, alliances, and material culture since the time of contact to promote their own ends, the use of an alien law designed to suppress cultural integrity is not a value-free adaptation. Any "empowering" potential here for Native individuals within the Canadian legal system could only have been used to the detriment of Native communities as a whole. Ultimately, this is a process from which only the colonizers have something to gain.

As Dan Cranmer and the others learned, the culture of argument of the Euro-Canadian legal system was (and is) unwilling to accommodate the viewpoint of aboriginal people. In a country still reeling from the revelations of several inquiries into the treatment of Native people by Canada's justice system, it seems ironic that an argument should be advanced for the empowering potential of the law for this same group. Like the accused in the Cranmer case, Delgam Uukw, along with the elders and chiefs of the Gitksan and Wet'suwet'en peoples, also made sophisticated, compelling arguments. And for a time, it seemed that they would be heard, that the legal system would make room for a new kind of argument, admit a new kind of evidence, view the past in a revivified way. But the arguments of the elders were ignored, and it was not merely the eccentricities of Chief Justice MacEachern's interpretation that determined this outcome. Fundamentally, the Delgam Uukw case, like the Cranmer prosecution before it, clearly demonstrates that, just as the law is not colour-blind, neither is its rhetoric able to accommodate all viewpoints regardless of location or origin. That is because the law, whether it be that concerning rights to the land and resources or that prohibiting the potlatch, is inseparable from its political context: it cannot be skeletonized.

The skeletonization of history is equally inadmissible. Clearly, MacEachern preferred the historians' "expert" testimony to that of anthropologists because he believed that history could be removed from politics (and, in making this belief explicit, proved the contrary). Given the way historical documents were presented in the courtroom, as evidentiary submissions cited not to the primary source from which they were taken but to other legal cases in which they had previously been used, MacEachern might have been justified in his perception. Assembled before him were fragmentary facts estranged from their historical context and lacking any sensitivity to the past, MacEachern simply added them to the lexicon of legal precedents generated by a judiciary devoted to the dominance of the imported cultural system. As historian Kerry Abel has pointed out: "Legal evidence and historical interpretation are not the same concepts; the perennial problem of distinguishing fact from interpretation can become both urgent and emotional in the courtroom. . . . On the other hand, historians can also educate the courts in the broader context of the issues at hand. Narrow interpretations of the law based on strict legal precedent will serve only to perpetuate past injustices."[29] As yet, the real value of the historian's testimony has not been realized.

MacEachern's example should serve as a reminder to historians that we disregard past and present politics at our peril. Employing the acknowledgment of Native agency as a means of depreciating the impact of colonialism does a disservice to our understanding of history and trivializes the continued response of the First Nations to the European "discovery" of the Americas. The fact that the colonial policies of coercive acculturation were not implemented as planned and/or did not produce assimilation can hardly be construed as meaning that they did not have a profound effect on the people to whom they were intended to apply. There is abundant evidence of their impact. The study of Aboriginal strategies for survival under alien rule is of critical importance and must necessarily be predicated on the recognition of Native agency. By the same token, Native agency will never be fully understood without an equal recognition of the oppressive forces that shaped every Native person's life. By way of analogy, when historians of the American South first started to study the world made by enslaved African-Americans, they introduced a picture of life under slavery that was nuanced, in which the traditional stereotypes were enervated. Yet never did they argue or even imply that the impact of slavery was diminished, or that its nefarious qualities were somehow lessened, by the resiliency of those enslaved.

Scholars of Canada's First Nations under colonialism would do well to learn from their example. When we look for Native agency, we must first be willing to recognize the right of First Nations people to political and moral self-determination before we can assess the impact of "wardship" on their societies and cultures. We must, further, be able to delineate in full the realm of colonial policy and practice before we can seek to understand the ways in which Native people mediated the impact of those governmental initiatives. Only then can we produce truly balanced and nuanced histories in which neither Native actors nor colonial power is ignored.

Finally, historians concerned with Aboriginal people must acknowledge that we write in a politically charged environment. Some of us work on land claims, others are not directly involved, but as the Gitksan and Wet'suwet'en case reveals, neither we nor our works are immune from use and misuse in Canadian courts of law. Before we apply theory generated in other contexts to the circumstances of Native-newcomer relations in Canada, we must be prepared to examine our basic premises as well as the possible implications that our work might have for Native people living today. We have, in fact, the potential to make a positive contribution not only to historical understanding but also to the process of redressing past injuries. In writing history, we simultaneously make it; this is a challenge and an opportunity which we cannot ignore.

NOTES

1. Supreme Court of British Columbia, *Delgamuukw vs. the Attorney-General of British Columbia*, "Reasons for Judgement of The Honourable Chief Justice Allan MacEachern," 8 March 1991, 50.

2. Ibid., 52.

3. Adrienne Rich, "Resisting Amnesia: History and Personal Life" in *Blood, Bread and Poetry: Selected Prose 1979–1985* (New York, 1986), 144.

4. R.A. Fisher, *Contact and Conflict: Indian-European Relations in British Columbia, 1774–1890* (Vancouver, 1977); A.J. Ray, *Indians in the Fur Trade: Their Role as Hunters, Trappers and Middlemen in the Lands Southwest of Hudson Bay, 1660–1870* (Toronto, 1974); A.J. Ray and D. Freeman, *"Give Us Good Measure": An Economic Analysis of Relations between the Indians and the Hudson's Bay Company before 1763* (Toronto, 1978); J.S.H. Brown, *Strangers in Blood: Fur Trade Company Families in Indian Country* (Vancouver, 1980); S. Van Kirk, *Many Tender Ties: Women in Fur Trade Society* (Winnipeg, 1980); B.G. Trigger, *Natives and Newcomers: Canada's "Heroic Age" Reconsidered* (Kingston, 1985).

5. Sarah Carter, *Lost Harvests: Prairie Indian Reserve Farmers and Government Policy* (Montreal, 1990); Clarence Bolt, *Shoes Too Small for Feet Too Large: Thomas Crosby and the Tsimshian* (Vancouver, 1992); Jo-Anne Fiske, "Gender and the Paradox of Residential Education in Carrier Society" in *Women and Education*, ed. Jane S. Gaskell and Arlene Tigar McLaren, 2nd ed. (Calgary, 1991), 131–46; Ken S. Coates, *"Best Left as Indians": Native-White Relations in the Yukon Territory, 1840–1973* (Montreal, 1991); Celia Haig-Brown, *Resistance and Renewal: Surviving the Indian Residential School* (Vancouver, 1988).

6. Here we are talking about scholarly works that carry within them their own values and uses. We are not speaking to the subject of authorial intent, though clearly context is as important an element in the evaluation of historical writing as it is to the study of any texts. Scholarship, when taken as a whole as it tends in a certain direction, can undoubtedly be interpreted and used in ways never intended by its authors. It is to such an identifiable trend in historical writing, not to particular authors, that we address our comments here.

7. G.M. Sproat, quoted in Douglas Cole and Ira Chaikin, *An Iron Hand upon the People: The Law against the Potlatch on the Northwest Coast* (Vancouver, 1990), 15.

8. On p. 182 appears the following appeal: "If the authors may be allowed some quite subjective judgements"; incredibly, it seems that the authors are unaware of the numerous "subjective judgements" that have been passed in the preceding 181 pages.

9. Cole and Chaikin, *An Iron Hand*, 181–82.

10. Ibid., 178.

11. Ibid., 177–78.

12. Ibid., 180.

13. Ibid., 1

14. J.R. Miller, "Owen Glendower, Hotspur, and Canadian Indian Policy" in *Sweet Promises: A Reader on Indian-White Relations in Canada* (Toronto, 1991), 340–41.

15. Learning a few Cree profanities and attending clandestine dance performances comprised this exposure and can hardly be seen to have restored her ancestral culture to her.

16. Eleanor Brass, *I Walk in Two Worlds* (Calgary, 1987), 13.

17. Celia Haig-Brown, *Resistance and Renewal: Surviving the Indian Residential School* (Vancouver, 1988), 15–21, 117, 120–21, 123.

18. Ibid., 15–16, 120–22.

19. National Archives of Canada (NA), Department of Indian Affairs, RG 10,

vol. 4037, file 317021, P.H. Bryce, "Report on Indian Residential Schools."

20. Miller, "Owen Glendower," 338.

21. Fiske, "Gender and the Paradox of Residential Education," 131–46.

22. Basil H. Johnston, *Indian School Days* (Toronto, 1988), 12.

23. Tina Loo, "Dan Cranmer's Potlatch: Law as Coercion, Symbol, and Rhetoric in British Columbia, 1884–1951," *Canadian Historical Review* 73, 2 (June 1992): 137.

24. Ibid., 128.

25. The provincial and federal governments considered the threat of armed struggle on the coast and in the interior of British Columbia real. In 1887, for instance, Prime Minister Macdonald appointed a royal commission of inquiry into the Northwest Coast Nations as a means of hearing grievances and thus forestalling the possibility of military conflict that would see the First Nations reject the authority of foreign governments on their lands. The fear of violence in Native territory was a persistent factor in "Indian" policy throughout the nineteenth century. See Jo–Anne Drake-Terry, *The Same as Yesterday: The Lillooet Chronicle the Theft of Their Lands and Resources* (Lillooet, 1989), 40–42, 45–47, 79, 83, 93–96, 110–11, 122, 163, 166, 169, 225.

26. Loo, "Dan Cranmer's Potlatch," 162.

27. Ibid., 162.

28. Ibid., 163, quoting Helen Codere in Franz Boas, *Kwakiutl Ethnography*, xxvii.

29. Kerry Abel, "Introduction" in *Aboriginal Resource Use in Canada: Historical and Legal Aspects*, ed. Kerry Abel and Jean Friesen (Winnipeg, 1991), 6.

THE DESTRUCTION OF AN OJIBWA COMMUNITY: RELATIONS WITH THE OUTSIDE SOCIETY[◇]

ANASTASIA M. SHKILNYK

ɔ

No community, however primitive or isolated, can be entirely free of influences from other communities and external institutions. For this reason, our portrait of the Grassy Narrows people must contain a discussion of their relationship, over time, to white society.

This relationship can best be described with reference to three distinct historical periods. The first, from the time of the treaty to the end of World War II (1873–1945), is characterized by the primacy of the Hudson's Bay Company and the missions in Indian life and by minimal state interference in community affairs. The second period, from the end of the war to the time of the relocation (1945–63), is marked by the beginning of provincial government involvement in land-use and resource-use regulations, the extension to Indians of certain universal federal government programs, and the beginning of a movement of Indian people off the reserve and into private sector wage jobs. The third period begins with the relocation to the new reserve and encompasses present-day Indian-white relationships. It is characterized by massive federal government intervention in band affairs, a sharp decline in the traditional mode of production, a surge in Indian alcoholism and social pathology, and an intensification of racism directed against Indian people in the town of Kenora.

FROM THE TREATY TO WORLD WAR II: 1873–1945

From the time of the treaty to the end of World War II, the Indians of northwestern Ontario were peripheral to the interests of the government and the white society. Even as resource development and white settlement

◇ Reprinted with permission from *A Poison Stronger Than Love: The Destruction of an Ojibwa Community* (New Haven: Yale University Press, 1985), 109–32.

expanded in the area of the Lake of the Woods, the Ojibwa did not participate in the booming economy of the new frontier.[1] They continued to live
on or near their reserve lands and trapping territories, and their traditional
means of livelihood, based on hunting, trapping, and gathering, remained
largely unthreatened. Their economic activities were not yet endangered by
significant competition from white people for resources or by government
regulations over land and resource use. The state as a whole, represented by
the governments of Ontario and Canada, played a marginal role in their
daily lives.

In contrast to the state apparatus, the Christian missions and the
Hudson's Bay Company were institutions of paramount importance in the
life of the Grassy Narrows people in the first half of the twentieth century.
In the geographically isolated regions of the north, the Bay found in Indian
people a captive market for its goods and established a monopoly in the
trade of furs. In many small settlements clustered around Bay trading posts,
the Hudson's Bay Company played god with the Indian people. The Bay's
tenacious hold over Indian trappers through their state of permanent
indebtedness to the company is well-known; there is no need to elaborate
on the basically exploitative nature of that relationship. At Grassy Narrows,
however, the people do not speak ill of the Company managers who lived
with them on the Bay island on the old reserve after 1911. They remember
the time "when the Bay still took care of the trappers and made a feast for
them at Christmas . . . and when the only wage jobs available were to haul
freight for the CNR or goods and supplies for the Bay, from the Jones Road
to the old reserve." They also remember that the Bay managers extended
credit for air transportation to those whose traplines were far from the old
reserve, that they provided rations in times of need or emergency, and that
the Bay was the only source of essential foodstuffs and implements. The
record of the Company in other parts of the north may be a cause for
shame; but in the minds of the Grassy Narrows people, the Hudson's Bay
Company does not touch the raw nerve of historical memory nearly as
acutely as the recall of the other controlling force in Indian life, the
Christian missions.

Historical accounts of early contact with Indian people are replete with
evidence that government representatives and missionaries regarded the
Indians as savages. They leave little doubt that the core message transmit-
ted to the indigenous people in the course of their colonization was that
their own culture was inferior, even barbaric, and that they should be
adopting the more civilized ways of the white society. Christianity was to
replace the ideology of the primitive man, just as the missionaries were to
serve as the agents of change. The entire process of "civilization" was to be
spearheaded by mission-run schools. The attitude of the government of
Canada, which was to prevail for almost three-quarters of a century after
the treaty, is well summed up in the following excerpt from the annual
report of John McIntyre, Indian Agent for reserves in Ontario. He is speaking of the establishment of schools run by missionaries for Indian children:
"By methods of this nature . . . the Indian would be gradually and permanently advanced to the scale of civil society; his migratory habits, and fond-

ness for roaming, would be cured, and an interesting class of our fellowmen rescued from degradation. . . . The aim of all these institutes [mission-run schools] is to train the Indian to give up his old ways, and to settle among his white brethren on equal terms and with equal advantage."[2]

The government relegated social and educational responsibilities to the missions because no "decent white teachers" could be expected to live under the primitive conditions of Indian life: "It is evident . . . that efficient teachers cannot be induced to isolate themselves from congenial society and other comforts of civilized life to undertake to teach schools among savages in remote localities."[3]

The ideology of colonization, of a linear advance "up the scale of civil society," and the alliance of convenience between the government and the Christian missions continued until the early 1950s. In northwestern Ontario, the Oblate Fathers, with financial assistance from the government of Canada, opened the first large residential school in the area at McIntosh in 1924. Young people from Grassy Narrows were boarded there along with Indian children from other northern Ontario reserves. Some Grassy Narrows people also attended St. Mary's Catholic residential school in Kenora, while others were sent to Presbyterian Cecilia Jeffreys, located on the outskirts of town. These residential schools became synonymous with Indian education until the late 1950s and early 1960s, when the federal government finally moved to secularize Indian education and bring it under the direct control of the Department of Indian Affairs and Northern Development. For a very long time, however, residential schools were seen as civilizing influences on the young generation of Indians, allowing the young to be educated in the values of the dominant society while the adults continued to live in the Indian way.

The residential schools paid little homage to education. Instead, the missionaries emphasized the virtues of a farming culture, the discipline of manual labor, strict adherence to regular hours, religious instruction, and the exclusive use of the English language. In the following passages, two Grassy Narrows band members, age sixty-one and forty-seven respectively, describe a day in school. Although more than a decade had passed before one followed the other into the McIntosh classroom, the curriculum had obviously changed very little:

In my generation, there wasn't too much resistance to residential school. We had it in our heads, but you couldn't say it out loud. We went along with it. The boys had to get up at 5:00 in the morning to clean the barn before breakfast. At 6:00 a.m. we had to be at Mass, and then we had to milk the cows. Sometimes during the day we had classes in English and arithmetic, but all I remember was the hard work, the chores . . . there was always work to do.

I went to grade two at McIntosh. There was only a couple of hours of teaching in the morning: one hour of catechism, one hour of English and arithmetic. At 10:00 o'clock, I had to go for the mail and returned about noon. Then, in the afternoon, I had to split wood until 3:00 p.m. Then I had to mend socks and do other chores like that. We had to take care of the horses, and the cows, and the garden. I was fourteen years old when I left school, and I know how to read and write just a little bit.

Aside from funding mission-run schools, the Department of Indian Affairs paid little heed to the content of the curriculum. It maintained a superficial and infrequent supervisory presence in the form of an inspector. One of the most revealing statements about the attitude of the federal government to Indian education comes from Father Lacelle, who served as administrator of the McIntosh school:

> I remember one time, the inspector was in to inspect the school. We had grade nine. I asked him if he was going to visit grade nine. He says no. He says that as a separate school in Ontario, we shouldn't have grade nine. Then he says that he isn't being paid for visiting grade nine, and then, to my great surprise, he added, "If we let them, the Indian people, go to grade nine, then they'll want to go to grade ten, and then they'll want to go to university. That's what we don't want."
>
> He said that right in front of me, and I told him that I was a witness to what he had said. But then he said, "If you try to do anything different, the higher-ups, they will shut you up. I have a family. I have to do what they say."
>
> What I'm trying to tell you is that there was a lot of pressure on people who worked with Indians not to rock the boat. The Department of Indian Affairs really didn't care about Indian education. We were getting the same grant for an eighteen-year-old teenager as for a six-year-old kid. This was still true in the 1950s. They also didn't care what was being taught, although in my time we tried to upgrade the curriculum. The attitude of the Indian Agents was very poor.

Although the residential school system was supposed to lead to the abandonment of traditional Ojibwa ways, and although every effort was made to denigrate Indian values and repress the Ojibwa language, the system did not have the same impact on every generation of the Grassy Narrows people. The first three generations of students at McIntosh, for example, did not experience the crushing blows to Indian identity that were felt by their successors. The reason for this is not difficult to understand: when these students returned to the old reserve from residential school, they could continue to live in the Indian way. The traditional mode of production was still intact, the social institutions were still functioning, and the elders of each family group made a special effort to reeducate the young people in the values of the Indian community and in the skills required to make a living from the land. The most devastating impact of residential schools on Indian culture and individual identity was felt by the generation that was caught in the transition from the old to the new way of life. This is the group that had neither the integrity of the old traditions and institutions nor the security of the white man's ways to guide it. People now in their mid-twenties represent the last cohort of students educated in residential schools. This speaker, twenty-two years old, feels especially bitter about the cultural deprivation sanctioned by these institutions:

> The missionaries had these big schools where they got paid by government. They took us away from our home life, they showed us their religion, and they brainwashed us in the values of capitalism and the industrial society. This was their definition of education. They forbid us to speak the Ojibwa language. They wanted assimilation. They weren't patient. We were immobilized. It was like a concentration camp.
>
> Then the definition of education was changed, and they put the children into schools on the reserves. But that meant that the parents had to stay on the reserve to take care of the children. There was no choice. You couldn't just leave for the trapline all winter. Everybody was trapped by this educational system. But the goal was still assimilation. . . . That goal was never changed.

The heritage of hostility to the Christian churches and the residue of raw, burning anger at the memory of the residential school experience remain the property of the younger generation of the Grassy Narrows people. The older people held on more tenaciously to their Indian language and identity, but they could not escape the gradual erosion of their culture by the relentless pressures from the state to limit their freedom to use the land.

FROM THE END OF THE WAR
TO RELOCATION: 1945–1963

Intervention by the government of Ontario in Indian life increased dramatically after the war, when the provincial government, with its constitutionally enshrined rights over land and resources, began to take a much more active role in the management of fur, fish, and game. The old Department of Game and Fisheries became part of the Department of Lands and Forests in 1946, and a new philosophy of "conservation and management" quickly took hold. Operating procedures included new regulations over access to resources, better record keeping on their use, regular reviews of licenses, and strategies for the scientific management of renewable resources.[4]

These changes affected Indian people in many ways. In the first place, the government established a system of registered traplines in 1947. Indians in northwestern Ontario received priority in the allocation of traplines, on the basis of historic use; however, they could lose their traplines if they did not meet annual harvest quotas set for certain species, particularly beaver. They also became subject to compulsory reporting procedures on the fur catch. Although these requirements were less strictly enforced for Treaty Indian trappers than for white trappers, Indian people nevertheless perceived them as intrusions on their treaty rights. Furthermore, the trapline registration served to fragment large tracts of territory held by the extended family into smaller individual units, making rotation of trapping areas more difficult and imposing a sense of privatization, of individual responsibility, on areas once managed communally.

The philosophy underlying provincial intervention in trapping was at odds with the Indians' point of view. For the government, the trapline was simply a convenient territorial unit, and trapping was basically a commercial activity. Through sound management principles, the fur could be exploited to yield the maximum return consistent with resource conservation goals. Access to the fur resource, by Indians or any other citizens of the province, was a privilege, not a right, which could be revoked at any time. In contrast, for the Indian people, the trapline was a place to live, raise children and teach life skills, obtain food, and harvest furs to exchange for other commodities. Trapping was not just a commercial activity; it was a way of life. Access to fur-bearing animals was a fundamental right guaranteed by the treaty. This divergence of views, here illustrated by reference to trapping, underlies contemporary struggles between the Indian people and the Ontario government over access to and use of natural resources.

The second area of Indian economic activity affected by the provincial government's postwar concern for resource management was commercial fishing. Licenses for commercial fishing had apparently been required since the turn of the century, but the province did not have an efficient system for controlling the fishery until 1947–48, when strict reporting requirements were imposed and a system of licenses was instituted for fishing specific lakes. In northwestern Ontario, Indian people didn't need licenses to fish for domestic consumption, for that was a fundamental right guaranteed by the treaty. Although the Grassy Narrows people dried fish for the winter, they did not use fish for trade until air transportation made it possible to deliver this perishable commodity to the market reliably and quickly. Thus, commercial fishing began much later at Grassy Narrows than at other Lake of the Woods reserves and was more closely associated with the opening of tourist camps for sports fishing. In 1957, the Ontario government issued a license to the Grassy Narrows band covering "the public waters of Indian Lake, Grassy Narrows Lake, and the waters lying between these lakes and adjacent to the Reserve."

Outside of reserve waters, this license was not valid from April 1 to September 30. According to provincial policy, sports fishing was to be given priority over commercial fishing in the Lake of the Woods and English River areas. The logic applied to the management of the fishery was identical to that governing the traplines: the fishery that yielded the highest economic return per dollar invested was the most deserving of government support. Since the sports fishery clearly generated more dollars per fish than the commercial fishery, its primacy became well established in government policy. Fortunately, the economy of Grassy Narrows in the postwar period had been more closely linked with the sports fishery in terms of the seasonal employment of guides by the fishing lodges. Nevertheless, this policy had an adverse impact on other Indian communities more dependent on the commercial fishery.

The third area of Indian economic activity affected by the new wave of provincial resource administration was the gathering of wild rice. Wild rice had always been an important food for the Ojibwa of northwestern Ontario. It also had a special place in the people's ceremonial and spiritual life. At Grassy Narrows, it was customary for the elders of the band to go into the fields to see if the crop was ready for picking. The fields ripened at different times, depending on water levels, weather, and location. Once the signal for a mature crop was given, the people assembled to begin the harvest with a thanksgiving feast. After the picking was over, the families returned to the old reserve to begin processing the green rice by drying, threshing, and roasting it. Most of the finished rice was stored for the winter. In the early 1940s, the processed rice began to be sold, in small quantities, to nonnative buyers. In the early 1950s, buyers began purchasing green rice directly from the pickers and sending it to processing plants in Manitoba and Minnesota.

As wild rice increased in importance as a cash crop, the Ontario government introduced a system of land-use permits, or "wild-rice license areas." The Grassy Narrows band received a certain block of land reserved for the exclusive use of band members; other tracts, containing actual or potential wild-rice fields, were to be accessible to nonnative harvesters. Indian people perceived this intervention by the state in regulating a resource they considered theirs by custom and treaty right as one more link in the chain that slowly strangulated their freedom to use the land in traditional ways.

More recently, another factor has stimulated government interest in wild rice. In the mid-1970s, the value of green rice quadrupled. The quick money that could be made by picking the rice with mechanical harvesters rather than by the Indian method of canoe and stick attracted the attention of white entrepreneurs. They organized to put pressure on the government of Ontario to open up access to the wild-rice fields, even in the areas licensed to Indian bands. The government prepared policy changes that would have effectively removed wild rice from Indian control. In 1978, however, a Royal Commission on the Northern Environment recommended that a moratorium of five years be placed on any changes to existing license areas. To date the moratorium is still in effect, but the Indian people have reason to doubt that the issue will be resolved in their favor. This issue has inflamed their anger and frustration against the relentless encroachment by the white society on their land and traditional resources.

The postwar period, which began with the registration of traplines and increasing provincial involvement in regulating access to off-reserve resources, also saw a major expansion of social welfare programs in Canada. Since these were based on universality of application, Indian people became eligible to receive regular monthly payments under the Family Allowance Act, passed in 1944. The Grassy Narrows people started to receive family allowance payments in 1946, consisting of $8 per school-aged child per month. In 1951, Indians seventy years of age and older began to receive Old Age Security Pensions. Other benefits administered by the provinces, and formerly available only to nonnative citizens, also began to flow to Indian people. Indians over sixty-five years of age became eligible to participate in the provincially administered Old Age Assistance Act, and blind persons could receive benefits under the Blind Persons Act. By the mid-1960s, Indian people in Ontario became eligible to receive welfare and other social assistance services comparable to those provided for the non-Indian population.

These categorical payments marked the transition from the rations of flour, tea, or lard delivered to widows and old people at Grassy Narrows at the discretion of the Indian Agent to regular transfer payments by check. For the Indian people, who were still largely outside the cash economy, these payments began to constitute an important source of income. Yet they were not of a scale to substitute for or otherwise displace the pursuits of hunting, trapping, and gathering. The corrosive effect of expanded government subsidies and social assistance measures on the traditional mode of production was to be felt in the late 1960s, after the community had been relocated to the new reserve.

At the national level, other winds of change were blowing that were to alter the context of Indian policy in Canada. Perhaps as a token of recognition of the contribution of Indian people to the war effort, in 1947–48 a Special Joint Committee of the Senate and House of Commons was appointed to reexamine the Indian Act, which defines the relationship between Indians and the broader Canadian society.[5] In the course of its deliberations, the committee heard shocking evidence concerning the depressed social and economic conditions on Indian reserves. It then produced a series of sweeping recommendations that were to guide the direction of public policy for the next decade. Among many other proposals, the committee recommended that Indian integration into Canadian society be accelerated; that separate schools for Indians be abolished and Indian education be placed under the direct and sole responsibility of the Indian Affairs Branch; that Indians be included in all "reconstruction" measures dealing with public health, unemployment, and social security; that Indians be accorded the same rights as other citizens with regard to the consumption of alcohol off the reserve; and that greater responsibility and more progressive measures of self-government of reserve and band affairs be granted to band councils.[6]

During the 1950s, the federal government gradually proceeded to take over direct responsibility for Indian health and education. Day schools on Indian reserves in northwestern Ontario were constructed as early as 1951 (at Whitedog, for example), and the Indian Affairs Branch began to be responsible for the selection and appointment of teachers. In 1960, Indian people were finally enfranchised to vote in federal elections. The Grassy Narrows people, however, remained isolated and removed from the mainstream of all these developments until their relocation. Band members working outside the old reserve in the postwar period were more immediately affected by a 1956 amendment to the Indian Act that permitted them to purchase and possess liquor.[7] Thus, the families who stayed on the old reserve for most of the period between the end of the war and the relocation continued a lifestyle undisturbed by interference from the federal government.

In this period, in contrast to the one following, the Department of Indian Affairs confined its relationship with the Grassy Narrows people to annual ceremonial visits on Treaty Day. During his visit, the Indian Agent was supposed to communicate to the people the policy of the department toward them, ensure that their children were attending school, legally sanction marriages, and help the Chief and Council in the administration of justice. An important place in the observance of Treaty Day was reserved for the distribution of indispensable tools and rations to the old and the disabled. Old people look back to this aspect of the Indian-government relationship and recall a not so distant time when conditions enabled families to provide for their own needs. In the words of a seventy-year-old man:

> On the old reserve, the Indian Agent used to supply us with all the things that we needed to make a living for ourselves—I mean garden tools and seeds, gill nets for fishing, shotgun shells, and things like that. This was good. Why did this stop? Everybody had enough, they could provide for their own potatoes and other vegetables. A lot of families had very good crops, enough to last the winter. They used to build a root house, put straw in it, and keep the vegetables there. People had enough to eat. They didn't need welfare.
>
> Now we can't make a living for ourselves anymore. The new reserve is on dirt and rock. We can't have gardens . . . the fish is poisoned, there are not as many moose and deer . . . and our people have to depend on government. This is not good. We used to be a proud and independent people. But everything has changed in my lifetime.

The contact of the Indian Agent with the people of Grassy Narrows may have been infrequent and limited to the transactions described, but the people remember well the attitude of the Department toward them: "At that time, Indians were treated like children. Indian Affairs wanted it that way. Indians had no voice at that time." Although the Indian Act gave the Department of Indian Affairs comprehensive authority to legislate on behalf of Indian people and to control their lives, the Indian Agents seem to have had little interest in "administering" day-to-day existence. According to Father Lacelle, their role in community life up to the time of the relocation was marginal:

> The change at Grassy Narrows had been very sudden. There was very little contact between the people there and the government until the government put them in villages. They resisted the move to the new reserve. That was against their grain. They were tribesmen, trappers, and hunters gathered in clans. Tribesmen, you know, are very independent.
>
> For years, the Department of Indian Affairs didn't know what was going on with the Indians at Grassy Narrows. We missionaries, we had to name people, keep a record of births, deaths, and marriages. The record keeping of Indian Agents was very poor. Also, at that time, the agents couldn't do anything anyway, because all policy came from above, from Ottawa.

The lack of access to the old reserve by road, the time and discomfort associated with travel by portage and canoe, and the expense of air transport served to insulate the Grassy Narrows people from unwanted visitors and even from well-intentioned civil servants. Their isolation alone, however, does not explain the undercurrent of unfriendliness to strangers.[8]

In the words of Father Lacelle:

The Grassy Narrows people, they used to tell me that they liked to be alone. They didn't like outsiders to get too close, and they most certainly didn't like anyone living on the reserve.

Indian people are certainly not all the same. Each community, even among the Ojibwa, is different. You can be accepted in one place and rejected in the next one. The Grassy Narrows people, they were always more unfriendly to outsiders.

In my opinion, of all the reserves that I ever visited and knew well, the Grassy Narrows people were closer to being primitive, in the sense of not being exposed to the outside society, than any other group I ever knew. They had related, historically, to the northern bands rather than to the Lake of the Woods bands, and they had kept to themselves more. This was certainly true of the group that had never moved outside the old reserve.

Even today, the people of Grassy Narrows continue to resent white people and government officials who come into the reserve. The sentiment of trespass, of violation of rights to domain supposedly protected by the treaty, no doubt has its roots in the extraordinary swiftness with which the protective cushion of isolation was broken down, especially with regard to interference from the state in reserve affairs. A respected elder in the community and former chief speaks to this point:

You have to remember that just twenty years ago our people saw no social workers, no welfare administrators. No police force was stationed on our reserve; no teachers lived on our reserve. The first white doctors started flying in to treat tuberculosis cases only in the 1950s, just before the Mennonites came.

Suddenly, after we moved to this new reserve, we saw government people all the time. They came to tell us how we should build our houses and where we should build them. They came to tell us how we should run our Chief and Council. They told us about local government, and they told us we had to have a band administration to take care of the money and the programs that were going to come from the government.

Within a few years of the move to the new reserve, we had social workers taking our children away to foster homes.

This statement supports the conclusion that in the period from World War II to the time of the relocation, the limited contact between the Grassy Narrows people and the state did not yet serve to undermine the social, economic, or political bases of the traditional Ojibwa way of life. Aside from the Hudson's Bay manager, the only other white people in the area of the old reserve were the Mennonite missionaries, who arrived in 1958 at the invitation of Chief Pierre Taypaywaykejick. Their influence on the community was a positive one. In 1961–62, they opened a little school on the Bay island and established themselves in the community by providing nursing services. Amazingly enough, the first nurses from the government's Indian Health Service began regular visits to Grassy Narrows only in the early 1970s, after the government recognized the risks to health posed by the mercury poisoning of the English-Wabigoon River. Until that time, medical treatment was administered mainly by the Mennonite nurses. A doctor had accompanied the Indian Agent only once a year, at Treaty time, in order to diagnose tuberculosis cases and send them to sanitariums.[9] The first resident physician, Peter Newberry, came to Grassy Narrows as a Quaker volunteer only in 1974. Contact between the Grassy Narrows people and the state medical authorities was, to say the least, occasional until the early 1970s.

In another sense, however, the absence of government involvement ensured that life on the old reserve was a constant struggle to eke out a subsistence living from the land. Though enveloped in a body of beliefs, customs, and institutions that lent it dignity and meaning, the way of life was not an easy one. So some people left the old reserve and journeyed to places like Dryden, Redditt, Farlane, Red Lake, and McIntosh in search of opportunities for wage employment. Those who wanted to be near their children in residential school settled around McIntosh. The trajectory of movement, and the reasons for the eventual return to reserve life, are illustrated here by the experiences of two families. The first speaker is a fifty-five-year-old man:

I was born on the old reserve, but my whole family moved to McIntosh in the 1930s. McIntosh at that time was like another settlement for Grassy people. We used it as a base camp and went winter trapping from there.

I went to McIntosh residential school for seven years. After that, I had many jobs. Like other people from Grassy, I worked on the railroad as a section man. I guided around McIntosh for about nine years. I worked at Red Lake in the mines, cut pulp for private contractors, and made a living in various jobs off the reserve. There was no welfare at that time on the old reserve, so some people had to go outside to work. But everyone used to come back for Treaty Day.

I came back to the old reserve in 1959. For two years, I was a commercial fisherman and fished year-round. I also had a trapline near Redditt, guided hunters, and worked on private pulp-cutting contracts. When they started building houses on the new reserve, I worked in construction. And when the training courses started with Manpower, I went on these courses.

When life became good on the new reserve, when people found out that the government was giving jobs and houses, they started coming back to Grassy Narrows.

The second speaker is forty-seven years old:

For a long time, the only job you could get on the old reserve was hauling goods from the CNR railway tracks for the Bay Company. You had to work hard for $2.50 a day. In 1943, my dad took the whole family and he went to work for the CNR railroad in the summertime. We lived at Brinka, close to Redditt, then at Farlane, and at Jones. In the wintertime, dad took us to his trapline and there he taught me how to trap. After working outside the reserve like this for seven years, dad got laid off, and we returned to the old reserve. He then got a job guiding at Ball Lake Lodge. I was a teenager then, but I worked there too, first as a cabin boy, and later as a guide.

Most people on the old reserve were very self-sufficient. They found work in trapping, guiding, fishing, or they went outside the reserve and found work on the railroad or in the mines. There was no such thing as unemployment. There was always work to do. But now on the new reserve, there is unemployment and even unemployment insurance.

At the time of the move to the new reserve, I was working for a mining company in Red Lake. I came back to Grassy Narrows, I think it was 1966, because we got a new house, and I heard that there were going to be jobs on the reserve.

Thus, there was a constant ebb and flow of people between the old reserve and the outside, and between seasonal work off the reserve and the winter sojourn on the traplines. Some chose to work outside the reserve in the wintertime and return to guide at the sports fishing lodges in the summertime. A survey of all heads of household carried out in 1977 at Grassy Narrows showed that about 51 percent always lived on or near the old reserve; about 18 percent moved to McIntosh and found work there while the children were in residential school; about 18 percent moved off the reserve in search of employment for periods of more than two years; and 13 percent moved to Grassy Narrows from other reserves.

But the people's migration did not last very long; it gained momentum in the early 1950s and ended in the middle 1960s, when people were induced to settle on the new reserve by the promise of houses, jobs, and welfare. Nevertheless, this brief off-reserve movement was an important aspect of the community's relations with the outside society in the postwar period. It exposed the Grassy Narrows people to the more negative aspects of life in the small railroad communities of northern Ontario. They returned to their community with ideas, conceptions, and habits that were inimical to the way of life of those who had never left the old reserve. Apparently this was particularly true of the people who lived around McIntosh. A former chief and elder of the community explains:

At one time, the people of Grassy Narrows were really split up. Those who went to McIntosh lived differently than the people who stayed on the old reserve. For one thing, the McIntosh people got exposed to welfare and cash. There was no welfare on the old reserve; only old people got rations, $8 a month in groceries. I think welfare spoils people. At the same time, families at McIntosh, whether they got cash from welfare or from work on the railroad, they learned to drink from the white people. The white people who worked on the railroads, they weren't the cream of Canadian society. There was a lot of violence around McIntosh.

When the Grassy Narrows people came back to the new reserve, they brought with them their way of life in McIntosh. There they got used to being on welfare, and in order to get us to move to the new reserve, the government promised us welfare.

The families on the old reserve, they had continued to live in the traditional way. They still lived an isolated life of hunting and trapping. They were not yet exposed to welfare or to drinking or to violence. This is where the bunching up of people on the new reserve, where the putting up of houses too close together and the mixing of clans, became really critical.

You had no sense of being with your own people any more; you had no sense of being in your own place. It started right after the move to the new reserve, but all the problems of the drinking and the worst of the violence really came in the 1970s.

THE NEW RESERVE AND INDIAN-WHITE RELATIONS: 1963-PRESENT

The third period in the history of the community's relations with the broader society begins with the relocation of the Grassy Narrows reserve in 1963. In general, this was a time of extraordinarily rapid change manifested by a dramatic alteration in settlement patterns, the breakup of the extended family and the shift to nuclear households, the beginning of dependency on social assistance, a change in the nature and functioning of band government, a sharp decline in the traditional mode of production, and the transformation of the economy to one based on the exploitation of government programs. . . . I propose now to examine an aspect of this third period that bears directly on the relations of the Grassy Narrows people to the broader society: the impact of the road connecting the new reserve with Kenora.

At first glance, Kenora seems like any other community in northern Ontario. Located 120 miles east of Winnipeg and about 300 miles west of Thunder Bay, it is far removed from large urban centers. On every side it is surrounded by a vast expanse of forests, lakes, and bush. This geographic situation provides an identity for the approximately 11 000 people who live there. They think of themselves as "Northerners"—people who can cope with a difficult physical environment, especially in the winter, who love the bush and have prized knowledge of it, who work hard and drink hard too. Kenora is an old town, as northern towns go. It was established with the building of the transcontinental railway in the late nineteenth century. Because of the town's strategic position in opening up the frontier to white settlement and resource expansion, two provinces fought for it. Kenora was first incorporated by the province of Manitoba in 1882 and then became formally incorporated by the province of Ontario in 1892. Most of its early inhabitants were recent immigrants who worked on railway construction crews: Norwegians, Finns, Ukrainians, Yugoslavs, Poles, Scots, Irish,

English, and Chinese. The various ethnic groups settled into little enclaves in the town, developing a definite pattern of residential segregation along ethnic lines. Almost from the very beginning, ethnicity was a tangible and significant facet of community life.

Socially, the character of the community was strongly influenced by the occupational structure and culture of the railroad and the pulp mill, each of which employed different classes of workmen, with different degrees of skill, responsibility, and status. Such differences were translated into social divisions that cut across ethnic origins. This patterning of social structure according to position in the occupational hierarchy was apparently characteristic of many single-industry, resource frontier communities in the Canadian north.[10]

During the first half of the twentieth century, the Indian presence in Kenora was welcomed. Only a handful of Indian people lived in town, simply because there were no real opportunities for Indians to participate in the economy of the frontier. Indians from the reserves around Kenora used to come into town for brief periods of time, primarily to trade or to have a holiday, but also to be educated or hospitalized. They constituted no threat to the social order of the town or to the economic security of its inhabitants. Their productive efforts, their harvest of fish, wild rice, or berries used in trade, were much appreciated by Kenora businessmen; in addition, Indians were "colorful" and "interesting." The memories of this earlier period of Indian–white contact in Kenora are no doubt romanticized, as is evident in this excerpt from a book about Indians by a Kenora resident:

> There were happier days for the Indians of Kenora. They used to come into town on holidays, and sit on the ground with their wares for sale, blueberries, bead work, beautiful art work, and leather work. They would pitch their tents in Ridout Bay and walk to town. Their babies were all decked out in beaded ticanoggans, and the Indian woman would strap the ticanoggan to her back and carry the baby around.
>
> Then when the holiday was over, they would all just disappear. In those days, the white man had respect for the Indian people, and the Indian people had respect for the white man.[11]

Certainly the construction of the Jones logging road in the late 1950s made it a little easier for the Grassy Narrows people to travel between the old reserve and the town of Kenora and thus to come to town more frequently than for special occasions only. However, two more fundamental and interrelated factors contributed to the significant increase in the transient Indian population in town and to the change in the attitude of the whites in Kenora toward Indians. These changes resulted, first, from the diversification of the town's economic base. In the decades following World War II, both federal and provincial governments established district or regional offices in Kenora. New jobs were created, oriented toward bureaucratic administration and service. Government became Kenora's second most important industry, after the Ontario-Minnesota Pulp and Paper Company. Second, this development coincided with the greater emphasis in public policy on providing services to native people in the area. Although the town did not need Indian people for their labor, in many ways it became heavily dependent upon them as various government agencies were established in town to serve the twelve Indian communities in the immediate vicinity.[12] Indian people began to come into town more frequently for medical treatment, schooling, court, and welfare.

With the provision of social assistance, unemployment insurance, family benefits, and other transfer payments in the form of checks, Indian people demonstrably had more cash to spend in Kenora's retail establishments, restaurants, and beer parlors than ever before. The white population of the town, uninformed about the internal changes in the economy and culture of many reserve communities, reacted only to the external manifestation of the "Indian presence" in town, a presence that rapidly began to be associated with the problem of "drunken Indians lying in the streets." By the early 1960s, a pattern of discrimination was well established in Kenora. Indians were tacitly forbidden to use certain hotels or restaurants, while those places that did accept Indians soon became branded as Indian hangouts. Even at the few bars and beverage rooms that were open to Indian customers, Indians and whites were spatially segregated. On the main streets of the town, Indians became an open target for sneering condescension, verbal abuse, or actual physical assault.

The law dealt unequally and unfairly with Indian people. The police would invariably arrest an Indian man or woman for intoxication in a public place; an equally inebriated white man or woman would receive a reprimand and might even be driven home. In cases of assault on Indians, white people expected no retribution from the law and rarely received it; Indians, on the other hand, if apprehended after a fight with a white person, would be tried and almost always found guilty of assault. Ultimately, the native person was helpless against the violence of the whites. This violence occurred among both adults and the young. Everywhere in town, Indians were confronted with white prejudice and open discrimination. Kenora became a hostile place, a racist community.

This very brief summary of the history of Kenora and of the evolution of Indian–white relationships in the town sets the stage for a description of what happened to the Grassy Narrows people after they were removed to the new reserve and connected to town by road. First of all, in a very short time, the Jones Road replaced canoe and portage routes as a means of travel between reserve communities. Indians began seeing each other more often in Kenora than on their reserves. The traditional orientation of the Grassy Narrows people to the more northern Ojibwa around Pekangikum shifted southward in a few short years to much closer contact with the Ojibwa around the Lake of the Woods. This development coincided with the cessation of seasonal migration to the northern traplines.

Second, the Jones Road not only enabled the Grassy Narrows people to get out of the new reserve but also enabled the more unsavory elements of white Kenora society to get in. "In the first year after the relocation, nobody bothered us too much. But then when the Kenora people heard that there was money, cash, on the new reserve, the taxi drivers became bootleggers.

They started coming in from town bringing a whole load of liquor in. First they asked you if you were drinking. If you said no, then they said, "Why don't you try it? Here, I'll give you a bottle free." Then they started to sell it. We had a dry reserve then, but it's amazing how much liquor started to get through."[13]

Third, because Kenora became the focal point for meeting Indians from other reserves and for doing business with government agencies in town, the Grassy Narrows people encountered the same prejudice and discrimination in town that faced all other Indians. The white society of Kenora did not make subtle distinctions between those Indians who had just come out of the bush, who were therefore perhaps more vulnerable to acts of overt or covert aggression, and those from other reserves who had been exposed to the disorganizing pressures of white contact sooner. "Good" and "bad" Indians were lumped together. Those Grassy Narrows people who never left the old reserve must have felt acutely the tension and hostility generated against them in town. In 1964, many of them came to Kenora to protest racial discrimination. This was the first time in the history of Indian–white contact in the town that Indians from different reserves organized a peaceful civil rights demonstration. A sixty-seven-year-old elder reminisces:

> The march of 1964 was organized by Peter Seymour, an Ojibwa from the Rat Portage reserve. He called all the chiefs together. He called the Director of the Ontario Human Rights Commission because he wanted to do things in a legal, peaceful way. About 400 Indian people made the march, about a week before Christmas. Six reserves in the Kenora area were involved. At Grassy Narrows, about half of all the old people went to this march. It started at the Holiday Inn and went by the church and the city council chambers. We made speeches to the mayor and his council.
>
> You see, at that time, Indians were turned out of stores and restaurants in town. There were very few places where Indians could go. It was time to protest the discrimination against our people in Kenora.
>
> Two weeks after the march, the politicians said that the march was organized by outside influences. But that's what they said in Georgia too, when the first civil rights marches started. Indians in Kenora were in the same position as the Negroes in the South in the early 1960s.

Indian–white relations in Kenora were not improved by the 1964 march. Paradoxically, racial tensions intensified as a result of the federal government's efforts to establish greater equivalence in medical, education, social, and employment services between the two races. The Kenora people saw only that taxpayers' dollars were going down the drain. They blamed the Indians themselves, not their status or conditions, and they blamed the government:

> You Ojibway are just as much to blame for discrimination as anyone. You're too busy crying over it to get out and do something about it. Let's see you work for a living and build and buy your own homes and pay for your own education. If you want equality

seriously, then cut your ties with the government and their juicy grants and free houses—step out into reality from your dream world. . . .

The blame according to the local [Kenora] people, lays on the shoulders of the federal government. The government pays them [the Indians] and pays them. It buys them . . . everything, and they still want more. If they hadn't given the Indian so much to begin with, the Indian would still retain his self-sufficiency, his self-reliance, and most important, his self-respect.[14]

Therein lies the crux of the matter. The Indians exchanged the intangible benefit of independence for the tangible benefits they received from the federal government (housing, schools, jobs, welfare, medical treatment). As the Indians accepted the goods and services offered to them by the government, they progressively lost their claim to being an independent people. Ultimately, they lost the ability to make decisions for themselves, at least within the context of the goods and services they accepted.[15]

The important aspect of this exchange is that the system intensifies the prejudice of the white community against Indians because they are seen not to be participating productively in the economy; rather, they are getting something for nothing, they are not working for a living, and, even worse, they are seen to be abusing property paid for by tax dollars. Thus, the Indians' participation in the system seems to be a total violation of the values and standards of the frontier society: hard work, paying your own way, and controlling your own life. The white people assert their moral superiority over the Indians in this regard, while at the same time they criticize the Indians for failing to live up to their own cultural traditions of self-sufficiency. They believe that Indians are poor because they are shiftless, lazy, unreliable, irresponsible, profligate with money and material goods. At the same time, they insist that Indians are this way because they have given up their old customs and values and have not yet adopted the new ones prized by the dominant society. White people ignore the historical evidence that it is the very geographic, legal, and economic segregation of Indian people from the mainstream society, combined with the erosion of the traditional economic base of Indian culture, that has led to their present dependence on government bureaucracies. They also ignore the fact that the very bureaucracies working to "help the Indians" are contributing millions of dollars and a substantial number of jobs to the economy of the Kenora community. An official of the district office of Indian Affairs ventures an estimate of the Indian contribution to the town:

I would say that the Indians spend one hell of a pile of money in this town [Kenora]. They keep a lot of businesses going here: supermarkets, car dealers, sports and hardware shops, taxis, clothing stores, you name it. All you have to do is look at one reserve, Grassy Narrows. The money paid out to that reserve by Indian Affairs alone is over a million and a half dollars a year. How much of that do you think stays in the community?

Sure, much of it gets spent on wages, but people spend their wages to buy from the Bay, and they spend an awful lot of money on taxis and airplane trips to town. They spend a great deal on booze, and all that money is spent in Kenora. Most of the money finds its way back to this town. And don't forget, all the construction materials and equipment come from Kenora.

Our Indian Affairs budget in this district, excluding capital but including staff costs, is about 5.4 million dollars, for Operations and Maintenance alone. Add capital, and our budget for the district may be in the neighborhood of ten million dollars a year. The fact is we have a budget equal to, or larger than, the town of Kenora! Where do you think all that money gets spent? I would say that Indians spend anywhere from seven to eight million dollars in the town of Kenora each year.

And how many white people do you think have jobs servicing the Indians? At one point, we counted twenty-eight different social agencies in Kenora who had something to do with Indians, excluding the Lake of the Woods Hospital. . . . Certainly, many of these jobs would not exist in the community without Indian people in the area. And that's about 600 jobs in total, at least half (and maybe more) of all the jobs in this town. In my opinion, if you took away the Indian reserves, you would close up Kenora.

The tragedy is that the town of Kenora is able to benefit economically from the poverty of Indian people that is ameliorated through government programs and services, but the entire social system of the town, and its social consciousness, in effect ensures that Indian people cannot escape from a life of economic deprivation on the reserves. Not only is it extremely difficult to find housing and employment in Kenora, but Indians are informally excluded from virtually every sector of the town's social life. Indians are valuable to Kenora only if they stay on the reserves and continue their dependence on the government, for only in this case can agencies based in town continue to provide services for them. "Prejudice and discrimination are important to the community, for whether or not the people are fully aware of it, the town as a whole is heavily dependent upon the existence of a separate, unequal, and adjacent native population."[16]

There are no easy solutions to the problem of white prejudice, because the feelings have gone far beyond resentment of the fact that Indians seem to have so much money that is not earned, or that they are spendthrifts and unreliable workers. The majority of whites in Kenora today think of Indians as untouchables, as profane persons. In matters of personal comportment, even cleanliness, whites feel that Indians are a contaminating presence in the town. The diverse manifestations of antisocial behavior exhibited by intoxicated Indians lead white people to generalize this behavior to all Indians. The most ordinary courtesies are neither expected of Indians nor extended to them. All Indians become outcasts; all are incriminated. The very category Indian is equated with a stigma, a moral destitution.

Indians react to their treatment as profane persons in various ways: by withdrawing from white society and seeking a measure of self-respect within the reserve community, by disguising certain essential characteristics of their Indianness, or by capitalizing on their situation to win small gains of money, resources, or services from the white society.[17] In Kenora, the Indians' reaction to the incessant undermining of a morally defensible self-image takes another, more self-destructive form. Rage and anger are turned inward and translated into violence against self or others. Louis Cameron, a young Ojibwa Indian, expresses this very well:

> You know, everybody knows that people have to be free to express human freedom. They have to laugh, they have to yell, and they have to be free to move around. But when you push people into a group like that, a lot of that expression turns inside. It's what you call internal aggression. And as a result of that, Indians live a dangerous style of life. They fight each other, they drink a lot. And the tendency to suicide is higher. . . .
> This is the crime, the injustice that is being committed by the government. . . . They are taking one segment of society and pushing it violently inward.[18]

In 1972, young Indians around Kenora decided that the strategy of non-violent protest advocated by their elders as a means to end racial discrimination in Kenora had to be changed. Led by Louis Cameron, they organized themselves into the Ojibway Warriors Society. In July 1974, armed with shotguns and rifles, young Warriors occupied Anishinabe Park in Kenora and held it as an armed camp, with barricades of barbed wire at the entrance to the park, for over four weeks. Under a poster bearing the following message:

THIS PIECE OF LAND

WE STAND ON, IS OUR

FLESH 'N BLOOD

BONE 'N MARROW

OF OUR BODIES, THIS

IS WHY WE CHOOSE

TO DIE HERE AT

ANISHINABE PARK

the Indians claimed that the land of the park was rightfully theirs.

In fact, the park had originally been purchased by Indian Affairs as a camping area for Indians travelling between the reserves and Kenora. But in 1959, the town bought the land from the government and developed it as a tourist area, without the permission of the Indian people. Therefore, the Indians claimed the park had been sold to Kenora illegally. In addition, they demanded more job opportunities for Indian people in the town, an end to discrimination by the townspeople, an end to police brutality and harassment of Indians, an overhaul of the operations of the Department of Indian Affairs, and a stronger voice by Indian people in the Department's decision making. According to Louis Cameron, the occupation of the park was a sign that Indian people were prepared to fight violence with violence: "We have to fight that style of life that is detrimental to human beings. So we, the

Ojibway Warriors Society, believe that the only way is to bring that internal aggression outwards. It must go out. We must break through the same way we got in. We got in by violence, we must go out by confrontation."[19]

The confrontation in the park was not well regarded by the old people of Grassy Narrows who had participated in the 1964 civil rights march. They felt that the end did not justify the means. They also felt that the situation was influenced too strongly by the leaders of the American Indian Movement (AIM). In the words of one of the leaders of the 1964 march: "Anishinabe Park. We did not feel, at Grassy Narrows, that it was the right thing to do at the time. Not even ten people from our reserve participated in the occupation of the park; it was only the young militants who went to the park. I also feel that the entire thing was too much influenced by Harvey Major and Dennis Banks of AIM, because they had been at Wounded Knee and they had their own ideas about how to do things in Kenora. The occupation of the park got out of control. All that happened was a backlash by the Kenora people."

The Kenora backlash came in the form of the book *Bended Elbow*, by Eleanor Jacobson. She wrote, "the United States have their 'Wounded Knee' but Canada has its 'Bended Elbow,' Kenora, Ontario."[20] Since the occupation of Anishinabe Park, very little has changed in Kenora. The town continues to exclude Indians from its economic and social life. For Indians locked into the reserve system, for the people of Grassy Narrows, the town's racism combined with government policies that sustain soul-destroying dependence may yet provoke a much wider conviction in the community that the Young Warriors were right. The time may yet come when the way out of the entrapment is the way in, when violence is answered by violence.

NOTES

1. These developments on the frontier included the building of a second transcontinental railway (the CNR line) in 1909, midway between the Grassy Narrows reserve and the CPR railway line, which passed through Kenora. In the 1920s, the lumbering industry was given a boost by the construction of a pulp mill in Kenora. Later in the same decade, a gold rush started around Red Lake, a town about 125 miles north of Grassy Narrows. Minaki Lodge, catering to wealthy tourists and sports fishermen, opened in 1916 near the rail crossing of the Winnipeg River. In the early 1930s, the Trans-Canada Highway was built through the town of Kenora, thus facilitating access to the region from points both east and west.

   For a more extensive discussion of the Indians' participation in the economy of northwestern Ontario before World War II, see an unpublished report prepared for the Anti-Mercury Ojibwa Group, the Islington Band, and the Grassy Narrows Band by Peter Usher, Patricia Anderson, Hugh Brody, Jennifer Keck, and Jill Torrie, "The Economic and Social Impact of Mercury Pollution on the Whitedog and Grassy Narrows Indian Reserves, Ontario," Ottawa, July 1979, 87–89.

2. Department of Indian Affairs and Northern Development, *Annual Reports*. Report of John McIntyre to the Superintendent-General of Indian Affairs in Ottawa, *Annual Reports*, 1885, 127.

3. Report of E. McColl to the Superintendent-General of Indian Affairs in Ottawa, *Annual Reports*, 1885, 127.

4. The description of provincial government policy regarding Indian land use presented on pp. 115 and 116 draws substantially on the more detailed analysis of this subject in Usher et al., "Economic and Social Impact," 90–91, 96–98, 106.

5. For a detailed examination of the evolution of the Indian Act, see "The Historical Development of the Indian Act" (Paper prepared by the Treaties and Historical Research Centre, Department of Indian Affairs and Northern Development, Ottawa, Aug. 1978).

6. Joint Committee of the Senate and the House of Commons, *Proceedings and Evidence* 16 (1961): 605–18.

7. This amendment to the Indian Act made it possible to sell beer and other liquor to the Grassy Narrows guides in the tourist camps, to the men on railway section gangs around McIntosh, and to those who worked in the mines around Red Lake. On-reserve alcohol consumption, however, remained prohibited until the mid-1970s.

8. The difference in hospitality between the Cree and the Ojibwa Indians, for example, was noted by early explorers as well as by contemporary scholars. The Cree were known for their hospitality, and yet both Cree and Ojibwa communities are geographically isolated, and both cultures are based on clan groups. Thus, isolation by itself does not explain hostility to strangers.

9. Tuberculosis was a cause of many deaths on the old reserve, especially among children. There was initial resistance to the sanitariums, because "some people never came back, and the Indians thought the white people were killing them there."

10. Ira M. Robinson, *New Industrial Towns on Canada's Resource Frontier* (Chicago: University of Chicago Department of Geography Research Paper, no. 73, 1962). Indeed, Kenora in its early days must have borne a striking resemblance to Sioux Lookout (Crow Lake) in its ethnic composition, association with the railroad, and social structure. An excellent exposition of the development of Crow Lake is given by David H. Stymeist, *Ethnics and Indians, Social Relations in a Northwestern Ontario Town* (Toronto: Peter Martin Associates, 1975), 24–39.

11. Eleanor M. Jacobson, *Bended Elbow* (Kenora, ON: Central Publications, 1976), 37. This book is a highly partisan and harshly negative account of Indians in Kenora, but it expresses feelings and perceptions that are widely shared among white residents of the town.

12. The federal government agencies include Indian Affairs, the Department of Manpower, and the Department of National Health and Welfare; the provincial government agencies are the Ministry of Natural Resources, Ontario Provincial Police, and Community and Social Services. Other government offices (Justice, Liquor Control Board, Mines, Highways, Transport, Post Office, and so on) serve both the Indian and the white populations.

13. Long-time Kenora residents confirmed the activities of bootleggers on the new reserve and the impact of road access on drinking patterns. Stu Martin said in an interview: "The drinking at Grassy Narrows really started when they were moved to the road, when the liquor began coming in. The taxi people, they exploited the Indians; they could bring in the booze very easily. The trouble at Grassy was related to alcohol, to the road, and to the relocation and the disruption of their way of life."

14. Jacobson, *Bended Elbow*, 5, 7–8, 12.

15. See Stymeist, *Ethnics and Indians*, 84–85, for a good discussion of the

244 ANASTASIA M. SHKILNYK

dimensions and implications of the existing exchange system between Indian people and the white organizations that serve them.

16. Ibid., 93.

17. An extensive and insightful discussion of strategies used by Indians to cope with the image whites have of them can be found in Niels Winther Braroe, *Indian and White* (Stanford: Stanford University Press, 1975), chaps. 6–8.

18. Louis Cameron, Anishinabe interview, quoted in "Quicksilver and Slow Death" (Paper prepared for the Ontario Public Interest Research Group, Oct. 1976, 25).

19. Ibid., 26.

20. Jacobson, *Bended Elbow*, 33.

WHEN THE WORLD WAS NEW: STORIES OF THE SAHTÚ DENE ◇

GEORGE BLONDIN

○

FIRST YEARS

I was born near Horton Lake, at the edge of the Barrens east of K'áhbamįtúé, in May, 1922. After New Year's that winter, people from K'áhbamįtúé and Sahtú had gathered near Horton Lake in a place where there was a patch of trees. Later, when it was getting warm—but before the snow melted—the people began to move back to their own places to hunt beaver and muskrat in the spring.

My parents and other people from Sahtú travelled back on the snow crust in May. They stopped for two days when I was born, and then started moving again.

It was a time when Dene still lived by their own laws and within their own culture. Oldtime Dene taught their children the Dene law. Just as you read in the Bible that parents tried to save the birthright of the eldest son or daughter, the Dene tried to make sure their children had medicine power.

Because I was the eldest son, my parents and grandparents tried the best they could for me to get medicine power. When I was a baby, I was sent to stay in each of my grandfathers' tents for a time, so they could see if I had medicine powers of my own. If not, the grandfathers could transfer some of their own medicine to me. I spent almost all my early life with my two grandfathers, Paul Blondin and Karkeye.

I remember a time Paul took me hunting in his canoe. We were on the shore of a big lake. It was spring, and the water was clean and calm. You

◇ (Yellowknife: Outcrop, 1990), 203–46. Reprinted with permission.

could hear and see all kinds of waterfowl. Grandfather Paul told me the name of each one, pointing to them, so I could tell which bird made each call.

Later, as we paddled close to shore, my grandfather beached the canoe and stepped out. He called me over to him.

"Do you want to look at something good?"

He pointed under some willow leaves and I saw six small blue eggs. I wanted to put them in my pocket, but Grandfather told me not to touch them. He wanted me to know that all the birds at the lake in spring have eggs. If I touched the eggs, he told me, the mother birds would not come back to the nest.

"You need the birds," Grandfather Paul told me. "Their music makes you feel happy when you're alone. When you hear the robin singing early in the morning, you get up right away, and you feel better."

We kept on travelling, and Grandfather Paul kept on talking to me. When we stopped to camp, he told me to help him with little things I could do. My grandfather never let me sleep after he got up. He always dressed before he made the fire, so I had to get dressed as well. He always got me to help start the fire.

My grandfather Karkeye was the same. That was how the grandfathers taught the children.

There were no stores in those days, and the supplies people got in the summer had to last all winter. There were no children's toys to buy, so Grandfather Karkeye was always making bows and arrows, small drums, and toy boats for us to play with.

He always told me what not to do: don't eat hot food, don't eat marrow, don't eat fat, don't smoke. Later on it was: don't lie around.

When I was five years old, we were staying on the shore of a fish lake. We were all in one tent, with Mom and Dad on one side and my grandparents on the other side.

After I helped Grandfather make the fire, I always sat down close to my mom. One morning, the woodstove was so hot that she opened the tent flap. You could see the lake just below. The weather was calm, with no wind. It was still dark, although daylight was coming. Mom told me to get water with the small lard pail. I was scared, but I went down to the lake anyway.

When I got to the shore, I dipped the pail in the water. Then I looked out on the lake and saw a giant of a man, with white hair, walking on the water toward me. I dropped the pail and ran screaming to my mother. I jumped into her lap. She asked me what had happened, and I told her.

She said I wasn't to tell anyone else what I had seen.

"It's your grandfather trying to transfer medicine over to you, and now you've spoiled everything. Without medicine, you're going to be poor. You are going to need help from others all the time."

At breakfast, Paul told my father that he and my grandmother didn't want me to stay with them any longer.

"We tried everything to transfer medicine to him, because he has no medicine of his own," Paul said. "But the medicine we want to transfer won't get to him."

He told my dad to raise me as well as he could. "I've looked into his future, and he will live a long time. He will still be living when all of us are dead, and he will have a wife and children."

When I was seven years old, in 1929, I went to school. Five years of boarding at the Roman Catholic mission school in Kǫ́ǫ́ were hard, but I was too young to realize what was going on. There were only four schools in the entire Northwest Territories in those days, all of them operated by Roman Catholic or Anglican missions. The mission at Zhatí Kǫ́ǫ́ took care of about fifty boys and fifty girls.

There was also a small store at Zhatí Kǫ́ǫ́ that sold the food and equipment people needed in the bush. The Dene brought in fish, ducks, moose, caribou, bear, beaver and muskrat from the bush, and traded meat or pelts for food, cloth and tobacco. The missionaries kept a few cattle and chickens, and grew potatoes and other vegetables in their garden.

We students got to eat all kinds of wild game, but mostly we ate "stick fish." In the fall, the mission hired Dene fishermen to go out on the mission boat and bring in fish by the thousands, which were then hung to dry. These fish were tied by the tail to a stick, ten to each, on a rack about four and a half metres high. The fish dried in the air and didn't spoil. These dry fish fed the students until spring.

At school, teaching was done mostly on the blackboard and out of a few books. When I got there, I was forbidden to speak my own language. It was hard at first, because I didn't know how to speak English: I didn't even know how to say "yes" or ' no." But in time, I learned. At the end of five years, I had moved into what they called Grade Four then (it would be Grade Two today), although I had very low marks in English.

I had forgotten everything my grandfather taught me. During all the years I was at the mission school, I saw my parents only once—although students who lived around Zhatí Kǫ́ǫ́ saw their families almost every summer. When I had to go home, the Bishop of the Northwest Territories, who knew my father, made travel arrangements for me and my brother Frank.

One evening in the spring, Sister told us we were going. The nuns packed for us and took us to a small scow crewed by a priest and a missionary brother, with a small engine that made a popping noise as we set out on Dehcho. The boat was very slow, and my brother and I kept standing up, because we were tired of sitting. The old priest yelled at us to sit down.

After we'd travelled the river for a few hours, we camped on a small island, where we found seagull eggs. The brother said they were good food, so we filled up a small box and the brother boiled as many eggs as we wanted. They tasted like fish, but we hadn't seen eggs for a while, so we ate until our bellies were full. Before morning, our bellies were sore.

The weather was good the next morning, so we set out again We landed in Kátł'o Dehé. It was only a small village then, with a church and a few Dene homes. It was Sunday, so we went to church. Then we travelled on the lake towards Denínu. That evening, we got to Denínu, a big town with a mission school, and that's where they left us.

A month went by before we could get on a plane. It was the kind you had to crank to start, and it made a deafening noise. We stopped at

Bèhchokǫ̀ for supper, and then flew non-stop to Ɂtseretúe, where my father was working at a small mining camp. My mother cried with joy when she saw us.

That was in 1934. We had come back to our own way of life, but in the eyes of our people, my brother and I were like aliens from outer space. No one at home spoke more than a word or two of English. My brother and I could not speak Gokedé. Our family had to make signs to us.

Dad took us with him everywhere he went. Sometimes we visited the fish nets, and sometimes we went moose hunting. We went with Mom to pick berries. We learned slowly.

Mom didn't speak English at all, so sometimes she asked us to do something and we did the opposite without knowing it. Once, she told us to bring her an axe, so we went outside and brought in a bunch of wood. No, she said, by shaking her head. We went outside again and waited. She came out and pointed to the axe and said in Gokedé, "*kokwi.*"

We went to the rabbit snares every day, with either Mom or Dad. We saw them kill rabbits by pulling the rabbit's heart.

"You can visit the rabbit snares on your own now," Dad told us one day. "You can't get lost. Just follow the trail you took before. You can come back the same way."

We followed the marks on the trail and found the snares. In them there were dead rabbits, which we put into our sack. But one big rabbit had been caught by the hind legs and was still alive. We tried to find its heart, but we couldn't. We just put the live rabbit in the sack with the dead ones, and headed home.

When we got back, Mom hugged us with joy, proud that her boys could bring home game on their own. She started to take the rabbits out of the sack and out jumped the live one. It raced all over the tent, while Mom yelled at us. We chased the rabbit around the woodstove, spilling the water pail and breaking the dishes. Finally we caught it, and everybody had a good laugh.

THE DENE CYCLE

In the winter of 1935, we moved to Ɂtseretúe, where my brother and I saw caribou for the first time. Dad was selling meat to the people running a mine at Nágazideh. I learned to drive a team of four dogs, and I could haul caribou meat for short distances.

In April, there was a big gathering of the T'licho and Sahtú Dene at the end of Ɂtseretúe. Fifteen dog teams came up from Wekwèti. About fifty families enjoyed drum dances and feasting on caribou dry meat and bones, grease and pounded meat. There were also handgames. Once the people played three nights in a row, with thirty players on each side.

When it got close to Easter, the T'licho went back to Bèhchokǫ̀, about 300 kilometres away. Dad and some of the other Sahtú Dene went with them, while my brother and I stayed home to help Mom.

There was a lot of work to do. We had three dogs and a toboggan, and every day we hitched our dogs up first thing and went five or six kilometres to cut wood. We didn't have a saw, so we had to use a dull axe. Mom had sharpened it for us, but we kept hitting rocks. The dogs were old and slow, and they didn't listen to us. It took us half a day to cut wood.

Of course, we played in the bush, too, and that took time. It was noon before we got back. After we ate, we chopped up all the wood. Then we had to get water and spruce brush for inside the tent. We did this every day, but we still had time to play with the other kids.

After the people came back from Bèhchokǫ̀, the men hunted caribou and everyone helped make dry meat. Then we started back to Sahtú, going towards Déline. The snow was melting when we started to travel overland. We reached Sahtú at the end of May, and people began to hunt beaver and muskrat.

A year had gone by since I got out of school. I was beginning to recognize animals and birds of all kinds. My brother and I were surprised to see so many kinds of birds in the bush. We were happy in the spring, when daylight lasted longer and longer. On Sahtú, the water seeped through the surface ice, leaving it dry, and we could play on it if we wore moccasins and rubbers. Dad had set fish hooks through the ice, and we visited the hooks by ourselves. It was exciting to pull a big trout through the ice.

Later on, about twelve families travelled across the ice toward Déline. Some of the people carried their canoes on sleds that had steel runners.

My brother and I ran for many kilometres, and we rode as well. We had nine dogs, and all of them wore leather booties so the ice needles wouldn't cut their feet.

We camped at places where the big rivers ran into the lake making open water where the people could set fish nets. Some people also set hooks in ice cracks out on the lake. There were ducks on the open water, and beaver and muskrat inland. Sometimes we camped in one place for three or four nights.

It was a lot of fun for kids. The beach was clean. The leaves were coming out. The birds were singing, and the ducks were calling noisily. The people were happy. They felt free.

After we arrived at Déline, we went by boat from the head of Sahtú Dé to Tulít'a on the banks of Dehcho.

The Dene lived according to their own laws and culture. They went off in all directions to their hunting areas in winter, and some didn't get to Tulít'a till summer. When they did, the people gathered for a big feast and dance. There were Sahtú Dene, Shihta Got'ine K'achot'ine and Deh Gah Got'ine at Tulít'a, and they all enjoyed ten days of feasting and fun. Afterward, everybody got supplies and went back to their hunting lands. After they hunted, they would come and trade dry meat and fish for more supplies for the winter.

TRAVELLING SAHTÚ DÉ

A group of people from Déline started out on Sahtú Dé in a boat that had only a three-horsepower motor, which isn't very strong against Sahtú Dé's current. It takes at least three nights to go through the rapids, which widen between high cliffs, with no channels. There are shallow rocks everywhere.

Every time we travelled on Sahtú Dé, we hitched up our dogteam, tied a long line to the canoe, and drove the dogs along the shore to pull the canoe up the rapids. The people joked and sang songs. They took time for hunting. There was no hurry to get anywhere; they travelled all over the land, so every place was home. Sometimes they spent two or three nights on the banks of Sahtú Dé, hunting ducks and moose. If they got a moose, everybody ate well.

That was how it was to travel on Sahtú Dé every summer.

After we got back to Délįne, we went to a fishing place to make dried fish. Every morning, Dad and I went to visit the fish nets, and then my brother and I helped Mom work on the fish. We had to keep a smoky fire going all the time: if it went out, flies landed on the fish.

Every family was doing the same thing. The men hunted moose, ducks, rabbits, bear and ptarmigan, so we would have all kinds of food.

People were strong then; they never complained about working hard. They prayed every morning and evening, and children prayed with their parents. People respected each other. Kids didn't play after dark. There were no such things as alcohol and parties. People saw cash only at treaty time. They were wealthy if they stored plentiful supplies—fat, dry meat, berries and fish—for the winter. People worked hard every day. They got up at six in the morning and worked until late at night.

There was lots to do to keep everybody happy. Young people played a bow and arrow game, a stick game (they threw at a peg and counted up the points), hide and seek, and handgames. Girls had their own games, and they started sewing very young.

In the fall, a group went to Tulít'a to trade dry fish for goods. Some people still had credit from the spring hunt to use for supplies that fall. We got our supplies, enough to last until Christmas, and picked our trapping areas. Then the heavy work started, the hunting for moose and caribou while they were fat. Once the animals started mating, they got thin.

o

In the fall of 1936, our family moved with another one to a place eighty kilometres from Délįne, to put up fish. My brother was sick with tuberculosis, so he had to stay in bed.

By now, I was good at doing housework and spoke Gokedé well. Every morning, my dad and I visited the nets, got wood and piled it for the winter. Dad worked hard and expected me to do the same. I worked like an adult, hunting ptarmigan. He got me up early, and after a while I got used to it.

When open season came, we went trapping inland. We killed four woodland caribou, and I loaded the toboggan and brought the meat back home. My mother and brother were happy to see me come back with the meat. We were a close, united family, with so much love.

At Christmas that winter, Dad went to Tulít'a and brought back flour, tea, sugar, jam and dried fruit. We trapped for several weeks. Then, in April of 1937 my brother died.

My dad took his body to Délįne to be buried.

In the spring, we moved to Turílį on Sahtú, where many Dene were fishing and shooting ducks. After the spring hunt, we went with these people back to Délįne. We portaged overland for about 25 kilometres, hitching our dogs to the big sleds. One man was sick, so they made a stretcher and four people carried it.

We went to Délįne, we went to Tulít'a. It was the same cycle every summer. Around the middle of August, when it was hot, we moved early to a different trapping area north of Chukezedeh, about 145 kilometres inland from Délįne.

We used dog packs to carry our supplies: a dog could pack his own weight. My dad packed a canoe, I packed a stove, Mom packed, and all the nine dogs packed, too. It took seven days of hard travelling, and the dogs' feet got bloody because the ground was so dry. Dad killed ducks and beaver and small game along the way, so we ate well. But the dogs got tired of eating dry fish.

My parents never complained. They laughed and joked and told stories every night. Dad taught me safety rules all the time, every day something different. We prayed morning and evening.

The second day after we got to the place where the river flows into Chukezetúe, Dad shot two fat moose. We made dry meat and the dogs ate well. In three weeks, Dad shot fifteen moose altogether. It was hard work to pack meat to our main camp all the time. We all worked late every night. Life was just working and sleeping, but we didn't worry. The Elders always told us the Creator walks the land and takes care of us, and it gave the people confidence.

My parents made a good man out of me, although at the time I thought they were mean. It took me all these years to realize they talked roughly to me for my own good. Of their fifteen children, I was the only boy who survived—but they spoke to me as if they still had ten boys left.

Every day at breakfast, Dad drilled safety rules into my head. "Don't depend on anybody," he would say. "Every morning, thank God for the good night you slept. Then think about what I said about safety that'll fit in with your daily work. Think about that as long as you live, no matter what work you do."

That fall, I stayed with Mom while Dad went trapping across Sahtú for two months, until the middle of December. Mom treated me just the way Dad did. "Get up," she would say in the morning. "It's five o'clock." It was cold in the tent at that hour, but she made sure I stayed up, even if I was standing by the stove to keep from freezing. I'd cook whatever we had, and then she'd give me a job, cutting wood or visiting nets.

The day came when we were ready to go trapping. I went with an old man to set traps. We went along the shore of Sahtú for half a day, then inland, camping whenever we were tired. We ate fish and dry meat—we didn't have fresh meat, because we hadn't killed any moose yet.

I was walking ahead of the dogteam when I saw an old grizzly bear track, so I doubled back and told the old man.

"Good," he said. "Let's follow the bear. Bear meat is good, and we need fresh meat. The bear's probably not too far away."

We took our rifles and packs and followed the bear. The track was old and covered with snow in some places, and sometimes it disappeared. That surprised me, but not the old man. "I knew he was going to do that," he said.

When the bear got to dense bush, it backtracked for half a kilometre and then jumped sideways into a thick willow patch, so the track disappeared. The bear did that four times: we spent all day tracking it. As it got close to its den, it made many circles.

"It must be close," the old man said. "Look at that hill. You see that tree? That's a bear tree. Let's go over and have a look."

A bear usually has a tree close to its den to climb. The old people could recognize a bear tree from a long way off during the winter, and that's how they killed bears in their dens.

The old man told me to get my rifle out and stand guard. "You stand right here and look down that bear hole," he said.

To me it looked like ordinary ground, because the bear had closed the hole and snow had fallen on top of it.

"Stand there and be alert while I cut a log to block the hole," the man told me.

I stood there, not paying much attention. The old man cut down a small tree and trimmed it. He used this as a pole to poke at the ground where I was standing.

"Here is the hole," he said, and banged at the mouth of the den to wake the bear. Then he laid the pole across the opening.

He said it was Dene custom to wake a bear before killing it; otherwise the meat wouldn't taste good. But the old man was worried that the big grizzly would rush out of the den, breaking his pole.

"Stay there," he told me. "I will cut a bigger log. Block the den well." He went several metres down the hill. I was standing there watching the hole when suddenly I heard a loud growl.

The bear tried to run out, but the pole held him. With another growl, the grizzly stuck his head and one arm out. The log was between its head and arm, so the bear could almost grab me. He swiped, and barely missed me. I was frozen with fear, and just stood there while the old man shouted, "Shoot! Shoot!"

Finally, the old man came running up the hill, grabbed the gun and shot the bear right at my feet.

"If you'd been alone, the bear would have killed you," he yelled. "You're a man—that's why you carry a gun. But you stood there like a stone."

I didn't blame him for getting angry. I was ashamed of myself. But I hadn't expected anything to happen.

We went back to camp, and I hitched up my dogs to go to the den and get the bear meat that same night. The old man roasted fat bear ribs, which made a good meal.

The Dene usually don't eat bear meat, mostly because of old stories like the one about a talking bear that knows everybody's mind, and because of medicine talk. If you have a bit of bear medicine, they say, you can't eat bear, because you can't trust bear. Most medicine people won't eat bear. Also, people see bears eat dirty things close to camp. But there wasn't anything wrong with bear meat way out in the bush, where they ate only berries and roots.

I trapped with this old man throughout November. Close to Christmas, we were at Edacho. The point sticks out in the middle of Sahtú and makes the lake narrow in the middle. It's about ninety kilometres from Edacho to ?ehdaı́la. The narrows freeze during the last week in November, and the caribou herds go across the narrows on the ice.

The last time we visited our traps, we were surprised to see caribou tracks. Then we saw caribou on the big lake and started shooting. We got four of them. That evening we roasted caribou head on the open fire and feasted all night.

VISITING THE FISH NETS

It's a busy life on the land, with only a youngster to be the man of the family. My mother was happy to see me, her only son, taking responsibility.

After I returned from trapping, I went into the bush for wood early the next morning. My dogs were so tired that I had to pack the wood on my shoulders for nearly a kilometre. I worked about three hours, cutting enough wood to last two days. I then visited our nets, about six kilometres away. Evening drew in quickly, because the days were so short at that time of year. The nets had been in place for a week, so they were frozen in place by very thick ice, and I had to use a chisel. It was about twenty below zero.

When you set a fish net under the ice, you make two holes, many metres apart. The hole where you pull the net out has to be about a metre and a quarter long and over a half a metre wide; the other one should be about half a metre square. You stake the net at one hole and tie a long line to the other end of the net, so you can pull it right out, then set it again when you're finished. At one side of the hole, you make a shelf, so the nets sit in the water and don't freeze while you are tending them bare-handed.

I had caught about 150 fish—trout, whitefish, jackfish, suckers, and grayling. Some of the fish were dead and all tangled up, because the nets had been there for a week. It took a long time to get them out. Before I could go home, I had to make a hole in the snow to cache my fish. It was about ten o'clock at night by then, but this was an average day's work.

People expect to be paid for their work nowadays. But at that time, I didn't even know that people in other places worked for money. I was happy, singing to myself as I walked home that night. I had nothing to worry about. It's a big land, and there's plenty of food. You feel free, because nobody tells you what to do.

When I got home, Mom had dinner cooked for me. She was soft-hearted. She would come over and kiss me when I got home and say "Poor boy! What happened to you?" But she never said things like that in front of my dad. He would say, "Don't spoil him. He has to live longer than us, and I have to make a man out of him."

Mom woke me up early the next morning. "Eat and go to work," she said. It was still dark when I hitched my dogs up. I made five trips and got a week's wood so that Mom would have enough while I visited my traps and my nets.

Tending the nets was easier this time, because the ice was thin after the other night, and there were fewer fish, all of them still alive. I loaded up sixty fish and came home.

The next day the old man and I went to check our traps. It took three nights. I caught seven marten and he caught twelve. Then we took our traps out, because we were going to Tulít'a for supplies, and would not be back for a long time.

When we got back to camp, my work started all over again —cutting and hauling wood, checking the nets. I had to haul lots of wood, because we were getting ready to go to Tulít'a.

My dad decided to go across the lake with a man named McCauley. I was left alone with Mom and Grandfather McCauley next door. By the time the first snow came, we had run out of tea and sugar, so we went across the country to Délįne and traded our fur at a small trading outpost.

That fall of 1939, Hitler had invaded Poland, and Great Britain was at war. The manager of the Hudson's Bay Company post gave me some old newspapers that showed soldiers at war. I told my family that a big war was going on, but they didn't believe me. I showed them the pictures, and they still wouldn't believe me. How can people kill one another? they asked.

The Second World War didn't affect the Dene much. Most people lived off the land, spending their time in the bush. Few knew how to read, so they didn't know what was happening outside their homeland. Even our supplies were unaffected. Only sugar and shells were rationed—we got ten pounds (4.5 kilograms) of sugar and two boxes of shells per month.

No one in this part of the country spoke English anyway, so no one knew anything about the terrible disasters happening in other parts of the world. The Dene only worried about what they were going to eat each day. It wasn't until years later that everything from Outside began to affect our daily lives.

After we got back to our camp in the bush, my father returned from trapping, and we went to Tulít'a for supplies. My mother was pregnant, and while we were away she died in childbirth. I was seventeen years old. My dad took the coffin to Délįne for burial.

I was lonely; there was nobody to keep our home, and my dad was not the same as my mom. We kept busy all the time. When spring came, we went to Tulít'a and then back to Délįne.

GOING TRAPPING WITH PAUL

As fall got nearer, a man named Paul suggested that we go trapping together. I agreed. I was nineteen by then, old enough. My dad went trapping with another family, and Paul and I went to the north shore of Sahtú.

We were in a hurry, because it was getting late in September. It's dangerous to start out on Sahtú so late in the season, because it's windy every day and the waves are huge. The lake starts to freeze early.

We got stuck three times. The third time, we were windbound many kilometres from our destination, on an island about thirteen kilometres long. A north wind was blowing, and it got colder and colder. On the second day, it started snowing, and the snow was knee deep before it stopped. Luckily, we shot two caribou, which had stayed on the island all summer. There were also plenty of ptarmigan, so we ate well.

We were stuck for two weeks in the cold and wind, but finally we got across. We headed into a long bay that was already frozen. We went to the far end and set nets under the ice. We had a good supply of fish in no time.

Then we began trapping. On that shore, there were many rodents for the foxes to feed on, so there were many foxes. We trapped along the shoreline and then inland. We were busy every day.

One pitch-dark night, our dogs started barking. We thought they must have heard a grizzly bear. When we went outside, we were surprised to hear noises all over the bush. Paul said caribou must be passing.

In the morning, we found tracks everywhere, and when full daylight came, we saw the caribou. It was the first time I had seen so many all at once. We shot as many as we could.

We went inland to set more traps. It was hard to travel because there were so many caribou around. We tried travelling in the trees, but after a few kilometres, we had to go onto the open Barrenlands. The caribou had packed the snow down, and they were everywhere. The dogs were jumping at them all the time, so one of us had to hold onto both dog teams while the other set traps.

On one long inland lake, the caribou were so thick we couldn't move on until the herd had passed. The animals were nearly stampeding as they hurried in great masses toward their winter feeding area. They came to a ridge that had a snowdrift on the other side, and the first two or three caribou over it got stuck. The animals behind them were running so close together that they landed on top of the fallen leaders. Three or four were trampled to death.

The caribou kicked away all the traps we set. Sometimes they got a hoof caught in a trap and couldn't escape, so they died there. Instead of a fox, we would find a big caribou. We cut such animals up for dog food.

The caribou gave us so much trouble we didn't get many foxes. I got 32 foxes and five mink; Paul got 33 foxes. We were so busy, we lost track of time as the days passed. We didn't have watches or calendars, and we didn't own a radio.

We were supposed to go to Déline for Christmas, and we were ready early. We stored all our traps in our tent and set off the next day. When we got out onto Sahtú, we found that the ice was only thirteen centimetres thick. We were scared, but we knew the lake was frozen all the way across, because no steam was rising from open water. It was so cold that we could see for great distances. We kept going, watching carefully for cracks in the ice.

There are many pressure ridges on Sahtú in winter. Some people say pressure ridges are caused by tides. Others say air underneath the ice makes small cracks that fill with water and freeze, causing the ice to expand; the pressure gets so strong that something has to give way. In places, the pressure ridges piled ice as high as a two or three storey house, which stretched right across the lake. It was hard to cross such ridges: we would look for a low spot and chop a trail through it.

While travelling on the ice, we heard noises like thunder and the ice would shake and crack all over. It was frightening, but like most people who live near the giant lake, we were used to these things.

We crossed 64 kilometres of lake ice that day. There was no snow on the ice, and travelling was good. After four nights, we got to Délįne.

"Why did you come so early?" people asked. "Everybody's still trapping."

They didn't believe us when we told them we'd lost track of the days. They teased us, saying we'd come to meet girls.

TRAPPING ALONE FOR THE FIRST TIME

Just a few days before Christmas, five of us went to Tulít'a to sell our fur and get more supplies. It took us ten days to get back to Délįne. We were ready to go trapping again, when Paul told me his father was sick and he couldn't go out.

My own father, Edward, had an idea. "Go and get your traps," he said, "and trap for lynx at Turíli."

Turíli was at the other end of Sahtú, about 320 kilometres from where I had last been trapping. I would have to travel 640 kilometres to pick up my traps.

People thought I was too young to travel alone. But my father said, "I've taught him enough. He can look after himself. If something happens to him, it's his own fault."

The first night after I set off on the long journey, it was snowing and travel was hard. I started early in the morning—long before daylight—and kept moving until late at night. The first three nights were cold, but there was no wind. On the last night, it started to snow and storm, and I still had sixty kilometres to go across the channel. I couldn't see forty metres ahead, but I had to go on, because I had no dog food left. If I got lost, my dogs and I would starve.

When daylight came I took careful directions with my compass. I couldn't see the sun or the sky; all I could see was the ice I was travelling on.

In the old days before compasses, people used the stars, sun and wind to find their way. If they were travelling on a large lake and couldn't see the sun or the stars, they used snowdrifts.

Higher snowdrifts are usually formed in a north-south line, because the wind blows in that direction more often. People travelled straight across the snowdrifts, so there'd be no danger they would go in circles and get lost. Bigger and bigger snowdrifts, shaped like canoes placed upside down, blocked my way. I decided to travel at an angle over these rows of drifts. That would take me close to where my main camp was.

My sled load was light: I carried only my blanket, having left my tent behind. The wind was strong, and I had to keep stopping to take ice out of my dogs' eyes.

Travel was slow, but I couldn't cover myself with the blanket and ride in the sled, because I had to watch our direction carefully. I walked behind my dogs to keep warm. When I was tired I rested, fed the dogs my last bit of fresh fish, wrapped myself in my eiderdown and ate small bits of boiled meat and snow.

I travelled late into the night, and I began to think I was lost. If I was lost, I would have to sleep there on the ice and wait until daylight, in case the wind went down. Like the dogs, I was walking in slow motion.

Suddenly it felt like I was going uphill. Then I saw something ahead: a small willow. I was on the shore at last, but I didn't know where.

I started walking across the land. After an hour I recognized country I'd been to the previous fall, and even found a place where I'd set a trap. I was happy now that I knew I was close to my camp with its tent, stove, and meat. I pushed my dogs to go on.

Dogs are smart; they knew they were close to camp, and they moved faster. I rode on the toboggan most of the time.

I got to my camp very late that night. I built a fire, got meat from the cache, and had a good meal. My dogs did, too. I slept for a few hours, but got up just at daylight. I saw that I didn't have enough meat for the trip back, so I decided to go hunting, up a nearby hill. I soon spotted fresh tracks, and then caribou on a small lake. I shot six, skinned them, made a fire and ate a good meal. Then I walked back to camp.

I brought the caribou home the next day and got ready for my trip back to the Turílịdeh, at the other end of Sahtú. I started off early, with a big load. It was a good day for travelling, and I got as far as the tent I had left behind. The second day was easy too, travelling on the shoreline.

On the third day I had to cross the channel, which is about 67 kilometres wide. The weather was fairly good when I started off. I had enough wood to make two fires. After four hours, since it was turning light, I stopped and made a fire. But when I stopped again four hours later, it was getting cloudy and the snow was starting to blow.

I started again, without any wood. I knew my direction, but all I had to go by was the angle of the snowdrifts. I travelled late into the night. The fresh snow made it hard pulling, and the dogs were slow. I had to walk all the time, and it seemed at times as if this long journey would go on forever. But I wasn't prepared for worse hardships to come.

GETTING WATER WITH A GUN

It was dark and snowing on the vast ice of Sahtú. I couldn't see what was around me, and I was too tired to go on, anyway. So I stopped and tied the dogs to large chunks of rough ice. I chopped frozen meat and fed them. Without a fire to cook meat, all I had to eat myself was leftover boiled meat. I couldn't melt water. I covered myself in my eiderdown and tried to sleep, but I couldn't, because I was so thirsty. I would have to try to make a hole in the ice.

I got up and put my parka on. I didn't have an ice chisel, only an axe. I chopped and chopped until the hole was more than a metre deep, but I still hadn't broken through the ice to water. As I chopped, ice chips fell back into the hole, and I had to shovel them out with a snowshoe. The hole had to be long so I could get my axe into its centre to make the hole deeper. By the time I gave up, it was at least three and a half metres long.

Back inside my eiderdown, I was more tired than ever, but I still couldn't sleep. Hunger and thirst got the better of me. I had some dry meat, and I ate snow. The snow only made me thirstier.

Suddenly I had an idea. If I shot into the hole with my gun, I might manage to break the remaining ice at the bottom. I put my parka back on, loaded my gun, pointed it at the deepest part of the hole and fired. Water gushed out, filling the long hole. I scooped it into my cup and drank, then got back inside my eiderdown with another cup of water. I drank it and ate more dry meat, and then I slept.

When I woke up, it was daylight. The sky was clear, and I could see the land, about six kilometres away. I hitched up my dogs and started off.

When I got to shore, I made a fire, had a good meal, and fed the dogs. Then we travelled along the shore until late at night, when I made camp.

The next day, I travelled about two hours and then had to go inland on a trail. It was drifted in, but the travelling was fairly good. I covered forty kilometres on land, and about 25 on the ice. I reached Dad's camp late that night. The whole trip had taken twelve days.

I rested for about two days. There were many caribou, so we ate well.

We went inland for three days, to the fish lake where Dad had spent the fall. We had to feed twelve dogs, and that takes a lot of food every day. We set the nets, but there weren't any fish during the cold spell. Inland fish lakes are like that: when it's cold the fish don't swim much. We knew there were plenty of rabbits that winter, but rabbits are like fish. When it's cold, they stay in their burrows and don't run around very much. We also knew there were moose in the area. But the weather was so cold that even if we had seen moose tracks, we couldn't have hunted. The moose would hear us too easily.

A few days later, Dad and I started down a river to set traps. We didn't care what we got—lynx, mink, marten, weasel, or fox. All were worth money.

Two days later we arrived at a small fish lake and put two nets under the ice. Then we walked down the river, setting snares and traps as we went. We saw many moose tracks, so we stayed where we were.

"When it gets to be warm and windy, we'll hunt here," Dad said.

We went back to the fish lake, where we hunted, fished, and visited our traps every day. One day, I went back to the first fish lake to take our nets out. I had to camp there to dry my nets, fix my rabbit snares, and trap. A north wind came up, and I didn't get back to camp until the next day.

Dad and his dogs were gone, so I knew he was out hunting. I stayed up late that night. It was lonely with nobody to talk to, but sometime very late, my dogs started barking. They heard Dad coming back to camp. He had shot a cow moose, and that night we feasted on fat moose meat.

The next day the wind stayed the same. We went to the place where Dad had shot the moose and pitched our tent. We had a meal and then went hunting in different directions. I saw a fresh track right away, and shot a moose and skinned it. Then I walked farther along the lakeshore and met Dad. We made a fire, ate together, and then went hunting again.

Later that afternoon, I followed two moose tracks and caught up to the moose. They ran away, but it was open country with lots of drifting snow. I chased the moose for several kilometres before I caught up with them and shot them. When I got back, Dad was cooking. He had shot a moose as well. We'd gotten four moose that day, so we had a good supply of food.

Next day, we moved our camp down the river to where Dad had shot his moose. We gathered the meat, and then went trapping in different directions.

There was no such thing as government land or people owning land. We hunted and trapped, slept and ate wherever we felt like it. It was a good life.

The days were getting longer and the weather was warmer. I always carried a rifle when I went to tend the traplines, and sometimes I hunted. In many places, the country had burned years ago, and there were new jack-pines. There are always lots of rabbits in such places, and they get fat in March. When I roasted one on the fire, the grease flowed from the fat on its back. Good life, good food.

When it got warm, we packed our traps and fur, and moved to Sahtú. When we got there, a trader wanted to buy our fur, but Dad said we should get at least $1300, while the trader offered only $1000. The next day, a plane came in from Sòmbak'è carrying Sam Barr, who offered us $1500. We sold the furs to him.

The spring hunt wouldn't start for about two months. Dad said he was going to visit people in Bèhchokǫ̀, about 240 kilometres away. I decided to go to Déline, a trip of about 140 kilometres.

I stayed with a family who had a young daughter. They were good people, living by the Dene laws and culture. I tried to look good by getting up early, fetching wood, and hunting. Once, I shot a moose. It wasn't long before these people said, "You should marry our daughter." But I didn't.

It was May, the time to hunt beaver and muskrat. After my visit in Déline, my trapping partner and I went to get the canoe and other things I had left on the north shore of Sahtú. We stopped in a good place after two days' travel. The snow was melting, so we left the sled on the shore and travelled into the bush with our dogs, looking for a beaver lake. We ran into a herd of caribou, and the dogs took off after them with most of our sup-plies and our blankets. We made a fire and ran around calling our dogs, but they didn't come back. We had to camp and wait.

They came back in the morning, but our supplies were gone. The packs had caught on the brush, and the dogs had chewed off the strings. We had only a small bag of tea, some sugar, and ten boxes of shells. We had to use our jackets for blankets when we slept.

Before the snow melted completely, we began hunting beaver. The beaver makes a hole in front of his house, and comes out of it at about four in the afternoon. The hunter goes there early, finds a good spot and waits. Sometimes it's a long wait.

We hunted for two weeks and shot fifteen beavers each. Then we fished for dog food, and got ready for the long trip to the north shore to get the canoe I'd left there the previous fall.

After five nights, we met some families at a place about fifty kilometres from Déline. They didn't have any fish for their dogs. I said to my partner,

"Let's go back to the river that empties into the lake. It makes a big open water, and there could be lots of fish there." It was about 25 kilometres back.

At the river, it was less than two metres down to the sand bottom, and we could see hundreds of trout in the water. But we couldn't catch any: they swam around the net, not into it. We had run out of fish for our own dogs, and we were hungry ourselves.

"Let's make a harpoon to spear the fish," I suggested.

"How?" asked my friend. "We haven't got any tools."

"We've got two butcher knives," I said. "Let's toss one of them into the fire and use the blade to make a harpoon."

I filed the blade so that it was like an arrowhead, about seven centimetres long. I wrapped a wire around one end, so a pin would fit in, but would slip out easily when the spear hit a fish. The wooden handle we made had to be straight and light; we scorched it black so the fish wouldn't see it.

When our harpoon was finished, we got into the canoe to try our luck. The sun was shining, and it was easy to see the fish against the sand bottom. I tried spearing a trout, but missed many times before I got the hang of it. Then I speared about fifteen trout and was starting to enjoy it. My partner tried. He had the same trouble at first, but by the end he had caught many fish, too.

WORKING ON THE CANOL PIPELINE

My father and I found ourselves in Tulít'a in the summer of 1942. Edward had decided to get married again after three years of being alone, so I stayed with my uncle.

Communications were so poor that we didn't know Japan had declared war on the United States. The United States feared the Japanese would invade Alaska, so they had decided to build a pipeline from Łe Gǫ́hlįnį to Whitehorse, Yukon, which would supply oil to defend their northern outposts. They were bringing thousands of soldiers down Dehcho in boats and barges to build the line.

Early one morning, my aunt woke me up. "There are coloured people outside," she told me excitedly.

The Dene in the tiny community of Tulít'a had never seen a black person before. Some of the old women screamed and locked their doors. Other people hid and watched the strangers from a distance. Some ran away, into the bush.

An RCMP man came to my aunt's house. I wondered what I had done, because the Dene never saw the Mounties unless they had done something wrong.

"Are you George Blondin?" he asked. When I nodded, he told me the United States Army in Łe Gǫ́hlįnį needed guides for the bush, and they wanted to hire four young men who could speak English. "You're one of the ones they want," the Mountie told me.

Four of us went to Łe Gǫhłı̨nı̨ on a U.S. Army plane. We worked for the survey department all summer, cutting line through the thick bush. It was the first time I ever worked for wages.

I'd been working on the crews for a month when my dad, Edward Blondin, joined us. That fall, there was a lot of rain and we got wet every day, and my father got sick. Because we lived in a tent, we couldn't get warm at night and his cold turned into a bad case of pneumonia.

I told the boss that I couldn't work, because I had to take care of Dad. When my father got worse, I begged the boss to get an army doctor. We were across the river and over thirty kilometres into the bush, but the boss had a portable radio so he could talk to Łe Gǫhłı̨nı̨. That evening the army sent a helicopter with a young doctor, who told me that my dad was in very bad shape. He gave him some strong pills, and then set about explaining how I was to treat Dad.

The doctor asked me if I knew what pneumonia was. "No, I don't know," I said. He took a piece of paper and drew a diagram of a person's lungs. He showed how the lungs fill with thick mucous that's hard to cough out. "Your dad's lungs are just full of this thick muck," he said. "He only has a small portion of his lungs left to breathe with. If that fills up, he's going to die."

He demonstrated with his stethoscope. He took my shirt off and told me to listen to my chest, so I did.

"What do you hear?" he asked me.

"I hear clean breathing," I said.

"All healthy people sound like that," the doctor said. "Now listen to your father's chest."

I did as he said. When I placed the stethoscope on Dad's chest, I could hear a sound like thick porridge boiling.

"The muck is so thick it can't come out," said the doctor. "It just bubbles, and that's what the noise is."

He showed me the lung diagram again. "Your dad has a small end of his lung free of this muck. That's why he's alive, but it will fill up tonight and he'll die." He rose to leave. "I'm going now. If you want to tell your dad, it's up to you. I'll come back tomorrow, but he'll be dead by then."

After the doctor left I felt really bad. My father was so sick he didn't know I was there. I started to cry. I couldn't help it. My mother had died three years before and ever since, my father and I had had only each other. We lived together, trapped and hunted together. Now the doctor said he was going to die. He was all I had left and he was going to die.

I knew my father well. On many long nights he would tell me stories about the past, about strong medicine people and what they did with their medicine. He'd told me he was reincarnated, had been born twice, and that he possessed a bit of medicine power himself. Sitting there as he lay sick, I thought, "It won't hurt to tell him he's going to die. He might do something about it."

I sat close to him and tried to wake him up from his deep stupor. Finally he looked at me with weak eyes. I gave him the medicine the doctor had left. Then I spoke to him. "I want to talk to you. Can you hear me?" I asked.

He nodded his head.

"The doctor says you're going to die tonight. You can't make it to tomorrow." I began to cry and just sat there.

It seemed as if my father wanted to speak. I gave him some hot water to sip. After a moment, I could make out what he was saying.

"I think I am going to live longer yet," he told me. "Just sit there. I'll use my medicine to see whether I will die or not. I'm not scared. Why didn't the doctor tell me himself?"

He started singing a song and murmuring words I couldn't make out. He went on that way for about half an hour, while I said nothing and watched.

After a long time, I offered him some more hot water. He took a sip and began talking clearly. I could understand him again. He was talking about medicine.

"I asked my moose medicine to try to help me. The moose went away for a while and came back with my spirit and put it in my body. The moose told me I'd be OK now. 'Is there anything you want?' the moose asked me. I said, 'Yes. I want you to see into the future for me and my son.' The moose looked into the future and said, 'You don't have to worry about yourself for a long time yet. You will have many children with this woman you married. You will see your grandchildren. You'll have a long life yet. Don't worry about your son. When you are dead of old age your son will live a long time afterward.'"

Those were my father's words as I sat beside him. It's hard to believe a person with one foot in the grave could say the doctor was lying. But I felt better, because I am a Dene and I believe in medicine.

After a while I thought maybe I should try giving my father some soup. I went to the cook and brought back a hot bowl. I fed my dad half of it, then stayed up all night to make sure it was warm in the tent. I took good care of my father, and he slept well that night.

In the morning, I fed him soup again. He looked better and tried to talk. Late in the afternoon the doctor came into the tent. "How's your dad?" he asked.

"He's still alive," I told him.

The doctor took his stethoscope and listened to my dad's chest. "George," he said, "I'm surprised, but your dad is going to live. Here, listen to his chest."

I listened and could hear only clean breath.

"What happened to all the muck?" wondered the doctor. "Anyway, he's going to get better. That's what's important. I'll come back tomorrow." He gave me more pills.

When the doctor came the next day, my father was a lot better, and had started to eat. In four days he was back to work.

An ordinary person would have been dead, but my father had his medicine to help him. Edward Blondin lived to be 86 years old, and to see his second wife's grandchildren.

In the fall, the army wanted to hire five dogteams to find a right-of-way for the pipeline through the Mackenzie Mountains. My father, along with

Joe Blondin, Fred Andrew, Paul Wright, and I got our teams ready for the long trip. We were going to be travelling with the army engineer, the Mountie, and his interpreter Fred Gaudet through difficult mountain country. We planned to cover a distance of 560 kilometres, from Le Gǫ́hlı̨nı̨ to Sheldon Lake—halfway to Whitehorse.

We started out from Le Gǫ́hlı̨nı̨ on October 15, 1942. It was too early for a dogteam trip; the lakes and rivers weren't yet frozen, and there was no snow on the ground. The loads were so heavy that we had to make double trips all the time. On one big river we had to build a raft on which to go back and forth. We spent three days in this place.

In the mountain country, the land was all up and down, not flat like the country we were used to around Sahtú. The rivers were still open, and many creeks were overflowing. After three weeks' travel, we had made only 160 kilometres. But there was plenty of game, so at least we ate well.

The Mountie, Fred Gaudet and Paul Wright turned back. Our boss the army man, my father and I, Joe Blondin and Fred Andrew reached Sheldon Lake on December 18. A trader living there had a radio transmitter, so the boss decided to wire for a plane and go to Whitehorse. Fred Andrew decided to go back to Tulít'a. We later learned that it took him ten days. Dad and I travelled on to Ross Post, a small settlement 160 kilometres farther on, where we met the people we worked for. It was strange for us, since we had to speak English all the time.

We worked for about two months, cutting lines for the survey crew, and moving the surveyors around with our dogteams. In March, the boss said we could go home. Travelling was hard, because there were two metres of snow in the valley. We had to break trail and make double trips much of the time. It took us a month to get back to Tulít'a.

In May Le Gǫ́hlı̨nı̨ was crowded with people from all over the country—private contractors from the United States and Canada, and thousands of soldiers. Mines everywhere were shut down, so people came North to get jobs at Le Gǫ́hlı̨nı̨.

But the Dene didn't get jobs in spite of all this activity. Our way of life didn't change much—except that times were harder, because fur prices dropped during the War. The Hudson's Bay Company was paying $5 for mink, $7 for marten, $5 for red fox, $12 for beaver and 50 cents for muskrat. In the meantime, the price of food was going up. It was hard to make a good living.

Thousands of people came to the North on cat-trains, using Dehcho as a winter road. Thousands of trucks were brought in to build the pipeline. The new people brought sicknesses with them. The Dene suffered terribly; they had a hard time surviving those years.

Tuberculosis was the big killer; it wiped out whole families. The Dene didn't know what tuberculosis was or how it was spread, so if one person in a family got it, everyone did. Most Dene were poor and all the children slept together under one blanket.

There were no medical services in the Le Gǫ́hlı̨nı̨ area. The hospitals at Łíídlı̨ Kǫ́ę́, Tthebachaghé, and Tahkl'a were small, with just one doctor and a few nurses each. The government realized something would have to be done, or half the Dene would die. Money was found to build a forty-bed hospital at Tulít'a. As soon as it was finished it was crowded with patients, and it stayed crowded until it burned down four years later.

o

It was 1943, and I was 21 years old. I went back to guiding the survey crews. I flew to Sheldon Lake and found they had brought in 118 horses from Fort St. John, British Columbia. It was the first time I'd ever seen a horse, and the first day I rode I was so sore that at lunchtime I couldn't put my legs together. The whole camp laughed at me.

I worked all summer, and went back to Le Gǫhlįnį in September. My dad stayed in Le Gǫhlįnį, but I went on to Déline, and trapped around Nere?e on Sahtú.

I was back in Déline at Christmas. I spent two weeks in town, then went trapping again for the rest of the winter. The snow was so deep that I usually had to double-travel and double-trap. First thing after breakfast, I would put on my big snowshoes and make the trail for the next day. I had my gun and a pack full of food with me. It was slow work, but it was exciting, too. You always expect something new beyond the hills, and that makes you work harder—even thought you don't make money at it.

Wherever I saw a rabbit trail, I set a rabbit snare; wherever I saw other tracks, I set a trap. When I got to a high hill, I could see a long way and I sang my Dene song very loud, so the small animals nearby could hear me. That's the way my parents taught me. It you do that, the land will be happy and you will also be happy and lucky.

I walked all day, and didn't get back to my dogs until late at night. I fed them and went to sleep. The next day, I travelled with the dogs on the trail I'd made the day before. Sometimes I caught rabbits and other fur-bearing animals. By the time I got to the end of my trail, it would be noon. I'd pitch my tent, clean and cook the rabbits, and feed the dogs. Then I'd go off to break trail again.

I did this until I had set all my traps. I didn't have any company, but I wasn't lonely. Once I shot a big, fat cow moose. I ate the good parts, gave some to the dogs, made some dry meat and saved the marrow to eat with the dry meat.

I trapped many animals valuable for their fur, including three big wolverines. When the weather got warm, I went back to Déline for Easter, and then to Tulít'a to see my father, Edward. Later, we went spring hunting in K'alįtúe, about eighty kilometres south of Tulít'a, where there were many ducks, muskrats and beavers.

We went back to Tulít'a, then to Déline, and then to the north shore of Sahtú to trap fox. George Doctor's family came with us. It was early September, and we had plenty of time to get ready for trapping. There were many caribou, so we made dry meat. When winter came, we set traps for white fox, but didn't get any—although we caught many coloured foxes.

After New Year's Day, 1944, we decided to visit Port Radium. The Canadian government had taken over Eldorado, and the mine had just reopened after being closed for two years. It was now going all out to produce uranium.

The mine manager agreed to pay us fifty cents a pound for all the caribou meat we could get. There were many caribou nearby, and we were happy to make some money. In no time, we had six toboggan loads of meat, and made about $1000 each. We bought everything we needed and still had cash to take home.

After we got back home in March, George Doctor decided to go back to Délįne with his family. I travelled toward K'áhbamįtúé, staying close to the treeline and making a trail one day so I could travel on it the next, as I'd done before. This area was different: there were lots of caribou, and hunting was more fun.

One night as I was coming back to camp, I saw a light in my tent. My father was inside. He had followed me and I was glad, because he knew the country well.

Two nights later, he told me to go out and kill three caribou. When I got back to the tent the next afternoon, he wasn't there. I fed all the dogs and waited for him until midnight, but he didn't come back. I went to sleep. Later the dogs woke me up with their barking, and I lit the candle and went outside. I wasn't expecting anyone but my father, so I went back inside, made a fire and warmed up some soup for him. Then I heard a dogteam approaching.

Two boys came into the tent and sat down beside the stove to warm up, without speaking to me. All three of us put our heads down and didn't say a word for a long time because we were all so shy. (Later we had a big laugh about this.)

Suddenly, I said "Hello" and at the same time they said "Hello." We began to talk. The boys had both been to school, and they knew some English. I asked if they'd seen my father.

"He came to our tent late at night and sent us to get you," they told me.

"Good. We'll eat, and then we'll go," I said.

They told me about their good times and I told them about mine. After two hours of talking, I tied my dad's dogteam behind my sled, and took the tent down. We set out.

It took about two hours to get to their main camp, where there were two tents. A family stayed in one; in the other lived an old man with his son. It was the first time I had met K'achot'ine from Rádelį Kǫ́. They didn't act like my own people and their language was different, but they shared everything they had. There were many caribou around, so they had lots of dry meat.

The next day, my father and I broke trail to the Barrenlands, so Dad could go home that way. I stayed on with the K'achot'ine families. We travelled together to a fish lake farther south, close to the shore of Sahtú.

There were nine tents already at the fish lake. I hunted, gathered wood, and checked fish nets for the family I was staying with. For fun, we young people played hand games and chased girls in the bush. The K'achot'ine weren't very strict. Boys and girls could visit the fish nets and fetch wood together.

When the snow started to melt, l travelled to Sahtú. A trader named Ray Overvold was living on the shore, and I bought ammunition and supplies from him. He told me muskrat was worth $5 in the South. I went home along the shore of the lake, and in the spring hunt, my father and I got 1700 muskrats in addition to caribou. We made 20 bundles of dry meat.

After the ice was gone, we waited for Overvold to pick us up, because we had too much freight to carry. The weather was so good it only took us one night to get to Déline.

GETTING MARRIED

We hadn't seen our own people for a whole year, so my father decided to have a feast for them. I made a fire outdoors and borrowed lots of tea kettles. I put a large tarp on the ground and cut up plenty of dry meat, with fat and pounded meat and bone grease, and many whitefish and dry fish. We invited everybody from Déline. My dad made a long speech and everyone ate well.

I didn't have a girlfriend, but my father decided it was time for me to marry. He found me a girl named Julie Ayah. A friend of mine wanted to get married, too. Since there was no priest in Déline and we all were going to Tulít'a anyway, the four of us got married there. We had two days of feasting, drum dances, and fiddle dancing.

After we got back to Déline, the federal Department of Fisheries wanted to hire the boat I had just bought from Ray Overvold. It was about nine metres long, and had a 35-horsepower inboard engine. Three scientists were testing fish in Sahtú. If they decided the lake was good, there would be commercial fishing in the future. My father and I worked as guides and ran the boat for the government men.

The scientists set three nets and caught many fish. They operated on the fish to find out what they eat, how long they live, how quickly they grow and so on.

That job took us three weeks. Then we went from Déline to l'uedehk'aledeh, at the far end of Sahtú. The trip there and back took us a month. By then it was fall, and we planned to go to Port Radium. But three people had drowned in a storm at Déline, so we didn't start out until the middle of October. Even so, it was stormy and snowing. But we knew the country, and we got safely to Port Radium.

There were about 400 people in the mining camp. The mine manager said he would buy trout for thirty cents a pound, and there were plenty of trout to catch. We sold some to buy tea, shells and flour. We made money by selling moccasins, as well. That helped, because fur prices were poor.

In 1945, things got better for Dene around Port Radium. The mining people hired us to cut green wood at $6 a cord. The trees were scattered, and a man had to work hard to cut a cord of wood and pile it in one place.

That year, the mine went at full speed to produce the atomic bomb. Long before the white people came, there were stories about this place. A medicine man in early days prophesied that the mine would develop, and that the atomic bomb would kill many people.

○

We were young, and the country was healthy. I had good dogs and a big boat. I had no worries and I was happy. In April, 1946 I wanted to go spring hunting, so my father offered to look after my pregnant wife while I hunted with my friend Malo Bewule, an older bachelor.

There were no beavers or muskrats in the immediate area. We started out from Port Radium in early April, across Sahtú toward muskrat country, 160 kilometres away. We got there in about a week, but we still had to travel another eighty kilometres inland. We had nine dogs at first, but we had to shoot three of them.

Muskrats were plentiful and we got carried away. Instead of going back across the ice, we went farther and farther inland, until we realized we couldn't get back to the lake ice before it became too dangerous to cross. We were past Tachinetúe, at the head of Shalitúe, with no radio and no maps. We decided to travel toward K'áhbamįtúé, but we had to guess which direction to take, because we didn't know the country. We had 1600 muskrat and ten beaver, and they were heavy to pack.

We were in grizzly bear country, in mating season. We often came across three or four bears in one spot. Once, paddling a small but fast river, I came around a point of land and saw four grizzlies, one in the water and the other three on the shore. I was going too fast to turn back. All I could do was grab my rifle with one hand and steer the canoe with the paddle in my other hand.

The fast water floated me past the bear in the river. I kept my gun pointed at him, but he just watched me. When I was far enough away, I threw my gun into the canoe and paddled as fast as I could.

I'll never forget that trip to K'áhbamįtúé. I packed 200 muskrats and the bigger canoe overland, while my friend packed 800 muskrats. Our six dogs packed 100 muskrats each. We carried our traps and blankets in our heavy packs.

The land was swampy. We had to keep going back to rescue bogged-down dogs. When we came to a lake, we unpacked the dogs and loaded the canoe. It was big enough to hold all the packs, but there was no room for the dogs or my friend, and they had to walk along the shore. At the other end, we packed up again. The journey went on and on.

There were millions of mosquitoes. Sometime their eyes were so swollen. We were afraid they would die, and we couldn't afford to lose any more dogs. We rubbed mosquito dope from a quart can into their coats, and when we made camp, we covered them with a tarp or made a fire near them to protect them.

When we came over a hill and saw the blue land still stretching far away, I sang my Dene song as loud as possible. I tried to laugh. My friend looked at me with a sad face. "Do you think that will help?" he asked. I told him it helped me to be happier and stronger.

At last we were nearing K'áhbamįtúé. There were signs of people all along the shore, because the Dene have used the area for thousands of years.

We got into the canoe with the packs and the dogs. It was riding with its gunwhales only a little above the water, but the lake was calm and there was no wind. We travelled east, following the shore. Just before we came to a long point of land, we saw a net in the water, so we knew we were close to people.

When we got around the point, we saw a canoe coming toward us. We called out, but the man seemed afraid of us and didn't reply. As we paddled closer to him, we explained who we were and why we were travelling in this place.

"Oh, you're Edward Blondin's son," the man exclaimed. "My dad travelled all over the country, and everyone knew him. "At first, I thought you were Inuit, and I got scared. You know, we used to fight wars a long time ago and we're enemies. That's why I wouldn't talk to you at first."

The Dene sometimes used to have strange ideas about other people. A long time ago, there were lots of different groups speaking different languages; they lived hundreds of kilometres apart, and never saw one another. The people passed down stories about using medicine power against other groups or of wars fought a long time ago.

Our new friend called out to his people, saying he'd met some Sahtú Dene, and they came down to meet us. I unpacked the canoe and asked where we could stay. After much talk, the K'áhbamįtúé people decided we should stay with a certain couple.

"If there's something you don't eat, just tell us," the woman said as she started cooking for us. In the old days, many people didn't eat certain foods because their medicine didn't allow them to. That's why she asked me that question. I told her I ate anything.

"Don't be shy," the woman told me. "You are a Blondin. You come from strong medicine people, and our people think you are the same. That's why they talked so much about who you could stay with."

We stayed with them for five days. The people showed us how to get home, travelling a lake about 32 kilometres long and then a summer trail they'd used for hundreds of years. It went 96 kilometres to the Rabbitskin River, which flows into Dehcho eight kilometres below Rádęlį Kǫ́.

We paddled all night and throughout the next day. We made three fires and rested each time, because we were so tired. At last, we got to Dehcho. We were sitting on the beach when a Dene family came in a boat to visit their nets. They took us back to Rádęlį Kǫ́, where I heard that the RCMP were looking for me.

The Mounties told me that everyone in Port Radium was worried about me. They thought I had drowned somewhere.

"You'd better go over to the signal boys and wire the RCMP at Port Radium to give a message to your father and your wife, telling them you're all right."

So I went to see the men from the Signals Corps. They had many messages for me. "They're wiring here every day," the officer in charge said. "I'm glad you're here; it will make everyone happy."

Because there were only two scheduled flights a month, I had to wait fifteen days to get on a plane. I flew to Tulít'a, then went by canoe to Déline, and by freight boat across Sahtú to Port Radium.

I got back to my family in the middle of August, and found that my first daughter, Evelyn, had been born while I was away. I brought back $4000, so I hadn't worked hard all that time for nothing.

A YEAR IN DÉLĮNE

By Dene custom, you stayed with your father for the first year after you married, then with your father-in-law for the next year. Because of this, I had to go to Délįne for a year.

At that time, there were only a few log houses and two small stores in Délįne. Most people lived in tents, with a stage outside where supplies were stored. You couldn't leave anything on the ground, because of all the dogs running around. Everyone in the village had dogs.

On maps, this settlement at the head of Sahtú De is called Fort Franklin after Sir John Franklin, who camped there in the last century. But the Dene have lived for thousands of years along the river between Little Lake and the headwaters. Our fathers and grandfathers told us how it often took a family a week to travel this stretch, which is only about ten kilometres or so, because they stopped at the hundreds of tents along the way to visit other families.

The Dene were attracted to this country by the abundant food supply. There were plenty of caribou and fur-bearing animals, and people could fish all year round for trout, whitefish, herring and grayling in the water that stayed open even in winter at the head of Sahtú Dé.

In the past, Dene used to catch fish by harpooning them. The people fishing made a hole close to the open water, covered themselves with hide, and waited for the fish to swim by. People took turns sitting there all day. They also caught fish in nets they made by weaving strips of willow bark together.

Because so many people lived at Délįne, many strong medicine people came here. Our stories say strong fish-medicine people always put out bait at Franklin Bay for herring and trout, so the fish would stay fat and never leave the people.

In 1957, researchers found dinosaur bones just across the lake from these traditional fishing and hunting grounds. Our Elders and prophets had always told us stories of how these large animals which we called Naʔácho, killed and ate our people, and about how hard it was for hunters to kill such animals.

Délįne became important to travellers when the Hudson's Bay Company set up a fur-trading post at Tulít'a. People who passed through Délįne on the way to the post shared the resources of the Sahtú Dene, the Bear Lake People.

In spite of these abundant resources, it was hard work for a man to take care of his family. Dry wood was at least eleven kilometres away, and the nets at the head of Sahtú Dé were across the lake. You got up at six o'clock in the morning to check your nets and get fish for yourself and your dogs. When you got back, it was dinnertime, but you still had to go out and get enough wood for a week. Then you went trapping for weeks at a time.

People helped one another, but some Dene who didn't fish well couldn't feed their dogs, so their teams were thin; this meant that they couldn't go for wood. If the head of a family was sick, the family had to depend on others. That's the way it was in Délı̨ne in 1947.

I stayed all winter, working hard. There were caribou nearby, so we ate well, but fur prices were low. In May, my daughter Georgina was born, and in August we went back to Port Radium.

When I got there, I made a deal with the Eldorado Mine to cut wood for their boiler, at $6 a cord. It wasn't much, but I could hunt and trap when I felt like it, so it was a fair living. There were many caribou that winter. The company plane went to Edmonton every two weeks, which meant we had good mail service. The company sold groceries to us at wholesale prices. 1948 was a good year. A few other families were at Port Radium, and they worked for us. We provided credit so they could buy their groceries. We sold fish to the company but we couldn't sell meat. That summer, more people from Délı̨ne came to work for me because fur prices were so low. In the fall, we made a trip to Hornby Bay to hunt caribou.

The winter of 1949 was good, too. There were lots of moose and caribou. People made extra money cutting wood, and they hunted, trapped, and tanned moose hide. The women sold moccasins to the mining people.

We were fairly prosperous, but tuberculosis and other health problems stayed with the Dene. A doctor took X-rays of us on instructions from the Department of Indian Affairs. Sick people were sent to the Charles Camsell Hospital in Edmonton, the only place where Northerners were treated for tuberculosis in those days. That was the extent of our medical services.

Our lives were becoming more complicated in other ways. Now that the war was over, the Canadian government decided it had to develop the North. This was all new to the Dene, and many things were imposed on us. These changes were hard and we couldn't fight back, because we were used to working in small groups. These changes meant we had to work together and we had to have guidance. Few of us were educated, and there was little money to fund schooling or political organizations.

The government started by setting up a small centre of administration at Tthebachaghé. But Sòmbak'è kept getting bigger as people came from the South looking for jobs in mining, and in 1967 it was decided to move the government to this town on the north shore of Tucho. Sòmbak'è—Yellowknife on maps—became the capital of the Northwest Territories.

At first, there were many meetings. The Dene had never been to such meetings before. The government decided to do something about health, education and housing for the Dene. Tuberculosis had wiped out many of our people by this time. Now the people in every settlement were checked by resident nurses and had X-rays taken.

Once the government put schools in all the settlements, parents had to stay in town so their children wouldn't miss school. Moving to settlements changed our way of life. In the past, the Dene had gone far out on the land, hunting and trapping in areas we had used for centuries. If an area was used too much, we left it for a few years so the animals had a chance to recover. Now the Dene couldn't roam the land the way we used to—but we still hunted every day. Soon there was hardly any game around the settlements. The government made new game laws, set up game warden's offices, and introduced closed seasons for game. This completely disrupted our traditional way of earning a living.

In the past, money hadn't been important to Dene. We knew what cash was, but we hadn't used it much. We had traded our fur for supplies, and it was part of our culture to share what we had. Living in settlements changed all this. Now you needed a steady income. Old age pensions and family allowances helped, but it wasn't enough to live on in town. People tried to get short-term jobs in the summer and trap in the winter. They did the best they could, but they had problems. The welfare system was created and people became dependent on it.

Dene living on the land carried their homes with them. We lived year-round in tents. But in a settlement, you needed a house. At first, the government gave out materials and told each family to build their own.

"We can't pay you," the government people said, "but we'll give you a box of groceries." There was no town planning, so people built their houses where they liked. No trucks hauled water or took away garbage; people did that themselves.

Then the government decided to build log houses for the Dene. Families cut the logs for their houses themselves and in payment the welfare people again gave them groceries. The families hauled their logs to town and peeled off the bark so they were ready for the builders. The new log houses had one big room, with a woodstove in the middle. When the families were ready to move in, the government housing agents told them they would have to pay money for rent. "One dollar a month," they said. The people were happy, because we thought this was cheap.

But things gradually changed. The government decided to build better houses. All the new houses were the same: two bedrooms, a kitchen, and a living room. Inside each house there was a water tank, an oil-burning stove for heat, an electric cooking stove, a fridge, a bathroom with a bathtub, and a pressure water system. People had to buy their own tables and chairs.

These were good houses, and people got jobs building them. But when the families were ready to move in, the government held a meeting. Rents would be higher, said the officials, because the houses had been expensive to build and were heated by oil, not wood. Each new house would rent for $30 a month. This wasn't bad, but they kept raising the rents, and in 1982, I paid $150 a month for a house in Délįne built back then.

The result of all this was that people couldn't pay the rents, so they got into debt.

The education system didn't work well, either. Many children dropped out of school, but their schooling had changed their attitudes. They didn't think the same way as their parents did. There were problems in every household.

Some young people found jobs, got married and made a good living for themselves, but many others did not. It might have been different if there were enough jobs. But most Northern jobs went to people from the South, because they were skilled in ways the Dene were not.

The older people changed, too. Alcohol made a big difference in their lives. Many people drank too much, and found themselves paying fines or going to jail.

THE PROPHECY OF AYAH

The changes in the lives of the Dene were predicted by a wonderful old man named Ayah, who was born around 1850, and lived in Délįne all his life. He died in 1941, when he was 91 years old.

Ayah lived according to the Dene way, just as Karkeye and Paul Blondin did. He was born with medicine to help others and when necessary to help himself. His medicine was not meant to be used for personal gain.

When he was nine years old, Ayah was living in the bush with his mother and her second husband—a harsh, rough man. It was December and very cold, but his stepfather chased Ayah out of the tent first thing every morning to start the fire.

One morning, Ayah put a pail of water on the fire so he could cook fish for breakfast. He put the fish down beside the stove and went to relieve himself. While he was gone, a neighbour's dog stole the fish. Ayah chased the dog and gave it a good beating, but it was too late. The dog had eaten the fish, and there was nothing left. Ayah went back to the tent.

By this time, his stepfather was up and sitting by the stove.

"What are you doing, chasing that dog so early in the morning?" he demanded. "It's not your dog—it belongs to the next tent. You might have killed it. If you want to act so smart, take my muzzle loader and go out in the bush and hunt. Come back here when you've killed something yourself."

Children didn't talk back to their parents in those days, so Ayah headed off into the bush without anything to eat. After he had walked for a while, he sat down and did some thinking.

He had been born with medicine but hadn't ever used it. Now he thought he should try moose medicine. He filled his pipe with tobacco and smoked with moose breath. After he did this he thought, "I want the moose to come." He loaded his gun, smoked and wished for moose.

Immediately, a cow and a calf appeared. Ayah shot the cow, which fell right beside him. He reloaded the gun and shot the calf. He used his knife to cut off the heads and take the guts out. Then he took some of the meat back to camp so he and his parents could eat. All this took twenty minutes. His family hadn't even cooked breakfast by the time he came back.

From then on, Ayah's stepfather treated him with great respect, because he knew the boy had strong medicine.

o

Young Ayah had a vision. A voice told him the vision would return if he was a good man and taught his people, so he made up his mind to be as good as possible.

Ayah grew up to be a good hunter, and he helped people when they needed help. He was respected by his people. The girls all chased Ayah, but he didn't pay any attention to them, and by the time he was forty years old, people wondered why he hadn't married. The reason was that Ayah was still waiting for the vision to return.

Priests had come into Denendeh, but not to the Sahtú area, when Ayah saw the vision again. The voice told him he would marry a woman from downriver, and it told him to get "words written on paper" from the priest. The voice said this would help him and give him the wisdom to teach his people. Ayah had his own rosary even before the priests came. He got his information from this vision.

Ayah didn't know any woman like the one the voice had spoken of. But when some Dene from Rádelį Kǫ visited the place where he was hunting and trapping, he was attracted to one of the women. He took this as a sign, and he asked her to marry him.

After his marriage, Ayah began to teach the people about God. He had never learned to read, yet he was able to read all the stories in the Bible. The people had usually heard a priest only twice a year, when they went to trade at Tulít'a, so they travelled great distances to listen to Ayah. They brought their children to him, so he could pray over them.

Ayah taught about what would happen if people didn't behave themselves. He told them not to drink alcohol. "It changes people's minds," he warned. He told them not to gamble. "The gains you made from hunting and trapping have been given to you by our Creator," he said. "Don't gamble them away."

My father and I often listened to Ayah. He spoke about the future, about how the Dene way of life would change. There would be more crime, he said, and people would drink alcohol. The Dene would not stick together, Ayah told us. "These are things that are going to happen to us in the future," Ayah warned. "We should be prepared."

Because my father and I had always taken a lot of trouble to hear him and had done favours for him, Ayah told us he would let us bury him when he died. And that was what happened.

In September, 1940, we were travelling through Délįne to go trapping around Sahtú. The wind had died down, so we loaded our boat with a sled, plenty of groceries, and our dogs. Our outboard engine was new and we'd never had problems with it, but when we pushed off, the motor wouldn't start. I pulled the starter cord for half an hour. Nothing happened. The wind started to get strong again, and it was getting dark. We went ashore and took the motor apart to find out what was wrong. After we pitched our tent, people came running to say that Ayah was sick. He had told them to repeat this message to my dad: "You'll have to bury me now, as I promised you could, a long time ago."

Ayah got together with the people for one last time. He shook hands with everyone, then fell asleep and died.

My father and I spent three days making Ayah's coffin and building a fence out of hardwood for his grave. It's still there today.

That was the last of Ayah, whose voice was so powerful that the Dene followed his teachings. Because of Ayah, people were religious, worked hard, and shared everything. As long as this great teacher lived, life was like that. But after he was gone, things started to change—just as Ayah had foretold.

Today, people still talk about Ayah's prophecies, which are proving to be true. To show respect for him, the Dene named the school in Délįne after him.

o

By 1950, we were poor. Fur prices were low, and the Dene had to keep moving all over the country in order to trap enough furs to survive. People were often sick, but the company doctor at Port Radium had a hard time treating us, since we moved on the land all the time, living in tents in the bush and travelling in cold weather. Some got so sick we had to go to the Camsell Hospital in Edmonton.

A priest visited the Dene in hospital and found that their clothes were old. He told the Edmonton welfare office, and people Outside donated big boxes of clothing.

In the fall, my own, Dad's, and another family moved to the head of Nágazideh, about eighty kilometres east of Port Radium. We set up a camp to fish and hunt, and cut wood for the mine. We killed a couple of moose. Then my father decided to move to a better fishing area, so he and the other family could start trapping by Christmas.

After they left, I kept on hunting, fishing and cutting wood. I got up very early to visit my five fish nets. I needed a great deal of fish, because I had many dogs to feed. By the time I visited the nets and fed the dogs and put the fish away, it was dinner time. I still had to cut two cords of wood that day, so I worked late into the night.

When I think about it now, I remember how wonderful it was to have my children around. When I was cutting wood, my two older daughters brought me a lunch and we sat on a log and joked as I ate. When I was older and had problems, I often thought that if I could change things, I wouldn't mind living in that time again.

When the lake started to freeze, I took my nets out of the water and waited until I could set them through the ice. In the meantime, I was busy cutting wood. I had all kinds of wild meat, whitefish and trout. My wife Julie visited the rabbit snares, but she couldn't stay away from the tent long, because we had four small children—Evelyn, Georgina, Walter and Bertha. The oldest was six years, the youngest eight months.

After the ice froze, I decided to set five nets. My wife and I worked late into the night to get them ready, putting the floats and sinkers on and wrapping them in tarpaulin so I could carry them.

I hitched my old dogs up and started out early the next morning. The ice was only twelve centimetres thick, but it was good enough to travel on.

My wife had to help me set the nets, so we took the children as well. The older ones took care of the younger ones inside the toboggan.

After our nets were in, I spent two nights setting traps. The first night I camped and slept under a tree. When I set out on the trail the next morning, the dogs suddenly began barking and running as fast as they could, just as if they were chasing a caribou herd. Dogs can smell caribou eight kilometres away if the wind is right, and the wind was right then. I let the team go.

The dogs ran hard for five or six kilometres. They took me to a fair-sized lake where many caribou were gathered. I shot six, all I needed. I camped at the lake, then returned home the next day.

Just a day after I got home, my oldest daughter came running into the tent. "Daddy, what's out there?" she cried.

I went outside and saw caribou all over the lake. They stayed for a week, and I was kept so busy that it seemed no time at all before it was the first week of December.

We decided to go to Port Radium for supplies. It took us a whole day to get there. When we arrived, the RCMP had a message from Délįne: my wife's brother was sick, and they wanted me to fetch him and bring him to Port Radium. It was 250 kilometres to Délįne, but my father said I should go.

I travelled with another man. There wasn't much snow on the ice and I had three older dogs who were good leaders, along with four pups. It took us two nights to get to Délįne, and we stayed two weeks. We travelled back with two other families. The boy was sick in the chest, and after we got him to Port Radium, he had to go on to the Camsell Hospital in Edmonton for treatment.

I wasn't healthy myself. My brother had died of tuberculosis when we were youngsters. I had slept with him until the day he died, so I was carrying TB. Finally it had caught up with me.

When I got sick the doctor thought I had kidney trouble, and decided he would have to send me Out to Edmonton. I was sad to leave my wife and four small children, and I grew very worried when the doctor in Edmonton told me I had tuberculosis. I would have to stay there for at least two years, he said.

I remembered that my grandfather Paul had told me I would live longer than all my relatives. I was only 35 years old then, and I was sure I would live, but the doctor wasn't. "If you're lucky, you might make it," he said.

At that time, people around Sahtú were poor, and many had been attracted to Port Radium by my contract with the mine, so that while I was in hospital there were lots of people from Délįne to cut the wood we had promised to the mine. My dad took care of the business, and he and my father-in-law took care of my family.

After I had spent nine months in the hospital, they let me go home. I had to take it easy for at least a year, but after six months, I was strong enough to hunt and fish, and by fall, I could go trapping. But I couldn't cut wood, because I couldn't lift heavy things.

Then my children all got sick. My son, Walter, died in the hospital. Shortly after, my wife got tuberculosis and she had to go to the Camsell

Hospital as well. They had found a better treatment by that time. When my daughters, Georgina and Bertha, got better, I asked Indian Affairs if there were any boarding schools I could send my children to. I sent Georgina and Bertha to the Mission School in Zhatí Kǫ́ę́.

I decided I couldn't live the old kind of life any more. Moving all around the country in cold weather wasn't good for me or my family. I'd already lost my oldest boy. I needed to live near a doctor and I wanted to be near the children's schools. I thought maybe I could live the same way as people did in large centres. I would work for wages.

I couldn't do that at Port Radium. I would have to move somewhere else. I decided to go to Sòmbak'è. Changing my way of life wouldn't be easy, but I had to do it for my children.

When I told my father what I wanted to do, he flew into a rage. "That's all the teaching your grandfather and I gave you? You're going to throw it aside and live the other way?"

I replied that the Dene would have to change their way of life sooner or later, because the world around them was changing all the time. By then the federal government had set up schools and people were starting to live in settlements. That was the real start of the change. If parents were travelling in the bush, how would their children get properly educated? Besides, getting medical attention was difficult if you lived in the bush. The Dene were now in contact with many new diseases that they had not known before. It seemed easier to move from the bush to the settlements than to travel long distances when people fell ill.

My father was stubborn, and I couldn't convince him with that kind of talk. He thought his way was right, that the Dene would never change, that the world would never change.

But I was stubborn, too. I didn't want to lose any more of my children. "My mother had fifteen children and fourteen of them died in the bush," I said to my father. "I don't want that to happen to my children. I will go somewhere where I can have them near me, with a hospital also nearby, and get a job for maybe twenty years. Later, I can go back to the bush."

My father didn't say anything for a long time. Finally, he asked, "Where are you going?"

I told him the closest big town was Sòmbak'è, 480 kilometres away, and that was where I would go.

My wife came back from Edmonton in the fall. In the spring, I sold everything I could and gave the rest to my dad. I shipped most of our stuff to Sòmbak'è on the barge, and we took a plane.

It was hard, being new in a town that size. I had to get a job right away. I got one in a sawmill on Desnedé, and worked there until Christmas. Then I went back to Sòmbak'è. That year, there were lots of claims being staked around Tsąmba K'é. My dad came in from Sahtú by dogteam, and a mining company asked us to stake for them. We loaded the dogs onto their plane and went out staking. My dad cut line and I wrote on the posts. We worked as a team for a month and a half and made a lot of money.

When it got warm, I got a contract to cut 750 cords of wood at a new development north of Sòmbak'è called Rayrock Mine. I got people to cut wood for me and made good money on the job.

In the spring of 1956, I got a job at Giant Yellowknife Mines and worked for straight wages—for someone else—for the first time. My best friend had introduced me to the mine superintendent.

"It's our policy not to hire native people in this area," the superintendent told me. "But since you've come such a long way, we'll try you out."

In the early days, some small companies had bribed native people with low wages and whiskey, in order to use their dogteams to stake claims and move camp cheaply. When Sòmbak'è got larger, these people didn't need the Dene anymore, and they didn't want anything to do with them. I was the only Dene then working for Giant Mine. It was hard at first, but I got better at it as time went by.

There were still few Dene who worked for wages. As more people moved to town, they trapped a bit to earn cash and a few young people got short-term jobs.

In the summer, the Dene were hired by the commercial fishing outfits to fish for them in their own canoes. Some native fishermen got rich this way, and that helped a bit. But the Dene living in town generally couldn't get jobs, and it was hard to get welfare. Some of them moved to the bush in the fall, came back for Christmas, and then went on their spring hunt as they had always done. But they found it hard, because there were so many new things to spend money on: rent, taxis, buses, shows, cafes, alcohol.

Changing my way of life was just as hard for me as it was for other Dene. When I had lived at Sahtú, life was simple. My elders had taught me to share; cash money hadn't meant much to me. In Sòmbak'è, I didn't know the value of money at first and I didn't know how to save. There were so many new things I had to buy. I worked for $1.49 an hour, and I had to pay for our power, phone, rent, oil and groceries.

I lived in the old part of town, on Latham Island. I shared things just as I was taught to do, so there were many Dene coming to the house and I fed them. I guess I couldn't change. I learned too late that it is hard to live two different ways of life at the same time.

That's why I prepared all my children to live and survive in this new way of life. I made sure that all my kids went to school every day. I told my son, "I didn't want to take you into the bush too often, because you might like that way of life." Sometimes I took my sons hunting, but I concentrated on teaching them to work for wages. At the same time, my children were told stories about their families, about ravens, about the land, the past, and our Dene culture. All my children are now independent.

I'd been working for the mine for fourteen years when my wife got sick with cancer of the blood. After four years in and out of hospital, Julie died. After I lost her, I couldn't work in the mine any more. My children were adults, able to look after themselves, so I decided to go back to Déline to hunt and trap the way I used to.

o

Some Dene say the Earth is our body. Others say the land is like a big warehouse. In the old days, they thought things would never change. But the change that came was so strong that it changed the Dene way of life. It was a change that went its own way without any control by Dene.

The government started the change in order to help people. But the problems have gotten bigger and bigger. Education has meant that children don't listen to their parents. Family relationships are changing constantly. This is hard for everyone. Few Dene hunt and trap full time, so their relationship to the land is also changing. They live in communities, so they need jobs to make money. But there aren't many jobs.

The government isn't to be blamed for everything that changed our people's lives. All kinds of things worked together to change the Dene, but the government started the process of change.

Some things do not change. Many younger Dene no longer live the traditional life, but they know it and understand its values. They try to use this heritage in their work, and to maintain control over the changes that affect our land and people. They are creating Dene lives in new ways.

It may be that in future the important values of Dene—respect for the land and respect for one another—will endure, both here in Denendeh and all over the world.

CUT-OFFS, CLAIMS PROHIBITION, AND THE ALLIED TRIBES, 1916-27 ◇

PAUL TENNANT

◦

The decade commencing in 1916 was a fateful one for the Indian land question and for Indian political activity. It began with the Allied Tribes united in representing the majority of tribal groups. It brought momentous judicial decisions in London, reduction of reserves and further suppression of Indian rights in British Columbia, and a full-blown parliamentary investigation of the land question and the claims of the Allied Tribes in Ottawa. It ended with the outlawing of claims-related activities and the disappearance of the Allied Tribes.

The McKenna-McBride Commission[1] spent 1913 and the next two years holding hearings and examining reserves throughout the province. Many Indians spoke at the hearings, frequently expressing fear that reserves would be reduced without Indian consent. McKenna and the other commissioners just as frequently reminded them that the Indian Act guaranteed that no reduction, or "surrender," of any reserve could occur without the consent of a majority of the adult males of the band affected. Nevertheless, the commissioners took the approach that they could recommend reductions without taking account of the views of Indians and that it would be up to the federal government to obtain Indian consent.

The verbatim transcripts of the hearings provide a wealth of information about Indian views and concerns. In the central and southern interior there was much complaint and worry about reserve size, the unsuitability of reserve land for agriculture, and the frequent lack of access to water for irrigating crops and raising stock. There were also frequent assertions of

---

Indian title and demands for treaties. John Chillihitza, for example, still the leading Okanagan chief, explained that his father had allowed Peter O'Reilly and G.M. Sproat to lay out reserves on the understanding that compensation would be paid later for lands occupied by settlers. "My father said 'All right, we will take our small piece where we are going to live, and we will talk about our interests in the big outside lands," and [O'Reilly and later Sproat] said 'All right'."[2] On the coast the primary concerns were aboriginal title and the need for treaties, and demands for these were expressed again and again. The Indian Rights Association wrote to a number of communities urging them to boycott the hearings because title was being ignored; some did so, while spokesmen for others appeared at the hearings but insisted on speaking about title.

McKenna and the other commissioners became adept at turning references to original ownership into questions relating to current reserves and current needs. When unsuccessful they would dismiss a witness or close the hearings, as they did, for example, at Hazelton, when the commission was hearing from Gitksan spokesmen. House chiefs from the community of Kuldoe sought to speak about title and self-government, but they were cut short by the chairman. William Jackson, a house chief in the Kisgegas community, then came to the witness table and insisted, apparently heatedly, on raising the same issues.[3]

Jackson:
We are asking to get back the land of our grandfathers—we want our places, and we want our places to be free as they were before; as our fathers had a free living in their own land, we want to be the same way. God gave us this land where we were brought up, and it was free. There was no one bothering us and we want the land just as it was before the white man ever came into this country.

Commissioner:
William Jackson and Indians of the Kisgegas Tribe: You need not speak to us about holding this land the same as your grandfathers did—the world moves along, and you in your lifetime must move with it.

Jackson:
What is moving this world?

Commissioner:
You will have to go to a wiser lot of men than the Kuldoes to find that out—but you will have to move with the world. If you don't you will be wiped out.

Jackson:
Who gave us this land—it was God. We heard it and all we know is that you people are taking away our land. This is our land—our own. No one [from] one house [can] serve as boss in the other house.

Chairman:
We are sorry you have not seen fit to answer our questions, and all that remains to be done is to wish you Good Bye.[4]

In June 1916, when the commission made its report (only days after the founding meeting of the Allied Tribes), Indian reserves in the province totalled 713 699 acres (or 1115 square miles). The commission recommended that 666 640 acres (1042 square miles) be confirmed as existing reserve lands and that 87 291 acres (136 square miles) be added as additions and as new reserves. This added land was valued at $444 838.80 or $5.10 an acre. The commission recommended that a total of 47 058 acres (74 square miles) be "cut-off" from existing reserves. This land to be cut off was almost entirely land regarded as highly desirable by white farmers, ranchers, developers, speculators, and municipal officials. It was mostly on the south coast and in the southern interior. Its value was appraised at between $1.2 and $1.5 million or upwards of $26.52 an acre.[5]

While it could be, and was, contended that Indians in general would be gaining more reserve land than they were losing, it could not be denied that the land to be cut off was worth much more than that to be added. There was, however, no attempt to balance losses and gains for each Indian community; most of those to experience cut-offs (some twenty-two communities were principally affected) were to gain little or no land in return. With the registered Indian population now less than twenty-four thousand, the commission's recommendations provided for a province-wide average reserve allocation of just over 150 acres for each family of five. But the average meant little, for there remained marked disparities among communities and tribal groups. The Kamloops band, for example, would have 688 acres for each family, while some other communities would have less than one-tenth that amount. In 1916, however, federal officials still maintained that no cut-offs would occur without the consent of the band affected.

Fortunately, or so it must have seemed to the Indians, the governments took no immediate action to implement the report. Premier McBride had retired in 1915, and H.C. Brewster and his Liberals came to power in September 1916. Ignorant of Indian matters and aware of white complaints about some of the proposed new reserves, Brewster resisted Duncan Campbell Scott's attempts to arrange a secret agreement in which both governments would approve and implement the commission's recommendations.[6] Brewster died in 1918 and was replaced as premier by John Oliver. Oliver and his minister of lands, Duff Pattullo, who was from Prince Rupert on the north coast, remained in charge of provincial policy on land and Indians over the next decade. While both would prove "hostile to Indians,"[7] their early actions were cause for some optimism within the Allied Tribes.

One of Pattullo's first acts was to write to Arthur Meighen, the Conservative minister of Indian affairs, to see whether Indian consent would indeed be required for the cut-offs. Meighen replied that it would, but he expressed confidence that his department would be able to obtain it.[8] In March 1919 the provincial legislature passed the Indian Affairs Settlement Act. Section 3 authorized the provincial government to "carry on such further negotiations and enter into such further agreements, whether with the Dominion Government or with the Indians" as were necessary to implement the report. Oliver seemed to take the provision seriously, for he proceeded to ask the Allied Tribes for its views on the commission's report. Scott took great exception to section 3 and to Oliver's request. He regarded the province as trespassing onto the exclusive right of the federal government to deal with Indians, and as events would soon make clear, he did not want any suggestion that Indians would have any say in the fate of the commission's proposals. In response, the deputy attorney-general of the province informed Scott that section 3 could be repealed if the dominion did not intend to obtain Indian consent to the proposed cut-offs.[9]

In responding to Oliver's request the Allied Tribes held a general assembly at Spences Bridge in June 1919. Although Peter Kelly, Andrew Paull, and other members of the executive committee had been actively lobbying against the proposed cut-offs, there had been no assembly since the founding of the organization in 1916. At Spences Bridge the Allied Tribes confirmed Peter Kelly as chairman of the executive committee, elected Andrew Paull as "recording secretary" of the organization, and authorized the committee (of which James Teit remained secretary) to prepare the statement requested by Oliver. As part of its preparation the committee held "various large inter-tribal meetings . . . in different parts of the Province."[10] It was through these meetings, rather than general assemblies, that local support for the Allied Tribes and its goals could be gauged, both by the leaders themselves and by Department of Indian Affairs officials in the various agencies.

Having approved a statement drafted by Kelly and Teit, the executive committee presented it to Oliver in a meeting with him in December 1919. The statement, some six thousand words long, was both a comprehensive claim to aboriginal title and a detailed rejection of the McKenna-McBride Commission's report. In the view of the Allied Tribes, the commission's terms of reference ignored the title question, the added lands were worth little while the cut-offs were valuable, inequities between tribes were not addressed, and the commission had ignored important matters, such as water rights, which were within its terms of reference. The statement was widely distributed among British Columbia Indians and appears to have superseded the Nisga'a petition of 1913 as the authoritative statement of British Columbia Indian claims. Like the Nisga'a petition, the statement affirmed that British Columbia Indians would "continue pressing our case in the Privy Council."[11]

In Ottawa members had now taken an ominous turn. In November Scott had recommended to Meighen that the Conservative government seek authority from Parliament to override the Indian veto, and in January 1920, Scott provided his detailed rationale.

> It is just possible that in some instances the Indians might, through some influence or prejudice, refuse to give the necessary consent. I think we should provide against such a contingency in our legislation confirming that all reductions and cut-offs should be effected without the consent of the Indians. I do not see that any injustice would be done to any band by such a provision. These reductions or cut-offs are recommended only where the Indians held more land than they required. When these cut-offs are sold, half of the proceeds will go to the Indians of the band and will be of more real benefit to them than would the land which they do not use.[12]

Meighen agreed. Bill 13, as it was labelled, was soon introduced. The Allied Tribes promptly turned its attention back to Ottawa, lobbying MPs and submitting a petition to the government pointing out the unfairness of cancelling the much vaunted and so frequently reaffirmed promise that Indian consent would be required for cut-offs. Opposition MPs were highly critical of the bill, but Meighen pressed ahead, repeating Scott's rationale.

Bill 13 was signed into law on Dominion Day 1920 as The British Columbia Indian Lands Settlement Act. It authorized the federal cabinet to implement the McKenna-McBride Commission recommendations by ordering "reductions or cutoffs to be effected without surrenders of the same by the Indians, notwithstanding any provisions of the Indian Act to the contrary." The government and Parliament of Canada thus broke repeated official promises. The act also authorized the federal government to proceed to "the full and final adjustment and settlement . . . respecting Indian lands and Indian affairs in the Province." No mention was made of the Indian concerns of title, treaties, and self-government, which Scott and Meighen clearly intended to ignore.

Meighen, who soon became prime minister, allowed Scott to move against Indian interests on several additional fronts. One assumption underlying the federal policy of Indian assimilation had been that the more intelligent, able, and educated Indians would wish to give up Indian status and leave the reserves in order to acquire the rights of full British subjects, that is, to accept "enfranchisement." By 1920 it was abundantly evident that few Indians wanted to take the step. Scott's answer was Bill 14, which was introduced and passed as the companion piece to Bill 13. It allowed the government to enfranchise any Canadian Indian without his or her consent. Enfranchised Indians could neither live on nor be buried on reserves. The bill also strengthened government powers to take custody of Indian children in order to compel school attendance.[13] British Columbia Indians regarded Bill 14 as even more offensive than Bill 13. The Allied Tribes spokesmen complained strenuously. Scott and Meighen remained adamant that compulsory enfranchisement was in the Indians' own best interest.

Although it had been in place since 1884, the anti-potlatch provision of the Indian Act, section 140, had been enforced only sporadically. After Scott became deputy superintendent, it was amended in 1914 and 1918 to expand the definition of prohibited activities and to make prosecution easier. Now the prohibition applied to "any Indian festival, dance or other ceremony of which the giving away or paying or giving back of money, goods or articles of any sort forms a part." The definition was so broad that it could apply to virtually any gathering organized by Indians themselves, including not only the traditional potlatch but also, in the hands of zealous missionaries or Indian agents, meetings to discuss land claims. The penalty for violating the potlatch prohibition did not include the option of a fine; it was jailing for at least two months and a maximum of six.[14]

It was in January 1920, precisely as Bills 13 and 14 were being developed, that Indian agents and police commenced the major wave of potlatch arrests, charges, prosecutions, convictions, and jailings in British Columbia.[15] In some cases agents or missionaries were local justices of the peace and were able to expedite legal proceedings. The Kwagiulth, under the thumb of an especially zealous anti-potlatch Indian agent, were at the forefront of the resistance to the law and its enforcement.[16] A number of prominent chiefs, Kwagiulth as well as others, were convicted and brought to Oakalla Penitentiary to serve their sentences. The jailings added fuel to the political opposition to Bills 13 and 14 and left a legacy of shame and bitterness evident decades later among the children and grandchildren of those imprisoned.[17] One immediate effect, however, was the decision of a number of the Kwagiulth chiefs to participate in the Allied Tribes.

In 1921 there occurred in London an event having critical relevance to aboriginal title throughout the British Empire, but especially in places, such as British Columbia, where title had not been explicitly extinguished. In a case arising in Southern Nigeria, Viscount Haldane affirmed, on behalf of the Judicial Committee of the Privy Council, that aboriginal title was a pre-existing right that "must be presumed to have continued unless the contrary is established by the context or the circumstances."[18] Should the British Columbia land claim get to the Judicial Committee, there was now a substantial possibility that the committee would rule that Indian title had not been extinguished. It is highly unlikely that either Arthur O'Meara or Scott remained unaware of Haldane's ruling or its implications. Scott, as the 1914 order-in-council had shown, was already aware of the danger of allowing the claim into the courts unless the government kept tight control of Indian actions. Now the Haldane ruling would cause Scott and the federal politicians to resolve at all costs to keep the British Columbia claim from getting into the courts and on to the Judicial Committee.

Despite the possible encouragement provided by Haldane's ruling in London, matters were not going well for the Allied Tribes. One persistent problem was the shortage of adequate and accurate information. Inevitably, it was government officials who controlled the most valuable documentary evidence. In their internal correspondence federal officials at times discussed the benefits of withholding information from Kelly and Paull,[19] and the two were in fact prevented by Scott and others from obtaining a copy of the vitally informative *Papers Connected with the Indian Land Question*, the compilation of documents published in 1875 that provided the authoritative record of the land question's early years.[20]

Kelly and Paull could point to no success whatever in their attempts to influence Scott and Meighen in Ottawa, and in Victoria, Oliver and Pattullo were now ignoring the Allied Tribes. In London the British government seemed oblivious to the issue. On the British Columbia coast the enforcement of the potlatch law was inhibiting the holding of local meetings to demonstrate support for the Allied Tribes, and during 1921 Indian opposition to Kelly, Paull, and O'Meara came into the open.

The third assembly of the Allied Tribes was held in January 1922 in North Vancouver; that an assembly was called in mid-winter, the most awkward time for travel, was itself an indication of difficulties. Later, Kelly and Paull described the meeting as having been "a general meeting of all B.C. Indians" at which the Allied Tribes joined with unaffiliated or "independent" Indians to form a "a larger alliance."[21] An examination of an attendance list, prepared five years after the event by Paull,[22] shows that only ten or so tribal groups were represented—compared to the sixteen at the founding meeting in 1916. The Nisga'a, Tsimshian, Gitksan, Carrier, Tahltan, Kaska-Dana, and Kootenay were not represented, perhaps more because of the time of year than because of discontent. In any event, the meeting can hardly have been in any position to form a "larger alliance."

The 1922 meeting appears, rather, to have been an attempt to prevent secession from the Allied Tribes by interior Indians. Chillihitza was present and acted as the main dissident spokesman, or so later events would suggest. Possibly the Interior Salish sentiments were affected by the absence of James Teit[23] or by hostility to O'Meara. But outright lack of support for Kelly and Paull was also evident. To counter the dissent, they agreed to reconstitute the executive committee to "consist of Indians and others deemed acceptable by Interiors."[24] While Kelly later stated that the meeting did herald a lesser role for white advisers, there is no evidence that the executive was reformed to the satisfaction of Chillihitza and his followers. Moreover, the only new support claimed after this time by Kelly and Paull was on the coast.[25]

Accounts of the 1922 meeting suggest not only declining unity but also a declining role for tribal groups. In describing the meeting Kelly and Paull enumerated those present not in terms of tribal groups, as they had done for the 1916 meeting, but in terms of bands or local communities.[26] There were some fifty Indians at the meeting, representing about half that number of communities.[27] From 1922 onward tribal groups as such do not appear to have been important elements within the Allied Tribes, nor do the bands and communities seem to have played any active part. Undoubtedly, most Indians endorsed the goals of the organization, but for practical purposes Kelly, Paull, and O'Meara were the organization.

In late 1921 the defeat of Meighen and the Conservatives by Mackenzie King and the Liberals brought about a slightly more sympathetic outlook in Ottawa, even though Scott continued as the senior appointed official in the Department of Indian Affairs. The legislation resulting from Bill 14, however, was soon repealed, and in 1923, with Scott's approval and support, a longstanding grievance was resolved with the granting to Indians of the right to hold commercial ocean-fishing licences. In British Columbia, some of the coastal fishermen soon became financial backers of the Allied Tribes.

The Allied Tribes executive committee resumed its lobbying, sending letters to King and obtaining meetings in 1922 and 1923 with both Scott and Charles Stewart, the minister of Indian affairs. The principal meeting with Scott occurred in August 1923, just after the provincial government had provided for its half of the final implementation of the McKenna-McBride recommendations. Kelly and Paull put forward the 1919 Allied Tribes statement as still valid and urged Scott to recommend that the federal cabinet not proceed to finalize the recommendations. Scott was surprised to find the Indians still committed to the pursuit of aboriginal title. He gave them no assurances.[28]

In 1924 the federal cabinet passed the order-in-council implementing the McKenna-McBride recommendations. The cut-off lands thus ceased to be part of Indian reserves in British Columbia. The action of the government gave an ironic twist to the common white phrase "Indian giver," meaning one who takes back something which has been given to keep. Among British Columbia Indians the cut-off lands remained a major symbol of white injustice.[29]

Defeated on the reserve question, the executive committee redoubled its efforts to get to the Judicial Committee in London. Now there was no ambiguity as to the meaning of "privy council." Kelly and Paull wanted it to rule on the legality of ignoring aboriginal title, and they did not want the federal authorities to block their way to London. In late 1925 the executive committee approved a petition to the Canadian Parliament, drafted by Kelly, asking that it establish a special committee as the first step in getting the proceedings underway. W.G. McQuarrie, MP for New Westminster, submitted the petition in June 1926, but it received little attention for the rest of the year as the King-Byng Affair unfolded and the Liberals again defeated the Conservatives in a general election.

In February 1927, H.H. Stevens, Conservative MP for Vancouver Centre, raised the matter again, asking King and Stewart if the government would not approve a "select committee to hear the representatives of the Indians and give the [land] question study." While he had "not much sympathy with some of the views entertained by those who are agitating," he did think it "desirable to satisfy and quiet the Indians" and so was "anxious to co-operate in giving them every opportunity to have the question settled" and not to have it "drift any longer."[30] On 8 March Stewart introduced, and the House passed, a motion that a special joint Senate-House committee be established "to enquire into the claims of the Allied Indian Tribes of British Columbia as set forth in their petition."[31] In going ahead with the motion, Stewart acted against Scott's advice, but he did so with the "covert intention" that the committee would in fact serve to keep the British Columbia land claim from getting to court and so to the Judicial Committee.[32]

The hearings of the special joint committee, which took place exactly forty years after the north coast enquiry,[33] finally gave Kelly and Paull the opportunity they had been seeking to present their case. The hearings also forced politicians and officials to make some sort of response. The Indians and the federal government had both hoped that the British Columbia government would send a spokesman to take part in the hearings, but Premier Oliver refused the federal invitation to do so.[34] Perhaps the Indians were optimistic that a favourable response was more likely since the committee was federal rather than provincial and since it had a Liberal rather than a Conservative majority. As matters turned out, however, the committee did not divide on partisan lines, and the outlook of white British Columbians was well represented on the committee by H.H. Stevens, by Senator Hewitt Bostock, the Kamloops rancher who was Senate co-chairman of the committee, and by three other senators from the province (G.H. Barnard, R.F. Green, and J.D. Taylor). Also among the fourteen members were Charles

Stewart and future prime minister R.B. Bennett. The committee commenced immediately and completed its hearings on 6 April.

During the initial closed meeting of the committee it was agreed that Scott would testify first, allowing him to argue against the case of the Allied Tribes before Kelly and Paull were given a chance to present it. Stevens went so far as to propose, unsuccessfully, that the Indians and other witnesses be excluded during Scott's testimony and thus be prevented from knowing the government's argument.[35] At the start of the open sessions, Scott presented a lengthy statement. He did not deny the existence of aboriginal title, but he argued that awarding reserves and spending federal money on Indian health, welfare, and education, which by that time totalled $10.8 million in British Columbia, was adequate compensation and that no further claim need be entertained. Nor did he believe that the Indians had come to the demands on their own or that their motives were to be respected:

> A few interviews with the advisers of the Indians convinced me that they were in possession of erroneous ideas about the nature of the Indian title and exaggerated views of the value of title, and had in fact not fully grasped the conditions under which the Crown had made treaties with the Indians in other parts of the Dominion. I became convinced that the expectation of receiving compensation of very large value either in money or privileges was influencing to a great extent the strength of the pressure being brought to bear on the Government, and I found the idea prevailing that the improvements made by white citizens to provincial lands . . . had enhanced the value of the Indian title.[36]

The only other federal official to take any major part was W.E. Ditchburn, the Indian commissioner for British Columbia. In his view, the matter of aboriginal title was "a canker in the minds of the Indians today. If it were removed . . . it would go very far towards a more satisfactory working out of the administration of the affairs by this Department." When a committee member asked, "Do the young people still harbour the thought that the land ownership will ultimately be vested in them?" Ditchburn replied, "They read as they run, of course, and their idea of the aboriginal title is much more exaggerated than that of the old people."[37]

Paull, Kelly, and O'Meara appeared for the Allied Tribes. They laid out the principles of the Royal Proclamation of 1763; they described accurately and in detail the course of events in British Columbia; they explained patiently and consistently their belief that British Columbia Indians should be dealt with on the same basis as had others in Canada. Aboriginal title was, in Kelly's words, the "fundamental issue" separate from but underlying all the particular grievances, such as those relating to reserves.[38]

While holding fast to the principle that the dollar amount of compensation for lands taken from Indians must be a matter of negotiation, Kelly amply confirmed the consistent Indian position that the whole point of payment was to acknowledge original Indian ownership and not to make

Indians rich. It was also clear that the Indians agreed that suitable treaties would serve to extinguish aboriginal title forever.[39] Simple fairness was raised several times by Kelly: "Why not keep unblemished the record of British fair dealing with native races? Why refuse to recognize the claim of certain tribes of Indians in one corner of the British Dominions, when it has been accorded to others in another part of the same Dominion?"[40]

Throughout the hearings H.H. Stevens was particularly vehement in badgering witnesses, especially O'Meara, whom he blamed for the whole issue. At one point when Kelly was testifying, Stevens referred to the claim as a bone that Kelly would not let go of; when Kelly objected, Stevens made fun of him in asides to other members of the committee.[41] Stevens also asserted that Indians were not farming effectively and were allowing orchard diseases to spread onto white farms. Ditchburn refuted the allegations.[42] Stevens believed that enfranchisement was the only appropriate path for Indians, and he rejected claims to aboriginal title, which, he insisted, were a recent invention, thought-up not by the Indians but by O'Meara:

> That is one thing I never did agree to in the last twenty years, or the nineteen years since I heard Mr. O'Meara first moot this claim for an aboriginal title. I never admitted it, and I never could bring my mind to see any solid ground for the aboriginal title. I do say this, that the Indians deserve, and we ought to accord them, the most generous treatment that we possibly can, and I have always advocated that we should try to bring the Indians to the position of independent citizenship as quickly as we can. That is my position, and has been throughout my whole life in British Columbia; but I have never yet been able to see any sound ground for admitting the existence of an aboriginal title, and the evidence we have received here up to the moment, has only confirmed my views.[43]

"Generous treatment" was a stock phrase among white politicians of the period when discussing Indian affairs. In practice the phrase meant allowing Indians full and equal rights providing they ceased to be Indians. It obviously did not mean generosity in such matters as initial reserve acreage or allowing Indians a say in the cut-off issue.

Nor were the Indians to have "generous treatment" in access to vital information about the fate of their aboriginal title. O'Meara attempted to present quotations from the instructions to Governor Douglas of 1858, in which Sir Edward Lytton alluded to treaties and to the Indians' possession of the land. Stevens objected to quotations from documents not placed in evidence and told O'Meara that "I have had twenty years of your nonsense, and I am tired of it."[44] The chairman informed O'Meara that he must produce the original document. Kelly interjected that O'Meara had been striving "to support his contention by making quotations from this authority and from that authority" as lawyers ordinarily did, and asked, "Why is it objected to in this case?" Stevens promptly replied, "Because he does not quote correctly."[45]

At that moment Stevens himself had in his hands a copy of the *Papers Connected with the Indian Land Question,*[46] which he had just sought to prevent O'Meara from quoting on the grounds that it was not available to the committee. Paull now interrupted: "There is a book that has been published many years ago, which contains all the dispatches in colonial days with the Imperial Government. All of those dispatches are contained in that book and we have been trying all the time since I have been associated with this matter to get a copy of it. I have been to the Department, and Dr. Scott could not let me have it. I have been to the Library, and they have not got it there. I know that Commissioner Ditchburn has that book; and I would ask to have access to it." Stevens again stated that O'Meara "ought to know, as your counsel, that he should not quote from something which he cannot produce."

Charles Murphy, one of the Senate members, asked the pivotal question. "Is the book in this room?" Scott replied, "I have no copy of this book, but this one for myself. I have no objection to allowing them to look at this book. I thought Mr. O'Meara was referring to something original from the Imperial Government." Ditchburn also had a copy with him, but he felt it would be more useful where it was than as evidence for the committee (in which case the Indians would have access to it). "I do not want this book to be put in and impounded. It is my personal copy and I do not know where to get another copy of it." Stevens, seeking to keep the cat in the bag, now suggested that Ditchburn do what Stevens had prevented O'Meara from doing. "Read the section into the record, then you will have it," said Stevens.

The committee chairman could at this point have had the book put in evidence, but instead he agreed only that O'Meara, not Ditchburn, should read the relevant section. "We want you to read what you are referring to now, Mr. O'Meara, into the record, because the book from which you are taking it belongs to the Indian Department, and they have only one copy of it, and they cannot let it go."[47] The Indians were thus once again, and for the Allied Tribes for the final time, denied access to the documents which they knew were important to their case. White politicians and officials, in contrast, including Stevens, Scott, and Ditchburn, could routinely possess copies and found it useful to carry them for ready reference.

Chief Chillihitza appeared before the committee, along with a lawyer, stating that he represented some thirty interior chiefs of the Okanagan, Shuswap, and Nlaka'pamux tribal groups. Chillihitza and Basil David, the Shuswap chief, who also spoke, provided a marked contrast to Kelly and Paull. They were still very much the traditional leaders, speaking their own languages through interpreters and showing little interest in legal or political details. At times Chillihitza rambled on about his conversations with G.M. Sproat and with the King in London in 1906, and he even complained about the presence of an unwanted individual on a particular reserve. While both Chillihitza and David sought more land for their peoples, they stressed reserve issues more than "aboriginal title"; indeed, the interpreters did not use the phrase, and the lawyer expressed his view that aboriginal title was not of concern to the interior Indians. In fact, however, Chillihitza did assert aboriginal title in asking, as he had before the McKenna-McBride Commission, that the governments live up to their promise to pay the Indians for lands not included in reserves.[48] Chillihitza and David also made clear that the Allied Tribes did not speak for the interior tribal groups.

After the two old interior chiefs had spoken, Kelly was asked by Stevens, "Supposing the aboriginal title is not recognized? Suppose recognition is refused, what position do you take then?" Kelly's response was prophetic:

> Then the position that we would have to take would be this: that we are simply dependent people. Then we would have to accept from you, just as an act of grace, whatever you saw fit to give us. Now that is putting it in plain language. The Indians have no voice in the affairs of this country. They have not a solitary way of bringing anything before the Parliament of this country, except as we have done last year by petition, and it is a mighty hard thing. If we press for that, we are called agitators, simply agitators, trouble makers, when we try to get what we consider to be our rights. It is a mighty hard thing, and as I have said, it has taken us between forty and fifty years to get to where we are to-day. And, perhaps, if we are turned down now, if this Committee see fit to turn down what we are pressing for, it might be another century before a new generation will rise up and begin to press this claim.[49]

Kelly was too pessimistic. It would be only four decades until a new generation rose up and began again to press the claim.

In its report, which was submitted five days after the completion of its hearings and which was immediately concurred in by both Commons and Senate, the committee unanimously rejected all the claims of the Allied Tribes. The committee went beyond the enquiry of 1887 by presenting six reasoned arguments for the rejection. The committee argued, first, that British exploration of the territory and subsequent exertion of sovereignty were evidence that Britain recognized "the lands as belonging to the Crown."[50] The committee ignored completely the acknowledgement of Indian title by colonial secretaries, by James Douglas, and by the island legislature. It did not even consider whether Indian title had existed prior to the advent of colonial government. It took for granted that extension of British sovereignty was in itself evidence that no prior title could have continued or been acknowledged. It did not discuss why the assumptions and procedures that had applied east of the Rockies did not apply in British Columbia. In this first and most basic argument, the committee essentially accepted the views prevailing among British Columbia Whites.

In its second argument the committee turned to revising history by asserting that the Hudson's Bay Company had achieved the "conquest" of "the territory of British Columbia." In support of this assertion, the committee noted that company posts were "fortified and the officers and servants of the Company were prepared to resist hostile attacks." The committee, however, chose to mention only two "attacks." In one, a band of Cowichan Indians "seized and slaughtered several animals belonging to the whites"; in the other, supposedly an aftermath of the first, a Songish group attacked Fort Victoria but was "easily over-awed by artillery."[51]

James Douglas would have been astounded to learn that a military conquest had occurred under his administration, as would he have been to know that it had been achieved by means of a dispute over straying livestock. Wisely, the committee did not dig itself deeper by trying to deal with such questions as how the *defensive* actions of the Company could amount to conquest or how even the "defeat" of two local Indian communities, had it occurred, could be taken to wipe out the land ownership on the rest of Vancouver Island. An even more serious question was how any action involving the company on Vancouver Island, to which its jurisdiction was confined, could be taken as affecting Indian title on the Mainland, which was not yet a colony. Absurd though it was, the conquest argument did have one slight redeeming feature; it contradicted the first argument by implicitly assuming that the prior inhabitants had existed in units recognizable in international law and that the units were in possession of land whose ownership could be transferred by conquest.

As its third argument the committee pointed out that "the Indians were not in agreement as to the nature of their claims" and asserted (wrongly, as has been suggested) that "the representatives of the Indian Tribes in the interior of British Columbia did not make any claim to any land of the Province based on an aboriginal title."[52]

Fourth, in rejecting the aboriginal title claim of the Allied Tribes, the committee went beyond historical exaggeration into falsification and misrepresentation:

> Early in the proceedings it developed that the aboriginal title claimed was first presented as a legal claim against the Crown about fifteen years ago. The claim then began to take form as one which should be satisfied by a treaty or agreement with the Indians in which conditions and terms put forward by them or on their behalf must be considered and agreed upon before a cession of the alleged title would be granted. Tradition forms so large a part of Indian mentality that if in pre-Confederation days the Indians considered they had an aboriginal title to the lands of the Province, there would have been tribal records of such being transmitted from father to son, either by word of mouth or in some other customary way. But nothing of the kind was shown to exist.[53]

This was the falsification. There was abundant evidence that Indians had claimed title from the beginning and had demanded treaties as early as 1887 in the north coast hearings. The *Papers Connected with the Indian Land Question*, which the officials had kept away from the Indians, showed that both Douglas and colonial secretaries had considered the Indians to have title. The despatch from Edward Lytton, which Stevens had sought to keep out of the proceedings, confirmed this fact, as did the Douglas treaties, one of which Kelly had read into the record. The *Papers* also provided evidence of numerous instances before 1875 in which Indians had considered themselves to have title. The transcripts of the 1887 hearings contained explicit examples of transmission of title. Even Scott had told the committee that "from the year 1875 until the present time there has been a definite claim, growing in clearness as years went by."[54]

The committee went on to assert that the Indians had, prior to the supposed fifteen-year period, consented to the denial of aboriginal title and that this consent had been demonstrated by their complete acceptance of the governments' reserve policies. "The evidence of Mr. Kelly goes to confirm the view that the Indians were consenting parties to the whole policy of the government both as to reserves and other benefits which they accepted for years without demur."[55] This was both falsification and misrepresentation. It even contradicted Scott's opening statements to the committee that from the earliest British Columbia Indians "had complained constantly of the insufficiency of land allotments for reserves."[56]

Fifth, the committee blamed white agitators.

> The Committee note with regret the existence of agitation, not only in British Columbia, but with Indians in other parts of the Dominion, which agitation may be called mischievous, by which the Indians are deceived and led to expect benefits from claims more or less fictitious. Such agitation, often carried out by designing white men, is to be deplored, and should be discountenanced, as the Government of the country is at all times ready to protect the interests of the Indians and to redress real grievances where such are shown to exist.[57]

Finally, the committee argued that the Indians had given up the right to serious consideration, since they had rejected the conditions set out in the 1914 order-in-council and had continued to take up the time of the government and of Parliament with "irrelevent issues."[58]

The arguments of the special committee are easily characterized. They were quick and casual, displaying no concern for reasoned explanation that could withstand serious scrutiny. It is noteworthy that the committee did *not* raise two particular arguments. It did not suggest that the Proclamation of 1763 had not extended westward to the Pacific, and it did not assert that the passage of legislation in the colonies prior to 1871 had served to extinguish any aboriginal title that might have existed.[59]

The committee made two main recommendations. First, although it recognized no need for treaties in British Columbia, it suggested that the Indians should receive an annual allotment of $100 000 "in lieu of" treaty payments.[60] (The committee made no mention of other treaty benefits, such as greater reserve acreage.) The government implemented the $100 000 allocation, which became known as the "B.C. special."

The other, more sinister, recommendation has already been referred to; it was that land claim agitation should be "discountenanced." As early as 1924 Scott had proposed prohibiting Indians from paying lawyers to pursue claims without government approval.[61] Now Scott prepared an amendment to the Indian Act which Stewart introduced, and it was quickly passed by Parliament. Appropriately, it was inserted as section 141, next to section 140, the anti-potlatch provision. The amendment stated that

> Every person who, without the consent of the Superintendent General expressed in writing, receives, obtains, solicits or requests from any Indian any payment or contribution or promise of any payment or contribution for the purpose of raising a fund or providing money for the prosecution of any claim which the tribe or band of Indians to which such Indian belongs, or of which he is a member, has or is represented to have for the recovery of any claim or money for the benefit of the said tribe or band, shall be guilty of an offence and liable upon summary conviction for each such offence to a penalty not exceeding two hundred dollars and not less than fifty dollars or to imprisonment for any term not exceeding two months.

The committee's recommendation had emphasized agitation by Whites, with persons such as O'Meara obviously in the thoughts of committee members. Section 141, however, applied to "every person," Indian or non-Indian. Had Scott and Stewart sought merely to prevent outside agitation, the amendment could easily have been phrased to apply only to persons who were not Indians. But their intent was to prevent all land claims activity and, above all, to block the British Columbia claim from getting to the Judicial Committee of the Privy Council. Striking at monetary exchanges, actual or promised, was chosen as the most expedient legal means to this end; monetary support was essential to land claims activities, and monetary exchanges could be identified and proven in court.

Without the minister's approval, no Indian or other person acting for the Allied Tribes or the Nisga'a Land Committee, for example, could now request or receive from any registered Indian any fee for legal or other services or any money for postage, travel, advertising, hall rental, refreshments, research expenses, legal fees, or court costs. The amendment quite simply made it impossible for any organization to exist if pursuing the land claim was one of its objectives.[62]

The addition of section 141 to the Indian Act evoked little discussion in Parliament or among white Canadians. It was taken for granted that Parliament had the right to curtail the rights and freedoms of Indians in ways that would not have been tolerated by Whites themselves. Much later, well after its repeal in 1951, the amendment was commonly looked back upon by British Columbia Whites, or at least by the few with reason to have heard of it, as having been merely intended to protect misguided Indians from conniving white lawyers.[63] Among British Columbia Indians the amendment is remembered much more intensely, and mention is often made of it in discussions of Indian political history. In Indian memories section 141 is usually linked with the potlatch prohibition, and the combination of the two produces the still common belief, which presumably existed from 1927 until 1951 as well, that any gathering of Indians or any discussion of land claims was illegal without the permission of a missionary, Indian agent, or police official.[64]

There is no certainty that the Allied Tribes would have survived 1927 even without the prohibition of claims activity. Section 141, however, was the hammer blow which abruptly ended the life of the organization. Nor is there certainty about the outcome had British Columbia Indians been free to pursue their claim through the courts. There was, however, some chance that the Judicial Committee of the Privy Council would have ruled that aboriginal title remained unextinguished in British Columbia, thus compelling the provincial and federal governments to negotiate agreements as stipulated in the Royal Proclamation of 1763. With the new amendment in place, however, it was illegal for the Indians to provide for any of the necessary steps to get their claims into court. From the white perspective, the Indian land question in British Columbia had been resolved.

NOTES

1. The origins of the commission are described in Paul Tennant, *Aboriginal People and Politics: The Indian Land Question in British Columbia, 1849–1989* (Vancouver: University of British Columbia Press, 1990), chap. 7.

2. BC, Royal Commission on Indian Affairs for the Province of British Columbia, *Evidence* (Victoria: Acme Press, 1916), hearings of 18 Oct. 1913 at Douglas Lake, 1–2 (cited hereafter as McKenna-McBride Commission, *Evidence*).

3. Kuldoe and Kisgegas no longer exist, having merged with other communities.

4. McKenna-McBride Commission, *Evidence*, Hearings of 13 July 1915 at New Hazelton, 4–5.

5. BC, Royal Commission on Indian Affairs for the Province of British Columbia, *Report* (Victoria: Acme Press, 1916), 1:177.

6. E. Brian Titley, *A Narrow Vision: Duncan Campbell Scott and the Administration of Indian Affairs in Canada* (Vancouver: University of British Columbia Press, 1986), 145. Titley presents a comprehensive treatment of the actions of the two governments after 1916 (145–61).

7. Ibid., 145.

8. Darcy Mitchell, "The Allied Indian Tribes of British Columbia: A Study in Pressure Group Behaviour" (MA thesis, University of British Columbia, 1977), 42.

9. Ibid., 43.

10. Canada, House of Commons, Special Committees of the Senate and House of Commons ... to Inquire into the Claims of the Allied Indian Tribes of British Columbia ..., *Proceedings, Reports and the Evidence* (Ottawa, King's Printer, 1927), 38 (cited hereafter as Special Committee [1927], *Proceedings*).

11. Allied Tribes, "Statement of the Allied Indian Tribes of British Columbia for the Government of British Columbia [Dec. 1919]." The full text is presented in Special Committee (1927), *Proceedings* 31–38.

12. NAC, RG10, vol. 3820, Scott to Meighen, 9 Jan. 1920, quoted in Darcy Mitchell, "The Allied Indian Tribes," 49. See also Titley, *A Narrow Vision*, 147ff.

13. Titley, *A Narrow Vision*, 49–51.

14. There were two further prohibitions contained in section 140. One was

aimed specifically at the sundance of plains Indians. The other was more general; without the permission of the minister, no Indian in any of the four western provinces could participate "in any show, exhibition, performance, stampede or pageant in aboriginal costume" or "in any Indian dance outside the bounds of his own reserve."

15. Daisy Sewid-Smith, *Prosecution or Persecution* (Campbell River, BC: Nu-Yim-Baleess Society, 1979).

16. Forrest LaViolette, *The Struggle for Survival: Indian Cultures and the Protestant Ethic in British Columbia* (Toronto: University of Toronto Press, 1961), 83ff.

17. The jailings are often mentioned today, even by young Indians.

18. *Amodu Tijani v. Secretary, Southern Nigeria* (1921), 2 AC, 409–10, quoted in *Calder v. Attorney-General of BC* (1973), 34 *Dominion Law Reports* (3d) [1973], 208 [Supreme Court of Canada].

19. Edwin May, "The Nishga Land Claim, 1873–1973" (MA thesis, Simon Fraser University, 1979), 110.

20. Special Committee (1927), *Proceedings*, 225–56. The compilation is BC, *Papers Connected with the Indian Land Question, 1850–1875* (Victoria: Government Printer, 1875) (cited hereafter as BC, *Papers*).

21. Special Committee (1927), *Proceedings*, 175–76. Cf. Titley, *A Narrow Vision*, 151.

22. Special Committee (1927), *Proceedings*, 175–76.

23. Teit was ill at this time; he died in Oct. 1922. Kathleen Mooney, "James Alexander Teit," *Canadian Encyclopedia*, 2nd ed. (Edmonton: Hurtig, 1988), 2121.

24. Special Committee (1927), *Proceedings*, 176.

25. Ibid.

26. Cf. Mitchell, "The Allied Indian Tribes," 64ff.

27. Special Committee (1927), *Proceedings*, 175–76. The numerous misspellings of both personal and place names as well as several errors in linking persons with places suggest that the list presented by Paull to the Special Committee in 1927 was not an original list filled out at the time of the meeting or by those who actually attended.

28. Titley, *A Narrow Vision*, 148.

29. Fifty years later both governments did agree that the cut-offs had been unjust, and arrangements were made to return the lands or to compensate the Indians for them.

30. House of Commons, *Debates*, 9 Feb. 1927, 174, quoted in Mitchell, "The Allied Indian Tribes," 80–81.

31. Ibid., 8 March 1927, 985, quoted in Mitchell, "The Allied Indian Tribes," 82.

32. Titley, *A Narrow Vision*, 154.

33. Cf. above.

34. Special Committee (1927), *Proceedings*, 2.

35. Ibid., 4.

36. Ibid., 12–13. In fact, as Kelly soon confirmed to the committee, the Allied Tribes had avoided presenting any dollar figure and continued to insist that any monetary aspect of settlement would be modest.

37. Ibid., 187.

38. Ibid., 146.

39. Ibid., 153–69.

40. Ibid., 160.

41. Ibid., 15.

42. Ibid., 155, 184.

43. Ibid., 161.

44. Ibid., 223.

45. Ibid., 225.

46. BC, *Papers*.

47. Special Committee (1927), *Proceedings*, 225–26. There is some suggestion in the committee discussion that O'Meara had been able to examine

the *Papers* in the Parliamentary library before they were borrowed or removed.

48. Ibid., 141ff.

49. Ibid., 160.

50. Ibid., viii.

51. Ibid.

52. Ibid.

53. Ibid.

54. Ibid., 6.

55. Ibid., viii.

56. Ibid., 6.

57. Ibid., viii–ix.

58. Ibid., ix–xi.

59. These were arguments advanced by the province in the 1960s as it sought to defend its denial of title.

60. Ibid., xviii.

61. Titley, *A Narrow Vision*, 59.

62. Organizations relying on white support were not affected but Scott and Stewart had no worries that such support would be significant. O'Meara did appear to be continuing to raise funds among the Nisga'a, and Scott considered prosecuting him, but his death in 1928 ended any concern in Ottawa (Titley, *A Narrow Vision*, 157). The amendment was not restricted to land claims. Except with the minister's approval, no chief or band council could now use funds contributed by band members to pursue claims of the everyday sort that might arise against persons harming band property, persons doing business with the band, or the department itself.

63. I base this observation upon the responses of white lawyers and government officials whom I interviewed or discussed the matter with during the 1980s.

64. Daniel Raunet, relying on his Nisga'a informants, writes that "There was a time, before the fifties, when the mere mention of the land issue was unlawful." Daniel Raunet, *Without Surrender Without Consent: A History of the Nishga Land Claims* (Vancouver: Douglas & McIntyre, 1984), 15. In 1988 the editor of *Kahtou* wrote that "the federal government passed legislation prohibiting the right for chiefs to gather for the discussion of the settlement of land issues in BC" (7 Nov. 1988).

JUSTA: A FIRST NATIONS LEADER
(DAKELHNE BUTSOWHUDILHZULH'UN) ◇

BRIDGET MORAN

◯

So there I was in September of 1956, nearly fourteen years old and on the run from the RCMP and the priests because I didn't want to go back to Lejac. When the hunt for me was finally over and there was no danger that I would be taken back to the school, I returned to my parents in Camp 24. I found a change in my dad. Before I started school he wanted me to stay home with him but now, four years later, he thought I should go back and finish my education. He talked and talked to me, but my mind was made up. Finally he said, "Well, if you're man enough to quit school, you're man enough to work."

With that my parents started back to Nakalat Lodge at the end of North Arm where Dad was working. They left me a little package of rice—I don't think it weighed a pound.

Although my parents were gone I wasn't really alone. I had my two brothers with me in Camp 24 and many relatives and friends. Maybe it was my parents' training or the discipline I had at Lejac, or a combination of both, but it never occurred to me to bum around or to steal. I knew that in order to live I had to work. Fortunately for me there were many mills operating in and around The Fort in those days. Today everything is computerized and you need your high school to get any kind of work, but back in the fifties and sixties a millworker never needed to be out of a job. You quit work one day and the next day, you were hired on somewhere else. So finding a job was easy, but the fact that I was underage was a problem. I needed someone over twenty-one to sign for me. I was lucky—I had two brothers, John and Teddy, and both were working. They signed for me and before I

◇ (Vancouver: Arsenal Pulp Press, 1994), 58–73, 116–123. Reprinted with permission.

knew it I had a job at the Fort St. James sawmill where they worked. My first job in the mill was a tough one, and dangerous too—I was working on the jack ladder where the logs are sent up to be cut—but the main thing was that I had work.

I remember the day I got my first pay-cheque. I went to the store and bought everything I needed for life in Camp 24. At last, I thought, I'm making it—I've got a job, a place to live, and I'm paying my own way.

o

For the next seven years I worked in mills in and around The Fort, and I worked hard, winter and summer. Mostly I lived in Camp 24, but I spent as much time as I could in the village of Tachie. My parents had moved across the lake from Portage in 1954 because by then most of my brothers and sisters had married and were raising families in Tachie village. Mom and Dad wanted to be where they could watch their grandchildren grow up.

In those seven years I tried just once to break away from mill work. I had always wanted to join the RCMP but when I realized I didn't have the education, the next best thing seemed to be the army. In 1962 I rode the bus to Vancouver with two of my friends with the intention of joining the army. One of my friends made it, but I was rejected along with my other friend, who later became my brother-in-law. He was deaf in one ear, and I was rejected because of the old knee trouble that had put me in a cast for nearly a year in Lejac. So much for joining the army. Back I went to The Fort and to mill work.

When I first worked in mills in and around The Fort, I had no thoughts about the future. I was young and I had many friends and relatives in my life in those years. My brother Teddy was the person who was closest to me. He was only two years older than me and had been with me in Lejac, and because we were about the same build and looked alike, strangers often thought we were twins. Teddy was a lot like me; in Lejac he liked sports, and when he got into the work force, he was a hard worker. He played just as hard too. He had a sense of humour like mine, he was a big tease and along with that, he liked to help others and was always really concerned about what happened to people. And we were alike in one other way—we both got into booze when we were still in our teens.

I modelled myself on my brothers and my friends—like them I was a hard worker and I played just as hard. I was young and tough, but work was never enough to burn all the energy that was stored up in me. Parties, music, girls—lots of girls and lots of beds—and eventually booze took care of the energy left over from my work in the mills.

Those years in the 1950s when I started working marked the final years when the Indian Act prohibited First Nations people from buying or drinking alcohol. In 1960 the Act was changed to allow us to consume alcohol and in 1961 we were allowed to vote on whether or not alcohol would be permitted on individual reserves. Portage, Tachie, and the Necoslie Reserve in Fort St. James voted 'yes,' which meant that now we could walk into a liquor store and buy what we liked. Before that time there was only home brew or liquor bought illegally for us by our non-Native friends. I had tried home brew a time or two but it made me sick. When we were in Lejac my friends and I sometimes sneaked into the chapel and drank Mass wine. It was very weak but if we drank enough of it we got high. Then we added water in the bottle so we wouldn't get caught. Until I was seventeen, apart from those times in Lejac, I had never tasted wine, beer or whiskey from a liquor store. But my brothers and my friends were all hard drinkers and it was almost a foregone conclusion that before I was eighteen years old, I would be one of the gang.

I've heard some of my people say that they started drinking because that made them feel they were as good as the white man. I never felt that way. I was always proud to be a member of the Carrier Nation and, apart from Lejac where our language and our way of life were treated like something inferior, I never felt that I was in a situation where I was discriminated against because of my Native heritage. Before I went back to my village to work in 1971, I always worked in the white world and I didn't have any problems with the white people who worked with me. I knew that my people had been and still were treated like second-class citizens—I would have had to be deaf and blind and dumb not to know that—but in those days I didn't think I could do anything to change it so I left it alone.

I drank because, to begin with, before the blackouts started, it was fun. It was party time. Early in my drinking days it was also illegal and that might have added something to the enjoyment. One time before the Indian Act was changed, when I was seventeen and still not drinking, I was with a group of friends in the bush. A white man we worked with bought a bottle of wine and the party was going strong when two RCMP officers walked into the middle of our circle in the bush. "Holy Christ!" said one of my friends, and he threw the bottle of wine away as fast as he could. The goldarn thing hit a tree and it bounced right back into the middle of our circle. Of course we were all hauled off to jail, me included, even though I hadn't been drinking.

That was only one of many times when I spent a night in jail. In time it became a pretty regular thing—working all week, living from pay-cheque to pay-cheque, never going near a bank to open an account or anything sensible like that, drinking and partying and fooling around with girls all weekend and then ending up in jail with Teddy and John, without any idea of what I had done or why I was there. On Monday mornings either the boss of the mill where I was working or one of the storekeepers, L.R. Dickinson, or the manager of Hudson's Bay, who knew me and knew that my dad was good for repayment, would come up with the $14.50 fine (it was either that or spend ten days in jail) and back I'd go to work, feeling like hell with a terrible hangover.

There were times when Teddy and I and some of our friends went to jail almost every weekend. I was usually picked up for fighting. When I was sober I was like my brothers John and Teddy—we never looked for a fight.

Apart from Father Allison who tried to sell me a Bible and Sister Alphonse who caught me kissing a girl, I never fought with anyone in Lejac. It wasn't in my nature in those days. I think alcohol was never meant for me—it seemed to give me false courage and a temper that I didn't have except when I was drinking. At a certain point in my partying I'd drop anyone for anything—a wrong word and pow! There's hardly a knuckle in my hands that isn't broken, a reminder of the hundreds of weekends and fights and blackouts and hangovers and waking up in jail cells wondering, "Where in heck am I?"

Of course we did more than party and fight and drink. My brothers and I worked hard at hard jobs. We stayed as close to our parents as we could and we still followed our traditional way of life, hunting and fishing and trapping, in between everything else. But it was the drinking, and for Teddy and me, what went with it—women, fights, jail, wasting money— that worried my mother and dad. They tried to reason with us, to warn us. "Something terrible is going to happen if you don't leave that booze alone," they said to us month after month, year after year. We didn't listen. It was as if we were on a treadmill and we didn't know how to stop it—we didn't even know if we wanted to stop it. Did I think I was having a good time? I don't know—maybe at the beginning of every party, but there was no fun in having blackouts and waking up in jail wondering, "Where am I? What have I done this time?" and seeing my dad's face as he bailed Teddy and John and me out one more time.

o

In July of 1963, when I was twenty-one years old, I left sawmill work and joined my dad at Nakalat Lodge at the end of North Arm. He had been employed there since it was first built as a hunting and fishing lodge by Mr. McKelvey in 1946.

Nakalat Lodge—what a role it has played in the life of our family! For sixteen years my dad worked there for part of every year. My brothers and sisters worked there, and I worked there for years after I quit mill work. Very often when my dad was there our whole family would join him, if not right at the lodge, then in our cabin just across the bay from Nakalat. Nakalat Lodge is on the edge of our hunting and fishing territory and our trapline, so at the same time that some of us were working at the lodge, we were also able to live off the land. That was very important to our family life.

To this day there is no road into the lodge; it is reached only by plane or boat. Nowadays from miles away as you approach the end of the North Arm by boat, you begin to see a blur on the horizon that is separate from trees and water. As you move closer, you see a dock, and in a semi-circle that hugs the bay, there are cabins, rusty brown in colour, that are as welcoming and snug as they look.

There was a time before 1946 when the approach was different, when waves broke against the shore and only the forest was to be seen. My family had a lot to do with clearing the bay, building the dock and putting up the main lodge and the cabins. Dad worked at both Nakalat Lodge and Douglas Lodge just outside of Fort St. James. In those years he was a guide, carpenter and labourer. When I joined him in the summer of 1963 at Nakalat, I followed in his footsteps. In the summer I was a guide, carpenter and labourer. When I joined him in the summer of 1963 at Nakalat, I followed in his footsteps. In the summer I was a guide for fishermen, in the fall I guided the hunters, and in the winter I looked after the grounds, built and maintained the cabins, and worked on the water system.

For years the manager was Mr. Wooten who now lives in Wyoming and still comes up to Nakalat in the summer. He was like a second father to me. Whether I worked at the lodge for a few months or all the year round, he paid me wages for twelve months. We did everything together, and between him and my dad, I learned a lot about construction and carpentry.

One summer I remember Mr. Wooten, his son Chuck, and I knocked down a cabin Dad had built years before. We kept the logs and rebuilt it and in the process, we decided to build a fireplace. John, Teddy, and Louis Murdock helped.

"Do any of you know how to build a fireplace?" Mr. Wooten asked us. We shook our heads.

"Well," he said "someone gave me a plan for a fireplace that might help us. We'll follow it and see what happens."

We did that—step by step we followed Mr. Wooten's print. That stone fireplace is still there, still throwing out heat on a cold winter's day.

I spent several winters alone in Nakalat Lodge as a caretaker, keeping myself busy with carpentry, working inside the cabins, and on the grounds. Those were good times. In the summer everyone was busy—all day and into the night there were the sounds of people arriving and leaving. In the long days of summer and early fall, Mr. Wooten and his wife were at the lodge, girls were working in the kitchen, and there were guides and tourist and planes and boats making Nakalat a hive of activity. In the winter, though, it was different. Only the sounds of the wind cracking bare branches in the frosty air and the birds who stayed with me all through the cold months broke the silence. I loved listening to the sounds of the wolves on the lake. Whenever I had free time I would hunt and trap, and everyday I was learning more about the land and its creatures.

○

The time alone never seemed long to me, but about the time when supplies were running low or I was beginning to long for a little company, I'd hear someone call out in the winter night, "Justa! Justa! Are you there?" It would be my dad, who worried about me when I was alone, or one of my brothers or friends like Moise Alexis, Walter, or Victor Joseph. I had booze with me in the winters in Nakalat, but the drinking never seemed to be as important or as much a part of my life at the lodge as it became when I was in Tachie or The Fort. I was never alone for more than a month without someone appearing, but when spring came, travelling on the ice was unpredictable, and then I would begin to wonder if I was ever going to leave. If it was a late spring, the ice wouldn't go out until late May or early June and that would mean I didn't see the bright lights of The Fort or Vanderhoof until the middle of June.

In those years I would come out of Nakalat in the spring after months by myself, or in the fall after a summer of guiding, and I would start the partying and the drinking again as if there had been no break for work or the peace of winter. And by now something else had come into my life—my parents started pushing me to marry. They wanted to follow the old ways and choose a wife for me, but I was having none of that. I told them I would do my own picking! And so I did. I had lots of girlfriends. But towards the end of those years, in 1965, 1966, 1967, almost without me realizing it, one woman began to stand out from the many women I danced and partied with—Theresa Pierre, from the village of Tachie. She was married, fourteen years older than me, and the mother of several children.

ɔ

I believe that all of my girlfriends, Theresa, the woman I married in 1973, had the toughest life.

She was born October 17, 1929, in the Carrier village of Grand Rapids, two-thirds of the way along the Tachie River towards Trembleur Lake. She was one of about twelve children born to her parents, Cecile and William Austin. William had a sister and brother-in-law, Agnes and August Mattess, who had no children, so Theresa was given to them to raise as their own child when she was a baby. This sharing of children was not unusual in our culture, but what was unusual was that for a long time Theresa wasn't told that the Austin boys and girls she knew and sometimes stayed with were really her brothers and sisters.

"I remember," Theresa told me, "sitting beside my foster mother one time when she was sewing. In my language I asked her how come she doesn't have babies like other women. I told her that I wouldn't mind to have a sister to play with. She told me that she couldn't have any babies, but I didn't really understand what she meant. She didn't explain that I wasn't her true daughter."

It was only when Theresa was in her early teens that a sister of hers, Mary Austin, told her the truth about her parents. They were playing together when Mary said to her, "Did you know you are my sister?"

"How can that be?" Theresa asked her. "My parents are over there," she said, pointing to the Mattess house.

"No," said Mary, "you're my mom and dad's daughter."

Then Theresa was really confused because she still didn't understand and there was no one she could ask.

Theresa says that she was very lonely as a child. Her foster parents didn't want her to go to school; they wanted to keep her at home and teach her their way of life and the Carrier culture. So instead of playing with toys, she would sit in the smokehouse with Agnes Mattess, and while watching what she was doing with the fish, she would take a little piece of skin or fish, and would try to do the same thing. And when her foster mother was making moccasins or baskets, Theresa sat beside her and watched her and soon she could make moccasins and baskets too.

The Mattesses moved from Grand Rapids to Tachie when Theresa was very young, but they still returned to their old home in the springtime for several weeks to trap beaver. Her foster parents also had a cabin across the lake from Tachie and they took the boat there every fall to fish and hunt. Theresa was with them when they went into the bush, no matter how long the walk. "It was really tiresome," she says, "but I couldn't stay in the cabin by myself. We stayed away from Tachie in the cabin for a few weeks. When the lake was calm and it wasn't windy, we would go across the lake, pick up what we needed in Tachie, and go back and camp out again until freeze-up."

When Theresa was twelve years old her parents were pressured by Indian Affairs and the priest into letting her go to Lejac. "I was really scared," she says. "I didn't understand the sisters when they talked to me because I didn't know how to speak English. When I spoke my own language they got mad at me, but they never touched me."

She was in Lejac for just over two months when tests showed that she had tuberculosis. "It was November," she told our daughter Sharon, "and it was cold and the girls had to go outside and dig up turnips and carrots in the garden. I was really cold and that night I started coughing up blood. A cousin of mine told Sister Catherine, who was really old and cranky, that I was spitting blood. Sister was mad at me for getting sick and told me to go to the laundry and help the other girls wash clothes. I was still coughing and bringing up blood. Another cousin took me to sister Catherine who got mad at me again, but she let me go to bed. I cried and cried—I was homesick for my mom and dad and I was scared and I couldn't speak the language to find out if I was going to die. The working girls brought me tea and soup and in about a week I was up again. Then someone came and took x-rays and that's when they found out I had TB."

She and two other girls from Lejac who also had tuberculosis went by train to the Coqualeetza Hospital in Sardis near Hope. She felt really lost then. She didn't know where she was and because of language nobody told her anything. "I just cried," she says. "I didn't even feel like eating. I didn't know what I was there for." A teacher came every day and taught her English and she learned to read and write. Then the doctors and nurses could explain her disease to her. "They were nice," she says.

After a year and a half the hospital said she was cured and she went back to Lejac. She was glad to return to school. By then she was older and she could speak and understand English, so life there wasn't so tough for her.

⊃

When Theresa was sixteen she came back to Tachie. Her education was finished; Lejac didn't keep students when they reached sixteen years of age. She had been away from home for almost four years and in all that time, she did not see the people she regarded as her mother and dad.

Once she was back in her home village, like many of the young people in Tachie, she found her parents very strict, even more strict than most of our parents were. When she was eighteen and their strictness got too much for her, she married a man from Tachie who was seven years older than Theresa. "I thought he was a nice guy," she says, "but I soon found out different. I married him mostly to get away from the strictness at home but I found I was worse off afterwards. Whenever he had money he drank, and then he would beat me. He never touched the kids—they were scared of him—but he used to buy home brew and that and other booze made him crazy. He beat on me all the time."

Theresa complained to the police, but they didn't do much to help her and her kids. One time, though, they did come through when she needed them. Her husband had beaten her unconscious and her foster parents put her in a boat to take her to The Fort. Halfway there a police boat caught up with them and took her the rest of the way. She was in the Vanderhoof Hospital for nearly two weeks. Her husband went to jail for it, but before long he was out and carrying on the same as before.

By 1956, when Theresa had five children, Kenny, Rita, Irene, William and Ruby, she woke upon morning and couldn't move—she said it felt like there was something tight around her chest. Tests showed that the disease had come back. She went to Miller Bay Hospital near Prince Rupert. For nearly two years she was treated there and in Coqualeetza. Then in July 1957 she had an operation to remove one lung. The operation was successful; the tuberculosis has never come back, but the surgery left her frail and thin.

Theresa left the hospital and returned to Tachie and her children who had been cared for by relatives when she was away. Her husband was still drinking and beating on her—between him and TB it's a wonder she lived to talk about it. The end came one day not long after she came back to Tachie. He was beating her, a cousin heard her screaming and he and a friend tried to get in the house to help her. Her husband heard them at the door and grabbed a gun. He fired the gun and killed the cousin, who was only twenty-two years old at the time.

"When he got out of jail he wanted me and the kids to leave Tachie and come to him," says Theresa, "but I refused. He was still drinking and I thought that sooner or later he would kill me and I knew the kids wouldn't have a chance if I was dead."

ɔ

When her husband was out of her life for good, Theresa and her kids survived on welfare. "The welfare was building me a house in Tachie, just boards, not like the houses today," she says. "They deducted half my welfare to pay for the house so my monthly cheque was only eighty-six dollars for me and my kids. It was a really hard time. To try to make some extra money I used to go out in the bush with my cousins, trap and work with the skins." One thing about Agnes and August Mattess—they might have been too strict, but they taught Theresa the Carrier ways when she was growing up and in those days when she was stronger, she could just about live off the land if she had to.

Theresa says that it was sometime during those hard years when she first noticed me. She was sitting outside on the porch of her mother-in-law's house in Tachie when she saw me walking towards the hall. I was going to a dance. "I thought he looked cute," Theresa tells people. "I had never talked to him or met him, but I thought someday I might get to know him."

We finally met sometime in the early sixties. I used to play the accordion and at a few of the parties Theresa would be there with her relatives and they would coax me to give them some music. It's at those parties I first remember seeing her. I was a real womanizer and Theresa was just one of my many girlfriends for a long time. Then one night when I was walking home from a party, she followed me and she said, "Look, I want to talk to you." She told me then that she was very serious about me, and for some reason that made me think more about her.

I began to spend more time with her. In 1965 and 1966, I was working at Nakalat Lodge. When I came home to Tachie in the spring and the fall, sometimes I would stay with my parents and sometimes I would stay with Theresa or some other girl. By the beginning of 1967 I was spending more and more time with Theresa. My parents didn't approve of her. They didn't like the fact that she was married, fourteen years older than me, and had several children. I didn't listen to them. I wasn't committed to Theresa at that time but I knew that she cared about me and besides, I wasn't going to let my parents choose my girlfriends or my wife for me.

By the first day of October 1967 Theresa was pregnant and due to have my baby at any moment. That day I was back in Tachie from Nakalat Lodge after the summer's work. I was twenty-four years old and I felt pretty good about everything when I got up that morning in Theresa's house. We talked about how she was feeling and then I said, "I'm going over to Mom and Dad's for a few minutes. I haven't seen them since I got back."

I wasn't thinking about the future as I covered the short distance between the houses—I don't suppose I was thinking about anything much at all. But the future was waiting for me; that short walk changed my life forever.

o

On a reserve as isolated and needy as Tachie, the job of band manager was a tough one, especially in the early and mid-1970s.

My biggest struggle was to get the members what they needed and at the same time keep spending within the budget we were given by Indian Affairs. If we ran a deficit the band was declared insolvent; Indian Affairs would give us hell and one way or the other they would recover the money. Everybody came to the band manager with their needs. There were many times when I had to refuse my own people something they badly needed— repairs to their houses, a cookstove or heater, tools, a motor. If the band members didn't know government policies and didn't get what they asked for, they would take it out on me. They knew that we got money from the government. They figured it was their money and sometimes it was impossible to convince them that there were hundreds of guidelines attached to every penny that came on to the reserve and that I had to follow those guidelines or the reserve would be in trouble.

I lived among my people, I knew them and yet I couldn't fulfill their needs, either because of a shortage of funds or a policy laid down in Ottawa. Sometimes when I had to say "No," or "Wait," or "I'll try but I don't think we have a hope in hell," I would be threatened. I had guns pulled on me and knives and axes thrown at me, but these threats were never the hardest part of the job. One way or another I knew my people and I could handle whatever came at me from them.

What took up my time, frustrated me, and by the 1980s almost drove me to suicide was trying to work around the bureaucracy in the Department of Indian Affairs. I often wondered if part of their job training was a course in delaying tactics. It was like pulling teeth to get the smallest thing out of their officials.

I only have to think back on our fight to have a water and sewer system installed in Tachie village to remember the frustration and anger I felt year after year when Indian Affairs bureaucrats put the chief, the councillors and me through the hoops. When I think about water and sewage, I think about endless meetings. We never got anything on the spur of the moment on our reserve. Years and years of our time, our energy, were used up in meeting after meeting after meeting.

The need for water and sewage systems had been documented by previous chiefs and councillors, but when we approached the Department of Indian Affairs in 1973 and 1974, once again we had to prove need. We had to show that village water and the outhouses were affecting our people. In the summer the outdoor toilets filled up with flies and in the spring the runoff in the drinking water made everybody in the village sick. We had to tell Indian Affairs every goldarn thing that was happening in our personal lives, down to how many times we ran to the toilet. Year after year we had to keep repeating that we were losing our band members to sickness, that the little kids had sores around their mouths, stomach upsets, and diarrhea. The public health nurses only had to look at the flies in the outdoor toilets on a hot summer day or to test the water we were drinking, especially in the springtime, to know where the infections were coming from.

It's not easy to get what you need on a reservation.

It took years of meetings to convince Indian Affairs that there was a health problem, a serious health problem, in Tachie. Month after month, year after year, the facts were presented to the government, health officials flew into the reserve and made inspections and conducted tests, reports were written, letters were sent off, replies were received, and still we had the overflowing toilets and the flies, the drinking water full of germs—and then another round of meetings and reports and letters would start up as if nothing had ever been said or written before.

I'd sit in the little ten-by-twelve band office after another letter or another meeting and God knows how many swear words I would use in every sentence I spoke—I would be so frustrated that it took all my control not to scream. The worst meetings, the ones that really drove me right up the wall, were the ones when Indian Affairs officials from Vancouver attended. They held the purse strings, so while we had them with us we would try to squeeze something out of them. The whole time we were trying to get answers to our questions they were watching the clock. "Hey," they would say, "we can't miss our flight, our plane leaves in an hour." They didn't give a hell, all they worried about was catching that goddamn flight. We couldn't afford to meet them in Vancouver, and so we were at the mercy of their timetable. It would have been easier if we could have dealt with department officials in the Prince George office, but when big expenditures were discussed we had to work through the regional bureaucrats in Vancouver. Compared to them the people in the Prince George office were just flunkies—we called them mopboys.

Finally after what seemed like a thousand meetings, Indian Affairs came to the conclusion that, "Yes, Tachie village does have some very. serious health problems which appear to be connected to the lack of proper water and sewage system."

Now the real tough part began—we started to negotiate about dollars. When anything was going to cost money we found ourselves having to suck up to department officials—we sucked up to get the agreement for a water system in the first place, we sucked up to get them to agree to some kind of a dollar figure, we sucked up to get them to raise the ante when we found the funds released were not enough to do the job adequately. Suck! That's what half the meetings were about.

As band manager, once the project began, I watched over the day-by-day progress from start to finish. Along with the chief and sometimes one or two of the councillors, I contacted engineers to design the systems. Then we had to get an estimate to cover the cost. Finally came the signing of the agreement between the band and the regional office in Vancouver. I kept a close watch on the actual work to make sure that the contractors didn't take any shortcuts, since outside contractors sometimes tried to cut a few corners. One contractor was laying pipes and his backhoe man, an honest guy, a non-Indian, came up to me and said quietly, "Justa, you're going to have to live with this for a long time and these guys are not doing it right." He showed me how the pipes were being laid without sand or bedding of any kind. I made them dig up the whole line they had completed and redo it.

Installing the systems was more complicated because we needed two—one for Old Tachie and one for Sunnyside—as there are two miles between the communities. And it wasn't long before the water systems in both communities broke down. I wasn't surprised. Indian Affairs took every cut they could find to keep costs down. They had no long-term vision; as long as they could save a penny here, a dollar there, they didn't give a heck about the future. In the old village the well went dry within a couple of years because too many people used it. In Sunnyside, as houses kept going up, the well eventually went dry too—an increase in population was not taken into account when the systems were designed. Finally we abandoned the wells and water was piped in from Stuart Lake. Then we had all the water we needed and to this day it's the best water in Canada. It is tested regularly to make sure it is kept that way.

o

Installation of the water and sewage systems in Tachie was the toughest and most time-consuming undertaking of my early years as a band manager, and what made it tougher was that other changes were going on at the same time.

The band members were pushing for many things—electricity, television, a new school, improvements in the roads inside the village and in the highway to The Fort. We had nothing; we needed everything. As time passed and the people of Tachie Reserve had more contact with the modern world beyond their villages, they wanted a share in what they believe was the good life. I was right in there with them—I was tired of coal oil lamps. I wanted to watch hockey games on TV and I was sick of my truck sliding down Pinchi Hill sideways in the fall and spring when the mud was a foot deep. All around us in Fort St. James and Vanderhoof and Burns Lake, people took for granted the very things we were still begging for. "For God's sake," we said to Indian Affairs and to anyone else in authority who would listen to us, "we're into the 1970s and our wives and mothers are still lighting lamps and washing clothes by hand."

When I took over as band manager, change was in the air. Many of our people, especially the young, were ready to throw out whatever was old and traditional and replace it with the new, the modern. I never saw this attitude in action more clearly than in 1972 when electricity finally came to Tachie Village. How the people celebrated when the lights came on and there was an end to lamps and lanterns and gas fixtures and coal oil!

As soon as we had power I drove around the village with a truck to collect what was thrown out so that the ground wouldn't be littered with discarded lamps. I couldn't believe what people threw away—old lamps, new lamps, and everything in between. There was no feeling for history or for the fact these same lamps had served the village in the old days. Everything went into my truck—I could almost hear people saying, "Good riddance!" as they flung away a lantern or a gas lamp that had served their grandparents for years.

My dad refused to throw away his lamps. He said, "You know that what you've got is not going to last forever. Someday it will break down and then where will we be for lights?" Nobody paid any attention to him. What the heck, they thought, we've got power and we'll never need these old lamps again! Of course, Dad was right—the first big storm dropped trees on to power lines and suddenly the village was in darkness again. I kept some of the newer lamps that had been thrown away and when there was this first power outrage, I had a light shining out of my windows; it was almost the only light in Tachie. I got a kick out of that.

And then there was the telephone.

When I was hired as band manager our only connection with the outside world was a radio telephone. I was determined to improve communications. Over the years we had lost too many of our people when we couldn't get a call through to the RCMP or to a doctor. Almost the first thing I said to the chief and councillors when I was made band manager was, "I'm going to darn well get a telephone system into Tachie!"

"You'll never do it!" they said. "You'll see—the telephone company won't go for it."

"Watch me! What's going to stop me?" I asked them.

I went to B.C. Telephone and asked what was needed to bring the phone system into our village.

"You need a population of five hundred people or more," I was told.

I went back to Tachie and did my homework. I counted everything that had two legs and was moving. I drew a map for the company showing every household in Tachie and the number of people in each house. Housing was in short supply, but not people. I came up with a count of seven hundred; that was all that was needed. A telephone system was installed and it was goodbye to the old radio telephone.

Next I was ready to try for television. Once again people said to me, "You're crazy. You're just the band manager. How the hell are you going to do it?" and once again I said, "Watch me!"

I talked to a number of non-Indians in Fort St. James who were in the television field. From there I prepared a request to The First Citizens Fund asking for money to purchase the necessary equipment. We were granted enough money to buy what was needed. With the help of technical people in The Fort we set up our equipment on Murray Ridge near Fort St. James and before long BCTV was beamed into our village.

o

The water and sewage systems were a real necessity for the health of our people and I've always been proud I helped to get them. The frustration, the endless meetings and the sucking up to Indian Affairs bosses were worth it, because the systems made all the difference between life and death in our village.

I wish I could feel the same about my part in getting telephone services and television into Tachie. To me they are like the road that links us with Fort St. James—mixed blessings. I often wonder if what we gained makes up for what we lost when we went modern, because I know we lost many things. Now with the telephone one person calls another person who has a telephone and they talk. The visiting between households that we used to have, the group discussions, these are gone from our village forever. We have improved communication with the outside world, but we don't communicate with each other as we used to before the telephone was in every house. Our television sets entertain us in our own homes, so we sit in front of the tube instead of calling on our neighbours. The feeling of community is gone.

Tachie was such a beautiful place before we tried to catch up with the rest of the world. Then people got together to help one another and to work and visit and discuss. Sometimes I'm not very proud that I'm partly to blame for that beautiful place being so changed that it's almost not there anymore.

MARKETING THE IMAGINARY INDIAN*

DANIEL FRANCIS

o

In 1929, when Buffalo Child Long Lance was living in New York, the B.F. Goodrich Company introduced a new type of canvas running shoe. The "Chief Long Lance Shoe" was modelled on an Indian moccasin and endorsed by Long Lance in an extensive advertising campaign. "In our primitive life, nothing was more important than our feet," Long Lance is quoted as saying in one magazine advertisement. "I wonder if the white race would not be sturdier if they took better care of their feet in childhood—by wearing shoes that allow free exercise of the foot and leg muscles." As part of the publicity for the new sneakers, Goodrich published a booklet, *How to Talk in Indian Sign Language*, featuring photographs of a bare-chested Long Lance, in breechcloth and headband, manipulating his hands.[1]

B.F. Goodrich wished to associate its shoes with speed, strength and durability. There was no better way to do this than to associate them with the Indian, known for his ability to run like the wind for hours at a time. Of course, shoes were not the first products to be marketed with the help of the Indian image. The association of Indians and products was a venerable one, going back at least to the travelling medicine shows of the late eighteenth century, in which potions and elixirs were peddled on the strength of their connection with Indian healing practices. The first decades of the twentieth century saw the appearance of dozens and dozens of products which tried to find favour with consumers by identifying with the Indian: Pocahontas perfume, Red Indian motor oil, Iroquois beer, Squaw Brand canned vegetables—the list goes on and on. For some products, the Indian was used as an all-purpose symbol of Canada. For others the Indian image was used to associate a product with the out-of-doors, or with strength and courage, or with the simple innocence of nature.

⬦ Reprinted with permission from *The Imaginary Indian: The Image of the Indian in Canadian Culture* (Vancouver: Arsenal Pulp Press, 1992), 169–90.

This tradition continued in the naming of sports teams after Indian groups—the Braves, the Redskins, the Indians. It represented an attempt to link the team with the courage, ferocity, strength and agility of the Indian. For the same reasons, audiences at sporting events occasionally utilized the Imaginary Indian. In 1916, for example, students at the University of British Columbia came up with the following chant:

Kitsilano, Capilano, Siwash, Squaw,
Kla-How-ya, Tillicum, Skookum, Wah,
Hiyu Mamook! Muck-a-Muck-a, Zip!
B.C. Varsity. Rip! Rip! Rip!
V-A-R-S-I-T-Y. Varsity.

Later the university adopted the Thunderbird as the name for its athletic teams.[2] More recently, the Atlanta Braves baseball team had an Indian mascot named Chief Noc-a-homa who inhabited a tipi just beyond the outfield fence. When Native groups complained, the team retired the Chief, but during the 1991 World Series, Braves' fans angered aboriginal Americans once again by using fake tomahawks and the so-called "tomahawk chop" to urge on the team.

The irony of seeking victory by invoking the totemic power of a socially oppressed people was apparently not recognized. But a grasp of irony has never been the strong suit of White society when it wishes to appropriate elements of Native culture.

Advertising relies on a simple message to make a point. It deals in stereotypes. Once it began using images of Native people, advertising created a whole new context for the Imaginary Indian. Suddenly images of the Indian were appearing on the pages of mass-circulation magazines, on billboards, on the shelves at the local supermarket. The Imaginary Indian became one of the icons of consumer society. The result was a reduction of aboriginal cultures to a series of slogans, a set of simplistic and patronizing attitudes.

Take, for example, this jingle used by General Motors to promote the Pontiac in 1927:

Heap Big Injun,
Pontiac a warrior brave was he,
One day he met Miss Sleeping Fawn
and fell in love you see,
Now, Sleeping Fawn was up to date,
No birch canoe will do,
You get a car and take me for a riding when you woo,
Pontiac, Pontiac, Heap Big Injun Brave . . .[3]

Many of the images of Indians which appeared in advertisements were intended to be positive. They reveal a widespread admiration for certain qualities which the public associated with "Indianness": bravery, physical prowess, natural virtue. Of course, these were qualities Indians were thought to have possessed in the distant past, before contact with the White Man. Advertisements did not feature Indians in suits or dresses; they did not highlight life on the reserve or on the other side of the tracks. Instead they showed the classic Indian head in feather headdress or the Indian princess in beaded doeskin. Advertising reinforced the belief that the best Indian was the historical Indian. It used the Indian as a symbol to appeal to modern consumers who admired values they associated with pre-industrial society.

○

The marketing of the Imaginary Indian reached its peak not with a product but an experience, the experience of railway travel. More than any other single aspect of White civilization, the railway transformed the world of the Indian, especially in Western Canada. It was the railway which conveyed the hundreds of thousands of new settlers into the West. It was the railway which kept these settlers supplied with everything they needed to establish the new grain economy. And it was the railway which transported the products of the new economy to market. Ironic, then, that the railway should lead the way in marketing the image of the Indian to sell its services to travellers.

The settlement of the West did not happen all at once. The Canadian Pacific Railway was completed in 1885, but the flood of immigrants into the new land did not begin for another decade. Meanwhile, the CPR had to find some way of paying for itself. Tourism was one answer. Cornelius Van Horne, the CPR's first general manager, determined to attract travellers by offering them first-class accommodation on his transcontinental trains.[4] Sleeping cars were fitted out with oversize berths, richly upholstered seats, mahogany and satinwood panelling, polished brass fittings, and bathrooms in every car. Elegant dining cars offered sumptuous meals and imported wines at tables set with white linen and gleaming silver. But comfort was not enough: travellers had to be offered spectacle. And here the CPR capitalized on one of its greatest assets—the magnificent beauty of the western landscape. Company officials recognized that the West could be sold as one great tourist attraction. The Rocky Mountains especially offered travellers some of the most spectacular scenery in the world. "1001 Switzerlands Rolled Into One" was how Van Horne described them.

The railway's publicity department began churning out posters, books and pamphlets extolling the natural wonders of Canada's West. No less an authority than the governor-general, the Marquis of Lorne, was enlisted in the cause. "Nowhere can finer scenery be enjoyed from the window of a car than upon this line," Lorne enthused in an article published by the CPR as its first promotional effort.[5] Some of the country's leading painters and photographers received free passes on the trains to go west and record the scenery. The CPR then used these scenes in its publicity material, or sold them along the route as postcards, viewbooks and individual prints.

At about the same time in the United States, the Santa Fe Railway began using artists to create a marketable image of the American southwest which would appeal to travellers.[6] Several painters concentrated on producing scenes of the Pueblo Indians which were reproduced on the railway company's calendar and distributed all over America. The "Santa Fe Indian" became a well-known symbol of the railway, and of the exotic, picturesque desert southwest. In Canada, on the other hand, artists remained mesmerized by the mountains to the exclusion of anything else. Lucius O'Brien, John Fraser, Thomas Mower Martin and F.M. Bell-Smith were just a few of the members of the "Railway School" of painters who made lush, dramatic portraits of towering peaks. They did not see the same artistic potential in the Indians of the West as their American counterparts did in the Southwest. Photographers, however, tended to pay more attention to the Indian. William Notman, Alexander Henderson, Oliver Buell and scores of less well-known photographers aimed their primitive equipment at the Native villages beside the CPR mainline, capturing images of the Native people going about their daily activities. These photographs sold briskly to passengers wanting mementoes of their trip.[7] At Banff, reported the English writer Douglas Sladen in his account of a cross-Canada train ride in 1894, "you can hire a fly, for all the world like a Brighton fly, with a pair of horses, to drive you over excellent gravelled roads to the Devil's Lake, or to very near the top of the big mountain. The American cockney spends all day driving about in these flies, and all night in buying ten-by-eight photographs."[8] Photographs were reproduced and distributed widely as part of the company's propaganda. In this form, they were the first encounter many eastern Canadians would have with the Indians of the frontier.

Following the example of their southern counterparts, the CPR gradually realized that the Indians were a surefire tourist attraction. "The Indians and the bears were splendid stage properties to have at a station where both the east and west bound trains . . . stop for lunch," remarked Sladen.[9] It was not entirely by accident then, that in 1894, when floods washed out the track, the company sent local guide and outfitter Tom Wilson down to the Stoney reserve at Morley to invite the Indians back to Banff to entertain the marooned travellers. The Indians performed traditional dances and competed in a number of rodeo events for prizes put up by the railway company. The whole affair turned out to be so popular that the CPR and local businesses decided to make Banff Indian Days an annual summer event.[10] The railway sponsored a similar pageant in Desbarats, Ontario, each summer with actors in Native costume performing scenes from a version of Longfellow's popular long poem, "Hiawatha."[11]

Travel on the CPR boomed in the years before World War I. In 1913, fifteen and a half million passengers rode the train. Encouraged by the railway's publicity machine, many of them went west to discover the much-heralded beauty of plains and mountains. Tourists were excited at the possibility of seeing wild Indians in their natural setting from the safety and convenience of a railcar. It was every bit as exotic as visiting the depths of Africa or some distant island in the Pacific.

Reality did not always measure up, however, as the British traveller Edward Roper discovered on his cross-Canada excursion in 1890. Pausing at Maple Creek, Saskatchewan, Roper observed a group of Blackfoot lingering around the railway station. "Many of them were partly civilized in dress, though ragged and dirty, and there was very little of the picturesque about them. Some few had good faces, but the ideal Red Man was not there." Later, at Gleichen, Alberta, Roper was pleased to have a chance to see some less "civilized" Natives, who impressed him with their paint and feathers and decorated clothing. These were much closer to the wild Indians of his imagination and he admired their animated good looks and clean appearance. Roper enjoyed throwing coins and oranges from the back of the train to watch young Natives scramble in the dust for them.[12] In B.C., he was surprised to find Indians occupying prominent places in White society. "I conclude that there must be something really good in a race which can, if only here and there, produce such specimens." However, he was impressed mainly by the indifference with which Canadians seemed to view the Indians. "The Canadians," he told his readers, "seemed to regard them as a race of animals which were neither benefit nor harm to anyone, mentioning that they were surely dying out, and that when they were all gone it would be a good thing."[13] Of course, the fact that the Indians were vanishing added an urgency to the tourists' quest for novelty. If they didn't see them soon, they might never see them.

o

Once the West was settled, the Indians lost some of their appeal as advertising devices. Western Canada was no longer promoted as a wild frontier. Tourists came west for the scenery and the hiking and the skiing, not to see the primitive Red Man. Still, there remained among travellers a fascination with Indians and their exotic culture and railways continued to capitalize on it whenever they could. One such opportunity arose in the 1920s in northern British Columbia.

For several decades, collectors had been stripping coastal villages of native artifacts and selling them to museums around the word. Most highly prized were the giant totem poles which over time had come to symbolize the people of the Northwest Coast. By 1920, hardly any of the huge monuments remained in their village settings, and those that did were in a sorry state of natural decay. A large cache of about seventy poles stood in the Indian villages along the Skeena River. During World War I, the construction of the Grand Trunk Pacific Railway through the river valley to Prince Rupert placed these villages right on the mainline of a transcontinental railway. As a result, the poles became a major tourist attraction. One Montreal newspaper calculated that they were the most photographed spot in Canada after Niagara Falls.[14]

Canadian National Railways, the publicly-owned corporation which took over the Grand Trunk after the war, recognized the value of the poles and took a leading role in their preservation, along with the Indian Department, the Parks Branch and the Victoria Memorial Museum in Ottawa. The expense of the project was justified mainly as a stimulus to tourism and therefore to the business of the CNR, though several of the officials involved were serious ethnologists who had more scientific reasons for preserving the poles. The Skeena Valley line was advertised as the railway to totem-pole land and thought was given to the creation of a major tourist resort. The initiative for the project came from government and railway officials, not the local Gitksan people who owned the poles. The Natives were not very interested in marketing their culture for tourists, and some of their chiefs asked the government to stop meddling with the poles. Harlan Smith, an official with the museum, reported that the Gitksan asked why a government which a few years earlier had banned the erection of new poles now wanted to preserve old ones. The Natives believed that their monuments were being used to put rail fares into the pockets of the CNR and wondered why they should co-operate. When the project finished in 1930, only about one-third of the Skeena Valley poles were restored. Still, the result was a benefit to the railway which highlighted the totems in its publicity material.

During the summer of 1926, the artists A.Y. Jackson and Edwin Holgate visited the Skeena to sketch the poles and the Native villages. Both men believed they were witnessing the remains of a culture in decline. Jackson later wrote that "the big powerful tribes . . . have dwindled to a mere shadow of their former greatness."[15] Wanting to take advantage of public interest in the poles, and in West Coast Natives generally, the CNR installed a "Totem Pole Room" for dining and dancing in the Chateau Laurier, its hotel in Ottawa, and commissioned Holgate to design it. The finished product, which opened in 1929, featured columns done up to resemble totem poles, large murals, and Native masks and designs festooning the walls.[16]

The marketing of the Skeena Valley poles as a tourist attraction by the CNR was part of a curious phenomenon—the appropriation of the totem pole as an unofficial symbol of British Columbia. The trend began in the 1920s, when various public bodies became alarmed at the rapid disappearance of poles from Native villages into the hands of museums and collectors, mainly outside Canada. As the number of poles dwindled, their value as works of art rose in public estimation. White British Columbians, and Canadians generally, decided that they were an important national treasure, a visible link with the country's first peoples and a part of its heritage which had to be preserved.

In Vancouver, the Art, Historical and Scientific Association was at the forefront of this movement. Founded in 1889, the AHS created the original Vancouver Museum to hold its growing collection of historical art and artifacts, including "a representative collection of native relics and handicrafts." Later, the AHS conceived the idea of erecting a model Indian village in Stanley Park "to give to the present and succeeding generations an adequate conception of the work and social life of the aborigines before the advent of the white man." The village did not materialize, and the association began collecting totem poles instead. The congregation of poles which now attracts the attention of so many visitors at Brockton Point in the park originated with these early efforts of the AHS.[17]

Since the 1920s, totem poles have appeared at a large number of public buildings, hotels, parks and shopping plazas in British Columbia. Almost every provincial milestone has been celebrated with the raising of a pole. Immediately following World War II, the BC Electric Company, owners of public transit systems on the Lower Mainland and Vancouver Island, altered the insignia on its vehicles to feature a large, spread-winged thunderbird, familiar from the top of so many totems. A tall Haida pole welcomes people entering Canada at the Peace Arch border crossing south of Vancouver. In 1958, when B.C. celebrated its centennial, the province presented Queen Elizabeth with a Kwakiutl pole which now stands in Windsor Great Park in England. In 1966, to celebrate the centennial of the union of the colonies of British Columbia and Vancouver Island, the province inaugurated the "Route of the Totems," a series of poles erected along highways and at ferry terminals from Victoria to Prince Rupert. In the mid-1980s, Duncan, a small town on Vancouver Island, declared itself the "City of Totem Poles" and commissioned a group of poles as a way of encouraging travellers to visit.[18] While Native people venerate totem poles for social and historical reasons, many non-Natives apparently share a more superstitious belief that poles have the power to make people stop and spend their money.

The totem pole is just one aspect of Native culture that has been adopted by non-Native Canadians as a symbol of their own. In 1991, the federal government unveiled a huge sculpture at the entrance to the new Canadian embassy building in Washington, D.C. The "Spirit of Haida G'waii" is a five-ton bronze statue depicting a canoe spilling over with Haida myth figures, carved by the renowned West Coast artist, Bill Reid, who is part Haida himself. Reid and his work are acclaimed worldwide. He ranks among the top monumental artists in Canada. However, it must be assumed that a sculpture in such a prestigious public location is intended to be not only a work of art but more than that, a symbol for Canada itself. The choice of a giant Haida canoe is an interesting attempt by the government to absorb Haida mythology into a more general mythology of relevance to all Canadians.

These attempts are ubiquitous. Recently I opened an American magazine to discover a government advertisement encouraging tourists to visit Canada.[19] A bold headline ran across two pages: "Only in God's Country could you meet such interesting souls." A stunning photograph shows two figures, presumably Native people, seated on a sandy beach. They are both wearing large raven's head masks, brightly painted, with long beaks. In the background, a third figure, carrying a ceremonial drum and wrapped in what appears to be a Chilkoot blanket, emerges from the mist at the water's edge. Offshore, islands melt into a blue haze.

The text, which begins by informing readers that "our native peoples have been entertaining visitors for centuries," incorporates a version of a creation myth. Raven beats his wings and brings the world into being. "The most revered of spirits and master of ceremonies, the Raven embodies what this land is today," continues the text. "Magic. For here the supernatural abides in all that is living." The advertisement is promoting Canada but refers specifically to British Columbia, where apparently everyone is a pantheist and the "Animal People" are "our link to another realm."

Needless to say, this is not a British Columbia I recognize, and I grew up there. Nor is it a British Columbia which any visitor should have any reasonable expectation of encountering. The Animal People do not show themselves to tourists. This British Columbia is the fabulation of an advertising copy-writer with a vivid Imaginary Indian.

The Indians in the advertisement are familiar enough. They are spiritual, mysterious Indians. They are a part of the land, like the animals, in touch with the unseen forces of nature. They appeal to the widespread conviction on the part of non-Natives that Native people experience the natural world in a way that is qualitatively different from the rest of us. As well, the Indians in the advertisement belong to history. Dressed in traditional costumes and placed in a context that evokes the past, they are not Indians as they appear to us in modern life. They are thoroughly exotic and otherworldly.

The advertisement is only indirectly interested in the Indian, however. It is more interested in making the Indian a symbol for Canada. It is telling potential visitors that Canada is an extraordinary, even supernatural, place where they are going to have unusual experiences. Like the Indians in the photograph, Canada is presented as embodying a sense of the mystery of the natural world. Indians are used to represent not a place that is modern and familiar, but rather a place that exists outside of time in another reality. There is really no difference between this advertisement and the photographs of Plains people used by the CPR to attract customers west a hundred years ago: Canada is still Indian country.

○

Many aspects of Native culture have been appropriated over the years and turned into commodities to help sell products in the marketplace. These products range from running shoes to cars to the country itself. Indian heroes like Pontiac, Indian artifacts like totem poles, Indian attitudes like the stoicism of the cigar-store Indian have all been invoked. Products are linked to the Indian in the expectation that some supposedly Native virtues will rub off. Indians themselves become commodities in the marketplace. The advertising image is based on stereotypes of the Imaginary Indian already abroad in the culture. In turn, advertising reinforces the stereotype by feeding it back into the mainstream culture in a self-repeating loop.

It may seem unimportant that images of Indians have appeared in tourist brochures and on tins of canned vegetables, coins and hood ornaments. But the phenomenon is not a trivial one. Many writers have observed that non-Natives have experienced a persistent sense of alienation in North America ever since the first Europeans arrived here. "Americans are really aliens in North America," says Vine Deloria, the American Sioux writer, "and try as they might they seem incapable of adjusting to the continent." In their search for ways to feel at home, Deloria continues, the newcomers have looked to the first inhabitants of the continent: "Indians, the original possessors of the land, seem to haunt the collective unconscious of the white man, and to the degree that one can identify the conflicting images of the Indian which stalk the white man's waking perception of the world one can outline the deeper problems of identity and alienation that trouble him."[20] One response to this dilemma is to "go Native," to become an Indian, or at least to take on Indian identities, either directly, as Archie Belaney did when he turned into Grey Owl, or spuriously, by appropriating elements of Indianness and making them representative of mainstream society.

Since the beginning of the country, non-Native Canadians have wanted Indians to transform themselves into Whites, to assimilate to the mainstream. But there has also been a strong impulse among Whites, less consciously expressed perhaps, to transform themselves into Indians. Grey Owl simply acted out the fantasy. Each time they respond to a sales pitch which features an Indian image, each time they chant an Indian slogan from their box seats, each time they dress up in feathers for a costume party or take pride in the unveiling of yet another totem pole as a symbol of the country, non-Native Canadians are trying in a way to become indigenous people themselves and to resolve their lingering sense of not belonging where they need to belong. By appropriating elements of Native culture, non-Natives have tried to establish a relationship with the country that pre-dates their arrival and validates their occupation of the land.

NOTES

1. Donald B. Smith, *Long Lance: The True Story of an Imposter* (Toronto: Macmillan, 1982), 180–81.

2. I am grateful to my friend Jim Taylor for this reference.

3. Quoted in Deborah Doxtator, *Fluffs and Feathers: An Exhibit on the Symbols of Indianness* (Brantford, ON: Woodland Cultural Centre, 1988), 46.

4. E.J. Hart, *The Selling of Canada* (Banff: Altitude Publishing, 1983), 12ff.

5. Cited in ibid., 23.

6. T.C. McLuhan, *Dream Tracks: The Railroad and the American Indian, 1890–1930* (New York: Harry N. Abrams, 1985).

7. Margery Tanner Hadley, "Photography, Tourism and the CPR" in *Essays on the Historical Geography of the Canadian West*, ed. L.A. Rosenvall and S.M. Evans (Calgary: University of Calgary Press, 1987), 58.

8. Douglas Sladen, *On the Cars and Off* (London: Ward, Lock and Bowden, 1895).

9. Ibid., 306.

10. Hart, *The Selling of Canada*, 59.

11. Leslie Monkman, *A Native Heritage* (Toronto: University of Toronto Press, 1981), 129.

12. Edward Roper, *By Track and Trail: A Journey Through Canada* (London: W.H. Allen and Co., 1891), 118, 120.

13. Ibid., 118, 244.

14. This discussion was based on David Darling and Douglas Cole, "Totem Pole Restoration on the Skeena, 1925–30," *BC Studies* 47 (Autumn 1980): 29–48.

15. A.Y. Jackson, *A Painter's Country* (Toronto: Clark, Irwin and Co., 1958), 111.

16. Dennis Reid, *Edwin Holgate* (Ottawa: National Gallery of Canada, 1976), 14–15.

17. John C. Goodfellow, *The Totem Poles in Stanley Park* (Vancouver: Art, Historical and Scientific Association of Vancouver, n.d.).

18. Hilary Stewart, *Totem Poles* (Vancouver: Douglas & McIntyre, 1990).

19. "The Sophisticated Traveller," *The New York Times Magazine*, pt. 2 (17 May 1992), 2–3.

20. Vine Deloria, "American Fantasy," foreword to *The Pretend Indians: Images of Native Americans in the Movies*, ed. Gretchen M. Bataille and Charles L.P. Silet (Ames, IA: Iowa State University Press, 1980), x.

THE TWENTIETH CENTURY AND THE FAILURE OF CENTRALIZATION: A MICMAC PERSPECTIVE *

DANIEL PAUL

o

"The twentieth century belongs to Canada" was a phrase coined near the turn of the century. In many ways this prediction came true: Canada became a prosperous country, with the second highest living standard in the world. However, an exception should have stated: "except for the Aboriginals, Black, and other people of colour."

In Nova Scotia, both the Blacks and the Micmac have been subjected to degrading discrimination and poverty. The Nova Scotia of 1901 was not a bastion of human rights. The Micmac and Blacks were regularly denied entrance to hotels, restaurants, and other public places with impunity until the late 1960s. After Confederation, apart from the indifferent and paternalistic application of the Indian Act, things did not improve appreciably for the Micmac or other Tribes in the new Canada. The only apparent change was that the Micmac now had to look to Ottawa instead of Halifax for subsistence allowances.

Victimization by racism was still their daily experience. Although overt persecution eased somewhat, the federal government's agenda for the Tribes was almost a mirror image of what the colonial governments had desired: extinction by assimilation became the prime objective of the new political establishment.

The civil and human rights of the Tribes were not seriously considered by the new political order for another century or so, and then only at the insistence of the United Nations. Racist attitudes among nearly all segments

* Reprinted with permission from *We Were Not Savages: A Micmac Perspective on the Collision of European and Aboriginal Civilization* (Halifax: Nimbus, 1993), 264–93.

of the dominant Canadian society have kept the Tribes in abject poverty right up to the present time.

Education, which would have given the Tribes the ability to prepare, strengthen, transform, and modernize their cultures for survival in the new order was all but denied until recent times. Educational opportunities for the good of the Aboriginals was espoused but its attendant requirements made it unacceptable: "You may have an education, but only if you assimilate and accept the eventual extinction of your race!"

As a result of the efforts of Joseph Howe and the Catholic Church, by 1867 some Micmac were able to read and write. However, no real effort to educate them was made until the passage of the Indian Act in 1876, and then this effort was hampered by the provision for the enfranchisement of every Aboriginal who graduated from a university.

The education of Indians beyond grade school, up until very recent times, when First Nations governments began to assume control and administration of so-called "Indian programs," has always been a low priority of government and, by the mandatory enfranchisement of university graduates, discouraged.

At the turn of the twentieth century, the Micmac and other Tribes of Canada found themselves in a country that really did not want them. They continued to suffer the pains of unbridled racism and the despair it engenders. The only difference was that in the twentieth century the Department of Indian Affairs was the main persecutor.

During the first half of the 1900s, Indian Affairs made no real effort to assist the Micmac to overcome the destitution and poverty of the preceding century and a half. The government's main concern was whether the Micmac on the mainland should be forced onto Reserves or forced off. This problem occupied their thinking for at least thirty years before they came up with their "ultimate solution": *centralization*. This plan called for all Aboriginals living in the Maritimes to relocate to four central locations for administrative purposes. This move was to please the bureaucrats, who were inconvenienced by having to provide services at nineteen different locations in Nova Scotia alone. Needless to say, the wishes of the Aboriginals were not taken into account in the formulation of this policy.

By the early part of the century, many Indian Reserves on the mainland had been surrendered, either conditionally or absolutely. Government spokesmen have insisted that this was done for the benefit of the Micmac, to provide an economic base for the Bands. But since no economic base ever developed, one must conclude that this effort failed miserably. The only real beneficiaries were the families and friends of politicians and bureaucrats involved in the administration of Indian Affairs. Political interference in Indian Affairs has traditionally been the norm rather than the exception.

During the twentieth century, the Micmac language became the target for assimilation. At school and other public institutions the People were forbidden to speak Micmac. At the residential school established at Shubenacadie in the late 1920s, it was a cardinal offense to speak the traditional language. This policy was followed in other Micmac communities outside the mainland, but not usually with the same dogged determination.

Despite this kind of assault, the Micmac language is still alive and healthy today throughout Cape Breton, New Brunswick, and Prince Edward Island. And, surprisingly, almost half of the Micmac on the mainland can still converse in their mother tongue, another example of the Micmac's dauntless spirit.

The residential schools, like all schools for the supposed education of Aboriginal children, were operated by the religious order of the denomination the Tribe adhered to—Roman Catholic in the case of the Micmac. These institutions were used by the Department of Indian Affairs for many purposes besides education: enforcement, punishment, and terrorism, to name a few. Reading about this era, one must remember that the Tribes in Canada had no access to human or civil rights procedures. The fights by parents and other relatives for access to their own children that will be described below, for example, were taken on without the assistance of laws that protected other Canadians.

Marilyn Millward wrote in an article entitled "Clean Behind the Ears?":

> Many of the students who attended the old Shubenacadie Indian Residential School carry with them the scars of that experience. But they were not the only ones to suffer. A look at surviving records reveals the anguish many parents endured, and shows the determination to speak and be heard that was their reaction to the way the educational and governmental bureaucracy dealt with them and their children.
>
> The Indian Residential School at Shubenacadie, Nova Scotia, operated between February 1930 and June 1967. It was intended to accommodate Micmac children who were deemed to be "underprivileged," defined by the Federal Department of Indian Affairs as orphaned, neglected, or living too distant to permit attendance at any day school. While children who were orphaned or remote from schools could be easily identified, it was more difficult to interpret the term "neglected." This was a matter to be determined by the local Indian Agent.
>
> Here, the Department intended to "consolidate Indian educational work in the Maritimes" and planned to "mould the lives of the young Aborigines and aid them in their search towards the goal of complete Canadian Citizenship." Duncan C. Scott, then Deputy Superintendent General of the Department of Indian Affairs, told the Halifax-Chronicle that their object and desire in establishing the new school was that its graduates should become self-supporting and *"not return to their old environment and habits."*[1]

The Department had first toyed with the idea of a residential school in 1892, but the decision to build a "school farm" was not taken until 1927. The school opened in 1930, staffed by members of Roman Catholic religious orders. The principal was a priest and the teachers were nuns. The curriculum was the same as that prescribed by the Nova Scotia Department of Education for the provincial school system, except for the courses in religion and in "how to be ashamed to be an Indian." Children were taught about all the advantages of White life and all the "evils" of Aboriginal isolation, language, and culture.

Ms. Millward states that parental permission was necessary for admission. Although she later qualifies this statement, the fact is she is mistaken. She may not have been aware of the law as it then stood. Aboriginals at that time were considered "wards of the Crown" and were at the complete mercy of the Department of Indian Affairs. The parental permission portions of the forms for admission to the school that Ms. Millward refers to were simply window dressing. The Indian Agents, who had been given complete control over Aboriginals, did not need the permission of the Micmac to do anything they wanted to do, and they used these powers at will.

Ms. Millward substantiates this fact when describing how a Micmac parent tried to keep a child home:

> A mother wanted to keep her children home after their vacation, and believed that only a note to her agent to that effect was necessary. When she learned *"it wasn't her decision to make,"* she had a justice of the peace write to the Department on her behalf. His help consisted of a note saying that this mother "says she 'loves' her children"—the word "loves" was belittled and negated by quotation marks. The agent wrote that she wanted them home only to take care of the house and their younger siblings, and so her request was apparently unsuccessful.[2]

The Department's control was all-encompassing. Ms. Millward reports of vacations:

> Perhaps because of the difficulty in having some of the children returned to the school after summer vacations, holidays at home were not allowed for any children during Christmas. Although specific reasons for this policy are not clear from the existing records, they are implied in a 1938 letter from the Department to an agent in the Annapolis Valley: "For many reasons which will no doubt suggest themselves to you, the Department does not allow holidays at Christmas, and I might say further that no valid reason has yet been given to us why holidays should be allowed at that period of the year. There is no question that the children attending the Shubenacadie Residential School receive every possible care and attention, and in addition at Christmas time there are always special festivities which the children enjoy."

In 1939, the parents at the Cambridge Reserve in Nova Scotia were determined to have their children home for Christmas, but the agent refused their request and advised them of the Department's rules. Reporting on the matter to the Department, he wrote: "These people went so far as to have a man go to the school for their children, they did not get the children. The Principal would not let them take them."

When one of these parents then sent her request to the Department herself, the agent reported: "She thought by writing she would be able to get her children home for Christmas. These people think that they can have their own way and would like to do so and when they find out they cannot they get mad."[3]

Indian Agents, officials of the Department and the school, and many other non-Aboriginals as well, failed to appreciate that Aboriginals experience all the emotions of human beings everywhere. The reason parents want their children home is because *they love them.*

Because our community lacked education facilities at the time, my parents sent two of my older brothers to the residential school, where they were kept until a small day school was located on-Reserve. During that time they experienced much abuse. From then on, when we were misbehaving, my mother would say, "If you don't behave, I'll put you in the residential school."

Ms. Millward reports many instances of abuse, including the denial of permission to keep children home when they were sick:

A former pupil of the school retained a lawyer in an attempt to keep his younger siblings from being returned to the school following their summer vacation in 1936. The lawyer contacted the agent, saying the complainant had related: "A very hard story of the treatment young Indian children receive there. It would appear that his own experience has been so hard that he dreads very much the idea of going back there, and naturally, feels it hard to see his younger brother and sister taken there, where they will receive similar treatment."

The agent did not believe there were grounds for complaint, but forwarded the lawyer's letter to the school principal who, in his written reply to the agent, seemed quite unsettled by it. "To let them get away with their lies doesn't seem the right thing to do—to keep them from spreading falsehoods about those who try to do something for them seems hopeless. And why white people fall for such stories is hard to explain. *For myself I never hope to catch up with him and his lies.* . . . I think the best thing to do is write to the Department and since we have a full school, request a few more beds and insist upon them coming back. *I am getting a bit tired of playing square with the Indian and in turn have him cut my throat.*"

He added that the lawyer didn't understand the regulations, which called for one half day in the classroom and the other half in labour, and recalled that the former pupil who had hired him was merely: "a big body with the mind of a ten year old child. . . . To play a game of baseball was work for him; he would rather sit in the sun and pester a bumble bee or a fly, by pulling off one wing and one leg at a time. *To make an Indian work is the unpardonable sin among them.*"

The principal called the allegations of hard treatment "ridiculous," and could not understand how a lawyer could be *"duped by an Indian."* The Department decided not to insist upon the return of the children, but also denied any financial aid that would allow them to pursue an education elsewhere.[4]

The racist statements of this priest show just what Aboriginals were up against in trying to acquire civil rights in a prejudiced society. The cutting off of financial aid was a tool used liberally by the Department to obtain compliance. As mentioned, this was the fear that compelled the Micmac at Pictou Landing to do what the politicians and bureaucrats wanted with Boat Harbour. Ms. Millward provides another example:

> The same year a fifteen-year-old girl from the nearby Shubenacadie Reserve refused to return to the school and gave the following statement to the agent and the Royal Canadian Mounted Police:
> "I have been going to Indian school for the past five years. . . . Before my holidays this year I was employed in kitchen for eleven weeks. . . . In the eleven weeks . . . I spent a total of two weeks in school. The Sister has beaten me many times over the head and pulled my hair and struck me on the back of neck with a ruler and at times grabbed ahold of me and beat me on the back with her fists.
> I have also been ordered to stand on the outside of the windows with a rope around my waist to clean windows on the fourth floor with a little girl holding the rope. When I told the Sister I was afraid to go out the window she scolded me and made me clean the window and threatened to beat me if I did not do it. This is being done to other children.
> After we get a beating we are asked what we got the beating for and if we tell them we do not know we get another beating. The Sisters always tell us not to tell our parents about getting a beating."[5]

The following incident Ms. Millward relates is one of the many my brother and cousins told me had happened during their incarcerations:

> One student remembers a particularly cruel incident, which took place at meal-time. The top of a salt shaker became loose, and when one boy used it to spice his porridge, the entire contents fell in a pile onto his meal: "He started to spoon it back into the salt shaker, at least the dry stuff. The Sister was watching . . . she came over to see what was going on. She found the fellow spooning the salt back. She told him to stop that. 'Since you like salt on your porridge, you might as well eat what's in your bowl.'
> He wouldn't. There was just too much salt in it. Nobody would. So she hit him in the back of the neck. 'Eat it!' So he finally took his spoon and took a mouthful of the stuff. It didn't stay down long. It came back up into his bowl. So she whacked him in the back of the head and said, 'I told you to eat it!'
> So he started to cry, took the spoon and tried to eat some more, and that came back up. About the third time he fainted. Instead of picking him up off the floor to help him up onto the bench, she picked him up by the neck and threw him out to the centre aisle. That Nun was full of that kind of stuff."[6]

I went to the day school located on the Shubenacadie Indian (now Indian Brook) Reserve during my elementary grades. We were taught by the Sisters of Charity and had a priest as a principal. I will mention two of many incidents that have left a lifelong impression upon me.

The first was the scene of a Sister dragging one girl, who was very frightened at the prospect of visiting a dentist, by her hair to meet an appointment. The second was when a Sister became so frightened of Aboriginals that she had to be sent back to the Mother House in Halifax and did not return. Although many of these people were kind and treated the children in the residential and day schools decently, they were just as guilty as the cruel ones, because they tolerated their sadism and did nothing to stop it.

The most insidious use of these institutions was in the attempt to wipe out tribal cultures in this country. Churches and governments must be condemned for their participation in this despicable assault upon Aboriginal civilizations.

The government hoped these schools would assimilate Aboriginal children. This plan was to wipe out their traditional languages by forbidding the children to speak them, and to imprint in the children's minds a picture of their cultures as inferior to White civilization. Both efforts failed miserably. They did succeed in increasing the resentment and hatred among Aboriginals toward their prosecutors including the federal government whose motto was: "We know best, take and be thankful."

During the time I attended the day school at Indian Brook, I cannot recall any effort being made to teach us about our heritage and culture. I do vividly recall that we were subjected to daily indoctrinations on religion. It was emphasized that if we failed our religious examinations we would not receive one grade at the end of term.

One positive thing that these educational institutions did do was to provide daily doses of vitamins to students. In the long run this proved most beneficial. The incidence of death among young children dropped dramatically and the Micmac population began to increase. For almost a hundred years the population in Nova Scotia had remained virtually static at around 2000; by 1950 it had reached only about 2600.

Another despicable practice used by the dominant society to demoralize the Tribes in the Americas was negative brainwashing. Movies, radio, television, magazines, newspapers, books, and advertisements all depicted the Aboriginals as wanton, cruel, and heartless animals. Religious sermons, textbooks, and every other means was used to convey the message: "*Indians are murderous, lazy, and worthless drunken savages.*"

This misinformation created a crisis of self-esteem and confidence among Aboriginal peoples. It reinforced the false and negative stereotype images the White population held of Aboriginal peoples and encouraged more racist persecution. A negative feeling about themselves was instilled in the subconscious of Aboriginals. It was not unusual to go to a movie during the thirties, forties, or fifties and find a large group of Aboriginal children cheering on the cowboys against the bad guys, "the Indians."

Fortunately, this stereotyping is being negated by the Aboriginal peoples themselves who have learned how to research and rediscover the true histories of their ancestors in their encounters with Europeans.

Around 1900, government officials decided to move the Micmac Band of Halifax County to the Truro (now Millbrook) Reserve. They proposed the surrender of three Reserves in Halifax County, supposedly to finance the move and buy land to add to the existing land base at Truro. This was one of many attempts in the twentieth century to force the mainland Micmac to leave their *traditional camping grounds* and move to a Reserve. The People resisted until the Great Depression persuaded some of them to make the move.

Did the Micmac initiate the move to surrender and sell their land holdings in Halifax County? Definitely not! Government bureaucrats had applied pressure for the surrender of their lands for more than forty years before they finally accomplished this objective. Members of Parliament (for example, M.B. Daley, MP for Halifax) were waiting in the wings to request purchase of the land.[7]

There was good reason for such great interest in purchasing surrendered Indian Reserve land: it could be bought for a song. The Department wasn't concerned with how much it could get for the land; its main concern was to get rid of it.

The documents concerning the Halifax County surrenders of 1919, infer that the land belonged to the members of the Shubenacadie Micmac District, but one certainly cannot conclude that all the Micmac were members of one Band, as some historians, politicians, and Ottawa lawyers believe. This notion flies in the face of historical documentation that shows that the British were at times at peace with some of the Bands under treaty, while at the same time at war with others.

Micmac Districts had not disappeared entirely, for even as late as 1910 the Chief of Bear River was recognized as the Chief of Annapolis, Digby, Yarmouth, Shelburne, and Queens counties and half of Lunenburg County; the Chief of Eskasoni was recognized as the Chief of Cape Breton; and the Chief at Shubenacadie was recognized as the Chief of the rest of the mainland. By 1919 the Chief at Shubenacadie was recognized as the Chief of the entire mainland and remained so until 1958, when the Department reorganized the Bands under the Indian Act.

What the Department did in the late 1950s simply reflected the reality of the existing Bands. A report on the Cape Breton Micmac coming to Halifax in 1861 to protest the use of their "trust fund moneys" to purchase land for the Pictou Landing Band shows that the Micmac Bands viewed themselves as separate entities:

> Your committee had before them Indian delegates, representing the views of their tribe, from the Island of Cape Breton (the Delegates were: Paul Christmas, Michael Christmas and Paul Andrews) . . . the Cape Breton Indians disapprove of the funds arising from the sale of their lands being used for the purchase of lands for the Pictou Indians. Your committee would therefore recommend that the purchase of said land become a charge upon the Province, and the amount paid out of the Indian reserve fund to be again restored as part of said fund.[8]

One of the main reasons some members of Indian Affairs wanted to impose the one Band concept is that in 1919 the federal government, irresponsibly, upon the recommendation of Superintendent Bouy, dumped the accumulated money of the separate Bands into one pot and then spent it without exercising its responsibility to expend the moneys *solely* for the Bands the funds had been held in trust for.

In New Brunswick, trust funds transferred to the federal government were done so in the name of the specific Band. In his report to the government in 1936, Dr. Thomas Robertson lists all the Bands in New Brunswick from Big Cove to Woodstock and shows to the penny just how much each Band had in its trust account. For Nova Scotia he simply shows a lump sum.[9]

There were many complaints from the Micmac about this state of affairs in the 1920s. The government lied to convince the Micmac of Halifax County that their funds were being held separately, when in fact they were not.

If the preposterous proposition that the Micmac of Nova Scotia formed only one Band is true, then it stands to reason that the Micmac of New Brunswick, Prince Edward Island, and Quebec are part of that one Band, instead of being divided into many. It seems, and time will tell, that the government mishandled the "trust fund moneys" of the Nova Scotia Bands and quite possibly is looking for a way out. When one calculates the principal, and compound interest, on the moneys the Bands had from Confederation to now, the amount owing to them is staggering. If the Bands could mount a successful lawsuit, based on the mismanagement of their trust funds, the future well-being of they and their children would be assured.

When at Eskasoni, Dr. Robertson met the Grand Chief of the Micmac and referred to him as the "Chief of Nova Scotia," he was, in fact, the spiritual leader of all the Micmac scattered throughout the eastern provinces. The Bands each had their own Chiefs and were protective of their individual identities, which later spelled bad news for the government's centralization policy. Dr. Robertson's misleading statement that he had met with the "Chief of Nova Scotia" may have been the basis for the assumption that there was only one Band in Nova Scotia. Interestingly, Dr. Robertson reported that during his visit to Cape Breton he asked the Grand Chief if he had anything to suggest for the betterment of his people. The Chief replied, "Yes, make my people work for everything they get. Make them break more land for cultivation in exchange for relief. You are ruining them."

The Micmac population of Nova Scotia continued to fluctuate for a long time after Confederation. From Joe Howe's estimate in 1843 of approximately 1300, the official population climbed to 1666 in 1871, and to 2076 in 1891, fell to 1542 in 1901, and then rose again to 2048 in 1921. In 1949 the population reached 2641; it then grew to 3561 in 1959, 4647 in 1970, 5868 in 1980, and 9242 by 1991.[10]

The drop between 1891 and 1901 of 534 persons can be explained by a smallpox epidemic and the migration of many families to the States. Although after 1921 the Micmac population held ground at the two thousand mark, it did not make any dramatic increases until the early 1950s.

Infant mortality and death from diseases such as consumption remained high throughout the first sixty years of the twentieth century. The root cause remained the same as it had been in the nineteenth and early twentieth centuries: substandard living conditions and malnutrition.

Micmac men, women, and children still went to bed in substandard housing and survived on substandard diets. Poverty and misery were still commonplace up to the 1960s.

The following is an extract from the report submitted to the Superintendent General of Indian Affairs by Dr. Robertson dated June 9, 1936, in response to the assignment given to him by the Privy Council to undertake an in-depth study of the living conditions of the Indians in the Maritimes:

HOUSING CONDITIONS

While there are a great many what we might call good houses among the Indians, while conditions vary in different districts, while better conditions exist among the Indians living on Reserves, more particularly those close to an Agent, yet in every district there are unsanitary houses, houses badly in need of repair and, in the great majority of districts, houses that are absolutely unfit for occupation.

HEALTH CONDITIONS

There is a lot of T.B. and venereal diseases. While there has been considerable improvement in the health of the Indians of late, this condition cannot hope to be continued under the present undernourished conditions, bad housing and the close contact of children with parents and other members of the family who are suffering from tuberculosis.

From the foregoing it will be seen that conditions among the Indians are very bad and many of them are depending wholly upon what they receive from the Government for their support.

The opinion of the man on the street is that the Indian is lazy, useless and himself responsible for his present conditions. However, a study of the record of each individual shows that the great majority of the Indians are good workers and that his present condition is due to matters over which he has little or no control.

For evidence of this we have but to look at conditions as they exist today in the activities by which he formerly obtained his livelihood, i.e., fishing, hunting, trapping, labour, etc. Hunting and trapping is a thing of the past. Very few are engaged in fishing, principally because today fishing is a deep water proposition and the Maritime Indian is not a deep water man. No one will employ an Indian today, he is a *"ward" of the Government*.

Farming: While this is not one of the methods by which he formerly obtained his living, it is one on which the Government has expended considerable money in breaking land and supplying him with fertilizer and seed. Before condemning the Indian for not increasing his farming operations, let us look at conditions under which he was asked to do so.

He knew nothing about farming, he needed instruction. He is a good worker only under supervision. He was given neither instruction nor supervision. His land was broken, he was given fertilizer

and seed and then left to his own devices. If he ate the seed potatoes and sold the fertilizer, as many of them did, he received his
full relief allowance, but if he produced a crop his allowance was
reduced. He was penalized for producing and bonused for non-
production.

With the exception of a little labour in the potato fields of Maine,
some pulp wood in parts of New Brunswick and Cape Breton and
some guiding in Nova Scotia, the only source of revenue the Indian
has today is from handles and baskets. Due to factory competition
reducing the price, the Indian finds that after paying the costs of
marketing his goods there is very little left for himself.

While the fact that the Indian population is increasing demands
that he be made self-supporting, and a study of the record of the
Indian as a worker shows that this can be done, many years have
elapsed under the Government of both political Parties but no plan
has been evolved whereby he may be placed in the position where
he could be made self-supporting.

The situation today is that the Indian is deteriorating and looking more and more to the Government for his support. That unless
some plan is formulated whereby he may be placed in the position
where he will be self-supporting, expenditures for the assistance of
the Indian will have to be greatly increased.

A search for means of increasing the Indian's earnings proves
there is nothing to be gained from hunting, fishing or trapping, nor
is there much to be hoped for in the realm of labour, but it does
show that his revenue from handles, baskets and craft wood could
be greatly increased.

With Indian goods superior as they are to the factory product,
there can be no doubt a proper organization could secure contracts
from consumers of these goods, such as governments, railways,
parks, potato companies, etc., and also find new markets among
tourists, merchants, etc., in this way saving of time and money now
spent by the Indian peddling his goods, as well as increasing his
sales.

While increased earning from handle and craft work would be
of great assistance, any plan in which there can be any hope for
success in the placing of the Indian in a position where he may be
made self-supporting must make agriculture its back-bone with
close and competent *supervision* its most vital essential.[11]

Dr. Robertson outlined what he viewed to be the major problems facing
Aboriginals in the Maritimes, but he left out the underlying reason for
all the problems plaguing the Micmac and all the rest of the Tribes in
Canada: *racism*.

Although Robertson identifies racism in his report by showing how it
prevents the Aboriginals from being self-sufficient, he, like his predecessors
and successors, does not call it by name or offer suggestions on how it
might be effectively dealt with. One should note here that the Department

of Indian Affairs has never set aside one cent to help Aboriginals combat racial discrimination.

Robertson suggests that an Indian can work "only under supervision" by a White person. Although he was probably one of the more liberal-minded officials at that time, he was not above making such stereotyped statements. Unfortunately, it became a by-word of the bureaucracy. They would mention "supervision" on a regular basis in their reports for decades to come.

Robertson mentions how Whites won't give the Aboriginals work, and then criticizes them as lazy, shiftless, and entirely responsible for their condition. It has become fashionable in this country to blame the victim for their problems. Remember that in the 1980s, the Nova Scotia Supreme Court Appeal Division's judges felt compelled to tell Junior Marshall that he was the author of his own misfortune.

The case of William G. Paul, my father and a member of the Shubenacadie Band, is a good example of how society dealt with Aboriginals in the 1930s.

Mr. Paul was working on the waterfront in Saint John, New Brunswick, in 1935, when he was laid off because of a shortage of work. Having a wife and family to support and no employment, he was forced to apply to the city for welfare assistance, which he initially received.

Then, someone complained to the city government that Mr. Paul was an "Indian" and as such should not receive city welfare. In spite of the fact that Mr. Paul had been a taxpayer until the time of his layoff, the city immediately took steps to right what they viewed as a wrong. It provided train fare for Mr. Paul, his wife, and their five small children and sent them packing to the Indian Brook Reserve near the village of Shubenacadie, Nova Scotia.

Mr. Paul had been born in the Sheet Harbour area of Nova Scotia, and his wife, Sarah, née Noel, had been born and raised near Enfield. Neither had ever been to the Indian Brook Reserve before; prior to moving to New Brunswick in the 1920s, he and his wife had lived on the Millbrook Reserve near Truro.

Upon his arrival at Indian Brook in November 1935, the Indian Agent gave Mr. Paul a few rolls of tar paper and some nails to build a tar paper shack in which he and his family spent the winter. The following year he built a small log cabin, in which his family increased by three before he built his own house in 1939. I was the last of the three children born in that log cabin. Like most other Aboriginal families of the day, poverty and hardship was part of our daily lives, well into the 1950s.

Many past reports, including Dr. Robertson's, have prominently mentioned that venereal disease was rampant among the Micmac and other Tribes. The answer to why the disease was so prevalent among them is obvious. When a person is starving and society doesn't respond, that person will do almost anything to survive. Some of the women, and no doubt some of the men, turned to prostitution for survival and, by participating in this activity, brought home the diseases.

To be forced to sell oneself for food is not a crime for the individual, it is a crime for the society he or she lives in. By its unrelenting discrimination and persecution, society forced the Aboriginal peoples to do everything in their power to survive. Today, with an adequate food supply, venereal disease among the Tribes has become rare.

Dr. Robertson outlined the steps of his plan to make the Maritime Aboriginals self-sufficient:

(a) Placing the Indians on reserves containing good agricultural land where he can be given a decent home. Instructions in farming and *proper supervision.*

(b) Direct relief to be discontinued and all able to work required to work for anything received.

(c) The appointment of full time agents whose duty will be not only supervision, but also to find markets for the Indian's products.

(d) The teaching of agriculture in the schools by school gardens and talks.

(e) The giving of short courses in agriculture to a few Indians boys who show interest in agriculture.

(f) The securing of the cooperation of the Indians by the holding of meetings for the purpose of discussing their problems with them.

(g) The full cooperation with the church in everything affecting the Indian.

(h) The encouragement of the Indian to produce by sharing with him any reduction in his allowance made possible by his own effort.

(i) The granting of no assistance to Indians living off their Reserve [to force them back onto the Reserve—the Department did not completely cut off Aboriginals living off Indian Reserves until 1967].

The adoption of this plan or policy would necessitate the securing of more Reserves as there is not enough good land on the present ones.[12]

Dr. Robertson then provides some explanations of his recommendations:

The moving of quite a number of Indians. In order to find the Indians feelings on this subject I spent considerable time discussing it with them in the different parts of the Province. All opposition disappeared when they found it would be to their own benefit.

The building of quite a number of homes. These houses should be built by the Indians themselves and they should not be finished on the inside for sanitary reasons. A house one and a half stories, twenty by thirty, with eight windows and two doors, sufficient for a family of five, built in this way should not cost more than one hundred and seventy-five to two hundred dollars in Nova Scotia (Yarmouth).

The appointment of full time competent Agents. It is impossible to give the necessary supervision with part time men and that supervision is absolutely necessary is amply evidenced by the fact that only at places where supervision is given is there any headway being made. On the appointment of competent Agents depends the success or failure of the plan, for we cannot have proper supervision without competent men. These Agents would not only supervise but they would also find markets for the Indian's products. In the appointment of these Agents no matter of any kind should be considered except the fitness of the man for the position. It should not be forgotten in the appointment of these men that they are to deal with human beings, whose bodily and spiritual welfare depends to a large extent upon the sympathetic execution of their duty.

The securing of the Indians' cooperation through meetings. This in my opinion is another vital matter. No organization is ever of any force or effect unless the members feel they are a vital part of it and are consulted re. its affairs. This is true of the White man and that it is also true of the Red is demonstrated by the fact that at Truro where this system has been adopted this year the Agent is getting full cooperation and is making real headway.

The full cooperation with the Church. This is another vital matter as both are working for the same object, the welfare of the Indian, and any friction would injure the cause.

Encouraging the Indian to produce. There is no question of the necessity of this as if there is no incentive there is not much work.

The giving of no assistance to Indians off the Reserve. While this would be the rule, there would be exceptions as there would be a number of cases where Indians had work for the greater part of the year and would require very little assistance to carry them through. In cases of that kind it would be folly to force them to return to the Reserve.[13]

Thus Dr. Robertson set the stage for the further humiliation and degradation of the Micmacs and Maliseets. The government used his report to formulate its new policy of "centralization," and in so doing virtually ignored his good recommendations and quickly implemented the bad.

Positive changes for the Tribes were difficult to come by because of the moronic attitudes prevalent in the Department towards their Aboriginal charges. The following letter sent out from Ottawa to all Indian Agents by the Superintendent General of Indian Affairs, Duncan Elliott, on December 15, 1921 is a case in point:

Sir:

It is observed with alarm that the holding of dances by the Indians on their reserves is in the increase, and that these practices tend to disorganize the efforts which the Department is putting forth to make them self-supporting.

I have, therefore, to direct you to use your utmost endeavours to dissuade the Indians from excessive indulgence in the practice of dancing. You should suppress any dances which cause waste of time, interfere with the occupations of the Indians, unsettle them for serious work, injure their health or encourage them in sloth and idleness.

You should also dissuade, and, if possible, prevent them from leaving their reserves for the purpose of attending fairs, exhibitions, etc., when their absence would result in their own farming and other interests being neglected. It is realized that reasonable amusement and recreation should be enjoyed by Indians, but they should not be allowed to dissipate their energies and abandon themselves to demoralizing amusements. By the use of tact and firmness, you can control and keep it, and this obstacle to continued progress will then disappear.

The rooms, halls or other places in which Indians congregate should be under constant inspection. They should be scrubbed, fumigated, cleansed or disinfected to prevent the dissemination of disease. The Indians should be instructed in regard to the matter of proper ventilation and the avoidance of overcrowded rooms where public assemblies are being held, and proper arrangement should be made for the shelter of their horses and ponies. The Agent will avail himself of the services of the medical attendant of his agency in the connection.[14]

Mr. Elliott's mentality was symptomatic of the prevailing attitudes among the majority of Canadians towards the Tribes at that time, as the following provision of the Indian Act of 1927 also attests:

SECTION 140—DANCES AND FESTIVALS

1. Every Indian or other person who engages in, or assists in celebrating or encourages either directly or indirectly another to celebrate any Indian Festival, dance or other ceremony of which the giving away or paying or giving back of money, goods or articles of any sort forms a part, or is a feature, whether such gift of money, goods or articles takes place before, at, or after the celebration of the same or who engages or assists in any celebration or dance of which the wounding or mutilation of the dead or living body of any human being or animal forms a part or is a feature, is guilty of an offence and is liable on summary conviction to imprisonment for a term not exceeding six months and not less than two months.

2. Nothing in this section shall be construed to prevent the holding of any agricultural show or exhibition or the giving away of prizes for exhibits thereat.

3. Any Indian in the provinces of Manitoba, Saskatchewan, Alberta or British Columbia or in the Territories who participates in any Indian Dance outside the bounds of his own reserve, or who participates in any show, exhibition, performance, stampede or pageant in aboriginal costume without the consent of the Superintendent General or his authorized agent, and any person

who induces or employs any Indian to take part in such dance, show, exhibition, performance, stampede or pageant, *or induces any Indian to leave his reserve or employs any Indian for such a purpose,* whether the dance, show, exhibition, stampede or pageant has taken place or nor, shall on summary conviction be liable to a penalty not exceeding twenty five dollars, or to imprisonment for one month, or to both penalty and imprisonment.[15]

This section of the Act directly attacks the traditions of the Tribes and, in the process, denies them the opportunity to earn a living. In the minds of a good many Whites, the provision that forbids the employment of Aboriginals was construed as a prohibition against employing Aboriginals, period. To demand that permission must be obtained before one racial segment of the population can do something that another racial segment of the population does without restriction is not paternalism as some would like to believe. It is simply mindless racism. Never did legislation require, for instance, that Scottish Canadians had to receive government permission to entertain for pay.

The prohibition against mutilating the dead in Section 140 is particularly offensive, because the Aboriginal Tribes of Canada have always held their dead in the highest respect and would consequently never have mutilated their remains. Some rites performed by certain Tribes over their dead may have caused some people of European Christian extraction some discomfort, but the European practice of embalming, and performing autopsies on the dead caused some of the Tribes discomfort too. No motive other than racism can be found for the enactment of such outlandish laws: the government's motive was to destroy the remnants of tribal civilizations.

Another delightful example of enlightened European civilization at work is the following:

SECTION 140A—POOLROOMS

Where it is made to appear in open court that any Indian, summoned before such court, by inordinate frequenting of a poolroom either on or off a reserve, misspends or wastes his time or means to the detriment of himself, his family or household, of which he is a member, the police magistrate, stipendiary magistrate, Indian agent, or two justices of the peace holding such court, shall by writing under his or their hand or hands forbid the owner or person in charge of a poolroom which such Indian is in the habit of frequenting to allow such Indian to enter such poolroom for the space of one year from the date of such notice.

Any owner or person in charge of a poolroom who allows an Indian to enter a poolroom in violation of such notice, and any Indian who enters a poolroom where his admission has been so forbidden, shall be liable on summary conviction to a penalty not exceeding twenty five dollars and costs or to imprisonment for a term not exceeding thirty days.[16]

I attended business college in Truro during 1960–61 and was not permitted to enter the poolroom because I was an Aboriginal. I did not know that it had been mandated by statute. The poolroom operator's attitude was probably a combination of racism and fear of violating the law.

Another gem in the Indian Act of 1930 is a section that appears to have been enacted to stifle entrepreneurial initiative:

SECTION 120—PREVENTION OF TRADE

120. Every person who buys or otherwise acquires from any Indian or band or irregular band of Indians in the province of Manitoba, Saskatchewan, or Alberta, or the Territories any cattle or other animals or any grain, root crops or other produce or sells to any such Indian any goods or supplies, cattle or other animals contrary to the provisions of this Act, shall on summary conviction, be liable to a penalty not exceeding one hundred dollars, or to imprisonment for a term not exceeding three months, or to both.[17]

There are many more obnoxious former sections of the Indian Act and regulations that seem to have been enacted more for the purpose of demeaning and degrading the Aboriginal than for anything else. The Indian Act was used as a weapon to oppress the Tribes, rather than for tribal benefit. Sections 140, 140a, and 120, in one form or another, remained part of the Act until 1951.

At the time of Dr. Robertson's recommendations, there was no movement in this country to make positive changes for the Aboriginals. "Centralization" was not carried out for the benefit of the Micmac and Maliseet peoples, it was undertaken primarily for the convenience of the bureaucrats. With Bands scattered throughout the region, the poor bureaucrat had a difficult time performing his duties. In 1940, nineteen full- and part-time Indian Agents operated in Nova Scotia. Their appointments were made strictly on a political basis, although lip service was given towards fulfilling the meaning of the Public Service Employment Act.

In late 1940 the bureaucrats began to plan for the creation of two agencies in Nova Scotia, at Shubenacadie and Eskasoni, and to relocate all the Micmac in Nova Scotia onto two Reserves, Eskasoni and Indian Brook. To put their plan into action, they decided the land base of the two Reserves had to be increased substantially, so they immediately set about acquiring more land. They also planned to build compounds on the two Reserves to house agency staff and the teachers of an envisioned school.

The Department had a considerable problem acquiring the lands needed for the expansion of Indian Brook Reserve and the Assistant Deputy Minister wrote the following memo dated August 13, 1943, to the Deputy Minister to suggest a way to resolve the matter:

Further consideration has been given to the situation that has developed in connection with the Shubenacadie Indian Reserve and as a result I have been directed to suggest that expropriation be undertaken. If you concur I would ask that you supply me with a plan of survey and description by the surveyor covering the original Reserve and all properties acquired or desired to be acquired for extensions to the same.[18]

This memo shows how determined the government was to implement its Centralization plans, because it was willing to expropriate land to make the plan work.

In contrast, in the case of Grand Lake Indian Reserve, the Reserve without a right-of-way from the public road, Indian Affairs had been horrified at the suggestion that expropriation might be needed. They even tried to claim that expropriation could not be utilized for a right-of-way. The only reason there is still no right-of-way into the Grand Lake Reserve today is that the Band wants one and the Department does not. If the Department truly wanted one, it would simply utilize its powers of expropriation.

The administration compounds housed an elite group of people (from the Micmac viewpoint) who lived like kings and queens in comparison to themselves. The compound homes were furnished with all the modern conveniences, including insulation, central heating, electricity, and indoor plumbing, and were finished on the inside. To the Micmac, this was luxury beyond imagination.

I can remember walking by the convent in the 1940s and looking into the dining room, where the table would be set with sterling silver and bone china, with more food than I ever could have imagined.

This is how we lived in those days: our house was all uninsulated shell, with no services whatsoever. Heat was supplied by a cast-iron, wood-burning kitchen range and a tin stove. Water was carried from a hand-dug well, and lights were from kerosene lamps. Electricity was brought to the Reserve in 1945, but only to serve the Indian Affairs compound. It was not be extended to the entire Reserve until the early 1950s.

We did not purchase furniture for our house until Family Allowance was introduced in 1948. Until then, all our furniture had been made by my father out of rough lumber. Straw ticks were used for mattresses, made with coarse bags that had contained animal feed. Our sheets, if any, and our underwear were made out of Robin Hood flour bags.

Most of our clothing was second-hand; I can remember attending school one year wearing a girl's coat. Most of the men on the Reserve wore used RCMP clothing. I still can see my cousin wearing huge Mountie boots and coats.

There was no refrigeration in our homes. The men invariably carried the rations home on their backs from the village of Shubenacadie, a distance of five miles. Sometimes they made two trips: one to carry home the basic groceries and the second to carry a ninety-eight-pound bag of flour.

Milk was practically an unknown luxury in our household. Instead of drinking milk as a child, more often than not I drank black tea. Expensive cuts of meat such as steaks and roasts were also unknown; on more than one occasion a stuffed porcupine took the place of a turkey at a holiday meal. At one time, a live porcupine within a five-mile radius of the Shubenacadie Indian Reserve was a rare find.

Around 1946 the agents tried to make a farmer out of my father who has no formal education, can neither read nor write, and who had worked as a lumberman, rough carpenter, or labourer when work could be found.

Now, at the age of 46, he was expected to become a productive farmer. They gave him a loan out of the revolving fund to buy a cow and helped him to build a small barn. The Department also provided seed potatoes and vegetable seed for planting in the "fertile" soil where our home was located—it was clay and stone, not farmland. Amazingly, he did manage to grow some crops from this unfertile soil, although the fruit of his efforts were about 25 percent of what could be grown on good farmland.

I can remember walking down to the village on the rare Saturday we had a few cents to attend a movie. As I passed the homes and farms of the White people along the way, I would dream about someday being as rich as they were. It was not until years later that I realized that most of the people I had envied had in reality been poor themselves. Your poverty must be outstanding when you think the poor of another race are rich.

While the Department bureaucrats were planning the centralization policy, they gave no thought to the fact that it would threaten the *traditional Band or tribal village system* among the Micmac and Maliseet.

As it had done throughout its existence, the Department ignored the Aboriginal point of view and went ahead with its life-shattering policy. They did this because they felt they were more intelligent and knowledgeable than the Aboriginals and knew better what was best for them. This perspective is still present in the system today.

The centralization policy was implemented in the Maritimes in 1942. With the hiring of two full-time Indian Agents and the Privy Council's endorsement of the two new agencies at Eskasoni and Shubenacadie, a new type of hell was created for the Micmac of Nova Scotia. The Micmac of Prince Edward Island and the Micmac and Maliseet of New Brunswick were also pushed into a situation that tried their will to survive.

A review of the ration rates and relief allowances in 1940 indicates the "generosity" of the government of the day towards Aboriginals. The following memo went out from Ottawa to all inspectors and Indian Agents on May 22, 1940:

> Indian Agents throughout the Dominion are instructed to undertake a complete revision of their ration lists and relief allowances. It is desirable that this revision should be completed not later than June 15.
>
> It is not expected that drastic reductions can be made in the monthly rations authorized at present for the support of aged and physically incapacitated Indians. An attempt should be made, however, to reduce items such as tea or commodities imported from other Countries. The new lists should be submitted in due course for Departmental approval.
>
> Relief allowances in the case of physically fit, able-bodied Indians should be cancelled not later than July 1. It is not the policy of the Department to provide able-bodied Indians with relief. All such Indians must undertake certain tasks either on the reserves or off the reserves. The cultivation of gardens, farm work, clearing land, road construction, drainage projects, wood cutting, etc. in certain districts are all tasks that might be undertaken.

Rations may be supplied to Indians engaged in such work. In no case, however, will it be permissible to supply relief to an Indian who refuses to undertake the task assigned him by the Agent; and the character of the work in which the Indian is engaged must be clearly stated on relief vouchers sent forward to the Department for payment.

We are attaching hereto a ration list to which you must strictly adhere. No payments will be made in future for commodities other than those included in the official list, except in cases of sickness, where special authorization has been secured from the Department.

A number of Indians have enlisted in the Canadian Active Service Force and the wives and dependents of these men are in receipt of government allowances. Care should be exercised by our Agents to prevent overlapping and duplication in Indian welfare effort.

[Signed by the Director; signature illegible.]

SCALE OF MONTHLY RATIONS FOR INDIAN RELIEF

	ADULTS					
RATION	1	2	3	4	5	6
	Lbs.	Lbs.	Lbs.	Lbs.	Lbs.	Lbs.
Flour 2nd grade	24	36	49	61	80	98
Rolled Oats	6	9	12	15	18	18
Baking Powder	1	1 3/4	1 3/4	2	2	2
Tea	1	1 1/2	2	2	2	3
Sugar	2	4	5	7	8	10
Lard	3	5	8	10	10	13
Beans	5	5	7	7	8	8
Rice	2	3	5	5	7	7
Cheese	1	1 1/2	1 1/2	2	2	3
Meat or Fish	$1.00	$1.50	$1.75	$2.00	$2.00	$2.25
Salt	.10 or .15 per month per family.					
Matches	.10 to .20 per month per family.					

NOTE: Indians under the age of 12 years shall be considered children, and over that age as adults. Issues of rations for each child, of flour, rolled oats, sugar, lard, beans, rice, cheese and meat or fish, shall be one half of the ration for an Adult.

Departmental approval must be secured for special rations recommended by the Medical Health Officer in cases of sickness, and milk that may be necessary in the case of infants.

Storekeepers should be warned that if they vary without authority the items contained in this list they are subject to immediate removal from the list of firms authorized to do Government Business. [These rations were purchase orders made out to specific stores and there was to be no substitution.]

R.A. Hoey, Supt. Welfare and Training.[19]

Can you imagine this diet month after month, year after year, with very little variation? No milk for your children, no hope for the future, except bare survival? Malnutrition was common among Aboriginals of the Maritimes and would remain so, because of governmental practices, for many years to come.

I remember an event when I was four or five years old, in either 1942 or 1943, when we ran out of food on a Friday and would have to go without over the weekend. Early Monday morning I walked with my mother to the Indian Agency to ask the Agent for a special ration.

Before long, the Agent had her begging and crying. Then he told her she would have to wait while he thought it over. At about 11:50, ten minutes before his lunchtime, he called us in and gave my mother a $2.00 special order, but not before subjecting her to more humiliating verbal abuse. I remember the event so well, because on that day I made up my mind that when I grew up "no one would ever do to me what that bastard had done to my mother." And to this day, no one ever has.

One of the prime factors in choosing Eskasoni and Shubenacadie as centralization locations was to accommodate White populations. On November 15, 1944, the Member of Parliament for Antigonish–Guysborough wrote the following memo to Mr. Hoey, Director of Indian Affairs:

Would you be good enough to advise me as to whether or not the Department of Indian Affairs intends to take any move in the near future respecting the transfer of all Indians in Nova Scotia to one or two central places of habitation?

I have had inquires from some of my constituents, expressing the hope that the Indians living in the neighbourhood of Bayfield, N.S. would be moved away from there soon, and this leads me to inquire as to the present status of the Department's plans in this connection.

Your early reply re the matter will be much appreciated.
J. Ralph Kirk.[20]

In a letter dated January 6, 1945, responding to Mr. Kirk's inquiries, the Acting Director of the Department's welfare program penned the following:

As you are no doubt aware, for many years *the problem of how to administer* the affairs of the small group of Indians in Nova Scotia has been a matter of serious concern and in order to place it on the soundest possible basis a partial consolidation of the Reserves and the gradual centralization of the Indian population has been decided upon.

I am sure you will appreciate the difficulties and wasteful expenditure of public moneys that are involved in trying to educate, hospitalize, train and care for the relatively few Indians of your Province when they are scattered in small groups and on widely separated reserves selected with little regard either to adequacy of area, suitable as to character of the land, or to the amenities of the situation of important white settlements.

I am sure you will agree that the worst conditions prevail on those reserves that are located on the outskirts of important industrial cities and communities and in such locations it has been our experience that *vice, immorality and poverty* exist to a much greater degree than prevails where the Indians live closer to nature and in a less artificial environment

With the hope of improving conditions, plans were made toward consolidation and centralization of the reserves in the knowledge may I say, that under such a plan we would be able to offer the Indian better educational and vocational facilities, added attention to his physical, moral and spiritual welfare, and to create a condition more closely approaching a self-sustaining livelihood for him than is possible at present. It was felt that *we would also improve the amenities of the White communities which are not improved by the immediate presence of isolated groups of Indians.*[21]

The Department was quite interested in getting Aboriginals out of areas populated by White people. If the government had really had the best interests of the Tribes at heart during this exercise, it would have set up new Reserves in close proximity to large industrial centres where the drive by the Micmac to achieve self-reliance could have been sustained.

Mr. Kirk also received this assurance from the Director of the Branch in a memo dated November 16, 1944 "I can state, however, without hesitation, that there has been no change in the Government policy and that the work of centralization will be expedited by us to the utmost extent possible."[22]

The truth is that the Aboriginals living off-Reserve prior to centralization, even though impoverished by anyone's standards, were far better off than those living on-Reserve.

In proof of the fact that White considerations took priority over Aboriginal interests, a provision under the Indian Act could remove Aboriginals from their homes in or near White communities if that was the White's desire. Shortly after the turn of the century, this provision was used in Nova Scotia when the Micmac residing near Kings Road, Sydney, about where the Holiday Inn is today, were forcibly removed from their Reserve and moved to where Membertou Reserve is now located. The Whites residing close to the area had gone to court and had the following provision of the Indian Act enforced:

INQUIRY AND REPORT BY EXCHEQUER
COURT AS TO REMOVAL OF INDIANS
SECTION 52, INDIAN ACT

1. In the case of an Indian reserve which adjoins or is situated wholly or partly within an incorporated town or city having a population of not less than eight thousand, and which reserve has not been released or surrendered by the Indians, the Governor in Council may, upon the recommendation of the Superintendent General, refer to the judge of the Exchequer Court of Canada for inquiry and report the question as to whether it is expedient, having

regard to the *interest of the public* and of the Indians of the band for whose use the reserve is held, that *the Indians should be removed* from the reserve or any part of it.

2. The order in council made in the case shall be certified by the Clerk of the Privy Council to the Registrar of the Exchequer Court of Canada, and the judge of the court shall thereupon proceed as soon as convenient to fix a time and place, of which due notice shall be given by publication in the Canada Gazette, and otherwise as may be directed by the judge, for taking the evidence and hearing and investigating the matter.

3. The judge shall have the like powers to issue subpoenas, compel the attendance and examination of witnesses, take evidence, give directions, and generally to hear and determine the matter and regulate the procedure as in proceedings upon information by the Attorney General within the ordinary jurisdiction of the court, and shall assign counsel to represent and act for the Indians who may be opposed to the proposed removal.

4. If the judge finds that it is expedient that the band of Indians should be removed from the reserve or any part of it, he shall proceed, before making his report, to ascertain the amounts of compensation, if any, which should be paid respectively to individual Indians of the band for the special loss or damages which they will sustain in respect of the buildings or improvements to which they are entitled upon the lands of the reserve for which they are located, and the judge shall, moreover, consider and report upon any of the other facts or circumstances of the case which he may deem proper or material to be considered by the Governor in Council.

5. The judge shall transmit his findings, with the evidence and a report of the proceedings, to the Governor in Council, who shall lay a full report of the proceedings, the evidence and findings before Parliament at the then current or next ensuing session thereof, and upon such findings being approved by resolution of Parliament the Governor in Council may thereupon give effect to the said findings and cause the reserve, or any part thereof from which it is found expedient to remove the Indians, to be sold or leased by public auction after three months advertisement in the public press, upon the best terms which in the opinion of the Governor in Council, may be obtained therefor.

6. The proceeds of the sale or lease, after deducting the usual percentage for management fund, shall be applied in compensating individual Indians for their buildings or improvements as found by the judge, in purchasing a new reserve for the Indians removed, in transferring the said Indians with their effects thereto, in erecting building upon the new reserve, and in providing the Indians with such other assistance as the Superintendent General may consider advisable; and the balance of the proceeds, if any, shall be placed to the credit of the Indians; but the Governor in Council shall not cause the Indians to be removed or disturb their possession, until

suitable reserve has been obtained and set apart for them in lieu of the reserve from which the expediency of removing the Indians is so established as aforesaid.

7. For the purpose of selecting, appropriating and acquiring the lands necessary to be taken, or which it may be deemed to be expedient to take, for any new reserve to be acquired for the Indians as authorized by the last preceding subsection, whether they are Crown lands or not, the Superintendent General shall have all the powers conferred upon the Minister by the Expropriation Act, and such new reserve shall, for the purpose aforesaid, be deemed to be a public work within the definition of that expression in the Expropriation Act; and all the provisions of the Expropriation Act, in so far as applicable and not inconsistent with this Act, shall apply in respect of the proceedings for the selection, survey, ascertainment and acquisition of the lands required and the determination and payment of the compensation therefor.

8. The Superintendent General shall not exercise the power of expropriation unless authorized by the Governor in Council.[23]

This gave the bureaucrats an enormous club to wield in their efforts to force the Aboriginals to do their bidding. No appeal process was provided to have the "Sydney" decision set aside. It caused the Micmac to think twice before opposing the Department. Perhaps the most despicable part of Section 52 was that the Department could force the Aboriginals to pay for their own expulsion! This offensive part of the Act was finally repealed in 1951.

The assertion that there has been but little justice in Canada for Aboriginals from the onset of European colonization up until recent times is well supported by historical documentation. For the most part, up until the 1980s, the justice system was used by the dominant society to control and oppress Aboriginal peoples. It was rarely used to accord them justice. Section 52 was contrary to the provisions of the Royal Proclamation of 1763, which forbade the alienation of Aboriginal lands without Aboriginal consent.

During 1941, letters were exchanged between the Premier of Nova Scotia A.S. MacMillan and the federal Minister of Mines and Resources T.A. Crerar concerning the feasibility of a plan to centralize the Aboriginals of the province. In his memo to the Premier, dated April 24, 1941, the Minister provides an outline of the plan under consideration and asks for the Premier's support:

It is of course not my wish to make any radical changes in the administration of Indian Affairs in your Province without first letting you know what we plan to do. While the *Indians are the "Wards" of the dominion*, their welfare is a matter in which the Provinces are also interested. The co-operation we receive from the Provinces makes our task less difficult or, to put into other words, the more co-operation we receive from the Provinces the more quickly will it be possible to improve the physical welfare of the Indians.[24]

In his letter, the Minister informs the Premier that he will be appointing a bureaucrat to come to Nova Scotia and investigate the possibilities of acquiring additional lands for the implementation of centralization at Eskasoni and Shubenacadie. He advises that a W.S. Arneil, by reason of his experience in land settlement work with the "Soldier Settlement Board," is specially qualified.

Mr. Arneil, of course, actually knew nothing of Aboriginals or about the laws surrounding the administration of "Indian lands," but in their opinion he was eminently qualified. This is the way the Department has usually selected employees to provide services to Aboriginals.

The Minister wrote his letter on April 24, 1941, and the Premier gave his full support to the concept, without much review, only five days later, on April 29:

> Dear Mr. Grerar:
>
> I have your letter with regard to the Indian Reserves in this Province and note carefully all that you have to say. This is entirely a new departure and no doubt will meet with some opposition from the Indians themselves—this, due to the fact that a number of these reservations are located near towns, for instance Shubenacadie, Truro, etc. and being near of course the Indians have the habit of spending their time loafing around the towns. However, I think if an agreement could be reached that the idea is a practical one and there are plenty of vacant lands where they can be placed in this Province.
>
> I shall be glad to meet your representative when he comes, and go into the matter with him and shall also put him in touch with the proper persons in our Lands and Forests Department as well as with our Farm Loan Board which is also an operating body. Possibly when he comes to Halifax he had better see me before discussing this matter with others.
>
> A.S. MacMillan.[25]

It seems that Premier MacMillan may have also had hopes of putting the Micmac as far away from White settlements as the boundaries of Nova Scotia might permit. It was truly amazing how fast the province responded to this proposal. By comparison, the Shubenacadie Band has been unable to receive a positive response from the province for many decades to its request for a right-of-way into its Reserve at Grand Lake.

Mr. Arneil, with the impressive title of Inspector of Indian Agencies, soon began his inspections and appraisals of the Reserves and their inhabitants in the Maritime Provinces. He quickly began to issue short preliminary reports, and one of the first was on Eskasoni. His lack of experience regarding Nova Scotia winters is obvious when he states that because the houses there are mostly shells, they are very hard to heat, but adequate! As one who has lived in an uninsulated house during a Nova Scotia winter, I can attest to the fact that they are not adequate. I can remember waking up after a cold winter's night to find a considerable frost build-up around where my nose was sticking out of the blankets. To avoid freezing to death, we piled every coat in the house onto our beds.

Mr. Arneil also stated that more than 75 percent of the Aboriginals in the province of Nova Scotia were in favour of centralization. As he was in contact with only a few during his travels through the Maritimes, this is an outrageous assessment. It would appear that one of the most valued qualities sought in prospective employees of the Department is the ability to play fast and loose with the truth when it comes to statistics on Aboriginals.

During 1942, word began to leak into the Micmac communities in Nova Scotia about the plans to centralize the People. Opposition to the plan was very strong among some members of the Micmac communities. As time passed, this opposition was supported by the majority. As a matter of fact, the Agent at Eskasoni, J.A. MacLean, in a moment of truth, admitted to Mr. Hoey, National Superintendent of Welfare and Training, in a letter dated May 27, 1944, that approximately 75 percent of the Indians in Nova Scotia were *opposed* to centralization.[26]

In his response to Mr. MacLean, dated June 5, 1944, Mr. Hoey said: "The writer is of the opinion that you should not attach too much importance to this *nominal opposition*." If Mr. Hoey considered 75 percent of the Nova Scotia Micmac to be a small opposition, what would he have considered a large opposition? He went on to say: "It is altogether likely that the delay in moving these bands to Eskasoni has resulted in a certain amount of dissatisfaction."[27]

One of the most ardent and consistent opponents to the centralization plan was Ben Christmas, a member of the Membertou Band. Mr. Christmas was the President of the United General Indian Council of Nova Scotia at the time, and he also became the Chief of the Membertou Band as time went on. Chief Joseph Julien of Millbrook, Margaret Phillips of Cole Harbour, Noel Marshall of Chapel Island, Joseph Cope of Halifax County, and many others also opposed the plan until it was finally scuttled in 1950.

Mr. Christmas was a very articulate man. He would have been amused by a description of him written by an Indian Agent dated March 1, 1943, concerning his opposition to the Department's centralization plans. Mr. MacLean wrote: "It appears that Ben Christmas, an Indian of Membertou Reserve, Sydney, N.S., who is considered to be *somewhat more intelligent than the ordinary Indian....* " [Mr. MacLean obviously had a low opinion about the intelligence of Aboriginals and was amazed Mr. Christmas could rise above this standard.] He continued: "I have been asked to inform you that no notice should be taken of letters from Mr. Christmas regarding the centralization plan, or from others who may write in this regard, as regardless of whose name may be used as a signature, Mr. Christmas is *the man behind the gun*."[28]

To persuade members from other Nova Scotia Bands to move from elsewhere on Cape Breton Island to Eskasoni, or from homes on the mainland to Shubenacadie, the Department began a propaganda campaign. They told Band members that if they moved there would be jobs, houses, schools, and recreation facilities, food would be plentiful, there would be no more near famines, medical services would be available, and so on. They told the People that they would make them self-sufficient. Clearly, the Department deliberately lied to entice the Micmac to move. Everything they told them were lies and impossible dreams.

The promised land never materialized, but in the short run "unsustainable economic development" was in full swing. New houses were built; compounds for bureaucrats and the teachers were built on both Reserves, and so were sawmills. Tree cutting proceeded as if the wooded areas on both Reserves were inexhaustible, which of course they were not, and the two sawmills ran full blast. Both mills paid scab wages and were hit by labour unrest around 1946. After the strikes were over, the men were still paid scab wages.

In answer to inquiries from Ottawa regarding the strike, the Indian Agent wrote: "there didn't seem to be any communistic connotations to the strike at Eskasoni."[29] It is a testament to their level-headed thinking and intelligence, that in the early 1900s the Tribes in Canada did not turn, like other oppressed people in many parts of the world, to extremism to find solutions for their problems.

Many foolish undertakings were begun by the Department during this time. Perhaps the most incompetent was that all the houses they were so proud of were built with *green lumber*. When the lumber dried, the houses twisted and warped beyond repair. When they were later judged unfit for human habitation and torn down, cracks more than one inch wide were discovered between the boards. Inferior quality concrete was used to lay the foundations for these homes and it soon began to crack and crumble.

Of all the homes constructed during that period, no more than a half a dozen were still standing in 1993.

The efforts of Chief Christmas and others in their fight against centralization probably prevented the Department from taking a more forceful approach. However, it did not prevent the bureaucrats from using some unscrupulous methods to force compliance.

The residential school at Shubenacadie was again used. Many families had their children taken away from them and placed in this school for "protection." The Department's rationalization was that their dwellings were unfit for human habitation and the health of the children was at risk. The Micmac were told that, after moving to Shubenacadie or Eskasoni, their children would be returned to their care.

By 1949 the government and its bureaucracy were becoming increasingly nervous about the centralization policy. They had even tried to entice people from New Brunswick and Prince Edward Island to move to Nova Scotia in order to keep up a semblance of growth in the two centralized communities. At one time, the Shubenacadie Indian Reserve was populated by Micmac from at least two dozen different Bands. But opposition continued to build among the Bands in the province: Membertou, Chapel Island, Nyanza, Whycocomagh, Afton, Pictou Landing, Millbrook, Sheet Harbour, Cole Harbour, Horton, Cambridge, Bear River, Yarmouth, and so on. Not one Micmac community in Nova Scotia was cooperating with the Department in this effort by 1949.

It was becoming quite evident that the only way the government could hope to achieve centralization was by force, and this option was given some serious consideration. Word of mouth, or the "Indian telegraph," as it was commonly referred to among the People, had prevented any further voluntary movement to the centralized communities. The people had become fully aware that the false promises of economic miracles for those who made the move had not materialized: they were still caught in the same poverty cycle, just in a new location.

The policy of centralization was bankrupt from the day of its conception. It had not been well thought out, nor had any real dialogue taken place with the Aboriginal peoples of the Maritimes while the policy was being formulated. The ideas some of the bureaucrats had come up with were better applied to animals than human beings.

The practice of herding a race of people together in defiance of their wishes and for the convenience of another race was utilized during the same period by another dictator: Joseph Stalin. Stalin deported several nationalities to far-flung parts of the former Soviet Union in order to destroy their civilizations. However, he failed, just as the Department did in its attempt to destroy the Micmac and Maliseet Tribes. During the Department's attempts at centralization in New Brunswick, they even considered moving both of these Tribes into one community at Kingsclear Indian Reserve. If this move had not been vigorously resisted by both Tribes, it would have been cultural genocide, as both cultures would have disappeared in the process.

Perhaps the best testament to the failure and, unwittingly, the worst condemnation of the centralization policy was contained in a report to Indian Affairs, Ottawa, written by the Agent in charge of the Shubenacadie Indian Agency, H.C. Rice, dated March 23, 1949:

> It would appear that the time is past due when a *hard and fast policy* should be laid down respecting the position that the Centralized Reserve at Micmac (Shubenacadie), N.S., is to play in respect to the Indians on the Mainland of Nova Scotia.
>
> Here follows a summary of the conditions on the Mainland of Nova Scotia, by Reserves, commencing at the Strait of Canso and proceeding Westward:
>
> *Guysborough County: Cook's Cove and Dort's Cove.*
> 22 Indians—7 Families declared destitute by the Medical Officer and now receiving relief in its various forms. [This was one of the communities the Department did manage to wipe out.]
>
> *Antigonish County: Heatherton, Afton, Summerside, and South River.*
> 121 Indians—36 Families declared destitute by the Medical Officer and now receiving relief in its various forms. [The Department did manage to wipe out the settlements at Heatherton, Summerside, and South River. However, these people regrouped and now mostly reside on the Afton Reserve.]

Pictou County: Pictou Landing Reserve.
74 Indians—36 Families declared destitute by the Medical Officer and now receiving relief in its various forms.

Colchester County: Millbrook Reserve.
124 Indians—24 Families on relief.

Cumberland County: Halfway River and Squatters.
39 Indians—15 Persons on relief. [The settlement at Halfway River was wiped out, but the off-Reserve settlement of Springhill Junction still exists.]

*Hants County: Indian Brook Reserve, Micmac, N.S. . . . [will be discussed later]

Halifax county: Sheet Harbour and Squatters.
56 Indians—12 Families on relief. [This was a false report; the "squatters" he refers to owned the lots where they resided, but they are all deceased now. There were also two other occupied Reserves in the county that he does not list: Cole Harbour and Beaver Dam. Mrs. Margaret Phillips of Cole Harbour had taken the Department on with regard to the centralization of the residents of Cole Harbour at Shubenacadie and had won, with the assistance of local politicians, the right to remain in Cole Harbour.]

Lunenburg County: Gold River and Squatters.
16 Indians—6 Indians on relief (two wholly maintained). [Micmac were also living at New Ross Reserve at the time, but he makes no mention of them; probably they were all working.]

Queens County: Wildcat Reserve and Squatters.
45 Indians—19 Families on relief. [Again the "squatters" mostly owned their lots. These people or their descendants still reside in the same area.]

Shelburne County: Squatters.
32 Indians—15 persons on relief. [The Reserve these people had was alienated from them and today is a land claim. Like in Queens County, these Micmac or their descendants still reside in the area.]

Yarmouth County: Yarmouth Reserve and Squatters.
30 Indians—16 Indians on relief.

Digby County: Bear River Reserve.
76 Indians—35 Persons on relief.

Annapolis County: Lequille Reserve and Squatters.
69 Indians—13 Families on relief. [Again the "squatters" mainly · owned their lots.]

Kings County: Cambridge Reserve and Squatters.
112 Indians—37 Families on relief.

It will be noted that outside of Hants County where the Centralized Reserve is located we have a total of 816 Indians of which 271 Families or part thereof on relief. [The total outside the centralized Reserve was probably closer to one thousand, taking into consideration the people left outside his census.]

At Micmac, N.S., we have approximately 700 Indians, we have 88 persons on relief. Some of these persons have large families and the relief at times is very high, especially during the Winter months, when there is little or no sale for Indian Handicraft whereby they could supplement their income.

However, it must be borne in mind that the majority of those on relief here were destitute in their former abode and it was to supervise their relief as well as give their families the benefit of education, medical treatment, *spiritual guidance*, etc., that they were taken to this Centralized Reserve. The fact they are here has been a marvellous benefit to them and their families as well as to the staff here, whose duty it is to supervise their relief and look after their welfare.

As the situation now stands, it is costing the Federal Government thousands of dollars yearly in relief, groceries, milk, fuel and clothing, medical, dental and hospital services and it is personally felt that in the majority of cases the desired result is not being obtained.

The shacks, camps, etc., that the Indians off this Reserve are living in are beyond description. They are not fit in the majority of cases for human habitation, infested with all the various types of parasites, vermin etc., known to science. Under these circumstances, staple foods, milk and eggs are given these people [they were lucky; we did not get these groceries on-Reserve] and they live in filth and exposed to disease in its various forms.

The Medical Services are confined to calls when required and although the average Physician takes a conscientious view of each case, his work is hampered by the conditions under which these people live. The Indian has lived for years under these conditions and he now appears to be content with his lot.

However it must be borne in mind that the Indian is sick, not in the sense that the term is usually applied, but due to the fact that he has been undernourished, ill clad and forced to live under conditions only found in the lowest of slums, until the present generation and possibly a few generations to come, he will be susceptible to disease, lacking initiative and in general one that will take considerable supervision, encouragement and understanding if he is to become a useful citizen of this Country.

The situation as detailed herein is applicable to the Micmacs of Nova Scotia, and it is in their behalf that this letter is being written.

The question now presents itself, what is the best solution to such a case, both from the standpoint of the Federal Government and the Indians as a whole. Bearing in mind that throughout this

Province we have, exclusive of Micmac, N.S., 271 Families on relief, the majority of whom are aged, it would appear that they all should be taken to the Centralized Reserve, the benefits to them of this transfer is well known and it is not necessary to repeat.

Once we have them here, what then? Should they be given individual houses or should a home for the aged Indians be built? The latter is by far the more economical in the long run, and I personally believe more beneficial to the Indian. In old age, the Indian is no more capable of looking after themselves than any other Race, and living alone (as they prefer to do) is always a worry and expense, as almost constant supervision must be maintained to get the results desired.

In a home, which would be properly supervised by a Superintendent, they would be kept clean, well fed, warmly clothed, etc., and in general would live the remaining days of their lives in comfort. However, it is realized the Indians desire to be alone, to travel when he or she so wishes, and to be free from anything that pertained to regularity, and he might not be content for some time, but when the benefits of such an institution would become known to him, we might expect their co-operation. This is purely a thought, and may be of some value in arriving at the most logical conclusion to this problem.

The alternative is, as previously stated, to place them in individual welfare houses on this Reserve. The average welfare house costs the Federal Government approximately $1400.00. I have reference here to the three room bungalow. The larger welfare house costs approximately $1800.00. The former type is suitable for these aged people, but a quick calculation will show that it is going to cost in the vicinity of $300 000.00 to house these indigents individually. They of course prefer this arrangement, but is it wise to expend this amount of money, to house them individually, when a much more economical and satisfactory solution would be to house them under one roof.

It is felt, in view of the fact we are about to enter upon a new year, that this matter be given careful consideration, taking into consideration that the building programme on this Reserve must be governed by your recommendations regarding our indigents. A basic policy should be made regarding these people, if they are to be moved to Micmac, N.S., we can concentrate on houses for them, as distinct from the conventional welfare house for able bodied Indians.

The aged, sick and destitute Indian is of primary concern, and it is felt should receive priority over everything else pertaining to the administration of this Agency. Once we have this problem overcome, we can devote our undivided effort toward establishing industries, encouraging agriculture, advanced education and the various other projects that tend to raise the standard of living of these people.[30]

Mr. Rice, for some reason, misstated the population figures. In his report he says 816 Micmacs did not reside at Shubenacadie, and he gave the population at Indian Brook Reserve as 700. Adding 816 and 700, plus the 186 he left off his count for the province outside of Shubenacadie, gives a total of 1702 people.

But on March 31, 1950, he filed a report showing there were only 1373 Indians living on mainland Nova Scotia.[31] The difference of 329 gives the impression that someone was padding the figures. The practice of padding population figures in order to acquire more money from Ottawa became a common practice among bureaucrats. However, after the Indian Register was established in 1951, the practice had to be discontinued because figures could then be verified.

On October 16, 1949, Mr. Rice wrote to Ottawa once more: "Due to the curtailing of operations at Shubenacadie and the *inability of the Indians to secure employment outside of this Reservation,* I suggest that we allow the cutting of Christmas trees on this Reserve for sale."[32] For all intents and purposes the forced centralization was over.

The realities of life were fast becoming clear to the people who had been duped into giving up their homes and moving to Shubenacadie and Eskasoni. Suddenly they found themselves trying to live on rations once more. Many began to leave, in some cases returning to their former homes if they were still standing, or building shacks if they were not. The majority, however, started an exodus from the province that drew half of the Micmac from their homeland in search of a better life in the U.S. or Central Canada. This, like centralization, proved to be a hopeless dream.

I myself left Nova Scotia in search of a better life in 1953, when I was 15 years old. Up until that time I had worked full time for almost a year at the government-owned community store at Indian Brook. They were paying me ten dollars a week for working six and a half days (52 hours) a week when I resigned.

Boston is where most of the families of my childhood friends migrated. We all arrived there over a period of several years with great expectations. However the reality of how badly Canada had failed us soon became evident. With our lack of education, experience, and skills, all that was available to us were the most menial low-paying jobs. A few prospered, many took to alcohol and died from drinking Muscatel, but most of us reassessed our lives and returned home.

Colonization caused many hardships among the Micmac. It was a terrible assault upon the Band structure of Micmac civilization. The Aboriginal, as always, suffered the consequences of the games that bureaucrats played to secure their own futures. The one positive achievement of centralization for the Micmac was that it moved our People to realize that we can fight back and win.

The defeat of this insidious policy can be attributed to the efforts of many individuals, foremost among them Chief Ben Christmas, Chief Joe Julien, Margaret Phillips, Noel Marshall, Joseph Cope, and others who provided the leadership to protect what they believed in. With their efforts, the individuality of the Bands, although diminished in number, survived. The death of centralization caused no tears, but its disastrous effects are still felt to this day.

Most people couldn't conceive of having a plan for life mapped out and implemented for them by someone else without their consent or approval. But this is precisely what was done to the Micmac and the Maliseet!

NOTES

1. Marilyn Millward, "Clean Behind the Ears? Micmac Parents, Micmac Children, and the Shubenacadie Residential School," *New Maritimes* (March/April 1992). Emphasis added.

2. Ibid.

3. Ibid.

4. Ibid.

5. Ibid.

6. Canada, Indian Affairs, Shubenacadie Indian Agency, centralization correspondence, 1938–1952, Confederacy of Mainland Micmacs files, Truro, NS.

7. Cape Breton and Pictou Micmacs, Land for Pictou, *Nova Scotia Assembly Journals*, 1 Feb. 1864, Appendix 37—Indian Affairs, 1–7.

8. Canada, Indian Affairs, Atlantic Region, Centralization and other correspondence, 1936–1952, Confederacy of Mainland Micmacs files, Truro, NS.

9. The Canada Census is the source for population figures of 1871–1921; the figures after 1921 are derived from Band lists.

10. Centralization correspondence, Atlantic Region. Emphasis added.

11. Ibid.

12. Ibid.

13. Canada, Indian Affairs, Circular Letter (forbidding dancing), 15 Dec. 1921, Ottawa.

14. Indian Act, 1927. Emphasis added.

15. Ibid., 1930.

16. Ibid.

17. Canada, Indian Affairs, Shubenacadie Indian Agency, Centralization correspondence, 1938–1952, Confederacy of Mainland Micmacs files, Truro, NS.

18. Centralization correspondence, Atlantic Region.

19. Ibid.

20. Ibid.

21. Ibid.

22. Indian Act, 1930.

23. Centralization correspondence, Atlantic Region.

24. Ibid.

25. Indian Affairs, Eskasoni Indian Agency, Centralization correspondence, 1938–1952, Confederacy of Mainland Micmacs files, Truro, NS. Emphasis added.

26. Centralization correspondence, Eskasoni.

27. Ibid.

28. Ibid.

29. Centralization correspondence, Shubenacadie. Emphasis added.

30. Ibid.

31. Ibid.

32. Ibid.

RENEWAL OF THE POTLATCH
AT CAPE MUDGE *

HARRY ASSU WITH JOY INGLIS

o

Many of the Kwagiulth people were arrested for taking part in a big potlatch given by Dan Cranmer on Village Island in 1921. Dan's wife Emma
was from Village Island, and her family were giving away a lot of things
that went into that potlatch because that's what the family is expected to do
for the daughter who is married. My father and eldest brother Dan were
called to go there because my father was related to Emma. I don't know if
anyone else went from the villages around here.

My father and brother were arrested. Charges were laid against them
under a law that had been on the books for a long time. They were told they
would go to jail unless they signed a paper that said they wouldn't potlatch
any more. They were told that our people would have to hand over everything they used for the potlatch, whether they were there or not. Anybody
arrested who didn't give up their family's masks and other things went to
jail. Twenty-two of our Kwagiulth people went to Oakalla. They were prisoners from two months to six months.[1]

My father had to go to court in Alert Bay two or three times. I was only
a young fellow then, and I wasn't too concerned—older men were handling
it anyway; but I remember thinking, "Why would the Indian agent start all
that?" I was around seventeen at the time and walked every day to
Quathiaski Cove from the village and back home at night after spending all
day learning to use machine tools with W. E. Anderson. He was the manager and the best mechanic we had at the cannery. I felt lucky to learn and
was working hard at it. I didn't know what the government was doing to
our people, taking away our culture.

* This excerpt is reprinted with permission of the publisher from *Assu of Cape Mudge: Recollections of a Coastal Indian Chief* by Harry Assu with Joy Inglis. (Vancouver: UBC Press, 1989), 104–21. All rights reserved by the Publisher.

The scow came around from the cannery and put in at the village to pick up the big pile of masks and headdresses and belts and coppers—everything we had for potlatching. I saw it pull out across Discovery Passage to the Campbell River side where more stuff was loaded on the *Princess Beatrice* for the trip to Alert Bay. Alert Bay was where the Potlatch gear was gathered together. It came mainly from our villages around here and from Alert Bay and Village Island. It was sent to the museum in Ottawa from Alert Bay by the Indian agent. Our old people who watched the barge pull out from shore with all their masks on it said: "There is nothing left now. We might as well go home." When we say "go home," it means to die.

When that shipment went to Ottawa they were supposed to send $1415 to pay for all the things our Kwagiulth people had been forced to give up under threat of jail. But people are still alive who didn't get paid, and they never knew anybody who did get paid. You can't buy *one* of those old pieces now for $1415! They took away around six hundred pieces.

A collector named Heye turned up at Alert Bay, and the Indian agent Halliday sold him some of our stuff before he shipped off the rest to the museum in Ottawa.[2] Even the government who were getting all the rest didn't like that! They wanted it all for themselves, I guess. Heye had his pick of all those hundreds and hundreds of pieces. One of them belonged to my father; some to my grandfather, Jim Naknakim; to my wife's uncle, John Dick; and to other Lekwiltok men in this area, as well as people from farther north at Alert Bay and Village Island. None of the pieces that went to Heye's museum in New York were ever returned, though we sent a delegation there to negotiate with them.

In 1978 the National Museum in Ottawa returned the part of the collection they still held because they knew it was wrong to force us to stop our custom of potlatching and take all our goods away from us. But early on Indian Affairs had gone ahead and loaned around 135 pieces of our masks and regalia to the Royal Ontario Museum, and it took us much longer to get that museum to return what is ours. This is our family inheritance I am talking about. You don't give up on that! Finally, in 1987 the Royal Ontario Museum returned what they had taken.

Our people figured that all that potlatch gear that was taken away to museums was still theirs by rights and that they still owned it, so it would have to be given back. Those old people kept trying to have it returned to them. A lot of people worked to get it back. I know Jimmy Sewid went to Ottawa with Guy Williams in 1963, and he went into the museum for the Kwagiulth people and demanded our stuff back. He had his wife's mother with him to be sure of what was ours. He told them he was ready to buy it back for the $1415 they claimed to have paid for it and to bring a truck around and load it in; and he told them he was ready to go to the newspapers and tell how the museum had got hold of our stuff.

Back then, they wouldn't show us the potlatch regalia or listen. Finally, in 1973 they informed our chiefs' meeting in the Kwakiutl District Council that they were going to return the "Potlatch Collection." But they didn't want to give it back to the families who own it. They wanted it put in a museum. So it was voted that the museum should be built at Cape Mudge. Well, the Nimpkish band at Alert Bay wanted the museum to be built up there. So in the end two museums were built, and each museum could show what was taken away from their own area. Village Islanders had to decide where their goods would go because they didn't live on Village Island anymore.

Here at Cape Mudge we set up the Nuyumbalees Society to get a museum going and bring back the potlatch regalia. We chose the name Kwagiulth Museum because we wanted it to be for all our people not just our Lekwiltok tribe. At Cape Mudge we are located where all people can easily call in on their way down from our northern villages to the city— Victoria or Vancouver. It's a good place for getting together. Nuyumbalees means "the beginning of all legends." The legends are the history of our families. That is why the chiefs show our dances in the potlatch, so that our legends are passed on to the people.

It has all worked out pretty well. All our stuff that was brought back from Ottawa is in glass cases in the museum according to the family that owns them. That's what the masks and other things mean to us: family ownership. We are proud of that! It tells our family rights to the people. With our people you don't talk about what rights to dances you've got; you call the people and show them in the potlatch. A few families had only a few pieces of what was taken away from their family returned and put in the museum. That wasn't right, and they were really angry. That's another reason why *all* the pieces that were taken away in 1922 and are in museums in Canada and other countries have to be brought back.

On museum opening day, 29 June 1979, my son Don brought his seiner around to the beach in front of the museum. Chiefs of all our Kwagiulth villages were on board, drumming and singing. Jim Sewid was our speaker. He welcomed everybody from the beach. There were about five hundred people. He called to the chiefs of each band in our language, welcoming the people from that village.

That's when they threw "Klassila," the spirit of dancing, from the boat to the shore, where it was caught by a fellow who started up dancing. Then he threw it back up and into the museum.[3]

Everyone moved up the beach and around the ramp outside the museum doors. We didn't have a ribbon cutting. That's not our custom. We had a cedar-bark cutting. The chiefs were holding a long piece of dyed red cedar bark in a circle. I chose Colleen Dick from Cape Mudge to be our princess and stand in the middle of the ring. She is the daughter of two families with a lot of masks on display in the museum. Her father was Dick, and her mother is Assu.

All the important people pressed close in to the bark ring so that nobody saw the knife passed hand to hand. The cedar bark was slashed and there was a scream. All the chiefs got excited, and each shouted out the cries of the animals they can show in the potlatch: the Whales blew, the Bears growled, the Hamatsas cried out. It sounded like a big roar.

When the museum doors were opened, the chiefs came first, followed by the people. Everybody was given a piece of the cedar ring as they came inside, just the way it was done in the old days. Then our chiefs gathered in the open space in the middle of the museum. After fifty-seven years we had our family possessions back! A big shout went up. It was the sound of Klassila, the spirit of dancing, now back again in the house.

My boys and I put up a totem pole to my father inside the museum. Sam Henderson and his sons carved it with Assu family crests. It's big and heavy, around twenty-nine feet tall and fifteen hundred pounds. It had to be lowered in from above before the museum roof was put on. When you raise a pole you have to potlatch. I potlatched for all the tribes when they gathered here for the museum opening. Our fishermen donated the salmon we roasted over the open fires for everybody—fifteen hundred pounds.

A year later another pole was put out in the open area outside the museum and beside the entrance door. That pole was carved by Sam Henderson and his sons and has the crests of their family on it. Sam was from Blunden Harbour, but he married the oldest daughter of Johnny Quocksister of Campbell River, and they raised their family over there. When he put up that pole, there was another big celebration when the Hendersons called the people to the potlatch.

The museum has been good for the Kwagiulth people. Our people who want to learn about native customs come to the museum. When the Ainu or Hawaiians or other people come to visit, we bring the here. Many of our young people have been trained to teach school classes and the public in the museum. They are learning the Kwakwala language, and there is carving, dancing, button-blanket-making, and work with cedar bark. They learn about the potlatch and how everything was used. The elders teach it to the kids. One of the museum programs won first prize for a program in the schools.

I've been on the museum board from the start. I think that getting our potlatch goods back has done a lot to teach our youth who we really are. It will help us to hold on to our history.

My wife Ida and I raised seven children and have twenty-four grandchildren and thirty-one great-grandchildren. At my birthday on 14 February 1986, our family gave a dinner party and sixty-one relatives attended.

Back in May 1977, we held a feast and called all our family members to it. We gave out names to sons and daughters, grandsons and granddaughters, nieces and nephews, and great-grandchildren. These names had been passed down in our family for generations. Names came from our great-grandparents, our grandparents, and their sisters and brothers; some came from our nieces' and nephews' grandparents—from both sides of the family.

About a year after I was born, my people gave a small potlatch for me in my grandfather's house. When I was ten years old, more was given to me in a family potlatch, and I received my boy-name. This name is x̌aṅağəmaẏa, meaning "top giver." After my father's death, his name yax̌nəkʷaʔas came to me. I now hold the name ʔewanukʷ which came to me with the gift of a copper from Jim Sewid at my last potlatch.

To give our names we invited everybody in our family to a dinner in the community hall at Cape Mudge. Ida and I wore our Klassila headdresses and button blankets. Jim Sewid's daughter Daisy acted as our speaker in giving away the names. Those related to us like the Cliftons and the Sewids also gave some names to grandchildren related to them. After dinner, when all the family were still at the tables, the names were called out. Each person got a card with his name written on it. Special names are given to people who are in line for them in the family. I gave out quite a bit of money. That's our potlatch custom to do that.

When you continue the names of the people in the family who have gone before, you feel part of something bigger that goes way back in time. Some of our people believed in reincarnation. I know I still do. Maybe that is part of why this custom is so important to us. But mainly it is important because it keeps the family together, the way we want it to be. We want them to be strong in the Indian culture.

My biggest potlatch was a memorial potlatch to honour my wife Ida. After she died, our families spent a year getting ready to call all the people. The potlatch has different parts. It starts with the sad songs for those who have died, then if coppers are given, there is a really nice happy time. That is followed by the serious Red Cedar Bark Ceremonies.[4] People from different villages come to show the dances they have a right to. Next comes the Klassila where the chiefs from different tribes dance for the people, and there is a lot of fun. It is peaceful then. That's the part I always liked best. At the end we hand out all the money and goods that have been gathered together for the people who take part.

Our potlatches start with q̓asa. It means crying. My wife was loved and respected by all our family and everyone who knew her. Everyone feels sad to see the elders die because they are the ones who are carrying on our custom of the potlatch today. Ida's close friends and relatives were the mourners. These women wearing button blankets sat down in a line at the back of the hall facing the people.

During the year after Ida's death I didn't say her name. That's an old custom of our people, and I don't know how many others keep it still. Speaking the name brings that person too close for comfort—like calling them back. We had other customs here at time of death such as burning the things that belonged to the dead. They did that when I was a boy. Before my time, women used to meet in a secret place in the woods to cry and scratch their faces and tear out their hair. If a song-maker overheard this crying, he could make up a song out of the sounds, and that song would be sung when all the people gathered at the potlatch in her honour. When I was a boy, the women here still cut ten inches off their hair when one of their "sisters" died.

Some of these mourning songs are remembered in each tribe and sung every year at potlatches. Bill Hunt of Fort Rupert led off at my potlatch with the first song. All the singers were with him, and they followed him and beat time. That song was made to honour a great chief of that tribe, nəqaʔbənkəm. It is a name that later went to Mungo Martin. You can hear the word ʔum̓aⱡ repeated over and over in the song. It means "noble lady" because they were singing it for Ida. If a man had died, the word "gigəme" would have been used. Jim King thanked the Fort Ruperts for me. Adam Dick of Kingcome Inlet was my speaker for the night, but he came late, so at first Jimmy King thanked the singers and dancers and those who stood up to speak for Ida. Every village used to have a speaker for potlatches. At Cape Mudge it was Tom Wallace for our people.

One of the next mourning songs told about six noblemen who left Quatsino Sound on a sailing ship and never came back. J.J. Wallace of Quatsino led that song.

The third set of songs came from the West Coast people. Ron Hamilton led the singers. Everybody likes West Coast songs. They have a really good tune in them.

Next, the Campbell River people paid their respects to Ida with a song Sam Henderson had made up when his wife (May Quocksister) died. May and Sam are dead now, but the song had been taped so that Henry George of čəlgʷadi was able to sing along with it and lead the other singers.

Jim Sewid led off with the last of the mourning songs sung in honour of Ida. Jim's father was qʷiqʷəsutinux̌ʷ from Gilford Island, and his mother was məməliliqəla from Village Island. The song he sang came down from the Rivers Inlet people to the people of Village Island. It is called "Lament of the Nobles."[5] It is about the spirit of the loved one travelling all around the world. While this song was being sung, all the mourners stood up and swayed slowly. We call that X̌eq̓ʷala, meaning we will shake off our sorrows. Well, that's the time for everybody to change over. We have to cheer up now because all relatives and friends have come down here to be with our family in time of trouble.

After the mourning ceremony came the giving of coppers to me. I didn't know anything about it beforehand so I was really surprised! A "copper" is a big shield made of copper metal with a design on it. Every copper has a name. They are bought for a higher and higher price each time they are sold. It has gone on for so long that some are worth thousands of dollars. Jim Sewid gave me a copper.

The name of my copper is quluma. It is so old that the meaning has been lost. Jim Sewid got it from his uncle Henry Bell, who passed it on to Jim before he died a few years ago. Before that it belonged to Jim's grandfather, Jim Bell from Village Island.

Jim and Flora Sewid's daughter Louisa is married to our son Don, and she is a member of the Cape Mudge band. That is why her father gave me a copper. It honours Louisa among our people. It is not right for a father to give nothing to his daughter's husband and family. It would be a disgrace for her. Jim Sewid was giving to me and my family as a dowry for Louisa. That's the way we all back up the marriage.

Jim and Flora Sewid and Ida and I have four grandsons by Don and Louisa: Brian, Patrick, Michael, and Bradley. What is given to me by the Sewids will go to my son Don when I die and then on to our (mutual) grandchildren. So when you receive wealth in a potlatch, it is like making a will. You have to do that in front of all the people so that these rights are known.

Louisa and Don stood at the centre of our two families when the copper was given in her name. She was dressed with cedar bark headdress with ermine tails and button blanket. J.J. Wallace was speaker for Jim, so he announced the copper was given to me. A great name was given to me with the copper. The name is ʔewanukʷ. It means (a chief is) "watching the point" (for the arrival of his guests at the potlatch).

Then my son Don was given one of the greatest names the Sewids own. That name is X̣əliliX̣a. It is a Gilford Island name meaning "always inviting." My son will use that name, and it will be passed on to his sons.

Next Jim Sewid had it announced that he would supid a copper to me. Supid means "pass on." The copper is given to me and is then bought back by Jim so that it stays in his family. Every time the copper is bought its price goes up; so Jim gave me even more than the copper had been worth before, and that money went toward putting on this potlatch. The name of the copper supid to me is lubiłila. That means "every cent went to buying it." Jim Sewid's uncle Henry Bell had owned it before. He had bought it from yəqiX̣əsm̓e, the father-in-law of Harry Mountain.

The old ladies who know all about how these things are done were dancing. Now that coppers were given to honour my daughter-in-law, Louisa can wear copper shapes outlined in buttons on her blanket.

More coppers were supid to me. Willie Cranmer of Alert Bay came up and handed me a copper named ʔənqʷəla, meaning "Foggy." It used to belong to Wakius at Alert Bay. The copper was taken away with the rest of the stuff for potlatching in 1922, but it has been returned. When the copper was supid to me, it was bought back right then, and the money went into the bag with the rest to give out at this potlatch.

Paul Willie of Kingcome Inlet brought up another copper to supid to me. The name of this copper is ʔisəmala. That means "Abalone Face." It was bought back then and more money to be given away was paid over for it.

Adam Dick from Kingcome Inlet brought a copper to supid to me, but he arrived too late to hand it over, so his mother gave it to me and bought it back again, so all that went into putting on my potlatch.

All these chiefs who supid coppers are important to my family. At the end Louisa presented me with the copper quluma, which Jim Sewid gave me outright, while a special song was sung. It says how her "brothers" came from far away to give coppers to her father-in-law. Then the women danced. Only those who had been married in the Indian way danced out in front of the people.

In the old days the chiefs brought coppers to the potlatches in case they had to sue somebody who tried to take away their place and grab it for himself. Then the chief would break a copper, and if that man couldn't do the same, he would have to back down. It's a lot different now. Nowadays they bring their coppers to the potlatch to honour people.

The next part of the potlatch is the Red Cedar Bark Ceremony. It's the dark side of our history that is being danced. All the dancers come out from behind a painted cloth screen. Guests don't go there because you are not supposed to know who is dancing the masks (of supernatural beings). In our big family there were so many dancers we needed two screens. Dora Cook painted one screen especially for this potlatch. Dora was back there telling the people when to get dressed and when to come out. There were so many people, she said it only worked because four generations were working together. So many dances were shown that a list was made and pinned up on the back of a screen. That was the first time that was ever done. It will be hard to remember all the dances that were shown at my potlatch.[6]

The most important dance in the Red Cedar Bark Ceremony is Hamatsa. My eldest son Steve danced that—top dancer. It was the Hamatsa ritual that Jim Sewid gave me and the second time Steve danced it. Jim gave him the name ʔənqalis to go with the Hamatsa Dance. That's the name Jim was given when he first was made a hamatsa dancer when he was a boy. It means "opening the mouth for food."

When the Hamatsa begins, you hear the whistles blowing. That's the sound of the cannibal monster bəxbəxʷəlanusiwe.[7] Then the hamatsa dancer appears from behind the screen. The power of the monster is on him, and he is hungry for human flesh because that's the food of the cannibal he met on his spirit quest. He is wild and out of control and has to be caught and brought back to his senses.

Adam Dick came out carrying two red cedar bark neck-rings to use to capture the hamatsa when they found him. Jim Sewid walked slowly behind him, shaking the round rattle that gives power to the neck-rings. When they got to Steve, they threw the neck-rings over his head and Steve shouted "hap!" "hap!" (food, food) and plunged off into the four corners of the dance floor. He circled around four times before the singing and drumming and whistling ended. Then he went off behind the screens. For those Red Cedar Bark dances everyone whirls around on the spot as they go in or come out from the screens. It's our custom; you have to do that.

Then the whistles blew again, and the songs and drumming started up, and Steve came out for the second time as hamatsa. My speaker was calling out to him not to fall, or he would disgrace our family and a copper would have to be broken. His sister Audrey danced backward before him holding out her arms as if she was offering him food. She is his conscience—she is trying to cool him off. Audrey was his heligaʔ, his leader. Then other women joined Audrey in trying to bring the hamatsa back to his senses, and men went with him too because once in a while he would break away and cry out, crouch down, and struggle to get away.

Next time the hamatsa came again, he carried my copper quluma. The whistles were sounding, and in the loud singing and drumming and shouting, he started getting wild again. He put the copper in the middle of the floor, and all the high-ranking people who have been made hamatsas came out to dance with him around it and support him.

After that they showed the dance of the həmsəmł, the bird monsters who feed the cannibal bəxbəxʷəlanusiwe. First is hux̌ʷhuqʷ. You're not supposed to know who dances the masks, but you can guess because the Hendersons of Campbell River carved those masks. Bobby Joseph came out with the dancer to help him because it is hard to see behind the mask, and the mask is so heavy that the dancer might fall. Next came ǧaluqʷemł, crooked beak. Dick Joseph of Turnour Island was with the dancer to help. Next dancer was Raven. They all danced at the same time with their wooden beaks lifting and banging down. At the last another crooked beak came out—so there were four cannibal birds. This is the most exciting part of the Hamatsa ritual with singing, fast, hard drumming, whistles, and the birds all out on the floor together.[8]

After that was finished, Mrs. M. Cook of Alert Bay had it announced by Willie Cranmer that she would be giving the potlatch next year.

My eldest grandson, Rod Naknakim, came out next dancing the story of a man who came out of the sea. That spirit was afraid of fire so he was always trying to put out the fire. Rod wore a neck-ring of twisted yellow and red cedar bark. He was being attracted by fire, and his attendants had to hold on to him so that he didn't burn himself. He kept rushing at the fire to stamp on it, to put it out. The dance is really old and always shown with the hamatsa if the person giving the potlatch has the right to it.

Even a little child can be made hamatsa. Nicole Assu is Don and Louisa's granddaughter by their eldest son Brian and his wife Tami. She was brought out by Vera Cranmer and Ethel Alfred, and she danced around the floor. Agnes Alfred gave her the name yaqusəlagəlis. That was the name the old lady was given when she was made hamatsa as a young girl. She's over a hundred years old now. It is a Village Island name and was passed down to Dora Cook, then Dora gave up the name and her place in the Hamatsa to Nicole.

In the next dance, rich woman was shown. She is q̓uminəwag̱as, a spirit from the forest wearing hemlock branches on her head. Other women came out with her, and Bobby Joseph and Ron Hamilton came with her. My niece Violet Duncan from Campbell River was q̓uminəwag̱as. Violet is a high-ranking lady, the daughter of my sister Susan, who was married to Johnny Quocksister of Campbell River. The singers and drummers keep everything going, and every time a dance is over, the speaker announces how the right to show it came into the family, who owns the dance. The way these dances spread out to the Kwagiulth people was by marriage dowries.

The ghost dancer was next. My daughter Pearl danced that for the people. Older women were out on the floor to guide her.

Then five of my grandchildren did the Wolf Dance. Some wore wolf headdresses. They lined up in a row and danced up and down in their places. You can tell it is the Wolf Dance by the songs and because the dancers keep their thumbs up.

The Ghost Dance was followed by a dance that came into our family long ago by marriage to a family from the West Coast. It is called ʔaʔumalał. The high-ranking lady dancer, Deane Le Fleur, wore a big cedar hat. She can throw sickness into people and cure them again. Of course, after each dance, the speaker has to tell where the dance came from and the name that is given to the dancer with it. If he forgets, one of the old ladies will go over to him and get after him.

In the next performance, all the dancers wore white. It is called n̓ən̓alał, the Day Dance. The fringes on their costumes moved as they danced slowly in a line. They greet the day. This was danced by the wives of my grandsons. The speaker told where this dance came from and announced the names given to the dancers.

One of my young granddaughters, Wendy Dick, danced the tuʔxʷid. She turned her button blanket inside out because a plain blanket used to be used for this dance. She wore hemlock branches on her head. Katy Ferrie of

Campbell River guided her because she is so young and hadn't danced it before. The song sung for this dance is "I Have Been All over the Earth." The people tease the dancer because she claims she has gone all around the world and returned with a ƛugʷe (treasure) of magic. They try to get her to show it to them. Then she danced slowly backward toward the screens, and you could see a big wooden frog following her across the floor. That was a surprise, and everybody was laughing. She proved her magic power all right!

There were so many dances that I have lost track of them. My speaker, Adam Dick, asked the drummers to hang on to their sticks because at this rate they might all have to stay all night. I remember there was the Professional Dance, where the singers and drummers keep changing the beat so the line of women dancers have to know how to follow. That dance was led by Lucy Onley. All sides of our families joined in.

Another dance was the x̌ʷix̌ʷi. Two men came out shaking shell rattles and scattering coins to the kids. Their masks were carved by Bill Holm. That dance came to our people from the Comox.

After that there was the Paddle Dance. This is a women's dance, and all my relatives joined into it. After paddling all around the floor, they ended up by bailing at the stern with a plastic bucket. It's a lot of fun to see.

The ʔuniqʷa dancer is the one who doesn't want anyone else coming out and dancing with her. She stops dancing if they do. She can look into the future and heal the people. My granddaughter Colleen Dick danced that. Colleen has been given my mother's name, maxʷaʔugʷa.

Twenty-four grandchildren came out next dancing to the tune of a song composed by nəqaʔbənkəm of Fort Rupert. The speaker thanked them for dancing and told where that song had come from.

The Mountain Goat hunter came on next. It was danced by my grandson Rick. He went round the floor carrying a long pole with a noose on it. As the drums beat faster and faster, the head of a mountain goat shot up above the screens, and the hunter made a run at it. It's a very important dance, that dance, and Jim Sewid received it as dowry when he married his wife Flora. It came long ago from Jack Peters of New Vancouver village.

One of the last dances in the Cedar Bark Series was the Salmon Dance. Any family that has twins can do the Salmon Dance. Our people said that twins are salmon. My granddaughter Colleen Dick has twins, so she led out the dancers. The Sewids have twins, Emma and Mabel, so they were the body of the Salmon in the middle of the line. Their sister Lucy Onley led that Salmon Dance. After the Sewid twins were born, there were no other twins born, so this Salmon Dance does not have a tail. The Hendersons in Campbell River have two sets of twins, so they can dance the whole Salmon. Others joined into the line of dancers to show respect for the families giving the dance. J.J. Wallace led the song for the Salmon Dance.

Another very important dance was məʔdəm. It tells the story of a boy who went out alone along Woss Lake, where he was given a ƛugʷe (treasure). He saw crystals rolling down the mountain there. From them he got his power to fly. At one time, the man who could do this dance was pulled up to the beams of the big house with leather strips through cuts on his back and knees. That is why my grandson Patrick, kept looking up into the beams above while he was dancing. Long ago I saw them pulling up a dancer here at Cape Mudge. It was Paddy Grey's father. His grandfather too had the right to that.

The war dancer came on about that time. He was carrying a big sea-serpent board in his arms. It was danced by my grandson Michael; and he was the warrior spirit, sisiyuλ. Michael wore the headdress of a chief; ermine skins on a cedar bark band. This is an important dance.

A Grizzly Bear spirit came out next. This dance is high up too. It was danced by Bradley Assu, fourth son of Don and Louisa. He received a name from Jim Sewid, who owns this dance and has given me the right to have it shown by my family.

For the last great event in the Red Cedar Bark Ceremony, my son Mel came out in a black blanket, carrying my copper quluma. He is helagalis, and he is making Raven's cry. This tells the chiefs that Raven will peck the copper into pieces if my rights to the coppers, songs, dances, and names that have come down in the family are challenged. The challenger would have to break a copper too or lose out.

Well, the Red Cedar Bark Ceremony was over, and there was a big roar of drumming and shouting. The song leader was calling "Wa!" and the singers were shouting out "Yi!" Everyone was shouting it out! It means "let's roll over" from the dark side of the ċeʔqa to the λaʔsala.

The Kwagiulth people really love Klassila. That's when we do the "Peace Dance" or "Feather Dance." It came down to us from the northern people—Bella Bella and Bella Coola. Chiefs who have come to the potlatch to honour the host come out in long lines and dance with their families for the people. They wear the ermine headdresses and blankets and aprons. Each time a different family comes out to dance, and then they show some λugʷe (treasure) that they have a right to show the people.

Everybody used to be very quiet and respectful in the old days, and there was no talking or walking around the house at Klassilas. Nowadays everybody is enjoying themselves, and some of the dances are really funny, so that I don't think it is so serious any more, after the opening part.

Brian Assu, my grandson, who is the oldest of the four sons of Don and Louisa was holikəłał. He comes out first. He is the boss—leader of the Klassila and equal to the Hamatsa in the Red Cedar Bark Ceremony. Brian is kʷikʷ, Eagle of the tribe. Adam Dick came out with Brian. He was shaking the round rattles. That makes it sacred. Brian has been given the right to use that rattle. This privilege that Brian is showing came down from Rivers Inlet. Agnes Alfred came out to help Brian because he got this right through her. Jim Sewid led the song that was his grandfather Sewid's song.

When the rattles sounded, a line of chiefs from my family came out—all grandsons. Tony Roberts, my daughter Jean's son, led them in to dance the Feather Dance. J.J. Wallace led a song that says, "He is going around the house looking for a λugʷe." Mungo Martin made that song. After they danced the Feather Dance, one of the Webber boys from the Tsulquade tribe started pestering a chief in the line of dancers. The one they choose is some-one close to the family giving the potlatch. This time it was Bobby Assu, and he went out of the hall. You could hear noises outside the building. Webber came back carrying the chief's blanket and headdress—the chief had disappeared! Then in came ǧʷəyəm, a Whale. Drumming was kept up all the time the Whale was danced around the house. Adam Dick's father carved that Whale mask.

After that, the next line of chiefs came out to honour our family, and after they danced, they got teased by the two boys from Tsulquade, and Bobby Joseph left the hall. Somebody brought in his headdress and blanket and said he had gone. Then back came the λugʷe, out from behind the screens. It was Echo. Under his blanket the Echo had mouthpieces of Komoqua (rich ruler of the wealth of the sea), Grizzly Bear, Sea-Egg (Urchin), Starfish, Raven, and Thunderbird. Every time he turned away and turned back again, he showed a different animal face. This mask had been carved by Jimmy Dick too. Jim Sewid and J.J. Wallace led the songs.

So, that is the way Klassila is done. The Henderson family came in next to dance Klassila, and after Bill Henderson was taken away, his λugʷe was shown: dᶻunuq̓ʷa (wild woman of the woods).

In the dance that followed the full moon and the half moon fought over which should be in the sky. They danced for the people, and the winner was decided by which got the loudest applause. It was really funny. They even danced the Twist! Lelooska, an artist from the States, made those masks.

Agnes Cranmer and Margaret Cook and a group of women came and danced the Peace Dance for the people. Lisa Wells was taken away, and two dancers came back wearing a "mother" and a "father" mask. They carried a cradle. It had a wooden baby in it. The baby sat up in the cradle when strings were pulled.

After the next line of chiefs came in for the Peace Dance, everything was interrupted by some "visitors." These uninvited Gakula are clowns who haven't been invited. They can't seem to keep their pants up. After they warmed their backsides at the "fire," they were made to dance, and then they were kicked out. You can't Klassila with those clowns around.

Another line of nobles came out led by Bobby Joseph, and the λugʷe for this dance was a different dᶻunuq̓ʷa, wild woman of the woods.

Well, for the ending, I led out the line of my family to Klassila with me: Rod Naknakim, Mel, Don and Louisa, Shirley Vrable, and my eldest daughter Audrey, who held the talking stick. A song from the West Coast people was sung and led by Ron Hamilton, who later spoke highly of my father and our family. Then women were standing up speaking for Ida and her family. Jim Sewid spoke again for us, and others spoke of the important history of our family.

Then all our family and supporters danced around the floor. They were really happy. They were waving towels and pillows and money to be given away. That's when the big gift-giving starts. That's what the potlatch is famous for.

We give to those people who came to sing and dance and speak for us and to all those who came to the potlatch. Things to give away were stacked up in the middle of the hall, and our family carried them to the people. Usually the old people and those who have done most of the planning for the potlatch go with those who are handing out the money and goods to be sure that people who have helped the family most are taken care of: the singers and those who showed their dances and helped out with the whole thing. Some of those who helped most were women in our family, so I bought pearl necklaces for them when I was in Hong Kong. They were given bouquets of carnations.

Well it was around nine-thirty or ten o'clock when the potlatch was over. There was still light in the west. You know, some of our people used to wonder whether the potlatch was a good thing or not. When I think about that potlatch now, I know it was good.

NOTES

1. For the circumstances surrounding the potlatch suppression and its effects on the native people in the Kwagiulth area with evidence from native people involved in the proceedings of that time, see *Prosecution or Persecution* by Daisy (My-yah-nelth) Sewid-Smith (1979). For confiscation and return of Kwagiulth potlatch gear as part of an international trend to repatriation, see Stephen Inglis, "Cultural Readjustment, a Canadian Case Study" in *Gazette: Quarterly of the Canadian Museums Association* 12 (Summer 1979). See also, Marie Mauzé, "The Potlatch Law and the Confiscation of Ceremonial Property among the Kwakiutl" in *Bulletin Amérique Indienne* (July 1983), trans. Katherine Odgers, Kwagiulth Museum, Cape Mudge.

2. George M. Heye, founder and collector for the Museum of the American Indian, Heye Foundation, New York.

3. The Spirit of Dancing, referred to as "Klassila," had been imprisoned in Ottawa for many years and was not being released to the Kwagiulth people. The Power of the Spirit was symbolically thrown from ship to shore, where it was "caught" and set the catcher dancing. He in turn

hurled the spirit across the beach and through the museum doors. The spirit had entered the ceremonial house (museum).

4. The dances in the Red Cedar Bark series are said to be "serious" because they portray the suffering of the men and women who endured the struggle against death on the extended spirit quests once undertaken by the young initiates into the dancing societies of the Northwest Coast. Some dances depict this anguish of mind and body that was experienced in encounters with the supernaturals. Then life itself was at risk from devouring monsters or by drowning, fire, or war. It was the "dark side of life" that must be gone through to achieve full adult status. Its re-enactment could involve ritual torture. The relationship between tribal masks and exorcism of the fear of death has been pointed out by M.M. Halpin, MOA, *Museum Note* 18 (n.d.).

5. See Appendix 7 for "Lament of the Nobles," trans. Daisy Sewid-Smith and published in *Campbell River Salmon Festival Souvenir Booklet* (1973).

6. The events of this potlatch were video-taped and may be seen by

7. bəxbəxʷəlanusiwe is the cannibal monster whose name is translated as "Cannibal-at-the-north-end-of-the-world." His body is covered with dreadful mouths that emit a whistling sound. He desires human flesh to eat and is seeking it out. The supernatural birds—Hox Hox, Crooked Beak, and Raven—secure the food for bəxbəxʷəlanusiwe. The hamatsa dancer portrays a hunter who encountered the monster and his terrible attendants and returns to his home community in a state of frenzy with the power of the cannibal still upon him. It should be noted that cannibalism was so abhorrent to the Coastal Indian people that it clearly indicated a seizure by an inhuman and supernatural agency.

A Kwagiulth version of the myth of the Cannibal-at-the-north-end of the world, he who feasts himself upon the tribes but is outwitted by the brave hamatsas, is told by George Hunt for Franz Boas in *Thirty-fifth Annual Report of the Bureau of American Ethnology*, pt. 2, Smithsonian Institution (Washington, DC, 1921), 1222–48.

For definitive information on the traditional enactment of the Hamatsa ritual see Audrey Hawthorn, *Kwakiutl Art* (1979), 45, 46.

For photo illustration and explanation of the contemporary dances of the Kwagiulth including the myth of bəxbəxʷəlanusiwe, see Peter L. Macnair, "Kwakiutl Winter Dances: A Re-enactment" (Toronto: Arts-canada, 1977), 62–86.

See also "The Origin of the Hamat'sa," a clear account of the cannibal monster myth from the Indians of the Rivers Inlet, a region from which the Kwagiulth got this and many other of their dances. in Jay Powell, Vickie Jensen, Vera Cranmer, and Agnes Cranmer, *Yaxwatʃanʔs. Learning Kwakwala Series. Book 12* (Alert Bay: U'Mista Society, n.d.).

8. Animals shown in the performances are not common forest animals but representations of supernatural beings that can transform from aspects of other animals to human form and back again. This distinction is indicated here by capitalizing the names, for example, Raven, Bear, and Wolf. In the time prior to the transformation of earth to its present form, all animals, including man, lives in similar social arrangements with chiefs, houses, and treasures. Occasionally, a young person seeking spirit power would encounter a supernatural being who would remove scales, feathers, or fur and reveal his human aspect in order to communicate with the suppliant and grant that person some treasure such as hunting prowess. Seekers were provided with symbols of their newly acquired status: name, song, costume, or mask. It is the story of these encounters that families show in the potlatch to validate the crests, dances, and songs that they have acquired the right to show.

GREAT WHITE FATHER KNOWS BEST:
OKA AND THE LAND CLAIMS PROCESS [*]

J . R .   M I L L E R

o

In their 1961 presentation to the Joint Committee of the Senate and House of Commons on Indian Affairs, the Oka Indians made a simple request:

> The Oka Indians wish that the Oka lands be given the status of a reserve. It has all the characteristics of it, with a resident agent of the Department, but it has not the legal status that would enable the band to have a perpetual use vested in it for their enjoyment and that of their children and descendants. What future is there for the Oka Indian? [1]

Nothing was done about the Indians' request through the 1960s, Indian and Northern Affairs Canada taking the view that there was no serious problem because Ottawa was administering the Mohawk lands at Kanesatake as though they were a properly established reserve. [2] As the 1970s opened, there was "still a widespread feeling among Indian people that the problems of Oka are far from settled." [3]

[*] Reprinted with permission from *Native Studies Review* 7, 1 (1991): 23–52. The author is indebted to the Social Sciences and Humanities Research Council of Canada and to the Messer Fund of the University of Saskatchewan, each of which funded parts of the research for this paper. I am also appreciative of the advice and information provided by Robert S. Allen, Deputy Chief, Treaties and Historical Research Centre, Indian and Northern Affairs Canada. He is responsible for saving me from many errors, but not for the ones that remain in spite of his counsel. I have also benefited greatly by a paper by John Thompson, "A Brief History of the Land Dispute at Kanesatake [Oka] from Contact to 1961," and from a compilation of copies of documents by Mary Jane Jones, "Research Report on the History of Disputes at Oka/Kanesatake." Both these helpful reports have been mimeographed by the Treaties and Historical Research Centre under the title *Materials Relating to the History of Land Dispute at Kanesatake (Oka)* (Ottawa, Feb. 1991). Where documents cited in the notes have been examined in the corpus of material assembled by Ms Jones rather than in the original location or on microfilm, this is indicated by an asterisk (*) at the beginning of my citation.

As Canadians know all too well in 1991, the "widespread feeling among Indian people" was justified, while Ottawa's complacent self-confidence was not. Through the 1970s and 1980s the dispute over title to lands occupied by Mohawk Indians adjacent to the Quebec town of Oka went from bad to worse. The Indians took advantage of a new land claims process that the federal government had devised after the pivotal Calder decision of 1973; they registered a demand, not for the recognition of the lands at Kanesatake as a "reserve," as had been requested in 1961, but as unsurrendered land held by Aboriginal title. When that comprehensive claim was rejected in 1975 by the Office of Native Claims (ONC), the Kanesatake Mohawk then initiated another claim, a specific claim to the lands. This, too, was rejected by the federal authorities in 1986. However, the federal minister of Indian Affairs offered to look for alternative methods of redressing the band's grievance. The federal government "recognized that there is an historical basis for Mohawk claims related to land grants in the 18th century." In 1989 Ottawa proposed a framework agreement for bringing about land reunification.[4] That was rejected by the Kanesatake Indians because it did not seem likely to produce enough land to meet their needs and it appeared not to address either "the long standing problems or unique character of Kanesatake."[5]

Through the later 1980s the unresolved issue of title to the lands occupied by Mohawk on Lake of Two Mountains rapidly degenerated. On the Indian side, rising frustration was exacerbated by the growing influence of a new form of Native militancy, the Warrior Society. On the non-Native side, impatience and acquisitiveness combined to produce an attack on a disputed piece of land. In the Euro-Canadian community there was growing exasperation that the continuing dispute over lands adjacent to Oka was thwarting development. Specifically, a plan to expand a privately owned nine-hole golf course to eighteen holes by acquiring and incorporating a forested tract that the municipality owned, but that the Indians claimed as their own, became a source of contention. In preparation for a confrontation over the disputed land some Kanesatake Mohawk erected barricades in the contested area on 11 March 1990. In due course, the town and golf club decided to proceed, securing an injunction from Quebec's Superior Court on 26 April. The Mohawk ignored the court order. A second injunction procured on 26 June was also rejected by the Indians. And on 10 July Mayor Ouellette requested Quebec's provincial police force to enforce the injunction by tearing down the roadblock. An assault by one hundred police officers the next day resulted in an exchange of gunfire, the death of a police corporal, and an eleven-week stand-off that involved Mohawk, police and 2500 Canadian soldiers at Kanesatake and Kahnewake. The last of the hold-out Warriors, their Mohawk supporters and a few journalists walked out to waiting army and police on 26 September 1990. Canada, Quebec and the Mohawk of Kanesatake are still evaluating the consequences.

How did a dispute over a relatively small parcel of land culminate in violence, death and a demoralizing confrontation in a country that prides itself on acceptance of diversity, pursuit of accommodation and a long tradition of peaceful compromise? Much of the commentary since the end of the Oka crisis has concentrated on specific, local, immediate factors. The Mohawk Warrior Society is portrayed either as a collection of righteous militants pursuing a sacred constitutional principle or as a band of goons. The local residents of Oka and Châteauguay are longsuffering neighbours or red-necked hooligans. The Sûreté du Québec are uniformed thugs or inexperienced law-enforcement officers trying to mediate in a hopelessly polarized situation. Quebec is either the most tolerant and generous of provinces in its treatment of Aboriginal peoples or the home of a nationality becoming increasingly unwilling to permit dissent by distinctive ethnic and racial minorities. Ottawa is to blame either for mollycoddling the Mohawk with promises of accommodation after their claims were rejected, or for failing to act decisively after the rejection of the second, specific claim in 1986 to acquire and transfer to the Indians enough lands to accommodate their wishes. Where in this welter of charges and counter-charges do the roots of the exceptional and lamentable eleven-week stand-off at Kanesatake lie?

The origins of the events of the summer of 1990 at Oka lie in none of the immediate and local factors on which attention has focused since late September 1990. Rather, the violence over the land dispute at Oka is the product of an attitude or disposition on the part of the government of Canada that stretches back at least a century and a half—an outlook that it knows best what serves the interests of Indigenous peoples and that it alone can solve their problems. The implication of this, of course, is that the same sort of confrontation and possibly violence that disfigured life in Kahnewake and Kanesatake in 1990 can—and are likely to—happen elsewhere. If the real reason for the trouble is a long-standing approach by the federal government to relations with Native peoples, and if the origins of the violence lie not in specific and local factors but in national policy, then obviously there is great potential for a repetition of the Oka tragedy in other parts of the country where there is competition for land and resources between the First Peoples and the newcomers. To understand better both the general nature of the Oka problem and its potential to recur elsewhere, it is necessary to consider the aged, extensive and alarming roots of the conflict.

Prior to the invasion of the valley of the St. Lawrence by Europeans in the sixteenth century, the territory near what the intruders would call the Lac des Deux Montagnes, or Lake of Two Mountains, was used by some of the Indigenous people who are known to scholars as the St. Lawrence Iroquoians. In the opinion of the Assembly of First Nations there had been Aboriginal presence at Kanesatake since at least 1000 years before the birth of Christ, and in the seventeenth century the Five Nations "took the land from the french [sic] in retaliation for Champlain's raid on their territory."[6] Non-Native scholars hold that sometime in the latter part of the sixteenth century, between the explorations of Jacques Cartier and Samuel de Champlain, the so-called "St. Lawrence Iroquoians" withdrew from the St. Lawrence region, abandoning the area to a variety of Algonkian peoples. These dwellers of the Ottawa River valley, being nomadic hunter-gatherers, extensively used the territory in which Oka was later established. They travelled over it, fished in its waters, and hunted in its nearby woods. In general, there was little or no permanent occupation of the lands on the north side of Lake of Two Mountains by Indian groups.

By a grant in 1717, confirmed in 1718, a tract of land three and one-half leagues in front and three leagues deep was set aside by the French crown for the Gentlemen of St. Sulpice of Paris as a refuge for a mixed group of Indians to whom they had been ministering since the 1670s. (The parcel of land was augmented by an additional grant by the crown that was made in 1733 and confirmed in 1735.[7]) This mixed group of Nipissing, Algonkin and Mohawk had in 1696 reluctantly transferred from the Mission de la Montagne near Ville Marie (later Montreal) to the Sault au Recollet on the north side of Montreal Island as European settlement of the future Montreal began to present obstacles to successful evangelization of these mission Indians. But even the more northerly Sault au Recollet eventually came within the pernicious ambit of European influence, and the Sulpicians once more became anxious to move their charges to a more remote and less morally menacing location. Again with reluctance, the Indians relocated, being persuaded by the missionaries that the move was for their own good. The French, whose concept of divine-right kingship entailed a belief in the crown's ownership of all lands in New France, purported to grant the land on Lake of Two Mountains "in order to transfer there the mission of the said Indians of Sault au Recollet" on "condition that they shall bear the whole expense necessary for removing the said mission, and also cause a church and a fort to be built there of stone at their own cost, for the security of the Indians. . . ."[8] In 1743 there were approximately 700 Indians—mostly Six Nations Iroquois and Huron, but also including Algonkin and Nipissing—at the Lake of Two Mountains mission.[9]

Title to the lands to which the mixture of Mohawk and Algonkians repaired on Lake of Two Mountains was never free from challenge. Neither the terms of the Capitulation of Montreal nor the Royal Proclamation provided much protection to the Indian occupants. The Capitulation promisingly stated that the "Indian allies of his most Christian Majesty [France], shall be maintained in the Lands they inhabit; if they chuse to remain there; they shall not be molested on any pretence whatsoever, for having carried arms, and served his most Christian Majesty; they shall have, as well as the French, liberty of religion, and shall keep their missionaries."[10] The Royal Proclamation of 1763, whose definition of "Hunting Grounds" reserved for Indians did not include the area around the Lake of Two Mountains because it lay within Quebec, also contained provisions regulating purchase of Indian lands within existing colonies. However, this protection did not apply to the Oka lands either, because they were held by Europeans to have been allocated by seigneurial grant.[11] A brief and ineffective claim by Lord Jeffrey Amherst was laid after the transfer of Quebec to British rule in the period 1760–63. The so-called "conqueror of Montreal" argued that these lands should be given to him, inasmuch as the provisions of the Capitulation of Montreal, while they guaranteed free exercise of the Roman Catholic religion, explicitly excluded the Sulpicians from their protections of conscience, custom and lands. However, the British authorities saw no more reason to humour Amherst's pretensions to Sulpician or Indian lands than they did his preposterous desire for the Jesuits' estates.[12]

Amherst's claim came to nothing, but tension soon developed between the Sulpicians and their Indian charges over use of and title to the lands on which Natives and clerics resided. By 1781 a disagreement between the priest and Indians over division of revenue from non-Indians who kept their cattle on the lands at Oka led the Sulpicians to state bluntly that the Indians had no right to the lands. The resulting confrontation led the Natives to present their claims to the British authorities in 1781, 1787 and 1795.[13] The Indians' case rested on several bases. They had once possessed, they said, a document granting them the lands on Lake of Two Mountains, but they had surrendered it for safekeeping to the priests, who now denied all knowledge of it. Moreover, during the Seven Years' War their representatives had met with British Indian Superintendent Sir William Johnson at Oswegatchie to promise not to fight the British, and to receive confirmation of "our lands as granted by the King of France." They had a wampum belt that recorded their possession of the lands. When General Guy Carleton, on a visit, had asked who owned uncultivated lands on the north shore of the lake, the Indians had told him "that they belonged to the Indians of the Lake." No one contradicted them. Finally, they had been told during the American Revolutionary War that if they fought with the British they would "fight for your Land and when the War is over you shall have it." All these—missing deed, their own record of taking the land, Johnson's assurance, the lack of contradiction when they said the lands were theirs and British promises during the American Revolution—constituted good and sufficient "title" for the Indians on the Lake of Two Mountains.

The Indians' position and other factors began seriously to cloud the Sulpicians' title to the properties at Oka. In particular, in the early decades of the nineteenth century the view increasingly took hold that the Sulpicians' legal position was weak for a technical legal reason. The original seigneurial grant of 1717–18 (expanded by an additional grant in 1733–35) had been made to the Sulpicians of Paris, who transferred their rights to the Sulpicians of Montreal in 1784.[14] But since the Canadian missionary body had no legal existence—that is, it was not legally incorporated by positive law—the Order was legally barred from possessing estates in mortmain, or inalienable tenure. A challenge was raised in 1763 to the Sulpicians' title by an Indian's sale of property to a newcomer, but on that occasion the Governor upheld the order's claim and dispossessed the would-be purchaser.[15] In 1788 the Indians of Oka themselves raised the issue directly with the crown, claiming title to the lands on which they were located. However, Lord Dorchester's council concluded, on the advice of the colonial law officers, "That no satisfactory Evidence is given to the Committee of any Title to the Indians of the Village in Question, either by the French Crown or any Grantee of that Crown."[16] However, no evidence was adduced that either law officers or councillors had made any effort to ascertain what were the bases of the Indians' claim. The abrupt rejection of their case did not deter the Indians, and the dubious quality of the Sulpicians' title was regularly highlighted by a number of petitions from the Aboriginal inhabitants of Oka for the granting of title to them.[17]

Further complications developed in the nineteenth century, especially during a period of heavy settlement following the War of 1812. Often lands were granted to non-Native settlers in the lower Ottawa Valley without consideration of or compensation for the long-standing use of the territory for hunting by Algonkin and Nipissing with ties to Oka.[18] These encroachments led the Algonkin and Nipissing of Lake of Two Mountains in 1822 to register a claim to land on both sides of the Ottawa River from a point above the seigniory on Lake of Two Mountains as far north as Lake Nipissing.[19] The claim was rejected by British officials in 1827 even though the Superintendent General of Indian Affairs, Sir John Johnson, strongly supported their position, and was again dismissed by the Executive Council of Lower Canada in 1837.[20]

Still the Sulpicians were obviously worried. In June 1839 the superior of the seminary made a proposal to the Indians that was designed to regularize the Order's claim. The Indians' rights to use, expand, dispose of or build on the particular plots would be guaranteed, and the Sulpicians would continue to provide the Indians with wood, though it might be cut only where the priests said. The Indians of Oka accepted this proposition.[21] Nonetheless, in order to resolve any technical difficulty and remove any cloud on the title, the legislature in 1840 (reconfirmed in 1841) passed "An Ordinance to incorporate the Ecclesiastics of the Seminary of Saint Sulpice of Montreal, to confirm their title to the Fief and Seigniory of the Island of Montreal, the Fief and Seigniory of the Lake of the Two Mountains, and the Fief and Seigniory of Saint Sulpice, in this Province; to provide for the gradual extinction of Seigniorial Rights and Dues within the Seigniorial limits of the said Fiefs and Seigniories, and for other purposes."[22] The fact that the representative assembly had been suspended following the Rebellion of 1837–38 in Lower Canada meant that the critical measure could be passed by a small, appointed council. No doubt the authorities wished to reward the Sulpicians for their ostentatious and vocal loyalty during the troubled times in the Lake of Two Mountains region. No one bothered to note that the Indians at Oka had refused to join or aid the *Patriotes*, though pressed to do so.[23]

Legislative disposition of the question of title did nothing to still the rivalry and tension between Indians and priests at Oka. One basis for the quarrel was the Indians' view that the land was truly theirs, and that the Sulpicians were merely trustees for their lands. This fundamental difference of opinion was exacerbated by friction over access to resources in and on the territory, and the conflict worsened steadily through the nineteenth century because of the increasing pressure of settlement in the area. A further complication arose from the fact that different Indian groups at Kanesatake used the territory differently. While the Iroquois at Oka were inclined towards agriculture on lands made available to them by the Sulpicians without charge, the Algonkin and Nipissing tended more to rely upon a hunting economy for which they extensively used a large area of the Ottawa Valley, returning to the Oka area only for two months in the summer. Not surprisingly, then, it was these Algonkian groups that felt more severely the negative impact of inrushing settlers and lumber firms. Their petition to Lord Dalhousie in 1822 began by noting "That in Consequence of the Increase of Population and the Number of New Settlements on the Lands in which they were accustomed to hunt and the Game getting Scarcer in Consequence thereof" they were being hardpressed.[24]

The depletion of furs in the region severely affected the economic position of the Algonkians.[25] Major General Darling, Military Secretary to Governor General Dalhousie, had observed in the late 1820s that Algonkin and Nipissing presented "an appearance of comparative wealth and advancement in civilization," while the conditions in which the Iroquois lived "bespeak wretchedness and inactivity in the extreme."[26] By the 1840s the condition of the Iroquois was still "far from prosperous" because of their reliance on an uncertain horticulture. But that of the Algonkin and Nipissing had become "still more deplorable":

> ... their hunting grounds on the Ottawa, which were formerly most extensive, abounding with deer, and other animals, yielding the richest furs, and which their ancestors had enjoyed from time immemorial, have been destroyed for the purposes of the chase. A considerable part has been laid out into townships, and either settled or taken possession of by squatters. The operations of the lumber-men have either destroyed or scared away the game throughout a still more extensive region, and thus, as settlement advances, shey [sic] are driven further and further from their homes, in search of a scanty and precarious livelihood. Their case has been often brought before the Government, and demands early attention.[27]

The Algonkin responded to these adverse changes in some cases by migrating to the Golden Lake area west of Bytown, and in others by shifting into a trade in wood for local markets.[28] Their increasing use of the forest resources brought them into conflict with the Sulpician seigneurs, who eventually prohibited free access to wood for commercial purposes.[29]

Denominational conflict soon worsened the situation. The Mississauga minister Peter Jones visited the Lake of Two Mountains settlement in 1851 at the request of his church to try to convert the Indians there to Protestantism.[30] Jones's mission did not enjoy immediate success, but the Methodists continued to proselytize in the area by means of itinerant missionaries. After the Methodists established a mission at Oka in 1868 a large number of the Iroquois in particular converted to Methodism in a symbolic act of rejection and defiance.[31] (Such behaviour has parallels elsewhere: the Catholicism of the Micmac in the eighteenth century was a badge of their alliance with the French, as well as a creed.) Not surprisingly, given the Sulpicians' view of themselves as owners of the lands and the strong religious feelings of the time, the Order attempted to stomp out Protestantism among the Indians. As early as 1852 Bishop Bourget of Montreal had excommunicated four of the leaders of the Mohawk Indians.[32] In the 1870s excommunicated four of the leaders of the Mohawk Indians.[32] In the 1870s the Sulpicians applied pressure by demanding that the Methodist chapel that the Indians and their supporters had erected be torn down and the ringleaders among the Indians be arrested. By court order the Methodist chapel was dismantled in 1875. Bad feelings degenerated to the point that in June 1877 a fire of mysterious origins destroyed the Catholic church at Oka. The ensuing criminal prosecution of Methodist Indians embroiled the mission inhabitants and large numbers of non-Natives in Quebec and Ontario in bitter controversy for years. The quarrel even attracted the disapproving attention of the Aborigines Protection Society in London and led to inquiries from the Colonial Office.[33] The destruction, threat of violence and growing political complications finally pushed the government of Canada towards action on the troubled Oka situation.

By the 1870s there was a well-established governmental tradition of trying to solve the Oka problem by either or both of two means: relocating the Indians or resolving the dispute by litigation. In 1853, "16 000 acres of land, in Dorchester, North River, in rear of the Township of Wexford, have been set apart for the Iroquois of Caughnawaga and Two Mountains," and similar provision of new lands was made at Maniwaki for the Algonkians from Oka in 1853.[34] Many of the Algonkin, seeking new lands for hunting and trapping, removed to the Maniwaki area, but the Iroquois stayed at Oka.[35] As the Oka problem heated up in the late 1860s and 1870s, Ottawa was tempted to repeat such a "solution" elsewhere. Neither the federal government of Alexander Mackenzie (1873–78) nor those of Sir John Macdonald (1867–73, 1878–91) wanted to grapple seriously with the issue. There were many reasons for their attitude. First, Canadian governments of the nineteenth century could not conceive of Indians having title to lands once Europeans had intruded into an area and begun to use the resources. Furthermore, by the mid-1870s Ottawa was experiencing considerable difficulties in dealing with the settler society of British Columbia. The government there was recalcitrant and obdurate in its refusal to honour its pledges, made in the agreement by which it united with Canada in 1871, to appropriate land for Indians in that province.[36] No federal government wanted quarrels with other provinces, especially the large and powerful province of Quebec, with its French and Catholic majority and its prickly sensitivity on questions of religion and provincial rights. Consequently federal governments avoided dealing with the Oka issue head-on.

Remonstrances by both the Algonkin and Iroquois at Oka in 1868 quickly turned Ottawa's thought to the possibilities of removal.[37] The Indians' demand in a petition that they "should have the same privileges as enjoyed by white people" evoked an interesting response, one that captured perfectly the government's thinking about Indians:

> . . . the Indians cannot have the same privileges as the white man, as long as the law remains as it is, but it is the intention of the Department to submit a scheme by which Indians could, under certain conditions and with certain qualifications, obtain their emancipation, and become, to all intents and purposes, citizens, as the

white men are. But in order that such a measure may obtain the sanction of Parliament, and become law, Indians must not violate the law of the land, nor throw, otherwise, obstacles in the way. They must respect property, be content with their present condition, and be sure that the disposition of the Government is to improve their condition, elevate them in their social position, and prepare them for a complete emancipation.[38]

The petitioners were told that their complaints against the Sulpicians were not well founded, and an order-in-council reconfirming federal government support for the seminary's title was passed.[39] The Under-Secretary of State also informed the Indian complainants that "The government has your welfare at heart."[40] The removal in 1869 of some of the Oka Indians to the upper Ottawa eased the problem temporarily. However, the increasing religious animosity of the 1870s, which threatened to bring on an extended Catholic-Protestant clash as White Methodists rallied to their Red brothers' cause,[41] made it tempting to get the Methodist Indians away from Oka.

By 1877, with the Indians at Oka claiming that they owned the land and resorts to violence becoming increasingly common, matters had come to a head.[42] The government launched an investigation by the Reverend William Scott, a Methodist clergyman and father of a future deputy superintendent general of Indian Affairs, that upheld the position of the seminary.[43] The department also initiated steps in 1879 to remove many of the aggrieved Indians from Oka to the Muskoka district of Ontario. The establishment of the Gibson reserve, and removal of Oka Indians to it, turned out not to be the total solution that the government sought. Agreement was reached in 1881 for the province of Ontario to supply, and for the Sulpicians to pay for, sufficient land in the township of Gibson to settle 120 families numbering about 500 persons, and in 1882 some of the Oka Indians settled at Gibson.[44] However, nothing like the expected number relocated. Only about one-third of the Oka Indians moved, and not all of those stayed for long at Gibson.[45] The stay-at-homes remained obdurate even though the ever-helpful Reverend Scott remonstrated with them: "By moral suasion alone the Department endeavours to accomplish what is deemed best for you."[46] Since most of the Indians remained on the lands near the Sulpician mission, the Oka land dispute continued to fester during the 1880s and 1890s. The Methodists' continuing interest in the issue, during a time when there was a sufficiently large number of other irritants concerning creed and language, ensured that successive governments in this period remained sensitive to the matter, even if they did nothing effective about it.[47]

Sporadically throughout the 1870s and 1880s Ottawa explored the possibility of resolving the Oka dispute by its other preferred method, litigation. As early as January 1873 Joseph Howe, minister responsible for Indian matters, extended an offer to a Methodist clerical champion of the Oka Indians to have the government "pay the cost of the Defense" of "the Indian to whom you refer as having been imprisoned for cutting wood at Oka." The government, according to Howe, was "prepared to carry the case if necessary before the highest tribunals in order that the questions in controversy between the Two Mountains Indians and the Gentlemen of the Seminary may be judicially investigated and set finally at rest."[48] Apparently nothing came of this proposal, nor of another effort of the department in 1882 to settle the dispute with a test case before the courts. Although Ottawa offered to pay the costs, in 1882 the parties could not agree on facts to submit to the courts.[49] And so, amid bickering and sectarian strife, the Oka question lumbered on, unresolved, through the 1880s and 1890s.

By 1903 the Laurier government had tired of the dispute and its attendant political liabilities. Religious passions remained strong in the new century, and during the first decade the dispute at Oka over woodcutting continued to cause friction and political embarrassment for the government. In 1902, for example, Prime Minister Laurier arranged to have an Indian Affairs officer despatched to Oka, where the "Indians are becoming threatening," because "I am under great obligation to the Superior of the Sulpicians, Father Colin."[50] Petitions and confrontations continued steadily. Finally, in 1903 a representative of the government suggested to prominent Toronto lawyer N.W. Rowell, who represented the Methodist legal interest in the Oka affair, that "they were anxious that the matter should be settled, and were prepared that a stated case should be agreed upon between the Seminary and the Indians, and the matter referred to a Court for adjudication, the Department paying the expenses of the litigation." Official thinking was that "the Indians have a certain right of possession or use in the property," but the precise nature and extent of those rights or interests were not clear. It was best, therefore, to refer the contentious and complex matter to the courts at public expense.[51] Not for the last time, Indian Affairs opened its files to counsel for each side, and not for the last time Indian land claims litigation proved a boon to the historical research industry. The Rowell firm, no doubt making good use of taxpayers' dollars, despatched a legal researcher to Paris to uncover documents that might strengthen the Indians' argument that they were the true owners of the lands at Oka.[52]

Thus began the celebrated case of *Angus Corinthe et al v. The Ecclesiastics of the Seminary of St. Sulpice of Montreal*, which eventually emerged from the bowels of the Judicial Committee of the Privy Council in 1912.[53] The Indians' argument combined a number of propositions. The Sulpicians' interest in the lands was only that of a "trustee for the Plaintiffs"; and the Indians "have from time immemorial" enjoyed the right to use the commons, cut firewood and pasture stock. As their formal argument to the Privy Council put it, they claimed "to be the absolute owners by virtue of the unextinguished Aboriginal title, the Proclamation of 1763, and possession sufficient to create title by prescription [tradition]. Alternatively, the Indians have claimed qualified title under the French grants." The respondents, the Sulpicians, "rely mainly on these statutory titles and claim that under these titles, they are the absolute owners of the Seigniory of the Lake of Two Mountains and not merely the owners in trust for the Indians." In the unlikely event that the high court found that eighteenth-century Indians had possessed some form of title or interest, the present Oka claimants "could not be their representative as the Appellants are the chiefs of the

Iroquois tribe only, and the Iroquois tribe's territory was far from the Island of Montreal and the Lake of Two Mountains." The Algonkin, who were closest to the land in the eighteenth century, were not, the seminary's factum pointedly argued, suing.

The Corinthe appeal to the Privy Council epitomized the principal features of land claims, which at the beginning of this century were in a most rudimentary state. The Indians relied both on an embryonic notion of Aboriginal title ("from time immemorial" they had used the resources of the tract) and British common law (the Sulpicians exercised title "merely as trustee" for the Indians). The latter argument was buttressed with their oral tradition, which in many instances was supported by documents recently unearthed in Paris. Counsel for the Sulpicians similarly argued a two-part case. The Order was the proper owner by virtue of the original grant, and, in the event that there could be any dispute about that point, their title had been clarified, recognized and confirmed by legislative action in 1841.

The judgment—in favour of the Sulpicians—similarly represented the limited nature of Indigenous peoples' legal title eighty years ago. Speaking for the Privy Council, Lord Chancellor Viscount Haldane ruled that

> Their Lordships thought that the effect of this [1841] Act was to place beyond question the title of the respondents [Sulpicians] to the Seigniory, and to make it impossible for the appellants to establish an independent title to possession or control in the administration . . . neither by aboriginal title, nor by prescription, nor on the footing that they were *cestuis que trustent* of the corporation, could the appellants assert any title in an action such as that out of which this appeal had arisen.

However, the court did note that a condition of the 1841 legislative confirmation of Sulpician title had created what in common law parlance would be a charitable trust, an obligation to care for the souls and instruct the young of the Indians at Oka, and that there might be means by which the Indians through governments could force the priests to honour those requirements. In the opinion of the Methodists' legal advisor, given the unlikelihood of the province of Quebec's interesting itself in the matter on behalf of the Indians, serious consideration should be given to pressing Ottawa, "the guardian of the indians [sic] of Canada," to compel the Sulpicians to honour their obligations.[54]

The Judicial Committee's ruling, though perhaps appearing odd after the Supreme Court of Canada's finding in the 1990 Sparrow case, is understandable in the context of its times. Legally, the negative finding rested on the propositions enunciated in the important St. Catharines Milling case of 1889. In that instance the Privy Council had ruled that there was such a thing as Aboriginal title, but that it constituted merely a usufructuary right and that it was "dependent on the goodwill of the Sovereign."[55] This was a view of Indigenous people's rights that, like the federal government's decision to remove some of the Oka Indians to Gibson township, might reasonably by summed up as the view that the Great White Father knew best what was in the interests of his Red-Skinned Children. It assumed that Aboriginal title was limited to use because title inhered in the Crown, and it posited that the head of state could remove what it had graciously granted ("dependent on the goodwill of the Sovereign"). The implication of this latter point, obviously, was that parliament and the legislatures, of which the Crown was a part, of course, could also unilaterally extinguish even this limited Aboriginal title. And, with very few and limited exceptions, Indians could not vote for representatives to sit in those chambers.[56] That is what the Judicial Committee held had occurred in the case of the Oka lands by the 1841 statute.

The entire doctrine of a limited Aboriginal title that was dependent on the will of the majority population's political representatives was consistent with the approach that Ottawa took in Indian affairs. The government's assumption was that Indians were in a state of tutelage, were legally "wards" of Ottawa, and were to be encouraged and coerced by a variety of policies to grow into full Euro-Canadian adulthood. In the meantime, they were legally infantile; Great White Father knew best. The Privy Council decision in the Oka land case in 1912 was completely consistent with these legal and policy positions.

Needless to say, the Indians of Oka accepted neither the ruling nor the doctrine of Aboriginal infantilism that underlay it. In the immediate aftermath of the court ruling their chief "states that it will not be possible to restrain the people longer, as he has been holding them in check pending the judgment of the court in the matter."[57] Methodist petitioning of the federal government resulted in no observable consequences,[58] and at Oka conditions reverted to the state that had prevailed before the decision to take the Corinthe case through the courts. The principal reason for Ottawa's inaction was the fact that the legal advice it had received was that the Privy Council decision placed no particular obligations on either the Sulpicians or the federal government.[59] The Indians kept complaining to Ottawa after 1912, especially when the Sulpicians from time to time sold off part of the disputed lands.[60] For example, when the Sulpicians were unable to repay $1 025 000 they had borrowed in 1933 from the province of Quebec, the Order handed over one hundred lots to the province, which much later transferred some of the plots to the municipality of Oka for one dollar.[61] In the 1930s the Sulpicians sold their rights to a considerable area, including lands the Indians considered theirs, to a Belgian company that began to enforce its proprietary rights on the Indians with consequent friction.[62] As a result of these occasional sales, settlement at Oka came to resemble a racial checkerboard: Whites and Mohawk lived side by side. Moreover, since the lands at Oka that the Mohawk occupied were not a formal or legal "reserve" within the meaning of the *Indian Act*, Indian control was even more tenuous than it otherwise would have been.[63]

The next phase came to a head in 1945. Sulpician land sales having occasioned considerable Mohawk disquiet during the 1930s, Ottawa intervened in a bumbled effort to resolve the dispute and lower the tension between Indians and clergy. Again without consulting the Indians involved, the federal government negotiated an agreement with the Sulpicians, who were nearly bankrupt, to purchase land for the remaining

Mohawk at the mission.[64] Although this had the immediate effect of lowering the temperature of the quarrel, it by no means cleared up the underlying dispute over ownership of the whole tract. Non-Indians assumed that the sale meant that Indians in future would confine themselves to their small, scattered plots, which totalled 1556 acres.[65] The descendants of Indians who believed they once had possessed more than sixty-four square miles now found their holdings reduced to two and one-half square miles. As a western member of Parliament observed in 1961, "They certainly did get gypped, did they not?"[66] Moreover, since the government failed to follow the terms of the *Indian Act* by setting the purchased lands aside by order-in-council as a reserve for the benefit of the Indians, this newly acquired parcel still was not legally a reserve. In law it remained merely a settlement, an anomalous status that did nothing to reassure the Indians.

By the end of the 1950s, as noted at the outset, the dispute was becoming troublesome once again. In 1959 the municipality of Oka used a private member's bill in Quebec's legislature to establish a nine-hole golf course on some land that the Mohawk claimed as their own.[67] The town knew that such action was a legal possibility because Indians Affairs had thoughtfully announced in 1958 that the Indians' land at Oka was not a legal Indian reserve. "These lands do not comprise an Indian Reserve. . . . The right to occupy the individual parcels became involved over the years, and the Indian affairs branch has been attempting to straighten these matters out. The work is nearing completion."[68] Oka's ability to secure the special legislation was perhaps explained by the fact that the municipality and the tract in question lay in the premier's constituency.[69] Perhaps the same factor also explains why the Indians who resided at Oka were given no notice of the private measure and no opportunity to argue against it.[70] In any event, the private member's bill transferred some "common lands" that the Indians had long used for wood-cutting and cattle-grazing into land destined for recreation. "What was once reserved for Indian use and profit is now reserved for golf," noted their lawyer.[71] As the Indians said themselves, "We also consider the building of the clubhouse directly adjacent to our graveyard a desecration and an insult to our sensibilities."[72]

Once the private member's bill was passed, the Kanesatake Mohawk tried to resist. The Indians asked Ottawa to disallow the private Quebec statute, but John Diefenbaker's government refused.[73] The Mohawk remonstrated about the unsatisfactory status of their limited holdings before the Joint Parliamentary Committee in 1961, telling the parliamentarians that "We want tribal ownership of land, not the individual ownership which the white man favours."[74] Once more their protests had no apparent effect.[75] The Joint Committee considered their protests in 1961 and recommended establishing an Indian claims commission, such as the United States had, to deal with the British Columbia and Oka land questions. However, not even this could move either the bureaucratic or political levels of government to action.[76] Whatever Ottawa was doing in an attempt "to straighten these matters out" in any event was overtaken and rendered irrelevant in the 1970s.

As a result of the Nishga or Calder case in 1973, a new chapter on Inuit and Indian land claims opened. Prior to the court's finding that there was such a thing as Aboriginal title and that it extended well beyond the limited version that the Privy Council had defined in the St. Catharine's Milling case, the Prime Minister had rejected the notion. In Pierre Trudeau's view, "We can't recognize aboriginal rights because no society can be built on historical 'might-have-beens'."[77] However, in the Nishga case six of seven supreme court justices gave powerful support to the concept of Aboriginal title, while rejecting the Nishga suit itself. Three of the judges found that legislative action in British Columbia had extinguished Aboriginal title, while the other three did not agree. (The seventh judge found against the plaintiff on a technical point.) In the wake of the Calder decision Trudeau had to recognize that he faced a much more powerful adversary than some mere historical might-have-been in this Aboriginal title. He reportedly responded, "Perhaps you had more legal rights than we thought you had when we did the white paper."[78] Given the fact that the ramifications of Aboriginal title were enormous in an era when the Cree of Quebec were battling the James Bay hydroelectric project and a variety of Native groups in the Mackenzie Valley were voicing opposition to northern energy development, some concessions were essential. Trudeau and his government, already battered by the First Peoples' united and vehement rejection of the White Paper of 1969, backed away from the prime minister's rarefied individualist notions and prepared to deal with Aboriginal land claims on a collective, systematic basis.[79] In August 1973 Indian Affairs Minister Jean Chrétien announced that a new policy would soon be forthcoming.

Beginning in July 1974, Ottawa set up a claims resolution process. Government now recognized two categories of Indian claims, comprehensive and specific. Comprehensive claims were based on the contention that the claimant had an unextinguished Aboriginal right through possession of a territory since time immemorial. The Nishga case would have been such a comprehensive claim. Specific claims, which might be about a variety of topics including land, were demands for redress based on an argument that commitments or legal obligations on the part of the government to Indian groups had not been carried out fully and properly. The government would assist in the development of claims cases by funding research by Indian organizations. And an Office of Native Claims (ONC) would become the focal point in Indian Affairs for the claims resolution process for both comprehensive and specific claims. The ONC would investigate claims lodged by Indian organizations and advise the Indian Affairs minister on their strength. If it so advised and Indian Affairs accepted the advice, the claim could then be negotiated. In these negotiations the Office of Native Claims would represent the federal government, and, following conclusion of an agreement, the ONC would help to implement and monitor compliance with the claim settlement. Finally, the office was also responsible for formulating policies covering the Native claims area.

The claims resolution policy of 1973–74 had a chequered history, largely because it was—and remains—seriously flawed. First and foremost, it was, as usual, the product of the Ottawa bureaucracy. Since it had not resulted from consultation and negotiation, it was the object of suspicion and contained elements that were unacceptable to the Native organizations. Some of these problems concerned the criteria by which Ottawa decided if claims were valid. For example, for comprehensive claims it was necessary to demonstrate that the claim emanated from an organized group, that the group had occupied the territory in question exclusively and continuously from pre-contact times (from time immemorial) to the present, and that the claimant could demonstrate it was the legitimate descendant and representative of the original occupiers. Such criteria ignored both pre- and post-contact migrations of Native groups in response to environmental, economic and military factors. It appeared to rule out, for example, the claim of the Inland Tlingit to the territory in northern British Columbia and southern Yukon that they occupied in the late twentieth century because that group had migrated there in the nineteenth century.[80] And, of course, it worked against the arguments of a group such as the Oka Indians, who had been contending since at least 1781 that the land they occupied was theirs, because those Indians had taken up residence on the land they now claimed well after the European arrived.

Other difficulties stemmed largely from the legalistic approach that the Ottawa bureaucracy took to the claims resolution process. The governing principle in the ONC's evaluation of specific claims was the doctrine of "lawful obligation," a narrow gate through which not all worthy cases could squeeze. And government representatives proved themselves prone to argue technical objections, such as invalidity of oral history evidence and the doctrine of laches (barrier to litigation by passage of time). Such approaches were to be expected from a bureaucracy, but they caused enormous problems. As early as 1980 it was noted that bands and organizations were choosing litigation over negotiation with the Office of Native Claims.[81] The inordinately slow pace of Ottawa's work and the backlog that inevitably developed also contributed greatly to disenchantment with the claims resolution process. Since Ottawa limited the number of comprehensive claims negotiations in which it would engage at any one time, a logjam quickly developed. In 1981 a review of the comprehensive claims resolution process noted that the James Bay and Northern Quebec Agreement was the only such dispute that had been resolved. Thirteen others were in various stages of negotiation.[82] By 1985 a task force set up to review the comprehensive claims process noted that there were six comprehensive claims under negotiation, another fifteen (thirteen of them in British Columbia) that had been accepted by the department and awaited negotiation, seven that were under review and several more that were expected. As the assessors noted, "in spite of more than a decade of negotiating, little progress has been made in the settlement of claims." The task force chair, Murray Coolican, pointed out that "At the current rate of settlement it could be another 100 years before all the claims have been addressed."[83] Things were no better in the area of specific claims: at the end of December 1981, twelve specific claims had been resolved, and 250 more awaited resolution.[84]

The problems with the claims resolution process stemmed from more than just the slow pace and consequent frustration. Many Indian groups objected to the two-fisted role played by Indian and Northern Affairs after the process was formalized in 1973–74. The bureaucracy that granted funds for claims research was the same body that decided how much money would be available to bands and other organizations for a variety of social, political and economic activities. Many suspected that the arrangement was designed to discourage claimants from pressing their cases too aggressively. Moreover, since the Office of Native Claims both decided which claims were to be accepted for negotiation and then bargained on behalf of the federal government, the process was clearly in contravention of a major tenet of natural justice. If it was true that no one should be judge in his or her own cause, what did one say about the Canadian claims process? More generally, all the high cards were dealt to the government in this unequal game:

> Without exception, an aboriginal party has few resources other than the intelligence, commitment, and skill of its leaders, who must sit across the table from the representatives of the Government of Canada, with their apparently overwhelming resources and power. The government decides which claim is accepted, how much money will be made available to the claimant group for research and negotiation, when negotiations will begin, and the process for negotiations. Except where court action threatens a major development project, the government's patience for negotiation appears unlimited. It is hardly surprising that aboriginal groups have little confidence in the fairness of the process, or in the government's desire for early settlements.[85]

Delay, the double role of Indian Affairs and lack of progress all added up to a claims process that engendered suspicion and opposition in equal parts.

Because of these discontents, the claims resolution process has been under scrutiny through most of its existence. As early as April 1975, claims issues were part of the agenda of a joint National Indian Brotherhood (NIB)/Indian Affairs committee, a consultation that ended abruptly in 1978 when the NIB pulled out in protest.[86] A review of the comprehensive claims procedures led to a restatement of policy under the title of *In All Fairness* in 1981. This document showed little evidence of influence from the Native community, and it embodied no new thinking in any event.[87] In December of the same year *Outstanding Business*, a revised statement of specific claims policy, modified arrangements in this area slightly. Although this document observed that "Indian representatives all stated, in the strongest of terms, that Indian views must be considered in the development of any new or modified claims policy," there were few signs that Ottawa paid much attention.[88] The adoption of the Charter of Rights and Freedoms, with its clause recognizing and affirming "existing aboriginal and treaty rights" caused more uncertainty in the Native community about the land claims process.

Above all, Ottawa's constant search for and insistence upon extinguishment of all Aboriginal rights as part of claims resolution became particularly ominous. As the *Report of the Task Force on Comprehensive Claims Policy* (Coolican Report) noted, there were other Aboriginal rights—such as self-government, for example—that were not necessarily integral to a land claim. Why should Inuit and Indians give up whatever other Aboriginal rights they had to get their comprehensive claim settled?[89] When a parliamentary committee, known usually as the Penner Committee, supported First Nations' views on self-government in 1983 by advocating *recognition* of that right, the arguments against accepting extinguishment of Aboriginal rights in order to get a comprehensive claims settlement were strengthened still further.

An abortive attempt to come to grips with these objections was made in 1985 in the task force on Comprehensive Claims Policy. Although Chief Gary Potts of the Teme-Augama Anishnabai noted that this inquiry "marks the first time since 1763 that government has made an effort to hear from the First Nations of Canada" concerning treaty-making and claims, there was little evidence that that hearing led to acceptance.[90] The task force condemned the slow pace of comprehensive claims negotiations, blamed government insistence on extinguishment for much of the problem, and called for a new comprehensive claims policy that would speed up the process and largely shunt aside the troublesome extinguishment issue. However, the *Comprehensive Land Claims Policy* that emerged in 1986, though it claimed later to have dropped its aim of "blanket extinguishment," offered nothing concrete to avoid the problem. When all the verbiage was stripped away, Indian and Northern Affairs still had not committed itself to drop extinguishment, persisted in talking about "granting" rather than "recognizing" self-government and was still reserving for itself the role of judge of whether or not a comprehensive claim was worthy of proceeding to negotiation.[91] By the later 1980s the major difference in Ottawa's claims resolution process was one of structure: the Office of Native Claims had been replaced in the middle of the decade by a Comprehensive Claims Branch and a Specific Claims Branch.

In light of the unsatisfactory nature and evolution of the federal government's land claims procedures after 1973, the bitter disappointment of the Oka Indians is easier to understand. They, after all, had always been treated like credulous and dependent children for whom others—Sulpicians, legislature, Methodist clerics, judicial committee and certainly Indian and Northern Affairs Canada—knew best what was in their interest. After 1974 they found themselves enmeshed in a claims resolution process that was unilaterally created and largely operated by the Great White Father in Ottawa. Given the history of Oka-Kanesatake, it was not surprising that the comprehensive land claim that they launched early in 1975 was rejected a few months later.

On the advice of the department of justice, the Office of Native Claims found that the comprehensive claim of the Mohawk of Akwesasne (St. Regis), Kahnewake (Caughnawaga) and Kanesatake to a large portion of southwestern Quebec did not rest on unextinguished Aboriginal title. If the Mohawk had possessed the land being claimed when Europeans arrived (and the expert in the justice department was inclined to doubt that they had), they had since lost it or given it up. "[I]f the claimants ever did have aboriginal title to the land in question, this title has long been extinguished by the dispositions made of the land under the French regime, by the decision of the Sovereign, after the cession [Conquest], to open the territory to settlement and by the grants made over the years pursuant to this policy." The justice department also believed that the lands the Mohawk were claiming had not been protected by the Royal Proclamation of 1763. In short, "the native title alleged by the claimants, if it ever existed, was extinguished, first by the French Kings at least with respect to the grants made by them, and, after the cession, by the Sovereign by the exercise of complete dominion over the land adverse to the right of occupancy of the Indians." However, the same opinion that dismissed the extensive Mohawk comprehensive claim explicitly stated that it did not apply to any "specific claims which the Mohawks of Oka, St. Regis, and Caughnawaga may have with respect to lands contiguous or near their existing reserves."[92]

Such reasoning, which showed that in some respects the federal government had not advanced beyond the 1912 judicial committee rationale that was based on the 1889 ruling on St. Catharine's Milling, ignored several facts. Iroquoians had undoubtedly ranged through and extracted resources from the region at the time of European contact. Particularly the Algonkin and Nipissing at Oka had until at least the 1820s regularly hunted, trapped and fished in the lower Ottawa Valley from their base at the settlement. Finally, Ottawa has accepted or seems prepared to accept claims from other groups whose records of occupation are no lengthier than that of the Indians at Oka. For example, the Golden Lake band of Algonkin in Ontario are proceeding with a comprehensive claim despite the fact that many of them are the descendants of migrants from Oka.[93] Nevertheless, Ottawa rejected the Mohawk comprehensive claim that included lands at Kanesatake-Oka.

The Kanesatake Indians' specific claim fared no better. Lodged in June 1977, it languished until October 1986, when its contention that the Kanesatake Mohawk had an interest in the territory that should be addressed was rejected. Since "the Oka Band has not demonstrated any outstanding lawful obligation on the part of the Federal Crown," Indian and Northern Affairs would not accept the claim for negotiation. However, Ottawa "recognized that there is an historical basis for Mohawk claims related to land grants in the 18th century," and "I [minister Bill McKnight] am willing to consider a proposal for alternative means of redress of the Kanesatake Band's grievance. . . ."[94] As noted earlier, efforts to carry out a land consolidation scheme at Kanesatake failed in 1989–90. This last attempt at resolution fell afoul of fears that Ottawa was not willing to go far enough to meet Mohawk needs, of divisions within the Kanesatake community and of the impatience of a municipality and a golf club that wanted to expand the existing course by annexing lands that the Mohawk considered theirs. The result, of course, was the violence of the summer of 1990.

Subsequent to the eleven-week confrontation at Kanesatake, Ottawa behaved in its usual consistently inconsistent fashion. While speaking to the Federation of Saskatchewan Indian Nations in August on the error of using confrontation and violence, the minister of Indian and Northern Affairs Canada, Tom Siddon, observed helpfully that "while our specific claims process *is* working, it is *not* working to the satisfaction of Indian people or myself."[95] In September 1990, Siddon lectured Indian leaders assembled in Ottawa on how they would have behaved during the crisis had they been responsible, good little Indian leaders.[96] Having twice rejected Mohawk land claims, the minister announced during the stand-off at Kanesatake that Ottawa would purchase and hand over to the aggrieved Indians the terrain in question. Once Ottawa had acquired some, but not all, of the disputed land in the autumn of 1990, the minister's representatives proceeded to become embroiled in a frustrating round of talks that led nowhere. By February 1991 the minister, appearing before the Commons committee on Aboriginal affairs, argued that the villain in the Oka story was the traditional system of government by chiefs selected by the clan mothers, a system that one of his predecessors had agreed to have restored in 1969. "Since 1986, clan mothers have appointed six different councils at Kanesatake," with resulting instability. The indecisiveness that resulted from traditional Mohawk governance, said Siddon, had made it impossible for the federal negotiator, in spite of eighteen meetings with the band council and municipality after 1989, to reach an agreement. That was why there had been violence, destruction, and death at Oka in the summer of 1990.[97]

The real explanation of the Oka tragedy is not clan mothers. Rather it is the Great White Father, or more precisely the attitude that has long prevailed in Ottawa that government is a paternalistic and benevolent agent that knows better than anyone else what is best for its Red Children. This attitude is indistinguishable from that of the Sulpicians and French government officials who in the seventeenth and eighteenth centuries shifted Algonkin, Nipissing and Mohawk groups from La Montagne to Sault au Recollet to Oka. It underlay the rejection of repeated Oka Indian demands from the 1780s to the 1830s to regularize their title. It accounted for the legislative fiat of 1841 that registered the Sulpicians' title to the disputed lands, a unilateral declaration that was upheld in the Corinthe case in 1912 and, in part, in Ottawa's rejection of the comprehensive land claim of the 1970s. The assumption that Ottawa knew best accounted, too, for the repeated efforts to resolve the controversy at Oka by removing some or all of the Indians—to Maniwaki, to Gibson, anywhere away from the political flashpoint of the moment. And, finally, these attitudes explained the repeated failure of bureaucrats and politicians to respond to Indian petitions to the Governor in the nineteenth century, to the joint parliamentary inquiry of the 1940s, and to the inquiry of 1961 that something be done to clear up the mess of the land dispute at Oka-Kanesatake.

The Great White Father in Ottawa is responsible for the Oka crisis, and for the larger mess of the land claims resolution process across the country. Procedures decided on in Ottawa and imposed on Aboriginal organizations have responded to bureaucratic imperatives and ignored Native needs. The continuing, futile attempt to impose a doctrine of extinguishment on Aboriginal rights in the comprehensive claims process is the clearest, most and Inuit organizations, in spite of the collapse in 1990 of the tentative Dene-Métis comprehensive claim agreement, in spite of the Sparrow and Sioui decisions of 1990, and in spite of the 1982 Charter of Rights and Freedoms, Ottawa refuses to drop a requirement that stands in the way of clearing up an enormous backlog. Why? Presumably because Ottawa—the Great White Father—knows best.

Just ask the people at Oka.

NOTES

1. Emile Colas, Legal Counsel for the Oka Indians to the Joint Committee of Senate and House of Commons on Indian Affairs, *Minutes of Proceedings and Evidence*, no. 1 (Ottawa: Queen's Printer, 1961), 14 March 1961, 15.

2. Throughout this paper the contemporary designation, Indian and Northern Affairs Canada, is used for a department or branch that has been known by various titles since 1880.

3. Treaties and Historical Research Centre [hereinafter THRC], Indian and Northern Affairs Canada, document 0-44, "Land Title at Oka [1973]."

4. Indian and Northern Affairs Canada, press release 1-9029, 27 July 1990; and "An Overview of the Oka Issue," press release, July 1990.

5. Canada, House of Commons, Minutes and Proceedings and Evidence of the Standing Committee on Aboriginal Affairs, The Fifth Report to the House, *The Summer of 1990* (Ottawa: May 1991).

6. Assembly of First Nations, "Kanesatake Background & Chronology," *Kanesatake (Oka) Update*, 20 Nov. 1990.

7. THRC, document K-59, "Oka 1881–1950." According to M. Trudel, *Introduction to New France* (Toronto: Holt Rinehart and Winston, 1968), 221, a common league equalled 2.76 English miles, while an official league was 2.42 English miles. This paper assumes that the measure of

the eighteenth-century grant was in official leagues.

8. Title of concession, 27 April 1717 (trans.), document K-59, "Oka 1881–1950."

9. R. Cole Harris, ed., *Historical Atlas of Canada*, vol. 1, *From the Beginnings to 1800* (Toronto: University of Toronto Press, 1987), plate 47 (B.G. Trigger).

10. A. Shortt and A.G. Doughty, eds., "Article XL of Capitulation of Montreal, 1760" in *Documents Relating to the Constitutional History of Canada, 1759–1791* (Ottawa: King's Printer, 1918), 33.

11. Peter A. Cumming and Neil H. Mickenberg, *Native Rights in Canada*, 2nd ed. (Toronto: Indian-Eskimo Association, 1972), 85–86.

12. R.C. Dalton, *The Jesuits' Estates Question 1760–1888: A Study of the Background for the Agitation of 1889* (Toronto: University of Toronto Press, 1968), chaps. 2–4.

13. Speech of several Indian chiefs to Col Campbell, 7 Feb. 1781; speech by Principal Chiefs to Sir John Johnson, 8 Feb. 1787; and letter of Indians to Joseph Chew, 7 Aug. 1795; in Great Library, Osgoode Hall, "Privy Council vol. 32," containing "Factums and supporting documents for Angus Corinthe et al v. The Ecclesiastics of the Seminary of St Sulpice of Montreal" (hereinafter cited as Factums). The cited documents are in the first part (labelled Volume 1) at 93–96, 99–102 and 132–34 respectively.

OKA AND THE LAND CLAIMS PROCESS 387

14. Richard H. Bartlett, *Indian Reserves in Quebec*, Studies in Aboriginal Rights no. 8 (Saskatoon: University of Saskatchewan Native Law Centre, 1984), 6.

15. *Decision of General Gage, Military Governor, 4 Nov. 1763, G.M. Mathieson's "Blue Book," RG 10, vol. 10 024.

16. "Report of a Committee of the Whole Council, 21 April 1789, ibid.

17. Indian and Northern Affairs Canada, "Comprehensive Land Claim of Kanesatake Indians," press release, July 1990.

18. Daniel Francis, *A History of the Native Peoples of Quebec 1760–1867* (Ottawa: Indian and Northern Affairs Canada, 1985), 14.

19. National Archives of Canada (hereafter NA), RG 10, Series A3 (Administrative Records of the Military 1677–1857), vol. 492, 30248-51 claim of Algonkin and Nipissing chiefs, Lake of Two Mountains, 22 July 1822, in form of petition to Lord Dalhousie.

20. *John Johnson to Col Darling, April 1823; Darling to Oka Indians in council at Caughnawaga, 5 Oct. 1827; and Report of a Committee of the Executive Council, 13 June 1837—all in Mathieson's "Blue Book."

21. *"Propositions made by Messire Quiblier, Superior of the Seminary of Montreal, to the Iroquois Tribe stationed at the Lake of the Two Mountains, and accepted by them. . . . 11 June 1839," by Father Quiblier, enclosed in D.C. Napier to Governor General, 18 July 1839, ibid.

22. 2 Vict., c. 50, 8 April 1839; 3 Vict., c. 30, 8 June 1840; 4 Vict., c. 42 [1841] of Consolidated Statutes of Lower Canada 1861. See the memorandum re "Oka Indians" by A.E. St. Louis, Indian Affairs Branch, 26 May 1948, in THRC, document K-59, "Oka 1881–1950."

23. Thompson, "Brief History," 20–23.

24. RG 10, Series A3, vol. 492, 30251, petition of 22 July 1822.

25. J. McCann-Magill, "The Golden Lake Land Claim: A Case Study for the Comparison of the Litigation and Negotiation Processes" (BA thesis, Carleton University, reprinted by THRC, Summer 1990), 11.

26. Quoted in "Report on the Affairs of the Indians in Canada 1845," *Journals of the Legislature of the Province of Canada, 1844–45*, Appendix EEE, Section II, Pt. 3.

27. Ibid. Similarly see the testimony of James Hughes, Superintendent, Indian Department, 16 Jan. 1843, in Report on the Affairs of the Indians of Canada, Journals of the Legislative Assembly of the Province of Canada 1847, Appendix T.

28. THRC, document K-19, A.E. St. Louis, memorandum on "Early History of the Algonquin Indians of Golden Lake" [1947].

29. Concerning Indian complaints over wood, see "Chief Joseph Onasakenrat and 15 others to Hon. Joseph Howe, Superintendent of Indian Affairs, transmitting petition of 26 July 1868," in Canada *Sessional Papers* (No. 55), 1870, 32–33.

30. Donald B. Smith, *The Reverend Peter Jones (Kahkewaquonaby) and the Mississauga Indians* (Toronto: University of Toronto Press, 1987), 217.

31. NA, RG 10, Red Series, vol. 2029, file 8946, petition of 19 Aug. 1871.

32. Thompson, "Brief History," 25.

33. NA, CO 42, vol. 753 (reel B-590), Despatch 30, "Relations existing between Seminary of St Sulpice & Protestant Indians resident at Oka," 9 Feb. 1878.

34. Report on the Petition of the Iroquois Chiefs of the Iroquois Tribes of the Lake of Two Mountains, 9 Oct. 1868, Canada, *Sessional Papers* (No. 55) 1870, 42.

35. R.C. Daniel, *A History of Native Claims Processes in Canada, 1867–1979*

(Ottawa: Indian Affairs and Northern Development, 1980), 78; McCann-Magill, *Golden Lake Claim*, 12.

36. Robin Fisher, *Contact and Conflict: Indian-European Relations in British Columbia 1774–1890* (Vancouver: University of British Columbia Press, 1977), chap. 8.

37. Joseph Onasakenral [sic] and twelve others to Sir John Macdonald, 10 Dec. 1868, in *Sessional Papers* (No. 55) 1870, 4–5.

38. Report on the Petition of the Algonquin Indians of the Lake of Two Mountains, 26 Oct. 1868; ibid., 41.

39. Report on the Petition of the Iroquois Chiefs of the Iroquois Tribes of the Lake of Two Mountains, 9 Oct. 1979; ibid., 42; Daniel, *Claims*, 78.

40. Etienne Parent to Joseph Onasakenrat and other Chiefs, 15 March 1869, quoted in Thompson, "Brief History," 29.

41. See, for example, Rev. John Borland, *The Assumptions of the Seminary of St. Sulpice* (Montreal: Gazette Printing House, 1872).

42. *NA, RG 10, Red Series, vol. 2035, file 8946-4, #200285, Memorandum of Solicitor General 25 Dec. 1897, annex "a" to P.C. 1727, 1 July 1898.

43. NA, RG 10, Red Series, vol. 725, Rev. William Scott, *Report Relating to the Affairs of the Oka Indians, made to the Superintendent General of Indian Affairs* (Ottawa: MacLean, Roger & Co., 1883) is the published version. It is curious that the published report's preface (p. 3) claims that the pamphlet was printed at the author's expense because in Aug. 1883 the deputy superintendent general of Indian Affairs indicated that Scott's financial situation was not good. See NA, MG 26 A, Sir John A. Macdonald Papers, vol. 289, 132681-3, L. Vankoughnet to Macdonald, 4 Aug. 1883. Similarly see ibid., vol. 290, 133064-6, same to same, 28 April 1885; ibid., 133068-70, same to same, 4 May 1885; RG 10, Red Series, vol. 2203, file 40 584, Rev. William Scott to Sir John A. Macdonald, 28 Nov.

1882 and 18 April 1884; ibid., L. Vankoughnet to Sir John A. Macdonald, 27 Dec. 1882 and 23 April 1883.

44. Donald J. Bourgeois, "Research Report on the Mohawks of the Gibson Indian Land Claim," 21 April 1982, 6. I am grateful to Professor Donald B. Smith, who provided me with a copy of this report.

45. NA, Secretary of State Correspondence, RG 6, A1, vol. 54, #7539, Rev. L. Colin, Superior, Seminary of St Sulpice to J.-A. Chapleau, 6 Nov. 1883; Daniel, *Claims*, 79.

46. Scott, *Report*, 63, Appendix 2, W. Scott to Chiefs of Oka Indians, 18 Dec. 1882.

47. For example, *Christian Guardian*, 17 Sept. 1884, 31 Aug. 1887, 7 Sept. 1904; NA, MG 27, II B 1, Lord Minto Papers, vol. 10, 11, "Subjects brought before Lord Minto by the Indian delegation from St Regis and Oka, 1901"; Rev. John Borland, *An Appeal to the Montreal Conference and Methodists Generally* (Montreal: Witness Printing House, 1883) and Norman Murray, *The Oka Question* (n.p., n.d. [1886]); RG 10, Red Series, vol. 2034, file 8946-3, newspaper clippings 1890.

48. NA, RG 10, Red Series, vol. 2029, file 8946, (draft) Joseph Howe to Rev. John Borland, 24 Jan. 1873.

49. *Ibid., vol. 2035, file 8946-4, unidentified, unsigned memorandum, 13 Oct. 1890; Daniel, *Claims*, 79 and 172, n. 5.

50. NA, MG 26 G, Sir Wilfrid Laurier Papers, vol. 791G, 225747, (copy) W. Laurier to Clifford Sifton, 17 Nov. 1902.

51. United Church of Canada Archives [UCA], A. Carman Papers, box 11, file 59, N.W. Rowell to Rev. Dr. Henderson, 1 Aug. 1903; enclosed with Rowell to Rev. Dr Carman, 1 Aug. 1903.

52. I.S. Fairty, "Reminiscences [1947]," *The Law Society of Upper Canada Gazette* 12, 3 (Sept. 1978): 257–58; Daniel, *Claims*, 82.

53. Unless otherwise noted, this treatment of the case relies upon: *Dominion Law Reports* 5, "Corinthe et al. v. Seminary of St Sulpice of Montreal," 263–68; and "Factums."

54. UCA, T.E.E. Shore Papers (accession 78.093C), box 3, file 57, N.W. Rowell to Rev. T.E.E. Shore, 2 Oct. 1912.

55. As quoted in B. Morse, ed., *Aboriginal Peoples and the Law: Indian, Metis and Inuit Rights in Canada* (Ottawa: Carleton University Press, 1985), 58.

56. The 1885 Franchise Act extended the franchise in federal elections to Indians east of Manitoba. The provision was repealed in 1898.

57. Shore Papers, box 3, file 57, N.W. Rowell to T.E.E. Shore, 2 Oct. 1912.

58. Ibid., (copy) T.E.E. Shore to Col S. Hughes, 26 Nov. 1912.

59. *RG 10, Red Series, vol 2032, file 8946X, part 3, E. Lafleur, "Opinion as to the Rights of the Iroquois and Algonquin Indians of Oka," 21 June 1916.

60. *Records of Indian Affairs, file 373/1-1, Bernard Bourdon to W.M. Cory, Jan. 1951.

61. *Ibid., file 373/3-8, Memorandum by G. Boudreault, 18 April 1969.

62. *Ibid., file 373/1-1 Royal Werry to W.J.F. Pratt, 16 March 1938. The federal minister did criticize the seminary's disposal of property that the Indians used at one point, but the context suggested that the protest was a bargaining ploy aimed at reducing the amount that the Sulpicians wanted for their lands at Oka. See T.A. Crerar to Sulpicians, 10 Dec. 1941, in *Minutes of Proceedings and Evidence*, 31–32.

63. Although Bartlett, *Indian Reserves in Quebec*, 6, refers to the "reserve at Oka," it was not and is not now a reserve because the lands have never been "set aside by Order-in-Council as a reserve for the benefit" of the Indians. Daniel, *Claims*, 83.

64. Their lawyer later claimed that the Indians were not informed of the 1945 transaction until 1957. See *Records of Indian Affairs, file 373/30-2-16, Emile Colas to Ellen L. Fairclough, 9 Feb. 1960.

65. Emile Colas, counsel for Oka Indians, *Minutes of Proceedings and Evidence*, 14, 34.

66. Mr F.G. Fane, ibid., 34.

67. *Statutes of the Province of Quebec, 8-9 Elizabeth II, c. 181, *An Act respecting the Corporation of Oka*, 18 Dec. 1959.

68. Minister of Citizenship and Immigration to attorney for the Oka Indians, 27 May 1958, quoted in *Minutes of Proceedings and Evidence*, 15.

69. Assembly of First Nations, "Kanesatake Background & Chronology"; Joint Committee, *Minutes of Proceeding and Evidence*, 14.

70. Oka Chiefs to Joint Committee of Senate and House of Commons on Indian Affairs, 20 April 1961, *Minutes of Proceedings and Evidence*, 319.

71. Ibid., 14.

72. Oka Chiefs to Joint Committee of Senate and House of Commons on Indian Affairs, ibid., 319.

73. Ibid., 18; *Records of Indian Affairs, file 373/30-2-16, Guy Favreau, Assistant Deputy Minister of Citizenship and Immigration, to Emile Colas, 9 Aug. 1960.

74. Joint Committee, *Minutes of Proceedings and Evidence*, 14. Their lawyer also took pains to explain that the Indians did not regard themselves as Canadian citizens, did not recognize Canadian law, and especially did not accept the validity of the Indian Act. Ibid., 23–25.

75. Ibid., 14; Document 0-44, "Land Title at Oka [1973]."

76. Joint Committee, *Minutes of Proceedings and Evidence*, 614, 615.

77. Don Purich, *Our Land: Native Rights in Canada* (Toronto: Lorimer, 1986), 52.

78. P.E. Trudeau as quoted by Flora MacDonald, MP, 11 April 1973, House of Commons *Debates*, 3207.

79. On Trudeau, Aboriginal rights, and claims see J.R. Miller, *Skyscrapers Hide the Heavens: A History of Indian-White Relations in Canada* (Toronto: University of Toronto Press, 1989), 224, 254–56.

80. Catharine McClellan, *My Old People Say: An Ethnographic Survey of Southern Yukon Territory*, vol. 1 (Ottawa: National Museums of Canada, Publications in Ethnology no. 6, 1975), 45–50.

81. Daniel, *Claims*, 227.

82. *In All Fairness: A Native Claims Policy—Comprehensive Claims* (Ottawa: Supply and Services Canada, 1981), 29–30.

83. *Living Treaties: Lasting Agreements*, Report of the Task Force To Review Comprehensive Claims Policy [Coolican Report] (Ottawa: Indian Affairs and Northern Development, 1985): "Three claims have been rejected on the basis of their having been superseded by law," 13. As of 15 March 1991, according to the deputy chief of the Treaties and Historical Research Centre, nineteen comprehensive claims awaited settlement. During the winter of 1990–91 the federal government "announced the lifting of the six-claim limit on the number of comprehensive claims the government will negotiate at any time" and moved to set up a task force on "how tripartite negotiations" with Native groups and provinces might proceed. INAC, *Transition*, Special Edition, Feb. 1991.

84. *Outstanding Business: A Native Claims Policy—Specific Claims* (Ottawa: Indian Affairs and Northern Development, 1982), 13. "Twelve claims had been settled involving cash payments of some $2.3 million. Seventeen claims had been rejected and five had been suspended by the claimants. Negotiations were in progress on 73 claims and another 80 were under government review. Twelve claims had been filed in court and 55 others referred for

administrative remedy (e.g., return of surrendered but unsold land)."

85. Coolican Report, 78.

86. Daniel, *Claims*, 230–31.

87. *In All Fairness*, esp. 17.

88. *Outstanding Business*, 16. The document claimed, however, that Indians' "views have been taken into consideration by the government in developing new policy initiatives."

89. Coolican Report, iii, 30, 40, 43. See also p. 14 re impact of constitution of 1982.

90. Ibid., ii.

91. *Comprehensive Land Claims Policy* (Ottawa: Supply and Services, 1986 [the title page nonetheless bears the date "1987"]), 12, 18, 23. For the minister's claim that "blanket extinguishment" was dropped as a requirement in 1986, see his statement to the House of Commons in Sept. 1990 in *Transition* 3, 12 (Dec. 1990): 3.

92. Paul Ollivier, Associate Deputy Minister, Department of Justice, to P.F. Girard, Office of Claims Negotiation, INAC, 26 Feb. 1975. A photocopy of this document, which was obtained by means of an application under the *Access to Information Act*, is in the possession of the author.

93. McCann-Magill, *Golden Lake Land Claim*, esp. 11–12.

94. INAC press release, "An Overview of the Oka Issue," 3; Bill McKnight to Grand Chief Hugh Nicholas, 14 Oct. 1986, and R.M. Connelly, Specific Claims Branch, to Chief Nicholas, 10 May 1984. Photocopies of the Mcknight and Connelly letters were obtained via the *Access to Information Act* and are in the author's possession.

95. *Transition* 3, 9 (Sept. 1990): 1.

96. *Globe and Mail*, 11 Sept. 1990.

97. Ibid., 20 Feb. 1991.

JUDGING HISTORY:
REFLECTIONS ON THE REASONS FOR
JUDGMENT IN DELGAMUUKW V. B.C. ◇

ROBIN FISHER

○

So far, most of the running against Chief Justice Allan McEachern's findings in *Delgamuukw v. B.C.* has been made by native people and anthropologists. Both groups have, quite rightly, objected to the denigration of native cultures, to the fact that oral testimony was first admitted then dismissed, and to the assertion that anthropologists were largely unreliable witnesses. Lawyers have also commented on the case in print, and will do so in more detail when the argument is rejoined in the British Columbia Court of Appeal.[1] Without wishing to diminish the force of any of these criticisms, I want to look at the judgment from the point of view of an historian. McEachern's "Reasons for Judgment" is a "book" that also ought to be reviewed as a piece of historical writing in its historiographical context.

It is fitting that the judgment be evaluated as history because McEachern invokes the historical perspective and, at first glance, treats historians and their work with much more respect than anthropology. At the beginning of his "chapter" entitled "An Historical Overview," he notes: "It is not possible to discuss this case except in an historical context."[2] Later, as he evaluates the various forms of evidence presented to the court, he writes of historians that, "I accept just about everything they put before me . . ."[3] By contrast, the evidence presented by Native people and anthropologists is treated with great skepticism. McEachern thought that Gitksan and Wet'suwet'en people who testified had "a romantic view" of the past and, therefore, "much of the plantiffs' historical evidence is not literally true."[4] The anthropologists were alleged to have engaged in a "type of study . . . called participant observation" which brought them too close to

◇ Reprinted with permission from *BC Studies* 95 (Autumn 1992): 43–54.

their subjects (in this case the plaintiffs) and, in McEachern's view, was "fatal to the credibility and reliability of their conclusions."[5] The judge's rejection of one approach to the past, and apparent acceptance of another, was fundamental to his "Reasons for Judgment" and therefore bears closer scrutiny.

A more careful examination of the evidence provided in the judgment will show that McEachern, in fact, paid very little attention to historians. His rejection of their work is less blatant than his dismissal of anthropology and oral tradition, but it is no less thorough. The reasons for ruling out much of what the native people and anthropologists had to say are up front and clearly stated. Those groups can come to grips with the arguments against them and much of the thinking that lies behind it. History and historians are treated more shabbily by not even being given that opportunity. McEachern may appeal to history and uphold the reliability of historians, but he appears to have no understanding of either the historical methodology or the conclusions of historians who have written about Native people in Canada. For this historian, then, both the method of and the reasons for McEachern's judgment are seriously flawed.

In *Delgamuukw v. B.C.* the naïvety of the conclusions about history follow logically from the means by which they were reached. The judge's professed reliance on historians arises from his belief that they are "largely collections of archival, historical documents."[6] But if writing history involved ten steps, then the historian has only taken one with the acquisition of the documents. The real work of the historian begins with reading the documents and evaluating them for internal consistency as well as establishing the context in which they were written. Individual documents must be compared to the rest of the written record and, where appropriate, non-written sources. Then the historian develops an interpretation of the past that is logical and consistent with all of the available evidence. The final steps are to write an account of the past in clear, accessible prose, and to point out to the reader, through footnotes and bibliography, the sources that formed the basis for the conclusions.

McEachern, by contrast, adopts a hopelessly outmoded procedure which he describes as a "'scissors and paste' format. . . ." No lesser authority than R.G. Collingwood wrote nearly fifty years ago that "scissors and paste history . . . is not really history at all," and then went on to explain that approach to the past began to be superseded in the seventeenth century.[7] McEachern does seem to have some reservations about scissors and paste, as he allows that "it is not usually good practice," but he goes ahead and follows it nonetheless.[8]

Actually the McEachern methodology would be better described as xerox, scissors, and paste. For the first step in this procedure is to pull the documents out of their original context by use of the xerox machine. Thus, for example, a letter for Governor James Douglas to the British Colonial Secretary on Indian land policy is isolated from his numerous letters on other issues of the day. It is as if Douglas did his thinking in watertight compartments rather than as a busy governor dealing with a dozen overlapping questions at the same time. Individual documents are then cut to pieces so that excerpts can be quoted. The historical sections of the judgment consist of long successions of quotations from original sources strung together with commentary by the judge. The trouble with scissors and paste is that scissors cut things out of context and, once removed from their setting, all the bits of the document are of equal weight. After the individual pieces have been trimmed to a suitable shape, with the application of paste, the past can be stuck back together according to a new, and more acceptable, pattern.

Worse still, by failing to refer the reader to the original source of the document, McEachern makes it very difficult to follow his cutting and pasting. There are several instances where documents are quoted without any citation at all.[9] When a reference is provided, the citations are not to archival collections, but are either to the compilations of documents brought together for this case or to previous cases where they were used. These citations obscure the historical reasoning behind the judgment. For, unless one has access to the exhibits placed before the court, or is very familiar with the documentary record, checking the accuracy of the quotations and the extent to which lack of context distorts their meaning will be a complicated task. Because one cannot easily check McEachern's footnotes, the validity of his interpretation of history remains, at very least, an open question.

Not all of these shortcoming are unique to the McEachern judgment. Though this may be a particularly brazen example, other judgments are based on similar techniques. Combing the documents for suitable quotes, pulling them out of context, and then citing them to court exhibits or other judgments is common practice in legal circles. It is almost as if an historical document does not acquire legitimacy until it has been introduced in court. Thus the various enactments of the colonial legislature of British Columbia that are alleged by the province to have extinguished aboriginal title prior to 1871 are sometimes called "the Calder XIII" in legal circles because they are referred to in the *Calder* case.[10] This shorthand form of citation is undoubtedly more convenient than referring to a series of Acts, but having the legal system recreate the past in its own image is not good history. The drawbacks of this approach will be explained in any primer on the historical method.[11]

Also anachronistic is Chief Justice McEachern's belief that the documents are self-explanatory. He praises historians for providing "much useful information with minimal editorial comment." Their marvelous collections," he adds, largely spoke for themselves." If one accepts this premise, then it is logical "to allow the participants—those who were actually on the scene dealing with these problems—to be judged by their own words. . . ."[12] This notion is, at best, very innocent. For the meaning of documents is not self-evident: it can only be understood in context. A document cannot be properly evaluated until we know who wrote it, for whom it was written, and, most importantly, why it was written.[13] As McEachern inadvertently shows, it is not possible for judges, any more than historians, simply to allow figures from the past to speak for themselves. By giving, as he does, an individual like Joseph Trutch the benefit of every doubt, the chief justice make a very real judgment about the past. Again, these points are elementary to the process of writing history.

Less obvious, perhaps, are the consequences of McEachern's complete faith in the documentary record as the primary, if not the only, reliable source of insight into the past. He hearkens back to the old view that history, based on the study of written sources, is the appropriate discipline for understanding European cultures, whereas anthropology, based on the use of oral and material sources, is the discipline devoted to indigenous peoples. One of the many problems with this dichotomy is that exclusive reliance on written documents to interpret history confirms the hegemony of the colonizers. And that is part of the reason why historians have concluded that they must move beyond their traditional reliance on written words if they are ever to understand the indigenous past.

Ethnohistory is the technique that is now used to write native history. Recognizing that no single source provides the key to unlock the past, ethnohistorians use oral tradition, ethnography, and archaeology as well as the written record.[14] Even the earliest documents were written by Europeans who observed Native cultures that were changing, often very rapidly. Therefore oral tradition and archaeology are particularly important for understanding Native cultures prior to the arrival of Europeans in North America. All of these sources must be critically evaluated, for each one has its own particular power as well as its deficiencies. And all of these sources must be used in conjunction: each one used to verify the others. Bruce Trigger is one of the leading exponents of ethnohistory in Canada, and he is selectively quoted by McEachern on the limitations of oral history.[15] The judge does not, however, quote Trigger, or any other historian, on the limitations of the written record.[16] The point that he misses is that each one of these sources has its drawbacks, which is why they all have to be mined for all that they are worth. Since he places so little credence on oral tradition, ethnography, and archaeology—the evidence that could be used to reconstruct pre-contact Gitksan and Wet'suwet'en life—it is hardly surprising that he should have found that those people did not have cultures that were viable and long-standing enough to establish an Aboriginal title to their territory.

With so little understanding of the historical methodology, it is not surprising that the chief justice is also unable to discriminate between good and bad history. The views of particular historians are brought to bear on his judgment without regard for their competence on the subject at hand. The counsel for the plaintiffs were apparently very critical of Joseph Trutch, who was a major figure in the making of Indian land policy in British Columbia. As Chief Commissioner of Lands and Works between 1864 and 1871, Trutch entrenched the non-recognition of aboriginal title and drastically reduced the size of existing reserves. Yet McEachern observes that some historians have not "treated Trutch as unkindly as plaintiff's counsel."[17] In support of this claim he cites Margaret Ormsby, who in British Columbia: A History does not say a word about Trutch's Indian policy, and Robert Cail, whose two chapters on Indian land policy rely entirely on published sources.[18] Other historians, who have looked more carefully at the record of Trutch's dealings with Indian land, have concluded that, in the 1860s, he made many of the decisions that have led to today's impasse on native land claims.[19] But for McEachern, the best historians are not those who have done adequate research or drawn the most logical conclusions, but simply those who appear to support his views.

Having selected historians with compatible opinions, McEachern then goes on to use their work in slippery ways. In his discussion of British Columbia's entry into Confederation, for example, he quotes Cail's opinion that "it is possible" that neither Trutch and the other British Columbia delegates, nor the federal officials, "intended to be anything less than candid" when they met in Ottawa to negotiate the Terms of Union in 1870.[20] Even at face value, that is a meaningless statement. The "possibility" that they intended to be candid allows equally for the possibility that they did not, and the fact that they "intended" to be candid does not exclude the possibility that they were obscure about particular issues when it came to the point. More importantly, as Cail goes on to demonstrate, it is difficult to escape the conclusion that Trutch, who was the key negotiator for British Columbia, failed to explain colonial policy on Indian land in British Columbia clearly to the federal representatives. Admittedly, there is no verbatim record of the negotiations in Ottawa, but all the evidence points to that conclusion, as does the federal government's consternation when it later found out the true nature of Indian land policy in the westernmost province.[21] McEachern, however, then slips away from the issue by noting, I think incorrectly, that the evidence on the character of Trutch is equivocal and so he will not enter the controversy. "Such matters," he concludes, "are better left to historians." One can only wish that he really meant it.[22]

McEachern's smorgasbord approach to historical interpretation is not confined to Canadian history. At one point he digresses "for a moment to mention a few excerpts from history, not related to British Columbia. . . . " He then devotes a couple of paragraphs to pronouncing judgment on New Zealand history and law relating to Maori land. He refers briefly to the Treaty of Waitangi, which was signed in 1840 between representatives of the British government and the Maori people. Its provisions have not always been honoured, but the treaty was and is seen in New Zealand as the country's founding document. It provides an interesting contrast to Canadian treaties with Native people because, rather than extinguishing aboriginal title, it guaranteed Maori possession of their lands, forests, and fisheries for as long as they wished. Signed nine years before the founding of the colony of Vancouver Island, it might also be taken as an indication of British policy on aboriginal land rights. But McEachern passes quickly over the treaty itself, nothing that "it is not necessary to detail all the circumstances which arose in that colony as a result of the Treaty of Waitangi. . . ." Instead, he quotes at length from a report of a select committee of the British House of Commons to the effect that native people had only "a qualified dominion" over the country that was confined to a right of occupancy. This was the view of George Gipps, who as governor of New South Wales also served briefly from Sydney as governor of New Zealand. McEachern quotes Gipps' opinion because it is very close to his own view of Gitksan-Wet'suwet'en land rights. What he fails to mention is that Gipps' interpretation was unacceptable to the British Secretary of State for the Colonies as the basis for policy, partly because it contradicted the principles of the

Treaty of Waitangi.[23] There was, as McEachern observes, no similar treaty signed in British Columbia.

Not, one suspects, that it would have made much difference to the chief justice if there had been, since he does not set much store by treaties with indigenous peoples. Part of the argument for the claim that the Gitksan-Wet'suwset'en retain title to their land is that, unlike some other native people within British Columbia and throughout much of Canada, they have never surrendered it by treaty. McEachern responds to this assertion by denigrating the treaties signed with native people, referring to them as an "historical 'farce'. . . ." He is here echoing the views of Clement F. Cornwall, one of the most rabid of British Columbia's settler-politicians on the issue of Indian land, who noted in 1887 how, in other parts of Canada, Indian title was "extinguished by the farce of purchasing the same for infinitesimally small sums. . . ." Cornwall at least understood that treaties were to extinguish title. McEachern further undermines the importance of these agreements by describing them as merely a means of "buying peace. . . ."[24] Significantly, Joseph Trutch also attempted to diminish the Douglas treaties on Vancouver Island by claiming that they were simply "for the purpose of securing friendly relations" with the Indians and not, as the documents themselves clearly state, to extinguish title.[25] Whatever the defects and limitations of the Douglas treaties on Vancouver Island and Treaty 8 in the Peace River country, most historians would argue that they do at least represent moments when the government negotiated with Native people over their land. At the end of McEachern's brief discussion of treaties we are still left with the question of why the Gitksan-Wet'suwet'en should not be treated in the same way as, say, the Songhees or the Beaver Indians.

Each of these examples of loose and shoddy use of historical detail is bad enough on its own, but collectively they add up to a general and much more substantial point. No one who writes about the past, whether historian or judge, is perfect. We all make mistakes of fact and interpretation. Yet for most historians there is a threshold beyond which the proliferation of minor errors and distortions begins to add up to major doubts about the credibility of the entire piece of work. As an historian, I would also expect sloppy thinking about the past to be associated with unclear thinking about the law. I am not, of course, in a position to assess the judge's use of legal precedent, though one who is presumably qualified to comment has already suggested that he is as arbitrary in his use of the law as he is in his use of history.[26] It would be bad enough if the "Reasons for Judgment" in *Delgamuukw v. B.C.* were merely slipshod on matters of detail, but many of McEachern's general presumptions about the way native people responded to the coming of Europeans are also ahistorical. By viewing the past in terms of the present, he develops interpretations that are very different from those of most historians who write on First Nations peoples in Canada.

When McEachern reflects on "what really went wrong" in relations between natives and Europeans, he concludes that the indigenous people were unable to adapt to change because their "lack of cultural preparation for the new regime. . . ." Thus, as he puts it, "Indian dependence upon the white society was one of their greatest problems." This opinion is expressed in the judgment itself and repeated in the particularly offensive *ex cathedra* pronouncements at the end, which are innocuously entitled "Some Comments."[27] McEachern's cited authority for this view is George Woodcock, whose research on Native history in British Columbia seems to be largely confined to reading books written by himself.[28] It is a notion that is at least fifty years out of date in the historical literature.

Historical writing on native people in Canada goes back more than 250 years, but work by academic historians can probably be said to have begun in the 1930s.[29] Certainly the first university-trained historian to pay significant attention to the indigenous people of Canada was Harold Innis, whose book *The Fur Trade in Canada* was first published in 1930.[30] Later in the decade G.F.G. Stanley wrote *The Birth of Western Canada*, in which he argued that the Indians of the prairies were doomed because "the savage, centuries behind in mental and economic development, cannot readily adapt himself to meet the new conditions."[31] At the same time, in British Columbia another historian, who was also a judge, F.W. Howay, held similar views about the Native people of the west coast. According to Howay, the early fur trade "seriously dislocated the finely balanced economic and social fabric of the Indians."[32] The common thread running through these works was that Native cultures were unable to respond to the pressure of, first, the fur trade economy and, later, the coming of European settlers.

Recent historians, who have done more detailed and sophisticated research, have drastically revised these early views. They have shown that Native cultures were dynamic and evolving at the time of contact, and that they continued to adapt after the arrival of Europeans. Far from being passive, Indians responded rationally to the newcomers, devised strategies for coping with their demands, and even shaped the Europeans' interests to suit their own.[33] Most fur trade historians now argue that the trade was a co-operative economic and social system in which Native people played an integral and determining role. One of the leading exponents of this view of the fur trade is Arthur Ray, and his work also figures prominently in this judgment. Ray has already explained how his specific evidence on Gitksan-Wet'suwet'en as traders was mishandled by the judge.[34] The pressure on Native cultures increased immensely with the coming of settlement, and there can be no doubt about the oppression that the indigenous people suffered at the hands of Europeans. And yet, even in the face of this new onslaught, they remained adaptive. Opportunities were extremely limited, but that did not mean that Native people were not able to exploit the few that existed. Thus McEachern's opinion that "their culture had not prepared them for the disciplined life of a tax paying agriculturist" is not shared by historians.[35] They have shown that, on the contrary, some Native groups both in British Columbia and on the prairies, became very successful farmers, even to the point of producing a surplus.[36]

This promising development was nipped in the bud, however, as Indians were left with too little land and given too few opportunities by government policy-makers who, among other things, represented white settlers who feared competition from Native farmers. Thus ethnohistorians now argue that native people did not immediately become dependent on

Europeans, and, when they did, it was not because of their inability to cope with the new order, but because they were given no opportunity to adapt.

McEachern's view of Native history is still firmly entrenched in the nineteenth century as interpreted by the historians of the 1930s. Since his method of determining the past is very different from that used by today's historians, it is hardly surprising that his conclusions would be also outdated. First McEachern fails to understand that the pre-contact cultures were viable and dynamic, then he argues that they were unable to adapt to European pressure, all of which undermines any valid claim to jurisdiction over their territory. In British Columbia there is a long tradition of judicial and political leaders listening to, but not hearing, Native people. The McEachern judgment obviously falls within that tradition. What is startling about this judgment is its author's failure to listen to the custodians of the past in his own culture. But then again, perhaps it is not so surprising.

For there is also a developing tradition in this province of lawyers and judges presuming to be historians, whether in or out of the courtroom. Having made judgments about legal issues that have a historical dimension, they presumably feel that they are thereby qualified to write history. Sometimes, as in *Delgamuukw v. B.C.*, they write a version of history into legal judgments, and sometimes they write books about the past. The lawyer, David Ricardo Williams, for example, has written biographical studies of several British Columbia figures. His books are long on knowledge of the law, but short on research into the historical context in which these men operated. They are particularly inadequate when they deal with native culture and history. His account of the Gitksan fugitive, Simon Peter Gunanoot, is based on legal rather than ethnographic knowledge, and his chapter on Indians in his biography of Matthew Baillie Begbie contains a number of errors of fact and interpretation.[37] But perhaps the most egregious example of a former judge posing as an historian is Thomas R. Berger's recent book, *A Long and Terrible Shadow*.[38] Berger takes a little over 150 pages to pass judgment on 500 years of native history over an entire continent. He concludes that native history in North America has been an unwavering, downhill line from Columbus to the present day. The evidence for this generalization comes from personal experiences and the selective reading of a tiny fraction of the secondary works on Native history and culture. His notion, that by going into Native communities today he can read the past back in a direct line to the time of contact, is called the fallacy of the ethnographic present in anthropological circles.[39] His reading on Native history in North America includes virtually nothing on the fur trade in Canada—that 300-year period during which, many historians argue, Indians and Europeans had a co-operative rather than an antagonistic relationship.

What these judges and lawyers are often doing is shaping the past to serve the needs of the present, which is not quite the same thing as writing history. It is also an approach that obviates the need for detailed research. We can safely assume that none of these legal professionals, let alone the bar associations, would let an historian walk in off the street and take over one of these cases just for a change of pace. But then, of course, any one can be an historian—or thinks s/he can! Once in a position to judge the laws, evidently one may also judge history.

The interface between the discipline of history and the legal system is still a problematic one. The courts often expect historians to be merely collectors of documents. If judges do move beyond McEachern's idea that written documents are self-evident, then they tend to demand a greater certainty of interpretation than history can provide. Both professions need to think more clearly about these problems, and McEachern's judgment may at least serve the useful purpose of stimulating that debate. Academic historians are certainly partly to blame for the facile view of history expressed in *Delgamuukw v. B.C.* They need to find ways to get their work beyond the halls of academe. Judges and lawyers, on the other hand, should expect historians to have a higher function than the xerox machine. They should be called upon to provide a disciplined analysis of the past. If judges are going to use history as a basis for defining the law, then they need to listen to historians, and historians need to make themselves heard.

NOTES

1. Hamar Foster, "It Goes Without Saying: Precedent and the Doctrine of Extinguishment by Implication in Delgamuukw et al v. The Queen," *The Advocate* 49 (May 1991): 341–57; Leslie Hall Pinder, *The Carriers of No: After the Land Claims Trial* (Vancouver: Lazara Press, 1990).

2. Allan McEachern, *Reasons for Judgment, Delgamuukw v. BC*, Supreme Court of British Columbia (1991), 17.

3. Ibid., 52.

4. Ibid., 48–49.

5. Ibid., 50.

6. Ibid., 52.

7. R.G. Collingwood, *The Idea of History* (London: Oxford University Press, 1961 [1946]), 257–60.

8. *Delgamuukw v. BC*, 99.

9. See, for example, *Delgamuukw v. BC*, 110, 120–23, 158, and 181–82.

10. Foster, "It Goes Without Saying," 345ff.

11. See, for example, Norman F. Cantor and Richard I. Schneider, *How to Study History* (New York: Thomas Y. Crowell, 1967), 44–45.

12. *Delgamuukw v. BC*, 52, 99.

13. Cantor and Schneider, *How to Study History*, 47–48; Robert Jones Shafer,

A Guide to the Historical Method (Homewood, IL: The Dorsey Press, 1974), 141–61.

14. On the nature of ethnohistory, see Bruce G. Trigger, *The Children of Aataentsic: A History of the Huron People to 1660* (Montreal: McGill-Queen's University Press, 1976), 1:11–21; James Axtel, "Ethnohistory: An Historian's Viewpoint," *Ethnohistory* 26 (Winter 1979): 1–13.

15. *Delgamuukw v. BC*, 47–48. In this case McEachern does provide a citation, but alas the page number is incorrect and less than half of the following quote actually comes from the source cited, which is Bruce Trigger, *Time and Traditions: Essays in Archaeological Interpretation* (Edinburgh: Edinburgh University Press, 1978), 127–28.

16. Bruce G. Trigger, *Natives and Newcomers: Canada's "Heroic Age" Reconsidered* (Montreal: McGill-Queen's University Press, 1985), 168.

17. *Delgamuukw v. BC*, 132.

18. Margaret A. Ormsby, *British Columbia: A History* (Toronto: Macmillan, 1958), passim; and Robert E. Cail, *Land, Man, and the Law: The Disposal of Crown Lands in British Columbia, 1871–1913* (Vancouver: University of British Columbia Press, 1974), 169–243.

19. Robin Fisher, "Joseph Trutch and Indian Land Policy," *BC Studies* 12

(1971–72): 3–33, and *Contact and Conflict: Indian-European Relations in British Columbia, 1774–1890* (Vancouver: University of British Columbia Press, 1977), 162–68 and 171–72. See also Paul Tennant, *Aboriginal Peoples and Politics: The Indian Land Question in British Columbia, 1849–1989* (Vancouver: University of British Columbia Press, 1990), 39–44.

20. *Delgamuukw v. BC*, 132; and Cail, *Land, Man, and the Law*, 185.

21. Cail, *Land, Man, and the Law*, 185–88; Fisher, *Contact and Conflict*, 177, 186.

22. *Delgamuukw v. BC*, 132.

23. See *Delgamuukw v. BC*, 133–34, where McEachern gets the name of the governor of New South Wales wrong and, though it is difficult to be sure in the absence of an exact citation, seems to refer to the wrong select committee of the House of Commons. On the Treaty of Waitangi see Claudia Orange, *The Treaty of Waitangi* (Wellington: Allen & Unwin, 1987), passim; and, for a brief comparison between New Zealand and western Canada, see Robin Fisher, "With or Without Treaty: Indian Land Claims in Western Canada" in *Sovereignty and Indigenous Rights: The Treaty of Waitangi in International Contexts*, ed. William Renwick (Wellington: Victoria University Press, 1991), 49–66.

24. *Delgamuukw v. BC*, 165–66.

25. Joseph Trutch, memorandum, enclosure in Musgrave to Granville, 29 Jan. 1870, British Columbia, *Papers Connected with the Indian Land Question, 1850–1875* (Victoria: R. Wolfenden, 1875), appendix, 11.

26. See Foster, "It Goes Without Saying, esp. 349–51.

27. *Delgamuukw v. BC*, 128–29, 299.

28. See Delgamuukw v. BC, 129, where Woodcock's book is incorrectly cited as *History of British Columbia*; and cf. George Woodcock, *British Columbia: A History of the Province* (Vancouver: Douglas & McIntyre, 1990), 126ff. For a somewhat more detailed comment on the limitations of Woodcock's research see Robin Fisher, "To

See Ourselves," *The Beaver* 71 (Aug./Sept. 1991): 53–54.

29. Bruce G. Trigger, "The Historian's Indian: Native Americans in Canadian Historical Writing from Charlevoix to the Present," *Canadian Historical Review* 67 (Sept. 1986): 315–42.

30. Harold H. Innis, *The Fur Trade in Canada: An Introduction to Canadian Economic History* (Toronto: University of Toronto Press, 1956).

31. G.F.G. Stanley, *The Birth of Western Canada: A History of the Riel Rebellions* (Toronto: University of Toronto Press, 1960 [1936]), 194.

32. F.W. Howay, W.N. Sage, and H.F. Angus, *British Columbia and the United States: The North Pacific Slope from Fur Trade to Aviation* (Toronto: Ryerson, 1942), 13. Though this book was jointly authored, Howay wrote the section on the fur trade.

33. For a summary of these views, see Bruce G. Trigger, "Early Native North American Responses to European Contact: Romantic versus Rationalistic Interpretations," *Journal of American History* 77 (March 1991): 1195–215.

34. Arthur J. Ray, "Fur Trade History and the Gitksan-Wet'suwet'en Comprehensive Claim: Men of Property and the Exercise of Title" in *Aboriginal Resource Use in Canada: Historical and Legal Aspects*, ed. Kerry Abel and Jean Friesen (Winnipeg: University of Manitoba Press, 1991), 301–15.

35. *Delgamuukw v. BC*, 128.

36. Sarah Carter, *Lost Harvests: Prairie Indian Reserve Farmers and Government Policy* (Montreal: McGill-Queen's University Press, 1990), 36–49, 162–76; Rolf Knight, *Indians at Work: An Informal History of Native Indian Labour in British Columbia, 1858–1930* (Vancouver: New Star Books, 1978), 66–77.

37. David Ricardo Williams, *Simon Peter Gunanoot: Trapline Outlaw* (Victoria: Sono Nis Press, 1982) and *"...The Man For a New Country": Sir Matthew Baillie Begbie* (Sidney: Gray's Publishing, 1977), esp. 100–18.

38. Thomas R. Berger, *A Long and Terrible Shadow: White Values, Native Rights in the Americas 1492–1992* (Vancouver: Douglas & McIntyre, 1991).

39. This point is explained by Bruce Trigger in one of the few books on Canadian native history that Berger does cite in his notes, see Trigger, *Natives and Newcomers*, 114–18.

FURTHER READING

○

BIBLIOGRAPHIES AND HISTORIOGRAPHICAL ESSAYS

Abler, Thomas Struthers, Sally M. Weaver, et al. *A Canadian Indian Bibliography, 1960–1970*. Toronto: University of Toronto Press, 1974.

Annis, R.C., ed. *Abstracts in Native Studies*. Brandon.: Abstracts of Native Studies Press, 1984.

Fisher, Robin, "Historical Writing on Native Peoples in Canada." *History and Social Science Teacher* 17 (Winter 1982): 65–72.

Grumet, Robert Steven. *Native Americans of the Northwest Coast: A Critical Bibliography*. Bloomington: Indiana University Press, 1979.

Helm, June. *The Indians of the Subartic: A Critical Bibliography*. Bloomington: Indiana University Press, 1976.

Krech, Shepard III. *Native Canadian Anthropology and History: A Selected Bibliography*. Winnipeg: Rupert's Land Research Centre, 1986.

McGee, Harold Franklin. "No Longer Neglected: A Decade of Writing Concerning the Native Peoples of the Maritimes." *Acadiensis* 10 (Autumn 1980): 135–42.

Peterson, Jacqueline, with John Anfinson. "The Indian and the Fur Trade: A Review of the Recent Literature." *Manitoba History* No. 10 (Autumn 1980): 10–18.

Smith, Dwight, ed. *Indians of the United States and Canada. A Bibliography*. Santa Barbara: American Bibliographical Center, 1974.

Surtees, Robert J. *Canadian Indian Policy: A Critical Bibliography*. Bloomington: Indiana University Press, 1982.

Swagerty, W.R., ed. *Scholars and the Indian Experience: Critical Reviews of Recent Writing in the Social Sciences*. Bloomington: Indiana University Press, 1984.

Tooker, Elisabeth. *The Indians of the Northeast: A Critical Bibliography*. Bloomington: Indiana University Press, 1978.

Van Kirk Sylvia. "Fur Trade Social History: Some Recent Trends." In *Old Trails and New Directions: Papers of the Third North American Fur Trade Conference*, edited by Carol M. Judd and Arthur J. Ray, 160–73. Toronto: University of Toronto Press, 1980.

Walker, James W. St. G. "The Indian in Canadian Historical Writing." Canadian Historical Association, Historical Papers (1971): 21–51.

_____. "The Indian in Canadian Historical Writing, 1972–1982." In *As Long as the Sun Shines and Water Flows: A Reader in Canadian Native Studies*, edited by Ian A.L. Gerry and Antoine S. Lussier, 340–57. Vancouver: University of British Columbia Press.

JOURNALS

Below is a list of the journals devoted to native studies. Other national journals, such as the *Canadian Historical Review* and *Canadian Ethnic Studies* and regional journals, such as *Acadiensis, Ontario History,* and *BC Studies,* frequently contain articles on First Nations history.

Arctic Anthropology
Canadian Journal of Anthropology
Canadian Journal of Native Studies
Ethnohistory
Études/Inuit/Studies
Native Studies Review
Recherches Amérindiennes au Québec

COLLECTIONS OF ESSAYS

Much useful material on native history, which is all too often overlooked, is available in published collections of essays ad periodicals, the most important of which are identified here.

Axtell, James, ed. *The European and the Indian: Essays in the Ethnohistory of Colonial North America.* New York: Oxford University Press, 1981.

Barman, Jean, Yvonne Hébert, and Don McCaskill, eds. *Indian Education in Canada.* Vol. 1, *The Legacy.* Vancouver: University of British Columbia Press, 1986.

——. *Indian Education in Canada.* Vol. 2, *The Challenge.* Vancouver: University of British Columbia Press, 1987.

Barron, F. Laurie, and James B. Waldram, eds. *1886 and After: Native Society in Transition.* Regina: Canadian Plains Research Center, 1986.

Boldt, Menno, and J. Anthony Long, eds. *The Quest for Justice: Aboriginal Peoples and Aboriginal Rights.* Toronto: University of Toronto Press, 1985.

Bolus, Malvina, ed. *People and Pelts: Selected Papers of the Second North American Fur Trade Conference.* Winnipeg: Peguis Publishers, 1972.

Buckley, Thomas, ed. *Rendezvous: Selected Papers of the Fourth North American Fur Trade Conference, 1981.* St. Paul: Minnesota Historical Society, 1984.

Cassidy, Frank. *Aboriginal Title in British Columbia: Delgamuukw vs The Queen.* Lantzville: Oolichan Books, 1992.

Coates, Ken, ed. *Aboriginal Land Claims in Canada: A Regional Perspective.* Toronto: Copp Clark Pitman, 1992.

Damas, David, ed. *Handbook of North American Indians.* Vol. 5, *Arctic.* Washington: Smithsonian Institution, 1984.

Fitzhugh, William W., ed. *Cultures in Contact: The European Impact on Native Cultural Institutions in Eastern North America, A.D. 100–1800.* Washington: Smithsonian Institution, 1985.

Getty, Ian A.L., and Antoine S. Lussier, eds. *As Long as the Sun Shines and the Water Flows: A Reader in Canadian Native Studies.* Vancouver: University of British Columbia Press, 1983.

Getty, Ian A.L., and Donald B. Smith, eds. *One Century Later: Western Canadian Reserve Indians Since Treaty 7.* Vancouver: University of British Columbia Press, 1978.

Helm, June, ed. *Handbook of North American Indians*. Vol. 6, *Subarctic*. Washington: Smithsonian Institution, 1981.

Judd, Carol M., and Arthur J. Ray, eds. *Old Trails and New Directions: Papers of the Third North American Fur Trade Conference*. Toronto: University of Toronto Press, 1980.

Krech, Shepard III, ed. *Indians, Animals, and the Fur Trade: A Critique of Keepers of the Game*. Athens: University of Georgia Press, 1981.

_____. *The Subarctic Fur Trade: Native Social and Economic Adaptations*. Vancouver: University of British Columbia Press, 1984.

Lussier, Antoine S., and D. Bruce Sealey, eds. *The Other Natives: The-les Metis 1870–1885*. 3 vols. Winnipeg: Manitoba Metis Federation Press, 1978–1980.

McGee, Harold Franklin ed. *The Native Peoples of Atlantic Canada: A History of Ethnic Interaction*. Toronto: McClelland & Stewart, 1974.

Martin, Calvin, ed. *The America Indian and the Problem of History*. New York: Oxford University Press, 1987.

Miller, J. R. ed. *Sweet Promises: A Reader on Indian-White Relations in Canada*. Toronto: University of Toronto Press, 1991.

Mills, Antonia and Richard Slobodin eds. *Amerindian Rebirth: Reincarnation Belief among North American Indians and Inuit*. Toronto: University of Toronto Press, 1994.

Morrison, R. Bruce and C. Roderick Wilson. *Native Peoples: The Canadian Experience*. Toronto: McClelland & Stewart, 1986.

Morrison, David and Jean-Luc Pilon, eds. *Threads of Arctic Prehistory: Papers in Honour of William E. Taylor, Jnr*. Ottawa: Canadian Museum of Civilization, 1994.

Morse, Bradford W., ed. *Aboriginal Peoples and the Law: Indian, Metis and Inuit Rights in Canada*. Ottawa: Carleton University Press, 1985.

Muise, D.A., ed. *Approaches to Native History in Canada: Papers of a Conference Held at the National Museum of Man, October, 1975*. Ottawa: National Museum of Man, 1977.

Peterson, Jacqueline, and Jennifer S.H. Brown, eds. *The New Peoples: Being and Becoming Métis in North America*. Winnipeg: University of Manitoba Press, 1985.

Ponting, J. Rick, ed. *Arduous Journey: Canadian Indians and Decolonization*. Toronto: McClelland & Stewart, 1986.

Rogers, Edward S. and Donald B. Smith, eds. *Aboriginal Ontario: Historical Perspectives on the First Nations*. Toronto: Dundurn Press, 1994.

Smith, Derek G., ed. *Canadian Indians and the Law: Selected Documents, 1663–1972*. Toronto: McClelland & Stewart, 1975.

Trigger, Bruce G., ed. *Handbook of North American Indians*: Vol. 15, *Northeast*. Washington: Smithsonian Institution, 1978.

Date ⌐